get with the programming

Through the power of practice and immediate personalized

feedback, MyProgrammingLab improves your performance.

MyProgrammingLab™

Learn more at www.myprogramminglab.com

ALWAYS LEARNING   PEARSON

INTRODUCTION TO PROGRAMMING USING

PYTHON

Y. Daniel Liang

Armstrong Atlantic State University

PEARSON

Boston   Columbus   Indianapolis   New York   San Francisco   Upper Saddle River
Amsterdam   Cape Town   Dubai   London   Madrid   Milan   Munich   Paris   Montreal   Toronto
Delhi   Mexico City   Sao Paulo   Sydney   Hong Kong   Seoul   Singapore   Taipei   Tokyo

Editorial Director, ECS: Marcia Horton
Editor-in-Chief: Michael Hirsch
Executive Editor: Tracy Dunkelberger
Associate Editor: Carole Snyder
Director of Marketing: Patrice Jones
Marketing Manager: Yezan Alayan
Marketing Coordinator: Kathryn Ferranti
Director of Production: Vince O'Brien
Managing Editor: Jeff Holcomb
Production Project Manager: Heather McNally
Manufacturing Buyer: Lisa McDowell
Art Director and Cover Designer: Anthony Gemmellaro
Text Designer: Gillian Hall
Cover Art: "Life Aquatic" © Arthur Xanthopoulos from Damaged Photography
Media Editor: Daniel Sandin
Full-Service Project Management: Gillian Hall
Composition: Laserwords
Printer/Binder: Edwards Brothers
Cover Printer: Lehigh-Phoenix Color/Hagerstown

Library of Congress Cataloging-in-Publication Data on file.

Prentice Hall
is an imprint of

www.pearsonhighered.com

10 9 8 7 6 5 4 3 2 1

ISBN 13: 978-0-13-274718-9
ISBN 10:   0-13-274718-9

*This book is dedicated to my former colleagues
at the National Severe Storms Laboratory,
in Norman, Oklahoma.*

To Samantha, Michael, and Michelle

PREFACE

Dear Reader,

what is programming?

This book assumes that you are a new programmer with no prior knowledge of programming. So, what is programming? Programming solves problems by creating solutions—writing programs—in a programming language. The fundamentals of problem solving and programming are the same regardless of which programming language you use. You can learn programming using any high-level programming language such as Python, Java, C++, or C#. Once you know how to program in one language, it is easy to pick up other languages, because the basic techniques for writing programs are the same.

why Python?

So what are the benefits of learning programming using Python? Python is easy to learn and fun to program. Python code is simple, short, readable, intuitive, and powerful, and thus it is effective for introducing computing and problem solving to beginners.

graphics

Beginners are motivated to learn programming so they can create graphics. A big reason for learning programming using Python is that you can start programming using graphics on day one. We use Python's built-in Turtle graphics module in Chapters 1–6 because it is a good pedagogical tool for introducing fundamental concepts and techniques of programming. We introduce Python's built-in Tkinter in Chapter 9, because it is a great tool for developing comprehensive graphical user interfaces and for learning object-oriented programming. Both Turtle and Tkinter are remarkably simple and easy to use. More importantly, they are valuable pedagogical tools for teaching the fundamentals of programming and object-oriented programming.

optional Turtle

To give instructors flexibility to use this book, we cover Turtle at the end of Chapters 1–6 so they can be skipped as optional material.

problem-driven

The book teaches problem solving in a problem-driven way that focuses on problem solving rather than syntax. We stimulate student interests in programming by using interesting examples in a broad context. While the central thread of the book is on problem solving, appropriate Python syntax and library are introduced in order to solve the problems. To support the teaching of programming in a problem-driven way, the book provides a wide variety of problems at various levels of difficulty to motivate students. In order to appeal to students in all majors, the problems cover many application areas in math, science, business, financial management, gaming, animation, and multimedia.

All data in Python are objects. We introduce and use objects from Chapter 3, but defining custom classes are covered in the middle of the book starting from Chapter 7. The book focuses on fundamentals first: it introduces basic programming concepts and techniques on selections, loops, and functions before writing custom classes.

fundamentals first

examples and exercises

The best way to teach programming is *by example*, and the only way to learn programming is *by doing*. Basic concepts are explained by example and a large number of exercises with various levels of difficulty are provided for students to practice. Our goal is to produce a text that teaches problem solving and programming in a broad context using a wide variety of interesting examples and exercises.

Sincerely,

Y. Daniel Liang
y.daniel.liang@gmail.com
www.cs.armstrong.edu/liang
www.pearsonhighered.com/liang

Pedagogical Features

The book uses the following elements to get the most from the material:

■ **Objectives** list what students should learn in each chapter. This will help them determine whether they have met the objectives after completing the chapter.

■ The **Introduction** opens the discussion with representative problems to give the reader an overview of what to expect from the chapter.

■ **Key Points** highlight the important concepts covered in each section.

■ **Check Points** provide review questions to help students track their progress and evaluate their learning.

■ **Problems**, carefully chosen and presented in an easy-to-follow style, teach problem solving and programming concepts. The book uses many small, simple, and stimulating examples to demonstrate important ideas.

■ **Key Terms** are listed with a page number to give students a quick reference to the important terms introducd in the chapter.

■ The **Chapter Summary** reviews the important subjccts that students should understand and remember. It helps them reinforce the key concepts they have learned in the chapter.

■ **Test Questions** are available online, grouped by sections for students to do self-test on programming concepts and techniques.

■ **Programming Exercises** are grouped by sections to provide students with opportunities to apply on their own the new skills they have learned. The level of difficulty is rated as easy (no asterisk), moderate (*), hard (**), or challenging (***). The trick of learning programming is practice, practice, and practice. To that end, the book provides a great many exercises.

■ **Notes**, **Tips**, and **Cautions** are inserted throughout the text to offer valuable advice and insight on important aspects of program development.

Note
Provides additional information on the subject and reinforces important concepts.

Tip
Teaches good programming style and practice.

Caution
Helps students steer away from the pitfalls of programming errors.

Flexible Chapter Orderings

Graphics is a valuable pedagogical tool for learning programming. The book uses Turtle graphics in Chapters 1–6 and Tkinter in the rest of the book. However, the book is designed to give the instructors the flexibility to skip the sections on graphics or to cover them later. The following diagram shows the chapter dependencies.

Chapter 10, Lists can be covered right after Chapter 6, Functions. Chapter 14, Tuples, Sets, and Dictionaries can be covered after Chapter 10.

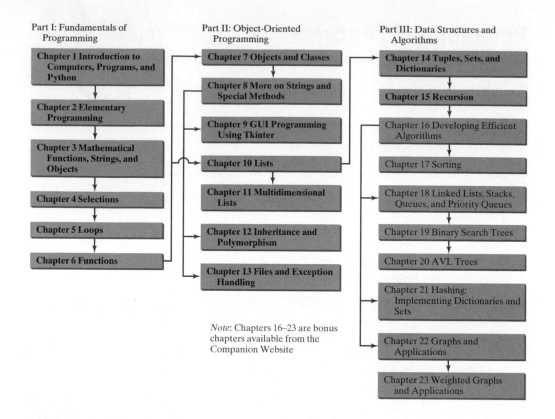

Part I: Fundamentals of Programming

- Chapter 1 Introduction to Computers, Programs, and Python
- Chapter 2 Elementary Programming
- Chapter 3 Mathematical Functions, Strings, and Objects
- Chapter 4 Selections
- Chapter 5 Loops
- Chapter 6 Functions

Part II: Object-Oriented Programming

- Chapter 7 Objects and Classes
- Chapter 8 More on Strings and Special Methods
- Chapter 9 GUI Programming Using Tkinter
- Chapter 10 Lists
- Chapter 11 Multidimensional Lists
- Chapter 12 Inheritance and Polymorphism
- Chapter 13 Files and Exception Handling

Part III: Data Structures and Algorithms

- Chapter 14 Tuples, Sets, and Dictionaries
- Chapter 15 Recursion
- Chapter 16 Developing Efficient Algorithms
- Chapter 17 Sorting
- Chapter 18 Linked Lists, Stacks, Queues, and Priority Queues
- Chapter 19 Binary Search Trees
- Chapter 20 AVL Trees
- Chapter 21 Hashing: Implementing Dictionaries and Sets
- Chapter 22 Graphs and Applications
- Chapter 23 Weighted Graphs and Applications

Note: Chapters 16–23 are bonus chapters available from the Companion Website

Organization of the Book

The chapters can be grouped into three parts that, taken together, form a comprehensive introduction to Python programming. Because knowledge is cumulative, the early chapters provide the conceptual basis for understanding programming and guide students through simple examples and exercises; subsequent chapters progressively present Python programming in detail, culminating with the development of comprehensive applications.

Part I: Fundamentals of Programming (Chapters 1–6)

The first part of the book is a stepping stone, preparing you to embark on the journey of learning programming. You will begin to know Python (Chapter 1) and will learn fundamental programming techniques with data types, variables, constants, assignments, expressions, operators, objects, and simple functions and string operations (Chapters 2–3), selection statements (Chapter 4), loops (Chapter 5), and functions (Chapter 6).

Part II: Object-Oriented Programming (Chapters 7–13)

This part introduces object-oriented programming. Python is an object-oriented programming language that uses abstraction, encapsulation, inheritance, and polymorphism to provide great flexibility, modularity, and reusability in developing software. You will learn object-oriented programming (Chapters 7–8), GUI programming using Tkinter (Chapter 9), lists (Chapter 10), multidimensional lists (Chapter 11), inheritance, polymorphism, and class design (Chapter 12), and files and exception handling (Chapter 13).

Part III: Data Structures and Algorithms (Chapters 14–15 and Bonus Chapters 16–23)

This part introduces the main subjects in a typical data structures course. Chapter 14 introduces Python built-in data structures: tuples, sets, and dictionaries. Chapter 15 introduces recursion to write functions for solving inherently recursive problems. Chapters 16–23 are bonus chapters on the Companion Website. Chapter 16 introduces measurement of algorithm efficiency and common techniques for developing efficient algorithms. Chapter 17 discusses classic sorting algorithms. You will learn how to implement linked lists, queues, and priority queues in Chapter 18. Chapter 19 presents binary search trees, and you will learn about AVL trees in Chapter 20. Chapter 21 introduces hashing, and Chapters 22 and 23 cover graph algorithms and applications.

Student Resource Website

The Student Resource Website (www.cs.armstrong.edu/liang/py) contains the following resources:

- Answers to review questions
- Solutions to even-numbered programming exercises
- Source code for the examples in the book
- Interactive self-test questions (organized by sections for each chapter)
- Supplements on using Python IDEs, advanced topics, etc.
- Resource links
- Errata

Additional Supplements

The text covers the essential subjects. The supplements extend the text to introduce additional topics that might be of interest to readers. The supplements listed in this table are available from the Companion Website.

Part I. General Supplements
  A. Glossary
  B. Installing and Using Python
  C. Python IDLE
  D. Python on Eclipse
  E. Python on Eclipse Debugging
  F. Python Coding Style Guidelines

Part II. Advanced Python Topics
  A. Regular Expressions
  B. Obtaining Date and Time
  C. The `str` Class's `format` Method
  D. Pass Arguments from Command Line
  E. Database Programming

Instructor Resource Website

The Instructor Resource Website, accessible from www.cs.armstrong.edu/liang/py, contains the following resources:

- Microsoft PowerPoint slides with interactive buttons to view full-color, syntax-highlighted source code and to run programs without leaving the slides.
- Solutions to all the review questions and exercises. Students will have access to the solutions of even-numbered programming exercises.
- Web-based quiz generator. (Instructors can choose chapters to generate quizzes from a large database of more than 800 questions.)

- Sample exams. In general, each exam has four parts:
  - Multiple-choice questions or short-answer questions
  - Correct programming errors
  - Trace programs
  - Write programs

- Projects. In general, each project gives a description and asks students to analyze, design, and implement the project.

Some readers have requested the materials from the Instructor Resource Website. Please understand that these are for instructors only. Such requests will not be answered.

MyProgrammingLab™

Online Practice and Assessment with MyProgrammingLab

MyProgrammingLab helps students fully grasp the logic, semantics, and syntax of programming. Through practice exercises and immediate, personalized feedback, MyProgrammingLab improves the programming competence of beginning students who often struggle with the basic concepts and paradigms of popular high-level programming languages.

A self-study and homework tool, a MyProgrammingLab course consists of hundreds of small practice problems organized around the structure of this textbook. For students, the system automatically detects errors in the logic and syntax of their code submissions and offers targeted hints that enable students to figure out what went wrong—and why. For instructors, a comprehensive gradebook tracks correct and incorrect answers and stores the code inputted by students for review.

MyProgrammingLab is offered to users of this book in partnership with Turing's Craft, the makers of the CodeLab interactive programming exercise system. For a full demonstration, to see feedback from instructors and students, or to get started using MyProgrammingLab in your course, visit www.myprogramminglab.com.

VideoNote

VideoNotes

VideoNotes are Pearson's new visual tool designed for teaching students key programming concepts and techniques. These short step-by-step videos demonstrate how to solve problems from design through coding. VideoNotes allow for self-placed instruction with easy navigation including the ability to select, play, rewind, fast-forward, and stop within each VideoNote exercise.

Margin icons in your textbook let you know when a VideoNote video is available for a particular concept or homework problem.

LiveLab

This book is accompanied by a complementary Web-based course assessment and management system for instructors. The system has four main components:

- The **Automatic Grading System** can automatically grade programs.

- The **Quiz Creation/Submission/Grading System** enables instructors to create and modify quizzes that students can take and be graded upon automatically.

- The **Peer Evaluation System** enables peer evaluations.

- **Checking plagiarisms, tracking grades, attendance, etc.,** lets students track their grades, and enables instructors to view the grades of all students, to check plagiarisms, and to track students' attendance.

The main features of the Automatic Grading System include:

- Students can run and submit exercises. (The system checks whether their program runs correctly—students can continue to run and resubmit the program before the due date.)
- Instructors can review submissions, run programs with instructor test cases, correct them, and provide feedback to students.
- Instructors can create/modify their own exercises, create public and secret test cases, assign exercises, and set due dates for the whole class or for individuals.
- All the exercises in the text can be assigned to students. Additionally, LiveLab provides extra exercises that are not printed in the text.
- Instructors can sort and filter all exercises and check grades (by time frame, student, and/or exercise).
- Instructors can check plagiarisms for a programming exercise.
- Instructors can delete students from the system.
- Students and instructors can track grades on exercises.

The main features of the Quiz System are:

- Instructors can create/modify quizzes from the test bank or a text file or create completely new tests online.
- Instructors can assign the quizzes to students and set a due date and test time limit for the whole class or for individuals.
- Students and instructors can review submitted quizzes.
- Instructors can analyze quizzes and identify students' weaknesses.
- Students and instructors can track grades on quizzes.

The main features of the Peer Evaluation System include:

- Instructors can assign/unassign exercises for peer evaluation.
- Instructors can view peer evaluation reports.

Acknowledgments

I would like to thank Armstrong Atlantic State University for enabling me to teach what I write and for supporting me in writing what I teach. Teaching is the source of inspiration for the book. I am grateful to the instructors and students who have offered comments, suggestions, bug reports, and praise.

This book has been greatly enhanced thanks to the outstanding reviewers. They are:

Claude Anderson – Rose-Hulman Institute of Technology
Lee Cornell – Minnesota State University – Mankato
John Magee – Boston University
Shyamal Mitra – University of Texas – Austin
Yenumula Reddy – Grambling State University
David Sullivan – Boston University
Hong Wang – University of Toledo

It is a great pleasure, honor, and privilege to work with Pearson. I would like to thank Tracy Dunkelberger, Marcia Horton, Michael Hirsch, Matt Goldstein, Carole Snyder, Tim Huddleston, Yez Alayan, Jeff Holcomb, Gillian Hall, Rebecca Greenberg, and their colleagues for organizing, producing, and promoting this project.

As always, I am indebted to my wife, Samantha, for her love, support, and encouragement.

BRIEF CONTENTS

CONTENTS

A detailed table of contents for the Web chapters is available on the companion Website:

APPENDIXES

CHAPTER
1

INTRODUCTION TO COMPUTERS, PROGRAMS, AND PYTHON

Objectives

- To demonstrate a basic understanding of computer hardware, programs, and operating systems (§§1.2–1.4).

- To describe the history of Python (§1.5).

- To explain the basic syntax of a Python program (§1.6).

- To write and run a simple Python program (§1.6).

- To explain the importance of, and provide examples of, proper programming style and documentation (§1.7).

- To explain the differences between syntax errors, runtime errors, and logic errors (§1.8).

- To create a basic graphics program using Turtle (§1.9).

1.1 Introduction

The central theme of this book is to learn how to solve problems by writing a program.

what is programming?
program

This book is about programming. So, what is programming? The term programming means to create (or develop) software, which is also called a *program*. In basic terms, software contains the instructions that tell a computer—or a computerized device—what to do.

Software is all around you, even in devices that you might not think would need it. Of course, you expect to find and use software on a personal computer, but software also plays a role in running airplanes, cars, cell phones, and even toasters. On a personal computer, you use word processors to write documents, Web browsers to explore the Internet, and e-mail programs to send messages. These programs are all examples of software. Software developers create software with the help of powerful tools called *programming languages*.

programming languages

This book teaches you how to create programs by using the Python programming language. There are many programming languages, some of which are decades old. Each language was invented for a specific purpose—to build on the strengths of a previous language, for example, or to give the programmer a new and unique set of tools. Knowing that there are so many programming languages available, it would be natural for you to wonder which one is best. But, in truth, there is no "best" language. Each one has its own strengths and weaknesses. Experienced programmers know that one language might work well in some situations, whereas a different language may be more appropriate in other situations. For this reason, seasoned programmers try to master as many different programming languages as they can, giving them access to a vast arsenal of software-development tools.

If you learn to program using one language, you should find it easy to pick up other languages. The key is to learn how to solve problems using a programming approach. That is the main theme of this book.

You are about to begin an exciting journey: learning how to program. At the outset, it is helpful to review computer basics, programs, and operating systems. If you are already familiar with such terms as CPU, memory, disks, operating systems, and programming languages, you may skip the review in Sections 1.2–1.4.

1.2 What Is a Computer?

A computer is an electronic device that stores and processes data.

hardware
software

A computer includes both *hardware* and *software*. In general, hardware comprises the visible, physical elements of the computer, and software provides the invisible instructions that control the hardware and make it perform specific tasks. Knowing computer hardware isn't essential to learning a programming language, but it can help you better understand the effects that a program's instructions have on the computer and its components. This section introduces computer hardware components and their functions.

A computer consists of the following major hardware components (Figure 1.1):

- A central processing unit (CPU)

- Memory (main memory)

- Storage devices (such as disks and CDs)

- Input devices (such as the mouse and keyboard)

- Output devices (such as monitors and printers)

- Communication devices (such as modems and network interface cards)

bus

A computer's components are interconnected by a subsystem called a *bus*. You can think of a bus as a sort of system of roads running among the computer's components; data and

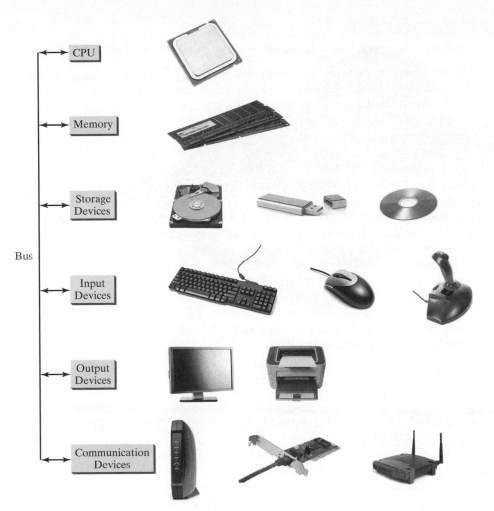

FIGURE 1.1 A computer consists of a CPU, memory, storage devices, input devices, output devices, and communication devices.

power travel along the bus from one part of the computer to another. In personal computers, the bus is built into the computer's *motherboard*, which is a circuit case that connects all of the parts of a computer together, as shown in Figure 1.2.

motherboard

1.2.1 Central Processing Unit

The *central processing unit (CPU)* is the computer's brain. It retrieves instructions from memory and executes them. The CPU usually has two components: a *control unit* and an *arithmetic/logic unit*. The control unit controls and coordinates the actions of the other components. The arithmetic/logic unit performs numeric operations (addition, subtraction, multiplication, division) and logical operations (comparisons).

CPU

Today's CPUs are built on small silicon semiconductor chips that contain millions of tiny electric switches, called *transistors*, for processing information.

Every computer has an internal clock, which emits electronic pulses at a constant rate. These pulses are used to control and synchronize the pace of operations. A higher clock *speed* enables more instructions to be executed in a given period of time. The unit of measurement of clock speed is the *hertz (Hz)*, with 1 hertz equaling 1 pulse per second. In the 1990s computers measured clocked speed in *megahertz*, but CPU speed has been improving continuously, and

speed

hertz

megahertz

CPU is placed
under the fan

Memory

Motherboard

FIGURE 1.2 The motherboard connects all parts of computer together.

gigahertz   the clock speed of a computer is now usually stated in *gigahertz (GHz)*. Intel's newest processors run at about 3 GHz.

core   CPUs were originally developed with only one core. The *core* is the part of the processor that performs the reading and executing of instructions. In order to increase CPU processing power, chip manufacturers are now producing CPUs that contain multiple cores. A multicore CPU is a single component with two or more independent processors. Today's consumer computers typically have two, three, and even four separate cores. Soon, CPUs with tens or even hundreds of cores will be affordable.

1.2.2 Bits and Bytes

Before we discuss memory, let's look at how information (data and programs) are stored in a computer.

A computer is really nothing more than a series of switches. Each switch exists in two states: on or off. Storing information in a computer is simply a matter of setting a sequence of switches on or off. If the switch is on, its value is 1. If the switch is off, its value is 0. These 0s and 1s are interpreted as digits in the binary number system and called *bits* (binary digits).

bits

byte   The minimum storage unit in a computer is a *byte*. A byte is composed of eight bits. A small number such as 3 can be stored as a single byte. To store a number that cannot fit into a single byte, the computer uses several bytes.

Data of various kinds, such as numbers and characters, are encoded as a series of bytes. As a programmer, you don't need to worry about the encoding and decoding of data, which the computer system performs automatically, based on the encoding scheme. An *encoding scheme* is a set of rules that govern how a computer translates characters, numbers, and symbols into data the computer can actually work with. Most schemes translate each character into a predetermined string of numbers. In the popular ASCII encoding scheme, for example, the character **C** is represented as **01000011** in one byte.

encoding scheme

A computer's storage capacity is measured in bytes and multiples of the byte, as follows:

- A *kilobyte (KB)* is about 1,000 bytes.

- A *megabyte (MB)* is about 1 million bytes.

- A *gigabyte (GB)* is about 1 billion bytes.

- A *terabyte (TB)* is about 1 trillion bytes.

kilobyte (KB)

megabyte (MB)

gigabyte (GB)

terabyte (TB)

A typical one-page word document might take 20 KB. So 1 MB can store 50 pages of documents and 1 GB can store 50000 pages of documents. A typical two-hour high-resolution movie might take 8 GB. So it would require 160 GB to store 20 movies.

1.2.3 Memory

A computer's *memory* consists of an ordered sequence of bytes for storing programs as well as data that the program is working with. You can think of memory as the computer's work area for executing a program. A program and its data must be moved into the computer's memory before they can be executed by the CPU.

memory

Every byte in the memory has a *unique address*, as shown in Figure 1.3. The address is used to locate the byte for storing and retrieving the data. Since the bytes in the memory can be accessed in any order, the memory is also referred to as *random-access memory (RAM)*.

unique address

RAM

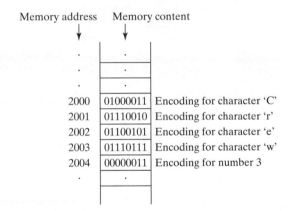

FIGURE 1.3 Memory stores data and program instructions in uniquely addressed memory locations. Each memory location can store one byte of data.

Today's personal computers usually have at least 1 gigabyte of RAM, but they more commonly have 2 to 4 GB installed. Generally speaking, the more RAM a computer has, the faster it can operate, but there are limits to this simple rule of thumb.

A memory byte is never empty, but its initial content may be meaningless to your program. The current content of a memory byte is lost whenever new information is placed in it.

Like the CPU, memory is built on silicon semiconductor chips that have millions of transistors embedded on their surface. Compared to CPU chips, memory chips are less complicated, slower, and less expensive.

1.2.4 Storage Devices

A computer's memory is a volatile form of data storage: any information that hasn't been stored in memory (that is, saved) is lost when the system's power is turned off. Programs and data are permanently stored on *storage devices* and are moved, when the computer actually uses them, to memory, which operates at much faster speeds than permanent storage devices can.

storage device

There are three main types of storage devices:

- Magnetic disk drives

- Optical disc drives (CD and DVD)

- USB flash drives

drive

Drives are devices for operating a medium, such as disks and CDs. A storage medium physically stores data or program instructions. The drive reads data from the medium and/or writes data onto the medium.

Disks

hard disk

A computer usually has at least one hard disk drive (Figure 1.4). *Hard disks* are used for permanently storing data and programs. Newer computers have hard disks that can store from 200 to 800 gigabytes of data. Hard disk drives are usually encased inside the computer, but removable hard disks are also available.

FIGURE 1.4 A hard disk is a device for permanently storing programs and data.

CDs and DVDs

CD-R

CD stands for compact disc. There are two types of CD drives: CD-R and CD-RW. A *CD-R* is for read-only permanent storage; the user cannot modify its contents once they are recorded. A *CD-RW* can be used like a hard disk; that is, you can write data onto the disc, and then overwrite that data with new data. A single CD can hold up to 700 MB. Most new PCs are equipped with a CD-RW drive that can work with both CD-R and CD-RW discs.

CD-RW

DVD

DVD stands for digital versatile disc or digital video disc. DVDs and CDs look alike, and you can use either to store data. A DVD can hold more information than a CD; a standard DVD's storage capacity is 4.7 GB. Like CDs, there are two types of DVDs: DVD-R (read-only) and DVD-RW (rewritable).

USB Flash Drives

Universal serial bus (USB) connectors allow the user to attach many kinds of peripheral devices to the computer. You can use a USB to connect a printer, digital camera, mouse, external hard disk drive, and other devices to the computer.

A USB *flash drive* is a device for storing and transporting data. A flash drive is small—about the size of a pack of gum, as shown in Figure 1.5. It acts like a portable hard drive that can be plugged into your computer's USB port. USB flash drives are currently available with up to 256 GB storage capacity.

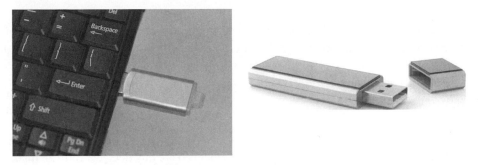

FIGURE 1.5   USB flash drives arc popular portable devices for storing data.

1.2.5   Input and Output Devices

Input and output devices let the user communicate with the computer. The most common input devices are *keyboards* and *mice*. The most common output devices are *monitors* and *printers*.

The Keyboard

A keyboard is a device for entering input. A typical keyboard is shown in Figure 1.6. *Compact keyboards are available without a numeric keypad.*

FIGURE 1.6   A computer keyboard consists of the keys for sending input to a computer.

Function keys are located across the top of the keyboard and are prefaced with the letter *F*.   function key
Their functions depend on the software currently being used.

modifier key

A *modifier key* is a special key (such as the *Shift*, *Alt*, and *Ctrl* keys) that modifies the normal action of another key when the two are pressed simultaneously.

numeric keypad

The *numeric keypad*, located on the right side of most keyboards, is a separate set of keys styled like a calculator to use for entering numbers quickly.

arrow keys

Arrow keys, located between the main keypad and the numeric keypad, are used to move the mouse pointer up, down, left, and right on the screen in many kinds of programs.

Insert key
Delete key
Page Up key
Page Down key

The *Insert*, *Delete*, *Page Up*, and *Page Down keys* are used in word processing and other programs for inserting text and objects, deleting text and objects, and moving up or down through a document one screen at a time.

The Mouse

A *mouse* is a pointing device. It is used to move a graphical pointer (usually in the shape of an arrow) called a *cursor* around the screen or to click on-screen objects (such as a button) to trigger them to perform an action.

The Monitor

The *monitor* displays information (text and graphics). The screen resolution and dot pitch determine the quality of the display.

screen resolution
pixels

The *screen resolution* specifies the number of pixels in horizontal and vertical dimensions of the display device. *Pixels* (short for "picture elements") are tiny dots that form an image on the screen. A common resolution for a 17-inch screen, for example, is 1024 pixels wide and 768 pixels high. The resolution can be set manually. The higher the resolution, the sharper and clearer the image is.

dot pitch

The *dot pitch* is the amount of space between pixels, measured in millimeters. The smaller the dot pitch, the sharper the display.

1.2.6 Communication Devices

modem

Computers can be networked through communication devices, such as a dial-up *modem* (*mo*dulator/*dem*odulator), a DSL or cable modem, a wired network interface card, or a wireless adapter.

- A dial-up modem uses a phone line and can transfer data at a speed up to 56,000 bps (bits per second).

digital subscriber line (DSL)

- A *digital subscriber line (DSL)* connection also uses a standard phone line, but it can transfer data 20 times faster than a standard dial-up modem.

cable modem

- A *cable modem* uses the cable TV line maintained by the cable company and is generally faster than DSL.

network interface card (NIC)
local area network (LAN)

- A *network interface card (NIC)* is a device that connects a computer to a *local area network (LAN)*, as shown in Figure 1.7. LANs are commonly used in universities, businesses, and government agencies. A high-speed NIC called *1000BaseT* can transfer data at 1,000 *million bits per second (mbps)*.

million bits per second (mbps)

- Wireless networking is now extremely popular in homes, businesses, and schools. Every laptop computer sold today is equipped with a wireless adapter that enables the computer to connect to a local area network and the Internet.

Note

Answers to checkpoint questions are on the Companion Website.

Check Point

1.1 What are hardware and software?

MyProgrammingLab™   **1.2** List five major hardware components of a computer.

1.3 What does the acronym "CPU" stand for?

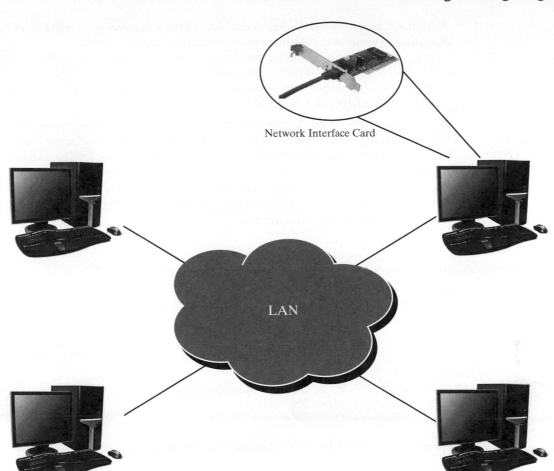

Network Interface Card

FIGURE 1.7 A local area network connects computers in close proximity to each other.

1.4   What unit is used to measure CPU speed?

1.5   What is a bit? What is a byte?

1.6   What is memory for? What does RAM stand for? Why is memory called RAM?

1.7   What unit is used to measure memory size?

1.8   What unit is used to measure disk size?

1.9   What is the primary difference between memory and a storage device?

1.3 Programming Languages

Computer programs, *known as* software, *are instructions that tell a computer what to do.*

Key Point

Computers do not understand human languages, so programs must be written in a language a computer can use. There are hundreds of programming languages, and they were developed to make the programming process easier for people. However, all programs must be converted into a language the computer can understand.

1.3.1 Machine Language

A computer's native language, which differs among different types of computers, is its *machine language*—a set of built-in primitive instructions. These instructions are in the form of binary code, so if you want to give a computer an instruction in its native language, you have to enter

machine language

the instruction as binary code. For example, to add two numbers, you might have to write an instruction in binary code, like this:

1101101010011010

1.3.2 Assembly Language

assembly language

Programming in machine language is a tedious process. Moreover, programs written in machine language are very difficult to read and modify. For this reason, *assembly language* was created in the early days of computing as an alternative to machine languages. Assembly language uses a short descriptive word, known as *mnemonic*, to represent each of the machine-language instructions. For example, the mnemonic **add** typically means to add numbers and **sub** means to subtract numbers. To add the numbers **2** and **3** and get the result, you might write an instruction in assembly code like this:

```
add 2, 3, result
```

assembler

Assembly languages were developed to make programming easier. However, because the computer cannot understand assembly language, another program—called an *assembler*—is used to translate assembly-language programs into machine code, as shown in Figure 1.8.

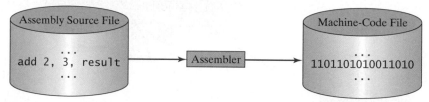

FIGURE 1.8 An assembler translates assembly-language instructions into machine code.

low-level language

Writing code in assembly language is easier than in machine language. However, it is still tedious to write code in assembly language. An instruction in assembly language essentially corresponds to an instruction in machine code. Writing in assembly requires that you know how the CPU works. Assembly language is referred to as a *low-level language*, because assembly language is close in nature to machine language and is machine dependent.

1.3.3 High-Level Language

high-level language

In the 1950s, a new generation of programming languages known as *high-level languages* emerged. They are platform-independent, which means that you can write a program in a high-level language and run it in different types of machines. High-level languages are English-like and easy to learn and use. The instructions in a high-level programming language are called *statements*. Here, for example, is a high-level language statement that computes the area of a circle with a radius of **5**:

statement

```
area = 5 * 5 * 3.1415
```

There are many high-level programming languages, and each was designed for a specific purpose. Table 1.1 lists some popular ones.

source program
source code

A program written in a high-level language is called a *source program* or *source code*. Because a computer cannot understand a source program, a source program must be translated into machine code for execution. The translation can be done using another programming tool called an *interpreter* or a *compiler*.

interpreter
compiler

- An interpreter reads one statement from the source code, translates it to the machine code or virtual machine code, and then executes it right away, as shown in Figure 1.9a.

TABLE 1.1 Popular High-Level Programming Languages

Language	Description
Ada	Named for Ada Lovelace, who worked on mechanical general-purpose computers. The Ada language was developed for the Department of Defense and is used mainly in defense projects.
BASIC	Beginner's All-purpose Symbolic Instruction Code. It was designed to be learned and used easily by beginners.
C	Developed at Bell Laboratories. C combines the power of an assembly language with the ease of use and portability of a high-level language.
C++	C++ is an object-oriented language, based on C.
C#	Pronounced "C Sharp." It is a hybrid of Java and C++ and was developed by Microsoft.
COBOL	COmmon Business Oriented Language. Used for business applications.
FORTRAN	FORmula TRANslation. Popular for scientific and mathematical applications.
Java	Developed by Sun Microsystems, now part of Oracle. It is widely used for developing platform-independent Internet applications.
Pascal	Named for Blaise Pascal, who pioneered calculating machines in the seventeenth century. It is a simple, structured, general-purpose language primarily for teaching programming.
Python	A simple general-purpose scripting language good for writing short programs.
Visual Basic	Visual Basic was developed by Microsoft and it enables the programmers to rapidly develop Windows-based applications.

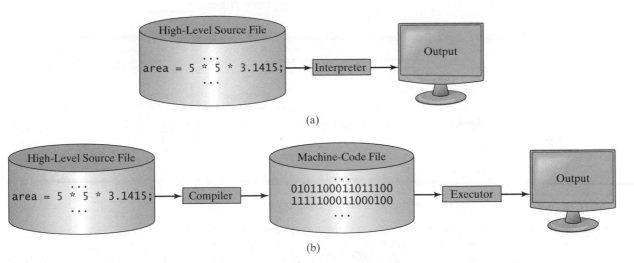

FIGURE 1.9 (a) An interpreter translates and executes a program one statement at a time. (b) A compiler translates the entire source program into a machine-language file for execution.

Note that a statement from the source code may be translated into several machine instructions.

■ A compiler translates the entire source code into a machine-code file, and the machine code file is then executed, as shown in Figure 1.9b.

Python code is executed using an interpreter. Most other programming languages are processed using a compiler.

1.10 What language does the CPU understand?

1.11 What is an assembly language?

✓Check
Point

MyProgrammingLab™

1.12 What is an assembler?

1.13 What is a high-level programming language?

1.14 What is a source program?

1.15 What is an interpreter?

1.16 What is a compiler?

1.17 What is the difference between an interpreted language and a compiled language?

1.4 Operating Systems

Key Point

The operating system (OS) *is the most important program that runs on a computer. The OS manages and controls a computer's activities.*

operating system (OS)

The popular operating systems for general-purpose computers are Microsoft Windows, Mac OS, and Linux. Application programs, such as a Web browser or a word processor, cannot run unless an operating system is installed and running on the computer. Figure 1.10 shows the interrelationship of hardware, operating system, application software, and the user.

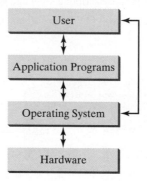

FIGURE 1.10 Users and applications access the computer's hardware via the operating system.

The major tasks of an operating system are:

■ Controlling and monitoring system activities

■ Allocating and assigning system resources

■ Scheduling operations

1.4.1 Controlling and Monitoring System Activities

Operating systems perform basic tasks, such as recognizing input from the keyboard, sending output to the monitor, keeping track of files and folders on storage devices, and controlling peripheral devices, such as disk drives and printers. An operating system must also ensure that different programs and users working at the same time do not interfere with each other. In addition, the OS is responsible for security, ensuring that unauthorized users and programs do not access the system.

1.4.2 Allocating and Assigning System Resources

The operating system is responsible for determining what computer resources a program needs (such as CPU time, memory space, disks, input and output devices) and for allocating and assigning them to run the program.

1.4.3 Scheduling Operations

The OS is responsible for scheduling programs' activities to make efficient use of system resources. Many of today's operating systems support such techniques as *multiprogramming*, *multithreading*, and *multiprocessing* to increase system performance.

Multiprogramming allows multiple programs to run simultaneously by sharing the same CPU. The CPU is much faster than the computer's other components. As a result, it is idle most of the time—for example, while waiting for data to be transferred from a disk or waiting for other system resources to respond. A multiprogramming OS takes advantage of this situation by allowing multiple programs to use the CPU when it would otherwise be idle. For example, multiprogramming enables you to use a word processor to edit a file at the same time as your Web browser is downloading a file.

Multithreading allows a single program to execute multiple tasks at the same time. For instance, a word-processing program allows users to simultaneously edit text and save it to a disk. In this example, editing and saving are two tasks within the same application. These two tasks may run concurrently.

Multiprocessing, or *parallel processing*, uses two or more processors together to perform subtasks concurrently and then combine solutions of the subtasks to obtain a solution for the entire task. It is like a surgical operation where several doctors work together on one patient.

multiprogramming

multithreading

multiprocessing

1.18 What is an operating system? List some popular operating systems.

1.19 What are the major responsibilities of an operating system?

1.20 What are multiprogramming, multithreading, and multiprocessing?

MyProgrammingLab™

1.5 The History of Python

Python is a general-purpose, interpreted, object-oriented programming language.

Python was created by Guido van Rossum in the Netherlands in 1990 and was named after the popular British comedy troupe *Monty Python's Flying Circus*. Van Rossum developed Python as a hobby, and Python has become a popular programming language widely used in industry and academia due to its simple, concise, and intuitive syntax and extensive library.

Python is a *general-purpose programming language*. That means you can use Python to write code for any programming task. Python is now used in the Google search engine, in mission-critical projects at NASA, and in transaction processing at the New York Stock Exchange.

Python is *interpreted*, which means that Python code is translated and executed by an interpreter, one statement at a time, as described earlier in the chapter.

Python is an *object-oriented programming (OOP)* language. Data in Python are objects created from classes. A *class* is essentially a type or category that defines objects of the same kind with properties and methods for manipulating objects. Object-oriented programming is a powerful tool for developing reusable software. Object-oriented programming in Python will be covered in detail starting in Chapter 7.

Python is now being developed and maintained by a large team of volunteers and is available for free from the Python Software Foundation. Two versions of Python are currently coexistent: Python 2 and Python 3. The programs written in Python 3 will not run in Python 2. Python 3 is a newer version, but it is not backward-compatible with Python 2. This means that if you write a program using the Python 2 syntax, it may not work with a Python 3 interpreter. Python provides a tool that automatically converts code written in Python 2 into syntax Python 3 can use. Python 2 will eventually be replaced by Python 3. This book teaches programming using Python 3.

general-purpose
   programming language

interpreted

object-oriented programming
   (OOP)

Python 2 vs. Python 3

MyProgrammingLab

1.21 Python is interpreted. What does that mean?

1.22 Can a program written in Python 2 run in Python 3?

1.23 Can a program written using Python 3 run in Python 2?

1.6 Getting Started with Python

A Python program is executed from the Python interpreter.

Key Point

Let's get started by writing a simple Python program that displays the messages **Welcome to Python** and **Python is fun** on the console. The word *console* is an old computer term that refers to the text entry and display device of a computer. Console input means to receive input from the keyboard and console output means to display output to the monitor.

console

console input

console output

Note

You can run Python on the Windows, UNIX, and Mac operating systems. For information on *installing Python*, see Supplement I.B, Installing and Using Python, on the Companion Website.

install Python

VideoNote

Start with Python

IDLE

1.6.1 Launching Python

Assume you have Python installed on the Windows OS. You can start Python in a command window by typing **python** at the command prompt, as shown in Figure 1.11, or by using IDLE, as shown in Figure 1.12. *IDLE* (*I*nteractive *DeveLopment Environment*) is an integrated development environment (IDE) for Python. You can create, open, save, edit, and run Python programs in IDLE. Both the command-line Python interpreter and IDLE are available after Python is installed on your machine. Note that Python (command line)

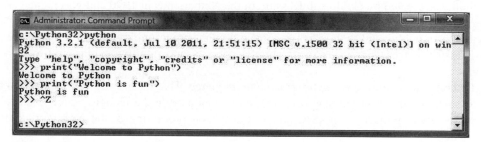

FIGURE 1.11 You can launch Python from the command window.

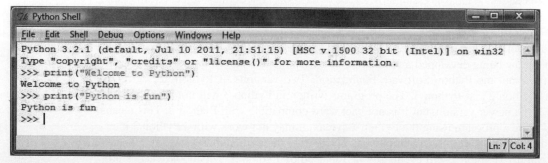

FIGURE 1.12 You can use Python from IDLE.

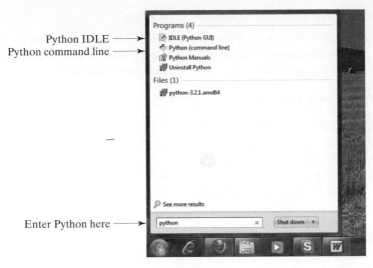

Python IDLE ⟶
Python command line ⟶

Enter Python here ⟶

FIGURE 1.13 You can launch the Python IDLE and command line from the Start button.

and IDLE can also be accessed directly from the Windows *Start* button by searching for **Python (command line)** or **IDLE (Python GUI)** on Windows 7 or Vista, as shown in Figure 1.13.

After Python starts, you will see the symbol >>>. This is the *Python statement prompt*, and it is where you can enter a Python statement.

Python statement prompt >>>

Note

Type the commands *exactly* as they are written in this text. Formatting and other rules will be discussed later in this chapter.

Now, type **print("Welcome to Python")** and press the *Enter* key. The string **Welcome to Python** appears on the console, as shown in Figure 1.11. *String* is a programming term meaning a sequence of characters.

string

Note

Note that Python requires double or single quotation marks around strings to delineate them from other code. As you can see in the output, Python doesn't display those quotation marks.

The **print** statement is one of Python's built-in *functions* that can be used to display a string on the console. A function performs actions. In the case of the **print** function, it displays a message to the console.

function

Note

In programming terminology, when you use a function, you are said to be *"invoking a function"* or *"calling a function."*

invoking a function
calling a function

Next, type **print("Python is fun")** and press the *Enter* key. The string **Python is fun** appears on the console, as shown in Figure 1.11. You can enter additional statements at the statement prompt >>>.

Note

To exit Python, press *CTRL+Z* and then the *Enter* key.

1.6.2 Creating Python Source Code Files

Entering Python statements at the statement prompt >>> is convenient, but the statements are not saved. To save statements for later use, you can create a text file to store the statements and use the following command to execute the statements in the file:

python *filename*.py

source file
script file
module
.py file
script mode
interactive mode

The text file can be created using a text editor such as Notepad. The text file, *filename*, is called a Python *source file* or *script file*, or *module*. By convention, Python files are named with the extension **.py**.

Running a Python program from a script file is known as running Python in *script mode*. Typing a statement at the statement prompt >>> and executing it is called running Python in *interactive mode*.

Note

Besides developing and running Python programs from the command window, you can create, save, modify, and run a Python script from IDLE. For information on using IDLE, see Supplement I.C on the Companion Website. Your instructor may also ask you to use Eclipse. Eclipse is a popular interactive development environment (IDE) used to develop programs quickly. Editing, running, debugging, and online help are integrated in one graphical user interface. If you want to develop Python programs using Eclipse, see Supplement I.D, on the Companion Website.

Python on Eclipse

Listing 1.1 shows you a Python program that displays the messages **Welcome to Python** and **Python is fun**.

LISTING 1.1 Welcome.py

comment
print a message

```
1  # Display two messages
2  print("Welcome to Python")
3  print("Python is fun")
```

line numbers

In this text, *line numbers* are displayed for reference purposes; they are not part of the program. So, don't type line numbers in your program.

execute the program

Suppose the statements are saved in a file named Welcome.py. To run the program, enter **python Welcome.py** at the command prompt, as shown in Figure 1.14.

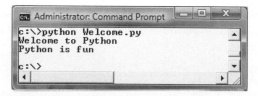

FIGURE 1.14 You can run a Python script file from a command window.

comment

In Listing 1.1, line 1 is a *comment* that documents what the program is and how it is constructed. Comments help programmers communicate and understand a program. They are not programming statements and thus are ignored by the interpreter. In Python, comments are preceded by a pound sign (#) on a line, called a *line comment*, or enclosed between three consecutive single quotation marks (' ' ') on one or several lines, called a *paragraph comment*.

line comment
paragraph comment

When the Python interpreter sees #, it ignores all text after # on the same line. When it sees ''', it scans for the next ''' and ignores any text between the triple quotation marks. Here are examples of comments:

```
# This program displays Welcome to Python

''' This program displays Welcome to Python and
    Python is fun
'''
```

Indentation matters in Python. Note that the statements are entered from the first column in the new line. The Python interpreter will report an error if the program is typed as follows:

indentation

```
# Display two messages
   print("Welcome to Python")
print("Python is fun")
```

Don't put any punctuation at the end of a statement. For example, the Python interpreter will report errors for the following code:

```
# Display two messages
print("Welcome to Python").
print("Python is fun"),
```

Python programs are *case sensitive*. It would be wrong, for example, to replace **print** in the program with **Print**.

case sensitive

You have seen several *special characters* (#, ", ()) in the program. They are used in almost every program. Table 1.2 summarizes their uses.

special characters

TABLE 1.2 Special Characters

Character	Name	Description
()	Opening and closing parentheses	Used with functions.
#	Pound sign	Precedes a comment line.
" "	Opening and closing quotation marks	Encloses a string (i.e., sequence of characters).
''' '''	Paragraph comments	Encloses a paragraph comment.

The program in Listing 1.1 displays two messages. Once you understand the program, it is easy to extend it to display more messages. For example, you can rewrite the program to display three messages, as shown in Listing 1.2.

LISTING 1.2 WelcomeWithThreeMessages.py

```
1  # Display three messages
2  print("Welcome to Python")
3  print("Python is fun")
4  print("Problem Driven")
```

comment
print statement

```
Welcome to Python
Python is fun
Problem Driven
```

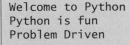

1.6.3 Using Python to Perform Mathematical Computations

Python programs can perform all sorts of mathematical computations and display the result. To display the addition, subtraction, multiplication, and division of two numbers, x and y, use the following code:

```
print(x + y)
print(x - y)
print(x * y)
print(x / y)
```

Listing 1.3 shows an example of a program that evaluates $\dfrac{10.5 + 2 \times 3}{45 - 3.5}$ and prints its result.

LISTING 1.3 ComputeExpression.py

comment
compute expression

```
1  # Compute expression
2  print((10.5 + 2 * 3) / (45 - 3.5))
```

```
0.397590361446
```

As you can see, it is a straightforward process to translate an arithmetic expression to a Python expression. We will discuss Python expressions further in Chapter 2.

MyProgrammingLab™

1.24 You can run Python in two modes. Explain these two modes.

1.25 Is Python case sensitive?

1.26 What is the Python source filename extension by convention?

1.27 What is the command to run a Python source file?

1.28 What is a comment? How do you denote a comment line and a comment paragraph?

1.29 What is the statement to display the message `Hello world` on the console?

1.30 Identify and fix the errors in the following code:

```
1  # Display two messages
2    print("Welcome to Python")
3  print("Python is fun").
```

1.31 Show the output of the following code:

```
print("3.5 * 4 / 2 - 2.5 is")
print(3.5 * 4 / 2 - 2.5)
```

1.7 Programming Style and Documentation

Good programming style and proper documentation make a program easy to read and prevents errors.

programming style

Programming style deals with what programs look like. When you create programs with a professional programming style, they not only execute properly but are easy for people to read and understand. This is very important if other programmers will access or modify your programs.

documentation

   Documentation is the body of explanatory remarks and comments pertaining to a program. These remarks and comments explain various parts of the program and help others understand its structure and function. As you saw earlier in the chapter, remarks and comments are embedded within the program itself; Python's interpreter simply ignores them when the program is executed.

Programming style and documentation are as important as coding. Here are a few guidelines.

1.7.1 Appropriate Comments and Comment Styles

Include a summary comment at the beginning of the program to explain what the program does, its key features, and any unique techniques it uses. In a long program, you should also include comments that introduce each major step and explain anything that is difficult to read. It is important to make comments concise so that they do not crowd the program or make it difficult to read.

1.7.2 Proper Spacing

A consistent spacing style makes programs clear and easy to read, debug (find and fix errors), and maintain.

A single space should be added on both sides of an operator, as shown in the following statement:

```
print(3+4*4)
```
◄──── Bad style

```
print(3 + 4 * 4)
```
◄──── Good style

More detailed guidelines can be found in Supplement I.F, Python Coding Style Guidelines, on the Companion Website.

1.8 Programming Errors

Programming errors can be categorized into three types: syntax errors, runtime errors, *and* logic errors.

Key Point

1.8.1 Syntax Errors

The most *common error* you will encounter are syntax errors. Like any programming language, Python has its own syntax, and you need to write code that obeys the *syntax rules*. If your program violates the rules—for example, if a quotation mark is missing or a word is misspelled—Python will report syntax errors.

common errors
syntax rules

Syntax errors result from errors in code construction, such as mistyping a statement, incorrect indentation, omitting some necessary punctuation, or using an opening parenthesis without a corresponding closing parenthesis. These errors are usually easy to detect, because Python tells you where they are and what caused them. For example, the following **print** statement has a syntax error:

syntax errors

```
>>> print("Programming is fun)
  File "<stdin>", line 1
    print("Programming is fun)
                              ^
SyntaxError: EOL while scanning string literal
>>>
```

The string **Programming is fun** should be closed with a closing quotation mark.

fix syntax errors

> **Tip**
> If you don't know how to correct a syntax error, compare your program closely, character by character, with similar examples in the text. In the first few weeks of this course, you will probably spend a lot of time fixing syntax errors. Soon, you will be familiar with Python syntax and will be able to fix syntax errors quickly.

1.8.2 Runtime Errors

runtime errors

input errors

Runtime errors are errors that cause a program to terminate abnormally. They occur while a program is running if the Python interpreter detects an operation that is impossible to carry out. Input mistakes typically cause runtime errors. An *input error* occurs when the user enters a value that the program cannot handle. For instance, if the program expects to read in a number, but instead the user enters a string of text, this causes data-type errors to occur in the program.

Another common source of runtime errors is division by zero. This happens when the divisor is zero for integer divisions. For example, the expression 1 / 0 in the following statement would cause a runtime error.

1.8.3 Logic Errors

logic errors

Logic errors occur when a program does not perform the way it was intended to. Errors of this kind occur for many different reasons. For example, suppose you wrote the program in Listing 1.4 to convert a temperature (35 degrees) from Fahrenheit to Celsius.

LISTING 1.4 ShowLogicErrors.py

```
1  # Convert Fahrenheit to Celsius
2  print("Fahrenheit 35 is Celsius degree ")
3  print(5 / 9 * 35 - 32)
```

```
Fahrenheit 35 is Celsius degree
-12.555555555555554
```

You will get Celsius −12.55 degrees, which is wrong. It should be 1.66. To get the correct result, you need to use 5 / 9 * (35 − 32) rather than 5 / 9 * 35 − 32 in the expression. That is, you need to add parentheses around (35 − 32) so Python will calculate that expression first before doing the division.

In Python, syntax errors are actually treated like runtime errors because they are detected by the interpreter when the program is executed. In general, syntax and runtime errors are easy to find and easy to correct, because Python gives indications as to where the errors came from and why they are wrong. Finding logic errors, on the other hand, can be very challenging.

1.32 What are three kinds of program errors?

1.33 If you forget to put a closing quotation mark on a string, what kind of error will be raised?

1.34 If your program needs to read data from a file, but the file does not exist, an error would occur when running this program. What kind of error is this?

1.35 Suppose you write a program for computing the perimeter of a rectangle and you mistakenly write your program so that it computes the area of a rectangle. What kind of error is this?

Check
Point

MyProgrammingLab

1.9 Getting Started with Graphics Programming

Turtle is Python's built-in graphics module for drawing lines, circles, and other shapes, including text. It is easy to learn and simple to use.

Key
Point

Beginners often enjoy learning programming by using graphics. For this reason, we provide a section on graphics programming at the end of most of the chapters in the first part of the book. However, these materials are not mandatory. They can be skipped or covered later.

There are many ways to write graphics programs in Python. A simple way to start graphics programming is to use Python's built-in **turtle** module. Later in the book, we will introduce *Tkinter* for developing comprehensive graphical user interface applications.

turtle
Tkinter

1.9.1 Drawing and Adding Color to a Figure

The following procedure will give you a basic introduction to using the **turtle** module. Subsequent chapters introduce more features.

1. Launch Python by choosing **Python** (command line) from the Windows *Start* button or by typing **python** at the command prompt.

2. At the Python statement prompt >>>, type the following command to import the **turtle** module. This command imports all functions defined in the **turtle** module and makes them available for you to use.

   ```
   >>> import turtle # Import turtle module
   ```

3. Type the following command to show the current location and direction of the turtle, as shown in Figure 1.15a.

   ```
   >>> turtle.showturtle()
   ```

   Graphics programming using the Python Turtle module is like drawing with a pen. The arrowhead indicates the current position and direction of the pen. **turtle** is initially positioned at the center of the window. Here, **turtle** refers to the object for drawing graphics (objects will be introduced in Chapter 3).

4. Type the following command to draw a text string:

   ```
   >>> turtle.write("Welcome to Python")
   ```

   Your window should look like the one shown in Figure 1.15b.

5. Type the following command to move the arrowhead **100** pixels forward to draw a line in the direction the arrow is pointing:

   ```
   >>> turtle.forward(100)
   ```

   Your window should now look like the one shown in Figure 1.15c.

   To draw the rest of Figure 1.15, continue with these steps.

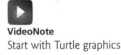

VideoNote
Start with Turtle graphics

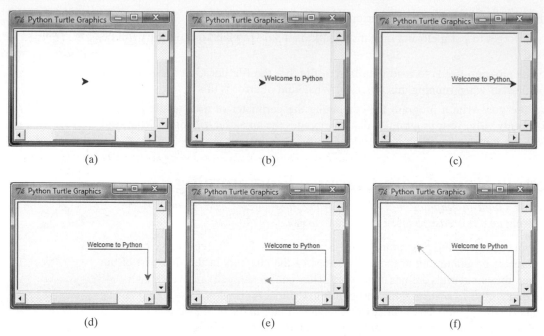

FIGURE 1.15 Graphics are dynamically displayed with each statement.

6. Type the following commands to turn the arrowhead right **90** degrees, change the **turtle**'s color to red, and move the arrowhead **50** pixels forward to draw a line, as shown in Figure 1.15d:

```
>>> turtle.right(90)
>>> turtle.color("red")
>>> turtle.forward(50)
```

7. Now, type the following commands to turn the arrowhead right **90** degrees, set the color to green, and move the arrowhead **100** pixels forward to draw a line, as shown in Figure 1.15e:

```
>>> turtle.right(90)
>>> turtle.color("green")
>>> turtle.forward(100)
```

8. Finally, type the following commands to turn the arrowhead right **45** degrees and move it **80** pixels forward to draw a line, as shown in Figure 1.15f:

```
>>> turtle.right(45)
>>> turtle.forward(80)
```

9. You can now close the Turtle Graphics window and exit Python.

1.9.2 Moving the Pen to Any Location

When the Turtle program starts, the arrowhead is at the center of the Python Turtle Graphics window at the coordinates (**0, 0**), as shown in Figure 1.16a. You can also use the **goto(x, y)** command to move the **turtle** to any specified point (**x, y**).

Restart Python and type the following command to move the pen to (**0, 50**) from (**0, 0**), as shown in Figure 1.16b.

```
>>> import turtle
>>> turtle.goto(0, 50)
```

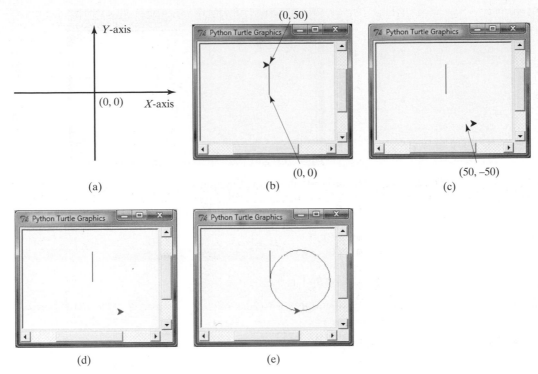

FIGURE 1.16 (a) The center of the Turtle Graphics window is at the coordinates (0, 0). (b) Move to (0, 50). (c) Move the pen to (50, –50). (d) Set color to red. (e) Draw a circle using the `circle` command.

You can also lift the pen up or put it down to control whether to draw a line when the pen is moved by using the **penup()** and **pendown()** commands. For example, the following commands move the pen to (**50, -50**), as shown in Figure 1.16c.

```
>>> turtle.penup()
>>> turtle.goto(50, -50)
>>> turtle.pendown()
```

You can draw a circle using the **circle** command. For example, the following commands set color red (Figure 1.16d) and draw a circle with radius **50** (Figure 1.16e).

```
>>> turtle.color("red")
>>> turtle.circle(50) # Draw a circle with radius 50
```

1.9.3 Drawing the Olympic Rings Logo

Listing 1.5 shows a program for drawing the Olympics rings logo, as shown in Figure 1.17.

LISTING 1.5 OlympicSymbol.py

```
1  import turtle
2
3  turtle.color("blue")                              draw blue circle
4  turtle.penup()
5  turtle.goto(-110, -25)
6  turtle.pendown()
7  turtle.circle(45)
8
9  turtle.color("black")                             draw black circle
```

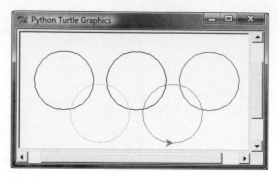

FIGURE 1.17 The program draws the Olympics rings logo.

```
10  turtle.penup()
11  turtle.goto(0, -25)
12  turtle.pendown()
13  turtle.circle(45)
14
15  turtle.color("red")
16  turtle.penup()
17  turtle.goto(110, -25)
18  turtle.pendown()
19  turtle.circle(45)
20
21  turtle.color("yellow")
22  turtle.penup()
23  turtle.goto(-55, -75)
24  turtle.pendown()
25  turtle.circle(45)
26
27  turtle.color("green")
28  turtle.penup()
29  turtle.goto(55, -75)
30  turtle.pendown()
31  turtle.circle(45)
32
33  turtle.done()
```

draw red circle (line 15)

draw yellow circle (line 21)

draw green circle (line 27)

pause (line 33)

The program imports the **turtle** module to use the Turtle Graphics window (line 1). It moves the pen to $(-110, -25)$ (line 5) and draws a blue circle with radius 45 (line 7). Similarly, it draws a black circle (lines 9–13), a red circle (lines 15–19), a yellow circle (lines 21–25), and a green circle (lines 27–31).

Line 33 invokes **turtle**'s **done()** command, which causes the program to pause until the user closes the Python Turtle Graphics window. The purpose of this is to give the user time to view the graphics. Without this line, the graphics window would be closed right after the program is finished.

Check Point

MyProgrammingLab™

1.36 How do you import the **turtle** module?

1.37 How do you display text in Turtle?

1.38 How do you move the pen forward?

1.39 How do you set a new color?

1.40 How do you move the pen without drawing anything?

1.41 How do you draw a circle?

1.42 What is the purpose of **turtle.done()** in line 33 in Listing 1.5?

KEY TERMS

.py file   16
assembler   10
assembly language   10
bit   4
bus   2
byte   4
cable modem   8
calling a function   15
central processing unit (CPU)   3
comment   16
compiler   10
console   14
dot pitch   8
DSL (digital subscriber line)   8
encoding scheme   4
function   15
hardware   2
high-level language   10
IDLE (Interactive DeveLopment
    Environment)   14
indentation   17
interactive mode   16
interpreter   10
invoking a function   15

line comment   16
logic error   20
low-level language   10
machine language   9
memory   5
modem   8
module   16
motherboard   3
network interface card (NIC)   8
operating system (OS)   12
pixel   8
program   2
runtime errors   20
screen resolution   8
script file   16
script mode   16
software   2
source code   10
source file   16
source program   10
statement   10
storage device   5
syntax errors   19
syntax rules   19

Note

The above terms are defined in the present chapter. Supplement I.A, Glossary, lists
all the key terms and descriptions in the book, organized by chapters.

Supplement I.A

CHAPTER SUMMARY

1. A computer is an electronic device that stores and processes data.

2. A computer includes both *hardware* and *software*.

3. Hardware is the physical aspect of the computer that can be touched.

4. Computer *programs*, known as *software*, are the invisible instructions that control the hardware and make it perform tasks.

5. *Computer programming* is the writing of instructions (i.e., code) for computers to perform.

6. The *central processing unit (CPU)* is a computer's brain. It retrieves instructions from memory and executes them.

7. Computers use zeros and ones because digital devices have two stable electrical states, off and on, referred to by convention as zero and one.

8. A *bit* is a binary digit 0 or 1.

9. A *byte* is a sequence of 8 bits.

10. A kilobyte is about 1,000 bytes, a megabyte about 1 million bytes, a gigabyte about 1 billion bytes, and a terabyte about 1,000 gigabytes.

11. *Memory* stores data and program instructions for the CPU to execute.

12. A *memory unit* is an ordered sequence of bytes.

13. Memory is volatile, because information that hasn't been saved is lost when the power is turned off.

14. Programs and data are permanently stored on *storage devices* and are moved to memory when the computer actually uses them.

15. The *machine language* is a set of primitive instructions built into every computer.

16. *Assembly language* is a low-level programming language in which a mnemonic is used to represent each machine-language instruction.

17. *High-level languages* are English-like and easy to learn and program.

18. A program written in a high-level language is called *source code*.

19. A *compiler* is a software program that translates the *source program* into a *machine-language* program.

20. The *operating system (OS)* is a program that manages and controls a computer's activities.

21. You can run Python on Windows, UNIX, and Mac.

22. Python is *interpreted*, meaning that Python translates each statement and processes it one at a time.

23. You can enter Python statements interactively from the Python statement prompt >>> or store all your code in one file and execute it using one command.

24. To run a Python *source file* from the command line, use the **python** *filename*.**py** command.

25. In Python, *comments* are preceded by a pound sign (#) on a line, called a *line comment*, or enclosed between triple quotation marks (''' and ''') on one or several lines, called a *paragraph comment*.

26. Python *source programs* are case sensitive.

27. Programming errors can be categorized into three types: syntax errors, runtime errors, and logic errors. *Syntax* and *runtime errors* cause a program to terminate abnormally. *Logic errors* occur when a program does not perform the way it was intended to.

TEST QUESTIONS

Do test questions for this chapter online at www.cs.armstrong.edu/liang/py/test.html.

PROGRAMMING EXERCISES

MyProgrammingLab™

 Note

Solutions to even-numbered exercises in this book are on the Companion Website. Solutions to all exercises are on the Instructor Resource Website. The level of difficulty is rated easy (no star), moderate (*), hard (**), or challenging (***).

level of difficulty

Section 1.6

1.1 (*Display three different messages*) Write a program that displays `Welcome to Python`, `Welcome to Computer Science`, and `Programming is fun`.

1.2 (*Display the same message five times*) Write a program that displays `Welcome to Python` five times.

*1.3 (*Display a pattern*) Write a program that displays the following pattern:

```
FFFFFFF   U     U   NN      NN
FF        U     U   NNN     NN
FFFFFFF   U     U   NN N    NN
FF         U   U    NN  N   NN
FF          UUU     NN      NNN
```

1.4 (*Print a table*) Write a program that displays the following table:

```
a      a^2    a^3
1      1      1
2      4      8
3      9      27
4      16     64
```

1.5 (*Compute expressions*) Write a program that displays the result of

$$\frac{9.5 \times 4.5 - 2.5 \times 3}{45.5 - 3.5}$$

1.6 (*Summation of a series*) Write a program that displays the result of $1 + 2 + 3 + 4 + 5 + 6 + 7 + 8 + 9$.

1.7 (*Approximate* π) π can be computed using the following formula:

$$\pi = 4 \times \left(1 - \frac{1}{3} + \frac{1}{5} - \frac{1}{7} + \frac{1}{9} - \frac{1}{11} + \ldots \right)$$

Write a program that displays the result of $4 \times \left(1 - \frac{1}{3} + \frac{1}{5} - \frac{1}{7} + \frac{1}{9} - \frac{1}{11} \right)$.

and $4 \times \left(1 - \frac{1}{3} + \frac{1}{5} - \frac{1}{7} + \frac{1}{9} - \frac{1}{11} + \frac{1}{13} - \frac{1}{15} \right)$.

1.8 (*Area and perimeter of a circle*) Write a program that displays the area and perimeter of a circle that has a radius of **5.5** using the following formulas:

$$area = radius \times radius \times \pi$$
$$perimeter = 2 \times radius \times \pi$$

1.9 (*Area and perimeter of a rectangle*) Write a program that displays the area and perimeter of a rectangle with the width of **4.5** and height of **7.9** using the following formula:

$$area = width \times height$$

1.10 (*Average speed*) Assume a runner runs **14** kilometers in **45** minutes and **30** seconds. Write a program that displays the average speed in miles per hour. (Note that **1** mile is **1.6** kilometers.)

*1.11 (*Population projection*) The US Census Bureau projects population based on the following assumptions:

> One birth every 7 seconds
> One death every 13 seconds
> One new immigrant every 45 seconds

Write a program to display the population for each of the next five years. Assume the current population is 312032486 and one year has 365 days. Hint: in Python, you can use integer division operator **//** to perform division. The result is an integer. For example, **5 // 4** is **1** (not **1.25**) and **10 // 4** is **2** (not **2.5**).

Section 1.9

1.12 (*Turtle: draw four squares*) Write a program that draws four squares in the center of the screen, as shown in Figure 1.18a.

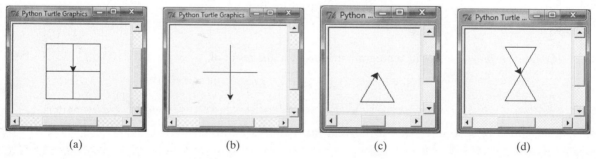

(a)   (b)   (c)   (d)

FIGURE 1.18 Four squares are drawn in (a), a cross is drawn in (b), a triangle is drawn in (c), and two triangles are drawn in (d).

1.13 (*Turtle: draw a cross*) Write a program that draws a cross as shown in Figure 1.18b.

1.14 (*Turtle: draw a triangle*) Write a program that draws a triangle as shown in Figure 1.18c.

1.15 (*Turtle: draw two triangles*) Write a program that draws two triangles as shown in Figure 1.18d.

1.16 (*Turtle: draw four circles*) Write a program that draws four circles in the center of the screen, as shown in Figure 1.19a.

1.17 (*Turtle: draw a line*) Write a program that draws a red line connecting two points (**-39, 48**) and (**50, -50**) and displays the coordinates of the two points, as shown in Figure 1.19b.

**1.18 (*Turtle: draw a star*) Write a program that draws a star, as shown in Figure 1.19c. (Hint: The inner angle of each point in the star is 36 degrees.)

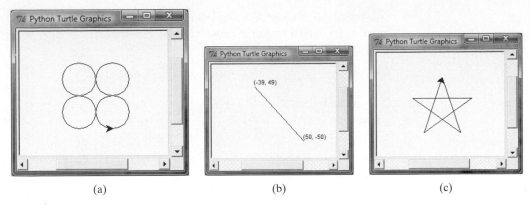

(a)   (b)   (c)

Figure 1.19 Four circles are drawn in (a), a line is drawn in (b), and a star is drawn in (c).

1.19 (*Turtle: draw a polygon*) Write a program that draws a polygon that connects the points (**40**, **-69.28**), (**-40**, **-69.28**), (**-80**, **-9.8**), (**-40**, **69**), (**40**, **69**), and (**80**, **0**) in this order, as shown in Figure 1.20a.

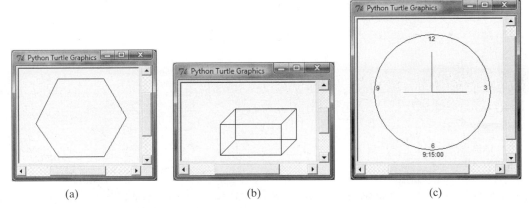

(a)   (b)   (c)

Figure 1.20 (a) The program displays a polygon. (b) The program displays a rectanguloid. (c) The program displays a clock for the time.

1.20 (*Turtle: display a rectanguloid*) Write a program that displays a rectanguloid, as shown in Figure 1.20b.

*__1.21__ (*Turtle: display a clock*) Write a program that displays a clock to show the time 9:15:00, as shown in Figure 1.20c.

CHAPTER

2

ELEMENTARY PROGRAMMING

Objectives

- To write programs that perform simple computations (§2.2).

- To obtain input from a program's user by using the **input** function (§2.3).

- To use identifiers to name elements such as variables and functions (§2.4).

- To assign data to variables (§2.5).

- To perform simultaneous assignment (§2.6).

- To define named constants (§2.7).

- To use the operators +, -, *, /, //, %, and ** (§2.8).

- To write and evaluate numeric expressions (§2.9).

- To use augmented assignment operators to simplify coding (§2.10).

- To perform numeric type conversion and rounding with the **int** and **round** functions (§2.11).

- To obtain the current system time by using **time.time()** (§2.12).

- To describe the software development process and apply it to develop a loan payment program (§2.13).

- To compute and display the distance between two points in graphics (§2.14).

2.1 Introduction

 Key Point

The focus of this chapter is on learning elementary programming techniques to solve problems.

In Chapter 1 you learned how to create and run very basic Python programs. Now you will learn how to solve problems by writing programs. Through these problems, you will learn fundamental programming techniques, such as the use of variables, operators, expressions, and input and output.

Suppose, for example, that you need to take out a student loan. Given the loan amount, loan term, and annual interest rate, can you write a program to compute the monthly payment and total payment? This chapter shows you how to write programs like this. Along the way, you learn the basic steps that go into analyzing a problem, designing a solution, and implementing the solution by creating a program.

2.2 Writing a Simple Program

 Key Point

Writing a program involves designing a strategy for solving the problem and then using a programming language to implement that strategy.

problem

Let's first consider the simple *problem* of computing the area of a circle. How do we write a program for solving this problem?

algorithm

Writing a program involves designing algorithms and then translating them into programming instructions, or code. When you *code*—that is, when you write a program—you translate an algorithm into a program. An *algorithm* describes how a problem is solved by listing the actions that need to be taken and the order of their execution. Algorithms can help the programmer plan a program before writing it in a programming language. Algorithms can be

pseudocode

described in natural languages or in *pseudocode* (natural language mixed with some programming code). The algorithm for calculating the area of a circle can be described as follows:

1. Get the circle's radius from the user.

2. Compute the area by applying the following formula:

$$area = radius \times radius \times \pi$$

3. Display the result.

 Tip
It's always good practice to outline your program (or its underlying problem) in the form of an algorithm before you begin coding.

In this problem, the program needs to read the radius, which the program's user enters from the keyboard. This raises two important issues:

- Reading the radius.

- Storing the radius in the program.

variable

Let's address the second issue first. The value for the radius is stored in the computer's memory. In order to access it, the program needs to use a *variable*. A variable is a name that references a value stored in the computer's memory. Rather than using **x** and **y** as variable names, choose *descriptive names*: in this case, for example, you can use the name

descriptive names

radius for the variable that references a value for radius and **area** for the variable that references a value for area.

The first step is to prompt the user to designate the circle's **radius**. You will learn how to prompt the user for information shortly. For now, to learn how variables work, you can assign a fixed value to **radius** in the program as you write the code.

The second step is to compute **area** by assigning the result of the expression **radius** *****
radius ***** **3.14159** to **area**.

In the final step, the program will display the value of **area** on the console by using
Python's **print** function.

The complete program is shown in Listing 2.1.

LISTING 2.1 ComputeArea.py

```
1  # Assign a value to radius
2  radius = 20 # radius is now 20          radius  ──►  20
3
4  # Compute area
5  area = radius * radius * 3.14159         area  ──►  1256.636
6
7  # Display results
8  print("The area for the circle of radius", radius, "is", area)
```

display result

```
The area for the circle of radius 20 is 1256.636
```

Variables such as **radius** and **area** reference values stored in memory. Every variable has
a name that refers to a value. You can *assign a value* to a variable using the syntax as shown
in line 2.

assign value

```
radius = 20
```

This statement assigns **20** to the variable **radius**. So now **radius** references the value
20. The statement in line 5

```
area = radius * radius * 3.14159
```

uses the value in **radius** to compute the expression and assigns the result into the variable
area. The following table shows the value for **radius** and **area** as the program is executed.
Each row in the table shows the values of variables after the statement in the corresponding
line in the program is executed. This method of reviewing how a program works is called
tracing a program. Tracing programs are helpful for understanding how programs work, and
they are useful tools for finding errors in programs.

trace a program

line#	radius	area
2	20	
5		1256.636

If you have programmed in other languages, such as Java, you know you have to declare a
variable with a *data type* to specify what type of values are being used, such as integers or text
characters. You don't do this in Python, however, because Python automatically figures out
the data type according to the value assigned to the variable.

data type

The statement in line 8 displays four items on the console. You can display any number of
items in a **print** statement using the following syntax:

```
print(item1, item2, ..., itemk)
```

print(item1, ...)

If an item is a number, the number is automatically converted to a string for displaying.

2.1 Show the printout of the following code:

```
width = 5.5
height = 2
print("area is", width * height)
```

2.2 Translate the following algorithm into Python code:

■ Step 1: Use a variable named **miles** with initial value **100**.

■ Step 2: Multiply miles by **1.609** and assign it to a variable named **kilometers**.

■ Step 3: Display the value of **kilometers**.

What is **kilometers** after Step 3?

2.3 Reading Input from the Console

Key
Point

Reading input from the console enables the program to accept input from the user.

In Listing 2.1, a radius is set in the source code. To use a different radius, you have to modify the source code. You can use the **input** function to ask the user to input a value for the radius. The following statement prompts the user to enter a value, and then it assigns the value to the variable:

```
variable = input("Enter a value: ")
```

eval function

The value entered is a string. You can use the function **eval** to evaluate and convert it to a numeric value. For example, **eval("34.5")** returns **34.5**, **eval("345")** returns **345**, **eval("3 + 4")** returns 7, and **eval("51 + (54 * (3 + 2))")** returns **321**.

Listing 2.2 rewrites Listing 2.1 to prompt the user to enter a radius.

LISTING 2.2 ComputeAreaWithConsoleInput.py

input radius

compute area

display result

```
1  # Prompt the user to enter a radius
2  radius = eval(input("Enter a value for radius: "))
3
4  # Compute area
5  area = radius * radius * 3.14159
6
7  # Display results
8  print("The area for the circle of radius", radius, "is", area)
```

```
Enter a value for radius: 2.5 ⏎Enter
The area for the circle of radius 2.5 is 19.6349375
```

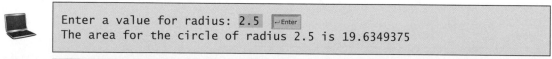

```
Enter a value for radius: 23 ⏎Enter
The area for the circle of radius 23 is 1661.90111
```

Line 2 prompts the user to enter a value (in the form of a string) and converts it to a number, which is equivalent to

```
s = input("Enter a value for radius: ")  # Read input as a string
radius = eval(s) # Convert the string to a number
```

After the user enters a number and presses the *Enter* key, the number is read and assigned to **radius**.

Listing 2.2 shows how to prompt the user for a single input. However, you can prompt for multiple inputs as well. Listing 2.3 gives an example of reading multiple inputs from the keyboard. This program reads three integers and displays their average.

LISTING 2.3 ComputeAverage.py

```
1   # Prompt the user to enter three numbers
2   number1 = eval(input("Enter the first number: "))
3   number2 = eval(input("Enter the second number: "))
4   number3 = eval(input("Enter the third number: "))
5
6   # Compute average
7   average = (number1 + number2 + number3) / 3
8
9   # Display result
10  print("The average of", number1, number2, number3,
11      "is", average)
```

input number1
input number2
input number3

```
Enter the first number: 1  ↵Enter
Enter the second number: 2  ↵Enter
Enter the third number: 3  ↵Enter
The average of 1  2  3 is 2.0
```

The program prompts the user to enter three integers (lines 2–4), computes their average (line 7), and displays the result (lines 10–11).

If the user enters something other than a number, the program will terminate with a *runtime error*. In Chapter 13, you will learn how to handle the error so that the program can continue to run.

runtime error

Normally a statement ends at the end of the line. In the preceding listing, the **print** statement is split into two lines (lines 10–11). This is okay, because Python scans the print statement in line 10 and knows it is not finished until it finds the closing parenthesis in line 11. We say that these two lines are *joined implicitly*.

joining lines explicitly

Note

In some cases, the Python interpreter cannot determine the end of the statement written in multiple lines. You can place the *line continuation symbol* (\) at the end of a line to tell the interpreter that the statement is continued on the next line. For example, the following statement

line continuation symbol

```
sum = 1 + 2 + 3 + 4 + \
      5 + 6
```

is equivalent to

```
sum = 1 + 2 + 3 + 4 + 5 + 6
```

split a long statement

Note

Most of the programs in early chapters of this book perform three steps: Input, Process, and Output, called *IPO*. Input is to receive input from the user. Process is to produce results using the input. Output is to display the results.

IPO

2.3 How do you write a statement to prompt the user to enter a numeric value?

2.4 What happens if the user enters **5a** when executing the following code?
```
radius = eval(input("Enter a radius: "))
```

2.5 How do you break a long statement into multiple lines?

✓**Check Point**

MyProgrammingLab™

2.4 Identifiers

Identifiers are the names that identify the elements such as variables and functions in a program.

identifiers

As you can see in Listing 2.3, **number1**, **number2**, **number3**, **average**, **input**, **eval**, and **print** are the names of things that appear in the program. In programming terminology, such names are called *identifiers*. All identifiers must obey the following rules:

identifier naming rules

- An identifier is a sequence of characters that consists of letters, digits, and underscores (_).

- An identifier must start with a letter or an underscore. It cannot start with a digit.

keyword
reserved word

- An identifier cannot be a keyword. (See Appendix A, Python Keywords, for a list of keywords.) *Keywords*, also called *reserved words*, have special meanings in Python. For example, **import** is a keyword, which tells the Python interpreter to import a module to the program.

- An identifier can be of any length.

For example, **area**, **radius**, and **number1** are legal identifiers, whereas **2A** and **d+4** are not because they do not follow the rules. When Python detects an illegal identifier, it reports a syntax error and terminates the program.

Note

case sensitive

Because Python is case sensitive, **area**, **Area**, and **AREA** are all different identifiers.

Tip

descriptive names

Descriptive identifiers make programs easy to read. Avoid using abbreviations for identifiers. Using complete words is more descriptive. For example, **numberOfStudents** is better than **numStuds**, **numOfStuds**, or **numOfStudents**. We use descriptive names for complete programs in the text. However, we will occasionally use variables names such as **i**, **j**, **k**, **x**, and **y** in the code snippets for brevity. These names also provide a generic tone to the code snippets.

Tip

variable naming convention

Use lowercase letters for variable names, as in **radius** and **area**. If a name consists of several words, concatenate them into one, making the first word lowercase and capitalizing the first letter of each subsequent word—for example, **numberOfStudents**. This naming style is known as the *camelCase* because the uppercase characters in the name resemble a camel's humps.

camelCase

MyProgrammingLab™

2.6 Which of the following identifiers are valid? Which are Python keywords (see Appendix A)?

```
·miles, ·Test, a+b, b-a, 4#R, $4, #44, ·apps
if, elif, x, y, radius
```

2.5 Variables, Assignment Statements, and Expressions

Variables are used to reference values that may be changed in the program.

why called variables?

As you can see from the programs in the preceding sections, variables are the names that reference values stored in memory. They are called "variables" because they may reference different values. For example, in the following code, **radius** is initially **1.0** (line 2) and then changed to **2.0** (line 7), and **area** is set to **3.14159** (line 3) and then reset to **12.56636** (line 8).

```
1   # Compute the first area
2   radius = 1.0
3   area = radius * radius * 3.14159
4   print("The area is", area, "for radius", radius)
5
6   # Compute the second area
7   radius = 2.0
8   area = radius * radius * 3.14159
9   print("The area is", area, "for radius", radius)
```

radius ⟶ 1.0
area ⟶ 3.14159

radius ⟶ 2.0
area ⟶ 12.56636

▶ VideoNote
Assignment statement

The statement for assigning a value to a variable is called an *assignment statement*. In Python, the equal sign (=) is used as the *assignment operator*. The syntax for assignment statements is as follows:

assignment statement
assignment operator

```
variable = expression
```

An *expression* represents a computation involving values, variables, and operators that, taken together, evaluate to a value. For example, consider the following code:

expression

```
y = 1                     # Assign 1 to variable y
radius = 1.0              # Assign 1.0 to variable radius
x = 5 * (3 / 2) + 3 * 2   # Assign the value of the expression to x
x = y + 1                 # Assign the addition of y and 1 to x
area = radius * radius * 3.14159 # Compute area
```

You can use a variable in an expression. A variable can also be used in both sides of the = operator. For example,

```
x = x + 1
```

In this assignment statement, the result of x + 1 is assigned to x. If x is 1 before the statement is executed, then it becomes 2 after the statement is executed.

To assign a value to a variable, you must place the variable name to the left of the assignment operator. Thus, the following statement is wrong:

```
1 = x     # Wrong
```

 Note

In mathematics, x = 2 * x + 1 denotes an equation. However, in Python, x = 2 * x + 1 is an assignment statement that evaluates the expression 2 * x + 1 and assigns the result to x.

If a value is assigned to multiple variables, you can use a syntax like this:

```
i = j = k = 1
```

which is equivalent to

```
k = 1
j = k
i = j
```

Every variable has a scope. The *scope of a variable* is the part of the program where the variable can be referenced. The rules that define the scope of a variable will be introduced gradually later in the book. For now, all you need to know is that a variable must be created before it can be used. For example, the following code is wrong:

scope of a variable

```
                          count is not defined yet.

>>> count = count + 1
NameError: count is not defined
>>>
```

To fix it, you may write the code like this:

```
>>> count = 1  # count is not created
>>> count = count + 1  # Now increment count
>>>
```

Caution

A variable must be assigned a value before it can be used in an expression. For example,

```
interestRate = 0.05
interest = interestrate * 45
```

This code is wrong, because **interestRate** is assigned a value **0.05**, but **interestrate** is not defined. Python is case-sensitive. **interestRate** and **interestrate** are two different variables.

2.6 Simultaneous Assignments

simultaneous assignment

Python also supports *simultaneous assignment* in syntax like this:

```
var1, var2, ..., varn = exp1, exp2, ..., expn
```

It tells Python to evaluate all the expressions on the right and assign them to the corresponding variable on the left simultaneously. Swapping variable values is a common operation in programming and simultaneous assignment is very useful to perform this operation. Consider two variables: **x** and **y**. How do you write the code to swap their values? A common approach is to introduce a temporary variable as follows:

```
>>> x = 1
>>> y = 2
>>> temp = x  # Save x in a temp variable
>>> x = y     # Assign the value in y to x
>>> y = temp  # Assign the value in temp to y
```

But you can simplify the task using the following statement to swap the values of **x** and **y**.

```
>>> x, y = y, x # Swap x with y
```

Simultaneous assignment can also be used to obtain multiple input in one statement. Listing 2.3 gives an example that prompts the user to enter three numbers and obtains their average. This program can be simplified using a simultaneous assignment statement, as shown in Listing 2.4.

LISTING **2.4** ComputeAverageWithSimultaneousAssignment.py

```
1   # Prompt the user to enter three numbers
2   number1, number2, number3 = eval(input(
3       "Enter three numbers separated by commas: "))
4
5   # Compute average
6   average = (number1 + number2 + number3) / 3
7
8   # Display result
9   print("The average of", number1, number2, number3
10      "is", average)
```

input numbers

```
Enter three numbers separated by commas: 1, 2, 3  ↵Enter
The average of 1  2   3 is 2.0
```

 enter input in one line

2.7   What is the naming convention for variables?

2.8   What is wrong in the following statement?

   2 = a

2.9   What is **x**, **y**, and **z** after the following statement?

   x = y = z = 0

2.10   Assume that **a = 1** and **b = 2**. What is **a** and **b** after the following statement?

   a, b = b, a

2.7 Named Constants

A named constant is an identifier that represents a permanent value.

 Key Point

The value of a variable may change during the execution of a program, but a *named constant* (or simply *constant*) represents permanent data that never changes. In our **ComputeArea** program, π is a constant. If you use it frequently, you don't want to keep typing **3.14159**; instead, you can use a descriptive name **PI** for the value. Python does not have a special syntax for naming constants. You can simply create a variable to denote a constant. However, to distinguish a constant from a variable, use all uppercase letters to name a constant. For example, you can rewrite Listing 2.1 to use a named constant for π, as follows:

constant naming convention

```
# Assign a radius
radius = 20 # radius is now 20

# Compute area
PI = 3.14159
area = radius * radius * PI

# Display results
print("The area for the circle of radius", radius, "is", area)
```

There are three benefits of using constants:

benefits of constants

1. You don't have to repeatedly type the same value if it is used multiple times.

2. If you have to change the constant's value (e.g., from **3.14** to **3.14159** for **PI**), you need to change it only in a single location in the source code.

3. Descriptive names make the program easy to read.

2.8 Numeric Data Types and Operators

Key Point

Python has two numeric types—integers and floating-point numbers—for working with the operators +, -, *, /, //, **, and %.

floating-point numbers

integer

int

float

VideoNote

Perform computation

literal

operands

operators +, -, *, /, //, **, %

The information stored in a computer is generally referred to as *data*. There are two types of numeric data: integers and real numbers. Integer types (*int* for short) are for representing whole numbers. Real types are for representing numbers with a fractional part. Inside the computer, these two types of data are stored differently. Real numbers are represented as floating-point (or *float*) values. How do we tell Python whether a number is an integer or a float? A number that has a decimal point is a float even if its fractional part is **0**. For example, **1.0** is a float, but **1** is an integer. These two numbers are stored differently in the computer. In the programming terminology, numbers such as **1.0** and **1** are called literals. A *literal* is a constant value that appears directly in a program.

The operators for numeric data types include the standard arithmetic operators, as shown in Table 2.1. The *operands* are the values operated by an operator.

TABLE 2.1 Numeric Operators

Name	Meaning	Example	Result
+	Addition	34 + 1	35
-	Subtraction	34.0 - 0.1	33.9
*	Multiplication	300 * 30	9000
/	Float Division	1 / 2	0.5
//	Integer Division	1 // 2	0
**	Exponentiation	4 ** 0.5	2.0
%	Remainder	20 % 3	2

The +, -, and * operators are straightforward, but note that the + and - operators can be both unary and binary. A *unary* operator has only one operand; a *binary* operator has two. For example, the - operator in **-5** is a unary operator to negate the number **5**, whereas the - operator in **4 - 5** is a binary operator for subtracting **5** from **4**.

unary operator

binary operator

2.8.1 The /, //, and ** Operators

/ operator

The / operator performs a float division that results in a floating number. For example,

```
>>> 4 / 2
2.0
>>> 2 / 4
0.5
>>>
```

// operator

The // operator performs an integer division; the result is an integer, and any fractional part is truncated. For example,

```
>>> 5 // 2
2
>>> 2 // 4
0
>>>
```

To compute a^b (**a** with an exponent of **b**) for any numbers **a** and **b**, you can write **a** `**` **b**   `**` exponent operator
in Python. For example,

```
>>> 2.3 ** 3.5
18.45216910555504
>>> (-2.5) ** 2
6.25
>>>
```

2.8.2 The % Operator

The **%** operator, known as *remainder* or *modulo* operator, yields the remainder after division.   % operator
The left-side operand is the dividend and the right-side operand is the divisor. Therefore, **7 %**
3 yields **1**, **3 % 7** yields **3**, **12 % 4** yields **0**, **26 % 8** yields **2**, and **20 % 13** yields **7**.

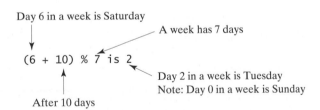

The remainder operator is very useful in programming. For example, an even number **% 2**
is always **0** and an odd number **% 2** is always **1**. Thus, you can use this property to determine
whether a number is even or odd. If today is Saturday, it will be Saturday again in 7 days. Suppose you and your friends are going to meet in 10 days. What day is in 10 days? You can find
that the day is Tuesday using the following expression:

Day 6 in a week is Saturday

A week has 7 days

(6 + 10) % 7 is 2

After 10 days

Day 2 in a week is Tuesday
Note: Day 0 in a week is Sunday

Listing 2.5 shows a program that obtains minutes and remaining seconds from an amount
of time in seconds. For example, **500** seconds contains **8** minutes and **20** seconds.

LISTING 2.5   DisplayTime.py

```
1  # Prompt the user for input
2  seconds = eval(input("Enter an integer for seconds: "))      input seconds
3
4  # Get minutes and remaining seconds
5  minutes = seconds // 60     # Find minutes in seconds         get minutes
6  remainingSeconds = seconds % 60   # Seconds remaining         get remainingSeconds
7  print(seconds, "seconds is", minutes,
8      "minutes and", remainingSeconds, "seconds")
```

```
Enter an integer for seconds: 500  ↵Enter
500 seconds is 8 minutes and 20 seconds
```

line#	seconds	minutes	remainingSeconds
2	500		
5		8	
6			20

Line 2 reads an integer for **seconds**. Line 5 obtains the minutes using **seconds // 60**. Line 6 (**seconds % 60**) obtains the remaining seconds after taking away the minutes.

2.8.3 Scientific Notation

scientific notation

Floating-point values can be written in *scientific notation* in the form of $a \times 10^b$. For example, the scientific notation for 123.456 is 1.23456×10^2 and for 0.0123456 is 1.23456×10^{-2}. Python uses a special syntax to write scientific notation numbers. For example, 1.23456×10^2 is written as **1.23456E2** or **1.23456E+2**, and 1.23456×10^{-2} as **1.23456E-2**. The letter **E** (or **e**) represents an exponent and can be in either lowercase or uppercase.

Note

why called floating point?

The float type is used to represent numbers with a decimal point. Why are they called *floating-point numbers*? These numbers are stored in scientific notation in memory. When a number such as **50.534** is converted into scientific notation, such as **5.0534E+1**, its decimal point is moved (floated) to a new position.

Caution

what is overflow?

When a variable is assigned a value that is too large (*in size*) to be stored in memory, it causes *overflow*. For example, executing the following statement causes overflow.

```
>>> 245.0 ** 1000
OverflowError: 'Result too large'
>>>
```

what is underflow?

When a floating-point number is too small (that is, too close to zero), it causes *underflow* and Python approximates it to zero. Therefore, usually you don't need to be concerned with underflow.

Check Point

MyProgrammingLab™

2.11 What are the results of the following expressions?

Expression	Result
42 / 5	_____
42 // 5	_____
42 % 5	_____
40 % 5	_____
1 % 2	_____
2 % 1	_____
45 + 4 * 4 - 2	_____
45 + 43 % 5 * (23 * 3 % 2)	_____
5 ** 2	_____
5.1 ** 2	_____

2.12 If today is Tuesday, what day of the week will it be in 100 days?

2.13 What is the result of **25 / 4**? How would you rewrite the expression if you wished the result to be an integer number?

2.9 Evaluating Expressions and Operator Precedence

Python expressions are evaluated in the same way as arithmetic expressions.

Key Point

Writing a numeric expression in Python involves a straightforward translation of an arithmetic expression using operators. For example, the arithmetic expression

$$\frac{3 + 4x}{5} - \frac{10(y - 5)(a + b + c)}{x} + 9\left(\frac{4}{x} + \frac{9 + x}{y}\right)$$

can be translated into a Python expression as:

```
(3 + 4 * x) / 5 - 10 * (y - 5) * (a + b + c) / x +
9 * (4 / x + (9 + x) / y)
```

Though Python has its own way to evaluate an expression behind the scene, the results of a Python expression and its corresponding arithmetic expression are the same. Therefore, you can safely apply the arithmetic rules for evaluating a Python expression. Operators contained within pairs of parentheses are evaluated first. Parentheses can be nested, in which case the expression in the inner parentheses is evaluated first. When more than one operator is used in an expression, the following operator precedence rule is used to determine the order of evaluation.

evaluate an expression

operator precedence rule

- Exponentiation (**) is applied first.

- Multiplication (*), float division (/), integer division (//) , and remainder operators (%) are applied next. If an expression contains several multiplication, division, and remainder operators, they are applied from left to right.

- Addition (+) and subtraction (-) operators are applied last. If an expression contains several addition and subtraction operators, they are applied from left to right.

Here is an example of how an expression is evaluated:

```
3 + 4 * 4 + 5 * (4 + 3) - 1
```
———— (1) inside parentheses first
```
3 + 4 * 4 + 5 * 7 - 1
```
———— (2) multiplication
```
3 + 16 + 5 * 7 - 1
```
———— (3) multiplication
```
3 + 16 + 35 - 1
```
———— (4) addition
```
19 + 35 - 1
```
———— (5) addition
```
54 - 1
```
———— (6) subtraction
```
53
```

2.14 How would you write the following arithmetic expression in Python?

$$\frac{4}{3(r + 34)} - 9(a + bc) + \frac{3 + d(2 + a)}{a + bd}$$

2.15 Suppose m and r are integers. Write a Python expression for mr^2.

2.10 Augmented Assignment Operators

Key Point

The operators +, -, *, /, //, %, and ** can be combined with the assignment operator (=) to form augmented assignment operators.

Very often the current value of a variable is used, modified, and then reassigned back to the same variable. For example, the following statement increases the variable **count** by **1**:

```
count = count + 1
```

augmented assignment
compound assignment

Python allows you to combine assignment and addition operators using an augmented (or compound) assignment operator. For instance, the preceding statement can be written as:

```
count += 1
```

addition assignment operator

The += operator is called the *addition assignment operator*. All augmented assignment operators are shown in Table 2.2.

TABLE 2.2 Augmented Assignment Operators

Operator	Name	Example	Equivalent
+=	Addition assignment	i += 8	i = i + 8
-=	Subtraction assignment	i -= 8	i = i - 8
*=	Multiplication assignment	i *= 8	i = i * 8
/=	Float division assignment	i /= 8	i = i / 8
//=	Integer division assignment	i //= 8	i = i // 8
%=	Remainder assignment	i %= 8	i = i % 8
**=	Exponent assignment	i **= 8	i = i ** 8

Caution

There are no spaces in the augmented assignment operators. For example, + = should be +=.

2.16 Assume that **a = 1**, and that each expression is independent. What are the results of the following expressions?

```
a += 4
a -= 4
a *= 4
a /= 4
a //= 4
a %= 4
a = 56 * a + 6
```

2.11 Type Conversions and Rounding

If one of the operands for the numeric operators is a float value, the result will be a float value.

Can you perform binary operations with two operands of different types? Yes. If an integer and a float are involved in a binary operation, Python automatically converts the integer to a float value. This is called *type conversion*. So, **3 * 4.5** is the same as **3.0 * 4.5**.

type conversion

Sometimes, it is desirable to obtain the integer part of a fractional number. You can use the **int(value)** function to return the integer part of a float value. For example,

int function

```
>>> value = 5.6
>>> int(value)
5
>>>
```

Note that the fractional part of the number is truncated, not rounded up.

You can also use the **round** function to round a number to the nearest whole value. For example,

round function

```
>>> value = 5.6
>>> round(value)
6
>>>
```

We will discuss the **round** function more in Chapter 3.

Note

The functions **int** and **round** do not change the variable being converted. For example, **value** is not changed after invoking the function in the following code:

```
>>> value = 5.6
>>> round(value)
6
>>> value
5.6
>>>
```

Note

The **int** function can also be used to convert an integer string into an integer. For example, **int("34")** returns **34**. So you can use the **eval** or **int** function to convert a string into an integer. Which one is better? The **int** function performs a simple conversion. It does not work for a non-integer string. For example, **int("3.4")** will cause an error. The **eval** function does more than a simple conversion. It can be used to evaluate an expression. For example, **eval("3 + 4")** returns **7**. However, there is a subtle "gotcha" for using the **eval** function. The **eval** function will produce an error for a numeric string that contains leading zeros. In contrast, the **int** function works fine for this case. For example, **eval("003")** causes an error, but **int("003")** returns **3**.

int vs. eval functions

Listing 2.6 shows a program that displays the sales tax with two digits after the decimal point.

LISTING 2.6 SalesTax.py

input purchaseAmount

compute tax

format

```
1  # Prompt the user for input
2  purchaseAmount = eval(input("Enter purchase amount: "))
3
4  # Compute sales tax
5  tax = purchaseAmount * 0.06
6
7  # Display tax amount with two digits after decimal point
8  print("Sales tax is", int(tax * 100) / 100.0)
```

```
Enter purchase amount: 197.55  ↵Enter
Sales tax is 11.85
```

line#	purchaseAmount	tax	output
2	197.55		
5		11.853	
8			11.85

format numbers

The value of the variable **purchaseAmount** is **197.55** (line 2). The sales tax is **6%** of the purchase, so the **tax** is evaluated as **11.853** (line 5). Note that

```
tax * 100 is 1185.3
int(tax * 100) is 1185
int(tax * 100) / 100.0 is 11.85
```

So, the statement in line 8 displays the tax **11.85** with two digits after the decimal point.

Check Point

2.17 What does a conversion from a float to an integer do with the fractional part of the float value? Does the **int(value)** function change the variable **value**?

MyProgrammingLab™

2.18 Are the following statements correct? If so, show their printout.

```
value = 4.6
print(int(value))
print(round(value))
print(eval("4 * 5 + 2"))
print(int("04"))
print(int("4.5"))
print(eval("04"))
```

2.12 Case Study: Displaying the Current Time

Key Point

You can use the **time()** *function in the* **time** *module to obtain the current system time.*

The problem is to develop a program that displays the current time in Greenwich Mean Time (GMT) in the format hour:minute:second, such as 13:19:18.

The **time()** function in the **time** module returns the current time in seconds with millisecond precision elapsed since the time **00:00:00** on January 1, 1970 GMT, as shown in Figure 2.1. This time is known as the *UNIX epoch*. The epoch is the point when time starts. **1970** was the year when the UNIX operating system was formally introduced. For

UNIX epoch

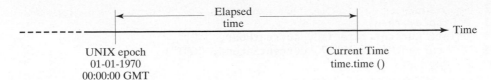

FIGURE 2.1   The `time.time()` function returns the seconds with millisecond precision since the UNIX epoch.

example, `time.time()` returns **1285543663.205**, which means **1285543663** seconds and **205** milliseconds.   `time.time()`

You can use this function to obtain the current time, and then compute the current second, minute, and hour as follows.

1. Obtain the current time (since midnight, January 1, 1970) by invoking `time.time()` (for example, **1203183068.328**).

2. Obtain the total seconds **totalSeconds** using the `int` function (`int(1203183068.328)` = **1203183068**).

3. Compute the current second from **totalSeconds % 60** (**1203183068** seconds % **60** = **8**, which is the current second).

4. Obtain the total minutes **totalMinutes** by dividing **totalSeconds** by **60** (**1203183068** seconds // **60** = **20053051** minutes).

5. Compute the current minute from **totalMinutes % 60** (**20053051** minutes % **60** = **31**, which is the current minute).

6. Obtain the total hours **totalHours** by dividing **totalMinutes** by **60** (**20053051** minutes // **60** = **334217** hours).

7. Compute the current hour from **totalHours % 24** (**334217** hours % **24** = **17**, which is the current hour).

Listing 2.7 gives the complete program.

LISTING 2.7   ShowCurrentTime.py

```
 1  import time                                              import time module
 2
 3  currentTime = time.time() # Get current time             currentTime
 4
 5  # Obtain the total seconds since midnight, Jan 1, 1970
 6  totalSeconds = int(currentTime)                           totalSeconds
 7
 8  # Get the current second
 9  currentSecond = totalSeconds % 60                         currentSecond
10
11  # Obtain the total minutes
12  totalMinutes = totalSeconds // 60                         totalMinutes
13
14  # Compute the current minute in the hour
15  currentMinute = totalMinutes % 60                         currentMinute
16
17  # Obtain the total hours
18  totalHours = totalMinutes // 60                           totalHours
19
20  # Compute the current hour
21  currentHour = totalHours % 24                             currentHour
```

display output

```
22
23  # Display results
24  print("Current time is", currentHour, ":",
25      currentMinute, ":", currentSecond, "GMT")
```

Current time is 17:31:8 GMT

variables	line# 3	6	9	12	15	18	21
currentTime	1203183068.328						
totalSeconds		1203183068					
currentSecond			8				
totalMinutes				20053051			
currentMinute					31		
totalHours						334217	
currentHour							17

Line 3 invokes **time.time()** to return the current time in seconds as a float value with millisecond precision. The seconds, minutes, and hours are extracted from the current time using the **//** and **%** operators (lines 6–21).

In the sample run, a single digit **8** is displayed for the second. The desirable output would be **08**. This can be fixed by using a function that formats a single digit with a prefix **0** (see Exercise 6.48).

✓Check
Point

MyProgrammingLab™

2.19 What is the UNIX epoch?

2.20 What does **time.time()** return?

2.21 How do you obtain the seconds from the returned value for **time.time()**?

2.13 Software Development Process

🔑 Key
Point

The software development life cycle is a multistage process that includes requirements specification, analysis, design, implementation, testing, deployment, and maintenance.

Developing a software product is an engineering process. Software products, no matter how large or how small, have the same life cycle: requirements specification, system analysis, system design, implementation, testing, deployment, and maintenance, as shown in Figure 2.2.

requirements specification

Requirements specification is a formal process that seeks to understand the problem that the software will address and to document in detail what the software system needs to do. This phase involves close interaction between users and developers. Most of the examples in

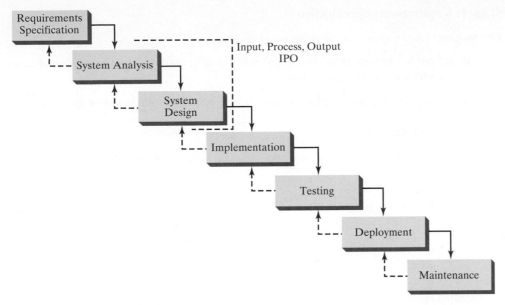

FIGURE 2.2   At any stage of the software development life cycle, it may be necessary to go back to a previous stage to correct errors or deal with other issues that might prevent the software from functioning as expected.

this book are simple, and their requirements are clearly stated. In the real world, however, problems are not always well defined. Developers need to work closely with their customers (the individuals or organizations that will use the software) and study the problem carefully to identify what the software needs to do.

System analysis seeks to analyze the data flow and to identify the system's input and output. When you do analysis, it helps to identify what the output is first, and then figure out what input data you need in order to produce the output.

System design is to design a process for obtaining the output from the input. This phase involves the use of many levels of abstraction to decompose the problem into manageable components, and design strategies for implementing each component. You can view a component as a subsystem that performs a specific function of the system. The essence of system analysis and design is input, process, and output (IPO).

Implementation involves translating the system design into programs. Separate programs are written for each component and then integrated to work together. This phase requires the use of a programming language such as Python. The implementation involves coding, self testing, and debugging (that is, finding errors, called *bugs*, in the code).

Testing ensures that the code meets the requirements specification and weeds out bugs. An independent team of software engineers not involved in the design and implementation of the product usually conducts such testing.

Deployment makes the software available for use. Depending on the type of the software, it may be installed on each user's machine or installed on a server accessible on the Internet.

Maintenance is concerned with updating and improving the product. A software product must continue to perform and improve in an ever-evolving environment. This requires periodic upgrades of the product to fix newly discovered bugs and incorporate changes.

To see the software development process in action, we will now create a program that computes loan payments. The loan can be a car loan, a student loan, or a home mortgage loan. For an introductory programming course, we focus on requirements specification, analysis, design, implementation, and testing.

system analysis

system design

IPO
implementation

testing

deployment

maintenance

Stage 1: Requirements Specification

The program must satisfy the following requirements:

- It must let the user enter the interest rate, the loan amount, and the number of years for which payments will be made.

- It must compute and display the monthly payment and total payment amounts.

Stage 2: System Analysis

The output is the monthly payment and total payment, which can be obtained using the following formula:

$$monthlyPayment = \frac{loanAmount \times monthlyInterestRate}{1 - \dfrac{1}{(1 + monthlyInterestRate)^{numberOfYears \times 12}}}$$

$$totalPayment = monthlyPayment \times numberOfYears \times 12$$

So, the input needed for the program is the annual interest rate, the length of the loan in years, and the loan amount.

Note

The requirements specification says that the user must enter the interest rate, the loan amount, and the number of years for which payments will be made. During analysis, however, it is possible that you may discover that input is not sufficient or that some values are unnecessary for the output. If this happens, you can go back to modify the requirements specification.

Note

In the real world, you will work with customers from all walks of life. You may develop software for chemists, physicists, engineers, economists, and psychologists and of course, you will not have (or need) the complete knowledge of all these fields. Therefore, you don't have to know how the mathematical formulas are derived. Nonetheless, given the annual interest rate, number of years, and loan amount, you can use this formula to compute the monthly payment. You will, however, need to communicate with the customers and understand how the mathematic model works for the system.

Stage 3: System Design

During system design, you identify the steps in the program:

Step 1.   Prompt the user to enter the annual interest rate, number of years, and loan amount.

Step 2.   The input for the annual interest rate is a number in percent format, such as 4.5%. The program needs to convert it into a decimal by dividing it by **100**. To obtain the monthly interest rate from the annual interest rate, divide it by 12, since a year has 12 months. So to obtain the monthly interest rate in decimal format, you need to divide the annual interest rate in percentage by **1200**. For example, if the annual interest rate is 4.5%, then the monthly interest rate is 4.5/1200 = 0.00375.

Step 3.   Compute the monthly payment using the formula given in Stage 2.

Step 4.   Compute the total payment, which is the monthly payment multiplied by **12** and multiplied by the number of years.

Step 5.   Display the monthly payment and total payment.

Stage 4: Implementation

Implementation is also known as *coding* (writing the code). In the formula, you have to compute $(1 + monthlyInterestRate)^{numberOfYears \times 12}$. You can use the exponentiation operator to write it as

```
(1 + monthlyInterestRate) ** (numberOfYears * 12)
```

Listing 2.8 gives the complete program.

LISTING 2.8 ComputeLoan.py

```
1   # Enter annual interest rate as a percentage, e.g., 7.25
2   annualInterestRate = eval(input(                          enter interest rate
3       "Enter annual interest rate, e.g., 7.25: "))
4   monthlyInterestRate = annualInterestRate / 1200           obtain monthly interest rate
5
6   # Enter number of years
7   numberOfYears = eval(input(                               enter years
8       "Enter number of years as an integer, e.g., 5: "))
9
10  # Enter loan amount
11  loanAmount = eval(input("Enter loan amount, e.g., 120000.95: "))   enter loan amount
12
13  # Calculate payment
14  monthlyPayment = loanAmount * monthlyInterestRate / (1     monthlyPayment
15      - 1 / (1 + monthlyInterestRate) ** (numberOfYears * 12))
16  totalPayment = monthlyPayment * numberOfYears * 12        totalPayment
17
18  # Display results
19  print("The monthly payment is", int(monthlyPayment * 100) / 100)   display result
20  print("The total payment is", int(totalPayment * 100) /100)
```

```
Enter annual interest rate, e.g., 7.25: 5.75  ↵Enter
Enter number of years as an integer, e.g., 5: 15  ↵Enter
Enter loan amount, e.g., 120000.95: 250000  ↵Enter
The monthly payment is 2076.02
The total payment is 373684.53
```

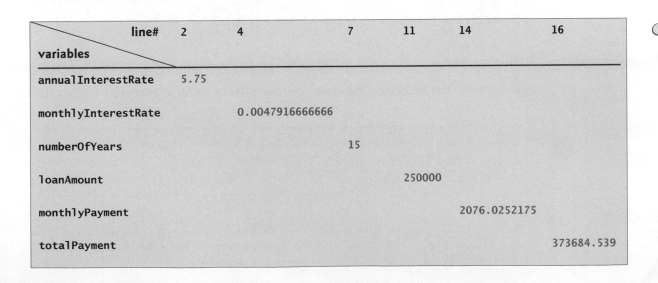

variables \ line#	2	4	7	11	14	16
annualInterestRate	5.75					
monthlyInterestRate		0.0047916666666				
numberOfYears			15			
loanAmount				250000		
monthlyPayment					2076.0252175	
totalPayment						373684.539

format numbers

Line 2 reads the annual interest rate, which is converted into the monthly interest rate in line 4.

The formula for computing the monthly payment is translated into Python code in lines 14–15.

The variable **monthlyPayment** is **2076.0252175** (line 14). Note that

```
int(monthlyPayment * 100) is 207602.52175
int(monthlyPayment * 100) / 100.0 is 2076.02
```

So, the statement in line 19 displays the tax **2076.02** with two digits after the decimal point.

Stage 5: Testing

After the program is implemented, test it with some sample input data and verify whether the output is correct. Some of the problems may involve many cases as you will see in later chapters. For this type of problems, you need to design test data that cover all cases.

incremental development and testing

Tip

The system design phase in this example identified several steps. It is a good approach to develop and test these steps incrementally by adding them one at a time. This process makes it much easier to pinpoint problems and debug the program.

2.14 Case Study: Computing Distances

 Key Point

This section presents two programs that compute and display the distance between two points.

Given two points, the formula for computing the distance is $\sqrt{(x_2 - x_1)^2 + (y_2 - y_1)^2}$. You can use **a ** **0.5** to compute $\sqrt{a}$. The program in Listing 2.9 prompts the user to enter two points and computes the distance between them.

LISTING 2.9 ComputeDistance.py

enter x1, y1

enter x2, y2

compute distance

```
 1  # Enter the first point with two float values
 2  x1, y1 = eval(input("Enter x1 and y1 for Point 1: "))
 3
 4  # Enter the second point with two float values
 5  x2, y2 = eval(input("Enter x2 and y2 for Point 2: "))
 6
 7  # Compute the distance
 8  distance = ((x1 - x2) * (x1 - x2) + (y1 - y2) * (y1 - y2)) ** 0.5
 9
10  print("The distance between the two points is", distance)
```

```
Enter x1 and y1 for Point 1: 1.5, -3.4 ↵Enter
Enter x2 and y2 for Point 2: 4, 5 ↵Enter
The distance between the two points is 8.764131445842194
```

The program prompts the user to enter the coordinates of the first point (line 2) and the second point (line 5). It then computes the distance between them (line 8) and displays it (line 10).

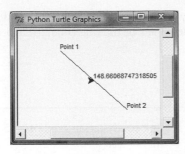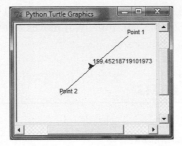

FIGURE 2.3   The program displays a line and its length.

Figure 2.3 illustrates the program in Listing 2.10. This program

1. Prompts the user to enter two points.

2. Computes the distance between the points.

3. Uses Turtle graphics to display the line that connects the two points.

4. Displays the length of the line at the center of the line.

Listing 2.10 gives the program.

LISTING 2.10   ComputeDistanceGraphics.py

```
 1  import turtle
 2
 3  # Prompt the user for inputting two points
 4  x1, y1 = eval(input("Enter x1 and y1 for point 1: "))
 5  x2, y2 = eval(input("Enter x2 and y2 for point 2: "))
 6
 7  # Compute the distance
 8  distance = ((x1 - x2) ** 2 + (y1 - y2) ** 2) ** 0.5
 9
10  # Display two points and the connecting line
11  turtle.penup()
12  turtle.goto(x1, y1) # Move to (x1, y1)
13  turtle.pendown()
14  turtle.write("Point 1")
15  turtle.goto(x2, y2) # Draw a line to (x2, y2)
16  turtle.write("Point 2")
17
18  # Move to the center point of the line
19  turtle.penup()
20  turtle.goto((x1 + x2) / 2, (y1 + y2) / 2)
21  turtle.write(distance)
22
23  turtle.done()
```

	import turtle
	enter x1, y1
	enter x2, y2
	compute distance
	move to point 1
	display point 1
	draw a line
	display point 2
	move to center
	display distance
	pause

```
Enter x1 and y1 for Point 1: -50, 34  ↵Enter
Enter x2 and y2 for Point 2: 49, -85  ↵Enter
```

The program prompts the user to enter the value for two points `(x1, y1)` and `(x2, y2)`, and computes their distance (lines 4–8). It then moves to `(x1, y1)` (line 12), displays the text `Point 1` (line 14), draws a line from (`x1, y1`) to (`x2, y2`) (line 15), and displays the text `Point 2` (line 16). Finally, it moves to the center of the line (line 20) and displays the distance (line 21).

Key Terms

algorithm 32	line continuation symbol 35
assignment operator (=) 37	literal 40
augmented assignment 44	operands 40
camelCase 36	operators 40
compound assignment 44	pseudocode 32
data type 33	reserved word 36
expression 37	scope of a variable 37
floating-point numbers 40	simultaneous assignment 38
identifiers 36	system analysis 49
incremental development and testing 52	system design 49
input, process, output (IPO) 35	type conversion 45
keyword 36	variable 32

Chapter Summary

1. You can get input using the `input` function and convert a string into a numerical value using the `eval` function.

2. *Identifiers* are the names used for elements in a program.

3. An identifier is a sequence of characters of any length that consists of letters, digits, underscores (_), and asterisk signs (*). An identifier must start with a letter or an underscore; it cannot start with a digit. An identifier cannot be a keyword.

4. *Variables* are used to store data in a program.

5. The equal sign (=) is used as the *assignment operator*.

6. A variable must be assigned a value before it can be used.

7. There are two types of numeric data in Python: integers and real numbers. Integer types (*int* for short) are for whole numbers, and real types (also called *float*) are for numbers with a decimal point.

8. Python provides *assignment operators* that perform numeric operations: + (addition), – (subtraction), * (multiplication), / (division), // (integer division), % (remainder), and ** (exponent).

9. The numeric operators in a Python expression are applied the same way as in an arithmetic expression.

10. Python provides augmented assignment operators: += (addition assignment), -= (subtraction assignment), *= (multiplication assignment), /= (float division assignment), //= (integer division assignment), and %= (remainder assignment). These operators combine the +, -, *, /, //, and % operators and the assignment operator into one augmented operators.

11. When evaluating an expression with values of an int type and a float type, Python automatically converts the int value to a float type value.

12. You can convert a float to an int using the **int(value)** function.

13. *System analysis* seeks to analyze the data flow and to identify the system's input and output.

14. *System design* is the stage when programmers develop a process for obtaining the output from the input.

15. The essence of system analysis and design is input, process, and output. This is called *IPO*.

TEST QUESTIONS

Do test questions for this chapter online at www.cs.armstrong.edu/liang/py/test.html.

PROGRAMMING EXERCISES

MyProgrammingLab™

Pedagogical Note

Instructors may ask you to document analysis and design for selected exercises. You should use your own words to analyze the problem, including the input, output, and what needs to be computed, and describe how to solve the problem in pseudocode.

document analysis and design

Debugging Tip

Python usually gives a reason for a syntax error. If you don't know how to correct it, compare your program closely, character by character, with similar examples in the text.

learn from examples

Sections 2.2–2.10

2.1 (*Convert Celsius to Fahrenheit*) Write a program that reads a Celsius degree from the console and converts it to Fahrenheit and displays the result. The formula for the conversion is as follows:

```
fahrenheit = (9 / 5) * celsius + 32
```

Here is a sample run of the program:

```
Enter a degree in Celsius: 43  ↵Enter
43 Celsius is 109.4 Fahrenheit
```

2.2 (*Compute the volume of a cylinder*) Write a program that reads in the radius and length of a cylinder and computes the area and volume using the following formulas:

```
area = radius * radius * π
volume = area * length
```

Here is a sample run:

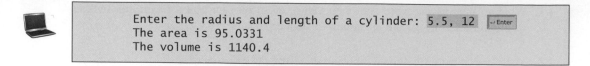

```
Enter the radius and length of a cylinder: 5.5, 12   ↵Enter
The area is 95.0331
The volume is 1140.4
```

2.3 (*Convert feet into meters*) Write a program that reads a number in feet, converts it to meters, and displays the result. One foot is **0.305** meters. Here is a sample run:

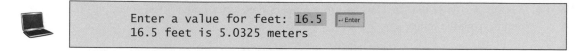

```
Enter a value for feet: 16.5   ↵Enter
16.5 feet is 5.0325 meters
```

2.4 (*Convert pounds into kilograms*) Write a program that converts pounds into kilograms. The program prompts the user to enter a value in pounds, converts it to kilograms, and displays the result. One pound is **0.454** kilograms. Here is a sample run:

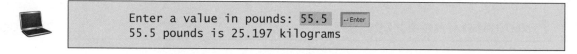

```
Enter a value in pounds: 55.5   ↵Enter
55.5 pounds is 25.197 kilograms
```

*2.5 (*Financial application: calculate tips*) Write a program that reads the subtotal and the gratuity rate and computes the gratuity and total. For example, if the user enters **10** for the subtotal and **15%** for the gratuity rate, the program displays **1.5** as the gratuity and **11.5** as the total. Here is a sample run:

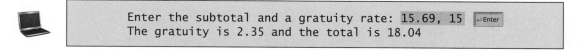

```
Enter the subtotal and a gratuity rate: 15.69, 15   ↵Enter
The gratuity is 2.35 and the total is 18.04
```

2.6 (*Sum the digits in an integer*) Write a program that reads an integer between **0 and **1000** and adds all the digits in the integer. For example, if an integer is **932**, the sum of all its digits is **14**. (Hint: Use the **%** operator to extract digits, and use the **//** operator to remove the extracted digit. For instance, **932 % 10 = 2** and **932 // 10 = 93**.) Here is a sample run:

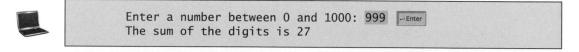

```
Enter a number between 0 and 1000: 999   ↵Enter
The sum of the digits is 27
```

2.7 (*Find the number of years and days*) Write a program that prompts the user to enter the minutes (e.g., 1 billion), and displays the number of years and days for the minutes. For simplicity, assume a year has **365 days. Here is a sample run:

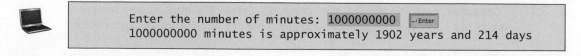

```
Enter the number of minutes: 1000000000   ↵Enter
1000000000 minutes is approximately 1902 years and 214 days
```

2.8 (*Science: calculate energy*) Write a program that calculates the energy needed to heat water from an initial temperature to a final temperature. Your program should prompt the user to enter the amount of water in kilograms and the initial and final temperatures of the water. The formula to compute the energy is

```
Q = M * (finalTemperature - initialTemperature) * 4184
```

where **M** is the weight of water in kilograms, temperatures are in degrees Celsius, and energy **Q** is measured in joules. Here is a sample run:

```
Enter the amount of water in kilograms: 55.5  ↵Enter
Enter the initial temperature: 3.5  ↵Enter
Enter the final temperature: 10.5  ↵Enter
The energy needed is 1625484.0
```

*2.9 (*Science: wind-chill temperature*) How cold is it outside? The temperature alone is not enough to provide the answer. Other factors including wind speed, relative humidity, and sunshine play important roles in determining coldness outside. In 2001, the National Weather Service (NWS) implemented the new wind-chill temperature to measure the coldness using temperature and wind speed. The formula is given as follows:

$$t_{wc} = 35.74 + 0.6215t_a - 35.75v^{0.16} + 0.4275t_a v^{0.16}$$

where t_a is the outside temperature measured in degrees Fahrenheit and v is the speed measured in miles per hour. t_{wc} is the wind-chill temperature. The formula cannot be used for wind speeds below 2 mph or for temperatures below $-58°F$ or above $41°F$.

Write a program that prompts the user to enter a temperature between $-58°F$ and $41°F$ and a wind speed greater than or equal to **2** and displays the wind-chill temperature. Here is a sample run:

```
Enter the temperature in Fahrenheit between -58 and 41: 5.3  ↵Enter
Enter the wind speed in miles per hour: 6  ↵Enter
The wind chill index is -5.56707
```

*2.10 (*Physics: find runway length*) Given an airplane's acceleration a and take-off speed v, you can compute the minimum runway length needed for an airplane to take off using the following formula:

$$length = \frac{v^2}{2a}$$

Write a program that prompts the user to enter v in meters/second (m/s) and the acceleration a in meters/second squared (m/s^2), and displays the minimum runway length. Here is a sample run:

```
Enter speed and acceleration: 60, 3.5  ↵Enter
The minimum runway length for this airplane is 514.286 meters
```

*2.11 (*Financial application: investment amount*) Suppose you want to deposit a certain amount of money into a savings account with a fixed annual interest rate. What amount do you need to deposit in order to have $5,000 in the account after three years? The initial deposit amount can be obtained using the following formula:

$$initialDepositAmount = \frac{finalAccountValue}{(1 + monthlyInterestRate)^{numberOfMonths}}$$

Write a program that prompts the user to enter final account value, annual interest rate in percent, and the number of years, and displays the initial deposit amount. Here is a sample run:

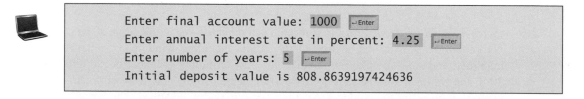

```
Enter final account value: 1000 ↵Enter
Enter annual interest rate in percent: 4.25 ↵Enter
Enter number of years: 5 ↵Enter
Initial deposit value is 808.8639197424636
```

2.12 (*Print a table*) Write a program that displays the following table:

```
a       b       a ** b
1       2       1
2       3       8
3       4       81
4       5       1024
5       6       15625
```

*2.13 (*Split digits*) Write a program that prompts the user to enter a four-digit integer and displays the number in reverse order. Here is a sample run:

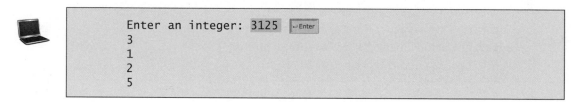

```
Enter an integer: 3125 ↵Enter
3
1
2
5
```

*2.14 (*Geometry: area of a triangle*) Write a program that prompts the user to enter the three points **(x1, y1)**, **(x2, y2)**, and **(x3, y3)** of a triangle and displays its area. The formula for computing the area of a triangle is

$$s = (side1 + side2 + side3) / 2$$

$$area = \sqrt{s(s - side1)(s - side2)(s - side3)}$$

Here is a sample run:

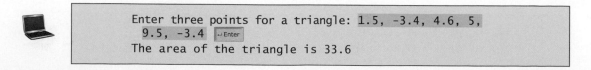

```
Enter three points for a triangle: 1.5, -3.4, 4.6, 5,
  9.5, -3.4 ↵Enter
The area of the triangle is 33.6
```

2.15 (*Geometry: area of a hexagon*) Write a program that prompts the user to enter the side of a hexagon and displays its area. The formula for computing the area of a hexagon is $Area = \dfrac{3\sqrt{3}}{2}s^2$, where s is the length of a side. Here is a sample run:

```
Enter the side: 5.5  ↵Enter
The area of the hexagon is 78.5895
```

2.16 (*Physics: acceleration*) Average acceleration is defined as the change of velocity divided by the time taken to make the change, as shown in the following formula:

$$a = \frac{v_1 - v_0}{t}$$

Write a program that prompts the user to enter the starting velocity v_0 in meters/second, the ending velocity v_1 in meters/second, and the time span t in seconds, and displays the average acceleration. Here is a sample run:

```
Enter v0, v1, and t: 5.5, 50.9, 4.5  ↵Enter
The average acceleration is 10.0889
```

*2.17 (*Health application: compute BMI*) Body mass index (BMI) is a measure of health based on weight. It can be calculated by taking your weight in kilograms and dividing it by the square of your height in meters. Write a program that prompts the user to enter a weight in pounds and height in inches and displays the BMI. Note that one pound is **0.45359237** kilograms and one inch is **0.0254** meters. Here is a sample run:

```
Enter weight in pounds: 95.5  ↵Enter
Enter height in inches: 50  ↵Enter
BMI is 26.8573
```

Sections 2.11–2.13

*2.18 (*Current time*) Listing 2.7, ShowCurrentTime.py, gives a program that displays the current time in GMT. Revise the program so that it prompts the user to enter the time zone in hours away from (offset to) GMT and displays the time in the specified time zone. Here is a sample run:

```
Enter the time zone offset to GMT: -5  ↵Enter
The current time is 4:50:34
```

*2.19 (*Financial application: calculate future investment value*) Write a program that reads in an investment amount, the annual interest rate, and the number of years, and displays the future investment value using the following formula:

$$futureInvestmentValue = investmentAmount \times (1 + monthlyInterestRate)^{numberOfMonths}$$

For example, if you enter the amount **1000**, an annual interest rate of **4.25%**, and the number of years as **1**, the future investment value is **1043.33**. Here is a sample run:

```
Enter investment amount: 1000 ⏎Enter
Enter annual interest rate: 4.25 ⏎Enter
Enter number of years: 1 ⏎Enter
Accumulated value is 1043.33
```

*2.20 (*Financial application: calculate interest*) If you know the balance and the annual percentage interest rate, you can compute the interest on the next monthly payment using the following formula:

```
interest = balance * (annualInterestRate / 1200)
```

Write a program that reads the balance and the annual percentage interest rate and displays the interest for the next month. Here is a sample run:

```
Enter balance and interest rate (e.g., 3 for 3%): 1000, 3.5 ⏎Enter
The interest is 2.91667
```

2.21 (*Financial application: compound value*) Suppose you save **$100 each month into a savings account with an annual interest rate of 5%. Therefore, the monthly interest rate is 0.05/12 = 0.00417. After the first month, the value in the account becomes

```
100 * (1 + 0.00417) = 100.417
```

After the second month, the value in the account becomes

```
(100 + 100.417) * (1 + 0.00417) = 201.252
```

After the third month, the value in the account becomes

```
(100 + 201.252) * (1 + 0.00417) = 302.507
```

and so on.

Write a program that prompts the user to enter a monthly saving amount and displays the account value after the sixth month. Here is a sample run of the program:

```
Enter the monthly saving amount: 100  ↵Enter
After the sixth month, the account value is 608.81
```

2.22 (*Population projection*) Rewrite Exercise 1.11 to prompt the user to enter the number of years and displays the population after that many years. Here is a sample run of the program:

```
Enter the number of years: 5  ↵Enter
The population in 5 years is 325932970
```

Section 2.14

2.23 (*Turtle: draw four circles*) Write a program that prompts the user to enter the radius and draws four circles in the center of the screen, as shown in Figure 2.4a.

2.24 (*Turtle: draw four hexagons*) Write a program that draws four hexagons in the center of the screen, as shown in Figure 2.4b.

**2.25 (*Turtle: draw a rectangle*) Write a program that prompts the user to enter the center of a rectangle, width, and height, and displays the rectangle, as shown in Figure 2.4c.

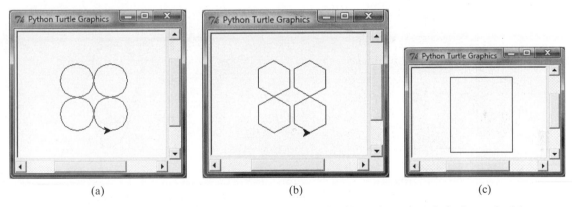

(a)   (b)   (c)

FIGURE 2.4 Four circles are drawn in (a), four hexagons are drawn in (b), and a rectangle is drawn in (c).

**2.26 (*Turtle: draw a circle*) Write a program that prompts the user to enter the center and radius of a circle, and then displays the circle and its area, as shown in Figure 2.5.

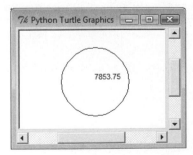

FIGURE 2.5 A circle and its area are displayed.

MATHEMATICAL FUNCTIONS, STRINGS, AND OBJECTS

Objectives

- To solve mathematics problems by using the functions in the **math** module (§3.2).

- To represent and process strings and characters (§§3.3–3.4).

- To encode characters using ASCII and Unicode (§§3.3.1–3.3.2).

- To use the **ord** function to obtain a numerical code for a character and the **chr** function to convert a numerical code to a character (§3.3.3).

- To represent special characters using the escape sequence (§3.3.4).

- To invoke the **print** function with the **end** argument (§3.3.5).

- To convert numbers to a string using the **str** function (§3.3.6).

- To use the + operator to concatenate strings (§3.3.7).

- To read strings from the keyboard (§3.3.8).

- To introduce objects and methods (§3.5).

- To format numbers and strings using the **format** function (§3.6).

- To draw various shapes (§3.7).

- To draw graphics with colors and fonts (§3.8).

3.1 Introduction

Key
Point

The focus of this chapter is to introduce functions, strings, and objects, and to use them to develop programs.

The preceding chapter introduced fundamental programming techniques and taught you how to write simple programs to solve basic problems. This chapter introduces Python functions for performing common mathematical operations. You will learn how to create custom functions in Chapter 6.

problem

Suppose you need to estimate the area enclosed by four cities, given the GPS locations (latitude and longitude) of these cities, as shown in the following diagram. How would you write a program to solve this problem? You will be able to write such a program after completing this chapter.

Charlotte (35.2270869, –80.8431267)

Atlanta
(33.7489954, –84.3879824)

Savannah (32.0835407, –81.0998342)

Orlando (28.5383355, –81.3792365)

Because all data in Python are objects, it is beneficial to introduce objects early so that you can begin to use them to develop useful programs. This chapter gives a brief introduction to objects and strings; you will learn more on objects and strings in Chapters 7 and 8.

3.2 Common Python Functions

Key
Point

Python provides many useful functions for common programming tasks.

function

A *function* is a group of statements that performs a specific task. Python, as well as other programming languages, provides a library of functions. You have already used the functions **eval**, **input**, **print**, and **int**. These are built-in functions and they are always available in the Python interpreter. You don't have to import any modules to use these functions. Additionally, you can use the built-in functions **abs**, **max**, **min**, **pow**, and **round**, as shown in Table 3.1.

TABLE 3.1 Simple Python Built-in Functions

Function	Description	Example
abs(x)	Returns the absolute value for **x**.	**abs(-2)** is **2**
max(x1, x2, ...)	Returns the largest among **x1, x2, ...**	**max(1, 5, 2)** is **5**
min(x1, x2, ...)	Returns the smallest among **x1, x2, ...**	**min(1, 5, 2)** is **1**
pow(a, b)	Returns a^b. Same as **a ** b**.	**pow(2, 3)** is **8**
round(x)	Returns an integer nearest to **x**. If **x** is equally close to two integers, the even one is returned.	**round(5.4)** is **5** **round(5.5)** is **6** **round(4.5)** is **4**
round(x, n)	Returns the float value rounded to **n** digits after the decimal point.	**round(5.466, 2)** is **5.47** **round(5.463, 2)** is **5.46**

For example,

```
>>> abs(-3) # Returns the absolute value
3
>>> abs(-3.5) # Returns the absolute value
3.5
>>> max(2, 3, 4, 6) # Returns the maximum number
6
>>> min(2, 3, 4) # Returns the minimum number
2
>>> pow(2, 3) # Same as 2 ** 3
8
>>> pow(2.5, 3.5) # Same as 2.5 ** 3.5
24.705294220065465
>>> round(3.51) # Rounds to its nearest integer
4
>>> round(3.4) # Rounds to its nearest integer
3
>>> round(3.1456, 3) # Rounds to 3 digits after the decimal point
3.146
>>>
```

Many programs are created to solve mathematical problems. The Python **math** module provides the mathematical functions listed in Table 3.2.

Two mathematical constants, **pi** and **e**, are also defined in the **math** module. They can be accessed using **math.pi** and **math.e**. Listing 3.1 is a program that tests some math functions. Because the program uses the math functions defined in the **math** module, the **math** module is imported in line 1.

TABLE 3.2   Mathematical Functions

Function	Description	Example
fabs(x)	Returns the absolute value for x as a float.	fabs(-2) is 2.0
ceil(x)	Rounds x up to its nearest integer and returns that integer.	ceil(2.1) is 3 ceil(-2.1) is -2
floor(x)	Rounds x down to its nearest integer and returns that integer.	floor(2.1) is 2 floor(-2.1) is -3
exp(x)	Returns the exponential function of x (e^x).	exp(1) is 2.71828
log(x)	Returns the natural logarithm of x.	log(2.71828) is 1.0
log(x, base)	Returns the logarithm of x for the specified base.	log(100, 10) is 2.0
sqrt(x)	Returns the square root of x.	sqrt(4.0) is 2
sin(x)	Returns the sine of x. x represents an angle in radians.	sin(3.14159 / 2) is 1 sin(3.14159) is 0
asin(x)	Returns the angle in radians for the inverse of sine.	asin(1.0) is 1.57 asin(0.5) is 0.523599
cos(x)	Returns the cosine of x. x represents an angle in radians.	cos(3.14159 / 2) is 0 cos(3.14159) is -1
acos(x)	Returns the angle in radians for the inverse of cosine.	acos(1.0) is 0 acos(0.5) is 1.0472
tan(x)	Returns the tangent of x. x represents an angle in radians.	tan(3.14159 / 4) is 1 tan(0.0) is 0
degrees(x)	Converts angle x from radians to degrees.	degrees(1.57) is 90
radians(x)	Converts angle x from degrees to radians.	radians(90) is 1.57

LISTING 3.1 MathFunctions.py

import math module

```
 1  import math # import math module to use the math functions
 2
 3  # Test algebraic functions
 4  print("exp(1.0) =", math.exp(1))
 5  print("log(2.78) =", math.log(math.e))
 6  print("log10(10, 10) =", math.log(10, 10))
 7  print("sqrt(4.0) =", math.sqrt(4.0))
 8
 9  # Test trigonometric functions
10  print("sin(PI / 2) =", math.sin(math.pi / 2))
11  print("cos(PI / 2) =", math.cos(math.pi / 2))
12  print("tan(PI / 2) =", math.tan(math.pi / 2))
13  print("degrees(1.57) =", math.degrees(1.57))
14  print("radians(90) =", math.radians(90))
```

exp
log
log10
sqrt

sin
cos
tan
degrees
radians

```
exp(1.0) = 2.71828182846
log(2.78) = 1.0
log10(10, 10) = 1.0
sqrt(4.0) = 2.0
sin(PI / 2) = 1.0
cos(PI / 2) = 6.12323399574e-17
tan(PI / 2) = 1.63312393532e+16
degrees(1.57) = 89.9543738355
radians(90) = 1.57079632679
```

You can use the math functions to solve many computational problems. Given the three vertices of a triangle, for example, you can compute the angles by using the following formula:

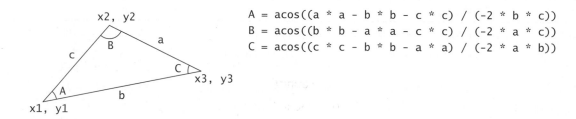

```
A = acos((a * a - b * b - c * c) / (-2 * b * c))
B = acos((b * b - a * a - c * c) / (-2 * a * c))
C = acos((c * c - b * b - a * a) / (-2 * a * b))
```

Don't be intimidated by the mathematic formula. As we discussed early in Listing 2.8, ComuteLoan.py, you don't have to know how the mathematical formula is derived in order to write a program for computing the loan payments. Here in this example, given the length of three sides, you can use this formula to write a program to compute the angles without having to know how the formula is derived. In order to compute the lengths of the sides, we need to know the coordinates of three corner points and compute the distances between the points.

Listing 3.2 is an example of a program that prompts the user to enter the x- and y-coordinates of the three corner points in a triangle and then displays the figure's angles.

LISTING 3.2 ComputeAngles.py

import math module

enter three points

compute edges

```
 1  import math
 2
 3  x1, y1, x2, y2, x3, y3 = eval(input("Enter three points: "))
 4
 5  a = math.sqrt((x2 - x3) * (x2 - x3) + (y2 - y3) * (y2 - y3))
 6  b = math.sqrt((x1 - x3) * (x1 - x3) + (y1 - y3) * (y1 - y3))
 7  c = math.sqrt((x1 - x2) * (x1 - x2) + (y1 - y2) * (y1 - y2))
```

```
 8
 9  A = math.degrees(math.acos((a * a - b * b - c * c) / (-2 * b * c)))    compute angles
10  B = math.degrees(math.acos((b * b - a * a - c * c) / (-2 * a * c)))
11  C = math.degrees(math.acos((c * c - b * b - a * a) / (-2 * a * b)))
12
13  print("The three angles are ", round(A * 100) / 100.0,               display result
14        round(B * 100) / 100.0, round(C * 100) / 100.0)
```

```
Enter three points: 1, 1, 6.5, 1, 6.5, 2.5  ↵Enter
The three angles are 15.26 90.0 74.74
```

The program prompts the user to enter three points (line 3). This prompting message is not clear. You should give the user explicit instructions on how to enter these points as follows:

```
input("Enter six coordinates of three points separated by commas\
like x1, y1, x2, y2, x3, y3: ")
```

The program computes the distances between the points (lines 5–7), and applies the formula to compute the angles (lines 9–11). The angles are rounded to display up to two digits after the decimal point (lines 13–14).

3.1   Evaluate the following functions:

(a) `math.sqrt(4)`

(b) `math.sin(2 * math.pi)`

(c) `math.cos(2 * math.pi)`

(d) `min(2, 2, 1)`

(e) `math.log(math.e)`

(f) `math.exp(1)`

(g) `max(2, 3, 4)`

(h) `abs(-2.5)`

(i) `math.ceil(-2.5)`

(j) `math.floor(-2.5)`

(k) `round(3.5)`

(l) `round(-2.5)`

(m) `math.fabs(2.5)`

(n) `math.ceil(2.5)`

(o) `math.floor(2.5)`

(p) `round(-2.5)`

(q) `round(2.6)`

(r) `round(math.fabs(-2.5))`

3.2   True or false? The argument for trigonometric functions represents an angle in radians.

3.3   Write a statement that converts **47** degrees to radians and assigns the result to a variable.

3.4   Write a statement that converts π / **7** to an angle in degrees and assigns the result to a variable.

3.3 Strings and Characters

A string (described in Chapter 1) is a sequence of characters. Python treats characters and strings the same way.

string

In addition to processing numeric values, you can process *strings* in Python. A *string* is a sequence of characters and can include text and numbers. *String* values must be enclosed in matching *single quotes* (') or *double quotes* ("). Python does not have a data type for characters. A single-character string represents a character. For example,

single quotes or double quotes

```
letter = 'A' # Same as letter = "A"
numChar = '4' # Same as numChar = "4"
message = "Good morning" # Same as message = 'Good morning'
```

The first statement assigns a string with the character **A** to the variable **letter**. The second statement assigns a string with the digit character **4** to the variable **numChar**. The third statement assigns the string **Good morning** to the variable **message**.

Note

For consistency, this book uses double quotes for a string with more than one character and single quotes for a string with a single character or an empty string. This convention is consistent with other programming languages, so it will be easy for you to convert a Python program to a program written in other languages.

3.3.1 ASCII Code

character encoding

Computers use binary numbers internally (see Section 1.2.2). A character is stored in a computer as a sequence of 0s and 1s. Mapping a character to its binary representation is called *character encoding*. There are different ways to encode a character. The manner in which characters are encoded is defined by an encoding scheme. One popular standard is ASCII (American Standard Code for Information Interchange), a 7-bit encoding scheme for representing all uppercase and lowercase letters, digits, punctuation marks, and control characters. ASCII uses numbers 0 through 127 to represent characters. Appendix B, The ASCII Character Set, shows the ASCII code for characters.

3.3.2 Unicode Code

Python also supports Unicode. Unicode is an encoding scheme for representing international characters. ASCII is a small subset of Unicode. Unicode was established by the Unicode Consortium to support the interchange, processing, and display of written texts in the world's diverse languages. A Unicode starts with **\u**, followed by four hexadecimal digits that run from **\u0000** to **\uFFFF**. (For information on hexadecimal numbers, see Appendix C.) For example, the word "welcome" is translated into Chinese using two characters, 欢 and 迎. The Unicode representations of these two characters are **\u6B22\u8FCE**.

The program in Listing 3.3 displays two Chinese characters and three Greek letters, as shown in Figure 3.1.

LISTING 3.3 DisplayUnicode.py

```
1  import turtle
2
3  turtle.write("\u6B22\u8FCE \u03b1 \u03b2 \u03b3")
4
5  turtle.done()
```

FIGURE 3.1 You can use Unicode to display international characters in a Python GUI program.

If no Chinese font is installed on your system, you will not be able to see the Chinese characters. In this case, delete **\u6B22\u8FCE** from your program to avoid errors. The Unicode codes for the Greek letters α, β, and γ are **\u03b1**, **\u03b2**, and **\u03b3**.

3.3.3 The **ord** and **chr** Functions

Python provides the **ord(ch)** function for returning the ASCII code for the character **ch** and the **chr(code)** function for returning the character represented by the code. For example,

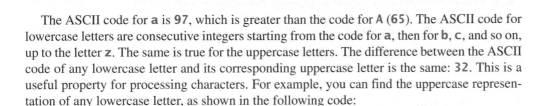

```
>>> ch = 'a'
>>> ord(ch)
97
>>> chr(98)
'b'
>>> ord('A')
65
>>>
```

The ASCII code for **a** is **97**, which is greater than the code for **A** (**65**). The ASCII code for lowercase letters are consecutive integers starting from the code for **a**, then for **b**, **c**, and so on, up to the letter **z**. The same is true for the uppercase letters. The difference between the ASCII code of any lowercase letter and its corresponding uppercase letter is the same: **32**. This is a useful property for processing characters. For example, you can find the uppercase representation of any lowercase letter, as shown in the following code:

```
 1  >>> ord('a') – ord('A')
 2  32
 3  >>> ord('d') – ord('D')
 4  32
 5  >>> offset = ord('a') – ord('A')
 6  >>> lowercaseLetter = 'h'
 7  >>> uppercaseLetter = chr(ord(lowercaseLetter) – offset)
 8  >>> uppercaseLetter
 9  'H'
10  >>>
```

Line 6 assigns a lowercase letter to variable **lowercaseLetter**. Line 7 obtains its corresponding uppercase letter.

3.3.4 Escape Sequences for Special Characters

Suppose you want to print a message with quotation marks in the output. Can you write a statement like this?

```
print("He said, "John's program is easy to read"")
```

No, this statement has an error. Python thinks the second quotation mark is the end of the string and does not know what to do with the rest of the characters.

To overcome this problem, Python uses a special notation to represent special characters, as shown in Table 3.3. This special notation, which consists of a *backslash* (\) followed by a letter or a combination of digits, is called an *escape sequence*.

The **\n** character is also known as a *newline*, *line break* or *end-of-line* (EOL) character, which signifies the end of a line. The **\f** character forces the printer to print from the next page. The **\r** character is used to move the cursor to the first position on the same line. The **\f** and **\r** characters are rarely used in this book.

backslash (\)

escape sequence

newline

line break

end-of-line (EOL) character

TABLE 3.3 Python Escape Sequences

Character Escape Sequence	Name	Numeric Value
\b	Backspace	8
\t	Tab	9
\n	Linefeed	10
\f	Formfeed	12
\r	Carriage Return	13
\\	Backslash	92
\'	Single Quote	39
\"	Double Quote	34

Now you can print the quoted message using the following statement:

```
>>> print("He said, \"John's program is easy to read\"")
He said, "John's program is easy to read"
```

Note that the symbols \ and " together represent one character.

3.3.5 Printing without the Newline

When you use the **print** function, it automatically prints a linefeed (**\n**) to cause the output to advance to the next line. If you don't want this to happen after the **print** function is finished, you can invoke the **print** function by passing a special argument **end = "anyendingstring"** using the following syntax:

```
print(item, end = "anyendingstring")
```

For example, the following code

```
1  print("AAA", end = ' ')
2  print("BBB", end = '')
3  print("CCC", end = '***')
4  print("DDD", end = '***')
```

displays

```
AAA BBBCCC***DDD***
```

Line 1 prints **AAA** followed by a space character ' ', line 2 prints **BBB**, line 3 prints **CCC** followed by ***, and line 4 prints **DDD** followed by ***. Note that '' in line 2 means an empty string. So, nothing is printed for ''.

You can also use the **end** argument for printing multiple items using the following syntax:

```
print(item1, item2, ..., end = "anyendingstring")
```

For example,

```
radius = 3
print("The area is", radius * radius * math.pi, end = ' ')
print("and the perimeter is", 2 * radius)
```

displays

```
The area is 28.26 and the perimeter is 6
```

3.3.6 The `str` Function

The **str** function can be used to convert a number into a string. For example,

```
>>> s = str(3.4) # Convert a float to string
>>> s
'3.4'
>>> s = str(3) # Convert an integer to string
>>> s
'3'
>>>
```

3.3.7 The String Concatenation Operator

You can use the + operator to add two numbers. The + operator can be used to concatenate two strings. Here are some examples:

```
1  >>> message = "Welcome " + "to " + "Python"
2  >>> message
3  'Welcome to Python'
4  >>> chapterNo = 3
5  >>> s = "Chapter " + str(chapterNo)
6  >>> s
7  'Chapter 3'
8  >>>
```

Line 1 concatenates three strings into one. In line 5, the **str** function converts the numeric value in variable **chapterNo** to a string. This string is concatenated with **"Chapter "** to obtain the new string **"Chapter 3"**.

The augmented assignment += operator can also be used for string concatenation. For example, the following code concatenates the string in **message** with the string **" and Python is fun"**.

```
>>> message = "Welcome to Python"
>>> message
'Welcome to Python'
>>> message += " and Python is fun"
>>> message
'Welcome to Python and Python is fun'
>>>
```

3.3.8 Reading Strings from the Console

To read a string from the console, use the **input** function. For example, the following code reads three strings from the keyboard:

```
s1 = input("Enter a string: ")
s2 = input("Enter a string: ")
s3 = input("Enter a string: ")
print("s1 is " + s1)
print("s2 is " + s2)
print("s3 is " + s3)
```

```
Enter a string: Welcome  ↵Enter
Enter a string: to  ↵Enter
Enter a string: Python  ↵Enter
s1 is Welcome
s2 is to
s3 is Python
```

✓Check Point

MyProgrammingLab™

3.5 Use the **ord** function to find the ASCII code for **1**, **A**, **B**, **a**, and **b**. Use the **chr** function to find the character for the decimal codes **40**, **59**, **79**, **85**, and **90**.

3.6 How do you display the characters \ and "?

3.7 How do you write a character in Unicode?

3.8 Suppose you entered **A** when running the following code. What is the output?
```
x = input("Enter a character: ")
ch = chr(ord(x) + 3)
print(ch)
```

3.9 Suppose you entered **A** and **Z** when running the following code. What is the output?
```
x = input("Enter a character: ")
y = input("Enter a character: ")
print(ord(y) - ord(x))
```

3.10 What is wrong in the following code? How do you fix it?
```
title = "Chapter " + 1
```

3.11 Show the result of the following code:
```
sum = 2 + 3
print(sum)
s = '2' + '3'
print(s)
```

3.4 Case Study: Minimum Number of Coins

Now let's look at a sample program that uses the features covered in this section. Suppose you want to develop a program that classifies a given amount of money into smaller monetary units. The program lets the user enter an amount as a floating-point value representing a total in dollars and cents, and then outputs a report listing the monetary equivalent in dollars, quarters, dimes, nickels, and pennies, as shown in the sample run.

minimum number of coins

Your program should report the maximum number of dollars, then the number of quarters, dimes, nickels, and pennies, in this order, to result in the minimum number of coins.

Here are the steps in developing the program:

1. Prompt the user to enter the amount as a decimal number, such as **11.56**.

2. Convert the amount (**11.56**) into cents (**1156**).

3. Divide the cents by **100** to find the number of dollars. Obtain the remaining cents using the cents remainder **% 100**.

4. Divide the remaining cents by **25** to find the number of quarters. Obtain the remaining cents using the remaining cents remainder **% 25**.

5. Divide the remaining cents by **10** to find the number of dimes. Obtain the remaining cents using the remaining cents remainder **% 10**.

6. Divide the remaining cents by **5** to find the number of nickels. Obtain the remaining cents using the remaining cents remainder **% 5**.

7. The remaining cents are the pennies.

8. Display the result.

The complete program is shown in Listing 3.4.

LISTING 3.4 ComputeChange.py

```
1  # Receive the amount
2  amount = eval(input("Enter an amount, for example, 11.56: "))     enter input
3
4  # Convert the amount to cents
5  remainingAmount = int(amount * 100)
6
7  # Find the number of one dollars
8  numberOfOneDollars = remainingAmount // 100                        dollars
9  remainingAmount = remainingAmount % 100
10
11 # Find the number of quarters in the remaining amount
12 numberOfQuarters = remainingAmount // 25                           quarters
13 remainingAmount = remainingAmount % 25
14
15 # Find the number of dimes in the remaining amount
16 numberOfDimes = remainingAmount // 10                              dimes
17 remainingAmount = remainingAmount % 10
18
19 # Find the number of nickels in the remaining amount
20 numberOfNickels = remainingAmount // 5                             nickels
21 remainingAmount = remainingAmount % 5
22
23 # Find the number of pennies in the remaining amount
24 numberOfPennies = remainingAmount                                  pennies
25
26 # Display the results
27 print("Your amount", amount, "consists of\n",                     output
28     "\t", numberOfOneDollars, "dollars\n",
29     "\t", numberOfQuarters, "quarters\n",
30     "\t", numberOfDimes,   "dimes\n",
31     "\t", numberOfNickels, "nickels\n",
32     "\t", numberOfPennies, "pennies")
```

```
Enter an amount, for example, 11.56: 11.56  ↵Enter
Your amount 11.56 consists of
     11 dollars
      2 quarters
      0 dimes
      1 nickels
      1 pennies
```

variables \ line#	2	5	8	9	12	13	16	17	20	21	24
amount	11.56										
remainingAmount		1156		56		6		6		1	
numberOfOneDollars			11								
numberOfQuarters					2						
numberOfDimes							0				
numberOfNickels									1		
numberOfPennies											1

The variable **amount** stores the amount entered from the console (line 2). This variable is not changed, because the amount has to be used at the end of the program to display the results. The program introduces the variable **remainingAmount** (line 5) to store the changing **remainingAmount**.

The variable **amount** is a float representing dollars and cents. It is converted to an integer variable **remainingAmount**, which represents all the cents. For instance, if **amount** is **11.56**, then the initial **remainingAmount** is **1156. 1156 // 100** is **11** (line 8). The remainder operator obtains the remainder of the division. So, **1156 % 100** is **56** (line 9).

The program extracts the maximum number of quarters from **remainingAmount** and obtains a new **remainingAmount** (lines 12–13). Continuing the same process, the program finds the maximum number of dimes, nickels, and pennies in the remaining amount.

As shown in the sample run, **0** dimes, **1** nickels, and **1** pennies are displayed in the result. It would be better not to display **0** dimes, and to display **1** nickel and **1** penny using the singular forms of the words. You will learn how to use selection statements to modify this program in the next chapter (see Exercise 4.7).

Caution

loss of precision

One serious problem with this example is the possible loss of precision when converting a float amount to the integer **remainingAmount**. This could lead to an inaccurate result. If you try to enter the amount **10.03**, **10.03 * 100** might be **1003.9999999999999**. You will find that the program displays **10** dollars and **2** pennies. To fix the problem, enter the amount as an integer value representing cents (see Exercise 3.8).

3.5 Introduction to Objects and Methods

Key Point

In Python, all data—including numbers and strings—are actually objects.

object

In Python, a number is an *object*, a string is an object, and every datum is an object. Objects of the same kind have the same type. You can use the **id** function and **type** function to get these pieces of information about an object. For example,

```
1  >>> n = 3  # n is an integer
2  >>> id(n)
3  505408904
4  >>> type(n)
5  <class 'int'>
6  >>> f = 3.0  # f is a float
```

```
 7  >>> id(f)
 8  26647120
 9  >>> type(f)
10  <class 'float'>
11  >>> s = "Welcome" # s is a string
12  >>> id(s)
13  36201472
14  >>> type(s)
15  <class 'str'>
16  >>>
```

VideoNote
String operations

The id for the object is automatically assigned a unique integer by Python when the program is executed. The id for the object will not be changed during the execution of the program. However, Python may assign a different id every time the program is executed. The type for the object is determined by Python according to the value of the object. Line 2 displays the id for a number object **n**, line 3 shows the id Python has assigned for the object, and its type is displayed in line 4.

In Python, an object's type is defined by a class. For example, the class for string is **str** (line 15), for integer is **int** (line 5), and for float is **float** (line 10). The term "class" comes from object-oriented programming, which will be discussed in Chapter 7. In Python, classes and types are synonymous.

 Note

The **id** and **type** functions are rarely used in programming, but they are good tools for learning more about objects.

id function
type function

A variable in Python is actually a reference to an object. Figure 3.2 shows the relationship between the variables and objects for the preceding code.

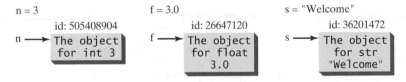

FIGURE 3.2 In Python, each variable is actually a reference to an object.

The statement **n = 3** in line 1 assigns value **3** to **n**, which actually assigns **3** to an **int** object referenced by variable **n**.

 Note

For **n = 3**, we say **n** is an integer variable that holds value **3**. Strictly speaking, **n** is a variable that references an **int** object for value **3**. For simplicity, it is fine to say **n** is an **int** variable with value **3**.

objects vs. object reference
variable

You can perform operations on an object. The operations are defined using functions. The functions for the objects are called *methods* in Python. Methods can only be invoked from a specific object. For example, the string type has the methods such as **lower()** and **upper()**,

methods

which return a new string in lowercase and uppercase. Here are some examples of how to invoke these methods:

```
1  >>> s = "Welcome"
2  >>> s1 = s.lower() # Invoke the lower method
3  >>> s1
4  'welcome'
5  >>> s2 = s.upper() # Invoke the upper method
6  >>> s2
7  'WELCOME'
8  >>>
```

Line 2 invokes **s.lower()** on object **s** to return a new string in lowercase and assigns it to **s1**. Line 5 invokes **s.upper()** on object **s** to return a new string in uppercase and assigns it to **s2**.

As you can see from the preceding example, the syntax to invoke a method for an object is **object.method()**.

strip()

Another useful string method is **strip()**, which can be used to remove (strip) the whitespace characters from both ends of a string. The characters **' '**, **\t**, **\f**, **\r**, and **\n** are known as the *whitespace characters*.

whitespace characters

For example,

```
>>> s = "\t Welcome \n"
>>> s1 = s.strip() # Invoke the strip method
>>> s1
'Welcome'
>>>
```

Note

Python on Eclipse

If you use Python on Eclipse, Eclipse automatically appends **\r** in the string entered from the **input** function. Therefore, you should use the **strip()** method to remove the **\r** character as follows:

```
s = input("Enter a string").strip()
```

More details on processing strings and on object-oriented programming will be discussed in Chapter 7.

3.12 What is an object? What is a method?

3.13 How do you find the id for an object? How do you find the type for an object?

3.14 Which of the following statements is the precise meaning for the statement **n = 3**?

    (a) **n** is a variable that holds **int** value **3**.

    (b) **n** is a variable that references an object that holds **int** value **3**.

3.15 Suppose **s** is "**\tGeorgia\n**". What is **s.lower()** and **s.upper()**?

3.16 Suppose **s** is " **\tGood\tMorning\n**". What is **s.strip()**?

3.6 Formatting Numbers and Strings

*You can use the **format** function to return a formatted string.*

Often it is desirable to display numbers in a certain format. For example, the following code computes interest, given the amount and the annual interest rate.

```
>>> amount = 12618.98
>>> interestRate = 0.0013
>>> interest = amount * interestRate
>>> print("Interest is", interest)
Interest is 16.404674
>>>
```

Because the interest amount is currency, it is desirable to display only two digits after the decimal point. To do this, you can write the code as follows:

```
>>> amount = 12618.98
>>> interestRate = 0.0013
>>> interest = amount * interestRate
>>> print("Interest is", round(interest, 2))
Interest is 16.4
>>>
```

However, the format is still not correct. There should be two digits after the decimal point like **16.40** rather than **16.4**. You can fix it by using the **format** function, like this:

format

```
>>> amount = 12618.98
>>> interestRate = 0.0013
>>> interest = amount * interestRate
>>> print("Interest is", format(interest, ".2f") )
Interest is 16.40                    16.404674
>>>
```

The syntax to invoke this function is

```
format(item, format-specifier)
```

where **item** is a number or a string and **format-specifier** is a string that specifies how the item is formatted. The function returns a string.

3.6.1 Formatting Floating-Point Numbers

If the item is a float value, you can use the specifier to give the width and precision of the format in the form of *width.precision*f. Here, **width** specifies the width of the resulting string, **precision** specifies the number of digits after the decimal point, and **f** is called the *conversion code*, which sets the formatting for floating point numbers. For example,

conversion code

```
print(format(57.467657, "10.2f"))
print(format(12345678.923, "10.2f"))
print(format(57.4, "10.2f"))
print(format(57, "10.2f"))
```

displays

```
|←— 10 —→|
□□□□□ 57.47
 123456782.92
□□□□□ 57.40
□□□□□ 57.00
```

where a square box (□) denotes a blank space. Note that the decimal point is counted as one space.

The `format("10.2f")` function formats the number into a string whose width is **10**, including a decimal point and two digits after the point. The number is rounded to two decimal places. Thus there are seven digits allocated before the decimal point. If there are fewer than seven digits before the decimal point, spaces are inserted before the number. If there are more than seven digits before the decimal point, the number's width is automatically increased. For example, `format(12345678.923, "10.2f")` returns **12345678.92**, which has a width of **11**.

You can omit the width specifier. If so, it defaults to **0**. In this case, the width is automatically set to the size needed for formatting the number. For example,

```
print(format(57.467657, "10.2f"))
print(format(57.467657, ".2f"))
```

displays

```
|←— 10 —→|
⊏⊐⊐⊐⊐ 57.47
57.47
```

3.6.2 Formatting in Scientific Notation

If you change the conversion code from **f** to **e**, the number will be formatted in scientific notation. For example,

```
print(format(57.467657, "10.2e"))
print(format(0.0033923, "10.2e"))
print(format(57.4, "10.2e"))
print(format(57, "10.2e"))
```

displays

```
|←— 10 —→|
⊏⊐ 5.75e+01
⊏⊐ 3.39e-03
⊏⊐ 5.74e+01
⊏⊐ 5.70e+01
```

The + and − signs are counted as places in the width limit.

3.6.3 Formatting as a Percentage

You can use the conversion code **%** to format a number as a percentage. For example,

```
print(format(0.53457, "10.2%"))
print(format(0.0033923, "10.2%"))
print(format(7.4, "10.2%"))
print(format(57, "10.2%"))
```

displays

```
|←— 10 —→|
⊏⊐⊐⊐ 53.46%
⊏⊐⊐⊐⊐ 0.34%
⊏⊐⊐ 740.00%
⊏⊐ 5700.00%
```

The format **10.2%** causes the number to be multiplied by 100 and displayed with a **%** sign following it. The total width includes the **%** sign counted as one space.

3.6.4 Justifying Format

By default, the format of a number is right justified. You can put the symbol < in the format specifier to specify that the item be left-justified in the resulting format within the specified width. For example,

```
print(format(57.467657, "10.2f"))
print(format(57.467657, "<10.2f"))
```

displays

```
|←——10——→|
□□□□□ 57.47
57.47
```

3.6.5 Formatting Integers

The conversion codes **d**, **x**, **o**, and **b** can be used to format an integer in decimal, hexadecimal, octal, or binary. You can specify a width for the conversion. For example,

```
print(format(59832, "10d"))
print(format(59832, "<10d"))
print(format(59832, "10x"))
print(format(59832, "<10x"))
```

displays

```
|←——10——→|
□□□□□ 59832
59832
□□□□□ e9b8
e9b8
```

The format specifier **10d** specifies that the integer is formatted into a decimal with a width of ten spaces. The format specifier **10x** specifies that the integer is formatted into a hexadecimal integer with a width of ten spaces.

3.6.6 Formatting Strings

You can use the conversion code **s** to format a string with a specified width. For example,

```
print(format("Welcome to Python", "20s"))
print(format("Welcome to Python", "<20s"))
print(format("Welcome to Python", ">20s"))
print(format("Welcome to Python and Java", ">20s"))
```

displays

```
|←————— 20 —————→|
Welcome to Python
Welcome to Python
□□□ Welcome to Python
Welcome to Python and Java
```

The format specifier **20s** specifies that the string is formatted within a width of 20. By default, a string is left justified. To right-justify it, put the symbol > in the format specifier. If the string is longer than the specified width, the width is automatically increased to fit the string.

Table 3.4 summarizes the format specifiers introduced in this section.

TABLE 3.4 Frequently Used Specifiers

Specifier	Format
"10.2f"	Format the float item with width 10 and precision 2.
"10.2e"	Format the float item in scientific notation with width 10 and precision 2.
"5d"	Format the integer item in decimal with width 5.
"5x"	Format the integer item in hexadecimal with width 5.
"5o"	Format the integer item in octal with width 5.
"5b"	Format the integer item in binary with width 5.
"10.2%"	Format the number in decimal.
"50s"	Format the string item with width 50.
"<10.2f"	Left-justify the formatted item.
">10.2f"	Right-justify the formatted item.

MyProgrammingLab™

3.17 What is the return value from invoking the **format** function?

3.18 What happens if the size of the actual item is greater than the width in the format specifier?

3.19 Show the printout of the following statements:

```
print(format(57.467657, "9.3f"))
print(format(12345678.923, "9.1f"))
print(format(57.4, ".2f"))
print(format(57.4, "10.2f"))
```

3.20 Show the printout of the following statements:

```
print(format(57.467657, "9.3e"))
print(format(12345678.923, "9.1e"))
print(format(57.4, ".2e"))
print(format(57.4, "10.2e"))
```

3.21 Show the printout of the following statements:

```
print(format(5789.467657, "9.3f"))
print(format(5789.467657, "<9.3f"))
print(format(5789.4, ".2f"))
print(format(5789.4, "<.2f"))
print(format(5789.4, ">9.2f"))
```

3.22 Show the printout of the following statements:

```
print(format(0.457467657, "9.3%"))
print(format(0.457467657, "<9.3%"))
```

3.23 Show the printout of the following statements:

```
print(format(45, "5d"))
print(format(45, "<5d"))
print(format(45, "5x"))
print(format(45, "<5x"))
```

3.24 Show the printout of the following statements:

```
print(format("Programming is fun", "25s"))
print(format("Programming is fun", "<25s"))
print(format("Programming is fun", ">25s"))
```

3.7 Drawing Various Shapes

The Python `turtle` *module contains methods for moving the pen, setting the pen's size, lifting, and putting down the pen.*

Key Point

Chapter 1 introduced drawing with the turtle. A turtle is actually an object that is created when you import the `turtle` module. You then invoke the turtle object's methods to perform operations. This section introduces more methods for the `turtle` object.

When a turtle object is created, its *position* is set at (**0, 0**)—the center of the window—and its *direction* is set to go straight to the right. The `turtle` module uses a pen to draw shapes. By default, the pen is down (like the tip of an actual pen touching a sheet of paper). When you move the turtle, it draws a line from the current position to the new position if the pen is down. Table 3.5 lists the methods for controlling the pen's drawing state; Table 3.6 lists the methods for moving the turtle.

turtle's position and direction

turtle's pen

VideoNote
Draw shapes

TABLE 3.5 Turtle Pen Drawing State Methods

Method	Description
`turtle.pendown()`	Pulls the pen down—drawing when moving.
`turtle.penup()`	Pulls the pen up—no drawing when moving.
`turtle.pensize(width)`	Sets the line thickness to the specified width.

TABLE 3.6 Turtle Motion Methods

Method	Description
`turtle.forward(d)`	Moves the turtle forward by the specified distance in the direction the turtle is headed.
`turtle.backward(d)`	Moves the turtle backward by the specified distance in the opposite direction the turtle is headed. The turtle's direction is not changed.
`turtle.right(angle)`	Turns the turtle right by the specified angle.
`turtle.left(angle)`	Turns the turtle left by the specified angle.
`turtle.goto(x, y)`	Moves the turtle to an absolute position.
`turtle.setx(x)`	Moves the turtle's x-coordinate to the specified position.
`turtle.sety(y)`	Moves the turtle's y-coordinate to the specified position.
`turtle.setheading(angle)`	Sets the orientation of the turtle to a specified angle. 0-East, 90-North, 180-West, 270-South.
`turtle.home()`	Moves the turtle to the origin (0, 0) and east direction.
`turtle.circle(r, ext, step)`	Draws a circle with the specified radius, extent, and step.
`turtle.dot(diameter, color)`	Draws a circle with the specified diameter and color.
`turtle.undo()`	Undo (repeatedly) the last turtle action(s).
`turtle.speed(s)`	Sets the turtle's speed to an integer between 1 and 10, with 10 being the fastest.

All these methods are straightforward. The best way to learn them is to write a test code to see how each method works.

The `circle` method has three arguments: The `radius` is required, and `extent` and `step` are optional. `extent` is an angle that determines which part of the circle is drawn. `step` determines the number of steps to use. If `step` is 3, 4, 5, 6, ..., the `circle` method will draw a maximum regular polygon with three, four, five, six, or more sides enclosed inside the circle (that is, a triangle, square, pentagon, hexagon, etc.). If `step` is not specified, the `circle` method will draw a circle.

Listing 3.5 shows sample code for drawing a triangle, a square, a pentagon, a hexagon, and a circle, as shown in Figure 3.3.

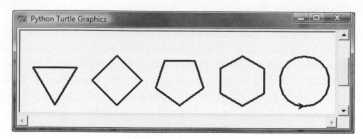

FIGURE 3.3 The program draws five shapes.

LISTING 3.5 SimpleShapes.py

| import turtle module | ```
 1  import turtle
 2
 3  turtle.pensize(3) # Set pen thickness to 3 pixels
 4  turtle.penup() # Pull the pen up
 5  turtle.goto(-200, -50)
 6  turtle.pendown() # Pull the pen down
 7  turtle.circle(40, steps = 3) # Draw a triangle
 8
 9  turtle.penup()
10  turtle.goto(-100, -50)
11  turtle.pendown()
12  turtle.circle(40, steps = 4) # Draw a square
13
14  turtle.penup()
15  turtle.goto(0, -50)
16  turtle.pendown()
17  turtle.circle(40, steps = 5) # Draw a pentagon
18
19  turtle.penup()
20  turtle.goto(100, -50)
21  turtle.pendown()
22  turtle.circle(40, steps = 6) # Draw a hexagon
23
24  turtle.penup()
25  turtle.goto(200, -50)
26  turtle.pendown()
27  turtle.circle(40) # Draw a circle
28
29  turtle.done()
``` |

set pen size (line 3)
penup (line 4)
move pen (line 5)
pendown (line 6)
draw a triangle (line 7)

pause (line 29)

Line 1 imports the **turtle** module. Line 3 sets the pen's thickness to **3** pixels. Line 4 pulls the pen up so that you can reposition it to (**-200, -50**) in line 5. Line 6 puts the pen down to draw a triangle in line 7. In line 7, the **turtle** object invokes the **circle** method with a radius of **40** and **3** steps to draw a triangle. Similarly, the rest of the program draws a square (line 12), a pentagon (line 17), a hexagon (line 22), and a circle (line 27).

Check Point

MyProgrammingLab™

3.25 How do you set the turtle to its original position (**0, 0**)?

3.26 How do you draw a red dot with diameter **3**?

3.27 What figure will the following method draw?

```
turtle.circle(50, step = 4)
```
```

3.28 How do you make the turtle move fast?

3.29 How do you undo the turtle's last action?

3.8 Drawing with Colors and Fonts

A turtle object contains the methods for setting colors and fonts.

Key Point

The preceding section showed you how to draw shapes with the **turtle** module. You learned how to use the motion methods to move the pen and use the pen methods to raise the pen up, set it down, and control its thickness. This section introduces more pen control methods and shows you how to set colors and fonts and write text.

Table 3.7 lists the pen methods for controlling drawing, color, and filling. Listing 3.6 is a sample program that draws a triangle, a square, a pentagon, a hexagon, and a circle in different colors, as shown in Figure 3.4. The program also adds text to the drawing.

TABLE 3.7 Turtle Pen Color, Filling, and Drawing Methods

Method	Description
turtle.color(c)	Sets the pen color.
turtle.fillcolor(c)	Sets the pen fill color.
turtle.begin_fill()	Calls this method before filling a shape.
turtle.end_fill()	Fills the shapes drawn before the last call to **begin_fill**.
turtle.filling()	Returns the fill state: **True** if filling, **False** if not filling.
turtle.clear()	Clears the window. The state and the position of the turtle are not affected.
turtle.reset()	Clears the window and reset the state and position to the original default value.
turtle.screensize(w, h)	Sets the width and height of the canvas.
turtle.hideturtle()	Makes the turtle invisible.
turtle.showturtle()	Makes the turtle visible.
turtle.isvisible()	Returns **True** if the turtle is visible.
turtle.write(s, font=("Arial", 8, "normal"))	Writes the string **s** on the turtle position. Font is a triple consisting of fontname, fontsize, and fonttype.

LISTING 3.6 ColorShapes.py

```
1  import turtle
2
3  turtle.pensize(3) # Set pen thickness to 3 pixels
4  turtle.penup() # Pull the pen up
5  turtle.goto(-200, -50)
6  turtle.pendown() # Pull the pen down
7  turtle.begin_fill() # Begin to fill color in a shape
8  turtle.color("red")
9  turtle.circle(40, steps = 3) # Draw a triangle
10 turtle.end_fill() # Fill the shape
11
12 turtle.penup()
13 turtle.goto(-100, -50)
14 turtle.pendown()
15 turtle.begin_fill() # Begin to fill color in a shape
16 turtle.color("blue")
17 turtle.circle(40, steps = 4) # Draw a square
```

import turtle module

set pen size
penup
move pen
pendown
begin_fill
set a color
draw a triangle
end_fill

```
18   turtle.end_fill() # Fill the shape
19
20   turtle.penup()
21   turtle.goto(0, -50)
22   turtle.pendown()
23   turtle.begin_fill() # Begin to fill color in a shape
24   turtle.color("green")
25   turtle.circle(40, steps = 5) # Draw a pentagon
26   turtle.end_fill() # Fill the shape
27
28   turtle.penup()
29   turtle.goto(100, -50)
30   turtle.pendown()
31   turtle.begin_fill() # Begin to fill color in a shape
32   turtle.color("yellow")
33   turtle.circle(40, steps = 6) # Draw a hexagon
34   turtle.end_fill() # Fill the shape
35
36   turtle.penup()
37   turtle.goto(200, -50)
38   turtle.pendown()
39   turtle.begin_fill() # Begin to fill color in a shape
40   turtle.color("purple")
41   turtle.circle(40) # Draw a circle
42   turtle.end_fill() # Fill the shape
43   turtle.color("green")
44   turtle.penup()
45   turtle.goto(-100, 50)
46   turtle.pendown()
```

write text

```
47   turtle.write("Cool Colorful Shapes",
48       font = ("Times", 18, "bold"))
49   turtle.hideturtle()
50
```

pause

```
51   turtle.done()
```

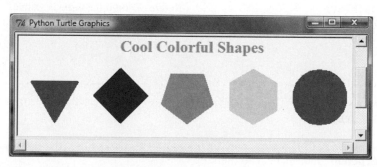

FIGURE 3.4 The program draws five shapes in different colors.

The program is similar to Listing 3.5. SimpleShapes.py, except that it fills each shape with a color and writes a string. The turtle object invokes the **begin_fill()** method in line 7 to tell Python to draw shapes filled with color. A triangle is drawn in line 9. Invoking the **end_fill()** method (line 10) completes the color filling for the shape.

The **write** method writes a string with the specified font at the current pen position (lines 47–48). Note that drawing takes place when the pen is moved if the pen is down. To avoid drawing, you need to pull the pen up. Invoking **hideturtle()** makes the turtle invisible (line 49) so you will not see the turtle in the window.

3.30   How do you set the turtle's color?

3.31   How do you fill a shape with color?

3.32   How do you make the turtle invisible?

KEY TERMS

backslash (\)   69
character encoding   68
end-of-line   69
escape sequence   69
line break   69

methods   75
newline   69
object   74
string   67
whitespace characters   76

CHAPTER SUMMARY

1.   Python provides the mathematical functions **abs**, **max**, **min**, **pow**, and **round** in the interpreter and the functions **fabs**, **ceil**, **floor**, **exp**, **log**, **sqrt**, **sin**, **asin**, **cos**, **acos**, **tan**, **degrees**, and **radians** in the **math** module.

2.   A *string* is a sequence of characters. String values can be enclosed in matching single quotes (') or double quotes ("). Python does not have a data type for characters; a single-character string represents a character.

3.   An *escape sequence* is a special syntax that begins with the character \ followed by a letter or a combination of digits to represent special characters, such as \', \", \t, and \n.

4.   The characters ' ', \t, \f, \r, and \n are known as the *whitespace characters*.

5.   All data including numbers and strings are *objects* in Python. You can invoke *methods* to perform operations on the objects.

6.   You can use the **format** function to format a number or a string and return the result as a string.

TEST QUESTIONS

Do test questions for this chapter online at www.cs.armstrong.edu/liang/py/test.html.

PROGRAMMING EXERCISES

MyProgrammingLab™

Section 3.2

3.1   (*Geometry: area of a pentagon*) Write a program that prompts the user to enter the length from the center of a pentagon to a vertex and computes the area of the pentagon, as shown in the following figure.

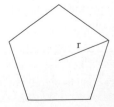

The formula for computing the area of a pentagon is $Area = \frac{3\sqrt{3}}{2}s^2$, where s is the length of a side. The side can be computed using the formula $s = 2r\sin\frac{\pi}{5}$, where r is the length from the center of a pentagon to a vertex. Here is a sample run:

```
Enter the length from the center to a vertex: 5.5  ↵Enter
The area of the pentagon is 108.61
```

*3.2 (*Geometry: great circle distance*) The great circle distance is the distance between two points on the surface of a sphere. Let $(x1, y1)$ and $(x2, y2)$ be the geographical latitude and longitude of two points. The great circle distance between the two points can be computed using the following formula:

$$d = radius \times \arccos(\sin(x_1) \times \sin(x_2) + \cos(x_1) \times \cos(x_2) \times \cos(y_1 - y_2))$$

Write a program that prompts the user to enter the latitude and longitude of two points on the earth in degrees and displays its great circle distance. The average earth radius is 6,371.01 km. Note that you need to convert the degrees into radians using the **math.radians** function since the Python trigonometric functions use radians. The latitude and longitude degrees in the formula are for north and west. Use negative to indicate south and east degrees. Here is a sample run:

```
Enter point 1 (latitude and longitude) in degrees:
39.55, -116.25  ↵Enter

Enter point 2 (latitude and longitude) in degrees:
41.5, 87.37  ↵Enter
The distance between the two points is 10691.79183231593 km
```

*3.3 (*Geography: estimate areas*) Find the GPS locations for Atlanta, Georgia; Orlando, Florida; Savannah, Georgia; and Charlotte, North Carolina from www.gps-data-team.com/map/ and compute the estimated area enclosed by these four cities. (Hint: Use the formula in Programming Exercise 3.2 to compute the distance between two cities. Divide the polygon into two triangles and use the formula in Programming Exercise 2.14 to compute the area of a triangle.)

3.4 (*Geometry: area of a pentagon*) The area of a pentagon can be computed using the following formula (s is the length of a side):

$$Area = \frac{5 \times s^2}{4 \times \tan\left(\dfrac{\pi}{5}\right)}$$

Write a program that prompts the user to enter the side of a pentagon and displays the area. Here is a sample run:

```
Enter the side: 5.5  ↵Enter
The area of the pentagon is 53.04444136781625
```

*3.5 (*Geometry: area of a regular polygon*) A regular polygon is an *n*-sided polygon in which all sides are of the same length and all angles have the same degree (i.e., the polygon is both equilateral and equiangular). The formula for computing the area of a regular polygon is

$$Area = \frac{n \times s^2}{4 \times \tan\left(\dfrac{\pi}{n}\right)}$$

Here, **s** is the length of a side. Write a program that prompts the user to enter the number of sides and their length of a regular polygon and displays its area. Here is a sample run:

```
Enter the number of sides: 5 ↵Enter
Enter the side: 6.5 ↵Enter
The area of the polygon is 73.69017017488385
```

Sections 3.3–3.6

*3.6 (*Find the character of an ASCII code*) Write a program that receives an ASCII code (an integer between **0** and **127**) and displays its character. For example, if the user enters **97**, the program displays the character **a**. Here is a sample run:

```
Enter an ASCII code: 69 ↵Enter
The character is E
```

3.7 (*Random character*) Write a program that displays a random uppercase letter using the **time.time()** function.

*3.8 (*Financial application: monetary units*) Rewrite Listing 3.4, ComputeChange.py, to fix the possible loss of accuracy when converting a float value to an int value. Enter the input as an integer whose last two digits represent the cents. For example, the input **1156** represents **11** dollars and **56** cents.

*3.9 (*Financial application: payroll*) Write a program that reads the following information and prints a payroll statement:

>   Employee's name (e.g., Smith)
>   Number of hours worked in a week (e.g., 10)
>   Hourly pay rate (e.g., 9.75)
>   Federal tax withholding rate (e.g., 20%)
>   State tax withholding rate (e.g., 9%)

A sample run is shown below:

```
Enter employee's name: Smith ↵Enter
Enter number of hours worked in a week: 10 ↵Enter
Enter hourly pay rate: 9.75 ↵Enter
Enter federal tax withholding rate: 0.20 ↵Enter
Enter state tax withholding rate: 0.09 ↵Enter

Employee Name: Smith
```

```
Hours Worked: 10.0
Pay Rate: $9.75
Gross Pay: $97.5
Deductions:
    Federal Withholding (20.0%): $19.5
    State Withholding (9.0%): $8.77
    Total Deduction: $28.27
Net Pay: $69.22
```

*3.10 (*Turtle: display Unicodes*) Write a program to display Greek letters $\alpha\beta\gamma\delta\epsilon\zeta\eta\theta$. The Unicode of these characters are **\u03b1 \u03b2 \u03b3 \u03b4 \u03b5 \u03b6 \u03b7 \u03b8**.

3.11 (*Reverse number*) Write a program that prompts the user to enter a four-digit integer and displays the number in reverse order. Here is a sample run:

```
Enter an integer: 3125  ↵ Enter
The reversed number is 5213
```

Sections 3.7–3.8

**3.12 (*Turtle: draw a star*) Write a program that prompts the user to enter the length of the star and draw a star, as shown in Figure 3.5a. (Hint: The inner angle of each point in the star is 36 degrees.)

(a)   (b)   (c)

FIGURE 3.5 The program (a) draws a star, (b) displays a STOP sign, and (c) draws an Olympic symbol.

*3.13 (*Turtle: display a STOP sign*) Write a program that displays a STOP sign, as shown in Figure 3.5b. The hexagon is in red and the text is in white.

3.14 (*Turtle: draw the Olympic symbol*) Write a program that prompts the user to enter the radius of the rings and draws an Olympic symbol of five rings of the same size with the colors blue, black, red, yellow, and green, as shown in Figure 3.5c.

*3.15 (*Turtle: paint a smiley face*) Write a program that paints a smiley face, as shown in Figure 3.6a.

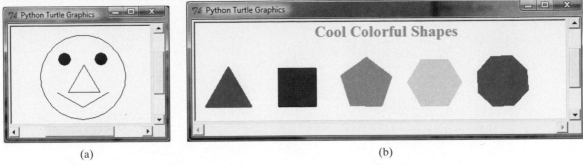

(a)   (b)

FIGURE 3.6   The program paints a smiley face in (a) and draws five shapes with bottom edges parallel to the *x*-axis in (b).

**3.16   (*Turtle: draw shapes*) Write a program that draws a triangle, square, pentagon, hexagon, and octagon, as shown in Figure 3.6b. Note that the bottom edges of these shapes are parallel to the *x*-axis. (Hint: For a triangle with a bottom line parallel to the *x*-axis, set the turtle's heading to 60 degrees.)

*3.17   (*Turtle: triangle area*) Write a program that prompts the user to enter the three points p1, p2, and p3 for a triangle and display its area below the triangle, as shown in Figure 3.7a. The formula for computing the area of a triangle is given in Exercise 2.14.

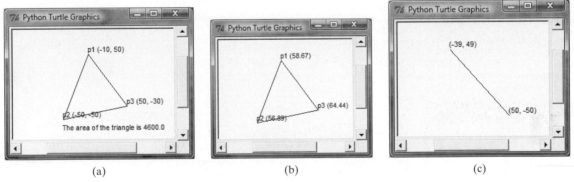

(a)   (b)   (c)

FIGURE 3.7   The program displays (a) the area of the triangle and (b) the angles for the triangle. (c) The program draws a line.

*3.18   (*Turtle: triangle angles*) Revise Listing 3.2, ComputeAngles.py, to write a program that prompts the user to enter the three points p1, p2, and p3 for a triangle and display its angles, as shown in Figure 3.7b.

**3.19   (*Turtle: draw a line*) Write a program that prompts the user to enter two points and draw a line to connect the points and displays the coordinates of the points, as shown in Figure 3.7c.

SELECTIONS

Objectives

- To write Boolean expressions using comparison operators (§4.2).
- To generate random numbers using the **random.randint(a, b)** or **random.random()** functions (§4.3).
- To program with Boolean expressions (**AdditionQuiz**) (§4.3).
- To implement selection control using one-way **if** statements (§4.4).
- To program with one-way **if** statements (**GuessBirthday**) (§4.5).
- To implement selection control using two-way **if-else** statements (§4.6).
- To implement selection control with nested **if** and multi-way **if-elif-else** statements (§4.7).
- To avoid common errors in **if** statements (§4.8).
- To program with selection statements (§§4.9–4.10).
- To combine conditions using logical operators (**and, or,** and **not**) (§4.11).
- To use selection statements with combined conditions (**LeapYear, Lottery**) (§§4.12–4.13).
- To write expressions that use the conditional expressions (§4.14).
- To understand the rules governing operator precedence and associativity (§4.15).
- To detect the location of an object (§4.16).

4.1 Introduction

Key
Point

A program can decide which statements to execute based on a condition.

problem

If you enter a negative value for **radius** in Listing 2.2, ComputeAreaWithConsoleInput.py, the program displays an invalid result. If the radius is negative, the program cannot compute the area. How can you deal with this situation?

selection statements

Like all high-level programming languages, Python provides *selection statements* that let you choose actions with two or more alternative courses. You can use the following selection statement to replace line 5 in Listing 2.2:

```python
if radius < 0:
    print("Incorrect input")
else:
    area = radius * radius * math.pi
    print("Area is", area)
```

Boolean expressions

Selection statements use conditions, which are *Boolean expressions*. This chapter introduces Boolean types, values, comparison operators, and expressions.

4.2 Boolean Types, Values, and Expressions

Key
Point

A Boolean expression is an expression that evaluates to a Boolean value **True** *or* **False***.*

comparison operators

How do you compare two values, such as whether a radius is greater than **0**, equal to **0**, or less than **0**? Python provides six *comparison operators* (also known as *relational operators*), shown in Table 4.1, which an be used to compare two values (the table assumes that a radius of **5** is being used).

VideoNote
Boolean expressions

TABLE 4.1 Comparison Operators

Python Operator	Mathematics Symbol	Name	Example (radius is 5)	Result
<	<	less than	radius < 0	False
<=	≤	less than or equal to	radius <= 0	False
>	>	greater than	radius > 0	True
>=	≥	greater than or equal to	radius >= 0	True
==	=	equal to	radius == 0	False
!=	≠	not equal to	radius != 0	True

== vs. =

> **Caution**
>
> The *equal to* comparison operator is two equal signs (==), not a single equal sign (=). The latter symbol is for assignment.

Boolean value

The result of the comparison is a *Boolean value*: **True** or **False**. For example, the following statement displays the result **True**:

```python
radius = 1
print(radius > 0)
```

A variable that holds a Boolean value is known as a Boolean variable. The Boolean data type is used to represent Boolean values. A Boolean variable can hold one of the two values: `True` or `False`. For example, the following statement assigns the value `True` to the variable `lightsOn`:

Boolean variable

```
lightsOn = True
```

`True` and `False` are literals, just like a number such as `10`. They are reserved words and cannot be used as identifiers in a program.

Boolean literals

Internally, Python uses `1` to represent `True` and `0` for `False`. You can use the `int` function to convert a Boolean value to an integer.

convert Boolean to `int`

For example,

```
print(int(True))
```

displays `1` and

```
print(int(False))
```

displays `0`.

You can also use the `bool` function to convert a numeric value to a Boolean value. The function returns `False` if the value is `0`; otherwise, it always returns `True`.

`bool` function

For example,

```
print(bool(0))
```

displays `False` and

```
print(bool(4))
```

displays `True`.

4.1 List six comparison operators.

4.2 Can the following conversions be allowed? If so, find the converted result.

```
i = int(True)
j = int(False)

b1 = bool(4)
b2 = bool(0)
```

Check Point

MyProgrammingLab™

4.3 Generating Random Numbers

The `randint(a, b)` *function can be used to generate a random integer between* `a` *and* `b`, *inclusively.*

Key Point

Suppose you want to develop a program to help a first grader practice addition. The program randomly generates two single-digit integers, `number1` and `number2`, and displays to the student a question such as `What is 1 + 7`, as shown in Listing 4.1. After the student types the answer, the program displays a message to indicate whether it is true or false.

To generate a random number, you can use the `randint(a, b)` function in the `random` module. This function returns a random integer `i` between `a` and `b`, inclusively. To obtain a random integer between `0` and `9`, use `randint(0, 9)`.

The program may be set up to work as follows:

Step 1: Generate two single-digit integers for **number1** (e.g., 4) and **number2** (e.g., 5)

Step 2: Prompt the student to answer, **"What is 4 + 5?"**

Step 3: Check whether the student's answer is correct.

LISTING 4.1 AdditionQuiz.py

import random module

```
 1  import random
 2
 3  # Generate random numbers
```
generate number1
generate number2
```
 4  number1 = random.randint(0, 9)
 5  number2 = random.randint(0, 9)
 6
 7  # Prompt the user to enter an answer
```
show question
```
 8  answer = eval(input("What is " + str(number1) + " + "
 9      + str(number2) + "? "))
10
11  # Display result
```
display result
```
12  print(number1, "+", number2, "=", answer,
13      "is", number1 + number2 == answer)
```

```
What is 1 + 7? 8  ↵Enter
1 + 7 = 8 is True
```

```
What is 4 + 8? 9  ↵Enter
4 + 8 = 9 is False
```

line#	number1	number2	answer	output
4	4			
5		8		
8			9	
12				4 + 8 = 9 is False

random module

The program uses the **randint** function defined in the **random** module. The **import** statement imports the module (line 1).

Lines 4–5 generate two numbers, **number1** and **number2**. Line 8 obtains an answer from the user. The answer is graded in line 12 using a Boolean expression **number1 + number2 == answer**.

randrange function

Python also provides another function, **randrange(a, b)**, for generating a random integer between **a** and **b** – **1**, which is equivalent to **randint(a, b** – **1)**. For example, **randrange(0, 10)** and **randint(0, 9)** are the same. Since **randint** is more intuitive, the book generally uses **randint** in the examples.

random function

You can also use the **random()** function to generate a random float **r** such that **0 <= r < 1.0**. For example

random.random()

random.random()

random.randint(a, b)

```
1  >>> import random
2  >>> random.random()
3  0.34343
4  >>> random.random()
5  0.20119
6  >>> random.randint(0, 1)
```

```
 7  0
 8  >>> random.randint(0, 1)
 9  1
10  >>> random.randrange(0, 1) # This will always be 0
11  0
12  >>>
```

random.randrange(a, b)

Invoking **random.random()** (lines 2 and 4) returns a random float number between **0.0** and **1.0** (excluding **1.0**). Invoking **random.randint(0, 1)** (lines 6 and 8) returns **0** or **1**. Invoking **random.randrange(0, 1)** (line 10) always returns **0**.

4.3   How do you generate a random integer i such that $0 \le i < 20$?

4.4   How do you generate a random integer i such that $10 \le i < 20$?

4.5   How do you generate a random integer i such that $10 \le i \le 50$?

4.6   How do you generate a random integer 0 or 1?

4.4 **if** Statements

A one-way **if** *statement executes the statements if the condition is true.*

The preceding program displays a message such as **6 + 2 = 7 is False**. If you wish the message to be **6 + 2 = 7 is incorrect**, you have to use a selection statement to make this minor change.

Python has several types of selection statements: one-way **if** statements, two-way **if-else** statements, nested **if** statements, multi-way **if-elif-else** statements and conditional expressions. This section introduces one-way **if** statements.

A one-way **if** statement executes an action if and only if the condition is true. The syntax for a one-way **if** statement is:

if statements

if statement

```
if boolean-expression:
    statement(s)  # Note that the statement(s) must be indented
```

The **statement(s)** must be indented at least one space to the right of the **if** keyword and each statement must be indented using the same number of spaces. For consistency, we indent it four spaces in this book.

The flowchart in Figure 4.1a illustrates how Python executes the syntax of an **if** statement. A *flowchart* is a diagram that describes an algorithm or process, showing the steps as boxes of various kinds, and their order by connecting these with arrows. Process operations are represented in these boxes, and arrows connecting them show flow of control. A diamond box is used to denote a Boolean condition and a rectangle box is for representing statements.

flowchart

If the **boolean-expression** evaluates to true, the statements in the **if** block are executed. The **if** block contains the statements indented after the **if** statement. For example:

if block

```
if radius >= 0:
    area = radius * radius * math.pi
    print("The area for the circle of radius", radius, "is", area)
```

The flowchart of the preceding statement is shown in Figure 4.1b. If the value of **radius** is greater than or equal to **0**, then the **area** is computed and the result is displayed; otherwise, these statements in the block are not executed.

The statements in the **if** block must be indented in the lines after the **if** line and each statement must be indented using the same number of spaces. For example, the following code is wrong, because the **print** statement in line 3 is not indented using the same number of spaces as the statement for computing area in line 2.

```
1  if radius >= 0:
2      area = radius * radius * math.pi  # Compute area
3    print("The area for the circle of radius", radius, "is", area)
```

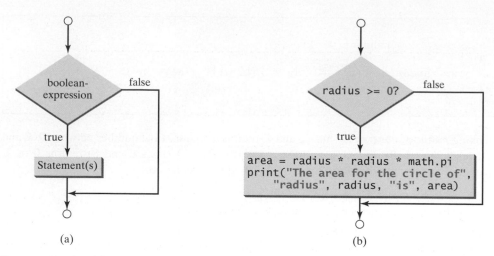

FIGURE 4.1 An **if** statement executes statements if the **boolean-expression** evaluates to **True**.

Listing 4.2 is an example of a program that prompts the user to enter an integer. If the number is a multiple of **5**, the program displays the result **HiFive**. If the number is divisible by **2**, the program displays **HiEven**.

LISTING 4.2 SimpleIfDemo.py

enter input

check 5

check even

```
1  number = eval(input("Enter an integer: "))
2
3  if number % 5 == 0:
4      print("HiFive")
5
6  if number % 2 == 0:
7      print("HiEven")
```

```
Enter an integer: 4  ↵Enter
HiEven
```

```
Enter an integer: 30  ↵Enter
HiFive
HiEven
```

The program prompts the user to enter an integer (line 1) and displays **HiFive** if it is divisible by **5** (lines 3–4) and **HiEven** if it is divisible by **2** (lines 6–7).

4.7 Write an **if** statement that assigns **1** to **x** if **y** is greater than **0**.

4.8 Write an **if** statement that increases **pay** by 3% if **score** is greater than **90**.

MyProgrammingLab™

4.5 Case Study: Guessing Birthdays

Guessing birthdays is an interesting problem with a simple program solution.

You can find out the date of the month when your friend was born by asking five questions. Each question asks whether the day is in one of the five sets of numbers.

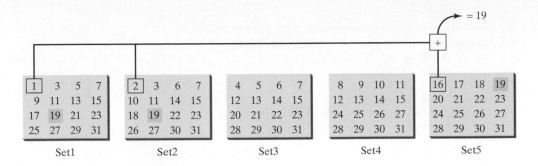

The birthday is the sum of the first numbers in the sets where the date appears. For example, if the birthday is **19**, it appears in Set1, Set2, and Set5. The first numbers in these three sets are **1**, **2**, and **16**. Their sum is **19**.

Listing 4.3 is a program that prompts the user to answer whether the day is in Set1 (lines 4–13), in Set2 (lines 16–25), in Set3 (lines 28–37), in Set4 (lincs 40–49), or in Set5 (lines 52–61). If the number is in the set, the program adds the first number in the set to **day** (lines 13, 25, 37, 49, and 61).

LISTING 4.3 GuessBirthday.py

```
1  day = 0 # birth day to be determined
2
3  # Prompt the user to answer the first question
4  question1 = "Is your birthday in Set1?\n" + \
5      " 1  3  5  7\n" + \
6      " 9 11 13 15\n" + \
7      "17 19 21 23\n" + \
8      "25 27 29 31" + \
9      "\nEnter 0 for No and 1 for Yes: "
10 answer = eval(input(question1))
11
12 if answer == 1:
13     day += 1
14
15 # Prompt the user to answer the second question
16 question2 = "Is your birthday in Set2?\n" + \
17     " 2  3  6  7\n" + \
18     "10 11 14 15\n" + \
19     "18 19 22 23\n" + \
20     "26 27 30 31" + \
21     "\nEnter 0 for No and 1 for Yes: "
22 answer = eval(input(question2))
23
24 if answer == 1:
25     day += 2
26
27 # Prompt the user to answer the third question
28 question3 = "Is your birthday in Set3?\n" + \
29     " 4  5  6  7\n" + \
30     "12 13 14 15\n" + \
31     "20 21 22 23\n" + \
32     "28 29 30 31" + \
33     "\nEnter 0 for No and 1 for Yes: "
34 answer = eval(input(question3))
35
36 if answer == 1:
37     day += 4
```

day to be determined

in question1?

in question2?

in question3?

in question4?

in question5?

```
38
39  # Prompt the user to answer the fourth question
40  question4 = "Is your birthday in Set4?\n" + \
41      " 8  9 10 11\n" + \
42      "12 13 14 15\n" + \
43      "24 25 26 27\n" + \
44      "28 29 30 31" + \
45      "\nEnter 0 for No and 1 for Yes: "
46  answer = eval(input(question4))
47
48  if answer == 1:
49      day += 8
50
51  # Prompt the user to answer the fifth question
52  question5 = "Is your birthday in Set5?\n" + \
53      "16 17 18 19\n"+ \
54      "20 21 22 23\n" + \
55      "24 25 26 27\n" + \
56      "28 29 30 31" + \
57      "\nEnter 0 for No and 1 for Yes: "
58  answer = eval(input(question5))
59
60  if answer == 1:
61      day += 16
62
63  print("\nYour birthday is "+ str(day) + "!")
```

```
Is your birthday in Set1?
 1  3  5  7
 9 11 13 15
17 19 21 23
25 27 29 31
Enter 0 for No and 1 for Yes: 1  ↵Enter

Is your birthday in Set2?
 2  3  6  7
10 11 14 15
18 19 22 23
26 27 30 31
Enter 0 for No and 1 for Yes: 1  ↵Enter

Is your birthday in Set3?
 4  5  6  7
12 13 14 15
20 21 22 23
28 29 30 31
Enter 0 for No and 1 for Yes: 0  ↵Enter

Is your birthday in Set4?
 8  9 10 11
12 13 14 15
24 25 26 27
28 29 30 31
Enter 0 for No and 1 for Yes: 0  ↵Enter
```

```
Is your birthday in Set5?
16 17 18 19
20 21 22 23
24 25 26 27
28 29 30 31
Enter 0 for No and 1 for Yes: 1   ↵Enter
Your birthday is 19!
```

line#	day	answer	output
1	0		
10		1	
13	1		
22		1	
25	2		
34		0	
46		0	
58		1	
61	19		
63			Your birthday is 19

The last character \ at the end of lines 4–8 is the line continuation symbol, which tells the interpreter that the statement is continued on the next line (see Section 2.3).

This game is easy to program. You may wonder how the game was created. The mathematics behind the game is actually quite simple. The numbers are not grouped together by accident. The way they are placed in the five sets is deliberate. The starting numbers in the five sets are **1**, **2**, **4**, **8**, and **16**, which correspond to **1**, **10**, **100**, **1000**, and **10000** in binary. A binary number for decimal integers between **1** and **31** has at most five digits, as shown in Figure 4.2a. Assume this number is $b_5b_4b_3b_2b_1$. So, $b_5b_4b_3b_2b_1 = b_50000 + b_4000 + b_300 + b_20 + b_1$, as shown in Figure 4.2b. If a day's binary number has a digit **1** in b_k, the number should appear in Set$k$. For example, number **19** is binary **10011**, so it appears in Set1, Set2, and Set5. It is binary **1** + **10** + **10000** = **10011** or decimal **1** + **2** + **16** = **19**. Number **31** is binary **11111**, so it appears in Set1, Set2, Set3, Set4, and Set5. It is binary **1** + **10** + **100** + **1000** + **10000** = **11111** or decimal **1** + **2** + **4** + **8** + **16** = **31**.

mathematics behind the game

Decimal	Binary
1	00001
2	00010
3	00011
...	
19	10011
...	
31	11111

(a)

$$
\begin{array}{rrr}
b_5\,0\,0\,0\,0 & & 10000 \\
b_4\,0\,0\,0 & & 1000 \\
b_3\,0\,0 & 10000 & 100 \\
b_2\,0 & 10 & 10 \\
+\quad b_1 & +\quad 1 & +\quad 1 \\
\hline
b_5b_4b_3b_2b_1 & 10011 & 11111 \\
& 19 & 31
\end{array}
$$

(b)

FIGURE 4.2 (a) A number between **1** and **31** can be represented using a 5-digit binary number. (b) A 5-digit binary number can be obtained by adding binary numbers **1**, **10**, **100**, **1000**, or **10000**.

4.6 Two-Way `if-else` Statements

Key Point

A two-way `if-else` statement decides which statements to execute based on whether the condition is true or false.

A one-way `if` statement takes an action if the specified condition is **True**. If the condition is **False**, nothing is done. But what if you want to take one or more alternative actions when the condition is **False**? You can use a two-way `if-else` statement. The actions that a two-way `if-else` statement specifies differ based on whether the condition is **True** or **False**.

Here is the syntax for a two-way `if-else` statement:

```
if boolean-expression:
    statement(s)-for-the-true-case
else:
    statement(s)-for-the-false-case
```

The flowchart of the statement is shown in Figure 4.3.

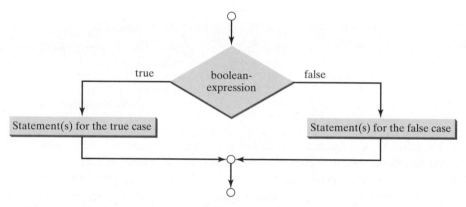

FIGURE 4.3 An `if-else` statement executes statements for the true case if the Boolean expression evaluates to **True**; otherwise, statements for the false case are executed.

If the **boolean-expression** evaluates to **True**, the statement(s) for the true case are executed; otherwise, the statement(s) for the false case are executed. For example, consider the following code:

two-way `if-else` statement

```
if radius >= 0:
    area = radius * radius * math.pi
    print("The area for the circle of radius", radius, "is", area)
else:
    print("Negative input")
```

If **radius >= 0** is true, **area** is computed and displayed; if it is false, the message **Negative input** is displayed.

Here is another example of the `if-else` statement. This one determines whether a number is even or odd, as follows:

```
if number % 2 == 0:
    print(number, "is even.")
else:
    print(number, "is odd.")
```

Suppose you want to develop a program for a first grader to practice subtraction. The program randomly generates two single-digit integers, **number1** and **number2**, with **number1 >= number2** and asks the student a question such as **"What is 9 - 2? "** After the student enters the answer, the program displays a message indicating whether it is correct.

The program may work as follows:

Step 1: Generate two single-digit integers for **number1** and **number2**.

Step 2: If **number1 < number2**, swap **number1** with **number2**.

Step 3: Prompt the student to answer, "What is number1 – number2?"

Step 4: Check the student's answer and display whether the answer is correct.

The complete program is shown in Listing 4.4.

LISTING 4.4   SubtractionQuiz.py

```
1   import random
2
3   # 1. Generate two random single-digit integers
4   number1 = random.randint(0, 9)
5   number2 = random.randint(0, 9)
6
7   # 2. If number1 < number2, swap number1 with number2
8   if number1 < number2:
9       number1, number2 = number2, number1  # Simultaneous assignment
10
11  # 3. Prompt the student to answer "What is number1 - number2?"
12  answer = eval(input("What is "+ str(number1) + " - " +
13      str(number2) + "? "))
14
15  # 4. Check the answer and display the result
16  if number1 - number2 == answer:
17      print("You are correct!")
18  else:
19      print("Your answer is wrong.\n", number1, '-',
20          number2, "is", number1 - number2, '.')
```

import random module

random numbers

swap if necessary

get answer

check the answer

```
What is 6 - 6? 0  ⏎Enter
You are correct!
```

```
What is 9 - 2? 5  ⏎Enter
Your answer is wrong.
9 - 2 is 7.
```

line#	number1	number2	answer	output
4	2			
5		9		
9	9	2		
12			5	
19				Your answer is wrong. 9 - 2 is 7.

If **number1 < number2**, the program uses simultaneous assignment to swap the two variables (lines 8–9).

4.9 Write an **if** statement that increases **pay** by 3% if **score** is greater than **90**, otherwise it increases **pay** by 1%.

Check
Point

MyProgrammingLab **4.10** What is the printout of the code in (a) and (b) if **number** is 30 and 35, respectively?

```
if number % 2 == 0:
    print(number, "is even.")

print(number, "is odd.")
```
(a)

```
if number % 2 == 0:
    print(number, "is even.")
else
    print(number, "is odd.")
```
(b)

4.7 Nested **if** and Multi-Way **if-elif-else** Statements

Key Point

One if *statement can be placed inside another* if *statement to form a nested* if *statement.*

The statement in an **if** or **if-else** statement can be any legal Python statement, including another **if** or **if-else** statement. The inner **if** statement is said to be *nested* inside the outer **if** statement. The inner **if** statement can contain another **if** statement; in fact, there is no limit to the depth of the nesting. For example, the following is a nested **if** statement:

nested if statement

```
if i > k:
    if j > k:
        print("i and j are greater than k")
else:
    print("i is less than or equal to k")
```

The **if j > k** statement is nested inside the **if i > k** statement.

The nested **if** statement can be used to implement multiple alternatives. The statement given in Figure 4.4a, for instance, assigns a letter value to the variable **grade** according to the score, with multiple alternatives.

```
if score >= 90.0:
    grade = 'A'
else:
    if score >= 80.0:
        grade = 'B'
    else:
        if score >= 70.0:
            grade = 'C'
        else:
            if score >= 60.0:
                grade = 'D'
            else:
                grade = 'F'
```
(a)

Equivalent

This is better

```
if score >= 90.0:
    grade = 'A'
elif score >= 80.0:
    grade = 'B'
elif score >= 70.0:
    grade = 'C'
elif score >= 60.0:
    grade = 'D'
else:
    grade = 'F'
```
(b)

FIGURE 4.4 A preferred format for multiple alternatives is shown in (b) using a multi-way *if-elif-else* statement.

The execution of how this **if** statement proceeds is shown in Figure 4.5. The first condition **(score >= 90)** is tested. If it is **True**, the grade becomes **A**. If it is **False**, the second condition **(score >= 80)** is tested. If the second condition is **True**, the grade becomes **B**. If that condition is **False**, the third condition and the rest of the conditions (if necessary) are tested until a condition is met or all of the conditions prove to be **False**. If all of the conditions are **False**, the grade becomes **F**. Note that a condition is tested only when all of the conditions that come before it are **False**.

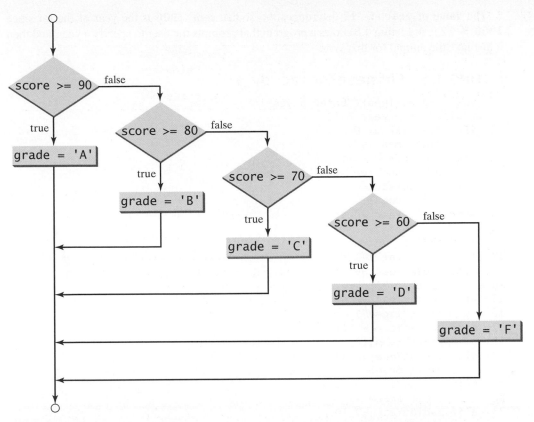

FIGURE 4.5 You can use a multi-way **if-elif-else** statement to assign a grade.

The **if** statement in Figure 4.4a is equivalent to the **if** statement in Figure 4.4b. In fact, Figure 4.4b is the preferred coding style for multiple alternative **if** statements. This style, called *multi-way* **if** *statements*, avoids deep indentation and makes the program easier to read. The multi-way **if** statements uses the syntax **if-elif-else**; **elif** (short for *else if*) is a Python keyword.

multi-way **if** statement

Now let's write a program to find out the Chinese zodiac sign for a given year. The Chinese zodiac sign is based on a 12-year cycle, and each year in this cycle is represented by an animal—monkey, rooster, dog, pig, rat, ox, tiger, rabbit, dragon, snake, horse, and sheep—as shown in Figure 4.6.

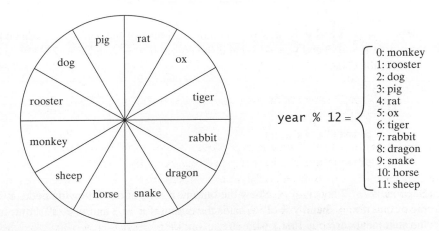

FIGURE 4.6 The Chinese zodiac is based on a 12-year cycle.

The value of **year % 12** determines the zodiac sign. **1900** is the year of the rat since **1900 % 12** is **4**. Listing 4.5 shows a program that prompts the user to specify a year, and then it displays the animal for that year.

LISTING 4.5 ChineseZodiac.py

enter year
12-year cycle
determine zodiac sign

```python
1  year = eval(input("Enter a year: "))
2  zodiacYear = year % 12
3  if zodiacYear == 0:
4      print("monkey")
5  elif zodiacYear == 1:
6      print("rooster")
7  elif zodiacYear == 2:
8      print("dog")
9  elif zodiacYear == 3:
10     print("pig")
11 elif zodiacYear == 4:
12     print("rat")
13 elif zodiacYear == 5:
14     print("ox")
15 elif zodiacYear == 6:
16     print("tiger")
17 elif zodiacYear == 7:
18     print("rabbit")
19 elif zodiacYear == 8:
20     print("dragon")
21 elif zodiacYear == 9:
22     print("snake")
23 elif zodiacYear == 10:
24     print("horse")
25 else:
26     print("sheep")
```

```
Enter a year: 1963  ↵Enter
rabbit
```

```
Enter a year: 1877  ↵Enter
ox
```

Check Point

MyProgrammingLab™

4.11 Suppose **x = 3** and **y = 2**; show the output, if any, of the following code. What is the output if **x = 3** and **y = 4**? What is the output if **x = 2** and **y = 2**? Draw a flowchart for the code.

```python
if x > 2:
    if y > 2:
        z = x + y
        print("z is", z)
    else:
        print("x is", x)
```

4.12 Suppose **x = 2** and **y = 4**. Show the output, if any, of the following code. What is the output if **x = 3** and **y = 2**? What is the output if **x = 3** and **y = 3**? (Hint: Indent the statement correctly first.)

```
if x > 2:
    if y > 2:
        z = x + y
        print("z is", z)
else:
    print("x is", x)
```

4.13 What is wrong in the following code?

```
if score >= 60.0:
    grade = 'D'
elif score >= 70.0:
    grade = 'C'
elif score >= 80.0:
    grade = 'B'
elif score >= 90.0:
    grade = 'A'
else:
    grade = 'F'
```

4.8 Common Errors in Selection Statements

Most common errors in selection statements are caused by incorrect indentation.

Key
Point

Consider the following code in (a) and (b).

```
radius = -20

if radius >= 0:
    area = radius * radius * math.pi
print("The area is", area)
```

(a) Wrong

```
radius = -20

if radius >= 0:
    area = radius * radius * math.pi
    print("The area is", area)
```

(b) Correct

In (a), the **print** statement is not in the **if** block. To place it in the **if** block, you have to indent it, as shown in (b).

Consider another example in the following code in (a) and (b). The code in (a) below has two **if** clauses and one **else** clause. Which **if** clause is matched by the **else** clause? The indentation indicates that the **else** clause matches the first **if** clause in (a) and the second **if** clause in (b).

```
i = 1
j = 2
k = 3

if i > j:
    if i > k:
        print('A')
else:
    print('B')
```

(a)

```
i = 1
j = 2
k = 3

if i > j:
    if i > k:
        print('A')
    else:
        print('B')
```

(b)

Since **(i > j)** is false, the code in (a) displays **B**, but nothing is displayed from the statement in (b).

assign Boolean variable

Tip

Often new programmers write the code that assigns a test condition to a Boolean variable, like the code in (a):

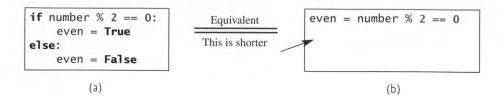

```
if number % 2 == 0:
    even = True
else:
    even = False
```
(a)

Equivalent
This is shorter

```
even = number % 2 == 0
```

(b)

The code can be simplified by assigning the test value directly to the variable, as shown in (b).

Check Point

MyProgrammingLab™

4.14 Which of the following statements are equivalent? Which ones are correctly indented?

```
if i > 0:
    x = 0
    y = 1
else:
    y = 0
    z = 0
```
(a)

```
if i > 0:
    x = 0
    y = 1
else:
    y = 0
    z = 0
```
(b)

```
if i > 0:
    x = 0
    y = 1
else:
    y = 0
    z = 0
```
(c)

```
if i > 0:
    x = 0
    y = 1
else:
    y = 0
    z = 0
```
(d)

4.15 Rewrite the following statement using a Boolean expression:

```
if count % 10 == 0:
    newLine = True
else:
    newLine = False
```

4.16 Are the following statements correct? Which one is better?

```
if age < 16:
    print("Cannot get a driver's license")
if age >= 16:
    print("Can get a driver's license")
```
(a)

```
if age < 16:
    print("Cannot get a driver's license")
else:
    print("Can get a driver's license")
```
(b)

4.17 What is the output of the following code if **number** is **14**, **15**, and **30**?

```
if number % 2 == 0:
    print(number, "is even")
if number % 5 == 0:
    print(number, "is multiple of 5")
```
(a)

```
if number % 2 == 0:
    print(number, "is even")
elif number % 5 == 0:
    print(number, "is multiple of 5")
```
(b)

4.9 Case Study: Computing Body Mass Index

You can use nested **if** *statements to write a program that interprets body mass index.*

Key Point

Body mass index (BMI) is a measure of health based on weight. It can be calculated by taking your weight in kilograms and dividing it by the square of your height in meters. The interpretation of BMI for people 16 years and older is as follows:

BMI	Interpretation
Below 18.5	Underweight
18.5–24.9	Normal
25.0–29.9	Overweight
Above 30.0	Obese

Write a program that prompts the user to enter a weight in pounds and height in inches and then displays the BMI. Note that one pound is **0.45359237** kilograms and one inch is **0.0254** meters. Listing 4.6 gives the program.

LISTING 4.6 ComputeBMI.py

```
1   # Prompt the user to enter weight in pounds
2   weight = eval(input("Enter weight in pounds: "))          input weight
3
4   # Prompt the user to enter height in inches
5   height = eval(input("Enter height in inches: "))          input height
6
7   KILOGRAMS_PER_POUND = 0.45359237   # Constant
8   METERS_PER_INCH = 0.0254           # Constant
9
10  # Compute BMI
11  weightInKilograms = weight * KILOGRAMS_PER_POUND
12  heightInMeters = height * METERS_PER_INCH
13  bmi = weightInKilograms / (heightInMeters * heightInMeters)   compute bmi
14
15  # Display result
16  print("BMI is", format(bmi, ".2f"))                      display output
17  if bmi < 18.5:
18      print("Underweight")
19  elif bmi < 25:
20      print("Normal")
21  elif bmi < 30:
22      print("Overweight")
23  else:
24      print("Obese")
```

```
Enter weight in pounds: 146 ↵Enter
Enter height in inches: 70 ↵Enter
BMI is 20.95
Normal
```

line#	weight	height	weightInKilograms	heightInMeters	bmi	output
2	146					
5		70				
11			66.22448602			
12				1.778		
13					20.9486	
16						BMI is 20.95
22						Normal

named constants

The two named constants, **KILOGRAMS_PER_POUND** and **METERS_PER_INCH**, are defined in lines 7–8. Named constants were introduced in Section 2.6. Using named constants here makes programs easy to read. Unfortunately, there is no special syntax for defining named constants in Python. Named constants are treated just like variables in Python. This book uses the format of writing constants in all uppercase letters to distinguish them from variables, and separates the words in constants with an underscore (_).

4.10 Case Study: Computing Taxes

Key
Point

You can use nested if *statements to write a program for computing taxes.*

The United States federal personal income tax is calculated based on filing status and taxable income. There are four filing statuses: single filers, married filing jointly, married filing separately, and head of household. The tax rates vary every year. Table 4.2 shows the rates for 2009. If you are, say, single with a taxable income of $10,000, the first $8,350 is taxed at 10% and the other $1,650 is taxed at 15%. So, your tax is $1,082.50.

TABLE 4.2   2009 U.S. Federal Personal Tax Rates

Marginal Tax Rate	Single	Married Filing Jointly	Married Filing Separately	Head of Household
10%	$0 – $8,350	$0 – $16,700	$0 – $8,350	$0 – $11,950
15%	$8,351 – $33,950	$16,701 – $67,900	$8,351 – $33,950	$11,951 – $45,500
25%	$33,951 – $82,250	$67,901 – $137,050	$33,951 – $68,525	$45,501 – $117,450
28%	$82,251 – $171,550	$137,051 – $208,850	$68,526 – $104,425	$117,451 – $190,200
33%	$171,551 – $372,950	$208,851 – $372,950	$104,426 – $186,475	$190,201 – $372,950
35%	$372,951+	$372,951+	$186,476+	$372,951+

You are to write a program to compute personal income tax. Your program should prompt the user to enter the filing status and taxable income and then compute the tax. Enter **0** for single filers, **1** for married filing jointly, **2** for married filing separately, and **3** for head of household.

Your program computes the tax for the taxable income based on the filing status. The filing status can be determined using **if** statements outlined as follows:

```
if status == 0:
    # Compute tax for single filers
elif status == 1:
    # Compute tax for married filing jointly
elif status == 2:
```

```
          # Compute tax for married filing separately
    elif status == 3:
          # Compute tax for head of household
    else:
          # Display wrong status
```

For each filing status there are six tax rates. Each rate is applied to a certain amount of taxable income. For example, of a taxable income of $400,000 for single filers, $8,350 is taxed at 10%, (33,950 – 8,350) at 15%, (82,250 – 33,950) at 25%, (171,550 – 82,250) at 28%, (372,950 – 171,550) at 33%, and (400,000 – 372,950) at 35%.

Listing 4.7 gives the solution to compute taxes for single filers. The complete solution is left as Programming Exercise 4.13 at the end of this chapter.

LISTING 4.7 ComputeTax.py

```
 1  import sys                                                         import sys module
 2
 3  # Prompt the user to enter filing status
 4  status = eval(input(                                              input status
 5      "(0-single filer, 1-married jointly,\n" +
 6      "2-married separately, 3-head of household)\n" +
 7      "Enter the filing status: "))
 8
 9  # Prompt the user to enter taxable income
10  income = eval(input("Enter the taxable income: "))                input income
11
12  # Compute tax
13  tax = 0
14
15  if status == 0:  # Compute tax for single filers                  compute tax
16      if income <= 8350:
17          tax = income * 0.10
18      elif income <= 33950:
19          tax = 8350 * 0.10 + (income - 8350) * 0.15
20      elif income <= 82250:
21          tax = 8350 * 0.10 + (33950 - 8350) * 0.15 + \
22              (income - 33950) * 0.25
23      elif income <= 171550:
24          tax = 8350 * 0.10 + (33950 - 8350) * 0.15 + \
25              (82250 - 33950) * 0.25 + (income - 82250) * 0.28
26      elif income <= 372950:
27          tax = 8350 * 0.10 + (33950 - 8350) * 0.15 + \
28              (82250 - 33950) * 0.25 + (171550 - 82250) * 0.28 + \
29              (income - 171550) * 0.33
30      else:
31          tax = 8350 * 0.10 + (33950 - 8350) * 0.15 + \
32              (82250 - 33950) * 0.25 + (171550 - 82250) * 0.28 + \
33              (372950 - 171550) * 0.33 + (income - 372950) * 0.35;
34  elif status == 1:  # Compute tax for married file jointly
35      print("Left as exercise")
36  elif status == 2:  # Compute tax for married separately
37      print("Left as exercise")
38  elif status == 3:  # Compute tax for head of household
39      print("Left as exercise")
40  else:
41      print("Error: invalid status")
42      sys.exit()                                                    exit program
43
44  # Display the result
45  print("Tax is", format(tax, ".2f"))                               display output
```

```
(0-single filer, 1-married jointly,
2-married separately, 3-head of household)
Enter the filing status: 0 ⏎Enter
Enter the taxable income: 400000 ⏎Enter
Tax is 117683.50
```

line#	status	income	tax	output
4	0			
10		400000		
13			0	
17			117683.5	
45				Tax is 117683.50

The program receives the filing status and taxable income. The multiple alternative **if** statements (lines 15, 34, 36, 38, and 40) check the filing status and compute the tax based on the filing status.

sys.exit()

sys.exit() (line 42) is defined in the **sys** module. Invoking this function terminates the program.

test all cases

To test a program, you need to provide input that covers all cases. For this program, your input should cover all statuses (**0**, **1**, **2**, and **3**). For each status, test the tax for each of the six brackets. So, there are a total of 24 cases.

Tip

For all programs, you should write a small amount of code and test it before moving on to add more code. This is called *incremental development and testing*. This approach makes debugging easier, because the errors are likely in the new code you just added.

incremental development and testing

✓Check Point

MyProgrammingLab™

4.18 Are the following two statements equivalent?

```
if income <= 10000:
    tax = income * 0.1
elif income <= 20000:
    tax = 1000 + \
        (income - 10000) * 0.15
```

```
if income <= 10000:
    tax = income * 0.1
elif income > 10000 and
        income <= 20000:
    tax = 1000 + \
        (income - 10000) * 0.15
```

4.19 What is wrong in the following code?

```
income = 232323

if income <= 10000:
    tax = income * 0.1
elif income > 10000 and income <= 20000:
    tax = 1000 + (income - 10000) * 0.15

print(tax)
```

4.11 Logical Operators

*The logical operators **not**, **and**, and **or** can be used to create a composite condition.*

Key Point

Sometimes, a combination of several conditions determines whether a statement is executed. You can use logical operators to combine these conditions to form a compound expression.

Logical operators, also known as *Boolean operators*, operate on Boolean values to create a new Boolean value. Table 4.3 lists the Boolean operators. Table 4.4 defines the **not** operator, which negates **True** to **False** and **False** to **True**. Table 4.5 defines the **and** operator. The **and** of two Boolean operands is true if and only if both operands are true. Table 4.6 defines the **or** operator. The **or** of two Boolean operands is true if at least one of the operands is true.

TABLE 4.3   Boolean Operators

Operator	Description
not	logical negation
and	logical conjunction
or	logical disjunction

TABLE 4.4   Truth Table for Operator **not**

p	not p	Example (assume **age = 24, gender = 'F'**)
True	False	**not (age > 18)** is **False**, because **(age > 18)** is **True**.
False	True	**not (gender == 'M')** is **True**, because **(gender == 'M')** is **False**.

TABLE 4.5   Truth Table for Operator **and**

p_1	p_2	p_1 and p_2	Example (assume **age = 24, gender = 'F'**)
False	False	False	**(age > 18) and (gender == 'F')** is **True**, because **(age > 18)** and **(gender == 'F')** are both **True**.
False	True	False	
True	False	False	**(age > 18) and (gender != 'F')** is **False**, because **(gender != 'F')** is **False**.
True	True	True	

TABLE 4.6   Truth Table for Operator **or**

p_1	p_2	p_1 and p_2	Example (assume **age = 24, gender = 'F'**)
False	False	False	**(age > 34) or (gender == 'F')** is **True**, because **(gender == 'F')** is **True**.
False	True	True	
True	False	True	**(age > 34) or (gender == 'M')** is **False**, because **(age > 34)** and **(gender == 'M')** are both **False**.
True	True	True	

The program in Listing 4.8 checks whether a number is divisible by **2** *and* **3**, by **2** *or* **3**, and by **2** *or* **3** but *not both*.

LISTING 4.8   TestBooleanOperators.py

```
1  # Receive an input
2  number = eval(input("Enter an integer: "))
3
4  if number % 2 == 0 and number % 3 == 0:
5      print(number, "is divisible by 2 and 3")
```

input

and

```
 6
 7   if number % 2 == 0 or number % 3 == 0:
 8       print(number, "is divisible by 2 or 3")
 9
10   if (number % 2 == 0 or number % 3 == 0) and \
11          not (number % 2 == 0 and number % 3 == 0):
12       print(number, "is divisible by 2 or 3, but not both")
```

or

```
Enter an integer: 18  ⏎Enter
18 is divisible by 2 and 3
18 is divisible by 2 or 3
```

```
Enter an integer: 15  ⏎Enter
15 is divisible by 2 or 3
15 is divisible by 2 or 3, but not both
```

In line 4, **number % 2 == 0 and number % 3 == 0** checks whether the number is divisible by **2** *and* **4**. **number % 2 == 0 or number % 3 == 0** (line 7) checks whether the number is divisible by **2** *or* **4**. The Boolean expression in lines 10–11

```
(number % 2 == 0 and number % 3 == 0) and
   not (number % 2 == 0 and number % 3 == 0)
```

checks whether the number is divisible by **2** or **3** but not both.

Note

De Morgan's law

De Morgan's law, named after Indian-born British mathematician and logician Augustus De Morgan (1806–1871), can be used to simplify Boolean expressions. The law states that:

```
not (condition1 and condition2)  is the same as
   not condition1 or not condition2
not (condition1 or condition2)  is the same as
   not condition1 and not condition2
```

So, line 11 in the preceding example,

```
not (number % 2 == 0 and number % 3 == 0)
```

can be simplified by using an equivalent expression:

```
(number % 2 != 0 or number % 3 != 0)
```

As another example,

```
not (number == 2 or number == 3)
```

is better written as

```
number != 2 and number != 3
```

If one of the operands of an **and** operator is **False**, the expression is **False**; if one of the operands of an **or** operator is **True**, the expression is **True**. Python uses these properties to improve the performance of these operators. When evaluating **p1 and p2**, Python first evaluates **p1** and then, if **p1** is **True**, evaluates **p2**; if **p1** is **False**, it does not evaluate **p2**. When evaluating **p1 or p2**, Python first evaluates **p1** and then, if **p1** is **False**, evaluates **p2**; if **p1** is **True**, it does not evaluate **p2**. Therefore, **and** is referred to as the *conditional* or *short-circuit AND* operator, and **or** is referred to as the *conditional* or *short-circuit OR* operator.

conditional operator
short-circuit evaluation

4.20 Assuming that **x** is **1**, show the result of the following Boolean expressions.

```
True and (3 > 4)
not (x > 0) and (x > 0)
(x > 0) or (x < 0)
(x != 0) or (x == 0)
(x >= 0) or (x < 0)
(x != 1) == not (x == 1)
```

4.21 Write a Boolean expression that evaluates to **True** if variable **num** is between **1** and **100**.

4.22 Write a Boolean expression that evaluates to **True** if variable **num** is between **1** and **100** or the number is negative.

4.23 Assuming **x** $=$ **4** and **y** $=$ **5**, show the result of the following Boolean expressions:

```
x >= y >= 0
x <= y >= 0
x != y == 5
(x != 0) or (x == 0)
```

4.24 Are the following expressions equivalent?

```
(a) (x >= 1) and (x < 10)
(b) (1 <= x < 10)
```

4.25 What is the value of the expression **ch >= 'A' and ch <= 'Z'** if **ch** is **'A'**, **'p'**, **'E'**, or **'5'**?

4.26 Suppose, when you run the following program, you enter input **2**, **3**, **6** from the console. What is the output?

```
x, y, z = eval(input("Enter three numbers: "))

print("(x < y and y < z) is", x < y and y < z)
print("(x < y or y < z) is", x < y or y < z)
print("not (x < y) is", not (x < y))
print("(x < y < z) is", x < y < z)
print("not(x < y < z) is", not (x < y < z))
```

4.27 Write a Boolean expression that evaluates true if **age** is greater than **13** and less than **18**.

4.28 Write a Boolean expression that evaluates true if **weight** is greater than **50** or **height** is greater than **160**.

4.29 Write a Boolean expression that evaluates true if **weight** is greater than **50** and **height** is greater than **160**.

4.30 Write a Boolean expression that evaluates true if either **weight** is greater than **50** or **height** is greater than **160**, but not both.

4.12 Case Study: Determining Leap Years

*A year is a leap year if it is divisible by **4** but not by **100** or if it is divisible by **400**.*

Key
Point

You can use the following Boolean expressions to determine whether a year is a leap year:

```
# A leap year is divisible by 4
isLeapYear = (year % 4 == 0)
# A leap year is divisible by 4 but not by 100
isLeapYear = isLeapYear and (year % 100 != 0)
```

```
# A leap year is divisible by 4 but not by 100 or divisible by 400
isLeapYear = isLeapYear or (year % 400 == 0)
```

or you can combine all these expressions into one, like this:

```
isLeapYear = (year % 4 == 0 and year % 100 != 0) or (year % 400 == 0)
```

Listing 4.9 is an example of a program that lets the user enter a year and then determines whether it is a leap year.

LISTING 4.9   LeapYear.py

input

leap year?

display result

```
1   year = eval(input("Enter a year: "))
2
3   # Check if the year is a leap year
4   isLeapYear = (year % 4 == 0 and year % 100 != 0) or \
5       (year % 400 == 0)
6
7   # Display the result
8   print(year, "is a leap year?", isLeapYear)
```

```
Enter a year: 2008  ⏎Enter
2008 is a leap year? True
```

```
Enter a year: 1900  ⏎Enter
1900 is a leap year? False
```

```
Enter a year: 2002  ⏎Enter
2002 is a leap year? False
```

4.13 Case Study: Lottery

Key Point

The lottery program in this case study involves generating random numbers, comparing digits, and using Boolean operators.

Suppose you want to develop a program to play a lottery. The program randomly generates a two-digit number, prompts the user to enter a two-digit number, and determines whether the user wins according to the following rules:

1. If the user's input matches the lottery in the exact order, the award is $10,000.

2. If all the digits in the user's input match all the digits in the lottery number, the award is $3,000.

3. If one digit in the user's input matches a digit in the lottery number, the award is $1,000.

The complete program is shown in Listing 4.10.

LISTING 4.10   Lottery.py

generate a lottery

enter a guess

```
1   import random
2
3   # Generate a lottery number
4   lottery = random.randint(0, 99)
5
6   # Prompt the user to enter a guess
7   guess = eval(input("Enter your lottery pick (two digits): "))
```

```
8
9   # Get digits from lottery
10  lotteryDigit1 = lottery // 10
11  lotteryDigit2 = lottery % 10
12
13  # Get digits from guess
14  guessDigit1 = guess // 10
15  guessDigit2 = guess % 10
16
17  print("The lottery number is", lottery)
18
19  # Check the guess
20  if guess == lottery:                          exact match?
21      print("Exact match: you win $10,000")
22  elif (guessDigit2 == lotteryDigit1 and \      match all digits?
23       guessDigit1 == lotteryDigit2):
24      print("Match all digits: you win $3,000")
25  elif (guessDigit1 == lotteryDigit1            match one digit?
26          or guessDigit1 == lotteryDigit2
27          or guessDigit2 == lotteryDigit1
28          or guessDigit2 == lotteryDigit2):
29      print("Match one digit: you win $1,000")
30  else:
31      print("Sorry, no match")
```

```
Enter your lottery pick (two digits): 45  ↵Enter
The lottery number is 12
Sorry, no match
```

```
Enter your lottery pick (two digits): 23  ↵Enter
The lottery number is 34
Match one digit: you win $1,000
```

variable \ line#	4	7	10	11	14	15	29
lottery	34						
guess		23					
lotteryDigit1			3				
lotteryDigit2				4			
guessDigit1					2		
guessDigit2						3	
output							Match one digit: you win $1,000

The program generates a lottery number using the **random.randint(0, 99)** function (line 4) and prompts the user to enter a guess (line 7). Note that **guess % 10** obtains the last digit from **guess** and **guess // 10** obtains the first digit from **guess**, since **guess** is a two-digit number (lines 14–15).

The program checks the guess against the lottery number in this order:

1. First check whether the guess matches the lottery number exactly (line 20).

2. If not, check whether the reversal of the guess matches the lottery number (lines 22–23).

3. If not, check whether one digit is in the lottery number (lines 25–28).

4. If not, nothing matches and display **Sorry, no match** (lines 30–31).

4.14 Conditional Expressions

Key Point

A conditional expression evaluates an expression based on a condition.

You might want to assign a value to a variable that is restricted by certain conditions. For example, the following statement assigns **1** to **y** if **x** is greater than **0**, and **-1** to **y** if **x** is less than or equal to **0**.

```
if x > 0:
    y = 1
else:
    y = -1
```

Alternatively, as in this next example, you can use a conditional expression to achieve the same result.

```
y = 1 if x > 0 else -1
```

conditional expression

Conditional expressions are in a completely different style. The syntax is:

```
expression1 if boolean-expression else expression2
```

The result of this conditional expression is **expression1** if **boolean-expression** is true; otherwise, the result is **expression2**.

Suppose you want to assign the larger number of variables **number1** and **number2** to **max**. You can simply write a statement using the conditional expression:

```
max = number1 if number1 > number2 else number2
```

For another example, the following statement displays the message **number is even** if **number** is even, and otherwise displays **number is odd**.

```
print("number is even" if number % 2 == 0 else "number is odd")
```

Check Point

MyProgrammingLab™

4.31 Suppose that when you run the following program you enter the input **2, 3, 6** from the console. What is the output?

```
x, y, z = eval(input("Enter three numbers: "))
print("sorted" if x < y and y < z else "not sorted")
```

4.32 Rewrite the following **if** statements using a conditional expression:

```
if ages >= 16:
    ticketPrice = 20
else:
    ticketPrice = 10
```

```
if count % 10 == 0:
    print(count)
else:
    print(count, end = " ")
```

4.33 Rewrite the following conditional expressions using **if/else** statements:

(a) score = 3 * scale if x > 10 else 4 * scale
(b) tax = income * 0.2 if income > 10000 else income * 0.17 + 1000
(c) print(i if number % 3 == 0 else j)

4.15 Operator Precedence and Associativity

Operator precedence and associativity determine the order in which operators are evaluated.

Key Point

Operator precedence and *operator associativity* determine the order in which Python evaluates operators. Suppose that you have this expression:

operator precedence
operator associativity

```
3 + 4 * 4 > 5 * (4 + 3) - 1
```

What is its value? What is the execution order of the operators?

Arithmetically, the expression in the parentheses is evaluated first. (Parentheses can be nested, in which case the expression in the inner parentheses is executed first.) When evaluating an expression without parentheses, the operators are applied according to the precedence rule and the associativity rule.

The precedence rule defines precedence for operators. Table 4.7 contains the operators you have learned so far, with the operators listed in decreasing order of precedence from top to bottom. The logical operators have lower precedence than the relational operators and the relational operators have lower precedence than the arithmetic operators. Operators with the same precedence appear in the same group.

precedence

TABLE 4.7 Operator Precedence Chart

Precedence	Operator
	+, - (Unary plus and minus)
	** (Exponentiation)
	not
	*, /, //, % (Multiplication, division, integer division, and remainder)
	+, - (Binary addition and subtraction)
	<, <=, >, >= (Comparison)
	==, != (Equality)
	and
	or
	=, +=, -=, *=, /=, //=, %= (Assignment operators)

If operators with the same precedence are next to each other, their *associativity* determines the order of evaluation. All binary operators are *left-associative*. For example, since + and – are of the same precedence and are left-associative, the expression

associativity

$$a - b + c - d \quad \text{is equivalent to} \quad ((a - b) + c) - d$$

Note

Python has its own way to evaluate an expression internally. The result of a Python evaluation is the same as that of its corresponding arithmetic evaluation.

behind the scenes

4.34 List the precedence order of the Boolean operators. Evaluate the following expressions:
```
True or True and False
True and True or False
```

Check Point

MyProgrammingLab™

4.35 True or false? All the binary operators except = are left-associative.

4.36 Evaluate the following expressions:

```
2 * 2 - 3 > 2 and 4 - 2 > 5
2 * 2 - 3 > 2 or 4 - 2 > 5
```

4.37 Is (x > 0 and x < 10) the same as ((x > 0) and (x < 10))? Is (x > 0 or x < 10) the same as ((x > 0) or (x < 10))? Is (x > 0 or x < 10 and y < 0) the same as (x > 0 or (x < 10 and y < 0))?

4.16 Detecting the Location of an Object

Detecting whether an object is inside another object is a common task in game programming.

In game programming, often you need to determine whether an object is inside another object. This section gives an example of testing whether a point is inside a circle. The program prompts the user to enter the center of a circle, the radius, and a point. The program then displays the circle and the point along with a message indicating whether the point is inside or outside the circle, as shown in Figure 4.7a–b.

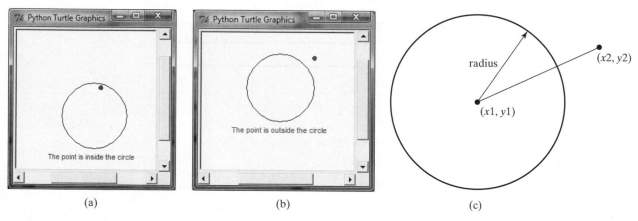

(a)   (b)   (c)

FIGURE 4.7 The program displays a circle, a point, and a message indicating whether the point is inside or outside the circle.

A point is in the circle if its distance to the center of the circle is less than or equal to the radius of the circle, as shown in Figure 4.7c. The formula for computing the distance is $\sqrt{(x_2 - x_1)^2 + (y_2 - y_1)^2}$. Listing 4.11 gives the program.

LISTING 4.11 PointInCircle.py

import turtle

enter input

draw a circle

```
1  import turtle
2
3  x1, y1 = eval(input("Enter the center of a circle x, y: "))
4  radius = eval(input("Enter the radius of the circle: "))
5  x2, y2 = eval(input("Enter a point x, y: "))
6
7  # Draw the circle
8  turtle.penup()           # Pull the pen up
9  turtle.goto(x1, y1 - radius)
10 turtle.pendown()         # Pull the pen down
11 turtle.circle(radius)
12 # Draw the point
```

```
13  turtle.penup()         # Pull the pen up
14  turtle.goto(x2, y2)
15  turtle.pendown()       # Pull the pen down
16  turtle.begin_fill()    # Begin to fill color in a shape
17  turtle.color("red")
18  turtle.circle(3)                                              draw a point
19  turtle.end_fill()      # Fill the shape
20
21  # Display the status
22  turtle.penup()         # Pull the pen up
23  turtle.goto(x1 - 70, y1 - radius - 20)
24  turtle.pendown()
25
26  d = ((x2 - x1) * (x2 - x1) + (y2 - y1) * (y2 - y1)) ** 0.5     compute distance
27  if d <= radius:
28      turtle.write("The point is inside the circle")            in the circle
29  else:
30      turtle.write("The point is outside the circle")           not in the circle
31
32  turtle.hideturtle()
33
34  turtle.done()                                                 pause
```

The program obtains the circle's center location and radius (lines 3–4) and the location of a point (line 5). It displays the circle (lines 8–11) and the point (lines 13–19). The program computes the distance between the center of the circle and the point (line 26) and determines whether the point is inside or outside the circle.

The code in lines 16–19 draws a dot, which can be simplified using the **dot** method, presented in Table 3.6, as follows:

```
turtle.dot(6, "red")
```

This method draws a red dot with diameter **6**.

KEY TERMS

Boolean expressions   92
Boolean value   92
operator associativity   117
operator precedence   117

random module   94
selection statements   92
short-circuit evaluation   113

CHAPTER SUMMARY

1. A Boolean type variable can store a **True** or **False** value.

2. The relational operators (<, <=, ==, !=, >, >=), which work with numbers and characters, yield a *Boolean value*.

3. The Boolean operators **and**, **or**, and **not** operate with Boolean values and variables.

4. When evaluating **p1 and p2**, Python first evaluates **p1** and then evaluates **p2** if **p1** is **True**; if **p1** is **False**, it does not evaluate **p2**. When evaluating **p1 or p2**, Python first evaluates **p1** and then evaluates **p2** if **p1** is **False**; if **p1** is **True**, it does not evaluate **p2**. Therefore, **and** is referred to as the conditional or *short-circuit* AND *operator*, and **or** is referred to as the conditional or short-circuit OR operator.

5. *Selection statements* are used for programming with alternative courses. There are several types of selection statements: **if** statements, **if-else** statements, nested **if-elif-else** statements, and conditional expressions.

6. The various **if** statements all make control decisions based on a *Boolean expression*. Based on the **True** or **False** evaluation of the expression, these statements take one of two possible courses.

7. The operators in arithmetic expressions are evaluated in the order determined by the rules of parentheses, *operator precedence*, and *operator associativity*.

8. Parentheses can be used to force the order of evaluation to occur in any sequence.

9. Operators with higher precedence are evaluated earlier. For operators of the same precedence, their associativity determines the order of evaluation.

TEST QUESTIONS

Do test questions for this chapter online at **www.cs.armstrong.edu/liang/py/test.html**.

PROGRAMMING EXERCISES

MyProgrammingLab™

Pedagogical Note

think before coding

For each exercise, you should carefully analyze the problem requirements and design strategies for solving the problem before coding.

Debugging Tip

Before you ask for help, read and explain the program to yourself, and trace it using several representative inputs by hand or using an IDE debugger. You learn how to program by debugging your own mistakes.

learn from mistakes

Section 4.2

*4.1 (*Algebra: solve quadratic equations*) The two roots of a quadratic equation, for example, $ax^2 + bx + c = 0$, can be obtained using the following formula:

$$r_1 = \frac{-b + \sqrt{b^2 - 4ac}}{2a} \quad \text{and} \quad r_2 = \frac{-b - \sqrt{b^2 - 4ac}}{2a}$$

$b^2 - 4ac$ is called the discriminant of the quadratic equation. If it is positive, the equation has two real roots. If it is zero, the equation has one root. If it is negative, the equation has no real roots.

Write a program that prompts the user to enter values for a, b, and c and displays the result based on the discriminant. If the discriminant is positive, display two roots. If the discriminant is **0**, display one root. Otherwise, display **The equation has no real roots**. Here are some sample runs.

```
Enter a, b, c: 1.0, 3, 1  ↵Enter
The roots are -0.381966 and -2.61803
```

```
Enter a, b, c: 1, 2.0, 1  ↵Enter
The root is -1
```

```
Enter a, b, c: 1, 2, 3  ↵Enter
The equation has no real roots
```

*4.2 (*Game: add three numbers*) The program in Listing 4.1 generates two integers and prompts the user to enter the sum of these two integers. Revise the program to generate three single-digit integers and prompt the user to enter the sum of these three integers.

Sections 4.3–4.8

*4.3 (*Algebra: solve 2 × 2 linear equations*) You can use Cramer's rule to solve the following 2 × 2 system of linear equation:

$$ax + by = e \qquad x = \frac{ed - bf}{ad - bc} \qquad y = \frac{af - ec}{ad - bc}$$
$$cx + dy = f$$

Write a program that prompts the user to enter a, b, c, d, e, and f and display the result. If $ad - bc$ is **0**, report that **The equation has no solution**.

```
Enter a, b, c, d, e, f: 9.0, 4.0, 3.0, -5.0, -6.0, -21.0  ↵Enter
x is -2.0 and y is 3.0
```

```
Enter a, b, c, d, e, f: 1.0, 2.0, 2.0, 4.0, 4.0, 5.0  ↵Enter
The equation has no solution
```

**4.4 (*Game: learn addition*) Write a program that generates two integers under 100 and prompts the user to enter the sum of these two integers. The program then reports true if the answer is correct, false otherwise. The program is similar to Listing 4.1.

*4.5 (*Find future dates*) Write a program that prompts the user to enter an integer for today's day of the week (Sunday is 0, Monday is 1, ..., and Saturday is 6). Also prompt the user to enter the number of days after today for a future day and display the future day of the week. Here is a sample run:

```
Enter today's day: 1  ↵Enter
Enter the number of days elapsed since today: 3  ↵Enter
Today is Monday and the future day is Thursday
```

```
Enter today's day: 0  ↵Enter
Enter the number of days elapsed since today: 31  ↵Enter
Today is Sunday and the future day is Wednesday
```

*4.6 (*Health application: BMI*) Revise Listing 4.6, ComputeBMI.py, to let users enter their weight in pounds and their height in feet and inches. For example, if a person is **5** feet and **10** inches, you will enter **5** for feet and **10** for inches. Here is a sample run:

```
Enter weight in pounds: 140  ↵Enter
Enter feet: 5  ↵Enter
Enter inches: 10  ↵Enter
BMI is 20.087702275404553
You are Normal
```

4.7 (*Financial application: monetary units*) Modify Listing 3.4, ComputeChange.py, to display the nonzero denominations only, using singular words for single units such as **1** dollar and **1** penny, and plural words for more than one unit such as **2** dollars and **3** pennies.

*4.8 (*Sort three integers*) Write a program that prompts the user to enter three integers and displays them in increasing order.

*4.9 (*Financial: compare costs*) Suppose you shop for rice and find it in two different-sized packages. You would like to write a program to compare the costs of the packages. The program prompts the user to enter the weight and price of each package and then displays the one with the better price. Here is a sample run:

```
Enter weight and price for package 1: 50, 24.59  ↵Enter
Enter weight and price for package 2: 25, 11.99  ↵Enter
Package 1 has the better price.
```

4.10 (*Game: multiplication quiz*) Listing 4.4, SubtractionQuiz.py, randomly generates a subtraction question. Revise the program to randomly generate a multiplication question with two integers less than **100**.

Sections 4.9–4.16

*4.11 (*Find the number of days in a month*) Write a program that prompts the user to enter the month and year and displays the number of days in the month. For example, if the user entered month **2** and year **2000**, the program should display that February 2000 has 29 days. If the user entered month **3** and year **2005**, the program should display that March 2005 has 31 days.

4.12 (*Check a number*) Write a program that prompts the user to enter an integer and checks whether the number is divisible by both **5** and **6**, divisible by **5** or **6**, or just one of them (but not both). Here is a sample run:

```
Enter an integer: 10  ↵Enter
Is 10 divisible by 5 and 6? False
Is 10 divisible by 5 or 6? True
Is 10 divisible by 5 or 6, but not both? True
```

*4.13 (*Financial application: compute taxes*) Listing 4.7, ComputeTax.py, gives the source code to compute taxes for single filers. Complete Listing 4.7 to give the complete source code for the other filing statuses.

VideoNote
Coffee price

4.14 (*Game: heads or tails*) Write a program that lets the user guess whether a flipped coin displays the head or the tail. The program randomly generates an integer **0** or **1**, which represents head or tail. The program prompts the user to enter a guess and reports whether the guess is correct or incorrect.

**4.15 (*Game: lottery*) Revise Listing 4.10, Lottery.py, to generate a three-digit lottery number. The program prompts the user to enter a three-digit number and determines whether the user wins according to the following rules:

1. If the user input matches the lottery number in the exact order, the award is $10,000.
2. If all the digits in the user input match all the digits in the lottery number, the award is $3,000.
3. If one digit in the user input matches a digit in the lottery number, the award is $1,000.

4.16 (*Random character*) Write a program that displays a random uppercase letter.

*4.17 (*Game: scissor, rock, paper*) Write a program that plays the popular scissor-rock-paper game. (A scissor can cut a paper, a rock can knock a scissor, and a paper can wrap a rock.) The program randomly generates a number **0**, **1**, or **2** representing scissor, rock, and paper. The program prompts the user to enter a number **0**, **1**, or **2** and displays a message indicating whether the user or the computer wins, loses, or draws. Here are sample runs:

```
scissor (0), rock (1), paper (2): 1  ↵Enter
The computer is scissor. You are rock. You won.
```

```
scissor (0), rock (1), paper (2): 2  ↵Enter
The computer is paper. You are paper too. It is a draw.
```

*4.18 (*Financials: currency exchange*) Write a program that prompts the user to enter the currency exchange rate between U.S. dollars and Chinese Renminbi (RMB). Prompt the user to enter **0** to convert from U.S. dollars to Chinese RMB and **1** for vice versa. Prompt the user to enter the amount in U.S. dollars or Chinese RMB to convert it to Chinese RMB or U.S. dollars, respectively. Here are some sample runs:

```
Enter the exchange rate from dollars to RMB: 6.81  ↵Enter
Enter 0 to convert dollars to RMB and 1 vice versa: 0  ↵Enter
Enter the dollar amount: 100  ↵Enter
$100.0 is 681.0 yuan
```

```
Enter the exchange rate from dollars to RMB: 6.81  ↵Enter
Enter 0 to convert dollars to RMB and 1 vice versa: 1  ↵Enter
Enter the RMB amount: 10000  ↵Enter
10000.0 yuan is $1468.43
```

```
Enter the exchange rate from dollars to RMB: 6.81  ↵Enter
Enter 0 to convert dollars to RMB and 1 vice versa: 5  ↵Enter
Incorrect input
```

**4.19 (*Compute the perimeter of a triangle*) Write a program that reads three edges for a triangle and computes the perimeter if the input is valid. Otherwise, display that the input is invalid. The input is valid if the sum of every pair of two edges is greater than the remaining edge. Here is a sample run:

```
Enter three edges: 1, 1, 1  ↵Enter
The perimeter is 3
```

```
Enter three edges: 1, 3, 1  ↵Enter
The input is invalid
```

*4.20 (*Science: wind-chill temperature*) Exercise 2.9 gives a formula to compute the wind-chill temperature. The formula is valid for temperatures in the range between $-58°F$ and $41°F$ and for wind speed greater than or equal to **2**. Write a program that prompts the user to enter a temperature and a wind speed. The program displays the wind-chill temperature if the input is valid; otherwise, it displays a message indicating whether the temperature and/or wind speed is invalid.

Comprehensive

**4.21 (*Science: day of the week*) Zeller's congruence is an algorithm developed by Christian Zeller to calculate the day of the week. The formula is

$$h = \left(q + \left\lfloor \frac{26(m + 1)}{10} \right\rfloor + k + \left\lfloor \frac{k}{4} \right\rfloor + \left\lfloor \frac{j}{4} \right\rfloor + 5j \right) \% 7$$

where

- **h** is the day of the week (0: Saturday, 1: Sunday, 2: Monday, 3: Tuesday, 4: Wednesday, 5: Thursday, 6: Friday).
- **q** is the day of the month.
- **m** is the month (3: March, 4: April, ..., 12: December). January and February are counted as months 13 and 14 of the previous year.
- **j** is the century (i.e., $\left\lfloor \frac{year}{100} \right\rfloor$).
- **k** is the year of the century (i.e., $year \% 100$).

Write a program that prompts the user to enter a year, month, and day of the month, and then it displays the name of the day of the week. Here are some sample runs:

```
Enter year: (e.g., 2008): 2013  ↵Enter
Enter month: 1-12: 1  ↵Enter
Enter the day of the month: 1-31: 25  ↵Enter
Day of the week is Friday
```

```
Enter year: (e.g., 2008): 2012  ↵Enter
Enter month: 1-12: 5  ↵Enter
Enter the day of the month: 1-31: 12  ↵Enter
Day of the week is Saturday
```

(Hint: $\lfloor n \rfloor$ = n//1 for a positive n. January and February are counted as **13** and **14** in the formula, so you need to convert the user input **1** to **13** and **2** to **14** for the month and change the year to the previous year.)

4.22 (*Geometry: point in a circle?*) Write a program that prompts the user to enter a point (x, y**) and checks whether the point is within the circle centered at (**0, 0**) with radius **10**. For example, (**4, 5**) is inside the circle and (**9, 9**) is outside the circle, as shown in Figure 4.8a.

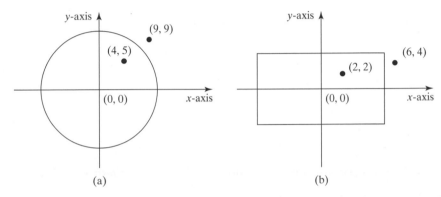

(a)   (b)

FIGURE 4.8   (a) Points inside and outside of the circle; (b) points inside and outside of the rectangle.

(Hint: A point is in the circle if its distance to (**0, 0**) is less than or equal to **10**. The formula for computing the distance is $\sqrt{(x_2 - x_1)^2 + (y_2 - y_1)^2}$. Test your program to cover all cases.) Two sample runs are shown next.

```
Enter a point with two coordinates: 4, 5  ↵Enter
Point (4.0, 5.0) is in the circle
```

```
Enter a point with two coordinates: 9, 9  ↵Enter
Point (9.0, 9.0) is not in the circle
```

4.23 (*Geometry: point in a rectangle?*) Write a program that prompts the user to enter a point (x, y**) and checks whether the point is within the rectangle centered at (**0, 0**) with width **10** and height **5**. For example, (**2, 2**) is inside the rectangle and (**6, 4**) is outside the rectangle, as shown in Figure 4.8b. (Hint: A point is in the rectangle if its horizontal distance to (**0, 0**) is less than or equal to **10 / 2** and its vertical distance to (**0, 0**) is less than or equal to **5.0 / 2**. Test your program to cover all cases.) Here are two sample runs:

```
Enter a point with two coordinates: 2, 2  ↵Enter
Point (2.0, 2.0) is in the rectangle
```

```
Enter a point with two coordinates: 6, 4  ⏎Enter
Point (6.0, 4.0) is not in the rectangle
```

4.24   (*Game: pick a card*) Write a program that simulates picking a card from a deck of 52 cards. Your program should display the rank (Ace**, **2**, **3**, **4**, **5**, **6**, **7**, **8**, **9**, **10**, **Jack**, **Queen**, **King**) and suit (**Clubs**, **Diamonds**, **Hearts**, **Spades**) of the card. Here is a sample run of the program:

```
The card you picked is the Jack of Hearts
```

*4.25   (*Geometry: intersecting point*) Two points on line 1 are given as (**x1, y1**) and (**x2, y2**) and on line 2 as (**x3, y3**) and (**x4, y4**), as shown in Figure 4.9a–b.

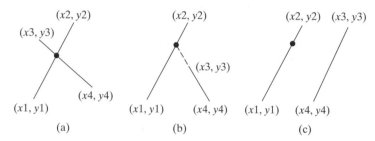

(a)   (b)   (c)

FIGURE 4.9   Two lines intersect in (a–b) and two lines are parallel in (c).

The intersecting point of the two lines can be found by solving the following linear equation:

$$(y_1 - y_2)x - (x_1 - x_2)y = (y_1 - y_2)x_1 - (x_1 - x_2)y_1$$

$$(y_3 - y_4)x - (x_3 - x_4)y = (y_3 - y_4)x_3 - (x_3 - x_4)y_3$$

This linear equation can be solved using Cramer's rule (see Exercise 4.3). If the equation has no solutions, the two lines are parallel (Figure 4.9c). Write a program that prompts the user to enter four points and displays the intersecting point. Here are sample runs:

```
Enter x1, y1, x2, y2, x3, y3, x4, y4:
2, 2, 5, -1, 4, 2, -1, -2  ⏎Enter
The intersecting point is at (2.88889, 1.1111)
```

```
Enter x1, y1, x2, y2, x3, y3, x4, y4:
2, 2, 7, 6, 4, 2, -1, -2  ⏎Enter
The two lines are parallel
```

4.26   (*Palindrome number*) Write a program that prompts the user to enter a three-digit integer and determines whether it is a palindrome number. A number is a palindrome if it reads the same from right to left and from left to right. Here is a sample run of this program:

```
Enter a three-digit integer: 121 ↵Enter
121 is a palindrome
```

```
Enter a three-digit integer: 123 ↵Enter
123 is not a palindrome
```

**4.27 (*Geometry: points in triangle?*) Suppose a right triangle is placed in a plane as shown below. The right-angle point is at (0, 0), and the other two points are at (200, 0), and (0, 100). Write a program that prompts the user to enter a point with x- and y-coordinates and determines whether the point is inside the triangle. Here are some sample runs:

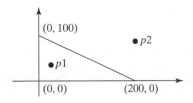

```
Enter a point's x- and y-coordinates: 100.5, 25.5 ↵Enter
The point is in the triangle
```

```
Enter a point's x- and y-coordinates: 100.5, 50.5 ↵Enter
The point is not in the triangle
```

**4.28 (*Geometry: two rectangles*) Write a program that prompts the user to enter the center x-, y-coordinates, width, and height of two rectangles and determines whether the second rectangle is inside the first or overlaps with the first, as shown in Figure 4.10. Test your program to cover all cases.

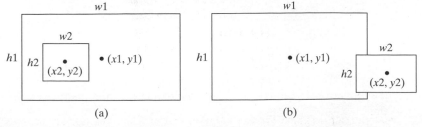

FIGURE 4.10 (a) A rectangle is inside another one. (b) A rectangle overlaps another one.

Here are some sample runs:

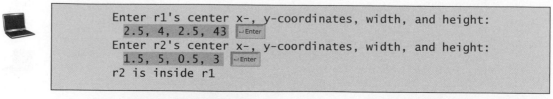

```
Enter r1's center x-, y-coordinates, width, and height:
2.5, 4, 2.5, 43 ⏎Enter
Enter r2's center x-, y-coordinates, width, and height:
1.5, 5, 0.5, 3 ⏎Enter
r2 is inside r1
```

```
Enter r1's center x-, y-coordinates, width, and height:
1, 2, 3, 5.5 ⏎Enter
Enter r2's center x-, y-coordinates, width, and height:
3, 4, 4.5, 5 ⏎Enter
r2 overlaps r1
```

```
Enter r1's center x-, y-coordinates, width, and height:
1, 2, 3, 3 ⏎Enter
Enter r2's center x-, y-coordinates, width, and height:
40, 45, 3, 2 ⏎Enter
r2 does not overlap r1
```

4.29 (*Geometry: two circles*) Write a program that prompts the user to enter the center coordinates and radii of two circles and determines whether the second circle is inside the first or overlaps with the first, as shown in Figure 4.11. (Hint: circle2 is inside circle1 if the distance between the two centers <= | **r1 - **r2**| and circle2 overlaps circle1 if the distance between the two centers <= **r1** + **r2**. Test your program to cover all cases.)

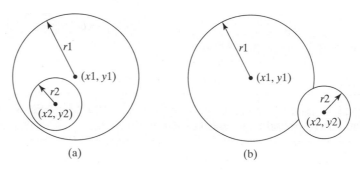

(a)   (b)

Figure 4.11 (a) A circle is inside another circle. (b) A circle overlaps another circle.

Here are some sample runs:

```
Enter circle1's center x-, y-coordinates, and radius:
0.5, 5.1, 13 ⏎Enter
Enter circle2's center x-, y-coordinates, and radius:
1, 1.7, 4.5 ⏎Enter
circle2 is inside circle1
```

```
Enter circle1's center x-, y-coordinates, and radius:
4.4, 5.7, 5.5 ⏎Enter
Enter circle2's center x-, y-coordinates, and radius:
6.7, 3.5, 3 ⏎Enter
circle2 overlaps circle1
```

```
Enter circle1's center x-, y-coordinates, and radius:
  4.4, 5.5, 1 ⏎Enter
Enter circle2's center x-, y-coordinates, and radius:
  5.5, 7.2, 1 ⏎Enter
circle2 does not overlap circle1
```

*4.30 (*Current time*) Revise Programming Exercise 2.18 to display the hour using a 12-hour clock. Here is a sample run:

```
Enter the time zone offset to GMT: -5 ⏎Enter
The current time is 4:50:34 AM
```

*4.31 (*Geometry: point position*) Given a directed line from point p0(x0, y0) to p1(x1, y1), you can use the following condition to decide whether a point p2(x2, y2) is on the left side of the line, on the right side of the line, or on the same line (see Figure 4.12):

$$(x1 - x0)*(y2 - y0) - (x2 - x0)*(y1 - y0) \begin{cases} >0 & \text{p2 is on the left side of the line} \\ =0 & \text{p2 is on the same line} \\ <0 & \text{p2 is on the right side of the line} \end{cases}$$

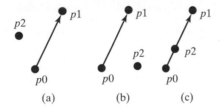

(a)   (b)   (c)

FIGURE 4.12 (a) p2 is on the left side of the line. (b) p2 is on the right side of the line. (c) p2 is on the same line.

Write a program that prompts the user to enter the x- and y-coordinates for the three points p0, p1, and p2 and displays whether p2 is on the left side of the line from p0 to p1, on the right side, or on the same line. Here are some sample runs:

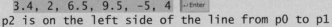

```
Enter coordinates for the three points p0, p1, and p2:
  3.4, 2, 6.5, 9.5, -5, 4 ⏎Enter
p2 is on the left side of the line from p0 to p1
```

```
Enter coordinates for the three points p0, p1, and p2:
  1, 1, 5, 5, 2, 2 ⏎Enter
p2 is on the same line from p0 to p1
```

```
Enter coordinates for the three points p0, p1, and p2:
  3.4, 2, 6.5, 9.5, 5, 2.5 ⏎Enter
p2 is on the right side of the line from p0 to p1
```

*4.32 (*Geometry: point on line segment*) Exercise 4.31 shows how to test whether a point is on an unbounded line. Revise Exercise 4.31 to test whether a point is on a line segment. Write a program that prompts the user to enter the x- and y-coordinates for the three points p0, p1, and p2 and displays whether p2 is on the line segment from p0 to p1. Here are some sample runs:

```
Enter coordinates for the three points p0, p1, and p2:
1, 1, 2.5, 2.5, 1.5, 1.5  ↵Enter
(1.5, 1.5) is on the line segment from (1.0, 1.0) to (2.5, 2.5)
```

```
Enter coordinates for the three points p0, p1, and p2:
1, 1, 2, 2, 3.5, 3.5  ↵Enter
(3.5, 3.5) is not on the line segment from (1.0, 1.0) to
(2.0, 2.0)
```

*4.33 (*Decimal to hex*) Write a program that prompts the user to enter an integer between **0** and **15** and displays its corresponding hex number. Here are some sample runs:

```
Enter a decimal value (0 to 15): 11  ↵Enter
The hex value is B
```

```
Enter a decimal value (0 to 15): 5  ↵Enter
The hex value is 5
```

```
Enter a decimal value (0 to 15): 31  ↵Enter
Invalid input
```

*4.34 (*Hex to decimal*) Write a program that prompts the user to enter a hex character and displays its corresponding decimal integer. Here are some sample runs:

```
Enter a hex character: A  ↵Enter
The decimal value is 10
```

```
Enter a hex character: a  ↵Enter
The decimal value is 10
```

```
Enter a hex character: 5  ↵Enter
The decimal value is 5
```

```
Enter a hex character: G  ⏎Enter
Invalid input
```

*4.35 (*Turtle: point position*) Write a program that prompts the user to enter the x- and y-coordinates for the three points p0, p1, and p2, and displays a message to indicate whether p2 is on the left side, the right side, or on the line from p0 to p1, as shown in Figure 4.13. See Exercise 4.31 for determining the point position.

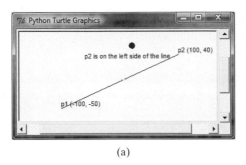
   (a)
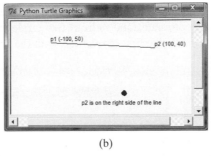
   (b)
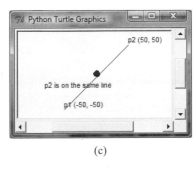
   (c)

FIGURE 4.13 The program displays the point position graphically.

**4.36 (*Turtle: point in a circle?*) Modify Listing 4.11 to let the program randomly generate a point within the square whose center is the same as the circle center and whose side is the diameter of the circle. Draw the circle and the point. Display a message to indicate whether the point is inside the circle.

**4.37 (*Turtle: point in a rectangle?*) Write a program that prompts the user to enter a point (x, y) and checks whether the point is within the rectangle centered at (0, 0) with width 100 and height 50. Display the point, the rectangle, and a message indicating whether the point is inside the rectangle in the window, as shown in Figure 4.14.

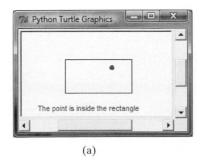
   (a)
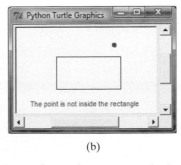
   (b)

FIGURE 4.14 The program displays the rectangle, a point, and a message whether a point is in or outside of the rectangle.

*4.38 (*Geometry: two rectangles*) Write a program that prompts the user to enter the center x-, y-coordinates, width, and height of two rectangles and determines whether the second rectangle is inside the first or overlaps with the first, as shown in Figure 4.15.

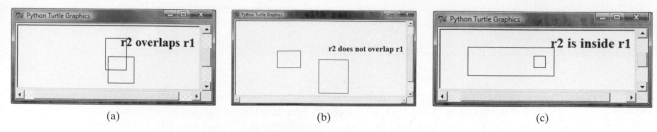

FIGURE 4.15 The program checks whether a rectangle is inside another one, overlaps another one, or does not overlap.

> ***4.39** (*Turtle: two circles*) Write a program that prompts the user to enter the center coordinates and radii of two circles and determines whether the second circle is inside the first or overlaps with the first, as shown in Figure 4.16.

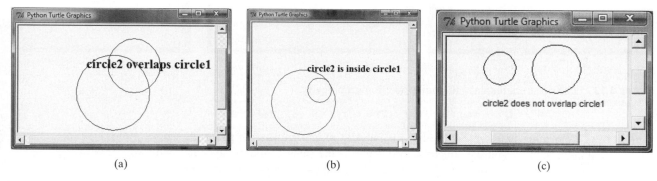

FIGURE 4.16 The program displays two circles and a status message.

CHAPTER

5

LOOPS

Objectives

- To write programs for executing statements repeatedly by using a **while** loop (§5.2).

- To develop loops following the loop design strategy (§§5.2.1–5.2.3).

- To control a loop with the user's confirmation (§5.2.4).

- To control a loop with a sentinel value (§5.2.5).

- To obtain a large amount of input from a file by using input redirection instead of typing from the keyboard and to save output to a file by using output redirection (§5.2.6).

- To use **for** loops to implement counter-controlled loops (§5.3).

- To write nested loops (§5.4).

- To learn the techniques for minimizing numerical errors (§5.5).

- To learn loops from a variety of examples (**GCD**, **FutureTuition**, **MonteCarloSimulation**, **PrimeNumber**) (§§5.6, 5.8).

- To implement program control with **break** and **continue** (§5.7).

- To use a loop to simulate a random walk (§5.9).

5.1 Introduction

Key Point

A loop can be used to tell a program to execute statements repeatedly.

Suppose that you need to display a string (e.g., **Programming is fun!**) 100 times. It would be tedious to type the statement 100 times:

100 times
```
print("Programming is fun!")
print("Programming is fun!")
...
print("Programming is fun!")
```

So, how do you solve this problem?

problem
why loop?
loop

Python provides a powerful construct called a *loop*, which controls how many times in succession an operation (or a sequence of operations) is performed. By using a loop statement, you don't have to code the print statement a hundred times; you simply tell the computer to display a string that number of times. The loop statement can be written as follows:

```
count = 0
while count < 100:
    print("Programming is fun!")
    count = count + 1
```

loop body

The variable **count** is initially **0**. The loop checks whether **count < 100** is true. If so, it executes the *loop body*—the part of the loop that contains the statements to be repeated—to display the message **Programming is fun!** and increments **count** by **1**. It repeatedly executes the loop body until **count < 100** becomes false (i.e., when **count** reaches **100**). At this point the loop terminates and the next statement after the loop statement is executed.

condition-controlled loop
count-controlled loop

A loop is a construct that controls the repeated execution of a block of statements. The concept of looping is fundamental to programming. Python provides two types of loop statements: **while** loops and **for** loops. The **while** loop is a *condition-controlled loop*; it is controlled by a true/false condition. The **for** loop is a *count-controlled loop* that repeats a specified number of times.

5.2 The **while** Loop

Key Point

*A **while** loop executes statements repeatedly as long as a condition remains true.*

The syntax for the **while** loop is:

while loop

```
while loop-continuation-condition:
    # Loop body
    Statement(s)
```

iteration
loop-continuation-
  condition

Figure 5.1a shows the **while**-loop flowchart. A single execution of a loop body is called an *iteration* (or repetition) of the loop. Each loop contains a **loop-continuation-condition**, a Boolean expression that controls the body's execution. It is evaluated each time to determine if the loop body should be executed. If its evaluation is **True**, the loop body is executed; otherwise, the entire loop terminates and the program control turns to the statement that follows the **while** loop.

VideoNote
while loop

The loop that displays **Programming is fun!** 100 times is an example of a **while** loop. Its flowchart is shown in Figure 5.1b. The **loop-continuation-condition** is **count < 100** and the loop body contains two statements:

```
count = 0
while count < 100:                      ┌── loop-continuation-condition
    print("Programming is fun!")
    count = count + 1
```
loop body

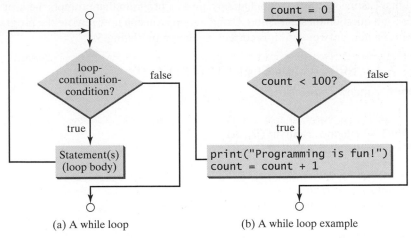

(a) A while loop   (b) A while loop example

Figure 5.1   The **while** loop repeatedly executes the statements in the loop body as long as the **loop-continuation-condition** evaluates to **True**.

Here is another example illustrating how a loop works:

```
sum = 0
i = 1
while i < 10:
    sum = sum + i
    i = i + 1
print("sum is", sum) # sum is 45
```

If **i** < **10** is true, the program adds **i** to **sum**. The variable **i** is initially set to **1**, then incremented to **2**, **3**, and so on, up to **10**. When **i** is **10**, **i** < **10** is false, and the loop exits. So **sum** is **1** + **2** + **3** + **...** + **9** = **45**.

Suppose the loop is mistakenly written as follows:

```
sum = 0
i = 1
while i < 10:
    sum = sum + i
i = i + 1
```

Note that the entire loop body must be indented inside the loop. Here the statement **i** = **i** + **1** is not in the loop body. This loop is infinite, because **i** is always **1** and **i** < **10** will always be true.

Note

Make sure that the **loop-continuation-condition** eventually becomes false so that the loop will terminate. A common programming error involves *infinite loops* (i.e., the loop runs forever). If your program takes an unusual long time to run and does not stop, it may have an infinite loop. If you run the program from the command window, press CTRL+C to stop it.

infinite loop

Caution

Programmers often mistakenly execute a loop one time more or less than intended. This kind of mistake is commonly known as the *off-by-one error*. For example, the following loop displays **Programming is fun** 101 times rather than 100 times. The error lies in the condition, which should be **count** < **100** rather than **count** <= **100**.

off-by-one error

```
count = 0
while count <= 100:
    print("Programming is fun!")
    count = count + 1
```

Recall that Listing 4.4, SubtractionQuiz.py, gives a program that prompts the user to enter an answer for a question on subtraction. Using a loop, you can now rewrite the program to let the user enter a new answer until it is correct, as shown in Listing 5.1.

LISTING 5.1 RepeatSubtractionQuiz.py

```
 1  import random
 2
 3  # 1. Generate two random single-digit integers
 4  number1 = random.randint(0, 9)
 5  number2 = random.randint(0, 9)
 6
 7  # 2. If number1 < number2, swap number1 with number2
 8  if number1 < number2:
 9      number1, number2 = number2, number1
10
11  # 3. Prompt the student to answer "What is number1 - number2?"
12  answer = eval(input("What is " + str(number1) + " - "
13      + str(number2) + "? "))
14
15  # 4. Repeatedly ask the question until the answer is correct
16  while number1 - number2 != answer:
17      answer = eval(input("Wrong answer. Try again. What is "
18          + str(number1) + " - " + str(number2) + "? "))
19
20  print("You got it!")
```

random number1
random number2

swap numbers

enter answer

check answer
enter answer again

```
What is 4 - 3? 4  ⏎Enter
Wrong answer. Try again. What is 4 - 3? 5  ⏎Enter
Wrong answer. Try again. What is 4 - 3? 1  ⏎Enter
You got it!
```

The loop in lines 16–18 repeatedly prompts the user to enter an answer when **number1 - number2 != answer** is true. Once **number1 - number2 != answer** is false, the loop exits.

5.2.1 Case Study: Guessing Numbers

The problem is to guess what number a computer has in mind. You will write a program that randomly generates an integer between **0** and **100**, inclusive. The program prompts the user to enter numbers continuously until it matches the randomly generated number. For each user input, the program reports whether it is too low or too high, so the user can choose the next input intelligently. Here is a sample run:

```
Guess a magic number between 0 and 100
Enter your guess: 50  ⏎Enter
Your guess is too high
Enter your guess: 25  ⏎Enter
Your guess is too low
Enter your guess: 42  ⏎Enter
Your guess is too high
Enter your guess: 39  ⏎Enter
Yes, the number is 39
```

intelligent guess

The magic number is between **0** and **100**. To minimize the number of guesses, enter **50** first. If your guess is too high, the magic number is between **0** and **49**. If your guess is too low, the magic number is between 51 and 100. So, after one guess, you can eliminate half the numbers from further consideration.

How do you write this program? Do you immediately begin coding? No. It is important to *think before coding*. Think about how you would solve the problem without writing a program. You need to first generate a random number between 0 and 100, inclusive, then prompt the user to enter a guess, and then compare the guess with the random number.

think before coding

It is a good practice to code *incrementally*—that is, one step at a time. For programs involving loops, if you don't know how to write a loop right away, you might first write the program so it executes the code once, and then figure out how to execute it repeatedly in a loop. For this program, you can create an initial draft, as shown in Listing 5.2.

code incrementally

N = eval(input("Enter N: "))
i = 1
while i < N
*i = i * 2*

LISTING 5.2 GuessNumberOneTime.py

```
 1  import random
 2
 3  # Generate a random number to be guessed
 4  number = random.randint(0, 100)
 5
 6  print("Guess a magic number between 0 and 100")
 7
 8  # Prompt the user to guess the number
 9  guess = eval(input("Enter your guess: "))
10
11  if guess == number:
12      print("Yes, the number is", number)
13  elif guess > number:
14      print("Your guess is too high")
15  else:
16      print("Your guess is too low")
```

generate a number

enter a guess

correct guess?

too high?

too low?

When this program runs, it prompts the user to enter a guess only once. To let the user enter a guess repeatedly, you can change the code in lines 11–16 to create a loop, as follows:

```
 1  while True:
 2      # Prompt the user to guess the number
 3      guess = eval(input("Enter your guess: "))
 4
 5      if guess == number:
 6          print("Yes, the number is", number)
 7      elif guess > number:
 8          print("Your guess is too high")
 9      else:
10          print("Your guess is too low")
```

This loop repeatedly prompts the user to enter a guess. However, the loop still needs to terminate; when **guess** matches **number**, the loop should end. So, revise the loop as follows:

```
 1  while guess != number:
 2      # Prompt the user to guess the number
 3      guess = eval(input("Enter your guess: "))
 4
 5      if guess == number:
 6          print("Yes, the number is", number)
 7      elif guess > number:
 8          print("Your guess is too high")
 9      else:
10          print("Your guess is too low")
```

The complete code is given in Listing 5.3.

LISTING 5.3 GuessNumber.py

generate a number

```
 1  import random
 2
 3  # Generate a random number to be guessed
 4  number = random.randint(0, 100)
 5
 6  print("Guess a magic number between 0 and 100")
 7
 8  guess = -1
 9  while guess != number:
10      # Prompt the user to guess the number
11      guess = eval(input("Enter your guess: "))
12
13      if guess == number:
14          print("Yes, the number is", number)
15      elif guess > number:
16          print("Your guess is too high")
17      else:
18          print("Your guess is too low")
```

enter a guess

too high?

too low?

	line#	number	guess	output
	4	39		
	8		−1	
iteration 1 {	11		50	
	16			Your guess is too high
iteration 2 {	11		25	
	18			Your guess is too low
iteration 3 {	11		42	
	16			Your guess is too high
iteration 4 {	11		39	
	14			Yes, the number is 39

The program generates the magic number in line 4 and prompts the user to enter a guess continuously in a loop (lines 9–18). For each guess, the program determines whether the user's number is correct, too high, or too low (lines 13–18). When the guess is correct, the program exits the loop (line 9). Note that **guess** is initialized to **-1**. This is to avoid initializing it to a value between **0** and **100**, because that could be the number to be guessed.

5.2.2 Loop Design Strategies

Writing a loop that works correctly is not an easy task for novice programmers. Consider the three steps involved when writing a loop:

Step 1: Identify the statements that need to be repeated.

Step 2: Wrap these statements in a loop like this:

```
while True:
    Statements
```

Step 3: Code the loop-continuation-condition and add appropriate statements for controlling the loop.

```
while loop-continuation-condition:
    Statements
    Additional statements for controlling the loop
```

5.2.3   Case Study: Multiple Subtraction Quiz

The subtraction quiz program in Listing 4.4, SubtractionQuiz.py, generates just one question for each run. You can use a loop to generate questions repeatedly. How do you write the code to generate five questions? Follow the loop design strategy. First, identify the statements that need to be repeated. These are the statements for obtaining two random numbers, prompting the user with a subtraction question, and grading the question. Second, wrap the statements in a loop. Third, add a loop-control variable and the loop-continuation-condition to execute the loop five times.

Listing 5.4 is a program that generates five questions and, after a student answers all of them, reports the number of correct answers. The program also displays the time spent on the test, as shown in the sample run.

LISTING 5.4   SubtractionQuizLoop.py

```
 1  import random
 2  import time
 3
 4  correctCount = 0   # Count the number of correct answers      correct count
 5  count = 0    # Count the number of questions                  total count
 6  NUMBER_OF_QUESTIONS = 5   # Constant
 7
 8  startTime = time.time() # Get start time                      get start time
 9
10  while count < NUMBER_OF_QUESTIONS:                            loop
11      # Generate two random single-digit integers
12      number1 = random.randint(0, 9)
13      number2 = random.randint(0, 9)
14
15      # If number1 < number2, swap number1 with number2
16      if number1 < number2:
17          number1, number2 = number2, number1
18
19      # Prompt the student to answer "What is number1 - number2?"
20      answer = eval(input("What is " + str(number1) + " - " +   display a question
21          str(number2) + "? "))
22
23      # Grade the answer and display the result
24      if number1 - number2 == answer:                          grade an answer
25          print("You are correct!")
26          correctCount += 1                                    increase correct count
27      else:
28          print("Your answer is wrong.\n", number1, "-",
29              number2, "is", number1 - number2)
30
31      # Increase the count
32      count += 1                                               increase control variable
33
34  endTime = time.time() # Get end time                         get end time
35  testTime = int(endTime - startTime) # Get test time          test time
36  print("Correct count is", correctCount, "out of",            display result
37      NUMBER_OF_QUESTIONS, "\nTest time is", testTime, "seconds")
```

```
What is 1 - 1? 0  [↵ Enter]
You are correct!

What is 7 - 2? 5  [↵ Enter]
You are correct!

What is 9 - 3? 4  [↵ Enter]
Your answer is wrong.
9 - 3 is 6

What is 6 - 6? 0  [↵ Enter]
You are correct!

What is 9 - 6? 2  [↵ Enter]
Your answer is wrong.
9 - 6 is 3

Correct count is 3 out of 5
Test time is 10 seconds
```

The program uses the control variable **count** to control the execution of the loop. **count** is initially **0** (line 5) and is increased by **1** in each iteration (line 32). A subtraction question is displayed and processed in each iteration. The program obtains the time before the test starts in line 8 and the time after the test ends in line 34, and computes the test time in seconds in line 35. The program displays the correct count and test time after all the quizzes have been taken (lines 36–37).

5.2.4 Controlling a Loop with User Confirmation

confirmation

The preceding example executes the loop five times. If you want the user to decide whether to take another question, you can offer a user *confirmation*. The template of the program can be coded as follows:

```
continueLoop = 'Y'
while continueLoop == 'Y' :
    # Execute the loop body once
    ...

    # Prompt the user for confirmation
    continueLoop = input("Enter Y to continue and N to quit: ")
```

You can rewrite Listing 5.4 with user confirmation to let the user decide whether to advance to the next question.

5.2.5 Controlling a Loop with a Sentinel Value

Another common technique for controlling a loop is to designate a special input value, known as a *sentinel value*, which signifies the end of the input. A loop that uses a sentinel value in this way is called a *sentinel-controlled loop*.

sentinel value
sentinel-controlled loop

The program in Listing 5.5 reads and calculates the sum of an unspecified number of integers. The input **0** signifies the end of the input. You don't need to use a new variable for each input value. Instead, use a variable named **data** (line 1) to store the input value and use a variable named **sum** (line 5) to store the total. Whenever a value is read, assign it to **data** (line 9) and add it to **sum** (line 7) if it is not zero.

LISTING 5.5   SentinelValue.py

```
1   data = eval(input("Enter an integer (the input ends " +
2       "if it is 0): "))
3
4   # Keep reading data until the input is 0
5   sum = 0
6   while data != 0:
7       sum += data
8
9       data = eval(input("Enter an integer (the input ends " +
10          "if it is 0): "))
11
12  print("The sum is", sum)
```

input data

loop

output result

```
Enter an integer (the input ends if it is 0): 2   ↵Enter
Enter an integer (the input ends if it is 0): 3   ↵Enter
Enter an integer (the input ends if it is 0): 4   ↵Enter
Enter an integer (the input ends if it is 0): 0   ↵Enter
The sum is 9
```

	line#	data	sum	output
	1	2		
	5		0	
iteration 1 {	7		2	
	9	3		
iteration 2 {	7		5	
	9	4		
iteration 3 {	7		9	
	9	0		
	12			The sum is 9

If **data** is not **0**, it is added to the **sum** (line 7) and the next item of input data is read (lines 9–10). If **data** is **0**, the loop body is no longer executed and the **while** loop terminates. The input value **0** is the sentinel value for this loop. Note that if the first input read is **0**, the loop body never executes, and the resulting sum is **0**.

Caution

Don't use floating-point values for equality checking in a loop control. Since those values are approximated, they could lead to imprecise counter values. This example uses **int** value for **data**. Consider the following code for computing $1 + 0.9 + 0.8 + \ldots + 0.1$:

numeric error

```
item = 1
sum = 0

while item != 0:   # No guarantee item will be 0
    sum += item
    item -= 0.1

print(sum)
```

The variable **item** starts with **1** and is reduced by **0.1** every time the loop body is executed. The loop should terminate when **item** becomes **0**. However, there is no guarantee that **item** will be exactly **0**, because the floating-point arithmetic is approximated. This loop seems okay on the surface, but it is actually an infinite loop.

5.2.6 Input and Output Redirections

In Listing 5.5, if you have a lot of data to enter, it would be cumbersome to type all the entries from the keyboard. You can store the data in a text file (named input.txt, for example) and run the program by using the following command:

```
python SentinelValue.py < input.txt
```

input redirection

This command is called *input redirection*. Instead of having the user type the data from the keyboard at runtime, the program takes the input from the file input.txt. Suppose the file contains the following numbers, one number per line:

```
2
3
4
0
```

The program should get **sum** to be **9**.

output redirection

Similarly, *output redirection* can send the output to a file instead of displaying it on the screen. The command for output redirection is:

```
python Script.py > output.txt
```

Input and output redirection can be used in the same command. For example, the following command gets input from input.txt and sends output to output.txt:

```
python SentinelValue.py < input.txt > output.txt
```

Run the program and see what contents show up in output.txt.

Check Point

MyProgrammingLab™

5.1 Analyze the following code. Is **count < 100** always **True**, always **False**, or sometimes **True** or sometimes **False** at Point A, Point B, and Point C?

```
count = 0
while count < 100:
    # Point A
    print("Programming is fun!")
    count += 1
    # Point B

# Point C
```

5.2 What is wrong if **guess** is initialized to **0** in line 8 in Listing 5.3?

5.3 How many times are the following loop bodies repeated? What is the printout of each loop?

```
i = 1
while i < 10:
    if i % 2 == 0:
        print(i)
```
(a)

```
i = 1
while i < 10:
    if i % 2 == 0:
        print(i)
        i += 1
```
(b)

```
i = 1
while i < 10:
    if i % 2 == 0:
        print(i)
    i += 1
```
(c)

5.4   Show the errors in the following code:

```
count = 0
while count < 100:
    print(count)
```
(a)

```
count = 0
while count < 100:
    print(count)
    count -= 1
```
(b)

```
count = 0
while count < 100:
count += 1
```
(c)

5.5   Suppose the input is **2 3 4 5 0** (one number per line). What is the output of the following code?

```
number = eval(input("Enter an integer: "))
max = number

while number != 0:
    number = eval(input("Enter an integer: "))
    if number > max:
        max = number

print("max is", max)
print("number", number)
```

5.3 The **for** Loop

*A Python **for** loop iterates through each value in a sequence.*

Key Point

Often you know exactly how many times the loop body needs to be executed, so a control variable can be used to count the executions. A loop of this type is called a counter-controlled loop. In general, the loop can be written as follows:

counter-controlled loop

```
i = initialValue  # Initialize loop-control variable
while i < endValue:
    # Loop body
    ...
    i += 1  # Adjust loop-control variable
```

VideoNote
for loop

A **for** loop can be used to simplify the preceding loop:

```
for i in range(initialValue, endValue):
    # Loop body
```

In general, the syntax of a **for** loop is:

for loop

```
for var in sequence:
    # Loop body
```

A sequence holds multiple items of data, stored one after the other. Later in the book, we will introduce strings, lists, and tuples. They are sequence-type objects in Python. The variable **var** takes on each successive value in the sequence, and the statements in the body of the loop are executed once for each value.

The function **range(a, b)** returns the sequence of integers a, a + 1, ..., b - 2, and b - 1. For example,

range(a, b) function

```
>>> for v in range(4, 8):
...     print(v)
...
4
5
6
7
>>>
```

range(a) function
range(a, b, k) function
step value

The **range** function has two more versions. You can also use **range(a)** or **range(a, b, k)**. **range(a)** is the same as **range(0, a)**. **k** is used as *step value* in **range(a, b, k)**. The first number in the sequence is **a**. Each successive number in the sequence will increase by the step value **k**. **b** is the limit. The last number in the sequence must be less than **b**. For example,

```
>>> for v in range(3, 9, 2):
...     print(v)
...
3
5
7
>>>
```

count backward

The step value in **range (3, 9, 2)** is **2**, and the limit is **9**. So, the sequence is **3**, **5**, and **7**.

The **range(a, b, k)** function can count backward if **k** is negative. In this case, the sequence is still **a, a + k, a + 2k**, and so on for a negative **k**. The last number in the sequence must be greater than **b**. For example,

```
>>> for v in range(5, 1, -1):
...     print(v)
...
5
4
3
2
>>>
```

Note

The numbers in the **range** function must be integers. For example, **range(1.5, 8.5)**, **range(8.5)**, or **range(1.5, 8.5, 1)** would be wrong.

Check
Point

MyProgrammingLab™

5.6 Suppose the input is **2 3 4 5 0** (one number per line). What is the output of the following code?

```
number = 0
sum = 0

for count in range(5):
    number = eval(input("Enter an integer: "))
    sum += number

print("sum is", sum)
print("count is", count)
```

5.7 Can you convert any **for** loop to a **while** loop? List the advantages of using **for** loops.

5.8 Convert the following **for** loop statement to a **while** loop:

```
sum = 0
for i in range(1001):
    sum = sum + i
```

5.9 Can you always convert any **while** loop into a **for** loop? Convert the following **while** loop into a **for** loop.

```
i = 1
sum = 0

while sum < 10000:
    sum = sum + i
    i += 1
```

5.10 Count the number of iterations in the following loops:

```
count = 0
while count < n:
    count += 1
```
(a)

```
for count in range(n):
    print(count)
```
(b)

```
count = 5
while count < n:
    count += 1
```
(c)

```
count = 5
while count < n:
    count = count + 3
```
(d)

5.4 Nested Loops

A loop can be nested inside another loop.

Key Point

nested loops

Nested loops consist of an outer loop and one or more inner loops. Each time the outer loop is repeated, the inner loops are reentered and started anew.

Listing 5.6 presents a program that uses nested **for** loops to display a multiplication table.

LISTING 5.6 MultiplicationTable.py

```
 1  print("          Multiplication Table")
 2  # Display the number title
 3  print("  |", end = '')
 4  for j in range(1, 10):
 5      print("  ", j, end = '')
 6  print()  # Jump to the new line
 7  print("----------------------------------------")
 8
 9  # Display table body
10  for i in range(1, 10):
11      print(i, "|", end = '')
12      for j in range(1, 10):
13          # Display the product and align properly
14          print(format(i * j, "4d"), end = '')
15      print()  # Jump to the new line
```

table title

table body

nested loop

display a line

```
               Multiplication Table
           1    2    3    4    5    6    7    8    9
    ------------------------------------------------------
    1 |    1    2    3    4    5    6    7    8    9
    2 |    2    4    6    8   10   12   14   16   18
    3 |    3    6    9   12   15   18   21   24   27
    4 |    4    8   12   16   20   24   28   32   36
    5 |    5   10   15   20   25   30   35   40   45
    6 |    6   12   18   24   30   36   42   48   54
    7 |    7   14   21   28   35   42   49   56   63
    8 |    8   16   24   32   40   48   56   64   72
    9 |    9   18   27   36   45   54   63   72   81
```

The program displays a title (line 1) on the first line in the output. The first **for** loop (lines 4–5) displays the numbers **1** through **9** on the second line. A line of dashes (-) is displayed on the third line (line 7).

The next loop (lines 10–15) is a nested **for** loop with the control variable **i** in the outer loop and **j** in the inner loop. For each **i**, the product **i * j** is displayed on a line in the inner loop, with **j** being **1, 2, 3, . . ., 9**.

To align the numbers properly, the program formats **i * j** using **format(i * j, "4d")** (line 14). Recall that **"4d"** specifies a decimal integer format with width **4**.

end = ''

Normally, the **print** function automatically jumps to the next line. Invoking **print(item, end = '')** (lines 3, 5, 11, and 14) prints the item without advancing to the next line. Note that the **print** function with the **end** argument was introduced in Section 3.3.5.

Note

Be aware that a nested loop may take a long time to run. Consider the following loop nested in three levels:

```
for i in range(1000):
    for j in range(1000):
        for k in range(1000):
            Perform an action
```

The action is performed 1,000,000,000 times. If it takes 1 millisecond to perform the action, the total time to run the loop would be more than 277 hours.

Check Point

MyProgrammingLab™

5.11 Show the output of the following programs. (Hint: Draw a table and list the variables in the columns to trace these programs.)

```
for i in range(1, 5):
    j = 0
    while j < i:
        print(j, end = " ")
        j += 1
```
(a)

```
i = 0
while i < 5:
    for j in range(i, 1, -1):
        print(j, end = " ")
    print("****")
    i += 1
```
(b)

```
i = 5
while i >= 1:
    num = 1
    for j in range(1, i + 1):
        print(num, end = "xxx")
        num *= 2
    print()
    i -= 1
```
(c)

```
i = 1
while i <= 5:
    num = 1
    for j in range(1, i + 1):
        print(num, end = "G")
        num += 2
    print()
    i += 1
```
(d)

5.5 Minimizing Numerical Errors

Using floating-point numbers in the loop-continuation-condition may cause numeric errors.

Key Point

Numerical errors involving floating-point numbers are inevitable. This section provides an example showing you how to minimize such errors.

The program in Listing 5.7 sums a series that starts with **0.01** and ends with **1.0**. The numbers in the series will increment by **0.01**, as follows: **0.01 + 0.02 + 0.03** and so on.

LISTING 5.7 TestSum.py

```
1  # Initialize sum
2  sum = 0
3
4  # Add 0.01, 0.02, ..., 0.99, 1 to sum
5  i = 0.01
6  while i <= 1.0:                          loop
7      sum += i
8      i = i + 0.01
9
10  # Display result
11  print("The sum is", sum)
```

```
The sum is 49.5
```

The result displayed is **49.5**, but the correct result is actually **50.5**. What went wrong? For each iteration in the loop, **i** is incremented by **0.01**. When the loop ends, the **i** value is slightly larger than **1** (not exactly **1**). This causes the last **i** value not to be added into **sum**. The fundamental problem is that the floating-point numbers are represented by approximation.

numeric error

To fix the problem, use an integer count to ensure that all the numbers are added to **sum**. Here is the new loop:

```
# Initialize sum
sum = 0

# Add 0.01, 0.02, ..., 0.99, 1 to sum
count = 0
i = 0.01
while count < 100:
    sum += i
    i = i + 0.01
    count += 1   # Increase count

# Display result
print("The sum is", sum)
```

Or, use a **for** loop as follows:

```
# Initialize sum
sum = 0

# Add 0.01, 0.02, ..., 0.99, 1 to sum
i = 0.01
for count in range(100):
    sum += i
    i = i + 0.01

# Display result
print("The sum is", sum)
```

After this loop, **sum** is **50.5**.

5.6 Case Studies

Key Point *Loops are fundamental in programming. The ability to write loops is essential in learning programming.*

If you can write programs using loops, you know how to program! For this reason, this section presents three additional examples of solving problems using loops.

5.6.1 Problem: Finding the Greatest Common Divisor

GCD

The greatest common divisor (GCD) of the two integers **4** and **2** is **2**. The greatest common divisor of the two integers **16** and **24** is **8**. How do you find the greatest common divisor? Let the two input integers be **n1** and **n2**. You know that number **1** is a common divisor, but it may not be the greatest common divisor. So you can check whether **k** (for **k** = **2**, **3**, **4**, and so on) is a common divisor for **n1** and **n2**, until **k** is greater than **n1** or **n2**. Store the common divisor in a variable named **gcd**. Initially, **gcd** is **1**. Whenever a new common divisor is found, it becomes the new **gcd**. When you have checked all the possible common divisors from **2** up to **n1** or **n2**, the value in the variable **gcd** is the greatest common divisor. The idea can be translated into the following loop:

```
gcd = 1 # Initial gcd is 1
int k = 2 # Possible gcd
while k <= n1 and k <= n2:
    if n1 % k == 0 and n2 % k == 0:
        gcd = k
    k += 1 # Next possible gcd

# After the loop, gcd is the greatest common divisor for n1 and n2
```

Listing 5.8 presents a program that prompts the user to enter two positive integers and finds their greatest common divisor.

LISTING 5.8 GreatestCommonDivisor.py

input
input

gcd

output

```
1  # Prompt the user to enter two integers
2  n1 = eval(input("Enter first integer: "))
3  n2 = eval(input("Enter second integer: "))
4
5  gcd = 1
6  k = 2
7  while k <= n1 and k <= n2:
8      if n1 % k == 0 and n2 % k == 0:
9          gcd = k
10     k += 1
11
12 print("The greatest common divisor for",
13     n1, "and", n2, "is", gcd)
```

```
Enter first integer: 125  ↵Enter
Enter second integer: 2525  ↵Enter
The greatest common divisor for 125 and 2525 is 25
```

think before you type

How would you approach writing this program? Would you immediately begin to write the code? No. It is important to *think before you type*. Thinking enables you to generate a logical solution for the problem without wondering how to write the code. Once you have a logical solution, type the code to translate the solution into a program.

A problem often has multiple solutions. The GCD problem can be solved in many ways. Exercise 5.16 at the end of this chapter suggests another solution. A more efficient solution is to use the classic Euclidean algorithm. See www.cut-the-knot.org/blue/Euclid.shtml for more information.

multiple solutions

5.12 If you think that a divisor for a number **n1** cannot be greater than **n1 / 2**, you might attempt to improve the program using the following loop:

```
k = 2
while k <= n1 / 2 and k <= n2 / 2:
    if n1 % k == 0 and n2 % k == 0:
        gcd = k
    k += 1
```

This revision is wrong. Can you find the reason?

Check Point

MyProgrammingLab

erroneous solutions

5.6.2 Problem: Predicting the Future Tuition

Suppose that the tuition for a university is **$10,000** this year and increases **7%** every year. In how many years will the tuition have doubled?

Before you attempt to write a program, first consider how to solve this problem by hand. The tuition for the second year is the tuition for the first year * **1.07**. The tuition for a future year is the tuition of its preceding year * **1.07**. So, the tuition for each year can be computed as follows:

```
year = 0  # Year 0
tuition = 10000

year += 1 # Year 1
tuition = tuition * 1.07

year += 1 # Year 2
tuition = tuition * 1.07

year += 1 # Year 3
tuition = tuition * 1.07
...
```

Keep computing **tuition** for a new year until it is at least **20000**. By then you will know how many years it will take for the tuition to be doubled. You can now translate the logic into the following loop:

```
year = 0  # Year 0
tuition = 10000
while tuition < 20000:
    year += 1
    tuition = tuition * 1.07
```

The complete program is shown in Listing 5.9.

LISTING 5.9 FutureTuition.py

```
1  year = 0  # Year 0
2  tuition = 10000  # Year 1
3
4  while tuition < 20000:
```

loop

next year's tuition

```
5          year += 1
6          tuition = tuition * 1.07
7
8   print("Tuition will be doubled in", year, "years")
9   print("Tuition will be $" + format(tuition, ".2f"),
10          "in", year, "years")
```

```
Tuition will be doubled in 11 years
Tuition will be $21048.52 in 11 years
```

The **while** loop (lines 4–6) is used to repeatedly compute the tuition for a new year. The loop terminates when **tuition** is greater than or equal to **20000**.

5.6.3 Problem: Monte Carlo Simulation

A Monte Carlo simulation uses random numbers and probability to solve problems. It has a wide range of applications in computational mathematics, physics, chemistry, and finance. We now look at an example of using a Monte Carlo simulation for estimating π.

First, draw a circle with its bounding square.

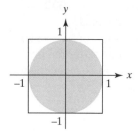

Assume the radius of the circle is **1**. So, the circle area is π and the square area is **4**. Randomly generate a point in the square. The probability that the point falls in the circle is **circleArea / squareArea** = π / **4**.

Write a program that randomly generates **1000000** points that fall in the square and let **numberOfHits** denote the number of points that fall in the circle. So, **numberOfHits** is approximately **1000000** * (π / **4**). π can be approximated as **4** * **numberOfHits** / **1000000**. The complete program is shown in Listing 5.10.

LISTING 5.10 MonteCarloSimulation.py

```
1   import random
2
3   NUMBER_OF_TRIALS = 1000000   # Constant
4   numberOfHits = 0
5
6   for i in range(NUMBER_OF_TRIALS):
7       x = random.random() * 2 - 1
8       y = random.random() * 2 - 1
9
10      if x * x + y * y <= 1:
11          numberOfHits += 1
12
13  pi = 4 * numberOfHits / NUMBER_OF_TRIALS
14
15  print("PI is", pi)
```

generate random points

check inside circle

estimate pi

```
PI is 3.14124
```

The program repeatedly generates a random point (**x**, **y**) in the square in lines 7–8:

```
x = random.random() * 2 - 1
y = random.random() * 2 - 1
```

Recall that **random()** returns a random float **r** such that **0 <= r < 1.0**.
If $x^2 + y^2 \leq 1$, the point is inside the circle and **numberOfHits** is incremented by **1**. π
is approximately **4 * numberOfHits / NUMBER_OF_TRIALS** (line 13).

5.7 Keywords **break** and **continue**

The **break** *and* **continue** *keywords provide additional controls to a loop.*

Key
Point

 Pedagogical Note

Two keywords, **break** and **continue**, can be used in loop statements to provide additional controls. Using **break** and **continue** can simplify programming in some cases. Overusing or improperly using them, however, can make programs difficult to read and debug. (*Note to readers*: You may skip this section without affecting your understanding of the rest of the book.)

You can use the keyword **break** in a loop to immediately terminate a loop. Listing 5.11 presents a program to demonstrate the effect of using **break** in a loop.

break keyword

LISTING 5.11 TestBreak.py

```
1    sum = 0
2    number = 0
3
4    while number < 20:
5        number += 1
6        sum += number
7        if sum >= 100:
8            break
9
10   print("The number is", number)
11   print("The sum is", sum)
```

break out of the loop

```
The number is 14
The sum is 105
```

The program adds integers from **1** to **20** in this order to **sum** until **sum** is greater than or equal to **100**. Without lines 7–8, this program would calculate the sum of the numbers from **1** to **20**. But with lines 7–8, the loop terminates when **sum** becomes greater than or equal to **100**. Without lines 7–8, the output would be:

```
The number is 20
The sum is 210
```

You can also use the **continue** keyword in a loop. When it is encountered, it ends the current iteration and program control goes to the end of the loop body. In other words, **continue** breaks out of an iteration, while the **break** keyword breaks out of a loop. The program in Listing 5.12 shows the effect of using **continue** in a loop.

continue statement

LISTING 5.12 TestContinue.py

```
1    sum = 0
2    number = 0
3
4    while number < 20:
5        number += 1
6        if number == 10 or number == 11:
7            continue
8        sum += number
9
10   print("The sum is", sum)
```

jump to the end of the
iteration

```
The sum is 189
```

The program adds all the integers from **1** to **20** except **10** and **11** to **sum**. The **continue** statement is executed when **number** becomes **10** or **11**. The **continue** statement ends the current iteration so that the rest of the statement in the loop body is not executed; therefore, **number** is not added to **sum** when it is **10** or **11**.

Without lines 6 and 7, the output would be as follows:

```
The sum is 210
```

In this case, all the numbers are added to **sum**, even when **number** is **10** or **11**. Therefore, the result is **210**.

You can always write a program without using **break** or **continue** in a loop (see Checkpoint Question 5.15). In general, it is appropriate to use **break** and **continue** if their use simplifies coding and makes programs easy to read.

Suppose you need to write a program to find the smallest factor other than **1** for an integer **n** (assume **n >= 2**). You can write a simple and intuitive code using the **break** statement as follows:

```
n = eval(input("Enter an integer >= 2: "))
factor = 2
while factor <= n:
    if n % factor == 0:
        break
    factor += 1
print("The smallest factor other than 1 for", n, "is", factor)
```

You may rewrite the code without using **break** as follows:

```
n = eval(input("Enter an integer >= 2: "))
found = False
factor = 2
while factor <= n and not found:
    if n % factor == 0:
        found = True
    else:
        factor += 1
print("The smallest factor other than 1 for", n, "is", factor)
```

Obviously, the **break** statement makes the program simpler and easier to read in this example. However, you should use **break** and **continue** with caution. Too many **break** and `continue` statements will produce a loop with many exit points and make the program difficult to read.

> **Note**
>
> Some programming languages have a **goto** statement. The **goto** statement indiscriminately transfers control to any statement in the program and executes it. This makes your program vulnerable to errors. The **break** and **continue** statements in Python are different from **goto** statements. They operate only in a loop statement. The **break** statement breaks out of the loop, and the **continue** statement breaks out of the current iteration in the loop.

goto

5.13 What is the keyword **break** for? What is the keyword **continue** for? Will the following program terminate? If so, give the output.

```
balance = 1000
while True:
    if balance < 9:
        break
    balance = balance - 9

print("Balance is", balance)
```
(a)

```
balance = 1000
while True:
    if balance < 9:
        continue
    balance = balance - 9

print("Balance is", balance)
```
(b)

5.14 The **for** loop on the left is converted into the **while** loop on the right. What is wrong? Correct it.

```
for i in range(4):
    if i % 3 == 0:
        continue
    sum += i
```
Converted

Wrong conversion

→

```
i = 0
while i < 4:
    if i % 3 == 0:
        continue
    sum += i
    i += 1
```

5.15 Rewrite the programs **TestBreak** and **TestContinue** in Listings 5.11 and 5.12 without using **break** and **continue** statements.

5.16 After the **break** statement in (a) is executed in the following loop, which statement is executed? Show the output. After the **continue** statement in (b) is executed in the following loop, which statement is executed? Show the output.

```
for i in range(1, 4):
    for j in range(1, 4):
        if i * j > 2:
            break

        print(i * j)

    print(i)
```
(a)

```
for i in range(1, 4):
    for j in range(1, 4):
        if i * j > 2:
            continue

        print(i * j)

    print(i)
```
(b)

5.8 Case Study: Displaying Prime Numbers

Key Point

This section presents a program that displays the first fifty prime numbers in five lines, each containing ten numbers.

An integer greater than **1** is *prime* if its only positive divisor is **1** or itself. For example, **2**, **3**, **5**, and **7** are prime numbers, but **4**, **6**, **8**, and **9** are not.

The problem can be broken into the following tasks:

■ Determine whether a given number is prime.

■ For **number** = **2, 3, 4, 5, 6, ...**, test whether the number is prime.

■ Count the prime numbers.

■ Display each prime number, and display ten numbers per line.

Obviously, you need to write a loop and repeatedly test whether a new number is prime. If the number is prime, increase the count by **1**. The count is **0** initially. When it reaches **50**, the loop terminates.

Here is the algorithm for the problem:

```
Set the number of prime numbers to be displayed as
    a constant NUMBER_OF_PRIMES
Use count to track the number of prime numbers and
    set an initial count to 0
Set an initial number to 2

while count < NUMBER_OF_PRIMES:
    Test if number is prime

    if number is prime:
        Display the prime number and increase count

    Increment number by 1
```

To test whether a number is prime, check whether it is divisible by **2, 3, 4, ...,** up to **number/2**. If a divisor is found, the number is not a prime. The algorithm can be described as follows:

```
Use a Boolean variable isPrime to denote whether
    the number is prime; Set isPrime to True initially

for divisor in range(2, number / 2 + 1):
    if number % divisor == 0:
        Set isPrime to False
        Exit the loop
```

The complete program is given in Listing 5.13.

LISTING 5.13 PrimeNumber.py

count prime numbers

```
1  NUMBER_OF_PRIMES = 50  # Number of primes to display
2  NUMBER_OF_PRIMES_PER_LINE = 10 # Display 10 per line
3  count = 0  # Count the number of prime numbers
4  number = 2  # A number to be tested for primeness
5
6  print("The first 50 prime numbers are")
7
8  # Repeatedly find prime numbers
```

```
 9  while count < NUMBER_OF_PRIMES:
10      # Assume the number is prime
11      isPrime = True  # Is the current number prime?
12
13      # Test if number is prime
14      divisor = 2
15      while divisor <= number / 2:                      check primeness
16          if number % divisor == 0:
17              # If true, the number is not prime
18              isPrime = False  # Set isPrime to false
19              break # Exit the for loop                 exit loop
20          divisor += 1
21
22      # Display the prime number and increase the count
23      if isPrime:
24          count += 1  # Increase the count
25
26          print(format(number, "5d"), end = '')        display if prime
27          if count % NUMBER_OF_PRIMES_PER_LINE == 0:
28              # Display the number and advance to the new line
29              print()  # Jump to the new line
30
31      # Check if the next number is prime
32      number += 1
```

```
The first 50 prime numbers are

   2    3    5    7   11   13   17   19   23   29
  31   37   41   43   47   53   59   61   67   71
  73   79   83   89   97  101  103  107  109  113
 127  131  137  139  149  151  157  163  167  173
 179  181  191  193  197  199  211  223  227  229
```

This is a complex example for novice programmers. The key to developing a programmatic solution for this problem—and for many other problems—is to break it into subproblems and develop solutions for each of them in turn. Do not attempt to develop a complete solution in the first trial. Instead, begin by writing the code to determine whether a given number is prime, and then expand the program to test whether other numbers are prime in a loop.

To determine whether a number is prime, check whether it is divisible by a number between 2 and **number/2** inclusive. If so, it is not a prime number; otherwise, it is a prime number. For a prime number, display it. If the count is divisible by **10**, advance to a new line. The program ends when the count reaches **50**.

The program uses the **break** statement in line 19 to exit the **for** loop as soon as the number is found to be a nonprime. You can rewrite the loop (lines 15–20) without using the **break** statement as follows:

```
while divisor <= number / 2 and isPrime:
    if number % divisor == 0:
        # If True, the number is not prime
        isPrime = False # Set isPrime to False
    divisor += 1
```

However, using the **break** statement makes the program simpler and easier to read in this case.

5.9 Case Study: Random Walk

Key Point

You can use Turtle graphics to simulate a random walk.

In this section, we will write a Turtle program that simulates a random walk in a lattice (e.g., like walking around a garden and turning to look at certain flowers) that starts from the center and ends at a point on the boundary, as shown in Figure 5.2. Listing 5.14 gives the program.

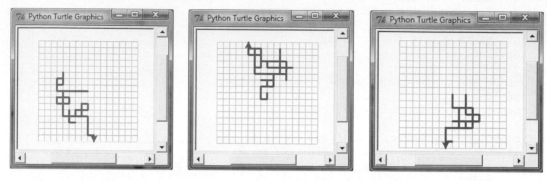

FIGURE 5.2   The program simulates random walks in a lattice.

LISTING 5.14   RandomWalk.py

import turtle	1	`import turtle`
import randint	2	`from random import randint`
	3	
set turtle speed	4	`turtle.speed(1)  # Set turtle speed to slowest`
	5	
	6	`# Draw 16-by-16 lattice`
set color	7	`turtle.color("gray")  # Color for lattice`
	8	`x = -80`
draw horizontal lines	9	`for y in range(-80, 80 + 1, 10):`
	10	`    turtle.penup()`
	11	`    turtle.goto(x, y)  # Draw a horizontal line`
	12	`    turtle.pendown()`
	13	`    turtle.forward(160)`
	14	
	15	`y = 80`
draw vertical lines	16	`turtle.right(90)`
	17	`for x in range(-80, 80 + 1, 10):`
	18	`    turtle.penup()`
	19	`    turtle.goto(x, y)  # Draw a vertical line`
	20	`    turtle.pendown()`
	21	`    turtle.forward(160)`
	22	
	23	`turtle.pensize(3)`
	24	`turtle.color("red")`
	25	
	26	`turtle.penup()`
move to center	27	`turtle.goto(0, 0)  # Go to the center`
	28	`turtle.pendown()`
	29	
current position	30	`x = y = 0 # Current pen location at the center of lattice`
check boundaries	31	`while abs(x) < 80 and abs(y) < 80:`
	32	`    r = randint(0, 3)`
	33	`    if r == 0:`
walk east	34	`        x += 10 # Walk right`

```
35              turtle.setheading(0)
36              turtle.forward(10)
37          elif r == 1:
38              y -= 10 # Walk down                          walk south
39              turtle.setheading(270)
40              turtle.forward(10)
41          elif r == 2:
42              x -= 10 # Walk left                          walk west
43              turtle.setheading(180)
44              turtle.forward(10)
45          elif r == 3:
46              y += 10 # Walk up                            walk north
47              turtle.setheading(90)
48              turtle.forward(10)
49
50  turtle.done()                                            pause
```

Assume the size of the lattice is **16** by **16** and the distance between two lines in the lattice is **10** pixels (lines 6–21). The program first draws the lattice in a gray color. It sets the color to gray (line 7), uses the **for** loop (lines 9–13) to draw the horizontal lines, and the **for** loop (lines 17–21) to draw the vertical lines.

The program moves the pen to the center (line 27), and starts to simulate a random walk in a **while** loop (lines 31–48). The variables x and y are used to track the current position in the lattice. Initially, it is at (**0, 0**) (line 30). A random number from **0** to **3** is generated in line 32. These four numbers each correspond to a direction: east, south, west, and north. Consider four cases:

- If a walk is to the east, x is increased by **10** (line 34) and the pen is moved to the right (lines 35–36).

- If a walk is to the south, y is decreased by **10** (line 38) and the pen is moved downward (lines 39–40).

- If a walk is to the west, x is decreased by **10** (line 42) and the pen is moved to the left (lines 43–44).

- If a walk is to the north, y is increased by **10** (line 46) and the pen is moved upward (lines 47–48).

The walk stops when **abs(x)** or **abs(y)** is **80** (i.e., the walk reaches the boundary of the lattice).

A more interesting walk is called a *self-avoiding walk*. It is a random walk in a lattice that does not visit the same point twice. You will learn how to write a program to simulate a self-avoiding walk later in the book.

KEY TERMS

break keyword   151
condition-controlled loop   134
continue keyword   151
count-controlled loop   134
infinite loop   135
input redirection   142
iteration   134
loop   134

loop body   134
loop-continuation-condition   134
nested loop   145
off-by-one error   135
output redirection   142
sentinel value   140

CHAPTER SUMMARY

1. There are two types of repetition statements: the `while` loop and the `for` loop.

2. The part of the *loop* that contains the statements to be repeated is called the *loop body*.

3. A one-time execution of a loop body is referred to as an *iteration of the loop*.

4. An *infinite loop* is a loop statement that executes infinitely.

5. In designing loops, you need to consider both the loop-control structure and the loop body.

6. The `while` loop checks the `loop-continuation-condition` first. If the condition is true, the loop body is executed; otherwise, the loop terminates.

7. A *sentinel value* is a special value that signifies the end of the input.

8. The `for` loop is a *count-controlled loop* and is used to execute a loop body a predictable number of times.

9. Two keywords, `break` and `continue`, can be used in a loop.

10. The `break` keyword immediately ends the innermost loop, which contains the break.

11. The `continue` keyword ends only the current iteration.

TEST QUESTIONS

Do test questions for this chapter online at www.cs.armstrong.edu/liang/py/test.html.

MyProgrammingLab

PROGRAMMING EXERCISES

read and think before coding

explore solutions

Pedagogical Note

For each problem, read it several times until you understand it. Think how to solve the problem before coding. Translate your logic into a program.

A problem often can be solved in many different ways. You should explore various solutions.

Sections 5.2–5.7

*5.1 (*Count positive and negative numbers and compute the average of numbers*) Write a program that reads an unspecified number of integers, determines how many positive and negative values have been read, and computes the total and average of the input values (not counting zeros). Your program ends with the input **0**. Display the average as a floating-point number. Here is a sample run:

```
Enter an integer, the input ends if it is 0: 1  ↵Enter
Enter an integer, the input ends if it is 0: 2  ↵Enter
Enter an integer, the input ends if it is 0: -1  ↵Enter
Enter an integer, the input ends if it is 0: 3  ↵Enter
```

```
Enter an integer, the input ends if it is 0: 0  ⏎Enter
The number of positives is 3
The number of negatives is 1
The total is 5
The average is 1.25
```

```
Enter an integer, the input ends if it is 0: 0  ⏎Enter
You didn't enter any number
```

5.2 (*Repeat additions*) Listing 5.4, SubtractionQuizLoop.py, generates five random subtraction questions. Revise the program to generate ten random addition questions for two integers between 1 and 15. Display the correct count and test time.

5.3 (*Conversion from kilograms to pounds*) Write a program that displays the following table (note that 1 kilogram is 2.2 pounds):

```
Kilograms    Pounds

1               2.2
3               6.6
...
197           433.4
199           437.8
```

5.4 (*Conversion from miles to kilometers*) Write a program that displays the following table (note that 1 mile is 1.609 kilometers):

```
Miles       Kilometers

1           1.609
2           3.218
...
9          15.481
10         16.090
```

*5.5 (*Conversion from kilograms to pounds and pounds to kilograms*) Write a program that displays the following two tables side by side (note that 1 kilogram is 2.2 pounds and that 1 pound is .45 kilograms):

```
Kilograms   Pounds   |   Pounds    Kilograms

1           2.2      |   20        9.09
3           6.6      |   25        11.36
...
197         433.4    |   510       231.82
199         437.8    |   515       235.09
```

*5.6 (*Conversion from miles to kilometers and kilometers to miles*) Write a program that displays the following two tables side by side (note that 1 mile is 1.609 kilometers and that 1 kilometer is .621 mile):

```
Miles       Kilometers   |   Kilometers    Miles

1           1.609        |   20            12.430
2           3.218        |   25            15.538
...
9          15.481        |   60            37.290
10         16.090        |   65            40.398
```

5.7   (*Use trigonometric functions*) Print the following table to display the **sin** value and **cos** value of degrees from 0 to 360 with increments of 10 degrees. Round the value to keep four digits after the decimal point.

Degree	Sin	Cos
0	0.0000	1.0000
10	0.1736	0.9848
...		
350	-0.1736	0.9848
360	0.0000	1.0000

5.8   (*Use the* **math.sqrt** *function*) Write a program that prints the following table using the **sqrt** function in the **math** module.

Number	Square Root
0	0.0000
2	1.4142
...	
18	5.2426
20	5.4721

**5.9   (*Financial application: compute future tuition*) Suppose that the tuition for a university is $10,000 this year and increases 5% every year. Write a program that computes the tuition in ten years and the total cost of four years' worth of tuition starting ten years from now.

5.10   (*Find the highest score*) Write a program that prompts the user to enter the number of students and each student's score, and displays the highest score. Assume that the input is stored in a file named score.txt, and the program obtains the input from the file.

*5.11   (*Find the two highest scores*) Write a program that prompts the user to enter the number of students and each student's score, and displays the highest and second-highest scores.

5.12   (*Find numbers divisible by 5 and 6*) Write a program that displays, ten numbers per line, all the numbers from 100 to 1,000 that are divisible by 5 and 6. The numbers are separated by exactly one space.

5.13   (*Find numbers divisible by 5 or 6, but not both*) Write a program that displays, ten numbers per line, all the numbers from 100 to 200 that are divisible by 5 or 6, but not both. The numbers are separated by exactly one space.

5.14   (*Find the smallest n such that $n^2 > 12,000$*) Use a **while** loop to find the smallest integer **n** such that n^2 is greater than 12,000.

5.15   (*Find the largest n such that $n^3 < 12,000$*) Use a **while** loop to find the largest integer **n** such that n^3 is less than 12,000.

*5.16   (*Compute the greatest common divisor*) For Listing 5.8, another solution to find the greatest common divisor of two integers **n1** and **n2** is as follows: First find **d** to be the minimum of **n1** and **n2**, and then check whether **d, d - 1, d - 2, ..., 2,** or **1** is a divisor for both **n1** and **n2** in this order. The first such common divisor is the greatest common divisor for **n1** and **n2**.

Section 5.8

*5.17   (*Display the ASCII character table*) Write a program that displays the characters in the ASCII character table from **!** to **~**. Display ten characters per line. The characters are separated by exactly one space.

**5.18 (*Find the factors of an integer*) Write a program that reads an integer and displays all its smallest factors, also known as *prime factors*. For example, if the input integer is 120, the output should be as follows:

```
2, 2, 2, 3, 5
```

**5.19 (*Display a pyramid*) Write a program that prompts the user to enter an integer from 1 to 15 and displays a pyramid, as shown in the following sample run:

```
Enter the number of lines: 7  ↵Enter
                    1
                  2 1 2
                3 2 1 2 3
              4 3 2 1 2 3 4
            5 4 3 2 1 2 3 4 5
          6 5 4 3 2 1 2 3 4 5 6
        7 6 5 4 3 2 1 2 3 4 5 6 7
```

*5.20 (*Display four patterns using loops*) Use nested loops that display the following patterns in four separate programs:

```
Pattern A        Pattern B        Pattern C        Pattern D

1                1 2 3 4 5 6              1        1 2 3 4 5 6
1 2              1 2 3 4 5             2 1         1 2 3 4 5
1 2 3            1 2 3 4            3 2 1          1 2 3 4
1 2 3 4          1 2 3           4 3 2 1          1 2 3
1 2 3 4 5        1 2          5 4 3 2 1           1 2
1 2 3 4 5 6      1         6 5 4 3 2 1            1
```

5.21 (*Display numbers in a pyramid pattern*) Write a nested **for loop that displays the following output:

```
                        1
                    1   2   1
                1   2   4   2   1
            1   2   4   8   4   2   1
        1   2   4   8  16   8   4   2   1
    1   2   4   8  16  32  16   8   4   2   1
1   2   4   8  16  32  64  32  16   8   4   2   1
1   2   4   8  16  32  64 128  64  32  16   8   4   2   1
```

*5.22 (*Display prime numbers between 2 and 1,000*) Modify Listing 5.13 to display all the prime numbers between 2 and 1,000, inclusive. Display eight prime numbers per line.

Comprehensive

**5.23 (*Financial application: compare loans with various interest rates*) Write a program that lets the user enter the loan amount and loan period in number of years and displays the monthly and total payments for each interest rate starting from 5% to 8%, with an increment of 1/8. Here is a sample run:

```
Loan Amount: 10000  ⏎Enter
Number of Years: 5  ⏎Enter
Interest Rate      Monthly Payment      Total Payment

5.000%             188.71               11322.74
5.125%             189.28               11357.13
5.250%             189.85               11391.59
...
7.875%             202.17               12129.97
8.000%             202.76               12165.83
```

For the formula to compute monthly payment, see Listing 2.8, ComputeLoan.py.

**5.24 (*Financial application: loan amortization schedule*) The monthly payment for a given loan pays the principal and the interest. The monthly interest is computed by multiplying the monthly interest rate and the balance (the remaining principal). The principal paid for the month is therefore the monthly payment minus the monthly interest. Write a program that lets the user enter the loan amount, number of years, and interest rate, and then displays the amortization schedule for the loan. Here is a sample run:

```
Loan Amount: 10000  ⏎Enter
Number of Years: 1  ⏎Enter
Annual Interest Rate: 7  ⏎Enter

Monthly Payment: 865.26
Total Payment: 10383.21

Payment#       Interest       Principal       Balance
1              58.33          806.93          9193.07
2              53.62          811.64          8381.43
...
11             10.00          855.26           860.27
12              5.01          860.25             0.01
```

Note

The balance after the last payment may not be zero. If so, the last payment should be the normal monthly payment plus the final balance.

Hint

Write a loop to display the table. Since the monthly payment is the same for each month, it should be computed before the loop. The balance is initially the loan amount. For each iteration in the loop, compute the interest and principal and update the balance. The loop may look like this:

```python
for i in range(1, numberOfYears * 12 + 1):
    interest = monthlyInterestRate * balance
    principal = monthlyPayment - interest
    balance = balance - principal
    print(i, "\t\t", interest, "\t\t", principal, "\t\t",
        balance)
```

*5.25 (*Demonstrate cancellation errors*) A *cancellation error* occurs when you are manipulating a very large number with a very small number. The large number may cancel out the smaller number. For example, the result of **100000000.0 + 0.000000001** is equal to **100000000.0**. To avoid cancellation errors and obtain more accurate results, carefully select the order of computation. For example, in computing the following series, you will obtain more accurate results by computing from right to left rather than from left to right:

$$1 + \frac{1}{2} + \frac{1}{3} + \ldots + \frac{1}{n}$$

Write a program that compares the results of the summation of the preceding series, computing both from left to right and from right to left with **n = 50000**.

*5.26 (*Sum a series*) Write a program to sum the following series:

$$\frac{1}{3} + \frac{3}{5} + \frac{5}{7} + \frac{7}{9} + \frac{9}{11} + \frac{11}{13} + \ldots + \frac{95}{97} + \frac{97}{99}$$

**5.27 (*Compute π*) You can approximate π by using the following series:

$$\pi = 4\left(1 - \frac{1}{3} + \frac{1}{5} - \frac{1}{7} + \frac{1}{9} - \frac{1}{11} + \ldots + \frac{(-1)^{i+1}}{2i - 1}\right)$$

Write a program that displays the π value for **i = 10000, 20000, . . .**, and **100000**.

5.28 (*Compute e*) You can approximate **e by using the following series:

$$e = 1 + \frac{1}{1!} + \frac{1}{2!} + \frac{1}{3!} + \frac{1}{4!} + \ldots + \frac{1}{i!}$$

Write a program that displays the **e** value for **i = 10000, 20000, . . .**, and **100000**. (Hint: Since $i! = i \times (i - 1) \times \ldots \times 2 \times 1$, then $\frac{1}{i!}$ is $\frac{1}{i(i - 1)!}$. Initialize **e** and **item** to be **1** and keep adding a new **item** to **e**. The new item is the previous item divided by **i** for **i = 2, 3, 4, ...**)

5.29 (*Display leap years*) Write a program that displays, ten per line, all the leap years in the twenty-first century (from year 2001 to 2100). The years are separated by exactly one space.

**5.30 (*Display the first days of each month*) Write a program that prompts the user to enter the year and first day of the year, and displays the first day of each month in the year on the console. For example, if the user entered year 2013, and 2 for Tuesday, January 1, 2013, your program should display the following output:

```
January 1, 2013 is Tuesday
...
December 1, 2013 is Sunday
```

**5.31 (*Display calendars*) Write a program that prompts the user to enter the year and first day of the year, and displays on the console the calendar table for the year. For example, if the user entered year 2005, and 6 for Saturday, January 1,

2005, your program should display the calendar for each month in the year, as follows:

January 2005

Sun	Mon	Tue	Wed	Thu	Fri	Sat
						1
2	3	4	5	6	7	8
9	10	11	12	13	14	15
16	17	18	19	20	21	22
23	24	25	26	27	28	29
30	31					

. . .

December 2005

Sun	Mon	Tue	Wed	Thu	Fri	Sat
				1	2	3
4	5	6	7	8	9	10
11	12	13	14	15	16	17
18	19	20	21	22	23	24
25	26	27	28	29	30	31

*5.32 (*Financial application: compound value*) Suppose you save $100 *each* month into a savings account with the annual interest rate 5%. So, the monthly interest rate is 0.05/12 = 0.00417. After the first month, the value in the account becomes

$$100 * (1 + 0.00417) = 100.417$$

After the second month, the value in the account becomes

$$(100 + 100.417) * (1 + 0.00417) = 201.252$$

After the third month, the value in the account becomes

$$(100 + 201.252) * (1 + 0.00417) = 302.507$$

and so on.

Write a program that prompts the user to enter an amount (e.g., 100), the annual interest rate (e.g., 5), and the number of months (e.g., 6), and displays the amount in the savings account after the given month.

*5.33 (*Financial application: compute CD value*) Suppose you put $10,000 into a CD with an annual percentage yield of 5.75%. After one month, the CD is worth

$$10000 + 10000 * 5.75 / 1200 = 10047.91$$

After two months, the CD is worth

$$10047.91 + 10047.91 * 5.75 / 1200 = 10096.06$$

After three months, the CD is worth

$$10096.06 + 10096.06 * 5.75 / 1200 = 10145.43$$

and so on.

Write a program that prompts the user to enter an amount (e.g., 10,000), the annual percentage yield (e.g., 5.75), and the number of months (e.g., 18), and displays a table as shown in the sample run.

```
Enter the initial deposit amount: 10000  ↵Enter
Enter annual percentage yield: 5.75  ↵Enter
Enter maturity period (number of months): 18  ↵Enter

Month  CD Value
1      10047.91
2      10096.06
...
17     10846.56
18     10898.54
```

**5.34 (*Game: lottery*) Revise Listing 4.10, Lottery.py, to generate a lottery of a two-digit number. The two digits in the number are distinct. (Hint: Generate the first digit. Use a loop to continuously generate the second digit until it is different from the first digit.)

**5.35 (*Perfect number*) A positive integer is called a *perfect number* if it is equal to the sum of all of its positive divisors, excluding itself. For example, 6 is the first perfect number, because 6 = 3 + 2 + 1. The next is 28 = 14 + 7 + 4 + 2 + 1. There arc four perfect numbers less than 10,000. Write a program to find these four numbers.

***5.36 (*Game: scissor, rock, paper*) Programming Exercise 4.17 gives a program that plays the scissor, rock, paper game. Revise the program to let the user play continuously until either the user or the computer wins more than two times.

*5.37 (*Summation*) Write a program that computes the following summation:

$$\frac{1}{1 + \sqrt{2}} + \frac{1}{\sqrt{2} + \sqrt{3}} + \frac{1}{\sqrt{3} + \sqrt{4}} + \ldots + \frac{1}{\sqrt{624} + \sqrt{625}}$$

*5.38 (*Simulation: clock countdown*) You can use the **time.sleep(seconds)** function in the **time** module to let the program pause for the specified seconds. Write a program that prompts the user to enter the number of seconds, displays a message at every second, and terminates when the time expires. Here is a sample run:

```
Enter the number of seconds: 3  ↵Enter
2 seconds remaining
1 second remaining
Stopped
```

*5.39 (*Financial application: find the sales amount*) You have just started a sales job in a department store. Your pay consists of a base salary plus a commission. The base salary is $5,000. The following scheme shows how to determine the commission rate:

Sales Amount	Commission Rate
$0.01–$5,000	8 percent
$5,000.01–$10,000	10 percent
$10,000.01 and above	12 percent

Your goal is to earn $30,000 a year. Write a program that finds out the minimum amount of sales you have to generate in order to make $30,000.

5.40 (*Simulation: heads or tails*) Write a program that simulates flipping a coin one million times and displays the number of heads and tails.

**5.41 (*Occurrence of max numbers*) Write a program that reads integers, finds the largest of them, and counts its occurrences. Assume that the input ends with number 0. Suppose that you entered 3 5 2 5 5 5 0; the program finds that the largest number is 5 and the occurrence count for 5 is 4. (Hint: Maintain two variables, max and count. The variable max stores the current maximum number, and count stores its occurrences. Initially, assign the first number to max and 1 to count. Compare each subsequent number with max. If the number is greater than max, assign it to max and reset count to 1. If the number is equal to max, increment count by 1.)

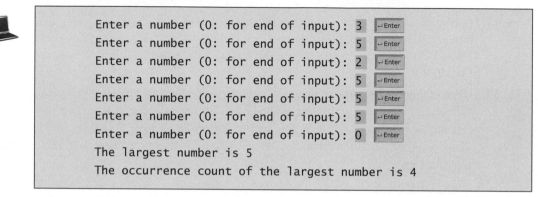

```
Enter a number (0: for end of input): 3  ↵Enter
Enter a number (0: for end of input): 5  ↵Enter
Enter a number (0: for end of input): 2  ↵Enter
Enter a number (0: for end of input): 5  ↵Enter
Enter a number (0: for end of input): 5  ↵Enter
Enter a number (0: for end of input): 5  ↵Enter
Enter a number (0: for end of input): 0  ↵Enter
The largest number is 5
The occurrence count of the largest number is 4
```

**5.42 (*Monte Carlo simulation*) A square is divided into four smaller regions as shown in (a). If you throw a dart into the square one million times, what is the probability for the dart to fall into an odd-numbered region? Write a program to simulate the process and display the result. (Hint: Place the center of the square in the center of a coordinate system, as shown in (b). Randomly generate a point in the square and count the number of times for a point to fall in an odd-numbered region.)

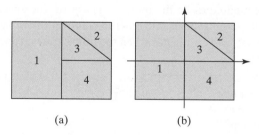

(a)   (b)

*5.43 (*Math: combinations*) Write a program that displays all possible combinations for picking two numbers from integers 1 to 7. Also display the total number of combinations.

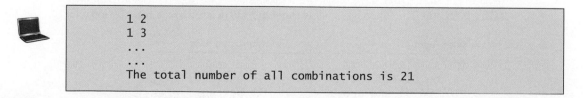

```
1 2
1 3
...
...
The total number of all combinations is 21
```

**5.44 (*Decimal to binary*) Write a program that prompts the user to enter a decimal integer and displays its corresponding binary value.

**5.45 (*Decimal to hex*) Write a program that prompts the user to enter a decimal integer and displays its corresponding hexadecimal value.

**5.46 (*Statistics: compute mean and standard deviation*) In business applications, you are often asked to compute the mean and standard deviation of data. The mean is simply the average of the numbers. The standard deviation is a statistic that tells you how tightly all the various data are clustered around the mean in a set of data. For example, what is the average age of the students in a class? How close are the ages? If all the students are the same age, the deviation is 0. Write a program that prompts the user to enter ten numbers, and displays the mean and standard deviations of these numbers using the following formula:

$$mean = \frac{\sum_{i=1}^{n} x_i}{n} = \frac{x_1 + x_2 + \ldots + x_n}{n} \qquad deviation = \sqrt{\frac{\sum_{i=1}^{n} x_i^2 - \frac{\left(\sum_{i=1}^{n} x_i\right)^2}{n}}{n - 1}}$$

Here is a sample run:

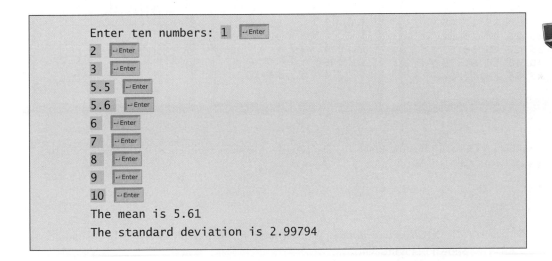

```
Enter ten numbers: 1 ↵Enter
2 ↵Enter
3 ↵Enter
5.5 ↵Enter
5.6 ↵Enter
6 ↵Enter
7 ↵Enter
8 ↵Enter
9 ↵Enter
10 ↵Enter
The mean is 5.61
The standard deviation is 2.99794
```

**5.47 (*Turtle: draw random balls*) Write a program that displays 10 random balls in a rectangle with width 120 and height 100, centered at (0, 0), as shown in Figure 5.3a.

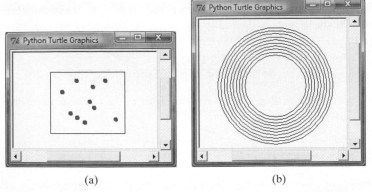

(a)   (b)

FIGURE 5.3   The program draws 10 random balls in (a), and 10 circles in (b).

**5.48 (*Turtle: draw circles*) Write a program that draws 10 circles with centers (0, 0), as shown in Figure 5.3b.

**5.49 (*Turtle: display a multiplication table*) Write a program that displays a multiplication table, as shown in Figure 5.4a.

**5.50 (*Turtle: display numbers in a triangular pattern*) Write a program that displays numbers in a triangular pattern, as shown in Figure 5.4b.

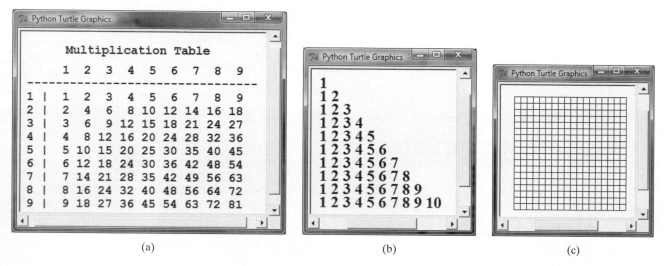

(a)   (b)   (c)

FIGURE 5.4 (a) The program displays a multiplication table. (b) The program displays numbers in a triangular pattern. (c) The program displays an 18-by-18 lattice.

**5.51 (*Turtle: display a lattice*) Write a program that displays an 18-by-18 lattice, as shown in Figure 5.4c.

**5.52 (*Turtle: plot the sine function*) Write a program that plots the sine function, as shown in Figure 5.5a.

Hint

The Unicode for π is **\u03c0**. To display -2π, use **turtle.write("-2\u03c0")**. For a trigonometric function like **sin(x)**, **x** is in radians. Use the following loop to plot the sine function:

```
for x in range(-175, 176):
    turtle.goto(x, 50 * math.sin((x / 100) * 2 * math.pi))
```

-2π is displayed at (−100, −15), the center of the axis is at (0, 0), and 2π is displayed at (100, −15).

FUNCTIONS

Objectives

- To define functions with formal parameters (§6.2).

- To invoke functions with actual parameters (i.e., arguments) (§6.3).

- To distinguish between functions that return and do not return a value (§6.4).

- To invoke a function using positional arguments or keyword arguments (§6.5).

- To pass arguments by passing their reference values (§6.6).

- To develop reusable code that is modular and is easy to read, debug, and maintain (§6.7).

- To create modules for reusing functions (§§6.7–6.8).

- To determine the scope of variables (§6.9).

- To define functions with default arguments (§6.10).

- To define a function that returns multiple values (§6.11).

- To apply the concept of function abstraction in software development (§6.12).

- To design and implement functions using stepwise refinement (§6.13).

- To simplify drawing programs with reusable functions (§6.14).

6.1 Introduction

problem

Functions can be used to define reusable code and organize and simplify code.

Suppose that you need to find the sum of integers from **1** to **10**, **20** to **37**, and **35** to **49**. If you create a program to add these three sets of numbers, your code might look like this:

```
sum = 0
for i in range(1, 11):
    sum += i
print("Sum from 1 to 10 is", sum)

sum = 0
for i in range(20, 38):
    sum += i
print("Sum from 20 to 37 is", sum)

sum = 0
for i in range(35, 50):
    sum += i
print("Sum from 35 to 49 is", sum)
```

why functions?

You may have observed that the code for computing these sums is very similar, except that the starting and ending integers are different. Wouldn't it be nice to be able to write commonly used code once and then reuse it? You can do this by defining a function, which enables you to create reusable code. For example, the preceding code can be simplified by using functions, as follows:

define `sum` function

```
1  def sum(i1, i2):
2      result = 0
3      for i in range(i1, i2 + 1):
4          result += i
5
6      return result
7
8  def main():
9      print("Sum from 1 to 10 is", sum(1, 10))
10     print("Sum from 20 to 37 is", sum(20, 37))
11     print("Sum from 35 to 49 is", sum(35, 49))
12
13 main() # Call the main function
```

define `main` function
invoke `sum`

Lines 1–6 define the function named `sum` with the two parameters `i1` and `i2`. Lines 8–11 define the `main` function that invokes `sum(1, 10)` to compute the sum from **1** to **10**, `sum(20, 37)` to compute the sum from **20** to **37**, and `sum(35, 49)` to compute the sum from **35** to **49**.

functions

A *function* is a collection of statements grouped together that performs an operation. In earlier chapters, you learned about such functions as `eval("numericString")` and `random.randint(a, b)`. When you call the `random.randint(a, b)` function, for example, the system actually executes the statements in the function and returns the result. In this chapter, you will learn how to define and use functions and apply function abstraction to solve complex problems.

6.2 Defining a Function

A function definition consists of the function's name, parameters, and body.

The syntax for defining a function is as follows:

```
def functionName(list of parameters)
    # Function body
```

VideoNote
Use functions

Let's look at a function created to find which of two numbers is bigger. This function, named **max**, has two parameters, **num1** and **num2**, the larger of which is returned by the function. Figure 6.1 illustrates the components of this function.

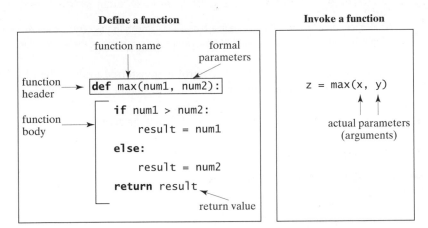

FIGURE 6.1   You can define a function and invoke it with arguments.

A function contains a header and body. The *header* begins with the **def** keyword, followed by the function's name and parameters, and ends with a colon.

function header

The variables in the function header are known as *formal parameters* or simply *parameters*. A parameter is like a placeholder: When a function is invoked, you pass a value to the parameter. This value is referred to as an *actual parameter* or *argument*. Parameters are optional; that is, a function may not have any parameters. For example, the **random.random()** function has no parameters.

formal parameters
parameters
actual parameter
argument

Some functions return a value, while other functions perform desired operations without returning a value. If a function returns a value, it is called a *value-returning function*.

value-returning function

The function body contains a collection of statements that define what the function does. For example, the function body of the **max** function uses an **if** statement to determine which number is larger and return the value of that number. A return statement using the keyword **return** is required for a value-returning function to return a result. The function terminates when a **return** statement is executed.

6.3 Calling a Function

Calling a function executes the code in the function.

Key Point

In a function's definition, you define what it is to do. To use a function, you have to *call* or *invoke* it. The program that calls the function is called a *caller*. There are two ways to call a function, depending on whether or not it returns a value.

caller

If the function returns a value, a call to that function is usually treated as a value. For example,

```
larger = max(3, 4)
```

calls **max(3, 4)** and assigns the result of the function to the variable **larger**.
    Another example of a call that is treated as a value is

```
print(max(3, 4))
```

which prints the *return value* of the function call **max(3, 4)**.

return value

If a function does not return a value, the call to the function must be a statement. For example, the **print** function does not return a value. The following call is a statement:

```
print("Programming is fun!")
```

Note

A value-returning function also can be invoked as a statement. In this case, the return value is ignored. This is rare but is permissible if the caller is not interested in the return value.

When a program calls a function, program control is transferred to the called function. A called function returns control to the caller when its return statement is executed or the function is finished.

Listing 6.1 shows a complete program that is used to test the **max** function.

LISTING 6.1 TestMax.py

define max function

main function

invoke max

```
1   # Return the max of two numbers
2   def max(num1, num2):
3       if num1 > num2:
4           result = num1
5       else:
6           result = num2
7
8       return result
9
10  def main():
11      i = 5
12      j = 2
13      k = max(i, j) # Call the max function
14      print("The larger number of", i, "and", j, "is", k)
15
16  main() # Call the main function
```

```
The larger number of 5 and 2 is 5
```

	Line#	i	j	k	num1	num2	result
	11	5					
	12		2				
Invoke max	2				5	2	
	4						5
	13			5			

main function

This program contains the **max** and **main** functions. The program script invokes the **main** function in line 16. By convention, programs often define a function named **main** that contains the main functionality for a program.

How is this program executed? The interpreter reads the script in the file line by line starting from line 1. Since line 1 is a comment, it is ignored. When it reads the function header in line 2, it stores the function with its body (lines 2–8) in the memory. Remember that a function's definition defines the function, but it does not cause the function to execute. The interpreter then reads the definition of the **main** function (lines 10–14) to the memory. Finally, the interpreter reads the statement in line 16, which invokes the **main** function and causes the **main** function to be executed. The control is now transferred to the **main** function, as shown in Figure 6.2.

execution

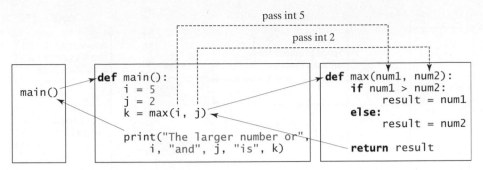

FIGURE 6.2   When a function is invoked, the control is transferred to the function. When the function is finished, the control is returned to where the function was called.

The execution of the **main** function begins in line 11. It assigns **5** to **i** and **2** to **j** (lines 11–12) and then invokes **max(i, j)** (line 13).

When the **max** function is invoked (line 13), variable **i**'s value is passed to **num1** and variable **j**'s value is passed to **num2**. The control is transferred to the **max** function, and the **max** function is executed. When the **return** statement in the **max** function is executed, the **max** function returns the control to its caller (in this case the caller is the **main** function).

After the **max** function is finished, the returned value from the **max** function is assigned to **k** (line 13). The **main** function prints the result (line 14). The **main** function is now finished, and it returns the control to its caller (line 16). The program is now finished.

>
> **Note**
> Here **main** is defined after **max**. In Python, functions can be defined in any order in a script file as long as the function is in the memory when it is called. You can also define **main** before **max**.

order of functions

6.3.1   Call Stacks

Each time a function is invoked, the system creates an *activation record* that stores its arguments and variables for the function and places the activation record in an area of memory known as a *call stack*. A call stack is also known as an execution stack, runtime stack, or machine stack, and is often shortened to just "the stack." When a function calls another function, the caller's activation record is kept intact and a new activation record is created for the new function call. When a function finishes its work and returns control to its caller, its activation record is removed from the call stack.

A call stack stores the activation records in a last-in, first-out fashion. The activation record for the function that is invoked last is removed first from the stack. Suppose function **m1** calls function **m2**, and then **m3**. The runtime system pushes **m1**'s activation record into the stack, then **m2**'s, and then **m3**'s. After **m3** is finished, its activation record is removed from the stack. After **m2** is finished, its activation record is removed from the stack. After **m1** is finished, its activation record is removed from the stack.

Understanding call stacks helps us comprehend how functions are invoked. When the **main** function is invoked, an activation record is created to store variables **i** and **j**, as shown in Figure 6.3a. Remember that all data in Python are objects. Python creates and stores objects in a separate memory space called *heap*. Variables **i** and **j** actually contain reference values to **int** objects **5** and **2**, as shown in Figure 6.3a.

Invoking **max(i, j)** passes the values **i** and **j** to parameters **num1** and **num2** in the **max** function. So now **num1** and **num2** reference **int** objects **5** and **2**, as shown in Figure 6.3b. The **max** function finds the maximum number and assigns it to **result**, so **result** now references **int** object **5**, as shown in Figure 6.3c. The result is returned to the **main** function

max function

activation record

stack

heap

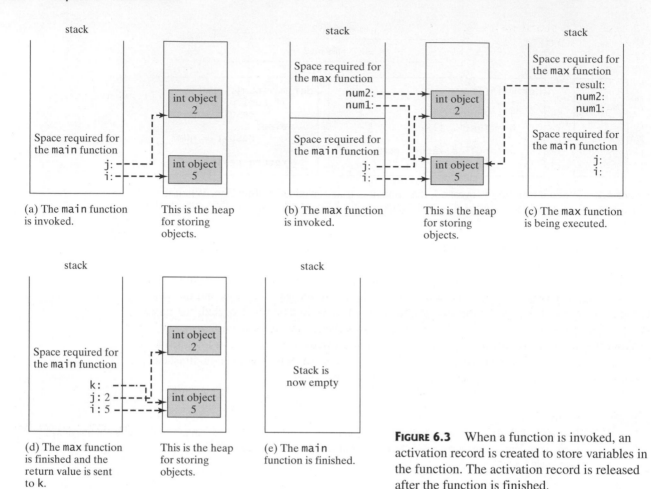

(a) The `main` function is invoked.

This is the heap for storing objects.

(b) The `max` function is invoked.

This is the heap for storing objects.

(c) The `max` function is being executed.

(d) The `max` function is finished and the return value is sent to `k`.

This is the heap for storing objects.

(e) The `main` function is finished.

FIGURE 6.3 When a function is invoked, an activation record is created to store variables in the function. The activation record is released after the function is finished.

and assigned to variable **k**. Now **k** references **int** object **5**, as shown in Figure 6.3d. After the **main** function is finished, the stack is empty, as shown in Figure 6.3e. The objects in the heap are automatically destroyed by the Python interpreter when they are no longer needed.

6.4 Functions with/without Return Values

Key Point

A function does not have to return a value.

The preceding section gives an example of a value-returning function. This section shows how to define and invoke a function that does not return a value. Such a function is commonly known as a *void function* in programming terminology.

void function

The program in Listing 6.2 defines a function named **printGrade** and invokes it to print the grade for a given score.

LISTING 6.2 PrintGradeFunction.py

printGrade function

```
1  # Print grade for the score
2  def printGrade(score):
3      if score >= 90.0:
4          print('A')
5      elif score >= 80.0:
6          print('B')
7      elif score >= 70.0:
8          print('C')
```

```
 9        elif score >= 60.0:
10            print('D')
11        else:
12            print('F')
13
14    def main():                                          main function
15        score = eval(input("Enter a score: "))
16        print("The grade is ", end = " ")
17        printGrade(score)                                invoke printGrade
18
19    main() # Call the main function
```

```
Enter a score: 78.5  ⏎Enter
The grade is C
```

The **printGrade** function does not return any value. So, it is invoked as a statement in line 17 in the **main** function.

To see the differences between a function that does not return a value and a function that returns a value, let's redesign the **printGrade** function to return a value. We call the new function that returns the grade, **getGrade**, as shown in Listing 6.3.

LISTING 6.3 ReturnGradeFunction.py

```
 1    # Return the grade for the score
 2    def getGrade(score):                                 getGrade function
 3        if score >= 90.0:
 4            return 'A'
 5        elif score >= 80.0:
 6            return 'B'
 7        elif score >= 70.0:
 8            return 'C'
 9        elif score >= 60.0:
10            return 'D'
11        else:
12            return 'F'
13
14    def main():                                          main function
15        score = eval(input("Enter a score: "))
16        print("The grade is", getGrade(score))           invoke getGrade
17
18    main() # Call the main function
```

```
Enter a score: 78.5  ⏎Enter
The grade is C
```

The **getGrade** function defined in lines 2–12 returns a character grade based on the numeric score value. It is invoked in line 16.

The **getGrade** function returns a character, and it can be invoked and used just like a character. The **printGrade** function does not return a value, and it must be invoked as a statement.

None function

Note

Technically, every function in Python returns a value whether you use **return** or not. If a function does not return a value, by default, it returns a special value **None**. For this reason, a function that does not return a value is also called a *None function*. The **None** value can be assigned to a variable to indicate that the variable does not reference any object. For example, if you run the following program:

```
def sum(number1, number2):
    total = number1 + number2

print(sum(1, 2))
```

you will see the output is **None**, because the **sum** function does not have a return statement. By default, it returns **None**.

return in None function

Note

A **return** statement is not needed for a **None** function, but it can be used for terminating the function and returning control to the function's caller. The syntax is simply

return

or

return None

This is rarely used, but it is sometimes useful for circumventing the normal flow of control in a function that does not return any value. For example, the following code has a return statement to terminate the function when the score is invalid.

```
# Print grade for the score
def printGrade(score):
    if score < 0 or score > 100:
        print("Invalid score")
        return # Same as return None

    if score >= 90.0:
        print('A')
    elif score >= 80.0:
        print('B')
    elif score >= 70.0:
        print('C')
    elif score >= 60.0:
        print('D')
    else:
        print('F')
```

MyProgrammingLab™

6.1 What are the benefits of using a function?

6.2 How do you define a function? How do you invoke a function?

6.3 Can you simplify the **max** function in Listing 6.1 by using a conditional expression?

6.4 True or false? A call to a **None** function is always a statement itself, but a call to a value-returning function is always a component of an expression.

6.5 Can you have a **return** statement in a **None** function? Does the **return** statement in the following function cause syntax errors?

```
def xFunction(x, y):
    print(x + y)
    return
```

6.6 Define the terms function header, parameter, and argument.

6.7 Write function headers for the following functions (and indicate whether the function returns a value):

- Computing a sales commission, given the sales amount and the commission rate.
- Printing the calendar for a month, given the month and year.
- Computing a square root.
- Testing whether a number is even, and returning true if it is.
- Printing a message a specified number of times.
- Computing the monthly payment, given the loan amount, number of years, and annual interest rate.
- Finding the corresponding uppercase letter, given a lowercase letter.

6.8 Identify and correct the errors in the following program:

```
1   def function1(n, m):
2   function2(3.4)
3
4   def function2(n):
5       if n > 0:
6         return 1
7    elif n == 0:
8       return 0
9     elif n < 0:
10      return -1
11
12  function1(2, 3)
```

6.9 Show the output of the following code:

```
1   def main():
2       print(min(5, 6))
3
4   def min(n1, n2):
5       smallest = n1
6       if n2 < smallest:
7           smallest = n2
8
9   main() # Call the main function
```

6.10 What error will occur when you run the following code?

```
def main():
    print(min(min(5, 6), (51, 6)))

def min(n1, n2):
    smallest = n1
    if n2 < smallest:
        smallest = n2

main() # Call the main function
```

6.5 Positional and Keyword Arguments

A function's arguments can be passed as positional arguments or keyword arguments.

The power of a function is its ability to work with parameters. When calling a function, you need to pass arguments to parameters. There are two kinds of arguments: *positional arguments* and *keyword arguments*. Using positional arguments requires that the arguments be passed in

Key Point

positional arguments

the same order as their respective parameters in the function header. For example, the following function prints a message **n** times:

```
def nPrintln(message, n):
    for i in range(n):
        print(message)
```

You can use **nPrintln('a', 3)** to print **a** three times. The **nPrintln('a', 3)** statement passes **a** to **message**, passes **3** to **n**, and prints **a** three times. However, the statement **nPrintln(3, 'a')** has a different meaning. It passes **3** to **message** and **a** to **n**. When we call a function like this, it is said to use *positional arguments*. The arguments must match the parameters in *order*, *number*, and *compatible type*, as defined in the function header.

keyword arguments

You can also call a function using *keyword arguments*, passing each argument in the form *name = value*. For example, **nPrintln(n = 5, message = "good")** passes 5 to **n** and **"good"** to **message**. The arguments can appear in any order using keyword arguments.

mixing keyword and positional arguments

It is possible to mix positional arguments with keyword arguments, but the positional arguments cannot appear after any keyword arguments. Suppose a function header is

```
def f(p1, p2, p3):
```

You can invoke it by using

```
f(30, p2 = 4, p3 = 10)
```

However, it would be wrong to invoke it by using

```
f(30, p2 = 4, 10)
```

because the positional argument **10** appears after the keyword argument **p2 = 4**.

Check Point

MyProgrammingLab™

6.11 Compare positional arguments and keyword arguments.

6.12 Suppose a function header is as follows:

```
def f(p1, p2, p3, p4):
```

Which of the following calls are correct?

```
f(1, p2 = 3, p3 = 4, p4 = 4)
f(1, p2 = 3, 4, p4 = 4)
f(p1 = 1, p2 = 3, 4, p4 = 4)
f(p1 = 1, p2 = 3, p3 = 4, p4 = 4)
f(p4 = 1, p2 = 3, p3 = 4, p1 = 4)
```

6.6 Passing Arguments by Reference Values

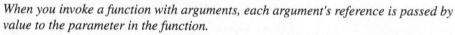
Key Point

When you invoke a function with arguments, each argument's reference is passed by value to the parameter in the function.

Because all data are objects in Python, a variable for an object is actually a reference to the object. When you invoke a function with arguments, the reference value of each argument is passed to the parameter. This is referred to as *pass-by-value* in programming terminology. For simplicity, we say that the value of an argument is passed to a parameter when invoking a function. The value is actually a reference value to the object.

pass-by-value

If the argument is a number or a string, the argument is not affected, regardless of the changes made to the parameter inside the function. Listing 6.4 gives an example.

LISTING 6.4 Increment.py

```
1  def main():
2      x = 1
3      print("Before the call, x is", x)
4      increment(x)                              invoke increment
5      print("After the call, x is", x)
6
7  def increment(n):
8      n += 1                                    increment n
9      print("\tn inside the function is", n)
10
11 main() # Call the main function
```

```
Before the call, x is 1
        n inside the function is 2
After the call, x is 1
```

As shown in the output for Listing 6.4, the value of **x** (**1**) is passed to the parameter **n** to invoke the **increment** function (line 4). The parameter **n** is incremented by **1** in the function (line 8), but **x** is not changed no matter what the function does.

The reason is that numbers and strings are known as *immutable objects*. The contents of immutable objects immutable objects cannot be changed. Whenever you assign a new number to a variable, Python creates a new object for the new number and assigns the reference of the new object to the variable.

Consider the following code:

```
>>> x = 4
>>> y = x
>>> id(x)   # The reference of x
505408920
>>> id(y) # The reference of y is the same as the reference of x
505408920
>>>
```

You assign **x** to **y**, and both **x** and **y** now point to the same object for integer value **4**, as shown in Figure 6.4a–b. But if you add **1** to **y**, a new object is created and assigned to **y**, as shown in Figure 6.4c. Now **y** refers to a new object, as shown in the following code:

```
>>> y = y + 1 # y now points to a new int object with value 5
>>> id(y)
505408936
>>>
```

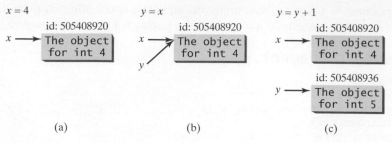

FIGURE 6.4   (a) **4** is assigned to **x**; (b) **x** is assigned to **y**; (c) **y + 1** is assigned to **y**.

6.13   What is pass-by-value?

6.14   Can the argument have the same name as its parameter?

6.15   Show the result of the following programs:

```python
def main():
    max = 0
    getMax(1, 2, max)
    print(max)

def getMax(value1, value2, max):
    if value1 > value2:
        max = value1
    else:
        max = value2

main()
```

(a)

```python
def main():
    i = 1
    while i <= 6:
        print(function1(i, 2))
        i += 1

def function1(i, num):
    line = ""
    for j in range(1, i):
        line += str(num) + " "
        num *= 2
    return line

main()
```

(b)

```python
def main():
    # Initialize times
    times = 3
    print("Before the call, variable",
        "times is", times)

    # Invoke nPrintln and display times
    nPrint("Welcome to CS!", times)
    print("After the call, variable",
        "times is", times)

# Print the message n times
def nPrint(message, n):
    while n > 0:
        print("n = ", n)
        print(message)
        n -= 1

main()
```

(c)

```python
def main():
    i = 0
    while i <= 4:
        function1(i)
        i += 1

        print("i is", i)

def function1(i):
    line = " "
    while i >= 1:
        if i % 3 != 0:
            line += str(i) + " "
        i -= 1

    print(line)

main()
```

(d)

6.16 For (a) in the preceding question, show the contents of the stack just before the function **max** is invoked, just as **max** is entered, just before **max** is returned, and right after **max** is returned.

6.7 Modularizing Code

Modularizing makes code easy to maintain and debug, and enables the code to be reused.

Key Point

Functions can be used to reduce redundant code and enable code reuse. Functions can also be used to modularize code and improve a program's quality. In Python, you can place the function definition into a file called *module* with the file-name extension **.py**. The module can be later imported into a program for reuse. The module file should be placed in the same directory with your other programs. A module can contain more than one function. Each function in a module must have a different name. Note that the **turtle**, **random**, and **math** are the modules defined in the Python library, and thus they can be imported into any Python program.

module

Listing 5.8, **GreatestCommonDivisor.py**, shows a program that prompts the user to enter two integers and displays their greatest common divisor. You can rewrite the program to use a function and place it into a module named **GCDFunction.py**, as shown in Listing 6.5.

LISTING 6.5 GCDFunction.py

```
1  # Return the gcd of two integers
2  def gcd(n1, n2):
3      gcd = 1 # Initial gcd is 1
4      k = 2   # Possible gcd
5
6      while k <= n1 and k <= n2:
7          if n1 % k == 0 and n2 % k == 0:
8              gcd = k # Update gcd
9          k += 1
10
11      return gcd # Return gcd
```

define gcd function

return gcd

Now we write a separate program to use the **gcd** function, as shown in Listing 6.6.

LISTING 6.6 TestGCDFunction.py

```
1  from GCDFunction import gcd # Import the gcd function
2
3  # Prompt the user to enter two integers
4  n1 = eval(input("Enter the first integer: "))
5  n2 = eval(input("Enter the second integer: "))
6
7  print("The greatest common divisor for", n1,
8      "and", n2, "is", gcd(n1, n2))
```

import gcd

get input

invoke gcd

```
Enter the first integer: 45  [↵Enter]
Enter the second integer: 75  [↵Enter]
The greatest common divisor for 45 and 75 is 15
```

Line 1 imports the **gcd** function from the **GCDFunction** module, which enables you to invoke **gcd** in this program (line 8). You can also import it using the following statement:

```
import GCDFunction
```

Using this statement, you would have to invoke **gcd** using **GCDFunction.gcd**.

By encapsulating the code for obtaining the gcd in a function, this program has several advantages:

1. It isolates the problem for computing the gcd from the rest of the code in the program. Thus, the logic becomes clear and the program is easier to read.

2. Any errors for computing the gcd are confined to the **gcd** function, which narrows the scope of debugging.

3. The **gcd** function now can be reused by other programs.

What happens if you define two functions with the same name in a module? There is no syntax error in this case, but the latter function definition prevails.

Listing 6.7 applies the concept of code modularization to improve Listing 5.13, **PrimeNumber.py**. The program defines two new functions, **isPrime** and **printPrimeNumbers**. The **isPrime** function determines whether a number is prime, and the **printPrimeNumbers** function prints prime numbers.

LISTING 6.7 PrimeNumberFunction.py

isPrime function

printPrimeNumbers function

invoke isPrime

```
 1  # Check whether number is prime
 2  def isPrime(number):
 3      divisor = 2
 4      while divisor <= number / 2:
 5          if number % divisor == 0:
 6              # If true, number is not prime
 7              return False # number is not a prime
 8          divisor += 1
 9
10      return True # number is prime
11
12  def printPrimeNumbers(numberOfPrimes):
13      NUMBER_OF_PRIMES = 50  # Number of primes to display
14      NUMBER_OF_PRIMES_PER_LINE = 10  # Display 10 per line
15      count = 0  # Count the number of prime numbers
16      number = 2  # A number to be tested for primeness
17
18      # Repeatedly find prime numbers
19      while count < numberOfPrimes:
20          # Print the prime number and increase the count
21          if isPrime(number):
22              count += 1 # Increase the count
23
24              print(number, end = " ")
25              if count % NUMBER_OF_PRIMES_PER_LINE == 0:
26                  # Print the number and advance to the new line
27                  print()
28
29          # Check if the next number is prime
30          number += 1
31
32  def main():
33      print("The first 50 prime numbers are")
```

```
34     printPrimeNumbers(50)                        invoke printPrimeNumbers
35
36  main()  # Call the main function
```

```
The first 50 prime numbers are

2    3    5    7    11   13   17   19   23   29
31   37   41   43   47   53   59   61   67   71
73   79   83   89   97   101  103  107  109  113
127  131  137  139  149  151  157  163  167  173
179  181  191  193  197  199  211  223  227  229
```

This program divides a large problem into two subproblems. As a result, the new program is easier to read and easier to debug. Moreover, the functions **printPrimeNumbers** and **isPrime** can be reused by other programs.

6.8 Case Study: Converting Decimals to Hexadecimals

This section presents a program that converts a decimal number to a hexadecimal number.

Key Point

Hexadecimal numbers (introduced in Chapter 3) are often used in computer systems programming (see Appendix C for information on number systems). To convert a decimal number d to a hexadecimal number, you have to find the hexadecimal digits $h_n, h_{n-1}, h_{n-2}, \ldots, h_2, h_1$, and h_0 such that

$$d = h_n \times 16^n + h_{n-1} \times 16^{n-1} + h_{n-2} \times 16^{n-2} + \ldots$$
$$+ h_2 \times 16^2 + h_1 \times 16^1 + h_0 \times 16^0$$

These hexadecimal digits can be found by successively dividing d by 16 until the quotient is 0. The remainders are $h_0, h_1, h_2, \ldots, h_{n-2}, h_{n-1}$, and h_n. The hexadecimal digits include the decimal digits 0,1,2,3,4,5,6,7,8,9 plus A which is the decimal value 10, B which is the decimal value 11, C which is 12, D which is 13, E which is 14, and F which is 15.

For example, the decimal number **123** is **7B** in hexadecimal. The conversion is done as shown below:

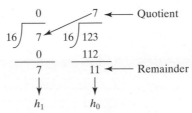

The remainder of dividing **123** by **16** is **11**, which is **B** in hexadecimal. The quotient of this division is **7**. The remainder of dividing **7** by **16** is **7** and the quotient is **0**. So, **7B** is the hexadecimal number for **123**.

The program in Listing 6.8 prompts the user to enter a decimal number and converts it into a hex number as a string.

LISTING 6.8 Decimal2HexConversion.py

```
1  # Convert a decimal to a hex as a string
2  def decimalToHex(decimalValue):                    define decimalToHex
```

```
 3        hex = " "
 4
 5        while decimalValue != 0:
 6            hexValue = decimalValue % 16
 7            hex = toHexChar(hexValue) + hex
 8            decimalValue = decimalValue // 16
 9
10        return hex
11
12    # Convert an integer to a single hex digit as a character
13    def toHexChar(hexValue):
14        if 0 <= hexValue <= 9:
15            return chr(hexValue + ord('0'))
16        else:  # 10 <= hexValue <= 15
17            return chr(hexValue - 10 + ord('A'))
18
19    def main():
20        # Prompt the user to enter a decimal integer
21        decimalValue = eval(input("Enter a decimal number: "))
22
23        print("The hex number for decimal",
24            decimalValue, "is", decimalToHex(decimalValue))
25
26    main() # Call the main function
```

define toHexChar

get a letter

input decimal

```
Enter a decimal number: 1234  ⏎ Enter
The hex number for decimal 1234 is 4D2
```

	line#	decimalValue	hex	hexValue	toHexChar(hexValue)
	21	1234			
	3		" "		
iteration 1	6			2	
	7		"2"		"2"
	8	77			
iteration 2	6			13	
	7		"D2"		"D"
	8	4			
iteration 3	6			4	
	7		"4D2"		"4"
	8	0			

The hex string is initially empty (line 3). The program uses the **decimalToHex** function (lines 2–10) to convert a decimal integer to a hex number as a string. The function gets the remainder of the division of the decimal integer by **16** (line 6). The remainder is converted into a character by invoking the **toHexChar** function and then appending to the hex string (line 7). Dividing the decimal number by **16** removes a hex digit from the number (line 8). The function repeatedly performs these operations in a loop until the quotient becomes **0** (lines 5–8).

The **toHexChar** function (lines 13–17) converts a **hexValue** between **0** and **15** into a hex character. If **hexValue** is between **0** and **9**, it is converted to **chr(hexValue + ord('0'))** (line 15). For example, if **hexValue** is **5, chr(hexValue + ord('0'))** returns **5.** Similarly, if

hexValue is between **10** and **15**, it is converted to **chr(hexValue - 10 + ord('A'))** (line 17). For example, if **hexValue** is **11**, **chr(hexValue - 10 + ord('A'))** returns **B**.

6.9 The Scope of Variables

The scope of a variable is the part of the program where the variable can be referenced.

Key Point

Chapter 2 introduced the scope of variables. This section discusses the scope of variables in the context of functions. A variable created inside a function is referred to as a *local variable*. Local variables can only be accessed within a function. The scope of a local variable starts from its creation and continues to the end of the function that contains the variable.

scope of a variable
local variable

In Python, you can also use *global variables*. They are created outside all functions and are accessible to all functions in their scope. Consider the following examples.

global variable

Example 1

```
1  globalVar = 1
2  def f1():
3      localVar = 2
4      print(globalVar)
5      print(localVar)
6
7  f1()
8  print(globalVar)
9  print(localVar) # Out of scope, so this gives an error
```

create a global variable

create a local variable

A global variable is created in line 1. It is accessed within the function in line 4 and outside the function in line 8. A local variable is created in line 3. It is accessed within the function in line 5. Attempting to access the variable from outside of the function causes an error in line 9.

Example 2

```
1  x = 1
2  def f1():
3      x = 2
4      print(x) # Displays 2
5
6  f1()
7  print(x) # Displays 1
```

create a global variable

create a local variable

Here a global variable **x** is created in line 1 and a local variable with the same name (**x**) is created in line 3. From this point on, the global variable **x** is not accessible in the function. Outside the function, the global variable **x** is still accessible. So, it prints **1** in line 7.

Example 3

```
1  x = eval(input("Enter a number: "))
2  if x > 0:
3      y = 4
4
5  print(y) # This gives an error if y is not created
```

create a variable

Here the variable **y** is created if **x > 0**. If you enter a positive value for **x** (line 1), the program runs fine. But if you enter a nonpositive value, line 5 produces an error because **y** is not created.

Example 4

```
1  sum = 0
2  for i in range(5):
```

variable i created

```
3        sum += i
4
5  print(i)
```

Here the variable **i** is created in the loop. After the loop is finished, **i** is **4**, so line 5 displays **4**.

global statement

You can bind a local variable in the global scope. You can also create a variable in a function and use it outside the function. To do either, use a **global** statement, as shown in the following example.

Example 5

global variable x

```
1  x = 1
2  def increase():
3      global x
4      x = x + 1
5      print(x) # Displays 2
6
7  increase()
8  print(x) # Displays 2
```

binding global variable

Here a global variable **x** is created in line 1 and **x** is bound in the function in line 3, which means that **x** in the function is the same as **x** outside of the function, so the program prints **2** in line 5 and in line 8.

 Caution

Although global variables are allowed and you may see global variables used in other programs, it is not a good practice to allow them to be modified in a function, because doing so can make programs prone to errors. However, it is fine to define global constants so all functions in the module can share them.

 Check Point

MyProgrammingLab™

6.17 What is the printout of the following code?

```
def function(x):
    print(x)
    x = 4.5
    y = 3.4
    print(y)

x = 2
y = 4
function(x)
print(x)
print(y)
```
(a)

```
def f(x, y = 1, z = 2):
    return x + y + z

print(f(1, 1, 1))
print(f(y = 1, x = 2, z = 3))
print(f(1, z = 3))
```
(b)

6.18 What is wrong in the following code?

```
1  def function():
2      x = 4.5
3      y = 3.4
4      print(x)
5      print(y)
6
7  function()
```

```
8   print(x)
9   print(y)
```

6.19 Can the following code run? If so, what is the printout?

```
x = 10
if x < 0:
    y = -1
else:
    y = 1

print("y is", y)
```

6.10 Default Arguments

Python allows you to define functions with default argument values. The default values are passed to the parameters when a function is invoked without the arguments.

Key Point

Listing 6.9 demonstrates how to define functions with *default argument* values and how to invoke such functions.

default argument

LISTING 6.9 `DefaultArgumentDemo.py`

```
1   def printArea(width = 1, height = 2):
2       area = width * height
3       print("width:", width, "\theight:", height, "\tarea:", area)
4
5   printArea() # Default arguments width = 1 and height = 2
6   printArea(4, 2.5) # Positional arguments width = 4 and height = 2.5
7   printArea(height = 5, width = 3) # Keyword arguments width
8   printArea(width = 1.2) # Default height = 2
9   printArea(height = 6.2) # Default width = 1
```

default argument

default arguments
positional arguments
keyword arguments
mixed arguments
mixed arguments

```
width: 1        height: 2       area: 2
width: 4        height: 2.5     area: 10.0
width: 3        height: 5       area: 15
width: 1.2      height: 2       area: 2.4
width: 1        height: 6.2     area: 6.2
```

Line 1 defines the **printArea** function with the parameters **width** and **height**. **width** has the default value **1** and **height** has the default value **2**. Line 5 invokes the function without passing an argument, so the program uses the default value **1** assigned to **width** and **2** to **height**. Line 6 invokes the function by passing **4** to **width** and **2.5** to **height**. Line 7 invokes the function by passing **3** to **width** and **5** to **height**. Note that you can also pass the argument by specifying the parameter name, as shown in lines 8 and 9.

Note

A function may mix parameters with default arguments and non-default arguments. In this case, the non-default parameters must be defined before default parameters.

Note

Many programming languages support a useful feature that allows you to define two functions with the same name in a module, but it is not supported in Python. With default arguments, you can define a function once, and call the function in many different ways. This achieves the same effect as defining multiple functions with the same name in other programming languages. If you define multiple functions in Python, the later definition replaces the previous definitions.

6.20 Show the printout of the following code:

```
def f(w = 1, h = 2):
    print(w, h)

f()
f(w = 5)
f(h = 24)
f(4, 5)
```

6.21 Identify and correct the errors in the following program:

```
1  def main():
2      nPrintln(5)
3
4  def nPrintln(message = "Welcome to Python!", n):
5      for i in range(n):
6          print(message)
7
8  main() # Call the main function
```

6.22 What happens if you define two functions in a module that have the same name?

6.11 Returning Multiple Values

The Python **return** *statement can return multiple values.*

Python allows a function to return multiple values. Listing 6.10 defines a function that takes two numbers and returns them in ascending order.

LISTING 6.10 MultipleReturnValueDemo.py

```
1  def sort(number1, number2):
2      if number1 < number2:
3          return number1, number2
4      else:
5          return number2, number1
6
7  n1, n2 = sort(3, 2)
8  print("n1 is", n1)
9  print("n2 is", n2)
```

return multiple values

receiving returned values

```
n1 is 2
n2 is 3
```

The **sort** function returns two values. When it is invoked, you need to pass the returned values in a simultaneous assignment.

6.23 Can a function return multiple values? Show the printout of the following code:

```
1  def f(x, y):
2      return x + y, x - y, x * y, x / y
3
4  t1, t2, t3, t4 = f(9, 5)
5  print(t1, t2, t3, t4)
```

6.12 Case Study: Generating Random ASCII Characters

A character is coded using an integer. Generating a random character is to generate an integer.

**Key
Point**

Computer programs process numeric data and characters. You have seen many examples involving numeric data. It is also important to understand characters and how to process them. This section gives an example of generating random ASCII characters.

As introduced in Section 3.3, every ASCII character has a unique ASCII code between **0** and **127**. To generate a random ASCII character, first generate a random integer between **0** and **127**, and then use the **chr** function to obtain the character from the integer using the following code:

```
chr(randint(0, 127))
```

Let's consider how to generate a random lowercase letter. The ASCII codes for lowercase letters are consecutive integers starting with the code for **a**, then for **b**, **c**, ..., and **z**. The code for **a** is

```
ord('a')
```

So a random integer between **ord('a')** and **ord('z')** is

```
randint(ord('a'), ord('z'))
```

Therefore, a random lowercase letter is

```
chr(randint(ord('a'), ord('z')))
```

Thus, a random character between any two characters **ch1** and **ch2** with **ch1 < ch2** can be generated as follows:

```
chr(randint(ord(ch1), ord(ch2)))
```

This is a simple but useful discovery. In Listing 6.11 we create a module named **RandomCharacter.py** with five functions that randomly generate specific types of characters. You can use these functions in your future projects.

LISTING 6.11 RandomCharacter.py

```python
 1  from random import randint # import randint
 2
 3  # Generate a random character between ch1 and ch2
 4  def getRandomCharacter(ch1, ch2):
 5      return chr(randint(ord(ch1), ord(ch2)))
 6
 7  # Generate a random lowercase letter
 8  def getRandomLowerCaseLetter():
 9      return getRandomCharacter('a', 'z')
10
11  # Generate a random uppercase letter
12  def getRandomUpperCaseLetter():
13      return getRandomCharacter('A', 'Z')
14
15  # Generate a random digit character
16  def getRandomDigitCharacter():
17      return getRandomCharacter('0', '9')
18
19  # Generate a random character
20  def getRandomASCIICharacter():
21      return chr(randint(0, 127))
```

Listing 6.12 is a test program that displays 175 random lowercase letters.

LISTING 6.12 TestRandomCharacter.py

```
1  import RandomCharacter
2
3  NUMBER_OF_CHARS = 175 # Number of characters to generate
4  CHARS_PER_LINE = 25 # Number of characters to display per line
5
6  # Print random characters between 'a' and 'z', 25 chars per line
7  for i in range(NUMBER_OF_CHARS):
8      print(RandomCharacter.getRandomLowerCaseLetter(), end = " ")
9      if (i + 1) % CHARS_PER_LINE == 0:
10         print()  # Jump to the new line
```

constants — lines 3–4

lowercase letter — line 8

```
gmjsohezfkgtazqgmswfclrao
pnrunulnwmaztlfjedmpchcif
lalqdgivxkxpbzulrmqmbhikr
lbnrjlsopfxahssqhwuuljvbe
xbhdotzhpehbqmuwsfktwsoli
cbuwkzgxpmtzihgatdslvbwbz
bfesoklwbhnooygiigzdxuqni
```

Line 1 imports the **RandomCharacter** module, because the program invokes the function defined in this module.

Invoking **getRandomLowerCaseLetter()** returns a lowercase letter (line 8).

parentheses required — Note that the function **getRandomLowerCaseLetter()** does not have any parameters, but you still have to use the parentheses when defining and invoking it.

✓ Check Point

MyProgrammingLab™

6.24 Write an expression that returns a random integer between **34** and **55**, inclusively.

6.25 Write an expression that returns a random character between **B** and **M**, inclusively.

6.26 Write an expression that returns a random number between **6.5** and **56.5** (excluding 56.5).

6.27 Write an expression that returns a random lowercase letter.

6.13 Function Abstraction and Stepwise Refinement

🔑 Key Point

Function abstraction is achieved by separating the use of a function from its implementation.

function abstraction

The key to developing software is to apply the concept of abstraction. You will learn many levels of abstraction from this book. *Function abstraction* separates the use of a function from its implementation. A client program, called simply the *client,* can use a function without knowing how it is implemented. The details of the implementation are encapsulated in the function and hidden from the client that invokes the function. This is known as *information*

information hiding

hiding or *encapsulation*. If you decide to change the implementation, the client program will not be affected, provided that you do not change the function header. The implementation of the function is hidden from the client in a "black box," as shown in Figure 6.5.

You have already used many of Python's built-in functions; you used these in client programs. You know how to write the code to invoke these functions in your program, but as a user of these functions, you are not required to know how they are implemented.

VideoNote
Divide and conquer

divide and conquer

The concept of function abstraction can be applied to the process of developing programs. When writing a large program, you can use the *"divide-and-conquer"* strategy, also known as

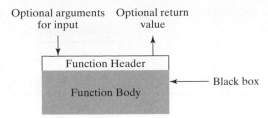

Optional arguments for input   Optional return value

Function Header

Function Body   ← Black box

FIGURE 6.5 The function body can be thought of as a black box that contains the detailed implementation of the function.

stepwise refinement, to break down the problem into subproblems. The subproblems can be further divided into smaller, more manageable ones.

stepwise refinement

Suppose you write a program that displays the calendar for a given month of the year. The program prompts the user to enter the year and the month, and then it displays the entire calendar for the month, as shown in the following sample run:

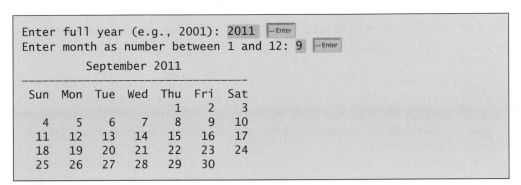

```
Enter full year (e.g., 2001): 2011  ↵Enter
Enter month as number between 1 and 12: 9  ↵Enter
            September 2011
-----------------------------------
 Sun  Mon  Tue  Wed  Thu  Fri  Sat
                          1    2    3
  4    5    6    7    8    9   10
 11   12   13   14   15   16   17
 18   19   20   21   22   23   24
 25   26   27   28   29   30
```

Let's use this example to demonstrate the divide-and-conquer approach.

6.13.1 Top-Down Design

How would you get started writing such a program? Would you immediately start coding? Beginning programmers often start by trying to work out the solution to every detail. Although details are important in the final program, concern for detail in the early stages may block the problem-solving process. To make problem solving flow as smoothly as possible, this example begins by using function abstraction to isolate details from design and only later implements the details.

For this example, the problem is first broken into two subproblems: (1) get input from the user and (2) print the calendar for the month. At this stage, you should be concerned with what the subproblems will achieve, not with how to get input and print the calendar for the month. You can draw a structure chart to help visualize the decomposition of the problem (see Figure 6.6a).

You can use the **input** function to read input for the year and the month. The problem of printing the calendar for a given month can be broken into two subproblems: (1) print the month title and (2) print the month body, as shown in Figure 6.6b. The month title consists of three lines: month and year, a dashed line, and the names of the seven days of the week. You need to get the month name (e.g., January) from the numeric month (e.g., 1). This is accomplished in **getMonthName** (see Figure 6.7a).

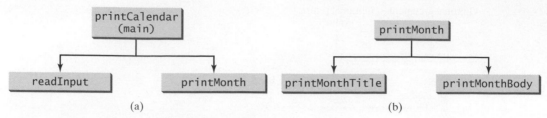

(a)   (b)

FIGURE 6.6 The structure chart shows that the **printCalendar** problem is divided into two subproblems, **readInput** and **printMonth**, and that **printMonth** is divided into two smaller subproblems, **printMonthTitle** and **printMonthBody**.

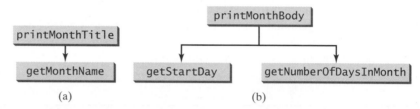

(a)   (b)

FIGURE 6.7 (a) To **printMonthTitle**, you need **getMonthName**. (b) The **printMonthBody** problem is refined into several smaller problems.

In order to print the month body, you need to know which day of the week is the first day of the month (**getStartDay**) and how many days the month has (**getNumberOfDaysInMonth**), as shown in Figure 6.7b. For example, December 2005 has 31 days, and December 1, 2005, is a Thursday.

How would you get the start day for the first date in a month? There are several ways to do so. Assume you know that the start day for January 1, 1800, was Wednesday (**START_DAY_FOR_JAN_1_1800 = 3**). You could compute the total number of days (**totalNumberOfDays**) between January 1, 1800, and the first date of the calendar month. The start day for the calendar month is **(totalNumberOfDays + startDay1800) % 7**, since every week has seven days. Thus, the **getStartDay** problem can be further refined as **getTotalNumberOfDays**, as shown in Figure 6.8a.

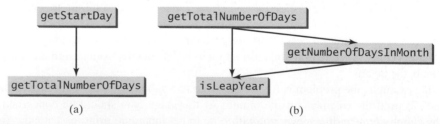

(a)   (b)

FIGURE 6.8 (a) To **getStartDay**, you need **getTotalNumberOfDays**. (b) The **getTotalNumberOfDays** problem is refined into two smaller problems.

To get the total number of days, you need to know whether the year is a leap year and the number of days in each month. Therefore, **getTotalNumberOfDays** needs to be further refined into two subproblems: **isLeapYear** and **getNumberOfDaysInMonth**, as shown in Figure 6.8b. The complete structure chart is shown in Figure 6.9.

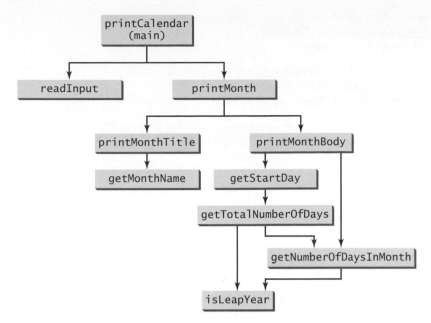

FIGURE 6.9   The structure chart shows the hierarchical relationship of the subproblems in the program.

6.13.2   Top-Down and/or Bottom-Up Implementation

Now let's turn our attention to implementation. In general, a subproblem corresponds to a function in the implementation, although some are so simple that this is unnecessary. You need to decide which modules to implement as functions and which to combine in other functions. Decisions of this kind should be based on the way that the overall program will be easier to read. In this example, the subproblem **readInput** can be simply implemented in the **main** function.

You can use either a "top-down" or a "bottom-up" approach. The top-down approach implements one function in the structure chart at a time from the top to the bottom. A *stub*, which is a simple but incomplete version of a function, can be used for the functions waiting to be implemented. Stubs enable you to build the framework of a program quickly. Implement the **main** function first, then use a stub for the **printMonth** function. For example, let **printMonth** display the year and the month in the stub. Thus, your program may begin like this:

top-down approach
stub

```
# A stub for printMonth may look like this
def printMonth(year, month):
    print(year, month)

# A stub for printMonthTitle may look like this
def printMonthTitle(year, month):
    print("printMonthTitle")

# A stub for getMonthBody may look like this
def getMonthBody(year, month):
    print("getMonthBody")

# A stub for getMonthName may look like this
def getMonthName(month):
    print("getMonthName")
```

```
# A stub for getStartDay may look like this
def getStartDay(year, month):
    print("getStartDay")

# A stub for getTotalNumberOfDays may look like this
def getTotalNumberOfDays(year, month):
    print("getTotalNumberOfDays")

# A stub for getNumberOfDaysInMonth may look like this
def getNumberOfDaysInMonth(year, month):
    print("getNumberOfDaysInMonth")

# A stub for isLeapYear may look like this
def isLeapYear(year):
    print("isLeapYear")

def main():
    # Prompt the user to enter year and month
    year = eval(input("Enter full year (e.g., 2001): "))
    month = eval(input((
        "Enter month as number between 1 and 12: ")))

    # Print calendar for the month of the year
    printMonth(year, month)

main() # Call the main function
```

Run and test the program, and fix any errors. You can now implement the **printMonth** function. For functions invoked from the **printMonth** function, you can again use stubs.

bottom-up approach
driver

The bottom-up approach implements one function in the structure chart at a time from the bottom to the top. For each function implemented, write a test program, known as the *driver*, to test it.

The top-down and bottom-up approaches are both fine. Both approaches implement functions incrementally, help to isolate programming errors, and make debugging easy. They can be used together.

6.13.3 Implementation Details

The **isLeapYear(year)** function can be implemented using the following code (see Section 4.12):

return year % 400 == 0 **or** (year % 4 == 0 **and** year % 100 != 0)

Use the following facts to implement **getTotalNumberOfDaysInMonth(year, month)**:

■ January, March, May, July, August, October, and December have 31 days.

■ April, June, September, and November have 30 days.

■ February has 28 days during a regular year and 29 days during a leap year. A regular year, therefore, has 365 days, and a leap year has 366 days.

To implement **getTotalNumberOfDays(year, month)**, you need to compute the total number of days (**totalNumberOfDays**) between January 1, 1800, and the first day of the calendar month. You could find the total number of days between the year 1800 and the calendar year and then figure out the total number of days prior to the calendar month in the calendar year. The sum of these two totals is **totalNumberOfDays**.

To print the calendar's body, first pad some space before the start day and then print the lines for every week.

The complete program is given in Listing 6.13.

LISTING 6.13   PrintCalendar.py

```
1   # Print the calendar for a month in a year
2   def printMonth(year, month):                                              printMonth
3       # Print the headings of the calendar
4       printMonthTitle(year, month)
5
6       # Print the body of the calendar
7       printMonthBody(year, month)
8
9   # Print the month title, e.g., May 1999
10  def printMonthTitle(year, month):                                         printMonthTitle
11      print("            ", getMonthName(month), " ", year)
12      print("—————————————————————————————————————————")
13      print(" Sun Mon Tue Wed Thu Fri Sat")
14
15  # Print month body
16  def printMonthBody(year, month):                                          printMonthBody
17      # Get start day of the week for the first date in the month
18      startDay = getStartDay(year, month)
19
20      # Get number of days in the month
21      numberOfDaysInMonth = getNumberOfDaysInMonth(year, month)
22
23      # Pad space before the first day of the month
24      i = 0
25      for i in range(0, startDay):
26          print("     ", end = " ")
27
28      for i in range(1, numberOfDaysInMonth + 1):
29          print(format(i, "4d"), end = " ")
30
31          if (i + startDay) % 7 == 0:
32              print() # Jump to the new line
33
34  # Get the English name for the month
35  def getMonthName(month):                                                  getMonthName
36      if month == 1:
37          monthName = "January"
38      elif month == 2:
39          monthName = "February"
40      elif month == 3:
41          monthName = "March"
42      elif month == 4:
43          monthName = "April"
44      elif month == 5:
45          monthName = "May"
46      elif month == 6:
47          monthName = "June"
48      elif month == 7:
49          monthName = "July"
50      elif month == 8:
51          monthName = "August"
52      elif month == 9:
53          monthName = "September"
54      elif month == 10:
55          monthName = "October"
56      elif month == 11:
57          monthName = "November"
```

```
58              else:
59                  monthName = "December"
60
61              return monthName
62
63  # Get the start day of month/1/year
64  def getStartDay(year, month):
65      START_DAY_FOR_JAN_1_1800 = 3
66
67      # Get total number of days from 1/1/1800 to month/1/year
68      totalNumberOfDays = getTotalNumberOfDays(year, month)
69
70      # Return the start day for month/1/year
71      return (totalNumberOfDays + START_DAY_FOR_JAN_1_1800) % 7
72
73  # Get the total number of days since January 1, 1800
74  def getTotalNumberOfDays(year, month):
75      total = 0
76
77      # Get the total days from 1800 to 1/1/year
78      for i in range(1800, year):
79          if isLeapYear(i):
80              total = total + 366
81          else:
82              total = total + 365
83
84      # Add days from Jan to the month prior to the calendar month
85      for i in range(1, month):
86          total = total + getNumberOfDaysInMonth(year, i)
87
88      return total
89
90  # Get the number of days in a month
91  def getNumberOfDaysInMonth(year, month):
92      if (month == 1 or month == 3 or month == 5 or month == 7 or
93          month == 8 or month == 10 or month == 12):
94          return 31
95
96      if month == 4 or month == 6 or month == 9 or month == 11:
97          return 30
98
99      if month == 2:
100         return 29 if isLeapYear(year) else 28
101
102     return 0 # If month is incorrect
103
104 # Determine if it is a leap year
105 def isLeapYear(year):
106     return year % 400 == 0 or (year % 4 == 0 and year % 100 != 0)
107
108 def main():
109     # Prompt the user to enter year and month
110     year = eval(input("Enter full year (e.g., 2001): "))
111     month = eval(input(("Enter month as number between 1 and 12: ")))
112
113     # Print calendar for the month of the year
114     printMonth(year, month)
115
116 main() # Call the main function
```

getStartDay

getTotalNumberOfDays

getNumberOfDaysInMonth

isLeapYear

This program does not validate user input. For instance, if the user enters either a month not in the range between **1** and **12** or a year before **1800**, the program displays an erroneous calendar. To avoid this error, add an **if** statement to check the input before printing the calendar.

This program prints calendars for a month but could easily be modified to print calendars for a whole year. Although it can print months only after January **1800**, it could be modified to print months before **1800**.

6.13.4 Benefits of Stepwise Refinement

Stepwise refinement breaks a large problem into smaller manageable subproblems. Each subproblem can be implemented using a function. This approach makes the program easier to write, reuse, debug, test, modify, and maintain.

Simpler Program

The print calendar program is long. Rather than writing a long sequence of statements in one function, stepwise refinement breaks it into smaller functions. This simplifies the program and makes the whole program easier to read and understand.

Reusing Functions

Stepwise refinement promotes code reuse within a program. The **isLeapYear** function is defined once and invoked from the **getTotalNumberOfDays** and **getNumberOfDasInMonth** functions. This reduces redundant code.

Easier Developing, Debugging, and Testing

Since each subproblem is solved in a function, a function can be developed, debugged, and tested individually. This isolates the errors and makes developing, debugging, and testing easier.

When implementing a large program, use the top-down and/or bottom-up approach. Do not write the entire program at once. Using these approaches seems to take more development time (because you repeatedly run the program), but it actually saves time and makes debugging easier.

incremental development and testing

Better Facilitating Teamwork

Since a large problem is divided into subprograms, the subproblems can be assigned to programmers. This makes it easier for programmers to work in teams.

6.14 Case Study: Reusable Graphics Functions

You can develop reusable functions to simplify coding in the **turtle** *module.*

Key Point

Often you need to draw a line between two points, display text or a small point at a specified location, depict a circle with a specified center and radius, or create a rectangle with a specified center, width, and height. It would greatly simplify programming if these functions were available for reuse. Listing 6.14 defines these functions in a module named **UsefulTurtleFunctions**.

LISTING 6.14 UsefulTurtleFunctions.py

```
1  import turtle
2
3  # Draw a line from (x1, y1) to (x2, y2)
4  def drawLine(x1, y1, x2, y2):
5      turtle.penup()
```

import turtle

function drawLine

```
 6      turtle.goto(x1, y1)
 7      turtle.pendown()
 8      turtle.goto(x2, y2)
 9
10  # Write a string s at the specified location (x, y)
11  def writeText(s, x, y):
12      turtle.penup() # Pull the pen up
13      turtle.goto(x, y)
14      turtle.pendown() # Pull the pen down
15      turtle.write(s) # Write a string
16
17  # Draw a point at the specified location (x, y)
18  def drawPoint(x, y):
19      turtle.penup() # Pull the pen up
20      turtle.goto(x, y)
21      turtle.pendown() # Pull the pen down
22      turtle.begin_fill() # Begin to fill color in a shape
23      turtle.circle(3)
24      turtle.end_fill() # Fill the shape
25
26  # Draw a circle centered at (x, y) with the specified radius
27  def drawCircle(x = 0, y = 0, radius = 10):
28      turtle.penup() # Pull the pen up
29      turtle.goto(x, y - radius)
30      turtle.pendown() # Pull the pen down
31      turtle.circle(radius)
32
33  # Draw a rectangle at (x, y) with the specified width and height
34  def drawRectangle(x = 0, y = 0, width = 10, height = 10):
35      turtle.penup() # Pull the pen up
36      turtle.goto(x + width / 2, y + height / 2)
37      turtle.pendown() # Pull the pen down
38      turtle.right(90)
39      turtle.forward(height)
40      turtle.right(90)
41      turtle.forward(width)
42      turtle.right(90)
43      turtle.forward(height)
44      turtle.right(90)
45      turtle.forward(width)
```

The margin notes on the left read: draw a line; function writeText; write string; function drawPoint; draw a tiny circle; function drawCircle; draw a circle; function drawRectangle.

Now that you have written this code, you can use these functions to draw shapes. Listing 6.15 gives a test program to use these functions from the **UsefulTurtleFunctions** module to draw a line, write some text, and create a point, a circle, and a rectangle, as shown in Figure 6.10.

LISTING 6.15 UseCustomTurtleFunctions.py

```
 1  import turtle
 2  from UsefulTurtleFunctions import *
 3
 4  # Draw a line from (-50, -50) to (50, 50)
 5  drawLine(-50, -50, 50, 50)
 6
 7  # Write text at (-50, -60)
 8  writeText("Testing useful Turtle functions", -50, -60)
 9
10  # Draw a point at (0, 0)
11  drawPoint(0, 0)
12
13  # Draw a circle at (0, 0) with radius 80
```

Margin notes: import turtle; import UsefulTurtleFunctions; draw a line; write text string; draw a point.

```
14  drawCircle(0, 0, 80)                                            draw a circle
15
16  # Draw a rectangle at (0, 0) with width 60 and height 40
17  drawRectangle(0, 0, 60, 40)                                     draw a rectangle
18
19  turtle.hideturtle()
20  turtle.done()                                                   pause
```

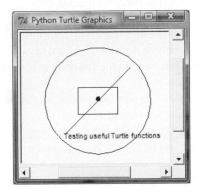

Figure 6.10   The program draws shapes using the custom functions.

The asterisk (*) in line 2 imports all functions from the **UsefulTurtleFunctions** module into the program. Line 5 invokes the **drawLine** function to draw a line, and line 8 invokes the **writeText** function to write a text string. The **drawPoint** function (line 11) draws a point, and the **drawCircle** function (line 14) draws a circle. Line 17 invokes the **drawRectangle** function to draw a rectangle.

Key Terms

actual parameter   173
argument   173
caller   173
default argument   189
divide and conquer   192
formal parameters (i.e., parameter)   173
functions   172
function abstraction   192
function header   173
global variable   187
immutable objects   181

information hiding   192
keyword arguments   180
local variable   187
None function   178
parameters   173
pass-by-value   180
positional arguments   179
return value   173
scope of a variable   187
stepwise refinement   193
stub   195

Chapter Summary

1.   Making programs modular and reusable is one of the central goals in software engineering. *Functions* can help to achieve this goal.

2.   A *function header* begins with the **def** keyword followed by function's name and *parameters*, and ends with a colon.

3.   Parameters are optional; that is, a function does not have to contain any parameters.

4. A function is called a *void* or *None function* if it does not return a value.

5. A **return** statement can also be used in a void function for terminating the function and returning to the function's caller. This is useful occasionally for circumventing the normal flow of control in a function.

6. The *arguments* that are passed to a function should have the same number, type, and order as the parameters in the function header.

7. When a program calls a function, program control is transferred to the called function. A called function returns control to the caller when its return statement is executed or when the last statement in the function is executed.

8. A value-returning function can also be invoked as a statement in Python. In this case, the function's return value is ignored.

9. A function's arguments can be passed as *positional arguments* or *keyword arguments*.

10. When you invoke a function with a parameter, the reference value of the argument is passed to the parameter. This is referred to as *pass-by-value* in programming terminology.

11. A variable created in a function is called a *local variable*. The scope of a local variable starts from its creation and exists until the function returns. A variable must be created before it is used.

12. *Global variables* are created outside all functions and are accessible to all functions in their scope.

13. Python allows you to define functions with *default argument* values. The default values are passed to the parameters when a function is invoked without the arguments.

14. The Python **return** statement can return multiple values.

15. *Function abstraction* is achieved by separating the use of a function from its implementation. The client can use a function without knowing how it is implemented. The details of the implementation are encapsulated in the function and hidden from the client that invokes the function. This is known as *information hiding* or *encapsulation*.

16. Function abstraction modularizes programs in a neat, hierarchical manner. Programs written as collections of concise functions are easier to write, debug, maintain, and modify than would otherwise be the case. This writing style also promotes function reusability.

17. When implementing a large program, use the top-down and/or bottom-up coding approach. Do not write the entire program at once. This approach may seem to take more time for coding (because you are repeatedly running the program), but it actually saves time and makes debugging easier.

TEST QUESTIONS

Do test questions for this chapter online at www.cs.armstrong.edu/liang/py/test.html.

PROGRAMMING EXERCISES

MyProgrammingLab™

Sections 6.2–6.9

6.1 (*Math: pentagonal numbers*) A pentagonal number is defined as $n(3n - 1)/2$ for $n = 1, 2, \ldots$, and so on. So, the first few numbers are 1, 5, 12, 22, ... Write a function with the following header that returns a pentagonal number:

```
def getPentagonalNumber(n):
```

Write a test program that uses this function to display the first 100 pentagonal numbers with 10 numbers on each line.

*6.2 (*Sum the digits in an integer*) Write a function that computes the sum of the digits in an integer. Use the following function header:

```
def sumDigits(n):
```

For example, **sumDigits(234)** returns **9** (2 + 3 + 4). (Hint: Use the **%** operator to extract digits, and the **//** operator to remove the extracted digit. For instance, to extract **4** from **234**, use **234 % 10** (= 4). To remove **4** from **234**, use **234 // 10** (= 23). Use a loop to repeatedly extract and remove the digits until all the digits are extracted.) Write a test program that prompts the user to enter an integer and displays the sum of all its digits.

**6.3 (*Palindrome integer*) Write the functions with the following headers:

```
# Return the reversal of an integer, e.g. reverse(456) returns
# 654
def reverse(number):

# Return true if number is a palindrome
def isPalindrome(number):
```

Use the **reverse** function to implement **isPalindrome**. A number is a palindrome if its reversal is the same as itself. Write a test program that prompts the user to enter an integer and reports whether the integer is a palindrome.

*6.4 (*Display an integer reversed*) Write the following function to display an integer in reverse order:

```
def reverse(number):
```

For example, **reverse(3456)** displays **6543**. Write a test program that prompts the user to enter an integer and displays its reversal.

*6.5 (*Sort three numbers*) Write the following function to display three numbers in increasing order:

```
def displaySortedNumbers(num1, num2, num3):
```

Write a test program that prompts the user to enter three numbers and invokes the function to display them in increasing order. Here are some sample runs:

```
Enter three numbers: 3, 2.4, 5  ↵Enter
The sorted numbers are 2.4 3 5
```

```
Enter three numbers: 31, 12.4, 15  ↵Enter
The sorted numbers are 12.4 15 31
```

*6.6 (*Display patterns*) Write a function to display a pattern as follows:

```
        1
      2 1
    3 2 1
...
n n-1 ... 3 2 1
```

The function header is

def displayPattern(n):

Write a test program that prompts the user to enter a number **n** and invokes **displayPattern(n)** to display the pattern.

*6.7 (*Financial application: compute the future investment value*) Write a function that computes a future investment value at a given interest rate for a specified number of years. The future investment is determined using the formula in Exercise 2.19.

Use the following function header:

def futureInvestmentValue(
    investmentAmount, monthlyInterestRate, years):

For example, **futureInvestmentValue(10000, 0.05/12, 5)** returns **12833.59**.

Write a test program that prompts the user to enter the investment amount and the annual interest rate in percent and prints a table that displays the future value for the years from 1 to 30. Here is a sample run:

```
The amount invested: 1000  ↵Enter
Annual interest rate: 9  ↵Enter

Years      Future Value
1             1093.80
2             1196.41
...
29           13467.25
30           14730.57
```

6.8 (*Conversions between Celsius and Fahrenheit*) Write a module that contains the following two functions:

```
# Converts from Celsius to Fahrenheit
def celsiusToFahrenheit(celsius):

# Converts from Fahrenheit to Celsius
def fahrenheitToCelsius(fahrenheit):
```

The formulas for the conversion are:

```
celsius = (5 / 9) * (fahrenheit - 32)
fahrenheit = (9 / 5) * celsius + 32
```

Write a test program that invokes these functions to display the following tables:

Celsius	Fahrenheit		Fahrenheit	Celsius
40.0	104.0	|	120.0	48.89
39.0	102.2	|	110.0	43.33
...				
32.0	89.6	|	40.0	4.44
31.0	87.8	|	30.0	-1.11

6.9 (*Conversions between feet and meters*) Write a module that contains the following two functions:

```
# Converts from feet to meters
def footToMeter(foot):

# Converts from meters to feet
def meterToFoot(meter):
```

The formulas for the conversion are:

```
foot = meter / 0.305
meter = 0.305 * foot
```

Write a test program that invokes these functions to display the following tables:

Feet	Meters		Meters	Feet
1.0	0.305	|	20.0	66.574
2.0	0.610	|	26.0	81.967
...				
9.0	2.745	|	60.0	196.721
10.0	3.050	|	66.0	213.115

6.10 (*Use the isPrime Function*) Listing 6.7, PrimeNumberFunction.py, provides the isPrime(number) function for testing whether a number is prime. Use this function to find the number of prime numbers less than 10,000.

6.11 (*Financial application: compute commissions*) Write a function that computes the commission, using the scheme in Exercise 5.39. The header of the function is:

```
def computeCommission(salesAmount):
```

Write a test program that displays the following table:

Sales Amount	Commission
10000	900.0
15000	1500.0
...	
95000	11100.0
100000	11700.0

6.12 (*Display characters*) Write a function that prints characters using the following header:

```
def printChars(ch1, ch2, numberPerLine):
```

This function prints the characters between **ch1** and **ch2** with the specified numbers per line. Write a test program that prints ten characters per line from **1** to **Z**.

*6.13 (*Sum series*) Write a function to compute the following series:

$$m(i) = \frac{1}{2} + \frac{2}{3} + \ldots + \frac{i}{i+1}$$

Write a test program that displays the following table:

i	m(i)
1	0.5000
2	1.1667
...	
19	16.4023
20	17.3546

*6.14 (*Estimate* π) π can be computed using the following series:

$$m(i) = 4\left(1 - \frac{1}{3} + \frac{1}{5} - \frac{1}{7} + \frac{1}{9} - \frac{1}{11} + \ldots + \frac{(-1)^{i+1}}{2i-1}\right)$$

Write a function that returns m(i) for a given i and write a test program that displays the following table:

i	m(i)
1	4.0000
101	3.1515
201	3.1466
301	3.1449
401	3.1441
501	3.1436
601	3.1433
701	3.1430
801	3.1428
901	3.1427

*6.15 (*Financial application: print a tax table*) Listing 4.7, ComputeTax.py, gives a program to compute tax. Write a function for computing tax using the following header:

def computeTax(status, taxableIncome):

Use this function to write a program that prints a tax table for taxable income from $50,000 to $60,000 with intervals of $50 for all four statuses, as follows:

Taxable Income	Single	Married Joint	Married Separate	Head of a House
50000	8688	6665	8688	7352
50050	8700	6673	8700	7365
...				
59950	11175	8158	11175	9840
60000	11188	8165	11188	9852

*6.16 (*Number of days in a year*) Write a function that returns the number of days in a year using the following header:

def numberOfDaysInAYear(year):

Write a test program that displays the number of days in the years from **2010** to **2020**.

Sections 6.10–6.11

*6.17 (*The MyTriangle module*) Create a module named **MyTriangle** that contains the following two functions:

```
# Returns true if the sum of any two sides is
#   greater than the third side.
def isValid(side1, side2, side3):

# Returns the area of the triangle.
def area(side1, side2, side3):
```

Write a test program that reads three sides for a triangle and computes the area if the input is valid. Otherwise, it displays that the input is invalid. The formula for computing the area of a triangle is given in Exercise 2.14. Here are some sample runs:

```
Enter three sides in double: 1, 3, 1  ↵Enter
Input is invalid
```

```
Enter three sides in double: 1, 1, 1  ↵Enter
The area of the triangle is 0.4330127018922193
```

*6.18 (*Display matrix of 0s and 1s*) Write a function that displays an *n*-by-*n* matrix using the following header:

```
def printMatrix(n):
```

Each element is 0 or 1, which is generated randomly. Write a test program that prompts the user to enter **n** and displays an *n*-by-*n* matrix. Here is a sample run:

```
Enter n: 3  ↵Enter
0 1 0
0 0 0
1 1 1
```

*6.19 (*Geometry: point position*) Exercise 4.31 shows how to test whether a point is on the left side of a directed line, on the right, or on the same line. Write the following functions:

```
# Return true if point (x2, y2) is on the left side of the
#   directed line from (x0, y0) to (x1, y1)
def leftOfTheLine(x0, y0, x1, y1, x2, y2):

# Return true if point (x2, y2) is on the same
#   line from (x0, y0) to (x1, y1)
def onTheSameLine(x0, y0, x1, y1, x2, y2):

# Return true if point (x2, y2) is on the
# line segment from (x0, y0) to (x1, y1)
def onTheLineSegment(x0, y0, x1, y1, x2, y2):
```

Write a program that prompts the user to enter the three points for p0, p1, and p2 and displays whether p2 is on the left of the line from p0 to p1, on the right, on the same line, or on the line segment. The sample runs of this program are the same as in Exercise 4.31.

*6.20 (*Geometry: display angles*) Rewrite Listing 2.9, ComputeDistance.py, using the following function for computing the distance between two points.

```
def distance(x1, y1, x2, y2):
```

6.21 (*Math: approximate the square root*) There are several techniques for implementing the **sqrt function in the **math** module. One such technique is known as the *Babylonian function*. It approximates the square root of a number, **n**, by repeatedly performing a calculation using the following formula:

```
nextGuess = (lastGuess + (n / lastGuess)) / 2
```

When **nextGuess** and **lastGuess** are almost identical, **nextGuess** is the approximated square root. The initial guess can be any positive value (e.g., **1**). This value will be the starting value for **lastGuess**. If the difference between **nextGuess** and **lastGuess** is less than a very small number, such as **0.0001**, you can claim that **nextGuess** is the approximated square root of **n**. If not, **nextGuess** becomes **lastGuess** and the approximation process continues. Implement the following function that returns the square root of **n**.

```
def sqrt(n):
```

Sections 6.12–6.13

**6.22 (*Display current date and time*) Listing 2.7, ShowCurrentTime.py, displays the current time. Enhance this program to display the current date and time. (Hint: The calendar example in Listing 6.13, PrintCalendar.py, should give you some ideas on how to find the year, month, and day.)

**6.23 (*Convert milliseconds to hours, minutes, and seconds*) Write a function that converts milliseconds to hours, minutes, and seconds using the following header:

```
def convertMillis(millis):
```

The function returns a string as hours:minutes:seconds. For example, **convertMillis(5500)** returns the string 0:0:5, **convertMillis(100000)** returns the string 0:1:40, and **convertMillis(555550000)** returns the string 154:19:10.

Write a test program that prompts the user to enter a value for milliseconds and displays a string in the format of hours:minutes:seconds.

6.24 (*Palindromic prime*) A *palindromic prime* is a prime number that is also palindromic. For example, **131 is a prime and also a palindromic prime, as are **313** and **757**. Write a program that displays the first 100 palindromic prime numbers. Display 10 numbers per line and align the numbers properly, as follows:

```
  2    3    5    7   11  101  131  151  181  191
313  353  373  383  727  757  787  797  919  929
```

6.25 (*Emirp*) An *emirp* (*prime* spelled backward) is a nonpalindromic prime number whose reversal is also a prime. For example, both **17 and **71** are prime numbers, so **17** and **71** are emirps. Write a program that displays the first 100 emirps. Display 10 numbers per line and align the numbers properly, as follows:

```
 13   17   31   37   71   73   79   97  107  113
149  157  167  179  199  311  337  347  359  389
. . .
```

**6.26 (*Mersenne prime*) A prime number is called a *Mersenne prime* if it can be written in the form $2^p - 1$ for some positive integer p. Write a program that finds all Mersenne primes with $p \leq 31$ and displays the output as follows:

```
p          2^p - 1
2             3
3             7
5            31
. . .
```

**6.27 (*Twin primes*) *Twin primes* are a pair of prime numbers that differ by 2. For example, 3 and 5, 5 and 7, and 11 and 13 are twin primes. Write a program to find all twin primes less than 1,000. Display the output as follows:

```
(3, 5)
(5, 7). . .
```

**6.28 (*Game: craps*) Craps is a popular dice game played in casinos. Write a program to play a variation of the game, as follows:

Roll two dice. Each die has six faces representing values 1, 2, ..., and 6, respectively. Check the sum of the two dice. If the sum is 2, 3, or 12 (called *craps*), you lose; if the sum is 7 or 11 (called *natural*), you win; if the sum is another value (i.e., 4, 5, 6, 8, 9, or 10), a *point* is established. Continue to roll the dice until either a 7 or the same point value is rolled. If 7 is rolled, you lose. Otherwise, you win.

Your program acts as a single player. Here are some sample runs.

```
You rolled 5 + 6 = 11
You win
```

```
You rolled 1 + 2 = 3
You lose
```

```
You rolled 4 + 4 = 8
point is 8
You rolled 6 + 2 = 8
You win
```

```
You rolled 3 + 2 = 5
point is 5
You rolled 2 + 5 = 7
You lose
```

**6.29 (*Financial: credit card number validation*) Credit card numbers follow certain patterns: It must have between 13 and 16 digits, and the number must start with:

- 4 for Visa cards
- 5 for MasterCard credit cards
- 37 for American Express cards
- 6 for Discover cards

In 1954, Hans Luhn of IBM proposed an algorithm for validating credit card numbers. The algorithm is useful to determine whether a card number is entered correctly or whether a credit card is scanned correctly by a scanner. Credit card numbers are generated following this validity check, commonly known as the *Luhn check* or the *Mod 10 check*, which can be described as follows (for illustration, consider the card number 4388576018402626):

1. Double every second digit from right to left. If doubling of a digit results in a two-digit number, add up the two digits to get a single-digit number.

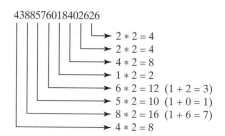

2. Now add all single-digit numbers from Step 1.

$$4 + 4 + 8 + 2 + 3 + 1 + 7 + 8 = 37$$

3. Add all digits in the odd places from right to left in the card number.

$$6 + 6 + 0 + 8 + 0 + 7 + 8 + 3 = 38$$

4. Sum the results from Steps 2 and 3.

$$37 + 38 = 75$$

5. If the result from Step 4 is divisible by 10, the card number is valid; otherwise, it is invalid. For example, the number 4388576018402626 is invalid, but the number 4388576018410707 is valid.

Write a program that prompts the user to enter a credit card number as an integer. Display whether the number is valid or invalid. Design your program to use the following functions:

```
# Return true if the card number is valid
def isValid(number):

# Get the result from Step 2
def sumOfDoubleEvenPlace(number):

# Return this number if it is a single digit, otherwise, return
# the sum of the two digits
def getDigit(number):

# Return sum of odd place digits in number
def sumOfOddPlace(number):
```

```
# Return true if the digit d is a prefix for number
def prefixMatched(number, d):

# Return the number of digits in d
def getSize(d):

# Return the first k number of digits from number. If the
# number of digits in number is less than k, return number.
def getPrefix(number, k):
```

**6.30 (*Game: chance of winning at craps*) Revise Exercise 6.28 to run it 10,000 times and display the number of winning games.

***6.31 (*Current date and time*) Invoking `time.time()` returns the elapsed time in seconds since midnight of January 1, 1970. Write a program that displays the date and time. Here is a sample run:

```
Current date and time is May 16, 2012 10:34:23
```

**6.32 (*Print calendar*) Exercise 4.21 uses Zeller's congruence to calculate the day of the week. Simplify Listing 6.13, PrintCalendar.py, using Zeller's algorithm to get the start day of the month.

**6.33 (*Geometry: area of a pentagon*) Rewrite Exercise 3.4 using the following function to return the area of a pentagon:

```
def area(s):
```

*6.34 (*Geometry: area of a regular polygon*) Rewrite Exercise 3.5 using the following function to return the area of a regular polygon:

```
def area(n, side):
```

*6.35 (*Compute the probability*) Use the functions in **RandomCharacter** in Listing 6.11 to generate 10,000 uppercase letters and count the occurrence of **A**.

*6.36 (*Generate random characters*) Use the functions in **RandomCharacter** in Listing 6.11 to print 100 uppercase letters and then 100 single digits, printing ten per line.

Section 6.14

*6.37 (*Turtle: generate random characters*) Use the functions in **RandomCharacter** in Listing 6.11 to display 100 lowercase letters, fifteen per line, as shown in Figure 6.11a.

6.38 (*Turtle: draw a line*) Write the following function that draws a line from point (x1, y1**) to (**x2, y2**) with color (default to black) and line size (default to 1).

```
def drawLine(x1, y1, x2, y2, color = "black", size = 1):
```

6.39 (*Turtle: draw a star*) Write a program that draws a star, as shown in Figure 6.11b. Use the **drawLine function defined in Exercise 6.38.

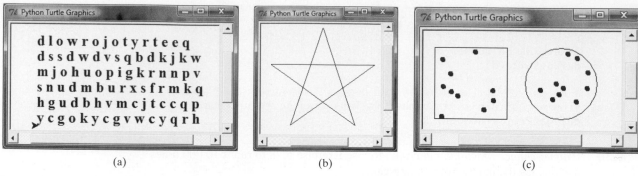

FIGURE 6.11   (a) The program displays random lowercase letters. (b) The program draws a star. (c) The program draws random points in a rectangle and in a circle.

**6.40   (*Turtle: filled rectangle and circle*) Write the following functions that fill a rectangle with the specified color, center, width, and height, and a circle with the specified color, center, and radius.

```python
# Fill a rectangle
def drawRectangle(color = "black",
    x = 0, y = 0, width = 30, height = 30):

# Fill a circle
def drawCircle(color = "black", x = 0, y = 0, radius = 50):
```

**6.41   (*Turtle: draw points, rectangles, and circles*) Use the functions defined in Listing 6.14 to write a program that displays a rectangle centered at $(-75, 0)$ with width and height 100 and a circle centered at $(50, 0)$ with radius 50. Fill 10 random points inside the rectangle and 10 inside the circle, as shown in Figure 6.11c.

**6.42   (*Turtle: plot the sine function*) Simplify the code for Exercise 5.52 by using the functions in Listing 6.14.

**6.43   (*Turtle: plot the sine and cosine functions*) Simplify the code for Exercise 5.53 by using the functions in Listing 6.14.

**6.44   (*Turtle: plot the square function*) Simplify the code for Exercise 5.54 by using the functions in Listing 6.14.

**6.45   (*Turtle: draw a regular polygon*) Write the following function to draw a regular polygon:

```python
def drawPolygon(x = 0, y = 0, radius = 50, numberOfSides = 3):
```

The polygon is centered at (x, y) with a specified radius for the bounding circle for the polygon and the number of sides. Write a test program that displays a triangle, square, pentagon, hexagon, heptagon, and octagon, as shown in Figure 6.12a.

*6.46   (*Turtle: connect all points in a hexagon*) Write a program that displays a hexagon with all the points connected, as shown in Figure 6.12b.

*6.47   (*Turtle: two chessboards*) Write a program that displays two chessboards, as shown in Figure 6.13. Your program should define at least the following function:

```python
# Draw one chessboard whose upper-left corner is at
# (startx, starty) and bottom-right corner is at (endx, endy)
def drawChessboard(startx, endx, starty, endy):
```

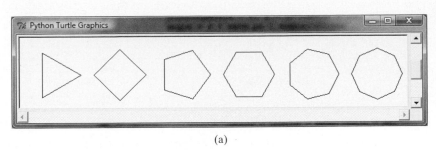

(a)

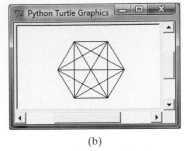

(b)

FIGURE 6.12 (a) The program displays several n-sided polygons. (b) The program displays a hexagon with all points connected.

FIGURE 6.13 The program draws two chessboards.

*6.48 (*Format an integer*) Write a function with the following header to format the integer with the specified width.

```python
def format(number, width):
```

The function returns a string for the number with prefix **0**s. The size of the string is the width. For example, **format(34, 4)** returns **"0034"** and **format(34, 5)** returns **"00034"**. If the number is longer than the width, the function returns the string representation for the number. For example, **format(34, 1)** returns **"34"**.

Write a test program that prompts the user to enter a number and its width and displays a string returned from invoking **format(number, width)**. Here is a sample run:

```
Enter an integer: 453 ↵Enter
Enter the width: 6 ↵Enter
The formatted number is 000453
```

OBJECTS AND CLASSES

Objectives

- To describe objects and classes, and use classes to model objects (§7.2).

- To define classes with data fields and methods (§7.2.1).

- To construct an object using a constructor that invokes the initializer to create and initialize data fields (§7.2.2).

- To access the members of objects using the dot operator (.) (§7.2.3).

- To reference an object itself with the self parameter (§7.2.4).

- To use UML graphical notations to describe classes and objects (§7.3).

- To distinguish between immutable and mutable objects (§7.4).

- To hide data fields to prevent data corruption and make classes easy to maintain (§7.5).

- To apply class abstraction and encapsulation to software development (§7.6).

- To explore the differences between the procedural paradigm and the object-oriented paradigm (§7.7).

7.1 Introduction

Object-oriented programming enables you to develop large-scale software and GUIs effectively.

Having learned the material in the preceding chapters, you are now able to solve many programming problems by using selections, loops, and functions. However, these features are not sufficient for developing a graphical user interface (GUI, pronounced *goo-ee*) or a large-scale software system. Suppose you want to develop the GUI shown in Figure 7.1. How would you program it?

why OOP?

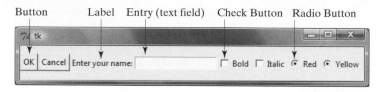

FIGURE 7.1   You can create GUI objects like this using object-oriented programming.

This chapter introduces object-oriented programming, which will build a foundation that enables you to develop GUIs and large-scale software systems in the upcoming chapters.

7.2 Defining Classes for Objects

A class defines the properties and behaviors for objects.

Section 3.5 introduced objects and methods, and showed you how to use objects. Objects are created from classes. This section shows you how to define custom classes.

object-oriented programming

object

Object-oriented programming (OOP) involves the use of objects to create programs. An *object* represents an entity in the real world that can be distinctly identified. For example, a student, a desk, a circle, a button, and even a loan can all be viewed as objects. An object has a unique identity, state, and behavior.

identity

- An object's *identity* is like a person's Social Security number. Python automatically assigns each object a unique id for identifying the object at runtime.

state
properties
attributes
data fields

- An object's *state* (also known as its *properties* or *attributes*) is represented by variables, called *data fields*. A circle object, for example, has a data field **radius**, which is a property that characterizes a circle. A rectangle object has the data fields **width** and **height**, which are properties that characterize a rectangle.

behavior
actions

- Python uses methods to define an object's *behavior* (also known as its *actions*). Recall that methods are defined as functions. You make an object perform an action by invoking a method on that object. For example, you can define methods named **getArea()** and **getPerimeter()** for circle objects. A circle object can then invoke the **getArea()** method to return its area and the **getPerimeter()** method to return its perimeter.

Objects of the same kind are defined by using a common class. The relationship between classes and objects is analogous to that between an apple-pie recipe and apple pies. You can make as many apple pies (objects) as you want from a single recipe (class).

class
contract

A Python *class* uses variables to store data fields and defines methods to perform actions. A class is a *contract*—also sometimes called a *template* or *blueprint*—that defines what an object's data fields and methods will be.

An object is an instance of a class, and you can create many instances of a class. Creating an instance of a class is referred to as *instantiation*. The terms *object* and *instance* are often used interchangeably. An object is an instance and an instance is an object.

Figure 7.2 shows a class named **Circle** and its three objects.

instantiation
object
instance

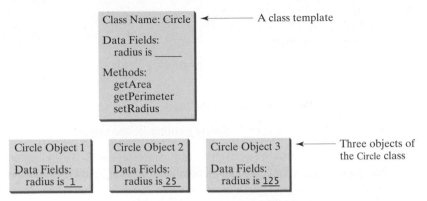

FIGURE 7.2 A class is a template—or contract—for creating objects.

7.2.1 Defining Classes

In addition to using variables to store data fields and define methods, a class provides a special method, `__init__`. This method, known as an *initializer*, is invoked to initialize a new object's state when it is created. An initializer can perform any action, but initializers are designed to perform initializing actions, such as creating an object's data fields with initial values.

Python uses the following syntax to define a class:

methods
initializer

class definition

```
class ClassName:
    initializer
    methods
```

Listing 7.1 defines the **Circle** class. The class name is preceded by the keyword **class** and followed by a colon (:). The initializer is always named `__init__` (line 5), which is a special method. *Note that init needs to be preceded and followed by two underscores.* A data field **radius** is created in the initializer (line 6). The methods **getPerimeter** and **getArea** are defined to return the perimeter and area of a circle (lines 8–12). More details on the initializer, data fields, and methods will be explained in the following sections.

VideoNote
Define and use classes

LISTING 7.1 `Circle.py`

```
1  import math
2
3  class Circle:
4      # Construct a circle object
5      def __init__(self, radius = 1):
6          self.radius = radius
7
8      def getPerimeter(self):
9          return 2 * self.radius * math.pi
10
11     def getArea(self):
12         return self.radius * self.radius * math.pi
13
14     def setRadius(self, radius):
15         self.radius = radius
```

class name

initializer
create data field

getPerimeter() method

getArea() method

Note

The naming style for class names in the Python library is not consistent. In this book, we will adopt a convention that capitalizes the first letter of each word in the class name. For example, **Circle**, **LinearEquation**, and **LinkedList** are correct class names according to our convention.

class naming convention

7.2.2 Constructing Objects

constructor

Once a class is defined, you can create objects from the class with a *constructor*. The constructor does two things:

■ It creates an object in the memory for the class.

■ It invokes the class's **__init__** method to initialize the object.

self parameter
__init__ method

All methods, including the initializer, have the first parameter **self**. This parameter refers to the object that invokes the method. The **self** parameter in the **__init__** method is automatically set to reference the object that was just created. You can specify any name for this parameter, but by convention **self** is usually used. We will discuss the role of **self** more in Section 7.2.4.

The syntax for a constructor is:

```
ClassName(arguments)
```

Figure 7.3 shows how an object is created and initialized. After the object is created, **self** can be used to reference the object.

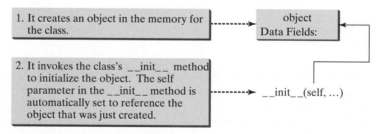

FIGURE 7.3 Constructing an object creates the object in the memory and invokes its initializer.

The arguments of the constructor match the parameters in the **__init__** method without **self**. For example, since the **__init__** method in line 5 of Listing 7.1 is defined as **__init__(self, radius = 1)**, to construct a **Circle** object with radius **5**, you should use **Circle(5)**. Figure 7.4 shows the effect of constructing a **Circle** object using **Circle(5)**. First, a **Circle** object is created in the memory, and then the initializer is invoked to set **radius** to **5**.

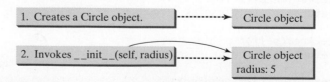

FIGURE 7.4 A circle object is constructed using **Circle(5)**.

The initializer in the **Circle** class has a default **radius** value of **1**. The following constructor creates a **Circle** object with default radius **1**:

default values

```
Circle()
```

7.2.3 Accessing Members of Objects

An object's member refers to its data fields and methods. Data fields are also called *instance variables*, because each object (instance) has a specific value for a data field. Methods are also called *instance methods*, because a method is invoked by an object (instance) to perform actions on the object such as changing the values in data fields for the object. In order to access an object's data fields and invoke an object's methods, you need to assign the object to a variable by using the following syntax:

instance methods

```
objectRefVar = ClassName(arguments)
```

For example,

```
c1 = Circle(5)
c2 = Circle()
```

You can access the object's data fields and invoke its methods by using the *dot operator (.),* also known as the *object member access operator.* The syntax for using the dot operator is:

dot operator (.)

```
objectRefVar.datafield
objectRefVar.method(args)
```

For example, the following code accesses the **radius** data field (line 3), and then invokes the **getPerimeter** method (line 5) and the **getArea** method (line 7). Note that line 1 imports the **Circle** class defined in the Circle module in Listing 7.1, Circle.py.

object member access
operator

```
1  >>> from Circle import Circle
2  >>> c = Circle(5)
3  >>> c.radius
4  5
5  >>> c.getPerimeter()
6  31.41592653589793
7  >>> c.getArea()
8  78.53981633974483
9  >>>
```

Note

Usually you create an object and assign it to a variable. Later you can use the variable to reference the object. Occasionally an object does not need to be referenced later. In this case, you can create an object without explicitly assigning it to a variable, as shown below:

```
print("Area is", Circle(5).getArea())
```

The statement creates a **Circle** object and invokes its **getArea** method to return its area. An object created in this way is known as an *anonymous object.*

anonymous object

7.2.4 The **self** Parameter

As mentioned earlier, the first parameter for each method defined is **self**. This parameter is used in the implementation of the method, but it is not used when the method is called. So, what is this parameter **self** for? Why does Python need it?

why **self**?

self is a parameter that references the object itself. Using **self**, you can access object's members in a class definition. For example, you can use the syntax **self.x** to access the instance variable **x** and syntax **self.m1()** to invoke the instance method **m1** for the object **self** in a class, as illustrated in Figure 7.5.

```
def ClassName:

    def __init__(self, ...):
        self.x = 1   # Create/modify x
        ...

    def m1(self, ...):
        self.y = 2   # Create/modify y
        ...
        z = 5 # Create/modify z
        ...                          Scope of z

    def m2(self, ...):
        self.y = 3   # Create/modify y
        ...
        u = self.x + 1 # Create/modify u
        self.m1(...) # Invoke m1
```

Scope of self.x
and self.y

Scope of z

FIGURE 7.5 The scope of an instance variable is the entire class.

scope of an instance variable

The scope of an instance variable is the entire class once it is created. In Figure 7.5, **self.x** is an instance variable created in the **__init__** method. It is accessed in method **m2**. The instance variable **self.y** is set to **2** in method **m1** and set to **3** in **m2**. Note that you can also create local variables in a method. The scope of a local variable is within the method. The local variable **z** is created in method **m1** and its scope is from its creation to the end of method **m1**.

7.2.5 Example: Using Classes

The preceding sections demonstrated the concept of class and objects. You learned how to define a class with the initializer, data fields, and methods, and how to create an object with constructor. This section presents a test program that constructs three circle objects with radii of **1**, **25**, and **125**, and then displays the radius and area of each circle in Listing 7.2. The program then changes the radius of the second object to **100** and displays its new radius and area.

LISTING 7.2 TestCircle.py

import Circle

main function

create object

invoke methods

create object

create object

```
1  from Circle import Circle
2
3  def main():
4      # Create a circle with radius 1
5      circle1 = Circle()
6      print("The area of the circle of radius",
7          circle1.radius , "is", circle1.getArea())
8
9      # Create a circle with radius 25
10     circle2 = Circle(25)
11     print("The area of the circle of radius",
12         circle2.radius , "is", circle2.getArea())
13
14     # Create a circle with radius 125
15     circle3 = Circle(125)
16     print("The area of the circle of radius",
17         circle3.radius , "is", circle3.getArea())
18
```

```
19      # Modify circle radius
20      circle2.radius = 100  # or circle2.setRadius(100)
21      print("The area of the circle of radius",
22          circle2.radius , "is" , circle2.getArea())
23
24  main() # Call the main function
```

set a new radius

```
The area of the circle of radius 1.0 is 3.141592653589793
The area of the circle of radius 25.0 is 1963.4954084936207
The area of the circle of radius 125.0 is 49087.385212340516
The area of the circle of radius 100.0 is 31415.926535897932
```

The program uses the **Circle** class to create **Circle** objects. Such a program that uses the class (such as **Circle**) is often referred to as a *client* of the class.

client

The **Circle** class is defined in Listing 7.1, Circle.py, and this program imports it in line 1 using the syntax **from Circle import Circle**. The program creates a **Circle** object with a default radius **1** (line 5) and creates two **Circle** objects with the specified radii (lines 10, 15), and then retrieves the **radius** property and invokes the **getArea()** method on the objects to obtain the area (lines 7, 12, and 17). The program sets a new **radius** property on **circle2** (line 20). This can also be done by using **circle2.setRadius(100)**.

Note

An variable that appears to hold an object actually contains a reference to that object. Strictly speaking, a variable and an object are different, but most of the time the distinction can be ignored. So it is fine, for simplicity, to say that "**circle1** is a **Circle** object" rather than use the longer-winded description that "**circle1** is a variable that contains a reference to a **Circle** object."

object vs. variable

7.1   Describe the relationship between an object and its defining class.

7.2   How do you define a class?

7.3   How do you create an object?

7.4   What is the name of the initializer method?

7.5   The first parameter in the initializer method is named **self** by convention. What is the role of **self**?

7.6   What is the syntax for constructing an object? What does Python do when constructing an object?

7.7   What are the differences between an initializer and a method?

7.8   What is the object member access operator for?

7.9   What problem arises in running the following program? How do you fix it?

Check
Point

MyProgrammingLab™

```
class A:
    def __init__(self, i):
        self.i = i

def main():
    a = A()
    print(a.i)

main() # Call the main function
```

7.10   What is wrong with the following programs?

```
1  class A:
2      # Construct an object of the class
3      def A(self):
4          radius = 3
```

(a)

```
1  class A:
2      # Construct an object of the class
3      def __init__(self):
4          radius = 3
5
6      def setRadius(radius):
7          self.radius = radius
```

(b)

7.3 UML Class Diagrams

UML class diagrams use graphical notation to describe classes.

UML

Key Point

The illustration of class templates and objects in Figure 7.2 can be standardized using UML (Unified Modeling Language) notation. This notation, as shown in Figure 7.6, called a *UML class diagram* or simply a *class diagram*, is language independent; that is, other programming languages use this same modeling and notation. In UML class diagrams, data fields are denoted as:

dataFieldName: dataFieldType

Constructors are shown as:

ClassName(parameterName: parameterType)

Methods are represented as:

methodName(parameterName: parameterType): returnType

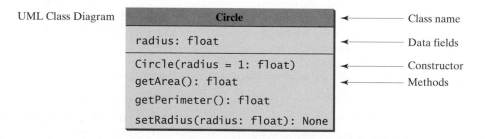

FIGURE 7.6 Classes and objects can be represented using UML notation.

The method definition in the class always has the special **self** parameter, but don't include it in the UML diagram, because the client does not need to know this parameter and does not use this parameter to invoke the methods.

The **__init__** method does not need to be listed in the UML diagram either, because it is invoked by the constructor and its parameters are the same as the constructor's parameters.

The UML diagram serves as the contract (template) for the client so that it will know how to use the class. The diagram describes for the client how to create objects and how to invoke the methods on the objects.

As an example, consider TV sets. Each TV is an object with states (that is, current channel, current volume level, and power on or off are its properties that are represented by data fields) and behaviors (change channels, adjust volume, and turn on/off are the actions each

TV object implements with methods). You can use a class to define TV sets. The UML diagram for the **TV** class is shown in Figure 7.7.

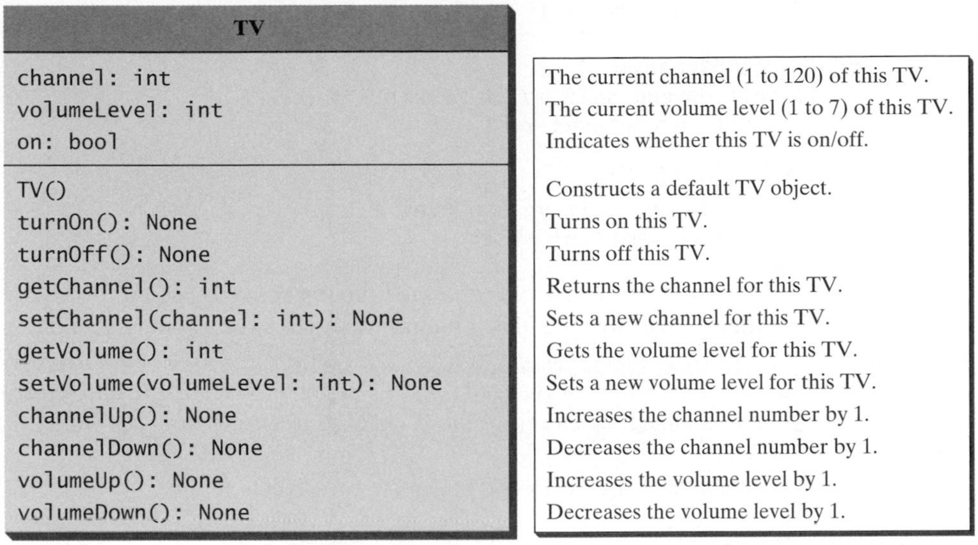

TV
channel: int
volumeLevel: int
on: bool
TV()
turnOn(): None
turnOff(): None
getChannel(): int
setChannel(channel: int): None
getVolume(): int
setVolume(volumeLevel: int): None
channelUp(): None
channelDown(): None
volumeUp(): None
volumeDown(): None

The current channel (1 to 120) of this TV.
The current volume level (1 to 7) of this TV.
Indicates whether this TV is on/off.

Constructs a default TV object.
Turns on this TV.
Turns off this TV.
Returns the channel for this TV.
Sets a new channel for this TV.
Gets the volume level for this TV.
Sets a new volume level for this TV.
Increases the channel number by 1.
Decreases the channel number by 1.
Increases the volume level by 1.
Decreases the volume level by 1.

FIGURE 7.7 The TV class defines TV sets.

Listing 7.3 gives the Python code for defining the **TV** class.

LISTING 7.3 TV.py

```python
 1  class TV:                                              # define a class
 2      def __init__(self):                                # define initializer
 3          self.channel = 1    # Default channel is 1     # create instance variables
 4          self.volumeLevel = 1   # Default volume level is 1
 5          self.on = False    # Initially, TV is off
 6
 7      def turnOn(self):                                  # turn on TV
 8          self.on = True
 9
10      def turnOff(self):                                 # turn off TV
11          self.on = False
12
13      def getChannel(self):                              # get the channel
14          return self.channel
15
16      def setChannel(self, channel):                     # set a new channel
17          if self.on and 1 <= self.channel <= 120:
18              self.channel = channel
19
20      def getVolumeLevel(self):                          # get the volume
21          return self.volumeLevel
22
23      def setVolume(self, volumeLevel):                  # set a new volume
24          if self.on and \
25              1 <= self.volumeLevel <= 7:
26              self.volumeLevel = volumeLevel
27
28      def channelUp(self):                               # increase channel
```

```
29          if self.on and self.channel < 120:
30              self.channel += 1
31
```
decrease channel
```
32      def channelDown(self):
33          if self.on and self.channel > 1:
34              self.channel -= 1
35
```
increase volume
```
36      def volumeUp(self):
37          if self.on and self.volumeLevel < 7:
38              self.volumeLevel += 1
39
```
decrease volume
```
40      def volumeDown(self):
41          if self.on and self.volumeLevel > 1:
42              self.volumeLevel -= 1
```

The initializer creates the instance variables **channel**, **volumeLevel**, and **on** for the data fields in a **TV** object (lines 2–5). Note that this initializer does not have any argument except **self**.

The channel and volume level are not changed if the TV is not on (lines 16–18 and 23–26). Before either of these is changed, its current value is checked to ensure that it is within the correct range.

Listing 7.4 is a program that uses the **TV** class to create two objects.

LISTING 7.4 TestTV.py

import TV class
```
1   from TV import TV
2
```
main function
create a TV
turn on
set a new channel
set a new volume
```
3   def main():
4       tv1 = TV()
5       tv1.turnOn()
6       tv1.setChannel(30)
7       tv1.setVolume(3)
8
```
create a TV
turn on
increase channel

increase volume
```
9       tv2 = TV()
10      tv2.turnOn()
11      tv2.channelUp()
12      tv2.channelUp()
13      tv2.volumeUp()
14
```
display state
```
15      print("tv1's channel is", tv1.getChannel(),
16          "and volume level is", tv1.getVolumeLevel())
17      print("tv2's channel is", tv2.getChannel(),
18          "and volume level is", tv2.getVolumeLevel())
19
20  main() # Call the main function
```

```
tv1's channel is 30 and volume level is 3
tv2's channel is 3 and volume level is 2
```

The program creates two **TV** objects **tv1** and **tv2** (lines 4 and 9), and invokes the methods on the objects to perform actions for setting channels and volume levels and for increasing channels and volumes. **tv1** is turned on by invoking **tv1.turnOn()** in line 5, its channel is set to **30** by invoking **tv1.setChannel(30)** in line 6, and its volume level is set to **3** in line 7. **tv2** is turned on in line 10, its channel is increased by **1** by invoking **tv2.channelUp()** in line 11, and again by another **1** in line 12. Since the initial channel is set to **1** (line 3 in

TV.py), **tv2**'s channel is now **3**. **tv2**'s volume is increased by **1** by invoking **tv2.volumeUp()** in line 13. Since the initial volume is set to **1** (line 4 in TV.py), **tv2**'s volume is now **2**.

The program displays the state of the objects in lines 15–18. The data fields are read using the **getChannel()** and **getVolumeLevel()** methods.

7.4 Immutable Objects vs. Mutable Objects

When passing a mutable object to a function, the function may change the contents of the object.

Key Point

Recall that numbers and strings are immutable objects in Python. Their contents cannot be changed. When passing an immutable object to a function, the object will not be changed. However, if you pass a mutable object to a function, the contents of the object may change. The example in Listing 7.5 demonstrates the differences between an immutable object and mutable object arguments in a function.

LISTING 7.5 TestPassMutableObject.py

```
 1  from Circle import Circle                                import Circle
 2
 3  def main():
 4      # Create a Circle object with radius 1
 5      myCircle = Circle()                                   create object
 6
 7      # Print areas for radius 1, 2, 3, 4, and 5
 8      n = 5
 9      printAreas(myCircle, n)                               invoke printAreas
10
11      # Display myCircle.radius and times
12      print("\nRadius is", myCircle.radius)                 display radius
13      print("n is", n)                                      display n
14
15  # Print a table of areas for radius
16  def printAreas(c, times):
17      print("Radius \t\tArea")
18      while times >= 1:
19          print(c.radius, "\t\t", c.getArea())
20          c.radius = c.radius + 1
21          times = times - 1
22
23  main() # Call the main function
```

```
Radius             Area

1                  3.141592653589793
2                  12.566370614359172
3                  29.274333882308138
4                  50.26548245743669
5                  79.53981633974483

Radius is 6
n is 5
```

The **Circle** class is defined in Listing 7.1. The program passes a **Circle** object **myCircle** and an **int** object **n** to invoke **printAreas(myCircle, n)** (line 9), which prints a table of areas for radii **1**, **2**, **3**, **4**, and **5**, as shown in the sample output.

When you pass an object to a function, the reference of the object is passed to the function. However, there are important differences between passing immutable objects and mutable objects.

- For an argument of an immutable object such as a number or string, the original value of the object outside the function is not changed.

immutable object vs. mutable object

- For an argument of a mutable object such as a circle, the original value of the object is changed if the contents of the object are changed inside the function.

In line 20, the **radius** property of the **Circle** object **c** is incremented by **1**. **c.radius + 1** creates a new **int** object, which is assigned to **c.radius**. **myCircle** and **c** both point to the same object. When the **printAreas** function is finished, **c.radius** is **6**. So, the printout for **myCircle.radius** is **6** from line 12.

In line 21, **times - 1** creates a new **int** object, which is assigned to **times**. Outside of the **printAreas** function, **n** is still **5**. So, the printout for **n** is **5** from line 13.

Check Point

MyProgrammingLab™

7.11 Show the output of the following program:

```python
class Count:
    def __init__(self, count = 0):
        self.count = count

def main():
    c = Count()
    times = 0
    for i in range(100):
        increment(c, times)

    print("count is", c.count)
    print("times is", times)

def increment(c, times):
    c.count += 1
    times += 1

main() # Call the main function
```

7.12 Show the output of the following program:

```python
class Count:
    def __init__(self, count = 0):
        self.count = count

def main():
    c = Count()
    n = 1
    m(c, n)

    print("count is", c.count)
    print("n is", n)

def m(c, n):
    c = Count(5)
    n = 3

main() # Call the main function
```

7.5 Hiding Data Fields

Making data fields private protects data and makes the class easy to maintain.

**Key
Point**

You can access data fields via instance variables directly from an object. For example, the following code, which lets you access the circle's radius from **c.radius**, is legal:

```
>>> c = Circle(5)
>>> c.radius = 5.4  # Access instance variable directly
>>> print(c.radius) # Access instance variable directly
5.4
>>>
```

However, direct access of a data field in an object is not a good practice—for two reasons:

- First, data may be tampered with. For example, **channel** in the **TV** class has a value between **1** and **120**, but it may be mistakenly set to an arbitrary value (e.g., **tv1.channel = 125**).

- Second, the class becomes difficult to maintain and vulnerable to bugs. Suppose you want to modify the **Circle** class to ensure that the radius is nonnegative after other programs have already used the class. You have to change not only the **Circle** class but also the programs that use it, because the clients may have modified the radius directly (e.g., **myCircle.radius = -5**).

VideoNote
Private data fields

To prevent direct modifications of data fields, don't let the client directly access data fields. This is known as *data hiding*. This can be done by defining *private data fields*. In Python, the private data fields are defined with two leading underscores. You can also define a *private method* named with two leading underscores.

data hiding
private data fields
private method

Private data fields and methods can be accessed within a class, but they cannot be accessed outside the class. To make a data field accessible for the client, provide a *get* method to return its value. To enable a data field to be modified, provide a *set* method to set a new value.

Colloquially, a **get** method is referred to as a *getter* (or *accessor*), and a **set** method is referred to as a *setter* (or *mutator*).

accessor
mutator

A **get** method has the following header:

def get*PropertyName*(self):

If the return type is Boolean, the **get** method is defined as follows by convention:

Boolean accessor

def is*PropertyName*(self):

A **set** method has the following header:

def set*PropertyName*(self, *propertyValue*):

Listing 7.6 revises the **Circle** class in Listing 7.1 by defining the **radius** property as private by placing two underscores in front of the property name (line 6).

LISTING 7.6 CircleWithPrivateRadius.py

```
1  import math
2
3  class Circle:
4      # Construct a circle object
5      def __init__(self, radius = 1):
6          self.__radius = radius
7
```

class name

initializer
private radius

getRadius()

```
8    def getRadius(self):
9        return self.__radius
10
11   def getPerimeter(self):
12       return 2 * self.__radius * math.pi
13
14   def getArea(self):
15       return self.__radius * self.__radius * math.pi
```

The **radius** property cannot be directly accessed in this new **Circle** class. However, you can read it by using the **getRadius()** method. For example:

```
1   >>> from CircleWithPrivateRadius import Circle
2   >>> c = Circle(5)
3   >>> c.__radius
4   AttributeError: no attribute '__radius'
5   >>> c.getRadius()
6   5
7   >>>
```

Line 1 imports the **Circle** class, which is defined in the **CircleWithPrivateRadius** module in Listing 7.6. Line 2 creates a **Circle** object. Line 3 attempts to access the property **__radius**. This causes an error, because **__radius** is private. However, you can use the **getRadius()** method to return the **radius** (line 5).

Tip
If a class is designed for other programs to use, to prevent data from being tampered with and to make the class easy to maintain, define data fields as private. If a class is only used internally by your own program, there is no need to hide the data fields.

Note
Name private data fields and methods with two leading underscores, but don't end the name with more than one underscores. The names with two leading underscores and two ending underscores have special meaning in Python. For example, **__radius** is a private data field, but, **__radius__** is not a private data field.

Check
Point

MyProgrammingLab™

7.13 What problem arises in running the following program? How do you fix it?

```
class A:
    def __init__(self, i):
        self.__i = i

def main():
    a = A(5)
    print(a.__i)

main() # Call the main function
```

7.14 Is the following code correct? If so, what is the printout?

```
1   def main():
2       a = A()
3       a.print()
4
```

```
 5   class A:
 6       def __init__(self, newS = "Welcome"):
 7           self.__s = newS
 8
 9       def print(self):
10           print(self.__s)
11
12   main()  # Call the main function
```

7.15   Is the following code correct? If not, fix the error.

```
class A:
    def __init__(self, on):
        self.__on = not on

def main():
    a = A(False)
    print(a.on)

main()  # Call the main function
```

7.16   What are the benefits of data hiding? How is it done in Python?

7.17   How do you define a private method?

7.6 Class Abstraction and Encapsulation

Class abstraction is a concept that separates class implementation from the use of a class. The class implementation details are invisible from the user. This is known as class encapsulation.

Key Point

There are many levels of abstraction in software development. In Chapter 6, you learned about function abstraction and used it in stepwise refinement. *Class abstraction* is the separation of class implementation from the use of a class. The creator of a class describes the class's functions and lets the client know how the class can be used. The class's collection of methods, together with the description of how these methods are expected to behave, serves as the *class's contract* with the client.

class abstraction

class's contract

As shown in Figure 7.8, the user of the class does not need to know how the class is implemented. The details of implementation are encapsulated and hidden from the user. This is known as *class encapsulation*. In essence, encapsulation combines data and methods into a single object and hides the data fields and method implementation from the user. For example, you can create a **Circle** object and find the area of the circle without knowing how the area is computed. For this reason, a class is also known as an *abstract data type* (ADT).

class encapsulation

abstract data type

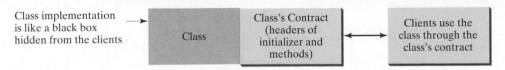

FIGURE 7.8   Class abstraction separates class implementation from the use of the class.

Class abstraction and encapsulation are two sides of the same coin. Many real-life examples illustrate the concept of class abstraction. Consider, for instance, building a computer system. Your personal computer has many components—a CPU, memory, disk, motherboard, fan, and so on. Each component can be viewed as an object that has properties and methods. To get the components to work together, you need to know only how each component is used and how it interacts with the others. You don't need to know how the components work internally. The internal implementation is encapsulated and hidden from you. You can even build a computer without knowing how a component is implemented.

The computer-system analogy precisely mirrors the object-oriented approach. Each component can be viewed as an object of the class for the component. For example, you might have a class that defines fans for use in a computer, with properties such as fan size and speed and methods such as start and stop. A specific fan is an instance of this class with specific property values.

As another example, consider getting a loan. A specific loan can be viewed as an object of a **Loan** class. The interest rate, loan amount, and loan period are its data properties, and computing monthly payment and total payment are its methods. When you buy a car, a loan object is created by instantiating the class with your loan interest rate, loan amount, and loan period. You can then use the methods to find the monthly payment and total payment of your loan. As a user of the **Loan** class, you don't need to know how these methods are implemented.

Listing 2.8, ComputeLoan.py, presented a program for computing loan payments. The program as it is currently written cannot be reused in other programs. One way to fix this problem is to define functions for computing monthly payment and total payment. However, this solution has limitations. Suppose you wish to associate a borrower with the loan. There is no good way to tie a borrower with a loan without using objects. The traditional procedural programming paradigm is action-driven; data are separated from actions. The object-oriented programming paradigm focuses on objects, so actions are defined along with the data in objects. To tie a borrower with a loan, you can define a loan class with borrower along with other properties of the loan as data fields. A loan object would then contain data and actions for manipulating and processing data, with loan data and actions integrated in one object. Figure 7.9 shows the UML class diagram for the **Loan** class. Note that the – (dash) in the UML class diagram denotes a private data field or method of the class.

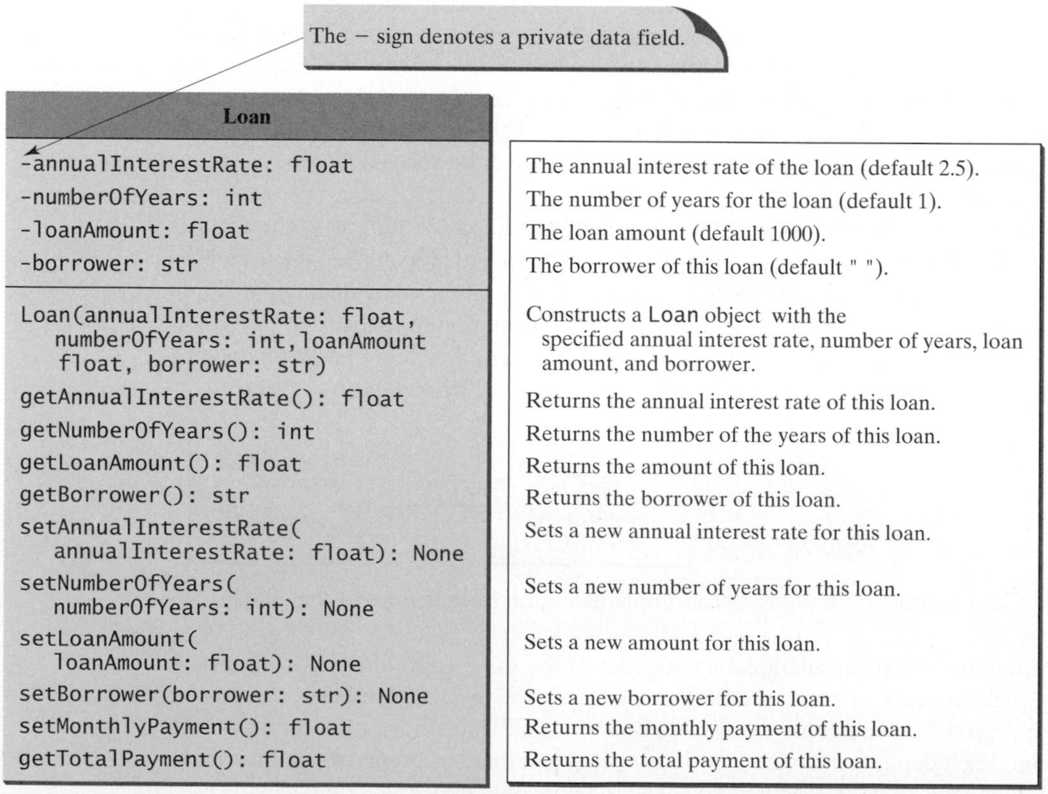

The − sign denotes a private data field.

Loan	
-annualInterestRate: float	The annual interest rate of the loan (default 2.5).
-numberOfYears: int	The number of years for the loan (default 1).
-loanAmount: float	The loan amount (default 1000).
-borrower: str	The borrower of this loan (default " ").
Loan(annualInterestRate: float, numberOfYears: int,loanAmount float, borrower: str)	Constructs a Loan object with the specified annual interest rate, number of years, loan amount, and borrower.
getAnnualInterestRate(): float	Returns the annual interest rate of this loan.
getNumberOfYears(): int	Returns the number of the years of this loan.
getLoanAmount(): float	Returns the amount of this loan.
getBorrower(): str	Returns the borrower of this loan.
setAnnualInterestRate(annualInterestRate: float): None	Sets a new annual interest rate for this loan.
setNumberOfYears(numberOfYears: int): None	Sets a new number of years for this loan.
setLoanAmount(loanAmount: float): None	Sets a new amount for this loan.
setBorrower(borrower: str): None	Sets a new borrower for this loan.
setMonthlyPayment(): float	Returns the monthly payment of this loan.
getTotalPayment(): float	Returns the total payment of this loan.

FIGURE 7.9 The UML diagram for the **Loan** class models (shows) the properties and behaviors of loans.

The UML diagram in Figure 7.9 serves as the contract for the **Loan** class. That is, the user can use the class without knowing how the class is implemented. Assume that the **Loan** class is available. We begin by writing a test program that uses the **Loan** class in Listing 7.7.

LISTING 7.7 TestLoanClass.py

```
1  from Loan import Loan
2
3  def main():
4      # Enter yearly interest rate
5      annualInterestRate = eval(input
6          ("Enter yearly interest rate, for example, 7.25: "))
7
8      # Enter number of years
9      numberOfYears = eval(input(
10         "Enter number of years as an integer: "))
11
12     # Enter loan amount
13     loanAmount = eval(input(
14         "Enter loan amount, for example, 120000.95: "))
15
16     # Enter a borrower
17     borrower = input("Enter a borrower's name: ")
18
19     # Create a Loan object
20     loan = Loan(annualInterestRate, numberOfYears,          create Loan object
21         loanAmount, borrower)
22
23     # Display loan date, monthly payment, and total payment
24     print("The loan is for", loan.getBorrower() )           invoke instance method
25     print("The monthly payment is",
26         format(loan.getMonthlyPayment() , ".2f"))           invoke instance method
27     print("The total payment is",
28         format(loan.getTotalPayment() , ".2f"))             invoke instance method
29
30  main() # Call the main function
```

```
Enter yearly interest rate, for example, 7.25: 2.5 ↵Enter
Enter number of years as an integer: 5 ↵Enter
Enter loan amount, for example, 120000.95: 1000 ↵Enter
Enter a borrower's name: John Jones ↵Enter
The loan is for John Jones
The monthly payment is 17.75
The total payment is 1064.84
```

The **main** function (1) reads the interest rate, payment period (in years), and loan amount, (2) creates a **Loan** object, and then (3) obtains the monthly payment (line 26) and total payment (line 28) using the instance methods in the **Loan** class.

The **Loan** class can be implemented as in Listing 7.8.

LISTING 7.8 Loan.py

```
1  class Loan :
2      def __init__(self, annualInterestRate = 2.5,           initializer
3          numberOfYears = 1, loanAmount = 1000, borrower = " "):
4          self.__annualInterestRate = annualInterestRate
5          self.__numberOfYears = numberOfYears
6          self.__loanAmount = loanAmount
```

```
 7              self.__borrower = borrower
 8
 9    def getAnnualInterestRate(self):
10        return self.__annualInterestRate
11
12    def getNumberOfYears(self):
13        return self.__numberOfYears
14
15    def getLoanAmount(self):
16        return self.__loanAmount
17
18    def getBorrower(self):
19        return self.__borrower
20
21    def setAnnualInterestRate(self, annualInterestRate):
22        self.__annualInterestRate = annualInterestRate
23
24    def setNumberOfYears(self, numberOfYears):
25        self.__numberOfYears = numberOfYears
26
27    def setLoanAmount(self, loanAmount):
28        self.__loanAmount = loanAmount
29
30    def setBorrower(self, borrower):
31        self.__borrower = borrower
32
33    def getMonthlyPayment(self):
34        monthlyInterestRate = self.__annualInterestRate / 1200
35        monthlyPayment = \
36          self.__loanAmount * monthlyInterestRate / (1 - (1 /
37          (1 + monthlyInterestRate) ** (self.__numberOfYears * 12)))
38        return monthlyPayment
39
40    def getTotalPayment(self):
41        totalPayment = self.getMonthlyPayment() * \
42            self.__numberOfYears * 12
43        return totalPayment
```

- get methods (lines 9–19)
- set methods (lines 21–31)
- getMonthlyPayment (line 33)
- getTotalPayment (line 40)

Because the data fields **annualInterestRate**, **numberOfYears**, **loanAmount**, and **borrower** are defined as private (with two leading underscores), they cannot be accessed from outside the class by a client program.

From a class developer's perspective, a class is designed for use by many different customers. In order to be useful in a wide range of applications, a class should provide a variety of ways for users to customize the class with methods.

Important Pedagogical Tip

The UML diagram for the **Loan** class is shown in Figure 7.9. You should first write a test program that uses the **Loan** class even though you don't know how the **Loan** class is implemented. This has three benefits:

- It demonstrates that developing a class and using a class are two separate tasks.
- It enables you to skip the complex implementation of certain classes without interrupting the sequence of the book.
- It is easier to learn how to implement a class if you are familiar with the class through using it.

For all the class development examples from now on, first create an object from the class and try to use its methods and then turn your attention to its implementation.

7.7 Object-Oriented Thinking

The procedural paradigm for programming focuses on designing functions. The object-oriented paradigm couples data and methods together into objects. Software design using the object-oriented paradigm focuses on objects and operations on objects.

Key Point

This book's approach is to teach problem solving and fundamental programming techniques before object-oriented programming. This section shows how procedural and object-oriented programming differ. You will see the benefits of object-oriented programming and learn to use it effectively. We will improve the solution for the BMI problem introduced in Chapter 4 by using the object-oriented approach. From the improvements, you will gain insight into the differences between procedural and object-oriented programming and see the benefits of developing reusable code using objects and classes.

Listing 4.6, ComputeBMI.py, presents a program for computing body mass index. The code as it is cannot be reused in other programs. To make it reusable, define a standalone function to compute body mass index, as follows:

def getBMI(weight, height):

This function is useful for computing body mass index for a specified weight and height. However, it has limitations. Suppose you need to associate the weight and height with a person's name and birth date. You could create separate variables to store these values, but these values are not tightly coupled. The ideal way to couple them is to create an object that contains them. Since these values are tied to individual objects, they should be stored in data fields. You can define a class named **BMI**, as shown in Figure 7.10.

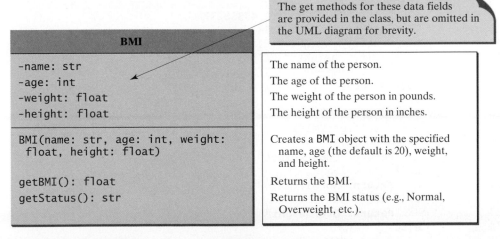

FIGURE 7.10 The **BMI** class encapsulates BMI data and methods.

Assume that the **BMI** class is available. Listing 7.9 is a test program that uses this class.

LISTING 7.9 UseBMIClass.py

```
1  from BMI import BMI
2
3  def main():
4      bmi1 = BMI("John Doe", 18, 145, 70)
5      print("The BMI for", bmi1.getName(), "is",
```

import BMI class

create an object
invoke method

```
 6            bmi1.getBMI(), bmi1.getStatus())
 7
 8    bmi2 = BMI("Peter King", 50, 215, 70)
 9    print("The BMI for", bmi2.getName(), "is",
10            bmi2.getBMI(), bmi2.getStatus())
11
12  main() # Call the main function
```

```
The BMI for John Doe is 20.81 Normal
The BMI for Peter King is 30.85 Obese
```

Line 4 creates an object **bmi1** for John Doe and line 8 creates an object **bmi2** for Peter King. You can use the methods **getName()**, **getBMI()**, and **getStatus()** to return the BMI information in a **BMI** object (lines 5 and 9).

The **BMI** class can be implemented as in Listing 7.10.

LISTING 7.10 BMI.py

```
 1  class BMI:
 2      def __init__(self, name, age, weight, height):
 3          self.__name = name
 4          self.__age = age
 5          self.__weight = weight
 6          self.__height = height
 7
 8      def getBMI(self):
 9          KILOGRAMS_PER_POUND = 0.45359237
10          METERS_PER_INCH = 0.0254
11          bmi = self.__weight * KILOGRAMS_PER_POUND /  \
12              ((self.__height * METERS_PER_INCH) * \
13              (self.__height * METERS_PER_INCH))
14          return round(bmi * 100) / 100
15
16      def getStatus(self):
17          bmi = self.getBMI()
18          if bmi < 18.5:
19              return "Underweight"
20          elif bmi < 25:
21              return "Normal"
22          elif bmi < 30:
23              return "Overweight"
24          else:
25              return "Obese"
26
27      def getName(self):
28          return self.__name
29
30      def getAge(self):
31          return self.__age
32
33      def getWeight(self):
34          return self.__weight
35
36      def getHeight(self):
37          return self.__height
```

The mathematical formula for computing the BMI using weight and height is given in Section 4.9. The method **getBMI()** returns the BMI. Since the weight and height are data fields in the object, the **getBMI()** method can use these properties to compute the BMI for the object.

The method **getStatus()** returns a string that interprets the BMI. The interpretation is also given in Section 4.9.

This example demonstrates the advantages of the object-oriented paradigm over the procedural paradigm. The object-oriented approach combines the power of the procedural paradigm with an added dimension that integrates data with operations into objects.

procedural vs. object-oriented paradigms

In procedural programming, data and operations are separate, and this methodology requires sending data to methods. Object-oriented programming places data and the operations that pertain to them together in an object. This approach solves many of the problems inherent in procedural programming. The object-oriented programming approach organizes programs in a way that mirrors the real world, in which all objects are associated with both attributes and activities. Using objects improves software reusability and makes programs easier to develop and easier to maintain. Programming in Python involves thinking in terms of objects; a Python program can be viewed as a collection of cooperating objects.

7.18 Describe the differences between procedural and object-oriented paradigms.

MyProgrammingLab™

KEY TERMS

abstract data type (ADT)   229
accessor (getter)   227
actions   216
anonymous object   219
attributes   216
behavior   216
class   216
class abstraction   229
class encapsulation   229
class's contract   229
client   221
constructor   218
data fields   216
data hiding   227
dot operator (.)   219

identity   216
initializer   217
instance   217
instance method   219
instance variable   220
instantiation   217
mutator (setter)   227
object-oriented programming
   (OOP)   216
private data fields   227
private method   227
property   216
state   216
Unified Modeling Language
   (UML)   222

CHAPTER SUMMARY

1. A *class* is a template, a blueprint, a contract, and a data type for objects. It defines the properties of objects and provides an *initializer* for initializing objects and methods for manipulating them.

2. The initializer is always named **__init__**. The first parameter in each method including the initializer in the class refers to the object that calls the method. By convention, this parameter is named **self**.

3. An object is an *instance* of a class. You use the *constructor* to create an object, and the *dot operator* (**.**) to access members of that object through its reference variable.

4. An instance variable or method belongs to an instance of a class. Its use is associated with individual instances.

5. *Data fields* in classes should be hidden to prevent data tampering and to make classes easy to maintain.

6. You can provide a **get** method or a **set** method to enable clients to see or modify the data. Colloquially, a **get** method is referred to as a *getter* (or *accessor*), and a **set** method as a *setter* (or *mutator*).

TEST QUESTIONS

Do test questions for this chapter online at www.cs.armstrong.edu/liang/py/test.html.

MyProgrammingLab™

PROGRAMMING EXERCISES

Sections 7.2–7.3

7.1 (*The* **Rectangle** *class*) Following the example of the **Circle** class in Section 7.2, design a class named **Rectangle** to represent a rectangle. The class contains:

- Two data fields named **width** and **height**.
- A constructor that creates a rectangle with the specified **width** and **height**. The default values are **1** and **2** for the **width** and **height**, respectively.
- A method named **getArea()** that returns the area of this rectangle.
- A method named **getPerimeter()** that returns the perimeter.

Draw the UML diagram for the class, and then implement the class. Write a test program that creates two **Rectangle** objects—one with width **4** and height **40** and the other with width **3.5** and height **35.7**. Display the width, height, area, and perimeter of each rectangle in this order.

Sections 7.4–7.7

7.2 (*The* **Stock** *class*) Design a class named **Stock** to represent a company's stock that contains:

- A private string data field named **symbol** for the stock's symbol.
- A private string data field named **name** for the stock's name.
- A private float data field named **previousClosingPrice** that stores the stock price for the previous day.
- A private float data field named **currentPrice** that stores the stock price for the current time.
- A constructor that creates a stock with the specified symbol, name, previous price, and current price.
- A get method for returning the stock name.
- A get method for returning the stock symbol.
- Get and set methods for getting/setting the stock's previous price.
- Get and set methods for getting/setting the stock's current price.
- A method named **getChangePercent()** that returns the percentage changed from **previousClosingPrice** to **currentPrice**.

Draw the UML diagram for the class, and then implement the class. Write a test program that creates a **Stock** object with the stock symbol INTC, the name Intel

Corporation, the previous closing price of **20.5**, and the new current price of **20.35**, and display the price-change percentage.

7.3 (*The Account class*) Design a class named **Account** that contains:

- A private **int** data field named **id** for the account.
- A private float data field named **balance** for the account.
- A private float data field named **annualInterestRate** that stores the current interest rate.
- A constructor that creates an account with the specified id (default 0), initial balance (default 100), and annual interest rate (default 0).
- The accessor and mutator methods for **id**, **balance**, and **annualInterestRate**.
- A method named **getMonthlyInterestRate()** that returns the monthly interest rate.
- A method named **getMonthlyInterest()** that returns the monthly interest.
- A method named **withdraw** that withdraws a specified amount from the account.
- A method named **deposit** that deposits a specified amount to the account.

Draw the UML diagram for the class, and then implement the class. (Hint: The method **getMonthlyInterest()** is to return the monthly interest amount, not the interest rate. Use this formula to calculate the monthly interest: **balance * monthlyInterestRate**. **monthlyInterestRate** is **annualInterestRate / 12**. Note that **annualInterestRate** is a percent (like 4.5%). You need to divide it by **100**.)

Write a test program that creates an **Account** object with an account id of 1122, a balance of $20,000, and an annual interest rate of 4.5%. Use the **withdraw** method to withdraw $2,500, use the **deposit** method to deposit $3,000, and print the id, balance, monthly interest rate, and monthly interest.

7.4 (*The Fan class*) Design a class named **Fan** to represent a fan. The class contains:

- Three constants named **SLOW**, **MEDIUM**, and **FAST** with the values **1**, **2**, and **3** to denote the fan speed.
- A private **int** data field named **speed** that specifies the speed of the fan.
- A private **bool** data field named **on** that specifies whether the fan is on (the default is **False**).
- A private **float** data field named **radius** that specifies the radius of the fan.
- A private string data field named **color** that specifies the color of the fan.
- The accessor and mutator methods for all four data fields.
- A constructor that creates a fan with the specified speed (default **SLOW**), radius (default **5**), color (default **blue**), and on (default **False**).

Draw the UML diagram for the class and then implement the class. Write a test program that creates two **Fan** objects. For the first object, assign the maximum speed, radius **10**, color **yellow**, and turn it on. Assign medium speed, radius **5**, color **blue**, and turn it off for the second object. Display each object's **speed**, **radius**, **color**, and **on** properties.

*7.5 (*Geometry: n-sided regular polygon*) An *n*-sided regular polygon's sides all have the same length and all of its angles have the same degree (i.e., the polygon is both equilateral and equiangular). Design a class named **RegularPolygon** that contains:

- A private **int** data field named **n** that defines the number of sides in the polygon.
- A private float data field named **side** that stores the length of the side.
- A private float data field named **x** that defines the *x*-coordinate of the center of the polygon with default value **0**.

- A private float data field named **y** that defines the y-coordinate of the center of the polygon with default value **0**.
- A constructor that creates a regular polygon with the specified n (default **3**), side (default **1**), x (default **0**), and y (default **0**).
- The accessor and mutator methods for all data fields.
- The method **getPerimeter()** that returns the perimeter of the polygon.
- The method **getArea()** that returns the area of the polygon. The formula for computing the area of a regular polygon is $Area = \dfrac{n \times s^2}{4 \times \tan\left(\dfrac{\pi}{n}\right)}$.

Draw the UML diagram for the class, and then implement the class. Write a test program that creates three **RegularPolygon** objects, created using **RegularPolygon()**, using **RegularPolygon(6, 4)** and **RegularPolygon(10, 4, 5.6, 7.8)**. For each object, display its perimeter and area.

*7.6 (*Algebra: quadratic equations*) Design a class named **QuadraticEquation** for a quadratic equation $ax^2 + bx + x = 0$. The class contains:
- The private data fields **a**, **b**, and **c** that represent three coefficients.
- A constructor for the arguments for **a**, **b**, and **c**.
- Three **get** methods for **a**, **b**, and **c**.
- A method named **getDiscriminant()** that returns the discriminant, which is $b^2 - 4ac$.
- The methods named **getRoot1()** and **getRoot2()** for returning the two roots of the equation using these formulas:

$$r_1 = \frac{-b + \sqrt{b^2 - 4ac}}{2a} \quad \text{and} \quad r_2 = \frac{-b - \sqrt{b^2 - 4ac}}{2a}$$

These methods are useful only if the discriminant is nonnegative. Let these methods return **0** if the discriminant is negative.

Draw the UML diagram for the class, and then implement the class. Write a test program that prompts the user to enter values for a, b, and c and displays the result based on the discriminant. If the discriminant is positive, display the two roots. If the discriminant is **0**, display the one root. Otherwise, display "The equation has no roots." See Exercise 4.1 for sample runs.

*7.7 (*Algebra: 2 × 2 linear equations*) Design a class named **LinearEquation** for a 2 × 2 system of linear equations:

$$\begin{array}{l} ax + by = e \\ cx + dy = f \end{array} \qquad x = \frac{ed - bf}{ad - bc} \qquad y = \frac{af - ec}{ad - bc}$$

The class contains:

- The private data fields **a**, **b**, **c**, **d**, **e**, and **f** with get methods.
- A constructor with the arguments for **a**, **b**, **c**, **d**, **e**, and **f**.
- Six **get** methods for **a**, **b**, **c**, **d**, **e**, and **f**.
- A method named **isSolvable()** that returns true if $ad - bc$ is not **0**.
- The methods **getX()** and **getY()** that return the solution for the equation.

Draw the UML diagram for the class, and then implement the class. Write a test program that prompts the user to enter **a**, **b**, **c**, **d**, **e**, and **f** and displays the result. If $ad - bc$ is **0**, report that "The equation has no solution." See Exercise 4.3 for sample runs.

*7.8 (*Stopwatch*) Design a class named **StopWatch**. The class contains:

- The private data fields **startTime** and **endTime** with get methods.
- A constructor that initializes **startTime** with the current time.
- A method named **start()** that resets the **startTime** to the current time.
- A method named **stop()** that sets the **endTime** to the current time.
- A method named **getElapsedTime()** that returns the elapsed time for the stop watch in milliseconds.

Draw the UML diagram for the class, and then implement the class. Write a test program that measures the execution time of adding numbers from 1 to 1,000,000.

7.9 (*Geometry: intersection*) Suppose two line segments intersect. The two endpoints for the first line segment are (x1, y1**) and (**x2, y2**) and for the second line segment are (**x3, y3**) and (**x4, y4**). Write a program that prompts the user to enter these four endpoints and displays the intersecting point. (Hint: Use the **LinearEquation** class from Exercise 7.7.)

```
Enter the endpoints of the first line segment: 2.0, 2.0, 0, 0  ↵Enter
Enter the endpoints of the second line segment: 0, 2.0, 2.0, 0  ↵Enter
The intersecting point is: (1.0, 1.0)
```

*7.10 (*The Time class*) Design a class named **Time**. The class contains:

- The private data fields **hour**, **minute**, and **second** that represent a time.
- A constructor that constructs a **Time** object that initializes **hour**, **minute**, and **second** using the current time.
- The **get** methods for the data fields **hour**, **minute**, and **second**, respectively.
- A method named **setTime(elapseTime)** that sets a new time for the object using the elapsed time in seconds. For example, if the elapsed time is **555550** seconds, the hour is **10**, the minute is **19**, and the second is **12**.

Draw the UML diagram for the class, and then implement the class. Write a test program that creates a **Time** object and displays its hour, minute, and second. Your program then prompts the user to enter an elapsed time, sets its elapsed time in the **Time** object, and displays its hour, minute, and second. Here is a sample run:

```
Current time is 12:41:6
Enter the elapsed time: 55550505  ↵Enter
The hour:minute:second for the elapsed time is 22:41:45
```

(Hint: The initializer will extract the hour, minute, and second from the elapsed time. The current elapsed time can be obtained using **time.time()**, as shown in Listing 2.7, ShowCurrentTime.py.)

MORE ON STRINGS AND SPECIAL METHODS

Objectives

- To learn how to create strings (§8.2.1).

- To use the `len`, `min`, and `max` functions to obtain the length of a string or the smallest or largest character in a string (§8.2.2).

- To access string elements by using the index operator (`[]`) (§8.2.3).

- To get a substring from a larger string by using the slicing `str[start : end]` operator (§8.2.4).

- To concatenate strings by using the + operator and to duplicate strings by using the * operator (§8.2.5).

- To use the `in` and `not in` operators to determine whether a string is contained within another string (§8.2.6).

- To compare strings by using comparison operators (==, !=, <, <=, >, and >=) (§8.2.7).

- To iterate characters in a string by using a for loop (§8.2.8).

- To test strings by using the methods `isalnum`, `isalpha`, `isdigit`, `isidentifier`, `islower`, `isupper`, and `isspace` (§8.2.9).

- To search for substrings by using the methods `endswith`, `startswith`, `find`, `rfind`, and `count` (§8.2.10).

- To convert strings by using the methods `capitalize`, `lower`, `upper`, `title`, `swapcase`, and `replace` (§8.2.11).

- To strip whitespaces from the left and/or right of a string by using the methods `lstrip`, `rstrip`, and `strip` (§8.2.12).

- To format strings by using the methods `center`, `ljust`, `rjust`, and `format` (§8.2.13).

- To apply strings in the development of applications (`CheckPalindrome`, `HexToDecimalConversion`) (§§8.3–8.4).

- To define special methods for operators (§8.5).

- To design the `Rational` class for representing rational numbers (§8.6).

8.1 Introduction

The focus of this chapter is on class design using Python's **str** *class as an example and exploring the role of special methods in Python.*

The preceding chapter introduced the important concepts of objects and classes. You learned how to define classes as well as how to create and use objects. The **str** class is not only useful for processing strings, but it is also a good example of class design. This class was introduced in Chapter 3. We will discuss the **str** class in depth in this chapter.

The special methods play an important role in Python. This chapter will also introduce special methods and operator overloading, and design classes using special methods.

8.2 The **str** Class

A **str** *object is immutable; that is, its content cannot be changed once the string is created.*

In Chapter 7, you learned how to define the classes **Loan** and **BMI** and create objects from these classes. You will frequently use the classes that come with the Python library to develop programs. This section introduces the Python **str** class.

Strings are fundamental in computer science, and processing strings is a common task in programming. Strings are the objects of the **str** class. So far, you have used strings in input and output. The **input** function returns a string from the keyboard and the **print** function displays a string on the monitor.

VideoNote

String methods

8.2.1 Creating Strings

You can create strings by using the constructor, as follows:

```
s1 = str() # Create an empty string object
s2 = str("Welcome") # Create a string object for Welcome
```

Python provides a simple syntax for creating a string object by using a string value. For example,

```
s1 = " " # Same as s1 = str()
s2 = "Welcome" # Same as s2 = str("Welcome")
```

A string object is immutable: once it is created, its contents cannot be changed. To optimize performance, Python uses one object for strings that have the same content. As shown in Figure 8.1, both **s1** and **s2** refer to the same string object and have the same id number.

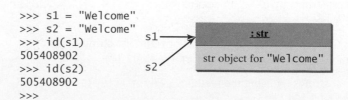

FIGURE 8.1 Strings with the same content are actually the same object.

This behavior is true for all immutable objects in the Python library. For example, **int** is an immutable class. Two **int** objects with the same value actually share the same object, as shown in Figure 8.2.

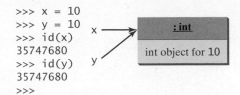

```
>>> x = 10
>>> y = 10
>>> id(x)
35747680
>>> id(y)
35747680
>>>
```

FIGURE 8.2 All immutable objects with the same content are stored in one object.

8.2.2 Functions for Strings

Several of Python's built-in functions can be used with strings. You can use the **len** function ~~len~~ len
to return the number of the characters in a string, and the **max** and **min** functions (introduced ~~max~~ max
in Chapter 3) to return the largest or smallest character in a string. Here are some examples: ~~min~~ min

```
1  >>> s = "Welcome"
2  >>> len(s)
3  7
4  >>> max(s)
5  'o'
6  >>> min(s)
7  'W'
8  >>>
```

Since **s** has **7** characters, **len(s)** returns **7** (line 3). Note that the lowercase letters have a higher ASCII value than the uppercase letters, so **max(s)** returns **o** (line 5) and **min(s)** returns **W** (line 7).

Here is another example:

```
s = input("Enter a string: ")
if len(s) % 2 == 0:
    print(s, "contains an even number of characters")
else:
    print(s, "contains an odd number of characters")
```

If you enter **computer** when running the code, it displays

```
computer contains an even number of characters
```

8.2.3 Index Operator [ ]

A string is a sequence of characters. A character in the string can be accessed through the index operator using the syntax:

```
s[index]
```

The indexes are **0** based; that is, they range from **0** to **len(s)-1**, as shown in Figure 8.3.   0 based

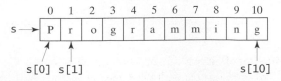

FIGURE 8.3 The characters in a string can be accessed via an index operator.

For example,

```
>>> s = "Welcome"
>>> for i in range(0, len(s), 2):
...     print(s[i], end = '')
Wloe
>>>
```

In the **for** loop, i is **0**, **2**, **4**, and **6**. So, **s[0]**, **s[2]**, **s[4]**, and **s[6]** are displayed.

Python also allows the use of negative numbers as indexes to reference positions relative to the end of the string. The actual position is obtained by adding the length of the string with the negative index. For example,

```
1  >>> s = "Welcome"
2  >>> s[-1]
3  'e'
4  >>> s[-2]
5  'm'
6  >>>
```

In line 2, **s[-1]** is the same as **s[-1 + len(s)]**, which is the last character in the string. In line 4, **s[-2]** is the same as **s[-2 + len(s)]**, which is the second last character in the string.

Note that since strings are immutable, you cannot change their contents. For example, the following code is illegal:

```
s[2] = 'A'
```

8.2.4 The Slicing Operator [start : end]

slicing operator

The *slicing operator* returns a slice of the string using the syntax **s[start : end]**. The slice is a substring from index **start** to index **end** – **1**. For example,

```
1  >>> s = "Welcome"
2  >>> s[1 : 4]
3  'elc'
```

s[1 : 4] returns a substring from index **1** to index **3**.

The starting index or ending index may be omitted. In this case, by default the starting index is **0** and the ending index is the last index. For example,

```
1  >>> s = "Welcome"
2  >>> s[ : 6]
3  'Welcom'
4  >>> s[4 : ]
5  'ome'
6  >>> s[1 : -1]
7  'elcom'
8  >>>
```

In line 2, **s[: 6]** is the same as **s[0 : 6]**, which returns a substring from index **0** to index **5**. In line 4, **s[4 :]** is the same as **s[4 : 7]**, which returns a substring from index **4** to index **6**. You can also use a negative index in slicing. For example, in line 6, **s[1 : -1]** is the same as **s[1 : -1 + len(s)]**.

negative index

> **Note**
> If index (**i** or **j**) in the slice operation **s[i : j]** is negative, replace the index with **len(s) + index**. If **j > len(s)**, **j** is set to **len(s)**. If **i >= j**, the slice is empty.

8.2.5 The Concatenation (+) and Repetition (*) Operators

You can join, or concatenate, two strings by using the *concatenation operator* (+). You can also use the *repetition operator* (*) to concatenate the same string multiple times. Here are some examples:

concatenation operator

repetition operator

```
1  >>> s1 = "Welcome"
2  >>> s2 = "Python"
3  >>> s3 = s1 + " to " + s2
4  >>> s3
5  'Welcome to Python'
6  >>> s4 = 3 * s1
7  >>> s4
8  'WelcomeWelcomeWelcome'
9  >>> s5 = s1 * 3
10 >>> s5
11 'WelcomeWelcomeWelcome'
12 >>>
```

Note that **3 * s1** and **s1 * 3** have the same effect (lines 6–11).

8.2.6 The **in** and **not in** Operators

You can use the **in** and **not in** operators to test whether a string is in another string. Here are some examples:

```
>>> s1 = "Welcome"
>>> "come" in s1
True
>>> "come" not in s1
False
>>>
```

Here is another example:

```
s = input("Enter a string: ")
if "Python" in s:
    print("Python", "is in", s)
```

```
    else:
        print("Python", "is not in", s)
```

If you run the program by entering `Welcome to Python` as the string, the program should display

```
python is in Welcome to Python.
```

8.2.7 Comparing Strings

You can compare strings by using the comparison operators (==, !=, >, >=, <, and <=, introduced in Section 4.2). Python compares strings by comparing their corresponding characters, and it does this by evaluating the characters' numeric codes. For example, **a** is larger than **A** because the numeric code for **a** is larger than the numeric code for **A**. See Appendix B, The ASCII Character Set, to find the numeric codes for characters.

Suppose you need to compare the strings **s1** ("**Jane**") with **s2** ("**Jake**"). The first two characters (**J** vs. **J**) from **s1** and **s2** are compared. Because they are equal, the second two characters (**a** vs. **a**) are compared. Because they are equal, the third two characters (**n** vs. **k**) are compared. Since **n** has a greater ASCII value than **k**, **s1** is greater than **s2**.

Here are some examples:

```
>>> "green" == "glow"
False
>>> "green" != "glow"
True
>>> "green" > "glow"
True
>>> "green" >= "glow"
True
>>> "green" < "glow"
False
>>> "green" <= "glow"
False
>>> "ab" <= "abc"
True
>>>
```

Here is another example:

```
1  s1 = input("Enter the first string: ")
2  s2 = input("Enter the second string: ")
3  if s2 < s1:
4      s1, s2 = s2, s1
5
6  print("The two strings are in this order:", s1, s2)
```

If you run the program by entering **Peter** and then **John**, **s1** is **Peter** and **s2** is **John** (lines 1–2). Since **s2 < s1** is **True** (line 3), they are swapped in line 4. Therefore the program displays the following message in line 6.

```
The two strings are in this order: John Peter
```

8.2.8 Iterating a String

A string is *iterable*. This means that you can use a for loop to traverse all characters in the string sequentially. For example, the following code displays all the characters in the string **s**:

for loop
iterable

```
for ch in s:
    print(ch)
```

You can read the code as "for each character **ch** in **s**, print **ch**."

The for loop does not use indexes to access characters. However, you still have to use indexes if you wish to traverse the characters in the string in a different order. For example, the following code displays the characters at odd-numbered positions in the string:

```
for i in range(0, len(s), 2):
    print(s[i])
```

The code uses variable **i** as the index for string **s**. **i** is initially **0**, then increment by **2** successively, before it reaches or exceeds **len(s)**. For each value **i**, **s[i]** is printed.

8.2.9 Testing Strings

The **str** class has many useful methods. The methods in Figure 8.4 test the characters in the string.

str	
isalnum(): bool	Returns True if characters in this string are alphanumeric and there is at least one character.
isalpha(): bool	Returns True if characters in this string are alphabetic and there is at least one character.
isdigit(): bool	Returns True if this string contains only number characters.
isidentifier(): bool	Returns True if this string is a Python identifier.
islower(): bool	Returns True if all characters in this string are lowercase lettters and there is at least one character.
isupper(): bool	Returns True if all characters in this string are uppercase lettters and there is at least one character.
isspace(): bool	Returns True if this string contains only whitespace characters.

FIGURE 8.4 The **str** class contains these methods for testing its characters.

Here are some examples of using the string testing methods:

```
1  >>> s = "welcome to python"
2  >>> s.isalnum()
3  False
4  >>> "Welcome".isalpha()
5  True
6  >>> "2012".isdigit()
7  True
8  >>> "first Number".isidentifier()
9  False
```

```
10  >>> s.islower()
11  True
12  >>> s.isupper()
13  False
14  >>> s.isspace()
15  False
16  >>>
```

s.isalnum() returns **False** (line 2), because **s** contains spaces, which are not letters or numerals. **Welcome** contains all letters (line 4), so **"Welcome".isalpha()** returns **True**. Since **2012** contains all numerals, **"2012".isdigit()** returns **True** (line 6). And because **first Number** contains a space, it is not an identifier, so **"first Number".isidentifier()** returns **False** (line 8).

Here is another example:

```
s = "2011"
if s.isdigit():
    print(s, "is a numeric string")
```

The code displays

```
2011 is a numeric string
```

8.2.10 Searching for Substrings

You can search for a substring in a string by using the methods in Figure 8.5.

str	
endswith(s1: str): bool	Returns True if the string ends with the substring s1.
startswith(s1: str): bool	Returns True if the string starts with the substring s1.
find(s1): int	Returns the lowest index where s1 starts in this string, or –1 if s1 is not found in this string.
rfind(s1): int	Returns the highest index where s1 starts in this string, or –1 if s1 is not found in this string.
count(substring): int	Returns the number of non-overlapping occurrences of this substring.

FIGURE 8.5 The **str** class contains these methods for searching substrings.

string search methods

Here are some examples of using the string search methods:

```
1  >>> s = "welcome to python"
2  >>> s.endswith("thon")
3  True
4  >>> s.startswith("good")
5  False
6  >>> s.find("come")
```

```
 7  3
 8  >>> s.find("become")
 9  -1
10  >>> s.rfind("o")
11  17
12  >>> s.count("o")
13  3
14  >>>
```

Since **come** is found in string **s** at index **3**, **s.find("come")** returns **3** (line 7). Because the first occurrence of substring **o** from the right is at index 17, **s.rfind("o")** returns **17** (line 11). In line 8, **s.find("become")** returns **−1**, since **become** is not in **s**. In line 12, **s.count("o")** returns **3**, because **o** appears three times in **s**.

Here is another example:

```
s = input("Enter a string: ")
if s.startswith("comp"):
    print(s, "begins with comp")
if s.endswith("er"):
    print(s, "ends with er")

print('e', "appears", s.count('e'), "time in", s)
```

If you enter **computer** when running the code, it displays

```
computer begins with comp
computer ends with er
e appears 1 time in computer
```

8.2.11 Converting Strings

You can make a copy of a string by using the methods shown in Figure 8.6. These methods let you control the capitalization of letters in the string's copy, or to replace the string entirely.

str	
capitalize(): str	Returns a copy of this string with only the first character capitalized.
lower(): str	Returns a copy of this string with all letters converted to lowercase.
upper(): str	Returns a copy of this string with all letters converted to uppercase.
title(): str	Returns a copy of this string with the first letter capitalized in each word.
swapcase(): str	Returns a copy of this string in which lowercase letters are converted to uppercase and uppercase to lowercase.
replace(old, new): str	Returns a new string that replaces all the occurrences of the old string with a new string.

FIGURE 8.6 The **str** class contains these methods for converting letter cases in strings and for replacing one string with another.

The **capitalize()** method returns a copy of the string in which the first letter in the string is capitalized. The **lower()** and **upper()** methods return a copy of the string in which all letters are in lowercase or uppercase. The **title()** method returns a copy of the string in which the first letter in each word is capitalized. The **swapCase()** method returns a copy of the string in which the lowercase letters are converted to uppercase and the uppercase letters are converted to lowercase. The **replace(old, new)** method returns a new string that replaces the substring **old** with substring **new**. Here are some examples of using these methods:

```
 1  >>> s = "welcome to python"
 2  >>> s1 = s.capitalize()
 3  >>> s1
 4  'Welcome to python'
 5  >>> s2 = s.title()
 6  >>> s2
 7  'Welcome To Python'
 8  >>> s = "New England"
 9  >>> s3 = s.lower()
10  >>> s3
11  'new england'
12  >>> s4 = s.upper()
13  >>> s4
14  'NEW ENGLAND'
15  >>> s5 = s.swapcase()
16  >>> s5
17  'nEW eNGLAND'
18  >>> s6 = s.replace("England", "Haven")
19  >>> s6
20  'New Haven'
21  >>> s
22  'New England'
23  >>>
```

 Note

As stated earlier, a string is immutable. None of the methods in the **str** class changes the contents of the string; instead, these methods create new strings. As shown in the preceding script, **s** is still **New England** (lines 21–22) after applying the methods **s.lower()**, **s.upper()**, **s.swapcase()**, and **s.replace("England", "Haven")**.

8.2.12   Stripping Whitespace Characters from a String

You can use the methods in Figure 8.7 to strip whitespace characters from the front, end, or both the front and end of a string. Recall that the characters **' '**, **\t**, **\f**, **\r**, and **\n** are called the *whitespace characters* (Section 3.5).

str	
lstrip(): str	Returns a string with the leading whitespace characters removed.
rstrip(): str	Returns a string with the trailing whitespace characters removed.
strip(): str	Returns a string with the starting and trailing whitespace characters removed.

FIGURE 8.7 The **str** class contains these methods for stripping leading and trailing whitespace characters.

Here are some examples of using the string stripping methods:

```
1  >>> s = "  Welcome to Python\t"
2  >>> s1 = s.lstrip()
3  >>> s1
4  'Welcome to Python\t'
5  >>> s2 = s.rstrip()
6  >>> s2
7  '  Welcome to Python'
8  >>> s3 = s.strip()
9  >>> s3
10  'Welcome to Python'
11  >>>
```

In line 2, **s.lstrip()** strips the whitespace characters in **s** from the left. In line 5, **s.rstrip()** strips the whitespace characters in **s** from the right. In line 8, **s.strip()** strips the whitespace characters in **s** from both the left and right.

 Note
The stripping methods only strip the whitespace characters in the front and end of a string. The whitespace characters surrounded by non-whitespace characters are not stripped.

 Tip
It is a good practice to apply the **strip()** method on an input string to ensure that any unwanted whitespace characters at the end of the input are stripped.

8.2.13 Formatting Strings

You can use the methods in Figure 8.8 to return a formatted string.

str	
center(width): str	Returns a copy of this string centered in a field of the given width.
ljust(width): str	Returns a string left justified in a field of the given width.
rjust(width): str	Returns a string right justified in a field of the given width.
format(items): str	Formats a string.

FIGURE 8.8 The **str** class contains these formatting methods.

Here are some examples that use the **center**, **ljust**, and **rjust** methods:

```
1  >>> s = "Welcome"
2  >>> s1 = s.center(11)
3  >>> s1
4  '  Welcome  '
5  >>> s2 = s.ljust(11)
6  >>> s2
7  'Welcome    '
8  >>> s3 = s.rjust(11)
9  >>> s3
10 '    Welcome'
11 >>>
```

In line 2, **s.center(11)** places **s** in the center of a string with **11** characters. In line 5, **s.ljust(11)** places **s** at the left of a string with **11** characters. In line 8, **s.rjust(11)** places **s** at the right of a string with **11** characters.

Section 3.6 introduced the **format** function for formatting a number or a string. The **str** class has a **format** method, covered in Supplement II.C, which is very similar to the **format** function.

8.1 Suppose that **s1**, **s2**, **s3**, and **s4** are four strings, given as follows:

```
s1 = "Welcome to Python"
s2 = s1
s3 = "Welcome to Python"
s4 = "to"
```

What are the results of the following expressions?

a. s1 == s2
b. s2.count('o')
c. id(s1) == id(s2)
d. id(s1) == id(s3)
e. s1 <= s4
f. s2 >= s4
g. s1 != s4
h. s1.upper()
i. s1.find(s4)
j. s1[4]
k. s1[4 : 8]

l. 4 * s4
m. len(s1)
n. max(s1)
o. min(s1)
p. s1[-4]
q. s1.lower()
r. s1.rfind('o')
s. s1.startswith("o")
t. s1.endswith("o")
u. s1.isalpha()
v. s1 + s1

8.2 Suppose that **s1** and **s2** are two strings. Which of the following statements or expressions are incorrect?

```
s1 = "programming 101"
s2 = "programming is fun"
s3 = s1 + s2
s3 = s1 - s2
s1 == s2
s1 >= s2
```

```
i = len(s1)
c = s1[0]
t = s1[ : 5]
t = s1[5 : ]
```

8.3 What is the printout of the following code?

```
s1 = "Welcome to Python"
s2 = s1.replace("o","abc")
print(s1)
print(s2)
```

8.4 Let **s1** be " Welcome " and **s2** be " welcome ". Write the code for the following statements:

(a) Check whether **s1** is equal to **s2** and assign the result to a Boolean variable **isEqual**.

(b) Check whether **s1** is equal to **s2**, ignoring case, and assign the result to a Boolean variable **isEqual**.

(c) Check whether **s1** has the prefix **AAA** and assign the result to a Boolean variable **b**.

(d) Check whether **s1** has the suffix **AAA** and assign the result to a Boolean variable **b**.

(e) Assign the length of **s1** to a variable **x**.

(f) Assign the first character of **s1** to a variable **x**.

(g) Create a new string **s3** that combines **s1** with **s2**.

(h) Create a substring of **s1** starting from index **1**.

(i) Create a substring of **s1** from index **1** to index **4**.

(j) Create a new string **s3** that converts **s1** to lowercase.

(k) Create a new string **s3** that converts **s1** to uppercase.

(l) Create a new string **s3** that trims whitespace characters on both ends of **s1**.

(m) Replace **e** with **E** in **s1**.

(n) Assign the index of the first occurrence of character **e** in **s1** to a variable **x**.

(o) Assign the index of the last occurrence of string **abc** in **s1** to a variable **x**.

8.5 Does any method in the string object change the contents of the string?

8.6 Suppose string **s** is an empty string; what is **len(s)**?

8.7 How do you determine whether a character is in lowercase or uppercase?

8.8 How do you determine whether a character is alphanumeric?

8.3 Case Study: Checking Palindromes

This section presents a program that checks whether a string is a palindrome.

Key Point

A string is a palindrome if it reads the same forward and backward. The words "mom," "dad," and "noon," for instance, are all palindromes.

The problem is to write a program that prompts the user to enter a string and reports whether the string is a palindrome. One solution is to have the program check whether the first character in the string is the same as the last character. If so, then the program can check whether the second character is the same as the second-to-last character. This process continues until a mismatch is found or all the characters in the string are checked, except for the middle character if the string has an odd number of characters.

To implement this idea, use two variables, say **low** and **high**, to denote the position of two characters at the beginning and the end in a string **s**, as shown in Listing 8.1 (lines 13 and 16). Initially, **low** is **0** and **high** is **len(s)** − **1**. If the two characters at these positions match, increment **low** by **1** and decrement **high** by **1** (lines 22–23). This process continues until (**low** >= **high**) or a mismatch is found.

LISTING 8.1 CheckPalindrome.py

input string

low index

high index

update indexes

```
 1  def main():
 2      # Prompt the user to enter a string
 3      s = input("Enter a string: ").strip()
 4
 5      if isPalindrome(s):
 6          print(s, "is a palindrome")
 7      else:
 8          print(s, " is not a palindrome")
 9
10  # Check if a string is a palindrome
11  def isPalindrome(s):
12      # The index of the first character in the string
13      low = 0
14
15      # The index of the last character in the string
16      high = len(s) - 1
17
18      while low < high:
19          if s[low] != s[high]:
20              return False # Not a palindrome
21
22          low += 1
23          high -= 1
24
25      return True # The string is a palindrome
26
27  main() # Call the main function
```

```
Enter a string: noon  ↵Enter
noon is a palindrome
```

```
Enter a string: moon  ↵Enter
moon is not a palindrome
```

The program prompts the user to enter a string into **s** (line 3), which uses the **strip()** method to remove any starting and ending whitespace characters, and then invokes **isPalindrome(s)** to determine whether **s** is a palindrome (line 5).

8.4 Case Study: Converting Hexadecimals to Decimals

 Key Point

This section presents a program that converts a hexadecimal number into a decimal number.

Section 6.8 illustrates a program that converts a decimal number to hexadecimal format. How do you convert a hex number into a decimal?

Given a hexadecimal number $h_n h_{n-1} h_{n-2} \ldots h_2 h_1 h_0$, the equivalent decimal value is

$$h_n \times 16^n + h_{n-1} \times 16^{n-1} + h_{n-2} \times 16^{n-2} + \ldots + h_2 \times 16^2 + h_1 \times 16^1 + h_0 \times 16^0$$

For example, the hex number **AB8C** is

$$10 \times 16^3 + 11 \times 16^2 + 8 \times 16^1 + 12 \times 16^0 = 43916$$

Our program will prompt the user to enter a hex number as a string and convert it into a decimal by using the following function:

def hexToDecimal(hex):

A brute-force approach is to convert each hex character into a decimal number, multiply it by 16^i for a hex digit at the i's position, and add all the items together to obtain the equivalent decimal value for the hex number.

Note that:

$$h_n \times 16^n + h_{n-1} \times 16^{n-1} + h_{n-2} \times 16^{n-2} + \ldots + h_1 \times 16^1 + h_0 \times 16^0$$
$$= (\ldots ((h_n \times 16 + h_{n-1}) \times 16 + h_{n-2}) \times 16 + \ldots + h_1) \times 16 + h_0$$

This observation, known as Honer's algorithm, leads to the following code for converting a hex string to a decimal number:

```
decimalValue = 0
for i in range(len(hex)):
    hexChar = hex[i]
    decimalValue = decimalValue * 16 + hexCharToDecimal(hexChar)
```

The following is a trace of the algorithm for hex number **AB8C**.

	i	hexChar	hexCharToDecimal (hexChar)	DecimalValue
before the loop				0
after the 1st iteration	0	A	10	10
after the 2nd iteration	1	B	11	10 * 16 + 11
after the 3rd iteration	2	8	8	(10 * 16 + 11) * 16 + 8
after the 4th iteration	3	C	12	((10 * 16 + 11) * 16 + 8) * 16 + 12

Listing 8.2 shows the complete program.

LISTING 8.2 HexToDecimalConversion.py

```
1  def main():
2      # Prompt the user to enter a hex number
3      hex = input("Enter a hex number: ").strip()
4
5      decimal = hexToDecimal(hex.upper())
6      if decimal == None:
7          print("Incorrect hex number")
8      else:
```

input string

hex to decimal

```
 9              print("The decimal value for hex number",
10                  hex, "is", decimal)
11
12     def hexToDecimal(hex):
13         decimalValue = 0
14         for i in range(len(hex)):
15             ch = hex[i]
16             if 'A' <= ch <= 'F' or '0' <= ch <= '9':
17                 decimalValue = decimalValue * 16 + \
18                     hexCharToDecimal(ch)
19             else:
20                 return None
21
22         return decimalValue
23
24     def hexCharToDecimal(ch):
25         if 'A' <= ch <= 'F':
26             return 10 + ord(ch) - ord('A')
27         else:
28             return ord(ch) - ord('0')
29
30     main() # Call the main function
```

cannot convert (margin note, line 20)

hex char to decimal (margin note, line 24)

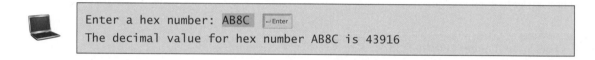

```
Enter a hex number: AB8C  ↵Enter
The decimal value for hex number AB8C is 43916
```

```
Enter a hex number: af71  ↵Enter
The decimal value for hex number af71 is 44913
```

```
Enter a hex number: ax71  ↵Enter
Incorrect hex number
```

The program reads a string from the console (line 3) and invokes the **hexToDecimal** function to convert a hex string to a decimal number (line 5). The characters can be entered in either lowercase or uppercase, and the program converts them to uppercase before invoking the **hexToDecimal** function.

The **hexToDecimal** function is defined in lines 12–22 to return an integer. The length of the string is determined by invoking **len(hex)** in line 14. This function returns **None** for an incorrect hex number (line 20).

None (margin note)

The **hexCharToDecimal** function is defined in lines 24–28 to return a decimal value for a hex character. The character can be in either lowercase or uppercase. Invoking **hex.upper()** converts the characters to uppercase. When invoking **hexCharToDecimal(ch)**, the character **ch** is already in uppercase. If **ch** is a letter between **A** and **F**, the program returns a decimal value **10 + ord(ch) - ord('A')** (line 26). If **ch** is a digit, the program returns a decimal value **ord(ch) - ord('0')** (line 28).

8.5 Operator Overloading and Special Methods

Python allows you to define special methods for operators and functions to perform common operations. These methods are named in a specific way for Python to recognize the association.

Key Point

In the preceding sections, you learned how to use operators for string operations. You can use the + operator to concatenate two strings, the * operator to concatenate the same string multiple times, the relational operators (==, !=, <, <=, >, and >=) to compare two strings, and the index operator [] to access a character. For example,

```
1  s1 = "Washington"
2  s2 = "California"
3  print("The first character in s1 is", s1[0])
4  print("s1 + s2 is", s1 + s2)
5  print("s1 < s2?", s1 < s2)
```

[] operator
+ operator
< operator

The operators are actually methods defined in the **str** class. Defining methods for operators is called *operator overloading*. Operator overloading allows the programmer to use the built-in operators for user-defined methods. Table 8.1 lists the mapping between the operators and methods. You name these methods with two starting and ending underscores so Python will recognize the association. For example, to use the + operator as a method, you would define a method named __**add**__. Note that these methods are not private, because they have two ending underscores in addition to the two starting underscores. Recall that the initializer in a class is named __**init**__, which is a special method for initializing an object.

operator overloading

For example, you can rewrite the preceding code using the methods as follows:

```
1  s1 = "Washington"
2  s2 = "California"
3  print("The first character in s1 is", s1.__getitem__(0))
```

__getitem__ method

TABLE 8.1 Operator Overloading: Operators and Special Methods

Operator/Function	Method	Description
+	__add__(self, other)	Addition
*	__mul__(self, other)	Multiplication
-	__sub__(self, other)	Subtraction
/	__truediv__(self, other)	Division
%	__mod__(self, other)	Remainder
<	__lt__(self, other)	Less than
<=	__le__(self, other)	Less than or equal to
==	__eq__(self, other)	Equal to
!=	__ne__(self, other)	Not equal to
>	__gt__(self, other)	Greater than
>=	__ge__(self, other)	Greater than or equal to
[index]	__getitem__(self, index)	Index operator
in	__contains__(self, value)	Check membership
len	__len__(self)	The number of elements
str	__str__(self)	The string representation

__add__ method
__lt__ method

```
4  print("s1 + s2 is", s1.__add__(s2))
5  print("s1 < s2?", s1.__lt__(s2))
```

s1.__getitem__(0) is the same as **s1[0]**, **s1.__add__(s2)** is the same as **s1 + s2**, and **s1.__lt__(s2)** is the same as **s1 < s2**. Now you can see the advantages of operator overloading. Using operators greatly simplifies programs, making them easier to read and maintain.

Python supports the **in** operator, which can be used to determine whether a character is in a string or an element is a member of a container. The corresponding method is named

__contains__ method
in operator

__contains__(self, e). You can use the method **__contains__** or the **in** operator to see if a character is in a string, as shown in the following code:

in operator
__contains__ method

```
1  s1 = "Washington"
2  print("Is W in s1?", 'W' in s1)
3  print("Is W in s1?", s1.__contains__('W'))
```

W in s1 is the same as **s1.__contains__('W')**.

__len__ method

If a class defines the **__len__(self)** method, Python allows you to invoke the method using a convenient syntax as a function call. For example, the **__len__** method is defined in the **str** class, which returns the number of characters in a string. You can use the method

len method

__len__ or the function **len** to get the number of characters in a string, as shown in the following code:

len function
__len__ method

```
1  s1 = "Washington"
2  print("The length of s1 is", len(s1))
3  print("The length of s1 is", s1.__len__())
```

len(s1) is the same as **s1.__len__()**.

Many of the special operators are defined in Python built-in types such as **int** and **float**. For example, suppose **i** is **3** and **j** is **4**. **i.__add__(j)** is the same as **i + j** and **i.__sub__(j)** is the same as **i - j**.

print object

 Note

You can pass an object to invoke **print(x)**. This is equivalent to invoking **print(x.__str__())** or **print(str(x))**.

 Note

The comparison operators **<**, **<=**, **==**, **!=**, **>**, and **>=** can also be implemented using the **__cmp__(self, other)** method. This method returns a negative integer if **self < other**, zero if **self == other**, and a positive integer if **self > other**. For two objects **a** and **b**, **a < b** calls **a.__lt__(b)** if the **__lt__** is available. If not, the **__cmp__** method is called to determine the order.

Check
Point

8.9 What is operator overloading?

8.10 What are the special methods for the operators **+**, **-**, *****, **/**, **%**, **==**, **!=**, **<**, **<=**, **>**, and **>=**?

MyProgrammingLab™

8.6 Case Study: The **Rational** Class

🔑 Key
Point

*This section shows how to design the **Rational** class for representing and processing rational numbers.*

VideoNote
Define classes

A rational number has a numerator and a denominator in the form **a/b**, where **a** is the numerator and **b** is the denominator. For example, **1/3**, **3/4**, and **10/4** are rational numbers.

A rational number cannot have a denominator of **0**, but a numerator of **0** is fine. Every integer **i** is equivalent to a rational number **i/1**. Rational numbers are used in exact computations involving fractions—for example, **1/3** = **0.33333....**. This number cannot be precisely represented in floating-point format using data type **float**. To obtain the exact result, we must use rational numbers.

Python provides data types for integers and floating-point numbers but not for rational numbers. This section shows how to design a class for rational numbers.

A rational number can be represented using two data fields: **numerator** and **denominator**. You can create a rational number with a specified numerator and denominator or create a default rational number with the numerator **0** and denominator **1**. You can add, subtract, multiply, divide, and compare rational numbers. You can also convert a rational number into an integer, floating-point value, or string. The UML class diagram for the **Rational** class is given in Figure 8.9.

Rational	
-numerator: int	The numerator of this rational number.
-denominator: int	The denominator of this rational number.
Rational(numerator = 0: int, denominator = 1: int)	Creates a rational number with a specified numerator (default 0) and denominator (default 1).
__add__(secondRational: Rational): Rational	Returns the addition of this rational number with another.
__sub__(secondRational: Rational): Rational	Returns the subtraction of this rational number with another.
__mul__(secondRational: Rational): Rational	Returns the multiplication of this rational number with another.
__truediv__(secondRational: Rational): Rational	Returns the division of this rational number with another.
__lt__(secondRational: Rational): bool	Compares this rational number with another.
Also __le__, __eq__, __ne__, __gt__, __ge__ are supported	
__int__(): int	Returns the numerator divided by denominator as an integer.
__float__(): float	Returns the numerator divided by denominator as a float.
__str__(): str	Returns a string in the form "numerator/denominator." Returns the numerator if the denominator is 1.
__getitem__(i)	Returns numerator using [0] and denominator using [1].

FIGURE 8.9 The UML diagram for the properties, initializer, and methods of the **Rational** class.

There are many equivalent rational numbers; for example, **1/3** = **2/6** = **3/9** = **4/12**. For convenience, **1/3** is used to represent all rational numbers that are equivalent to **1/3**. The numerator and the denominator of **1/3** have no common divisor except **1**, so **1/3** is said to be in lowest terms.

To reduce a rational number to its lowest terms, you need to find the greatest common divisor (GCD) of the absolute values of its numerator and denominator and then divide both numerator and denominator by this value. You can use the function for computing the GCD of two integers **n** and **d**, as suggested in Listing 5.8, GreatestCommonDivisor.py. The numerator and denominator in a **Rational** object are reduced to their lowest terms.

As usual, we first write a test program to create **Rational** objects and test the functions in the **Rational** class. Listing 8.3 is a test program.

LISTING 8.3 TestRationalClass.py

```
1  import Rational
2
3  # Create and initialize two rational numbers r1 and r2.
4  r1 = Rational.Rational(4, 2)
5  r2 = Rational.Rational(2, 3)
6
7  # Display results
8  print(r1, "+", r2, "=", r1 + r2)
9  print(r1, "-", r2, "=", r1 - r2)
10 print(r1, "*", r2, "=", r1 * r2)
11 print(r1, "/", r2, "=", r1 / r2)
12
13 print(r1, ">", r2, "is", r1 > r2)
14 print(r1, ">=", r2, "is", r1 >= r2)
15 print(r1, "<", r2, "is", r1 < r2)
16 print(r1, "<=", r2, "is", r1 <= r2)
17 print(r1, "==", r2, "is", r1 == r2)
18 print(r1, "!=", r2, "is", r1 != r2)
19
20 print("int(r2) is", int(r2))
21 print("float(r2) is", float(r2))
22
23 print("r2[0] is", r2[0])
24 print("r2[1] is", r2[1])
```

import Rational

create Rational

invoke add
invoke subtract
invoke multiply
invoke divide

compare two numbers

get int value

index operator

```
2 + 2/3 = 8/3
2 - 2/3 = 4/3
2 * 2/3 = 4/3
2 / 2/3 = 3
2 > 2/3 is True
2 >= 2/3 is True
2 < 2/3 is False
2 <= 2/3 is False
2 == 2/3 is False
2 != 2/3 is True
int(r2) is 0
float(r2) is 0.6666666666666666
r2[0] is 2
r2[1] is 3
```

The program creates two rational numbers, **r1** and **r2** (lines 4 and 5), and displays the results of **r1 + r2, r1 - r2, r1 * r2**, and **r1 / r2** (lines 8–11). **r1 + r2** is equivalent to **r1.__add__(r2)**.

The **print(r1)** function prints the string returned from **str(r1)**. Invoking **str(r1)** returns a string representation for the rational number **r1**, which is the same as invoking **r1.__str__()**.

Invoking **int(r2)** (line 20) returns an integer for the rational number **r2**, which is the same as invoking **r2.__int__()**.

Invoking **float(r2)** (line 21) returns a float for the rational number **r2**, which is the same as invoking **r2.__float__()**.

Invoking **r2[0]** (line 23) is the same as invoking **r2.__getitem__(0)**, which returns the numerator from **r2**.

The **Rational** class is implemented in Listing 8.4.

LISTING 8.4 Rational.py

```
1  class Rational:
2      def __init__(self, numerator = 1, denominator = 0):          initializer
3          divisor = gcd(numerator, denominator)                    gcd
4          self.__numerator = (1 if denominator > 0 else -1) \      initialize numerator
5              * int(numerator / divisor)
6          self.__denominator = int(abs(denominator) / divisor)     initialize denominator
7
8      # Add a rational number to this rational number
9      def __add__(self, secondRational):                           add
10         n = self.__numerator * secondRational[1] + \
11             self.__denominator * secondRational[0]
12         d = self.__denominator * secondRational[1]
13         return Rational(n, d)
14
15     # Subtract a rational number from this rational number
16     def __sub__(self, secondRational):                           subtract
17         n = self.__numerator * secondRational[1] - \
18             self.__denominator * secondRational[0]
19         d = self.__denominator * secondRational[1]
20         return Rational(n, d)
21
22     # Multiply a rational number by this rational number
23     def __mul__(self, secondRational):                           multiply
24         n = self.__numerator * secondRational[0]
25         d = self.__denominator * secondRational[1]
26         return Rational(n, d)
27
28     # Divide a rational number by this rational number
29     def __truediv__(self, secondRational):                       divide
30         n = self.__numerator * secondRational[1]
31         d = self.__denominator * secondRational[0]
32         return Rational(n, d)
33
34     # Return a float for the rational number
35     def __float__(self):                                         float
36         return self.__numerator / self.__denominator
37
38     # Return an integer for the rational number
39     def __int__(self):                                           int
40         return int(self.__float__())
41
42     # Return a string representation
43     def __str__(self):                                           str
44         if self.__denominator == 1:
45             return str(self.__numerator)
46         else:
47             return str(self.__numerator) + "/", self.__denominator)
48
49     def __lt__(self, secondRational):                            lt
50         return self.__cmp__(secondRational) < 0
51
52     def __le__(self, secondRational):
53         return self.__cmp__(secondRational) <= 0
54
```

The math expressions shown alongside the code:

add: $\frac{a}{b} + \frac{c}{d} = \frac{ad + bc}{bd}$

subtract: $\frac{a}{b} - \frac{c}{d} = \frac{ad - bc}{bd}$

multiply: $\frac{a}{b} \times \frac{c}{d} = \frac{ac}{bd}$

divide: $\frac{a}{b} \div \frac{c}{d} = \frac{ad}{bc}$

```
55        def __gt__(self, secondRational):
56            return self.__cmp__(secondRational) > 0
57
58        def __ge__(self, secondRational):
59            return self.__cmp__(secondRational) >= 0
60
61        # Compare two numbers
62        def __cmp__(self, secondRational):
63            temp = self.__sub__(secondRational)
64            if temp[0] > 0:
65                return 1
66            elif temp[0] < 0:
67                return -1
68            else:
69                return 0
70
71        # Return numerator and denominator using an index operator
72        def __getitem__(self, index):
73            if index == 0:
74                return self.__numerator
75            else:
76                return self.__denominator
77
78    def gcd(n, d):
79        n1 = abs(n)
80        n2 = abs(d)
81        gcd = 1
82
83        k = 1
84        while k <= n1 and k <= n2:
85            if n1 % k == 0 and n2 % k == 0:
86                gcd = k
87            k += 1
88
89        return gcd
```

cmp (line 62)

getitem (line 72)

gcd (line 78)

The rational number is encapsulated in a **Rational** object. Internally, a rational number is represented in its lowest terms (lines 4–6), and the numerator determines its sign (line 4). The denominator is always positive (line 6). The data fields **numerator** and **denominator** are defined as private with two leading underscores.

The **gcd()** is not a member method in the **Rational** class, but a function defined in the **Rational** module (Rational.py) (lines 78–89).

Two **Rational** objects can interact with each other to perform addition, subtraction, multiplication, and division operations. These methods return a new **Rational** object (lines 9–32). Note that **secondRational[0]** refers to the numerator of **secondRational** and **secondRational[1]** refers to the denominator of **secondRational**. The use of the index operator is supported by the **__getitem(i)__** method (lines 72–76), which returns the numerator and denominator of the rational number based on the index.

The **__cmp__(secondRational)** method (lines 62–69) compares this rational number to the other rational number. It first subtracts the second rational from this rational and saves the result in **temp** (line 63). The method returns **-1**, **0**, or **1** if **temp**'s numerator is less than, equal to, or greater than **0**.

The comparison method **__lt__**, **__le__**, **__gt__**, and **__ge__** are implemented using the **__cmp__** method (lines 49–59). Note that the methods **__ne__** and **__eq__** are not implemented explicitly, but they are implicitly implemented by Python if the **__cmp__** method is available.

You have used the **str**, **int**, and **float** functions to convert an object to a **str**, **int**, or **float**. The methods **__str__()**, **__int__()**, and **__float__()** are implemented in the

Rational class (lines 35–47) to return a **str** object, **int** object, or **float** object from a **Rational** object.

8.11 Will the program work if you replace line 63 in Rational.py with the following code?

```
temp = self - secondRational
```

8.12 Will the program work if you replace the **__str__** method in lines 43–47 as follows?

```
def __str__(self):
    if self.__denominator == 1:
        return str(self[0])
    else:
        return str(self[0]) + "/" + str(self[1])
```

KEY TERMS

CHAPTER SUMMARY

1. A string object is immutable. Its contents cannot be changed.

2. You can use the Python functions **len**, **min**, and **max** to return the length of a string, and the minimum and maximum elements in a string.

3. You can use the index operator **[]** to reference an individual character in a string.

4. You can use the concatenate operator + to concatenate two strings, the repetition operator * to duplicate strings, the slicing operator **[:]** to get a substring, and the **in** and **not in** operators to check whether a character is in a string.

5. The comparison operators (==, !=, <, <=, >, and >=) can be used to compare two strings.

6. You can use a *for* loop to *iterate* all characters in a string.

7. You can use the methods such as **endswith**, **startswith**, **isalpha**, **islower**, **isupper**, **lower**, **upper**, **find**, **count**, **replace**, and **strip** on a string object.

8. You can define special methods for *overloading the operators*.

TEST QUESTIONS

Do test questions for this chapter online at www.cs.armstrong.edu/liang/py/test.html.

PROGRAMMING EXERCISES

Sections 8.2–8.4

*8.1 (*Check SSN*) Write a program that prompts the user to enter a Social Security number in the format ddd-dd-dddd, where *d* is a digit. The program displays **Valid SSN** for a correct Social Security number or **Invalid SSN** otherwise.

8.2 (*Check substrings*) You can check whether a string is a substring of another string by using the **find method in the **str** class. Write your own function to implement **find**. Write a program that prompts the user to enter two strings and then checks whether the first string is a substring of the second string.

**8.3 (*Check password*) Some Web sites impose certain rules for passwords. Write a function that checks whether a string is a valid password. Suppose the password rules are as follows:

- A password must have at least eight characters.
- A password must consist of only letters and digits.
- A password must contain at least two digits.

Write a program that prompts the user to enter a password and displays **valid password** if the rules are followed or **invalid password** otherwise.

8.4 (*Occurrences of a specified character*) Write a function that finds the number of occurrences of a specified character in a string using the following header:

```
def count(s, ch):
```

The **str** class has the **count** method. Implement your method without using the **count** method. For example, **count("Welcome", 'e')** returns **2**. Write a test program that prompts the user to enter a string followed by a character and displays the number of occurrences of the character in the string.

8.5 (*Occurrences of a specified string*) Write a function that counts the occurrences of a specified non-overlapping string **s2 in another string **s1** using the following header:

```
def count(s1, s2):
```

For example, **count("system error, syntax error", "error")** returns **2**. Write a test program that prompts the user to enter two strings and displays the number of occurrences of the second string in the first string.

*8.6 (*Count the letters in a string*) Write a function that counts the number of letters in a string using the following header:

```
def countLetters(s):
```

Write a test program that prompts the user to enter a string and displays the number of letters in the string.

*8.7 (*Phone keypads*) The international standard letter/number mapping for telephones is:

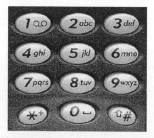

Write a function that returns a number, given an uppercase letter, as follows:

```
def getNumber(uppercaseLetter):
```

Write a test program that prompts the user to enter a phone number as a string. The input number may contain letters. The program translates a letter (uppercase or lowercase) to a digit and leaves all other characters intact. Here is a sample run of the program:

```
Enter a string: 1-800-Flowers  ↵Enter
1-800-3569377
```

```
Enter a string: 1800flowers  ↵Enter
18003569377
```

*8.8 (*Binary to decimal*) Write a function that parses a binary number as a string into a decimal integer. Use the function header:

def binaryToDecimal(binaryString):

For example, binary string 10001 is 17 ($1 \times 2^4 + 0 \times 2^3 + 0 \times 2^2 + 0 \times 2 + 1 = 17$). So, **binaryToDecimal("10001")** returns **17**.

Write a test program that prompts the user to enter a binary string and displays the corresponding decimal integer value.

**8.9 (*Binary to hex*) Write a function that parses a binary number into a hex number. The function header is:

def binaryToHex(binaryValue):

Write a test program that prompts the user to enter a binary number and displays the corresponding hexadecimal value.

**8.10 (*Decimal to binary*) Write a function that parses a decimal number into a binary number as a string. Use the function header:

def decimalToBinary(value):

Write a test program that prompts the user to enter a decimal integer value and displays the corresponding binary value.

Section 8.5

*8.11 (*Reverse a string*) Write a function that reverses a string. The header of the function is:

def reverse(s):

Write a test program that prompts the user to enter a string, invokes the **reverse** function, and displays the reversed string.

*8.12 (*Bioinformatics: find genes*) Biologists use a sequence of letters **A**, **C**, **T**, and **G** to model a *genome*. A *gene* is a substring of a genome that starts after a triplet **ATG** and ends before a triplet **TAG**, **TAA**, or **TGA**. Furthermore, the length of a gene string is a multiple of **3** and the gene does not contain any of the triplets **ATG**, **TAG**, **TAA**, and **TGA**. Write a program that prompts the user to enter a genome and displays all genes in the genome. If no gene is found in the input sequence, the program displays **no gene is found**. Here are the sample runs:

```
Enter a genome string: TTATGTTTTAAGGATGGGGCGTTAGTT  ↵Enter
TTT
GGGCGT
```

```
Enter a genome string: TGTGTGTATAT  ↵Enter
no gene is found
```

*8.13 (*Longest common prefix*) Write a method that returns the longest common prefix of two strings. For example, the longest common prefix of **distance** and **disinfection** is **dis**. The header of the method is:

```
def prefix(s1, s2)
```

If the two strings have no common prefix, the method returns an empty string.

Write a **main** method that prompts the user to enter two strings and displays their common prefix.

**8.14 (*Financial: credit card number validation*) Rewrite Exercise 6.29 using a string input for a credit card number.

**8.15 (*Business: check ISBN-10*) An *ISBN-10* (International Standard Book Number) consists of 10 digits: $d_1d_2d_3d_4d_5d_6d_7d_8d_9d_{10}$. The last digit, d_{10}, is a checksum, which is calculated from the other nine digits using the following formula:

$$(d_1 \times 1 + d_2 \times 2 + d_3 \times 3 + d_4 \times 4 + d_5 \times 5 + d_6 \times 6 + d_7 \times 7 + d_8 \times 8 + d_9 \times 9) \% 11$$

If the checksum is **10**, the last digit is denoted as X, according to the ISBN convention. Write a program that prompts the user to enter the first 9 digits as a string and displays the 10-digit ISBN (including leading zeros). Your program should read the input as a string. Here are sample runs:

```
Enter the first 9 digits of an ISBN-10 as a string:
  013601267  ↵Enter
The ISBN-10 number is 0136012671
```

```
Enter the first 9 digits of an ISBN-10 as a string:
  013031997  ↵Enter
The ISBN-10 number is 013031997X
```

**8.16 (*Business: check ISBN-13*) *ISBN-13* is a new standard for identifying books. It uses 13 digits: $d_1d_2d_3d_4d_5d_6d_7d_8d_9d_{10}d_{11}d_{12}d_{13}$. The last digit, d_{13}, is a checksum, which is calculated from the other digits using the following formula:

$$10 - (d_1 + 3d_2 + d_3 + 3d_4 + d_5 + 3d_6 + d_7 + 3d_8 + d_9 + 3d_{10} + d_{11} + 3d_{12}) \% 10$$

If the checksum is **10**, replace it with **0**. Your program should read the input as a string. Here are sample runs:

```
Enter the first 12 digits of an ISBN-13 as a string:
  978013213080  ↵Enter
The ISBN-13 number is 9780132130806
```

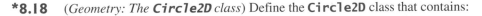

```
Enter the first 12 digits of an ISBN-13 as a string:
  978013213079  ↵Enter
The ISBN-13 number is 9780132130790
```

Section 8.6

8.17 (*The* **Point *class*) Design a class named **Point** to represent a point with **x**- and **y**-coordinates. The class contains:

- Two private data fields **x** and **y** that represent the coordinates with get methods.
- A constructor that constructs a point with specified coordinates with default point (**0, 0**).
- A method named **distance** that returns the distance from this point to another point of the **Point** type.
- A method named **isNearBy(p1)** that returns true if point **p1** is close to this point. Two points are close if their distance is less than **5**.
- Implement the **__str__** method to return a string in the form (x, y).

Draw the UML diagram for the class, and then implement the class. Write a test program that prompts the user to enter two points, displays the distance between them, and indicates whether they are near each other. Here are sample runs:

```
Enter two points x1, y1, x2, y2: 2.1, 2.3, 19.1, 19.2  ↵Enter
The distance between the two points is 23.97
The two points are not near each other
```

```
Enter two points x1, y1, x2, y2: 2.1, 2.3, 2.3, 4.2  ↵Enter
The distance between the two points is 1.91
The two points are near each other
```

*8.18 (*Geometry: The* **Circle2D** *class*) Define the **Circle2D** class that contains:

- Two private float data fields named **x** and **y** that specify the center of the circle with **get/set** methods.
- A private data field **radius** with **get/set** methods.
- A constructor that creates a circle with the specified **x**, **y**, and **radius**. The default values are all **0**.
- A method **getArea()** that returns the area of the circle.
- A method **getPerimeter()** that returns the perimeter of the circle.
- A method **containsPoint(x, y)** that returns **True** if the specified point (**x, y**) is inside this circle (see Figure 8.10a).
- A method **contains(circle2D)** that returns **True** if the specified circle is inside this circle (see Figure 8.10b).
- A method **overlaps(circle2D)** that returns **True** if the specified circle overlaps with this circle (see Figure 8.10c).
- Implement the **__contains__(another)** method that returns **True** if this circle is contained in another circle.

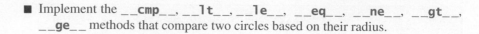

- Implement the **__cmp__**, **__lt__**, **__le__**, **__eq__**, **__ne__**, **__gt__**, **__ge__** methods that compare two circles based on their radius.

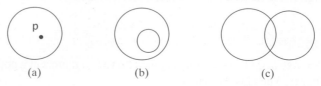

(a)   (b)   (c)

FIGURE 8.10 (a) A point is inside the circle. (b) A circle is inside another circle. (c) A circle overlaps another circle.

Draw the UML diagram for the class, and then implement the class. Write a test program that prompts the user to enter two circles with x- and y-coordinates and the radius, creates two **Circle2D** objects **c1** and **c2**, displays their areas and perimeters, and displays the result of **c1.containsPoint(c2.getX(), c2.getY())**, **c1.contains(c2)**, and **c1.overlaps(c2)**. Here is a sample run:

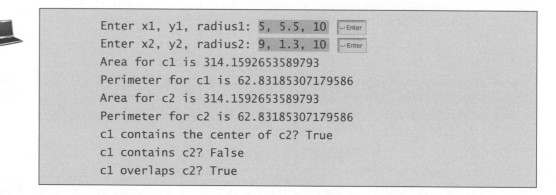

```
Enter x1, y1, radius1: 5, 5.5, 10  ↵Enter
Enter x2, y2, radius2: 9, 1.3, 10  ↵Enter
Area for c1 is 314.1592653589793
Perimeter for c1 is 62.83185307179586
Area for c2 is 314.1592653589793
Perimeter for c2 is 62.83185307179586
c1 contains the center of c2? True
c1 contains c2? False
c1 overlaps c2? True
```

*8.19 (*Geometry: The **Rectangle2D** class*) Define the **Rectangle2D** class that contains:

- Two float data fields named **x** and **y** that specify the center of the rectangle with **get/set** methods. (Assume that the rectangle sides are parallel to x- or y-axes.)
- The data fields **width** and **height** with **get/set** methods.
- A constructor that creates a rectangle with the specified **x**, **y**, **width**, and **height** with default values 0.
- A method **getArea()** that returns the area of the rectangle.
- A method **getPerimeter()** that returns the perimeter of the rectangle.
- A method **containsPoint(x, y)** that returns **True** if the specified point (**x, y**) is inside this rectangle (see Figure 8.11a).
- A method **contains(Rectangle2D)** that returns **True** if the specified rectangle is inside this rectangle (see Figure 8.11b).
- A method **overlaps(Rectangle2D)** that returns **True** if the specified rectangle overlaps with this rectangle (see Figure 8.11c).
- Implement the **__contains__(another)** method that returns **True** if this rectangle is contained in another rectangle.
- Implement the **__cmp__**, **__lt__**, **__le__**, **__eq__**, **__ne__**, **__gt__**, **__ge__** methods that compare two circles based on their areas.

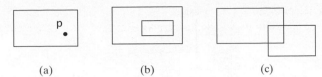

(a)   (b)   (c)

FIGURE 8.11 (a) A point is inside the rectangle. (b) A rectangle is inside another rectangle. (c) A rectangle overlaps another rectangle.

Draw the UML diagram for the class, and then implement the class. Write a test program that prompts the user to enter two rectangles with center x-, y-coordinates, width, and height, creates two **Rectangle2D** objects **r1** and **r2**, displays their areas and perimeters, and displays the result of **r1.containsPoint(r2.getX(), r2.getY())**, **r1.contains(r2)**, and **r1.overlaps(r2)**. Here is a sample run:

```
Enter x1, y1, width1, height1: 9, 1.3, 10, 35.3  ↵Enter
Enter x2, y2, width2, height2: 1.3, 4.3, 4, 5.3  ↵Enter
Area for r1 is 353.0
Perimeter for r1 is 90.6
Area for r2 is 21.2
Perimeter for r2 is 18.6
r1 contains the center of r2? False
r1 contains r2? False
r1 overlaps r2? False
```

8.20 (*Use the **Rational** class*) Write a program that computes the following summation series using the **Rational** class:

$$\frac{1}{2} + \frac{2}{3} + \frac{3}{4} + \ldots + \frac{8}{9} + \frac{9}{10}$$

*8.21 (*Math: The **Complex** class*) Python has the **complex** class for performing complex number arithmetic. In this exercise, you will design and implement your own **Complex** class. Note that the **complex** class in Python is named in lowercase, but our custom **Complex** class is named with C in uppercase.

A complex number is a number of the form $a + bi$, where a and b are real numbers and i is $\sqrt{-1}$. The numbers a and b are known as the real part and the imaginary part of the complex number, respectively. You can perform addition, subtraction, multiplication, and division for complex numbers using the following formulas:

$(a + bi) + (c + di) = (a + c) + (b + d)i$

$a + bi - (c + di) = (a - c) + (b - d)i$

$(a + bi)*(c + di) = (ac - bd) + (bc + ad)i$

$(a + bi)/(c + di) = (ac + bd)/(c^2 + d^2) + (bc - ad)i/(c^2 + d^2)$

You can also obtain the absolute value for a complex number using the following formula:

$$|a + bi| = \sqrt{a^2 + b^2}$$

(A complex number can be interpreted as a point on a plane by identifying the (a,b) values as the coordinates of the point. The absolute value of the complex number corresponds to the distance of the point to the origin, as shown in Figure 8.12.)

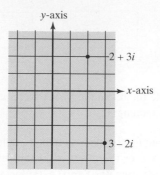

FIGURE 8.12 Point (2, 3) can be written as a complex number (2 + 3*i*) and (3, −2) as (3 − 2*i*).

Design a class named **Complex** for representing complex numbers and the methods **__add__**, **__sub__**, **__mul__**, **__truediv__**, and **__abs__** for performing complex-number operations, and override the **__str__** method by returning a string representation for a complex number. The **__str__** method returns **(a + bi)** as a string. If **b** is **0**, it simply returns **a**.

Provide a constructor **Complex(a, b)** to create a complex number *a* + *bi* with the default value of **0** for *a* and *b*. Also provide the **getRealPart()** and **getImaginaryPart()** methods for returning the real and imaginary parts of the complex number, respectively.

Write a test program that prompts the user to enter two complex numbers and displays the result of their addition, subtraction, multiplication, and division. Here is a sample run:

```
Enter the first complex number: 3.5, 6.5  ↵Enter
Enter the second complex number: -3.5, 1  ↵Enter
(3.5 + 6.5i) + (-3.5 + 1i) = (0.0 + 7.5i)
(3.5 + 6.5i) - (-3.5 + 1i) = (7.0 + 5.5i)
(3.5 + 6.5i) * (-3.5 + 1i) = (-18.75 - 19.25i)
(3.5 + 6.5i) / (-3.5 + 1i) = (-0.43396226415 - 1.981132075547i)
|(3.5 + 6.5i)| = 4.47213595499958
```

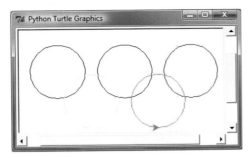

FIGURE 1.17 The program draws the Olympics rings logo.

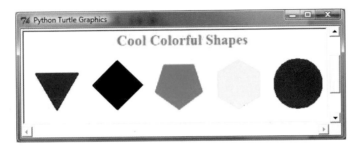

FIGURE 3.4 The program draws five shapes in different colors.

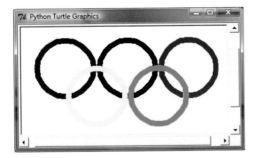

FIGURE 3.5 The program draws an Olympic symbol.

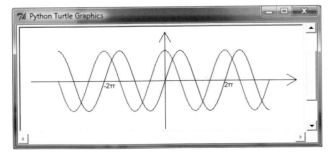

FIGURE 5.5 The program plots sine function in blue and cosine function in red.

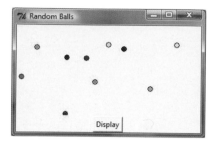

FIGURE 9.36 Ten balls with random colors are displayed at random locations.

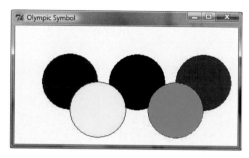 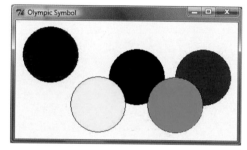

FIGURE 9.39 The blue circle is dragged with the mouse.

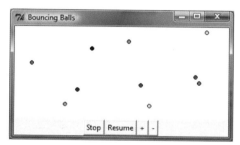

FIGURE 10.14 The program displays bouncing balls with control buttons.

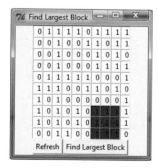

FIGURE 11.17 The program displays 0s and 1s randomly with a click of the Refresh button.

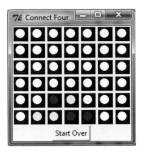 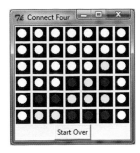

FIGURE 12.25 The program enables two players to play the Connect Four game.

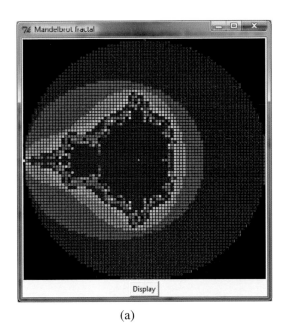

(a)

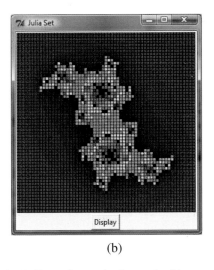

(b)

FIGURE 12.26 A Mandelbrot image is shown in (a) and a Julia set image is shown in (b).

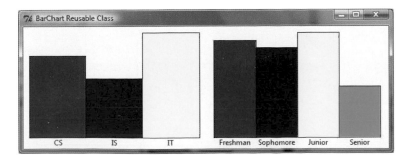

FIGURE 12.28 The program uses the **BarChart** class to display bar charts.

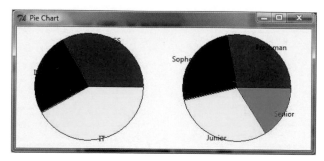

FIGURE 12.29 The program uses the `PieChart` class to display pie charts.

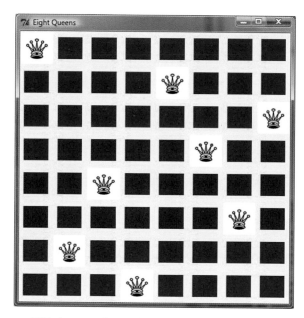

FIGURE 15.11 `queens[i]` denotes the position of the queen in row `i`.

GUI Programming Using Tkinter

Objectives

- To create a simple GUI application with Tkinter (§9.2).

- To process events by using callback functions that are bound to a widget's command option (§9.3).

- To use labels, entries, buttons, check buttons, radio buttons, messages, and text to create graphical user interfaces (§9.4).

- To draw lines, rectangles, ovals, polygons, and arcs and display text strings in a canvas (§9.5).

- To use geometry managers to lay out widgets in a container (§9.6).

- To lay out widgets in a grid by using the grid manager (§9.6.1).

- To pack widgets side by side or on top of each other by using the pack manager (§9.6.2).

- To place widgets in absolute locations by using the place manager (§9.6.3).

- To achieve a desired layout by using containers to group widgets (§9.7).

- To use images in widgets (§9.8).

- To create applications that contain menus (§9.9).

- To create applications that contain popup menus (§9.10).

- To bind a widget's mouse and key events to a callback function for processing events (§9.11).

- To develop animations (§9.12).

- To use scroll bars to scroll through the contents of a text widget (§9.13).

- To use standard dialog boxes to display messages and accept user input (§9.14).

9.1 Introduction

Key
Point

Tkinter enables you to develop GUI programs and is an excellent pedagogical tool for learning object-oriented programming.

There are many GUI modules available for developing GUI programs in Python. You have used the **turtle** module for drawing geometric shapes. Turtle is easy to use and is an effective pedagogical tool for introducing the fundamentals of programming to beginners. However, you cannot use turtle to create graphical user interfaces. This chapter introduces Tkinter, which will enable you to develop GUI projects. Tkinter is not only a useful tool for developing GUI projects, but it is also a valuable pedagogical tool for learning object-oriented programming.

what is Tkinter?

Note

Tkinter (pronounced T-K-Inter) is short for "Tk interface." Tk is a GUI library used by many programming languages for developing GUI programs on Windows, Mac, and UNIX. Tkinter provides an interface for Python programmers to use the Tk GUI library, and it is the de-facto standard for developing GUI programs in Python.

9.2 Getting Started with Tkinter

Key
Point

*The **tkinter** module contains the classes for creating GUIs. The **Tk** class creates a window for holding GUI widgets (i.e., visual components).*

Listing 9.1 introduces Tkinter with a simple example.

LISTING 9.1 SimpleGUI.py

```
1  from tkinter import *  # Import all definitions from tkinter
2
3  window = Tk()  # Create a window
4  label = Label(window, text = "Welcome to Python")  # Create a label
5  button = Button(window, text = "Click Me")  # Create a button
6  label.pack()  # Place the label in the window
7  button.pack()  # Place the button in the window
8
9  window.mainloop()  # Create an event loop
```

create a window
create a label
create a button
place label
place button

event loop

When you run the program, a label and a button appear in the Tkinter window, as shown in Figure 9.1.

FIGURE 9.1 The label and button are created in Listing 9.1.

Whenever you create a GUI-based program in Tkinter, you need to import the **tkinter** module (line 1) and create a window by using the **Tk** class (line 3). Recall that the asterisk (*) in line 1 imports all definitions for classes, functions, and constants from the **tkinter** module to the program. **Tk()** creates an instance of a window. **Label** and **Button** are Python Tkinter *widget classes* for creating labels and buttons. The first argument of a widget class is always the *parent container* (i.e., the container in which the widget will be placed). The statement (line 4)

widget class
parent container

```
label = Label(window, text = "Welcome to Python")
```

constructs a label with the text **Welcome to Python** that is contained in the window.

The statement (line 6)

```
label.pack()
```

places **label** in the container using a pack manager. In this example, the pack manager packs the widget in the window row by row. More on the pack manager will be introduced in Section 9.6.2. For now, you can use the pack manager without knowing its full details.

Tkinter GUI programming is event driven. After the user interface is displayed, the program waits for user interactions such as mouse clicks and key presses. This is specified in the following statement (line 9)

```
window.mainloop()
```

The statement creates an event loop. The event loop processes events continuously until you close the main window, as shown in Figure 9.2.

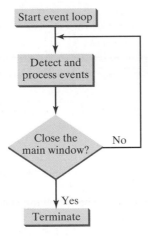

FIGURE 9.2 A Tkinter GUI program listens and processes events in a continuous loop.

9.1 What are turtle and Tkinter suitable for?

9.2 How do you create a window?

9.3 What is **window.mainloop()** for?

Check
Point
MyProgrammingLab™

9.3 Processing Events

A Tkinter widget can be bound to a function, which is called when an event occurs.

Key
Point

▶
VideoNote
Simple GUI

The **Button** widget is a good way to demonstrate the basics of event-driven programming, so we'll use it in the following example.

When the user clicks a button, your program should process this event. You enable this action by defining a processing function and binding the function to the button, as shown in Listing 9.2.

LISTING 9.2 ProcessButtonEvent.py

process OK

process Cancel

create a window
create a button
create a button

place button
place button

event loop

```
1  from tkinter import *  # Import all definitions from tkinter
2
3  def processOK():
4      print("OK button is clicked")
5
6  def processCancel():
7      print("Cancel button is clicked")
8
9  window = Tk() # Create a window
10 btOK = Button(window, text = "OK", fg = "red", command = processOK)
11 btCancel = Button(window, text = "Cancel", bg = "yellow",
12                   command = processCancel)
13 btOK.pack() # Place the OK button in the window
14 btCancel.pack() # Place the Cancel button in the window
15
16 window.mainloop()  # Create an event loop
```

When you run the program, two buttons appear, as shown in Figure 9.3a. You can watch the events being processed and see their associated messages in the command window in Figure 9.3b.

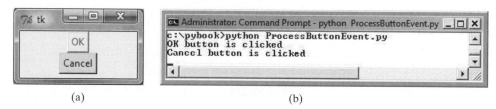

(a)   (b)

FIGURE 9.3   (a) Listing 9.2 displays two buttons in a window. (b) Watching events being processed in the command window.

callback functions
handlers

The program defines the functions **processOK** and **processCancel** (lines 3–7). These functions are bound to the buttons when the buttons are constructed. These functions are known as *callback functions*, or *handlers*. The following statement (line 10)

```
btOK = Button(window, text = "OK", fg = "red", command = processOK)
```

binds the *OK* button to the **processOK** function, which will be called when the button is clicked. The **fg** option specifies the button's foreground color and the **bg** option specifies its background color. By default, **fg** is black and **bg** is gray for all widgets.

You can also write this program by placing all the functions in one class, as shown in Listing 9.3.

LISTING 9.3 ProcessButtonEventAlternativeCode.py

initialize GUI

create a button

create a button

```
1  from tkinter import *  # Import all definitions from tkinter
2
3  class ProcessButtonEvent:
4      def __init__(self):
5          window = Tk() # Create a window
6          btOK = Button(window, text = "OK", fg = "red",
7                        command = self.processOK )
8          btCancel = Button(window, text = "Cancel", bg = "yellow",
9                            command = self.processCancel )
```

```
10          btOK.pack() # Place the OK button in the window              place button
11          btCancel.pack() # Place the Cancel button in the window      place button
12
13          window.mainloop() # Create an event loop                     event loop
14
15      def processOK(self):                                             process OK
16          print("OK button is clicked")
17
18      def processCancel(self):                                         process Cancel
19          print("Cancel button is clicked")
20
21  ProcessButtonEvent() # Create an object to invoke __init__ method
```

The program defines a class for creating the GUI in the __init__ method (line 4). The functions **processOK** and **processCancel** are now instance methods in the class, so they are called by **self.processOK** (line 7) and **self.processCancel** (line 9).

There are two advantages of defining a class for creating a GUI and processing GUI events. First, you can reuse the class in the future. Second, defining all the functions as methods enables them to access instance data fields in the class.

9.4 When you create a widget object from a widget class, what should be the first argument?

9.5 What is a widget's **command** option for?

✔ **Check Point**

MyProgrammingLab™

9.4 The Widget Classes

Tkinter's GUI classes define common GUI widgets such as buttons, labels, radio buttons, check buttons, entries, canvases, and others.

🔑 **Key Point**

Table 9.1 describes the core widget classes Tkinter provides.

TABLE 9.1   Tkinter Widget Classes

Widget Class	Description
Button	A simple button, used to execute a command.
Canvas	Structured graphics, used to draw graphs and plots, create graphics editors, and implement custom widgets.
Checkbutton	Clicking a check button toggles between the values.
Entry	A text entry field, also called a text field or a text box.
Frame	A container widget for containing other widgets.
Label	Displays text or an image.
Menu	A menu pane, used to implement pull-down and popup menus.
Menubutton	A menu button, used to implement pull-down menus.
Message	Displays a text. Similar to the label widget, but can automatically wrap text to a given width or aspect ratio.
Radiobutton	Clicking a radio button sets the variable to that value, and clears all other radio buttons associated with the same variable.
Text	Formatted text display. Allows you to display and edit text with various styles and attributes. Also supports embedded images and windows.

There are many options for creating widgets from these classes. The first argument is always the parent container. You can specify a foreground color, background color, font, and cursor style when constructing a widget.

color

To specify a color, use either a color name (such as red, yellow, green, blue, white, black, purple) or explicitly specify the red, green, and blue (RGB) color components by using a string **#RRGGBB**, where **RR**, **GG**, and **BB** are hexadecimal representations of the red, green, and blue values, respectively.

font

You can specify a font in a string that includes the font name, size, and style. Here are some examples:

```
Times 10 bold
Helvetica 10 bold italic
CourierNew 20 bold italic
Courier 20 bold italic overstrike underline
```

text formatting

By default, the text in a label or a button is centered. You can change its alignment by using the **justify** option with the named constants **LEFT**, **CENTER**, or **RIGHT**. (Remember, as discussed in Section 2.6, named constants are in all uppercase.) You can also display the text in multiple lines by inserting the newline character **\n** to separate lines of text.

mouse cursor

You can specify a particular style of mouse cursor by using the **cursor** option with string values such as **arrow** (the default), **circle**, **cross**, **plus**, or some other shape.

change properties

When you construct a widget, you can specify its properties such as **fg**, **bg**, **font**, **cursor**, **text**, and **command** in the constructor. Later in the program, you can change the widget's properties by using the following syntax:

```
widgetName["propertyName"] = newPropertyValue
```

For example, the following code creates a button and its **text** property is changed to **Hide**, **bg** property to **red**, and **fg** to **#AB84F9**. **#AB84F9** is a color specified in the form of RRGGBB.

```
btShowOrHide = Button(window, text = "Show", bg = "white")
btShowOrHide["text"] = "Hide"
btShowOrHide["bg"] = "red"
btShowOrHide["fg"] = "#AB84F9" # Change fg color to #AB84F9
btShowOrHide["cursor"] = "plus" # Change mouse cursor to plus
btShowOrHide["justify"] = LEFT # Set justify to LEFT
```

Each class comes with a substantial number of methods. The complete information about these classes is beyond the scope of this book. A good reference resource for Tkinter can be found at www.pythonware.com/library/tkinter. This chapter provides examples that show you how to use these widgets.

Listing 9.4 is an example of a program that uses the widgets **Frame**, **Button**, **Checkbutton**, **Radiobutton**, **Label**, **Entry** (also known as a text field), **Message**, and **Text** (also known as a text area).

LISTING 9.4 WidgetsDemo.py

```
1  from tkinter import * # Import all definitions from tkinter
2
3  class WidgetsDemo:
4      def __init__(self):
5          window = Tk() # Create a window
6          window.title("Widgets Demo") # Set a title
7
8          # Add a check button, and a radio button to frame1
9          frame1 = Frame(window) # Create and add a frame to window
10         frame1.pack()
11         self.v1 = IntVar()
```

create a window
window title

create frame

```
12        cbtBold = Checkbutton(frame1, text = "Bold",              create check button
13            variable = self.v1 , command = self.processCheckbutton)
14        self.v2 = IntVar()
15        rbRed = Radiobutton(frame1, text = "Red", bg = "red",     create radio button
16            variable = self.v2 , value = 1,
17            command = self.processRadiobutton)
18        rbYellow = Radiobutton(frame1, text = "Yellow",
19            bg = "yellow", variable = self.v2, value = 2,
20            command = self.processRadiobutton)
21        cbtBold.grid(row = 1, column = 1)                         grid manager
22        rbRed.grid(row = 1, column = 2)
23        rbYellow.grid(row = 1, column = 3)
24
25        # Add a label, an entry, a button, and a message to frame1
26        frame2 = Frame(window) # Create and add a frame to window  create frame
27        frame2.pack()
28        label = Label(frame2, text = "Enter your name: ")
29        self.name = StringVar()
30        entryName = Entry(frame2, textvariable = self.name )       create entry
31        btGetName = Button(frame2, text = "Get Name",
32            command = self.processButton)
33        message = Message(frame2, text = "It is a widgets demo")   create message
34        label.grid(row = 1, column = 1)
35        entryName.grid(row = 1, column = 2)
36        btGetName.grid(row = 1, column = 3)
37        message.grid(row = 1, column = 4)
38
39        # Add text
40        text = Text(window) # Create and add text to the window    create text
41        text.pack()
42        text.insert(END,                                           insert text
43            "Tip\nThe best way to learn Tkinter is to read ")
44        text.insert(END,
45            "these carefully designed examples and use them ")
46        text.insert(END, "to create your applications.")
47
48        window.mainloop() # Create an event loop                   event loop
49
50    def processCheckbutton(self):
51        print("check button is "
52            + ("checked " if self.v1.get() == 1 else "unchecked"))  check button status
53
54    def processRadiobutton(self):
55        print(("Red" if self.v2.get() == 1 else "Yellow")          radio button status
56            + " is selected " )
57
58    def processButton(self):
59        print("Your name is " + self.name.get())                   entry name
60
61 WidgetsDemo() # Create GUI                                        create GUI
```

When you run the program, the widgets are displayed as shown in Figure 9.4a. As you click the *Bold* button, select the *Yellow* radio button, and type in "Johnson," you can watch the events being processed and see their associated messages in the command window in Figure 9.4b.

The program creates the window (line 5) and invokes its **title** method to set a title (line 6). The **Frame** class is used to create a frame named **frame1** and the parent container for the frame is the window (line 9). This frame is used as the parent container for a check button and two radio buttons, created in lines 12, 15, and 18.

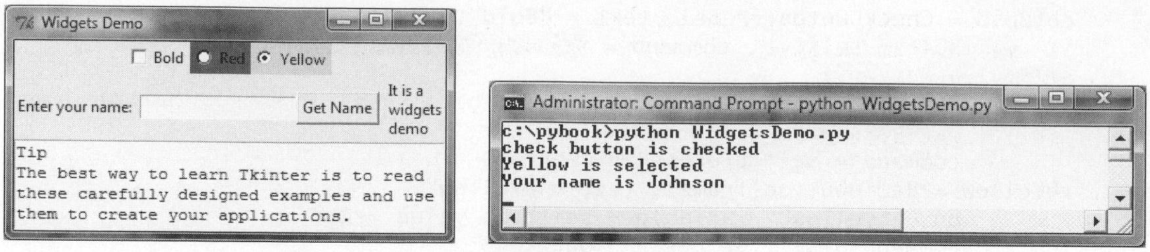

(a)   (b)

FIGURE 9.4 (a) The widgets are displayed in the user interface. (b) Watching events being processed.

IntVar
DoubleVar
StringVar

You use an entry (text field) for entering a value. The value must be an object of **IntVar**, **DoubleVar**, or **StringVar** representing an integer, a float, or a string, respectively. **IntVar**, **DoubleVar**, and **StringVar** are defined in the **tkinter** module.

The program creates a check button and associates it with the variable **v1**. **v1** is an instance of **IntVar** (line 11). **v1** is set to **1** if the check button is checked, or **0** if it isn't checked. When the check button is clicked, Python invokes the **processCheckbutton** method (line 13).

The program then creates a radio button and associates it with an **IntVar** variable, **v2**. **v2** is set to **1** if the *Red* radio button is selected, or **2** if the *Yellow* radio button is checked. You can define any integer or string values when constructing a radio button. When either of the two buttons is clicked, the **processRadiobutton** method is invoked.

geometry manager

The grid *geometry manager* is used to place the check button and radio buttons into **frame1**. These three widgets are placed in the same row and in columns 1, 2, and 3, respectively (lines 21–23).

The program creates another frame, **frame2** (line 26), for holding a label, an entry, a button, and a message widget. Like **frame1**, **frame2** is placed inside the window.

An entry is created and associated with the variable **name** of the **StringVar** type for storing the value in the entry (line 29). When you click the *Get Name* button, the **processButton** method displays the value in the entry (line 59). The **Message** widget is like a label except that it automatically wraps the words and displays them in multiple lines.

The grid geometry manager is used to place the widget in **frame2**. These widgets are placed in the same row and in columns 1, 2, 3, and 4, respectively (lines 34–37).

The program creates a **Text** widget (line 40) for displaying and editing text. It is placed inside the window (line 41). You can use the **insert** method to insert text into this widget. The **END** option specifies that the text is inserted into the end of the current content.

Listing 9.5 is a program that lets the user change the color, font, and text of a label, as shown in Figure 9.5.

LISTING 9.5 ChangeLabelDemo.py

```python
1  from tkinter import *  # Import all definitions from tkinter
2
3  class ChangeLabelDemo:
4      def __init__(self):
5          window = Tk()  # Create a window
6          window.title("Change Label Demo")  # Set a title
7
8          # Add a label to frame1
9          frame1 = Frame(window)  # Create and add a frame to window
10         frame1.pack()
11         self.lbl = Label(frame1, text = "Programming is fun")
12         self.lbl.pack()
13
```

window title

create frame1

create label

```
14              # Add a label, entry, button, two radio buttons to frame2
15              frame2 = Frame(window) # Create and add a frame to window
16              frame2.pack()
17              label = Label(frame2, text = "Enter text: ")
18              self.msg = StringVar()
19              entry = Entry(frame2, textvariable = self.msg)
20              btChangeText = Button(frame2, text = "Change Text",
21                  command = self.processButton)
22              self.v1 = StringVar()
23              rbRed = Radiobutton(frame2, text = "Red", bg = "red",
24                  variable = self.v1, value = 'R',
25                  command = self.processRadiobutton)
26              rbYellow = Radiobutton(frame2, text = "Yellow",
27                  bg = "yellow", variable = self.v1, value = 'Y',
28                  command = self.processRadiobutton)
29
30              label.grid(row = 1, column = 1)
31              entry.grid(row = 1, column = 2)
32              btChangeText.grid(row = 1, column = 3)
33              rbRed.grid(row = 1, column = 4)
34              rbYellow.grid(row = 1, column = 5)
35
36              window.mainloop() # Create an event loop
37
38      def processRadiobutton(self):
39          if self.v1.get() == 'R':
40              self.lbl["fg"] = "red"
41          elif self.v1.get() == 'Y':
42              self.lbl["fg"] = "yellow"
43
44      def processButton(self):
45          self.lbl["text"] = self.msg.get() # New text for the label
46
47  ChangeLabelDemo() # Create GUI
```

	create frame2
	create entry
	button callback
	radio button callback
	radio button callback
	event loop
	set a new fg
	set a new fg
	set new text
	create GUI

FIGURE 9.5   The program changes the label's **text** and **fg** properties dynamically.

When you select a radio button, the label's foreground color changes. If you enter new text in the entry field and click the *Change Text* button, the new text appears in the label.

The program creates the window (line 5) and invokes its **title** method to set a title (line 6). The **Frame** class is used to create a frame named **frame1** and the parent container for the frame is the window (line 9). This frame is used as the parent container for a label created in line 11. Because the label is a data field in the class, it can be referenced in a callback function.

The program creates another frame, **frame2** (line 15), for holding a label, an entry, a button, and two radio buttons. Like **frame1**, **frame2** is placed inside the window.

An entry is created and associated with the variable **msg** of the **StringVar** type for storing the value in the entry (line 19). When you click the *Change Text* button, the **processButton** method sets a new text entry for the label in **frame1**, using the text in the entry (line 45).

Two radio buttons are created and associated with a **StringVar** variable, **v2**. **v2** is set to **R** if the *Red* radio button is selected, or to **Y** if the *Yellow* radio button is clicked. When the user clicks either of the two buttons, Python invokes the **processRadiobutton** method to change the label's foreground color in **frame1** (lines 38–42).

9.6 How do you create a label with the text **Welcome**, a white foreground, and a red background?

9.7 How do you create a button with the text **OK**, a white foreground, a red background, and with the callback function **processOK**?

9.8 How do you create a check button with the text **apple**, a white foreground, a red background, associated with the variable **v1**, and with the callback function **processApple**?

9.9 How do you create a radio button with the text **senior**, a white foreground, a red background, associated with the variable **v1**, and with the callback function **processSenior**?

9.10 How do you create an entry with a white foreground, a red background, and associated with the variable **v1**?

9.11 How do you create a message with the text **programming is fun**, a white foreground, and a red background?

9.12 **LEFT**, **CENTER**, and **RIGHT** are named constants defined in the **tkinter** module. Use a **print** statement to display the values defined by **LEFT**, **CENTER**, and **RIGHT**.

9.5 Canvas

*You use the **Canvas** widget for displaying shapes.*

You can use the methods **create_rectangle**, **create_oval**, **create_arc**, **create_polygon**, or **create_line** to draw a rectangle, oval, arc, polygon, or line on a canvas.

Listing 9.6 shows how to use the **Canvas** widget. The program displays a rectangle, an oval, an arc, a polygon, a line, and a text string. The objects are all controlled by buttons, as shown in Figure 9.6.

LISTING 9.6 CanvasDemo.py

```
1  from tkinter import * # Import all definitions from tkinter
2
3  class CanvasDemo:
4      def __init__(self):
5          window = Tk() # Create a window
6          window.title("Canvas Demo") # Set title
7
8          # Place canvas in the window
9          self.canvas = Canvas(window, width = 200, height = 100,
10             bg = "white")
11          self.canvas.pack()
12
13          # Place buttons in frame
14          frame = Frame(window)
15          frame.pack()
16          btRectangle = Button(frame, text = "Rectangle",
17              command = self.displayRect)
```

create a window

create a canvas

create a frame

create buttons

```
18          btOval = Button(frame, text = "Oval",
19              command = self.displayOval)
20          btArc = Button(frame, text = "Arc",
21              command = self.displayArc)
22          btPolygon = Button(frame, text = "Polygon",
23              command = self.displayPolygon)
24          btLine = Button(frame, text = "Line",
25              command = self.displayLine)
26          btString = Button(frame, text = "String",
27              command = self.displayString)
28          btClear = Button(frame, text = "Clear",
29              command = self.clearCanvas)
30          btRectangle.grid(row = 1, column = 1)          place buttons
31          btOval.grid(row = 1, column = 2)
32          btArc.grid(row = 1, column = 3)
33          btPolygon.grid(row = 1, column = 4)
34          btLine.grid(row = 1, column = 5)
35          btString.grid(row = 1, column = 6)
36          btClear.grid(row = 1, column = 7)
37
38          window.mainloop() # Create an event loop          event loop
39
40      # Display a rectangle
41      def displayRect(self):
42          self.canvas.create_rectangle(10, 10, 190, 90, tags = "rect")     display rectangle
43
44      # Display an oval
45      def displayOval(self):
46          self.canvas.create_oval(10, 10, 190, 90, fill = "red",          display oval
47              tags = "oval")
48
49      # Display an arc
50      def displayArc(self):
51          self.canvas.create_arc(10, 10, 190, 90, start = 0,              display arc
52              extent = 90, width = 8, fill = "red", tags = "arc")
53
54      # Display a polygon
55      def displayPolygon(self):
56          self.canvas.create_polygon(10, 10, 190, 90, 30, 50,             display polygon
57              tags = "polygon")
58
59      # Display a line
60      def displayLine(self):
61          self.canvas.create_line(10, 10, 190, 90, fill = "red",          display line
62              tags = "line")
63          self.canvas.create_line(10, 90, 190, 10, width = 9,
64              arrow = "last", activefill = "blue", tags = "line")
65
66      # Display a string
67      def displayString(self):
68          self.canvas.create_text(60, 40, text = "Hi, I am a string",     display string
69              font = "Times 10 bold underline", tags = "string")
70
71      # Clear drawings
72      def clearCanvas(self):
73          self.canvas.delete("rect", "oval", "arc", "polygon",            clear canvas
74              "line", "string")
75
76  CanvasDemo() # Create GUI          create GUI
```

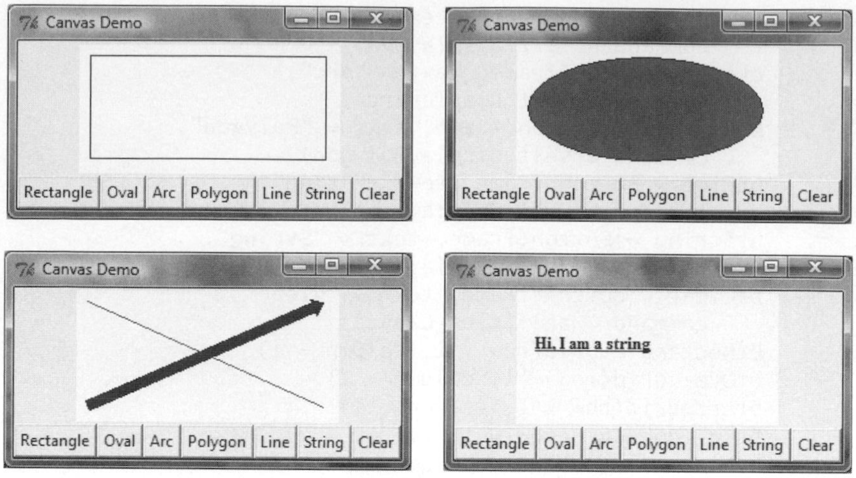

FIGURE 9.6 The geometrical shapes and strings are drawn on the canvas.

The program creates a window (line 5) and sets its title (line 6). A **Canvas** widget is created within the window with a width of **200** pixels, a height of **100** pixels, and a background color of **white** (lines 9–10).

Seven buttons—labeled with the text *Rectangle*, *Oval*, *Arc*, *Polygon*, *Line*, *String*, and *Clear*—are created (lines 16–29). The *grid manager* places the buttons in one row in a frame (lines 30–36).

grid manager

To draw graphics, you need to tell the widget where to draw. Each widget has its own coordinate system with the origin (0, 0) at the upper-left corner. The *x*-coordinate increases to the right, and the *y*-coordinate increases downward. Note that the Tkinter coordinate system differs from the conventional coordinate system, as shown in Figure 9.7.

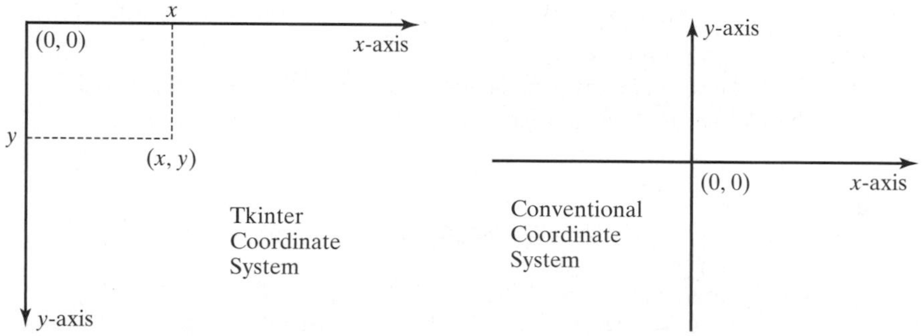

coordinate system

FIGURE 9.7 The Tkinter coordinate system is measured in pixels, with **(0, 0)** at its upper-left corner.

The methods **create_rectangle**, **create_oval**, **create_arc**, **create_polygon**, and **create_line** (lines 42, 46, 51, 56, and 61) are used to draw rectangles, ovals, arcs, polygons, and lines, as illustrated in Figure 9.8.

create_text

The **create_text** method is used to draw a text string (line 68). Note that the horizontal and vertical center of the text is displayed at (*x*, *y*) for **create_text(x, y, text)** as shown in Figure 9.8.

tags

All the drawing methods use the **tags** argument to identify the drawing. These tags are used in the **delete** method for clearing the drawing from the canvas (lines 73–74).

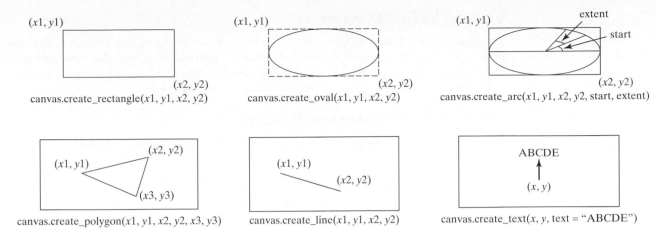

FIGURE 9.8 The **Canvas** class contains the methods for drawing graphics.

The **width** argument can be used to specify the pen size in pixels for drawing the shapes (lines 52 and 63).

width

The **arrow** argument can be used with **create_line** to draw a line with an arrowhead (line 64). The arrowhead can appear at the start, end, or both ends of the line with the argument value **first**, **end**, or **both**.

arrow

The **activefill** argument makes the shape change color when you move the mouse over it (line 64).

activefill

9.13 Write the code to draw a line from (**34**, **50**) to (**50**, **90**).

9.14 Write the code to draw a rectangle centered at (**70**, **70**) with a width of **100** and a height of **100**. Fill the rectangle with the color red.

9.15 Write the code to draw an oval centered at (**70**, **70**) with a width of **200** and a height of **100**. Fill the rectangle with red.

9.16 Write the code to draw an arc with a starting angle of **30**, with an extent angle of **45** in a bounding rectangle with its upper-left corner at (**10**, **10**) and bottom-right corner at (**80**, **80**).

9.17 Write the code to draw a polygon with points at (**10**, **10**), (**15**, **30**), (**140**, **10**), and (**10**, **100**). Fill the shape with red.

9.18 How do you draw a shape with a large pen size?

9.19 How do you draw a line with an arrowhead?

9.20 How do you make a shape change color when the mouse is moved over it?

✓**Check Point**

MyProgrammingLab™

9.6 The Geometry Managers

Tkinter uses a geometry manager to place widgets inside a container.

Key Point

Tkinter supports three geometry managers: the grid manager, the pack manager, and the place manager. You have already used the grid and pack managers. This section describes these managers and introduces some additional features.

 Tip
Since each manager has its own style of placing the widget, it is not a good practice to mix the managers for the widgets in the same container. You can use a frame as a sub-container to achieve the desired layout.

9.6.1 The Grid Manager

The grid manager places widgets into the cells of an invisible grid in a container. You can place a widget in a specified row and column. You can also use the **rowspan** and **columnspan** parameters to place a widget in multiple rows and columns. Listing 9.7 uses the grid manager to lay out a group of widgets, as shown in Figure 9.9.

rowspan
columnspan

LISTING 9.7 GridManagerDemo.py

```
1  from tkinter import * # Import all definitions from tkinter
2
3  class GridManagerDemo:
4      window = Tk() # Create a window
5      window.title("Grid Manager Demo") # Set title
6
7      message = Message(window, text =
8          "This Message widget occupies three rows and two columns")
9      message.grid(row = 1, column = 1, rowspan = 3, columnspan = 2)
10     Label(window, text = "First Name:").grid(row = 1, column = 3)
11     Entry(window).grid(row = 1, column = 4, padx = 5, pady = 5)
12     Label(window, text = "Last Name:").grid(row = 2, column = 3)
13     Entry(window).grid(row = 2, column = 4)
14     Button(window, text = "Get Name").grid(row = 3,
15         padx = 5, pady = 5, column = 4, sticky = E)
16
17     window.mainloop() # Create an event loop
18
19 GridManagerDemo() # Create GUI
```

rowspan (line 9)

padx (line 11)

sticky (line 15)

event loop (line 17)

create GUI (line 19)

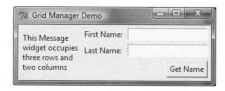

FIGURE 9.9 The grid manager was used to place these widgets.

The **Message** widget is placed in row 1 and column 1 and it expands to three rows and two columns (line 9). The *Get Name* button uses the **sticky** = **E** option (line 15) to stick to the east in the cell so that it is right aligned with the **Entry** widgets in the same column. The **sticky** option defines how to expand the widget if the resulting cell is larger than the widget itself. The **sticky** option can be any combination of the named constants **S**, **N**, **E**, and **W**, or **NW**, **NE**, **SW**, and **SE**.

sticky option

The **padx** and **pady** options pad the optional horizontal and vertical space in a cell (lines 11 and 15). You can also use the **ipadx** and **ipady** options to pad the optional horizontal and vertical space inside the widget borders.

padx option
pady option

9.6.2 The Pack Manager

pack manager
side
fill
expand

The *pack manager* can place widgets on top of each other or place them side by side. You can also use the **fill** option to make a widget fill its entire container.

Listing 9.8 displays three labels, as shown in Figure 9.10a. These three labels are packed on top of each other. The red label uses the option **fill** with value **BOTH** and **expand** with value **1**. The **fill** option uses named constants **X**, **Y**, or **BOTH** to fill horizontally, vertically, or both ways. The **expand** option tells the pack manager to assign additional space to the widget box. If the parent widget is larger than necessary to hold all the packed widgets, any extra space is distributed among the widgets whose **expand** option is set to a nonzero value.

LISTING 9.8 PackManagerDemo.py

```
1   from tkinter import * # Import all definitions from tkinter
2
3   class PackManagerDemo:
4       def __init__(self):
5           window = Tk() # Create a window
6           window.title("Pack Manager Demo 1") # Set title
7
8           Label(window, text = "Blue", bg = "blue").pack()
9           Label(window, text = "Red", bg = "red").pack(
10              fill = BOTH, expand = 1)                            expand
11          Label(window, text = "Green", bg = "green").pack(
12              fill = BOTH)                                        fill
13
14          window.mainloop() # Create an event loop
15
16  PackManagerDemo() # Create GUI                                  create GUI
```

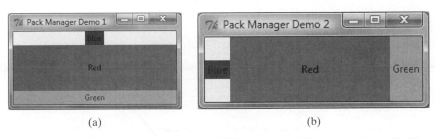

(a)   (b)

FIGURE 9.10   (a) The pack manager uses the `fill` option to fill the container. (b) You can place widgets side by side.

Listing 9.9 displays the three labels shown in Figure 9.10b. These three labels are packed side by side using the **side** option. The **side** option can be **LEFT**, **RIGHT**, **TOP**, or **BOTTOM**. By default, it is set to **TOP**.

LISTING 9.9 PackManagerDemoWithSide.py

```
1   from tkinter import * # Import all definitions from tkinter
2
3   class PackManagerDemoWithSide:
4       window = Tk() # Create a window
5       window.title("Pack Manager Demo 2") # Set title
6
7       Label(window, text = "Blue", bg = "blue").pack(side = LEFT)       side
8       Label(window, text = "Red", bg = "red").pack(
9           side = LEFT, fill = BOTH, expand = 1)
10      Label(window, text = "Green", bg = "green").pack(
11          side = LEFT, fill = BOTH)
12
13      window.mainloop() # Create an event loop
14
15  PackManagerDemoWithSide() # Create GUI                                create GUI
```

9.6.3 The Place Manager

place manager

The *place manager* places widgets in absolute positions. Listing 9.10 displays the three labels shown in Figure 9.11.

LISTING 9.10 PlaceManagerDemo.py

```
1  from tkinter import * # Import all definitions from tkinter
2
3  class PlaceManagerDemo:
4      def __init__(self):
5          window = Tk() # Create a window
6          window.title("Place Manager Demo") # Set title
7
8          Label(window, text = "Blue", bg = "blue").place(
9              x = 20, y = 20)
10         Label(window, text = "Red", bg = "red").place(
11             x = 50, y = 50)
12         Label(window, text = "Green", bg = "green").place(
13             x = 80, y = 80)
14
15         window.mainloop() # Create an event loop
16
17 PlaceManagerDemo() # Create GUI
```

place

create GUI

FIGURE 9.11 The place manager places widgets in absolute positions.

The upper-left corner of the blue label is at (**20, 20**). All three labels are placed using the place manager.

 Note

The place manager is not compatible with all computers. If you run this program on Windows with a screen monitor with 1024 × 768 resolution, the layout size is just right. When the program is run on Windows with a monitor with a higher resolution, the components appear very small and clump together. When it is run on Windows with a monitor with a lower resolution, they cannot be shown in their entirety. Because of these incompatibility issues, you should generally avoid using the place manager.

MyProgrammingLab™

9.21 What is wrong if you write the following code using the pack manager for a button?

```
button.pack(LEFT)
```

9.22 If you need to pad spaces between widgets, which geometry manager should you use?

9.23 Why should you avoid using the place manager?

9.24 X, Y, BOTH, S, N, E, and W, or NW, NE, SW, and SE are named constants defined in the **tkinter** module. Use a **print** statement to display the values defined in these constants.

9.7 Case Study: Loan Calculator

This section provides an example that uses GUI widgets, geometry layout managers, and events.

Key Point

VideoNote

Create GUI application

Listing 2.8 developed a console-based program for computing loans. This section develops a GUI application for computing loan payments, as shown in Figure 9.12a.

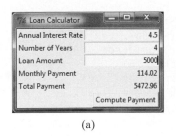
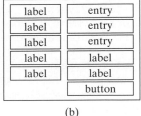

(a)   (b)

FIGURE 9.12 The program computes loan payments and provides a graphical user interface.

Developing a GUI application involves designing the user interface and writing the code to process the events. Here are the major steps in writing the program:

1. Design the user interface (UI) by drawing a sketch, as shown in Figure 9.12b. The UI consists of labels, text entry boxes, and a button. You can use the grid manager to position them in the window.

2. Process the event. When the button is clicked, the program invokes a callback function to obtain the user input for the interest rate, number of years, and loan amount from the text entries, computes the monthly and total payments, and displays the values in the labels.

Listing 9.11 shows the complete program.

LISTING 9.11 LoanCalculator.py

```
1  from tkinter import * # Import all definitions from tkinter
2
3  class LoanCalculator:
4      def __init__(self):
5          window = Tk() # Create a window
6          window.title("Loan Calculator") # Set title
7
8          Label(window, text = "Annual Interest Rate").grid(row = 1,
9              column = 1, sticky = W)
10          Label(window, text = "Number of Years").grid(row = 2,
11              column = 1, sticky = W)
12          Label(window, text = "Loan Amount").grid(row = 3,
13              column = 1, sticky = W)
14          Label(window, text = "Monthly Payment").grid(row = 4,
15              column = 1, sticky = W)
16          Label(window, text = "Total Payment").grid(row = 5,
17              column = 1, sticky = W)
18
19          self.annualInterestRateVar = StringVar()
20          Entry(window, textvariable = self.annualInterestRateVar,
21              justify = RIGHT).grid(row = 1, column = 2)
22          self.numberOfYearsVar = StringVar()
```

create window

create labels

create entries

```
23              Entry(window, textvariable = self.numberOfYearsVar,
24                  justify = RIGHT).grid(row = 2, column = 2)
25              self.loanAmountVar = StringVar()
26              Entry(window, textvariable = self.loanAmountVar,
27                  justify = RIGHT).grid(row = 3, column = 2)
28
29              self.monthlyPaymentVar = StringVar()
30              lblMonthlyPayment = Label(window, textvariable =
31                  self.monthlyPaymentVar).grid(row = 4, column = 2,
32                      sticky = E)
33              self.totalPaymentVar = StringVar()
34              lblTotalPayment = Label(window, textvariable =
35                  self.totalPaymentVar).grid(row = 5,
36                      column = 2, sticky = E)
```
create button
callback
```
37              btComputePayment = Button(window, text = "Compute Payment",
38                  command = self.computePayment).grid(
39                      row = 6, column = 2, sticky = E)
40
41              window.mainloop() # Create an event loop
42
```
computePayment
```
43          def computePayment(self):
44              monthlyPayment = self.getMonthlyPayment(
45                  float(self.loanAmountVar.get()),
46                  float(self.annualInterestRateVar.get()) / 1200,
47                  int(self.numberOfYearsVar.get()))
```
set monthlyPayment
```
48              self.monthlyPaymentVar.set(format(monthlyPayment, "10.2f"))
49              totalPayment = float(self.monthlyPaymentVar.get()) * 12 \
50                  * int(self.numberOfYearsVar.get())
```
set totalPayment
```
51              self.totalPaymentVar.set(format(totalPayment, "10.2f"))
52
```
getMonthlyPayment
```
53          def getMonthlyPayment(self,
54                  loanAmount, monthlyInterestRate, numberOfYears):
55              monthlyPayment = loanAmount * monthlyInterestRate / (1
56                  - 1 / (1 + monthlyInterestRate) ** (numberOfYears * 12))
57              return monthlyPayment;
58
```
create GUI
```
59  LoanCalculator()  # Create GUI
```

The program creates the user interface with labels, entries, and a button placed in the window using the grid manager (lines 8–39). The command option for the button is set to the **computePayment** method (line 38). When the *Compute Payment* button is clicked, its method is invoked, which obtains the user input for the annual interest rate, years for the loan, and loan amount to calculate the monthly payment and total payment (lines 43–51).

9.8 Displaying Images

Key Point

You can add an image to a label, button, check button, or radio button.

To create an image, use the **PhotoImage** class as follows:

```
photo = PhotoImage(file = imagefilename)
```

The image file must be in GIF format. You can use a conversion utility to convert image files in other formats into GIF format.

Listing 9.12 shows you how to add images to labels, buttons, check buttons, and radio buttons. You can also use the **create_image** method to display an image in a canvas, as shown in Figure 9.13.

LISTING 9.12 ImageDemo.py

```
1  from tkinter import * # Import all definitions from tkinter
2
3  class ImageDemo:
4      def __init__(self):
5          window = Tk() # Create a window                            create window
6          window.title("Image Demo") # Set title
7
8          # Create PhotoImage objects
9          caImage = PhotoImage(file = "image/ca.gif")               create image
10         chinaImage = PhotoImage(file = "image/china.gif")
11         leftImage = PhotoImage(file = "image/left.gif")
12         rightImage = PhotoImage(file = "image/right.gif")
13         usImage = PhotoImage(file = "image/usIcon.gif")
14         ukImage = PhotoImage(file = "image/ukIcon.gif")
15         crossImage = PhotoImage(file = "image/x.gif")
16         circleImage = PhotoImage(file = "image/o.gif")
17
18         # frame1 to contain label and canvas
19         frame1 = Frame(window)
20         frame1.pack()
21         Label(frame1, image = caImage).pack(side = LEFT)          image in label
22         canvas = Canvas(frame1)
23         canvas.create_image(90, 50, image = chinaImage)          image in canvas
24         canvas["width"] = 200
25         canvas["height"] = 100
26         canvas.pack(side = LEFT)
27
28         # frame2 contains buttons, check buttons, and radio buttons
29         frame2 = Frame(window)
30         frame2.pack()
31         Button(frame2, image = leftImage).pack(side = LEFT)       image in button
32         Button(frame2, image = rightImage).pack(side = LEFT)
33         Checkbutton(frame2, image = usImage).pack(side = LEFT)    image in check button
34         Checkbutton(frame2, image = ukImage).pack(side = LEFT)
35         Radiobutton(frame2, image = crossImage).pack(side = LEFT) image in radio button
36         Radiobutton(frame2, image = circleImage).pack(side = LEFT)
37
38         window.mainloop() # Create an event loop
39
40  ImageDemo() # Create GUI                                          create GUI
```

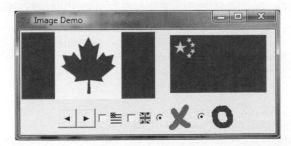

FIGURE 9.13 The program displays widgets with images.

The program places image files in the image folder in the current program directory, then creates **PhotoImage** objects for several images in lines 9–16. These objects are used in widgets. The image is a property in **Label**, **Button**, **Checkbutton**, and **RadioButton** (lines 21 and 31–36). Image is not a property for **Canvas**, but you can use the **create_image** method to display an image on the canvas (line 23). In fact, you can display multiple images in one canvas.

MyProgrammingLab™

9.25 What image format is supported in Python?

9.26 What is wrong with the following statement for creating a **PhotoImage**?

```
image = PhotoImage("image/us.gif")
```

9.27 How do you create a button that shows an image in c:\pybook\image\canada.gif?

9.9 Menus

You can use Tkinter to create menus, popup menus, and toolbars.

Tkinter provides a comprehensive solution for building graphical user interfaces. This section introduces menus, popup menus, and toolbars.

Menus make selection easier and are widely used in windows. You can use the **Menu** class to create a menu bar and a menu, and use the **add_command** method to add items to the menu.

Listing 9.13 shows you how to create the menus shown in Figure 9.14.

LISTING 9.13 MenuDemo.py

```
1    from tkinter import *
2
3    class MenuDemo:
4        def __init__(self):
5            window = Tk()
6            window.title("Menu Demo")
7
8            # Create a menu bar
9            menubar = Menu(window)
10           window.config(menu = menubar) # Display the menu bar
11
12           # Create a pull-down menu, and add it to the menu bar
13           operationMenu = Menu(menubar, tearoff = 0)
14           menubar.add_cascade(label = "Operation", menu = operationMenu)
15           operationMenu.add_command(label = "Add",
16               command = self.add)
17           operationMenu.add_command(label = "Subtract",
18               command = self.subtract)
19           operationMenu.add_separator()
20           operationMenu.add_command(label = "Multiply",
21               command = self.multiply)
22           operationMenu.add_command(label = "Divide",
23               command = self.divide)
24
25           # Create more pull-down menus
26           exitmenu = Menu(menubar, tearoff = 0)
27           menubar.add_cascade(label = "Exit", menu = exitmenu)
28           exitmenu.add_command(label = "Quit", command = window.quit)
29
30           # Add a tool bar frame
31           frame0 = Frame(window) # Create and add a frame to window
```

Margin notes:
create a menu bar (line 9)
display menu bar (line 10)
create a menu (line 13)
display a menu (line 14)
add menu item (line 15)
create a menu (line 26)
display a menu (line 27)
add menu item (line 28)

```
32              frame0.grid(row = 1, column = 1, sticky = W)
33
34              # Create images
35              plusImage = PhotoImage(file = "image/plus.gif")                   create an image
36              minusImage = PhotoImage(file = "image/minus.gif")
37              timesImage = PhotoImage(file = "image/times.gif")
38              divideImage = PhotoImage(file = "image/divide.gif")
39
40              Button(frame0, image = plusImage, command =                       create a button
41                  self.add).grid(row = 1, column = 1, sticky = W)
42              Button(frame0, image = minusImage,
43                  command = self.subtract).grid(row = 1, column = 2)
44              Button(frame0, image = timesImage,
45                  command = self.multiply).grid(row = 1, column = 3)
46              Button(frame0, image = divideImage,
47                  command = self.divide).grid(row = 1, column = 4)
48
49              # Add labels and entries to frame1
50              frame1 = Frame(window)
51              frame1.grid(row = 2, column = 1, pady = 10)
52              Label(frame1, text = "Number 1:").pack(side = LEFT)
53              self.v1 = StringVar()
54              Entry(frame1, width = 5, textvariable = self.v1,
55                  justify = RIGHT).pack(side = LEFT)
56              Label(frame1, text = "Number 2:").pack(side = LEFT)
57              self.v2 = StringVar()
58              Entry(frame1, width = 5, textvariable = self.v2,
59                  justify = RIGHT).pack(side = LEFT)
60              Label(frame1, text = "Result:").pack(side = LEFT)
61              self.v3 = StringVar()
62              Entry(frame1, width = 5, textvariable = self.v3,
63                  justify = RIGHT).pack(side = LEFT)
64
65              # Add buttons to frame2
66              frame2 = Frame(window) # Create and add a frame to window
67              frame2.grid(row = 3, column = 1, pady = 10, sticky = E)
68              Button(frame2, text = "Add", command = self.add).pack(
69                  side = LEFT)
70              Button(frame2, text = "Subtract",
71                  command = self.subtract).pack(side = LEFT)
72              Button(frame2, text = "Multiply",
73                  command = self.multiply).pack(side = LEFT)
74              Button(frame2, text = "Divide",
75                  command = self.divide).pack(side = LEFT)
76
77              mainloop()
78
79      def add(self):                                                           callback method
80          self.v3.set(eval(self.v1.get()) + eval(self.v2.get()))
81
82      def subtract(self):                                                      callback method
83          self.v3.set(eval(self.v1.get()) - eval(self.v2.get()))
84
85      def multiply(self):                                                      callback method
86          self.v3.set(eval(self.v1.get()) * eval(self.v2.get()))
87
88      def divide(self):                                                        callback method
89          self.v3.set(eval(self.v1.get()) / eval(self.v2.get()))
90
91  MenuDemo() # Create GUI                                                       create GUI
```

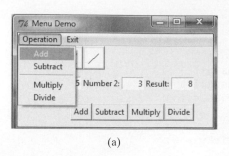
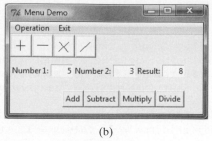

(a)   (b)   (c)

FIGURE 9.14   The program performs arithmetic operations using menu commands, toolbar buttons, and buttons.

The program creates a menu bar in line 9, and the menu bar is added to the window. To display the menu, use the **config** method to add the menu bar to the container (line 10). To create a menu inside a menu bar, use the menu bar as the parent container (line 13) and invoke the menu bar's **add_cascade** method to set the menu label (line 14). You can then use the **add_command** method to add items to the menu (lines 15–23). Note that the **tearoff** is set to **0**, which specifies that the menu cannot be moved out of the window. If this option is not set, the menu can be moved out of the window, as shown in Figure 9.14c.

The program creates another menu named **Exit** (lines 26–27) and adds the **Quit** menu item to it (line 28).

The program creates a frame named **frame0** (lines 31–32) and uses it to hold toolbar buttons. The toolbar buttons are buttons with images, which are created by using the **PhotoImage** class (lines 35–38). The command for each button specifies a callback function to be invoked when a toolbar button is clicked (lines 40–47).

The program creates a frame named **frame1** (lines 50–51) and uses it to hold labels and entries for numbers. Variables **v1**, **v2**, and **v3** bind the entries (lines 53, 57, and 61).

The program creates a frame named **frame2** (lines 66–67) and uses it to hold four buttons for performing *Add*, *Subtract*, *Multiply*, and *Divide*. The *Add* button, Add menu item, and Add tool bar button have the same callback function **add** (lines 79–80), which is invoked when any one of them—the button, menu item, or tool bar button—is clicked.

9.10 Popup Menus

Key Point

A popup menu, also known as a context menu, is like a regular menu, but it does not have a menu bar and it can float anywhere on the screen.

Creating a popup menu is similar to creating a regular menu. First, you create an instance of **Menu**, and then you can add items to it. Finally, you bind a widget with an event to pop up the menu.

The example in Listing 9.14 uses popup menu commands to select a shape to be displayed in a canvas, as shown in Figure 9.15.

LISTING 9.14   PopupMenuDemo.py

```
1  from tkinter import * # Import all definitions from tkinter
2
3  class PopupMenuDemo:
4      def __init__(self):
5          window = Tk() # Create a window
6          window.title("Popup Menu Demo") # Set title
7
```

```
 8              # Create a popup menu
 9              self.menu = Menu(window, tearoff = 0)                    create a menu
10              self.menu.add_command(label = "Draw a line",            add menu item
11                  command = self.displayLine)
12              self.menu.add_command(label = "Draw an oval",
13                  command = self.displayOval)
14              self.menu.add_command(label = "Draw a rectangle",
15                  command = self.displayRect)
16              self.menu.add_command(label = "Clear",
17                  command = self.clearCanvas)
18
19              # Place canvas in window
20              self.canvas = Canvas(window, width = 200,                create a canvas
21                  height = 100, bg = "white")
22              self.canvas.pack()
23
24              # Bind popup to canvas
25              self.canvas.bind("<Button-3>", self.popup)              bind popup menu
26
27              window.mainloop() # Create an event loop
28
29      # Display a rectangle
30      def displayRect(self):                                          display rectangle
31          self.canvas.create_rectangle(10, 10, 190, 90, tags = "rect")
32
33      # Display an oval
34      def displayOval(self):                                          display oval
35          self.canvas.create_oval(10, 10, 190, 90, tags = "oval")
36
37      # Display two lines
38      def displayLine(self):                                          display lines
39          self.canvas.create_line(10, 10, 190, 90, tags = "line")
40          self.canvas.create_line(10, 90, 190, 10, tags = "line")
41
42      # Clear drawings
43      def clearCanvas(self):                                          clear canvas
44          self.canvas.delete("rect", "oval", "line")
45
46      def popup(self, event):
47          self.menu.post(event.x_root, event.y_root)
48
49  PopupMenuDemo() # Create GUI                                         create GUI
```

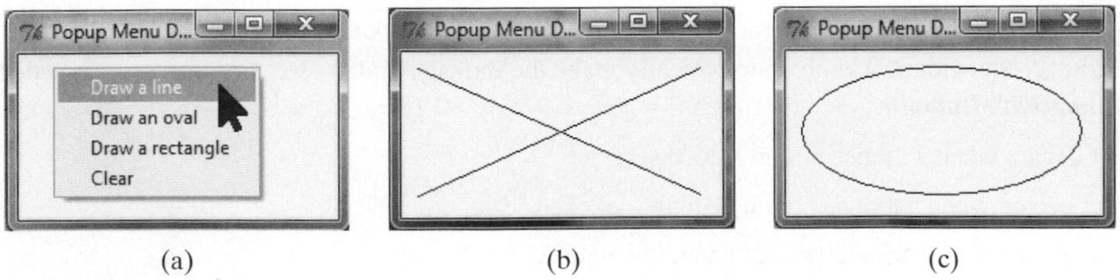

(a)   (b)   (c)

FIGURE 9.15   The program displays a popup menu when the canvas is clicked.

The program creates a menu to hold menu items (lines 9–17). A canvas is created to display the shapes. The menu items use callback functions to instruct the canvas to draw shapes.

Customarily, you display a popup menu by pointing to a widget and clicking the right mouse button. The program binds the right mouse button click with the popup callback function on the **canvas** (line 25). When you click the right mouse button, the **popup** callback function is invoked, which displays the menu at the location where the mouse is clicked.

9.28 What method do you use to display a menu bar?

9.29 How do you display a popup menu?

9.11 Mouse, Key Events, and Bindings

*You can use the **bind** method to bind mouse and key events to a widget.*

The preceding example used the widget's **bind** method to bind a mouse event with a callback handler by using the syntax:

```
widget.bind(event, handler)
```

If a matching event occurs, the handler is invoked. In the preceding example, the event is **<Button-3>** and the handler function is **popup**. The event is a standard Tkinter object, which is automatically created when an event occurs. Every handler has an event as its argument. The following example defines the handler using the event as the argument:

```
def popup(event):
    menu.post(event.x_root, event.y_root)
```

The **event** object has a number of properties describing the event pertaining to the event. For example, for a mouse event, the **event** object uses the **x**, **y** properties to capture the current mouse location in pixels.

Table 9.2 lists some commonly used events and Table 9.3 lists some event properties.

The program in Listing 9.15 processes mouse and key events. It displays the window as shown in Figure 9.16a. The mouse and key events are processed and the processing information is displayed in the command window, as shown in Figure 9.16b.

TABLE 9.2 Events

Event	Description
<B*i*-Motion>	An event occurs when a mouse button is moved while being held down on the widget.
<Button-*i*>	Button-1, Button-2, and Button-3 identify the left, middle, and right buttons. When a mouse button is pressed over the widget, Tkinter automatically grabs the mouse pointer's location. ButtonPressed-*i* is synonymous with Button-*i*.
<ButtonReleased-*i*>	An event occurs when a mouse button is released.
<Double-Button-*i*>	An event occurs when a mouse button is double-clicked.
<Enter>	An event occurs when a mouse pointer enters the widget.
<Key>	An event occurs when a key is pressed.
<Leave>	An event occurs when a mouse pointer leaves the widget.
<Return>	An event occurs when the *Enter* key is pressed. You can bind any key such as *A*, *B*, *Up*, *Down*, *Left*, *Right* in the keyboard with an event.
<Shift+A>	An event occurs when the *Shift+A* keys are pressed. You can combine *Alt*, *Shift*, and *Control* with other keys.
<Triple-Button-*i*>	An event occurs when a mouse button is triple-clicked.

TABLE 9.3 Event Properties

Event Property	Description
char	The character entered from the keyboard for key events.
keycode	The key code (i.e., Unicode) for the key entered from the keyboard for key events.
keysym	The key symbol (i.e., character) for the key entered from the keyboard for key events.
num	The button number (1, 2, 3) indicates which mouse button was clicked.
widget	The widget object that fires this event.
x and y	The current mouse location in the widget in pixels.
x__root and y_root	The current mouse position relative to the upper-left corner of the screen, in pixels.

LISTING 9.15 MouseKeyEventDemo.py

```python
 1  from tkinter import * # Import all definitions from tkinter
 2
 3  class MouseKeyEventDemo:
 4      def __init__(self):
 5          window = Tk() # Create a window
 6          window.title("Event Demo") # Set a title
 7          canvas = Canvas(window, bg = "white", width = 200, height = 100)
 8          canvas.pack()
 9
10          # Bind with <Button-1> event
11          canvas.bind("<Button-1>", self.processMouseEvent)
12
13          # Bind with <Key> event
14          canvas.bind("<Key>", self.processKeyEvent)
15          canvas.focus_set()
16
17          window.mainloop() # Create an event loop
18
19      def processMouseEvent(self, event):
20          print("clicked at", event.x, event.y)
21          print("Position in the screen", event.x_root, event.y_root)
22          print("Which button is clicked? ", event.num)
23
24      def processKeyEvent(self, event):
25          print("keysym? ", event.keysym)
26          print("char? ", event.char)
27          print("keycode? ", event.keycode)
28
29  MouseKeyEventDemo() # Create GUI
```

create a canvas

bind a mouse event

bind a key event
set focus

process mouse event

process key event

create GUI

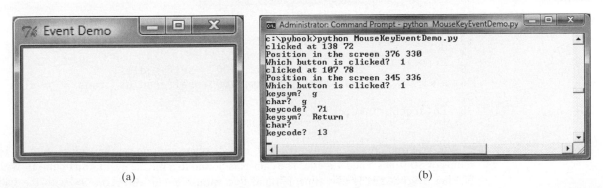

(a)   (b)

FIGURE 9.16 The program processes mouse and key events.

The program creates a canvas (line 7) and binds a mouse event **<Button-1>** with the call-back function **processMouseEvent** (line 11) on the canvas. Nothing is drawn on the canvas. So it is blank as shown in Figure 9.16a. When the left mouse button is clicked on the canvas, an event is created. The **processMouseEvent** is invoked to process an event that displays the mouse pointer's location on the canvas (line 20), on the screen (line 21), and which mouse button is clicked (line 22).

The **Canvas** widget is also the source for the key event. The program binds a key event with the callback function **processKeyEvent** on the canvas (line 14) and sets the focus on the canvas so that the canvas will receive input from the keyboard (line 15).

Listing 9.16 displays a circle on the canvas. The circle radius is increased with a left mouse click and decreased with a right mouse click, as shown in Figure 9.17.

LISTING 9.16 EnlargeShrinkCircle.py

```
 1  from tkinter import * # Import all definitions from tkinter
 2
 3  class EnlargeShrinkCircle:
 4      def __init__(self):
 5          self.radius = 50
 6
 7          window = Tk() # Create a window
 8          window.title("Control Circle Demo") # Set a title
 9          self.canvas = Canvas(window, bg = "white",
10              width = 200, height = 200)
11          self.canvas.pack()
12          self.canvas.create_oval(
13              100 - self.radius, 100 - self.radius,
14              100 + self.radius, 100 + self.radius, tags = "oval")
15
16          # Bind canvas with mouse events
17          self.canvas.bind("<Button-1>", self.increaseCircle)
18          self.canvas.bind("<Button-3>", self.decreaseCircle)
19
20          window.mainloop() # Create an event loop
21
22      def increaseCircle(self, event):
23          self.canvas.delete("oval")
24          if self.radius < 100:
25              self.radius += 2
26          self.canvas.create_oval(
27              100 - self.radius, 100 - self.radius,
28              100 + self.radius, 100 + self.radius, tags = "oval")
29
30      def decreaseCircle(self, event):
31          self.canvas.delete("oval")
32          if self.radius > 2:
33              self.radius -= 2
34          self.canvas.create_oval(
35              100 - self.radius, 100 - self.radius,
36              100 + self.radius, 100 + self.radius, tags = "oval")
37
38  EnlargeShrinkCircle() # Create GUI
```

Left margin annotations:
- initialize GUI (line 4)
- set radius property (line 5)
- create canvas (line 9)
- bind a mouse event (line 17)
- bind a mouse event (line 18)
- increase circle (line 22)
- decrease circle (line 30)
- create GUI (line 38)

The program creates a canvas (line 9) and displays a circle on the canvas with an initial radius of **50** (lines 5 and 12–14). The canvas is bound to a mouse event **<Button-1>** with the handler **increaseCircle** (line 17) and to a mouse event **<Button-3>** with the handler **decreaseCircle** (line 18). When the left mouse button is pressed, the **increaseCircle**

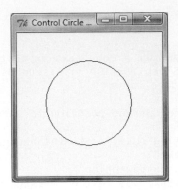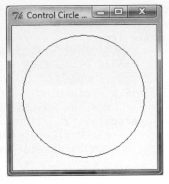

FIGURE 9.17   The program uses mouse events to control the circle's size.

function is invoked to increase the radius (lines 24–25) and redisplay the circle (lines 26–28). When the right mouse button is pressed, the **decreaseCircle** function is invoked to decrease the radius (lines 32–33) and redisplay the circle (lines 34–36).

9.30   How do you bind a canvas with the left mouse click event and callback function **p**?

9.31   What is the event for moving the mouse while pressing the right mouse button?

9.32   What is the event for clicking the left mouse button twice?

9.33   What is the event for clicking the middle mouse button three times?

9.34   What argument is automatically passed to an event-handling function?

9.35   How do you get the current mouse location from the event object?

9.36   How do you get the key character from the event object?

MyProgrammingLab™

9.12 Animations

Animations can be created by displaying a sequence of drawings.

The **Canvas** class can be used to develop animations. You can display graphics and text on the canvas and use the **move(tags, dx, dy)** method to move the graphic with the specified tags **dx** pixels to the right if **dx** is positive and **dy** pixels down if **dy** is positive. If **dx** or **dy** is negative, the graphic is moved left or up.

The program in Listing 9.17 displays a moving message repeatedly from left to right, as shown in Figure 9.18.

LISTING 9.17 AnimationDemo.py

```
1  from tkinter import * # Import all definitions from tkinter
2
3  class AnimationDemo:
4      def __init__(self):
5          window = Tk() # Create a window
6          window.title("Animation Demo") # Set a title
7
8          width = 250 # Width of the canvas
9          canvas = Canvas(window, bg = "white",
10             width = 250, height = 50)
11         canvas.pack()
12
13         x = 0 # Starting x position
14         canvas.create_text(x, 30,
15             text = "Message moving?", tags = "text")
```

create a canvas

create a text string

```
16
17            dx = 3
18            while True:
```

move text
```
19                canvas.move("text", dx, 0) # Move text dx unit
```
sleep
```
20                canvas.after(100) # Sleep for 100 milliseconds
```
update canvas
```
21                canvas.update() # Update canvas
22                if x < width:
23                    x += dx   # Get the current position for string
24                else:
```
restart from left
```
25                    x = 0 # Reset string position to the beginning
```
delete text
```
26                    canvas.delete("text")
27                    # Redraw text at the beginning
```
create a text string
```
28                    canvas.create_text(x, 30, text = "Message moving?",
29                        tags = "text")
30
31            window.mainloop() # Create an event loop
32
```
create GUI
```
33    AnimationDemo() # Create GUI
```

FIGURE 9.18   The program animates a moving message.

The program creates a canvas (line 9) and displays text on the canvas at the specified initial location (lines 13–15). The animation is done essentially in the following three statements in a loop (lines 19–21):

```
canvas.move("text", dx, 0) # Move text dx unit
canvas.after(100) # Sleep for 100 milliseconds
canvas.update() # Update canvas
```

The *x*-coordinate of the location is moved to the right **dx** units by invoking **canvas.move** (line 19). Invoking **canvas.after(100)** puts the program to sleep for **100** milliseconds (line 20). Invoking **canvas.update()** redisplays the canvas (line 21).

You can add tools to control the animation's speed, stop the animation, and resume the animation. Listing 9.18 rewrites Listing 9.17 by adding four buttons to control the animation, as shown in Figure 9.19.

LISTING 9.18   ControlAnimation.py

```
1    from tkinter import * # Import all definitions from tkinter
2
3    class ControlAnimation:
4        def __init__(self):
5            window = Tk() # Create a window
6            window.title("Control Animation Demo") # Set a title
7
8            self.width = 250 # Width of self.canvas
9            self.canvas = Canvas(window, bg = "white",
10               width = self.width, height = 50)
11           self.canvas.pack()
12
13           frame = Frame(window)
14           frame.pack()
15           btStop = Button(frame, text = "Stop", command = self.stop)
```

```
16          btStop.pack(side = LEFT)
17          btResume = Button(frame, text = "Resume",
18              command = self.resume)
19          btResume.pack(side = LEFT)
20          btFaster = Button(frame, text = "Faster",
21              command = self.faster)
22          btFaster.pack(side = LEFT)
23          btSlower = Button(frame, text = "Slower",
24              command = self.slower)
25          btSlower.pack(side = LEFT)
26
27          self.x = 0 # Starting x position                          starting position
28          self.sleepTime = 100 # Set a sleep time                   initial sleep time
29          self.canvas.create_text(self.x, 30,
30              text = "Message moving?", tags = "text")
31
32          self.dx = 3
33          self.isStopped = False
34          self.animate()
35
36          window.mainloop() # Create an event loop
37
38      def stop(self): # Stop animation                             stop
39          self.isStopped = True
40
41      def resume(self): # Resume animation                         resume
42          self.isStopped = False
43          self.animate()
44
45      def faster(self): # Speed up the animation                   faster
46          if self.sleepTime > 5:
47              self.sleepTime -= 20
48
49      def slower(self): # Slow down the animation                  slower
50          self.sleepTime += 20
51
52      def animate(self): # Move the message                        animate
53          while not self.isStopped:
54              self.canvas.move("text", self.dx, 0) # Move text
55              self.canvas.after(self.sleepTime) # Sleep
56              self.canvas.update() # Update canvas                 update
57              if self.x < self.width:
58                  self.x += self.dx  # Set new position
59              else:
60                  self.x = 0 # Reset string position to beginning
61                  self.canvas.delete("text")
62                  # Redraw text at the beginning
63                  self.canvas.create_text(self.x, 30,
64                      text = "Message moving?", tags = "text")
65
66  ControlAnimation() # Create GUI                                  create GUI
```

FIGURE 9.19   The program uses buttons to control the animation.

The program starts the animation by invoking **animate()** (line 34). The **isStopped** variable determines whether the animation continues to move. It is set to **False** initially (line 33). When it is false, the loop in the **animate** method executes continuously (lines 53–64).

Clicking the buttons *Stop*, *Resume*, *Faster*, or *Slower* stops, resumes, speeds up, or slows down the animation. When the *Stop* button is clicked, the **stop** function is invoked to set **isStopped** to **True** (line 39). This causes the animation loop to terminate (line 53). When the *Resume* button is clicked, the **resume** function is invoked to set **isStopped** to **False** (line 42) and resume animation (line 43).

The speed of the animation is controlled by the variable **sleepTime**, which is set to **100** milliseconds initially (line 28). When the *Faster* button is clicked, the **faster** method is invoked to reduce **sleepTime** by **20** (line 47). When the *Slower* button is clicked, the **slower** function is invoked to increase **sleepTime** by **20** (line 50).

MyProgrammingLab™

9.37 What method can you use to put the program to sleep?

9.38 What method can you use to update the drawing?

9.13 Scrollbars

A **Scrollbar** *widget can be used to scroll the contents in a* **Text**, **Canvas**, *or* **Listbox** *widget vertically or horizontally.*

Listing 9.19 gives an example of scrolling in a **Text** widget, as shown in Figure 9.20.

LISTING 9.19   ScrollText.py

```
 1  from tkinter import * # Import all definitions from tkinter
 2
 3  class ScrollText:
 4      def __init__(self):
 5          window = Tk() # Create a window
 6          window.title("Scroll Text Demo") # Set title
 7
 8          frame1 = Frame(window)
 9          frame1.pack()
10          scrollbar = Scrollbar(frame1)
11          scrollbar.pack(side = RIGHT, fill = Y)
12          text = Text(frame1, width = 40, height = 10, wrap = WORD,
13              yscrollcommand = scrollbar.set)
14          text.pack()
15          scrollbar.config(command = text.yview)
16
17          window.mainloop() # Create an event loop
18
19  ScrollText() # Create GUI
```

create a Scrollbar (line 10)

create Text (line 12)

tie scrollbar with text (line 15)

create GUI (line 19)

```
7½ Scroll Text Demo                    □ ▣ ✕
Four score and seven years ago our    ▲
fathers brought forth on this
continent, a new nation,
conceived in Liberty, and dedicated to
the proposition that all men are
created equal.                        ▼
```

FIGURE 9.20   You can use the scrollbar (on the far right) to scroll to see text not currently visible in the Text widget.

The program creates a **Scrollbar** (line 10) and places it to the right of the text (line 11). The scrollbar is tied to the **Text** widget (line 15) so that the contents in the **Text** widget can be scrolled through.

9.39 What widgets can be used with a scrollbar?

9.40 How do you associate a scrollbar with a view?

9.14 Standard Dialog Boxes

You can use standard dialog boxes to display message boxes or to prompt the user to enter numbers and strings.

Finally, let's look at Tkinter's standard dialog boxes (often referred to simply as *dialogs*). Listing 9.20 gives an example of using these dialogs. A sample run of the program is shown in Figure 9.21.

LISTING 9.20 DialogDemo.py

```
 1  import tkinter.messagebox
 2  import tkinter.simpledialog
 3  import tkinter.colorchooser
 4
 5  tkinter.messagebox.showinfo("showinfo", "This is an info msg")     showinfo
 6
 7  tkinter.messagebox.showwarning("showwarning", "This is a warning")  showwarning
 8
 9  tkinter.messagebox.showerror("showerror", "This is an error")       showerror
10
11  isYes = tkinter.messagebox.askyesno("askyesno", "Continue?")        askyesno
12  print(isYes)
13
14  isOK = tkinter.messagebox.askokcancel("askokcancel", "OK?")         askokcancel
15  print(isOK)
16
17  isYesNoCancel = tkinter.messagebox.askyesnocancel(                  askyesnocancel
18      "askyesnocancel", "Yes, No, Cancel?")
19  print(isYesNoCancel)
20
21  name = tkinter.simpledialog.askstring(                             askstring
22      "askstring", "Enter your name")
23  print(name)
24
25  age = tkinter.simpledialog.askinteger(                             askinteger
26      "askinteger", "Enter your age")
27  print(age)
28
29  weight = tkinter.simpledialog.askfloat(                            askfloat
30      "askfloat", "Enter your weight")
31  print(weight)
```

The program invokes the **showinfo**, **showwarning**, and **showerror** functions to display an information message (line 5), a warning (line 7), and an error (line 9). These functions are defined in the **tkinter.messagebox** module (line 1).

The **askyesno** function displays the *Yes* and *No* buttons in the dialog box (line 11). The function returns **True** if the *Yes* button is clicked or **False** if the *No* button is clicked.

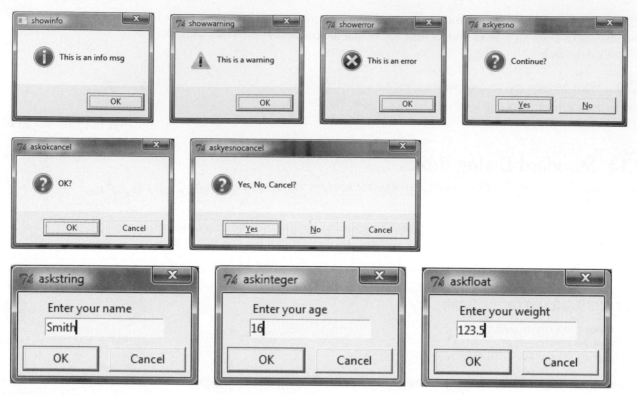

FIGURE 9.21 You can use the standard dialogs to display message boxes and accept input.

The **askokcancel** function displays the *OK* and *Cancel* buttons in the dialog box (line 14). The function returns **True** if the *OK* button is clicked or **False** if the *Cancel* button is clicked.

The **askyesnocancel** function displays the *Yes*, *No*, and *Cancel* buttons in the dialog box (line 17). The function returns **True** if the *Yes* button is clicked, **False** if the *No* button is clicked or **None** if the *Cancel* button is clicked.

The **askstring** function (line 21) returns the string entered from the dialog box after the *OK* button is clicked or **None** if the *Cancel* button is clicked.

The **askinteger** function (line 25) returns the integer entered from the dialog box after the *OK* button is clicked or **None** if the *Cancel* button is clicked.

The **askfloat** function (line 29) returns the float entered from the dialog box after the *OK* button is clicked or **None** if the *Cancel* button is clicked.

modal
    All the dialog boxes are *modal* windows, which means that the program cannot continue until a dialog box is dismissed.

 Check Point

9.41 Write a statement that displays "Welcome to Python" in a message dialog.

9.42 Write statements using a dialog box to prompt the user to enter an integer, a float, and a string.

MyProgrammingLab™

KEY TERMS

callback functions   274
geometry manager   278
grid manager   282
handlers   274

pack manager   284
parent container   273
place manager   286
widget class   273

CHAPTER SUMMARY

1. To develop a GUI application in Tkinter, first use the **Tk** class to create a window, then create widgets and place them inside the window. The first argument of each *widget class* must be the *parent container*.

2. To place a widget in a container, you have to specify its *geometry manager*.

3. Tkinter supports three geometry managers: pack, grid, and place. The *pack manager* places widgets side by side or on top of each other. The *grid manager* places widgets in grids. The *place manager* places the widget in absolute locations.

4. Many widgets have the command option for binding an event with a *callback function*. When an event occurs, the callback function is invoked.

5. The **Canvas** widget can be used to draw lines, rectangles, ovals, arcs, and polygons, and to display images and text strings.

6. Images can be used in many widgets such as labels, buttons, check buttons, radio buttons, and canvases.

7. You can use the **Menu** class to create menu bars, menu items, and popup menus.

8. You can bind mouse and key events to a widget with a callback function.

9. You can use canvases to develop animations.

10. You can use standard dialog boxes to display messages and receive input.

TEST QUESTIONS

Do test questions for this chapter online at www.cs.armstrong.edu/liang/py/test.html.

PROGRAMMING EXERCISES

MyProgrammingLab™

 Note
The image icons used in the exercises throughout the book can be obtained from
www.cs.armstrong.edu/liang/py/book.zip under the **image** folder.

download image files

Sections 9.2–9.8

*9.1 (*Move the ball*) Write a program that moves a ball in a panel. You should define a panel class for displaying the ball and provide the methods for moving the ball left, right, up, and down, as shown in Figure 9.22a. Check the boundaries to prevent the ball from moving out of sight completely.

*9.2 (*Create an investment-value calculator*) Write a program that calculates the future value of an investment at a given interest rate for a specified number of years. The formula for the calculation is as follows:

```
futureValue = investmentAmount * (1 + monthlyInterestRate)^(years * 12)
```

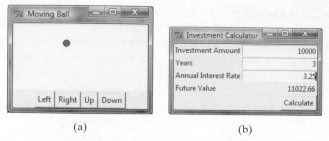

(a)   (b)

FIGURE 9.22 (a) You can click a button to move the ball. (b) You can obtain the future value by entering the investment amount, years, and annual interest rate.

Use text fields for users to enter the investment amount, years, and interest rate. Display the future amount in a text field when the user clicks the *Calculate* button, as shown in Figure 9.22b.

*9.3 (*Select geometric figures*) Write a program that draws a rectangle or an oval, as shown in Figure 9.23. The user selects a figure from a radio button and specifies whether it is filled by selecting a check button.

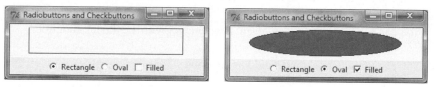

FIGURE 9.23 The program displays a rectangle or an oval when you select a shape type, and whether it is filled.

*9.4 (*Display rectangles*) Write a program that displays 20 rectangles, as shown in Figure 9.24.

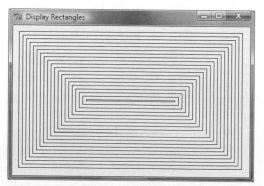

FIGURE 9.24 The program displays 20 rectangles.

9.5 (*Game: display a checkerboard*) Write a program that displays a checkerboard in which each white and black cell is a canvas with a background of black or white, as shown in Figure 9.25a.

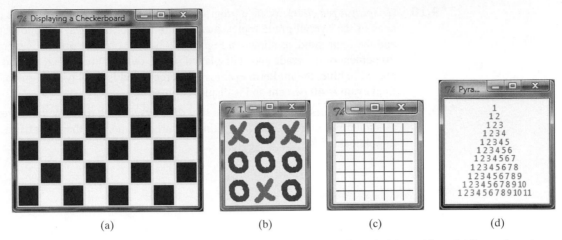

FIGURE 9.25   (a) The programs display a checkerboard, (b) a tic-tac-toe board, (c) a grid, and (d) numbers in a triangular formation.

9.6   (*Game: display a tic-tac-toe board*) Write a program that displays nine labels. Each label may display an image icon for an X or an image icon for an O, as shown in Figure 9.25b. What to display is randomly decided. Use the `random.randint(0, 1)` function to generate an integer **0** or **1**, which corresponds to displaying a cross image (X) icon or a not image (O) icon. The cross and not images are in the files **x.gif** and **o.gif**.

9.7   (*Display an 8 × 8 grid*) Write a program that displays an 8 × 8 grid, as shown in Figure 9.25c. Use red for vertical lines and blue for horizontal lines.

**9.8   (*Display numbers in a triangular pattern*) Write a program that displays numbers in a triangular pattern, as shown in Figure 9.25d. The number of lines in the display changes to fit the window as the window resizes.

9.9   (*Display a bar chart*) Write a program that uses a bar chart to display the percentages of the overall grade represented by the project, quizzes, the midterm exam, and the final exam, as shown in Figure 9.26a. Suppose that the project is **20 percent of the grade and its value is displayed in red, quizzes are **10** percent and are displayed in blue, the midterm exam is **30** percent and is displayed in green, and the final exam is **40** percent and is displayed in orange.

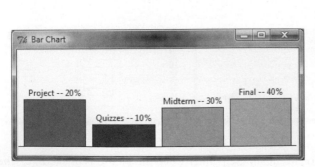

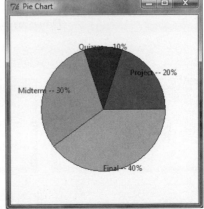

FIGURE 9.26   (a) The programs display a bar chart and (b) a pie chart.

9.10 (*Display a pie chart*) Write a program that uses a pie chart to display the percentages of the overall grade represented by the project, quizzes, the midterm exam, and the final exam, as shown in Figure 9.26b. Suppose that project is weighted as **20 percent of the grade and is displayed in red, quizzes are **10** percent and are displayed in blue, the midterm exam is **30** percent and is displayed in green, and the final exam is **40** percent and is displayed in orange.

9.11 (*Display a clock*) Write a program that displays a clock to show the current time, as shown in Figure 9.27a. To obtain the current time, use the **datetime class in Supplement II.B.

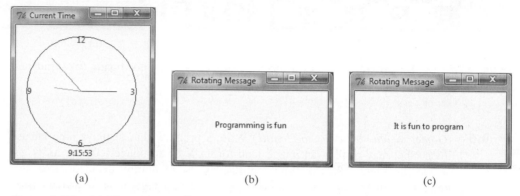

(a)   (b)   (c)

FIGURE 9.27 (a) The program displays a clock for the current time. (b–c) The program alternates between the display of two messages.

Sections 9.9–9.14

**9.12 (*Alternate two messages*) Write a program to change, with a left mouse click, between two messages displayed on a canvas, "Programming is fun" and "It is fun to program," as shown in Figure 9.27b–c.

*9.13 (*Display the mouse position*) Write two programs: one that displays the mouse position when the mouse is clicked (see Figure 9.28a–b), and the other displays the mouse position when the mouse button is pressed and ceases to display it when the mouse button is released.

*9.14 (*Draw lines using the arrow keys*) Write a program that draws line segments using the arrow keys. The line starts from the center of the frame and draws toward east, north, west, or south when the *Right* arrow key, *Up* arrow key, *Left* arrow key, or *Down* arrow key is clicked, as shown in Figure 9.28c.

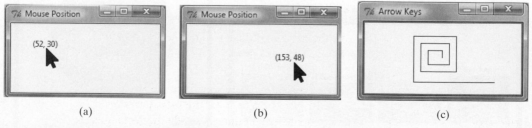

(a)   (b)   (c)

FIGURE 9.28 (a–b) The program displays the location of the mouse pointer when the mouse is clicked. (c) The program draws a line when the Up, Down, Left, and Right arrow keys are pressed.

**9.15 (*Display a still fan*) Write a program that displays a still fan, as shown in Figure 9.29a.

**9.16 (*Display a running fan*) Write a program that displays a fan running, as shown in Figure 9.29a.

**9.17 (*Racing car*) Write a program that simulates car racing, as shown in Figure 9.29b–d. The car moves from left to right. When it reaches the right end, it restarts from the left and continues the same process. Let the user increase and decrease the car's speed by pressing the *Up* and *Down* arrow keys.

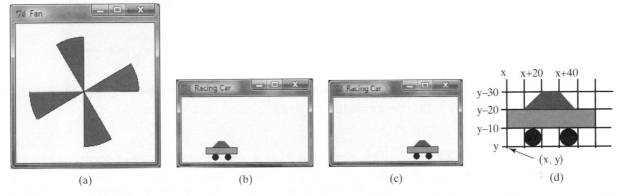

(a) (b) (c) (d)

FIGURE 9.29 (a) The programs display a fan and (b–c) a moving car. (d) You can redraw a car with a new base point.

*9.18 (*Display flashing text*) Write a program that displays the flashing text "Welcome," as shown in Figure 9.30a–b. (Hint: To make the text flash, you need to repeatedly draw it on the canvas or alternately delete it. Use a Boolean variable to control the alternation.)

*9.19 (*Move a circle using keys*) Write a program that moves a circle up, down, left, or right using the arrow keys, as shown in Figure 9.30c–d.

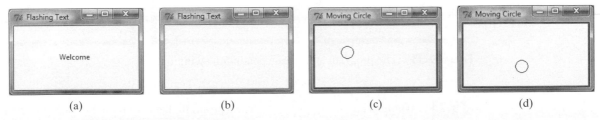

(a) (b) (c) (d)

FIGURE 9.30 (a–b) The program displays a flashing label with text. (c–d) The circle is moved when the arrow keys are pressed.

9.20 (*Geometry: inside a circle?*) Write a program that draws a fixed circle centered at (100**, **60**) with radius **50**. Whenever the mouse is moved while the left button is pressed, display the message indicating whether the mouse pointer is inside the circle, as shown in Figure 9.31.

9.21 (*Geometry: inside a rectangle?*) Write a program that draws a fixed rectangle centered at (100**, **60**) with width **100** and height **40**. Whenever the mouse is moved, display the message indicating whether the mouse pointer is inside the rectangle, as shown in Figure 9.32. To detect whether the pointer is inside a rectangle, use the **Rectangle2D** class defined in Exercise 8.19.

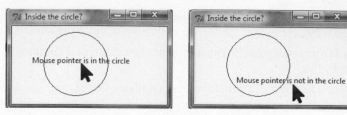

FIGURE 9.31 Detect whether the mouse pointer is inside a circle.

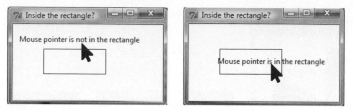

FIGURE 9.32 Detect whether the mouse pointer is inside a rectangle.

**9.22 (*Geometry: pendulum*) Write a program that animates a pendulum swinging, as shown in Figure 9.33. Press the *Up* arrow key to increase the speed and the *Down* arrow key to decrease it. Press the *S* key to stop the animation and the *R* key to resume it.

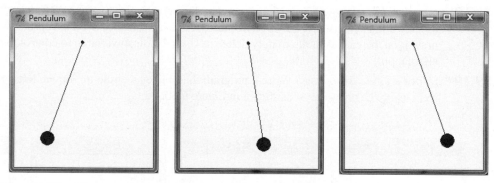

FIGURE 9.33 The program animates a pendulum swinging.

*9.23 (*Buttons and radio buttons*) Write a program that uses radio buttons to select background colors for text, as shown in Figure 9.34. The available colors are red, yellow, white, gray, and green. The program uses the buttons <= and => to move the text left or right.

FIGURE 9.34 The <= and => buttons move the message on the panel, and you can also set the background color for the message.

9.24   (*Display circles*) Write a program that displays a new larger circle with a left mouse click and removes the largest circle with a right mouse click, as shown in Figure 9.35.

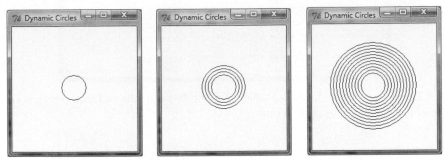

FIGURE 9.35   The program adds/removes circles with left/right mouse clicks.

**9.25   (*Traffic lights*) Write a program that simulates a traffic light. The program lets the user select one of three lights: red, yellow, or green. When a radio button is selected, the light is turned on, and only one light can be on at a time (see Figure 9.36a–b). No light is on when the program starts.

*9.26   (*Display balls with random colors*) Write a program that displays ten balls with random colors and placed at random locations, at shown in Figure 9.36c.

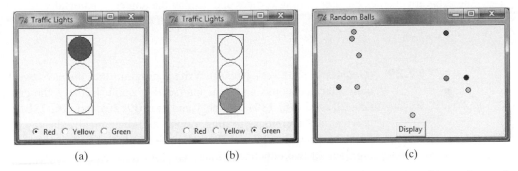

       (a)   (b)   (c)

FIGURE 9.36   (a–b) The radio buttons let the user choose a traffic light color. (c) Ten balls with random colors are displayed at random locations.

*9.27   (*Compare loans with various interest rates*) Rewrite Exercise 5.23 to create the user interface shown in Figure 9.37. Your program should let the user enter the loan amount and loan period in the number of years from a text field, and should display the monthly and total payments for each interest rate starting from **5** percent to **8** percent, with increments of one-eighth, in a text area.

**9.28   (*Geometry: display angles*) Write a program that enables the user to drag the vertices of a triangle and displays the angles dynamically, as shown in Figure 9.38a. Change the mouse cursor to the cross-hair shape when the mouse is moved close to a vertex. The formula to compute angles A, B, and C (see Figure 9.38b) is given in Listing 3.2.

Hint: Use the **Point** class to represent a point, as described in Exercise 8.17. Create three points at random locations initially. When the mouse is moved close to a point, change the cursor to a cross-hair pointer (+) and reset the point to where the mouse is. Whenever a point is moved, redisplay the triangle and the angles.

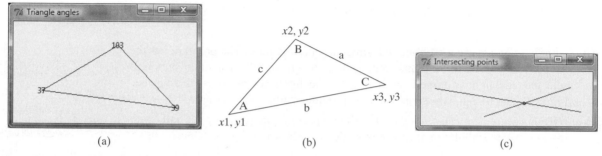

FIGURE 9.37 The program displays a table for monthly payments and total payments on a given loan based on various interest rates.

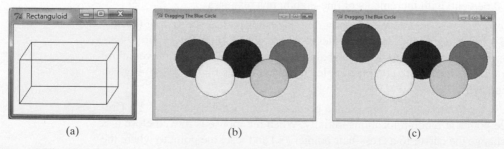

| (a) | (b) | (c) |

FIGURE 9.38 (a–b) The program enables the user to drag vertices and display the angles dynamically. (c) The program enables the user to drag vertices and display the lines and their intersecting point dynamically.

9.29 (*Geometry: intersecting point*) Write a program that displays two line segments with their end points and their intersecting point. Initially, the end points are at (20**, **20**) and (**56**, **130**) for line 1 and at (**100**, **20**) and (**16**, **130**) for line 2. The user can use the mouse to drag a point and dynamically display the intersecting point, as shown in Figure 9.38c. (Hint: See Exercise 4.25 for finding the intersecting point of two unbounded lines. The hint for Exercise 9.28 applies to this exercise as well.)

9.30 (*Display a rectanguloid*) Write a program that displays a rectanguloid, as shown in Figure 9.39a.

9.31 (*Display five filled circles*) Write a program that displays five filled circles, as shown in Figure 9.39b. Enable the user to drag the blue circle using the mouse, as shown in Figure 9.39c.

| (a) | (b) | (c) |

FIGURE 9.39 (a) The program displays a rectanguloid. (b–c) The blue circle is dragged with the mouse.

*9.32 (*Two movable vertices and their distances*) Write a program that displays two circles with radius **20** at locations (**20**, **20**) and (**120**, **50**) with a line connecting the two circles, as shown in Figure 9.40a. The distance between the circles is displayed along the line. The user can drag a circle. When that happens, the circle and its line are moved and the distance between the circles is updated. Your program should not allow the circles to get too close. Keep them at least **70** pixels apart between the two circles' centers.

**9.33 (*Draw an arrow line*) Write a program that randomly draws an arrow line when the *Draw a Random Arrow Line* button is clicked, as shown in Figure 9.40b.

**9.34 (*Address book*) Write a program that creates a user interface for displaying an address, as shown in Figure 9.40c.

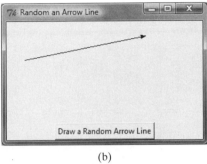

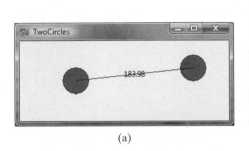

(a)

(b)

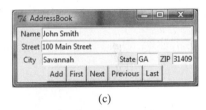

(c)

FIGURE 9.40 (a) The user can drag the circles and the program redisplays the distance. (b) The program draws an arrow line randomly. (c) The program creates a user interface for displaying addresses.

CHAPTER

10

LISTS

Objectives

- To describe why lists are useful in programming (§10.1).
- To learn how to create lists (§10.2.1).
- To explore common operations for sequences (§10.2.2).
- To use the `len`, `min`, `max`, `sum`, and `random.shuffle` functions with a list (§10.2.3).
- To access list elements by using indexed variables (§10.2.4).
- To obtain a sublist from a larger list by using the slicing operator `[start : end]` (§10.2.5).
- To use the `+` (concatenation), `*` (repetition), and `in/not in` operators on lists (§10.2.6).
- To traverse elements in a list using a `for` loop (§10.2.7).
- To compare the contents of two lists by using comparison operators (§10.2.8).
- To create lists by using list comprehension (§10.2.9).
- To invoke a list's `append`, `count`, `extend`, `index`, `insert`, `pop`, `remove`, `reverse`, and `sort` methods (§10.2.10).
- To split a string into a list using the `str`'s `split` method (§10.2.11).
- To read data from the console into a list (§10.2.12).
- To use lists in application development (§§10.3–10.5).
- To copy the contents of one list to another (§10.6).
- To develop and invoke functions that include list arguments and return lists (§§10.7–10.9).
- To search elements using the linear (§10.10.1) or binary (§10.10.2) search algorithm.
- To sort a list by using the selection sort (§10.11.1).
- To sort a list by using the insertion sort (§10.11.2).
- To develop a bouncing ball animation by using a list (§10.12).

10.1 Introduction

Key Point

why list?

A list can store a collection of data of any size.

Programs commonly need to store a large number of values. Suppose, for instance, that you need to read 100 numbers, compute their average, and then find out how many of the numbers are above the average. Your program first reads the numbers and computes their average, then compares each number with the average to determine whether it is above the average. In order to accomplish this task, the numbers must all be stored in variables. To do this, you would have to create 100 variables and repeatedly write almost identical code 100 times. Writing a program this way is impractical. So, how do you solve this problem?

An efficient, organized approach is needed. Python provides a type called a list that stores a sequential collection of elements. In our example, you can store all 100 numbers in a list and access them through a single list variable. The solution might look like Listing 10.1.

LISTING 10.1 DataAnalysis.py

create a list

store number in list

get average

above average?

```
 1  NUMBER_OF_ELEMENTS = 5 # For simplicity, use 5 instead of 100
 2  numbers = [] # Create an empty list
 3  sum = 0
 4
 5  for i in range(NUMBER_OF_ELEMENTS):
 6      value = eval(input("Enter a new number: "))
 7      numbers.append(value)
 8      sum += value
 9
10  average = sum / NUMBER_OF_ELEMENTS
11
12  count = 0 # The number of elements above average
13  for i in range(NUMBER_OF_ELEMENTS):
14      if numbers[i] > average:
15          count += 1
16
17  print("Average is", average)
18  print("Number of elements above the average is", count)
```

```
Enter a new number: 1  ↵Enter
Enter a new number: 2  ↵Enter
Enter a new number: 3  ↵Enter
Enter a new number: 4  ↵Enter
Enter a new number: 5  ↵Enter
Average is 3.0
Number of elements above the average is 2
```

The program creates an empty list (line 2). It repeatedly reads a number (line 6), appends it to the list (line 7), and adds it to **sum** (line 8). It obtains **average** in line 10. It then compares each number in the list with the average to count the number of values above the average (lines 12–15).

array

Note

In many other programming languages, you would use a type called an *array* to store a sequence of data. An array has a fixed size. A Python list's size is flexible. It can grow and shrink on demand.

10.2 List Basics

A list is a sequence defined by the `list` *class. It contains the methods for creating, manipulating, and processing lists. Elements in a list can be accessed through an index.*

10.2.1 Creating Lists

The `list` class defines lists. To create a list, you can use `list`'s constructor, as follows:

```
list1 = list() # Create an empty list
list2 = list([2, 3, 4]) # Create a list with elements 2, 3, 4
list3 = list(["red", "green", "blue"]) # Create a list with strings
list4 = list(range(3, 6)) # Create a list with elements 3, 4, 5
list5 = list("abcd") # Create a list with characters a, b, c, d
```

You can also create a list by using the following syntax, which is a little simpler:

```
list1 = [] # Same as list()
list2 = [2, 3, 4] # Same as list([2, 3, 4])
list3 = ["red", "green"] # Same as list(["red", "green"])
```

The elements in a list are separated by commas and are enclosed by a pair of brackets (`[]`).

 Note

A list can contain the elements of the same type or mixed types. For example, the following list is fine:

```
list4 = [2, "three", 4]
```

10.2.2 List Is a Sequence Type

Strings and lists are sequence types in Python. A string is a sequence of characters, while a list is a sequence of any elements. The common operations for sequences are summarized in Table 10.1. These operations for strings were introduced in Chapter 8. The sequence operations for lists are the same as for strings. Sections 10.2.3–10.2.8 give examples of using these operations for lists.

TABLE 10.1 Common Operations for Sequence s

Operation	Description
`x in s`	True if element x is in sequence s.
`x not in s`	True if element x is not in sequence s.
`s1 + s2`	Concatenates two sequences s1 and s2.
`s * n, n * s`	n copies of sequence s concatenated.
`s[i]`	ith element in sequence s.
`s[i : j]`	Slice of sequence s from index i to j − 1.
`len(s)`	Length of sequence s, i.e., the number of elements in s.
`min(s)`	Smallest element in sequence s.
`max(s)`	Largest element in sequence s.
`sum(s)`	Sum of all numbers in sequence s.
`for loop`	Traverses elements from left to right in a **for** loop.
`<, <=, >, >=, =, !=`	Compares two sequences.

len
max
min
sum
random.shuffle

10.2.3 Functions for Lists

Several Python built-in functions can be used with lists. You can use the **len** function to return the number of elements in the list, the **max/min** functions to return the elements with the greatest and lowest values in the list, and the **sum** function to return the sum of all elements in the list. You can also use the **shuffle** function in the **random** module to shuffle the elements randomly in the list. Here are some examples:

```
1  >>> list1 = [2, 3, 4, 1, 32]
2  >>> len(list1)
3  5
4  >>> max(list1)
5  32
6  >>> min(list1)
7  1
8  >>> sum(list1)
9  42
10  >>> import random
11  >>> random.shuffle(list1) # Shuffle the elements in list1
12  >>> list1
13  [4, 1, 2, 32, 3]
14  >>>
```

Invoking **random.shuffle(list1)** (line 11) randomly shuffles the elements in **list1**.

10.2.4 Index Operator [ ]

An element in a list can be accessed through the index operator, using the following syntax:

myList[index]

0 based

List indexes are **0** based; that is, they range from **0** to **len(myList)-1**, as illustrated in Figure 10.1.

myList = [5.6, 4.5, 3.3, 13.2, 4.0, 34.33, 34.0, 45.45, 99.993, 11123]

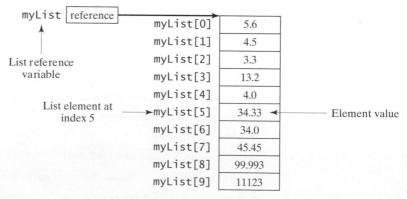

FIGURE 10.1 The list **myList** has 10 elements with indexes from **0** to **9**.

myList[index] can be used just like a variable, so it is also known as an *indexed variable*. For example, the following code adds the values in **myList[0]** and **myList[1]** to **myList[2]**.

```
myList[2] = myList[0] + myList[1]
```

The following loop assigns **0** to **myList[0]**, **1** to **myList[1]**, ..., and **9** to **myList[9]**:

```
for i in range(len(myList)):
    myList[i] = i
```

Caution

Accessing a list out of bounds is a common programming error that results in a run-time **IndexError**. To avoid this error, make sure that you do not use an index beyond **len(myList) – 1**.

Programmers often mistakenly reference the first element in a list with index **1**, but it should be **0**. This is called the *off-by-one error*. It is a common error in a loop to use <= where < should be used. For example, the following loop is wrong:

IndexError

off-by-one error

```
i = 0
while i <= len(myList):
    print(myList[i])
    i += 1
```

The <= should be replaced by <.

Python also allows the use of negative numbers as indexes to reference positions relative to the end of the list. The actual position is obtained by adding the length of the list with the negative index. For example:

negative index

```
1  >>> list1 = [2, 3, 5, 2, 33, 21]
2  >>> list1[-1]
3  21
4  >>> list1[-3]
5  2
6  >>>
```

In line 2, **list1[-1]** is same as **list1[-1 + len(list1)]**, which gives the last element in the list. In line 4, **list1[-3]** is same as **list1[-3 + len(list1)]**, which gives the third last element in the list.

10.2.5 List Slicing **[start : end]**

The index operator allows you to select an element at the specified index. The *slicing operator* returns a slice of the list using the syntax **list[start : end]**. The slice is a sublist from index **start** to index **end – 1**. Here are some examples:

slicing operator

```
1  >>> list1 = [2, 3, 5, 7, 9, 1]
2  >>> list1[2 : 4]
3  [5, 7]
4  >>>
```

The starting index or ending index may be omitted. In this case, the starting index is **0** and the ending index is the last index. For example:

```
1  >>> list1 = [2, 3, 5, 2, 33, 21]
2  >>> list1[ : 2]
3  [2, 3]
4  >>> list1[3 : ]
5  [2, 33, 21]
6  >>>
```

Note that **list1[: 2]** is the same as **list1[0 : 2]** (line 2), and that **list1[3 :]** is the same as **list1[3 : len(list1)]** (line 4).

negative index   You can use a negative index in slicing. For example:

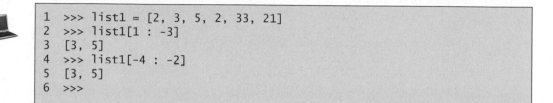

```
1  >>> list1 = [2, 3, 5, 2, 33, 21]
2  >>> list1[1 : -3]
3  [3, 5]
4  >>> list1[-4 : -2]
5  [3, 5]
6  >>>
```

In line 2, **list1[1 : -3]** is the same as **list1[1 : -3 + len(list1)]**. In line 4, **list1[-4 : -2]** is the same as **list1[-4 + len(list1) : -2 + len(list1)]**.

Note

If **start >= end**, **list[start : end]** returns an empty list. If **end** specifies a position beyond the end of the list, Python will use the length of the list for **end** instead.

10.2.6 The +, *, and **in/not in** Operators

concatenation operator +
repetition operator *

You can use the concatenation operator (+) to join two lists and the repetition operator (*) to replicate elements in a list. Here are some examples:

```
1   >>> list1 = [2, 3]
2   >>> list2 = [1, 9]
3   >>> list3 = list1 + list2
4   >>> list3
5   [2, 3, 1, 9]
6   >>>
7   >>> list4 = 3 * list1
8   >>> list4
9   [2, 3, 2, 3, 2, 3]
10  >>>
```

A new list is obtained by concatenating **list1** with **list2** (line 3). Line 7 duplicates **list1** three times to create a new list. Note that **3 * list1** is the same as **list1 * 3**.

You can determine whether an element is in a list by using the **in** or **not in** operator. For example:

```
>>> list1 = [2, 3, 5, 2, 33, 21]
>>> 2 in list1
True
```

```
>>> 2 not in list1
False
>>>
```

10.2.7 Traversing Elements in a **for** Loop

The elements in a Python list are iterable. Python supports a convenient **for** loop, which enables you to traverse the list sequentially without using an index variable. For example, the following code displays all the elements in the list **myList**:

```
for u in myList:
    print(u)
```

You can read the code as, "For each element **u** in **myList**, print it."

You still have to use an index variable if you wish to traverse the list in a different order or change the elements in the list. For example, the following code displays the elements at odd-numbered positions.

```
for i in range(0, len(myList), 2):
    print(myList[i])
```

10.2.8 Comparing Lists

You can compare lists using the comparison operators (>, >=, <, <=, ==, and !=). For this to work, the two lists must contain the same type of elements. The comparison uses *lexicographical* ordering: the first two elements are compared, and if they differ this determines the outcome of the comparison; if they are equal, the next two elements are compared, and so on, until either list is exhausted. Here are some examples:

```
 1  >>> list1 = ["green", "red", "blue"]
 2  >>> list2 = ["red", "blue", "green"]
 3  >>> list2 == list1
 4  False
 5  >>> list2 != list1
 6  True
 7  >>> list2 >= list1
 8  False
 9  >>> list2 > list1
10  False
11  >>> list2 < list1
12  True
13  >>> list2 <= list1
14  True
15  >>>
```

10.2.9 List Comprehensions

List comprehensions provide a concise way to create a sequential list of elements. A list comprehension consists of brackets containing an expression followed by a **for** clause, then zero or more **for** or **if** clauses. The list comprehension produces a list with the results from evaluating the expression. Here are some examples:

```
 1  >>> list1 = [x for x in range(5)] # Returns a list of 0, 1, 2, 3, 4
 2  >>> list1
 3  [0, 1, 2, 3, 4]
 4  >>>
 5  >>> list2 = [0.5 * x for x in list1]
 6  >>> list2
 7  [0.0, 0.5, 1.0, 1.5, 2.0]
 8  >>>
 9  >>> list3 = [x for x in list2 if x < 1.5]
10  >>> list3
11  [0.0, 0.5, 1.0]
12  >>>
```

In line 1, **list1** is created from an expression using a **for** clause. The numbers in **list1** are **0**, **1**, **2**, **3**, and **4**. Each number in **list2** is half of the corresponding number in **list1** (line 5). In line 9, **list3** consists of the numbers whose value is less than **1.5** in **list2**.

10.2.10 List Methods

Once a list is created, you can use the **list** class's methods (shown in Figure 10.2) to manipulate the list.

list
append(x: object): None
count(x: object): int
extend(l: list): None
index(x: object): int
insert(index: int, x: object): None
pop(i): object
remove(x: object): None
reverse(): None
sort(): None

Adds an element x to the end of the list.

Returns the number of times element x appears in the list.

Appends all the elements in l to the list.

Returns the index of the first occurrence of element x in the list.

Inserts an element x at a given index. Note that the first element in the list has index 0.

Removes the element at the given position and returns it. The parameter i is optional. If it is not specified, list.pop() removes and returns the last element in the list.

Removes the first occurrence of element x from the list.

Reverses the elements in the list.

Sorts the elements in the list in ascending order.

FIGURE 10.2 The **list** class contains methods for manipulating a list.

Here are some examples that use the **append**, **count**, **extend**, **index**, and **insert** methods:

```
 1  >>> list1 = [2, 3, 4, 1, 32, 4]
 2  >>> list1.append(19)
 3  >>> list1
 4  [2, 3, 4, 1, 32, 4, 19]
 5  >>> list1.count(4) # Return the count for number 4
 6  2
 7  >>> list2 = [99, 54]
 8  >>> list1.extend(list2)
 9  >>> list1
10  [2, 3, 4, 1, 32, 4, 19, 99, 54]
11  >>> list1.index(4) # Return the index of number 4
12  2
```

```
13  >>> list1.insert(1, 25) # Insert 25 at position index 1
14  >>> list1
15  [2, 25, 3, 4, 1, 32, 4, 19, 99, 54]
16  >>>
```

Line 2 appends **19** to the list, and line 5 returns the count of the number of occurrences of element **4** in the list. Invoking **list1.extend()** (line 8) appends **list2** to **list1**. Line 11 returns the index for element **4** in the list, and line 13 inserts **25** into the list at index **1**.

Here are some examples that use the **insert**, **pop**, **remove**, **reverse**, and **sort** methods:

```
1   >>> list1 = [2, 25, 3, 4, 1, 32, 4, 19, 99, 54]
2   >>> list1.pop(2)
3   3
4   >>> list1
5   [2, 25, 4, 1, 32, 4, 19, 99, 54]
6   >>> list1.pop()
7   54
8   >>> list1
9   [2, 25, 4, 1, 32, 4, 19, 99]
10  >>> list1.remove(32) # Remove number 32
11  >>> list1
12  [2, 25, 4, 1, 4, 19, 99]
13  >>> list1.reverse() # Reverse the list
14  >>> list1
15  [99, 19, 4, 1, 4, 25, 2]
16  >>> list1.sort() # Sort the list
17  >>> list1
18  [1, 2, 4, 4, 19, 25, 99]
19  >>>
```

Line 2 removes the element at index **2** from the list. Invoking **list1.pop()** (line 6) returns and removes the last element from **list1**. Line 10 removes element **32** from **list1**, line 13 reverses the elements in the list, and line 15 sorts the elements in the list in ascending order.

10.2.11 Splitting a String into a List

The **str** class contains the **split** method, which is useful for splitting items in a string into a list. For example, the following statement:

```
items = "Jane John Peter Susan".split()
```

splits the string **Jane John Peter Susan** into the list **['Jane', 'John', 'Peter', 'Susan']**. In this case the items are delimited by spaces in the string. You can use a nonspace delimiter. For example, the following statement:

```
items = "09/20/2012".split("/")
```

splits the string **09/20/2012** into the list **['09', '20', '2012']**.

regular expressions

Note

Python supports regular expressions, an extremely useful and powerful feature for matching and splitting a string using a pattern. Regular expressions are complex for beginning students. For this reason, we cover them in Supplement II.A, Regular Expressions.

10.2.12 Inputting Lists

You may often need code that reads data from the console into a list. You can enter one data item per line and append it to a list in a loop. For example, the following code reads ten numbers *one per line* into a list.

```
lst = [] # Create a list
print("Enter 10 numbers: ")
for i in range(10):
    lst.append(eval(input())
```

Sometimes it is more convenient to enter the data in one line separated by spaces. You can use the string's **split** method to extract data from a line of input. For example, the following code reads ten numbers separated by spaces from one line into a list.

```
# Read numbers as a string from the console
s = input("Enter 10 numbers separated by spaces from one line: ")
items = s.split() # Extract items from the string
lst = [eval(x) for x in items] # Convert items to numbers
```

Invoking **input()** reads a string. Using **s.split()** extracts the items delimited by spaces from string **s** and returns items in a list. The last line creates a list of numbers by converting the items into numbers.

10.2.13 Shifting Lists

Sometimes you need to shift the elements left or right. Python does not provide such a method in the **list** class, but you can write the following function to perform a left shift.

```
def shift(lst):
    temp = lst[0] # Retain the first element

    # Shift elements left
    for i in range(1, len(lst)):
        lst[i - 1] = lst[i]

    # Move the first element to fill in the last position
    lst[len(lst) - 1] = temp
```

10.2.14 Simplifying Coding

Lists can be used to greatly simplify coding for certain tasks. For example, suppose you wish to obtain the English month name for a given month in number. If the month names are stored in a list, the month name for a given month can be accessed simply via index. The following code prompts the user to enter a month number and displays its month name:

```
months = ["January", "February", "March", ..., "December"]
monthNumber = eval(input("Enter a month number (1 to 12): "))
print("The month is", months[monthNumber - 1])
```

If the **months** list is not used, you would have to determine the month name using a lengthy multi-way if-else statement as follows:

```
if monthNumber == 0:
    print("The month is January")
elif monthNumber == 1:
    print("The month is February")
...
else:
    print("The month is December")
```

10.1 How do you create an empty list and a list with the three integers 1, 32, and 2?

10.2 Given **lst = [30, 1, 12, 14, 10, 0]**, how many elements are in **lst**? What is the index of the first element in **lst**? What is the index of the last element in **lst**? What is **lst[2]**? What is **lst[-2]**?

10.3 Given **lst = [30, 1, 2, 1, 0]**, what is the list after applying each of the following statements? Assume that each line of code is independent.

```
lst.append(40)
lst.insert(1, 43)
lst.extend([1, 43])
lst.remove(1)
lst.pop(1)
lst.pop()
lst.sort()
lst.reverse()
random.shuffle(lst)
```

10.4 Given **lst = [30, 1, 2, 1, 0]**, what is the return value of each of the following statements?

```
lst.index(1)
lst.count(1)
len(lst)
max(lst)
min(lst)
sum(lst)
```

10.5 Given **list1 = [30, 1, 2, 1, 0]** and **list2 = [1, 21, 13]**, what is the return value of each of the following statements?

```
list1 + list2
2 * list2
list2 * 2
list1[1 : 3]
list1[3]
```

✓ **Check
Point**

MyProgrammingLab™

10.6 Given `list1 = [30, 1, 2, 1, 0]`, what is the return value of each of the following statements?

```
[x for x in list1 if x > 1]
[x for x in range(0, 10, 2)]
[x for x in range(10, 0, -2)]
```

10.7 Given `list1 = [30, 1, 2, 1, 0]` and `list2 = [1, 21, 13]`, what is the return value of each of the following statements?

```
list1 < list2
list1 <= list2
list1 == list2
list1 != list2
list1 > list2
list1 >= list2
```

10.8 Indicate true or false for the following statements:

(a) Every element in a list must have the same type.

(b) A list's size is fixed after it is created.

(c) A list can have duplicate elements.

(d) The elements in a list can be accessed via an index operator.

10.9 What are `list1` and `list2` after the following lines of code?

```
list1 = [1, 43]
list2 = list1
list1[0] = 22
```

10.10 What are `list1` and `list2` after the following lines of code?

```
list1 = [1, 43]
list2 = [x for x in list1]
list1[0] = 22
```

10.11 How do you obtain a list from a string? Suppose `s1` is `welcome`. What is `s1.split('o')`?

10.12 Write statements to do the following:

(a) Create a list with 100 Boolean `False` values.

(b) Assign the value `5.5` to the last element in the list.

(c) Display the sum of the first two elements.

(d) Compute the sum of the first five elements in the list.

(e) Find the minimum element in the list.

(f) Randomly generate an index and display the element of this index in the list.

10.13 What happens when your program attempts to access a list element with an invalid index?

10.14 What is the output of the following code?

```
lst = [1, 2, 3, 4, 5, 6]
```

```
for i in range(1, 6):
    lst[i] = lst[i - 1]

print(lst)
```

10.3 Case Study: Lotto Numbers

The problem is to write a program that determines whether all the input numbers cover 1 to 99.

Key Point

Each ticket for the Pick-10 lotto has 10 unique numbers ranging from **1** to **99**. Suppose you buy a lot of tickets and like to have them cover all the numbers from **1** to **99**. Write a program that reads the ticket numbers from a file and determines whether all numbers are covered. Assume the last number in the file is **0**. Suppose the file contains the following numbers:

```
80 3 87 62 30 90 10 21 46 27
12 40 83 9 39 88 95 59 20 37
80 40 87 67 31 90 11 24 56 77
11 48 51 42 8 74 1 41 36 53
52 82 16 72 19 70 44 56 29 33
54 64 99 14 23 22 94 79 55 2
60 86 34 4 31 63 84 89 7 78
43 93 97 45 25 38 28 26 85 49
47 65 57 67 73 69 32 71 24 66
92 98 96 77 6 75 17 61 58 13
35 81 18 15 5 68 91 50 76
0
```

Your program should display

```
The tickets cover all numbers
```

Suppose the file contains the numbers

```
11 48 51 42 8 74 1 41 36 53
52 82 16 72 19 70 44 56 29 33
0
```

Your program should display

```
The tickets don't cover all numbers
```

How do you mark a number as covered? You can create a list with 99 Boolean elements. Each element in the list can be used to mark whether a number is covered. Let the list be **isCovered**. Initially, each element is **False**, as shown in Figure 10.3a. Whenever a number is read, its corresponding element is set to **True**. Suppose the numbers entered are **1, 2, 3, 99**, and **0**. When number **1** is read, **isCovered[0]** is set to **True** (see Figure 10.3b). When number **2** is read, **isCovered[2 - 1]** is set to **True** (see Figure 10.3c). When number **3** is read, **isCovered[3 - 1]** is set to **True** (see Figure 10.3d). When number **99** is read, **isCovered[98]** is set to **True** (see Figure 10.3e).

The algorithm for the program can be described as follows:

```
for each number k read from the file,
    mark number k as covered by setting isCovered[k - 1] true
```

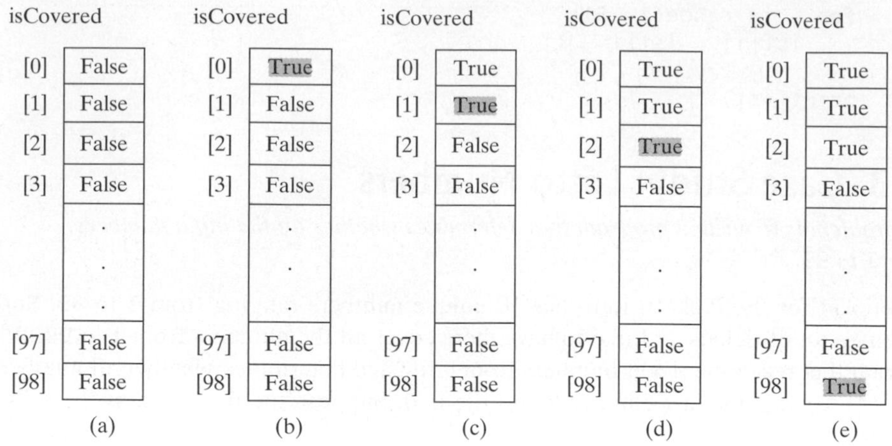

isCovered	isCovered	isCovered	isCovered	isCovered
[0] False	[0] True	[0] True	[0] True	[0] True
[1] False	[1] False	[1] True	[1] True	[1] True
[2] False	[2] False	[2] False	[2] True	[2] True
[3] False	[3] False	[3] False	[3] False	[3] False
.	.	.	.	.
.	.	.	.	.
.	.	.	.	.
[97] False	[97] False	[97] False	[97] False	[97] False
[98] False	[98] False	[98] False	[98] False	[98] True
(a)	(b)	(c)	(d)	(e)

FIGURE 10.3   If number **i** appears in a Lotto ticket, **isCovered[i - 1]** is set to true.

```
if every isCovered[i] is true:
    The tickets cover all numbers
else:
    The tickets don't cover all numbers
```

The complete program is given in Listing 10.2.

LISTING 10.2   LottoNumbers.py

```
 1  # Create a list of 99 Boolean elements with value False
 2  isCovered = 99 * [False]
 3  endOfInput = False
 4  while not endOfInput:
 5      # Read numbers as a string from the console
 6      s = input("Enter a line of numbers separated by spaces: ")
 7      items = s.split() # Extract items from the string
 8      lst = [eval(x) for x in items] # Convert items to numbers
 9
10      for number in lst:
11          if number == 0:
12              endOfInput = True
13          else:
14              # Mark its corresponding element covered
15              isCovered[number - 1] = True
16
17  # Check whether all numbers (1 to 99) are covered
18  allCovered = True # Assume all covered initially
19  for i in range(99):
20      if not isCovered[i]:
21          allCovered = False  # Find one number not covered
22          break
23
24  # Display result
25  if allCovered:
26      print("The tickets cover all numbers")
27  else:
28      print("The tickets don't cover all numbers")
```

create and initialize list

read input line

get input numbers

mark number covered

check allCovered?

```
Enter a line of numbers separated by spaces: 2 5 6 5 4 3 ↵Enter
Enter a line of numbers separated by spaces: 23 43 2 0 ↵Enter
The tickets don't cover all numbers
```

```
Enter a line of numbers separated by spaces: 1 2 3 4 5 6 ↵Enter
Enter a line of numbers separated by spaces: 7 8 9 10 11 ↵Enter
...
The tickets cover all numbers
```

Suppose you have created a text file named LottoNumbers.txt that contains the following input data: **2 5 6 5 4 3 23 43 2 0**

You can run the program by using the following command from the command window:

python LottoNumbers.py < LottoNumbers.txt

The program creates a list of 99 Boolean values with the initial value **False** (line 2). It repeatedly reads a line of numbers (line 6), extracts the numbers from the line (lines 7–8). For each number, the program performs the following operations in a loop:

- If the number is **0**, set **endOfInput True** (line 12).

- If the number is not zero, set its corresponding value for **isCovered** to **True** (line 15).

When the number is **0**, the input ends (line 4). The program determines whether all numbers are covered in lines 18–22 and displays the result in lines 25–28.

10.4 Case Study: Deck of Cards

The problem is to write a program that picks 4 cards randomly from a deck of 52 cards.

Key
Point

All the cards can be represented using a list named **deck**, filled with initial values **0** to **51**, as follows:

```
deck = [x for x in range(52)]
```

Or, you can use:

```
deck = list(range(52))
```

Card numbers **0** to **12**, **13** to **25**, **26** to **38**, and **39** to **51** represent 13 spades, 13 hearts, 13 diamonds, and 13 clubs, respectively, as shown in Figure 10.4. **cardNumber // 13** determines the suit of the card and **cardNumber % 13** determines the rank of the card, as shown in Figure 10.5. After shuffling the deck, pick the first four cards from deck. The program displays the cards from these four card numbers.

Listing 10.3 gives the solution to the problem.

LISTING 10.3 DeckOfCards.py

```
1  # Create a deck of cards
2  deck = [x for x in range(52)]
```

create list deck

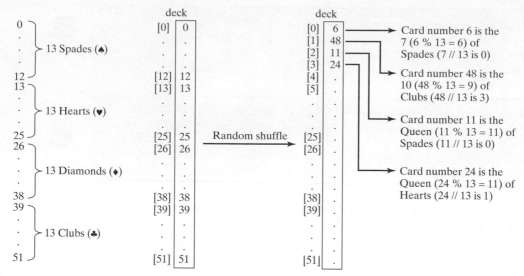

FIGURE 10.4 Fifty-two cards are stored in a list named **deck**.

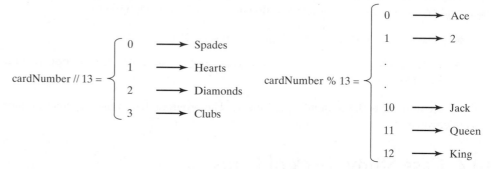

FIGURE 10.5 A card number identifies to a card.

```
3
4   # Create suits and ranks lists
5   suits = ["Spades", "Hearts", "Diamonds", "Clubs"]
6   ranks = ["Ace", "2", "3", "4", "5", "6", "7", "8", "9",
7       "10", "Jack", "Queen", "King"]
8
9   # Shuffle the cards
10  import random
11  random.shuffle(deck)
12
13  # Display the first four cards
14  for i in range(4):
15      suit = suits[deck[i] // 13]
16      rank = ranks[deck[i] % 13]
17      print("Card number", deck[i], "is the", rank, "of", suit)
```

list of strings (line 5)
list of strings (line 6)
shuffle deck (line 11)
suit of a card (line 15)
rank of a card (line 16)

```
Card number 6 is the 7 of Spades
Card number 48 is the 10 of Clubs
Card number 11 is the Queen of Spades
Card number 24 is the Queen of Hearts
```

The program creates a deck of 52 cards (line 2), a list `suits` for the four suits (line 5), and a list `ranks` for the 13 cards in a suit (lines 6–7). The elements in `suits` and `ranks` are strings.

The `deck` is initialized with the values `0` to `51`. A deck value `0` represents the ace of spades, `1` represents the 2 of spades, `13` represents the ace of hearts, and `14` represents the 2 of hearts.

Lines 10–11 randomly shuffle the deck. After the deck is shuffled, `deck[i]` contains an arbitrary value. `deck[i]  //  13` is `0`, `1`, `2`, or `3`, which determines the suit (line 15); `deck[i] % 13` is a value between `0` and `12`, which determines the rank (line 16).

If the `suits` list is not defined, you would have to determine the suit using a lengthy `if` statement as follows:

```
if deck[i] // 13 == 0:
    print("suit is Spades")
elif deck[i] // 13 == 1:
    print("suit is Hearts")
elif deck[i] // 13 == 2:
    print("suit is Diamonds")
else:
    print("suit is Clubs")
```

With `suits = ["Spades", "Hearts", "Diamonds", "Clubs"]` defined in a list, `suits[deck // 13]` gives the suit for the `deck`. Using lists greatly simplifies the solution for this program.

10.5 Deck of Cards GUI

The program picks 4 cards randomly from a deck of 52 cards and displays the cards.

Key Point

This section presents a GUI program that lets the user click the *Shuffle* button to display four random cards graphically on the console, as shown in Figure 10.6.

FIGURE 10.6 Clicking the Shuffle button displays four cards randomly.

You can use Turtle or Tkinter to develop GUI programs in Python. Turtle is a good pedagogical tool for introducing the fundamentals of programming, but its capability is limited to drawing lines, shapes, and text strings. For developing comprehensive GUI projects, you should use Tkinter. From now on, we will use Tkinter in our GUI examples. Listing 10.4 gives the GUI program for creating the *Shuffle* button and displaying the four cards randomly.

LISTING 10.4 DeckOfCardsGUI.py

```
1  from tkinter import * # Import all definitions from tkinter
2  import random
3
```

```
4   class DeckOfCardsGUI:
5       def __init__(self):
6           window = Tk() # Create a window
7           window.title("Pick Four Cards Randomly") # Set title
8
9           self.imageList = [] # Store images for cards
10          for i in range(1, 53):
11              self.imageList.append(PhotoImage(file = "image/card/"
12                  + str(i) + ".gif"))
13
14          frame = Frame(window) # Hold four labels for cards
15          frame.pack()
16
17          self.labelList = [] # A list of four labels
18          for i in range(4):
19              self.labelList.append(Label(frame,
20                  image = self.imageList[i]))
21              self.labelList[i].pack(side = LEFT)
22
23          Button(window, text = "Shuffle",
24              command = self.shuffle).pack()
25
26          window.mainloop() # Create an event loop
27
28      # Choose four random cards
29      def shuffle(self):
30          random.shuffle(self.imageList)
31          for i in range(4):
32              self.labelList[i]["image"] = self.imageList[i]
33
34  DeckOfCardsGUI() # Create GUI
```

Left margin annotations:
- image list (line 9)
- add images to list (line 11)
- label list (line 17)
- create labels (line 19)
- create a button (line 23)
- random shuffle (line 30)
- set new images (line 32)

The program creates 52 images from the image files stored in the **image/card** folder in the current program directory (lines 9–12). The files are named 1.gif, 2.gif, ..., and 52.gif. The images are added to **imageList**. Each image is an instance of the **PhotoImage** class.

The program creates a frame to hold four labels (lines 14–15). The labels are added to **labelList** (lines 17–21).

The program creates a button (line 23). When the button is clicked, the **shuffle** function is invoked to randomly shuffle the image list (line 30) and set the first four images in the list as the labels (lines 31–32).

10.6 Copying Lists

 Key Point

To copy the data in one list to another list, you have to copy individual elements from the source list to the target list.

You often need to duplicate a list or part of a list in a program. In such cases you could attempt to use the assignment statement (=), as follows:

```
list2 = list1
```

copy reference

garbage collection

However, this statement does not copy the contents of the list referenced by **list1** to **list2**; instead, it merely copies the reference value from **list1** to **list2**. After this statement, **list1** and **list2** refer to the same list, as shown in Figure 10.7. The list previously referenced by **list2** is no longer referenced; it becomes *garbage*. The memory space occupied by **list2** will be automatically collected and reused by the Python interpreter.

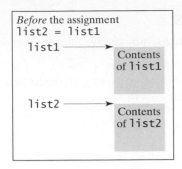 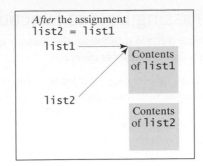

FIGURE 10.7 Before the assignment statement, `list1` and `list2` point to separate memory locations. After the assignment, the `list1` reference value is passed to `list2`.

Here is an example to illustrate the concept:

```
1  >>> list1 = [1, 2]
2  >>> list2 = [3, 4, 5]
3  >>> id(list1)
4  36207312
5  >>> id(list2)
6  36249848
7  >>>
8  >>> list2 = list1
9  >>> id(list2)
10 36207312
11 >>>
```

Two lists are created (lines 1–2) and each is an independent object with a different id (lines 4 and 6). After assigning `list1` to `list2`, `list2`'s id is the same as `list1`'s (line 10). `list1` and `list2` now refer to the same object.

To get a duplicate copy of `list1` into `list2`, you can use:

```
list2 = [x for x in list1]
```

or simply:

```
list2 = [] + list1
```

10.15 What is the output of the following code?

```
list1 = list(range(1, 10, 2))
list2 = list1
list1[0] = 111
print(list1)
print(list2)
```

10.16 What is the output of the following code?

```
list1 = list(range(1, 10, 2))
list2 = [] + list1
list1[0] = 111
print(list1)
print(list2)
```

Check Point

MyProgrammingLab™

10.7 Passing Lists to Functions

Key Point

When passing a list to a function, the contents of the list may change after the function call, since a list is a mutable object.

Since list is an object, passing a list to a function is just like passing an object to a function. For example, the following function displays the elements in a list:

```
def printList(lst):
    for element in lst:
        print(element)
```

You can invoke it by passing a list. For instance, the following statement invokes the **printList** function to display **3**, **1**, **2**, **6**, **4**, and **2**.

```
printList([3, 1, 2, 6, 4, 2])
```

Note

anonymous list

The preceding statement creates a list and passes it to the function. There is no explicit reference variable for the list. Such a list is called an *anonymous list*.

immutable vs. mutable

Since a list is a mutable object, the contents of a list may change in the function. Take the code in Listing 10.5, for example:

LISTING 10.5 PassListArgument.py

immutable object
mutable object

```
 1  def main():
 2      x = 1 # x is an int variable
 3      y = [1, 2, 3] # y is a list
 4
 5      m(x, y) # Invoke m with arguments x and y
 6
 7      print("x is", x)
 8      print("y[0] is", y[0])
 9
10  def m(number, numbers):
11      number = 1001 # Assign a new value to number
12      numbers[0] = 5555 # Assign a new value to numbers[0]
13
14  main() # Call the main function
```

```
x is 1
y[0] is 5555
```

In this sample run, you see that after **m** is invoked (line 5, **x** remains **1**, but **y[0]** is changed to **5555**. This is because **y** and **numbers** refer to the same list object. When **m(x, y)** is invoked, the reference values of **x** and **y** are passed to **number** and **numbers**. Since **y** contains the reference value to the list, **numbers** now contains the same reference value to the same list. Since **number** is immutable, altering it inside a function creates a new instance and the original instance outside the function is not changed. So, outside of the function, **x** is still **1**.

There is another issue we need to address regarding using a list as a default argument. Consider the code in Listing 10.6.

LISTING 10.6 DefaultListArgument.py

```
1   def add(x, lst = []):
2       if x not in lst:
3           lst.append(x)
4
5       return lst
6
7   def main():
8       list1 = add(1)
9       print(list1)
10
11      list2 = add(2)
12      print(list2)
13
14      list3 = add(3, [11, 12, 13, 14])
15      print(list3)
16
17      list4 = add(4)
18      print(list4)
19
20  main()
```

default argument

```
[1]
[1, 2]
[11, 12, 13, 14, 3]
[1, 2, 4]
```

The function **add** appends **x** to list **lst** if **x** is not in the list (lines 1–5). When the function is executed for the first time (line 8), the default value **[]** for the argument **lst** is created. This default value is created only once. **add(1)** adds **1** to **lst**.

When the function is called again (line 11), **lst** is now **[1]** not **[]**, because **lst** is created only once. After **add(2)** is executed, **lst** becomes **[1, 2]**.

In line 14, the list argument **[11, 12, 13, 14]** is given, and this list is passed to **lst**.

In line 17, the default list argument is used. Since the default list now is **[1, 2]**, after invoking **add(4)**, the default list becomes **[1, 2, 4]**.

If you want the default list to be **[]** for every function call, you can revise the function as shown in Listing 10.7.

LISTING 10.7 DefaultNoneListArgument.py

```
1   def add(x, lst = None):
2       if lst == None:
3           lst = []
4       if x not in lst:
5           lst.append(x)
6
7       return lst
8
```

default argument

new empty list

```
 9  def main():
10      list1 = add(1)
11      print(list1)
12
13      list2 = add(2)
14      print(list2)
15
16      list3 = add(3, [11, 12, 13, 14])
17      print(list3)
18
19      list4 = add(4)
20      print(list4)
21
22  main()
```

```
[1]
[2]
[11, 12, 13, 14, 3]
[4]
```

Here a new empty list is created every time the **add** function is called without a list argument (line 3). If the list argument is given when invoking the function, the default list is not used.

10.8 Returning a List from a Function

Key Point

When a function returns a list, the list's reference value is returned.

You can pass list arguments when invoking a function. A function can also return a list. For example, the following function returns a list that is the reversal of another list.

create a list

return list

```
1  def reverse(lst):
2      result = []
3
4      for element in lst:
5          result.insert(0, element)
6
7      return result
```

Line 2 creates a new list **result**. Lines 4–5 copy elements from the list named **lst** to the list named **result**. Line 7 returns the list. For example, the following statement returns a new list **list2** with the elements **6, 5, 4, 3, 2,** and **1**.

```
list1 = [1, 2, 3, 4, 5, 6]
list2 = reverse(list1)
```

Note that the **list** class has the method **reverse()** that can be invoked to reverse a list.

Check Point

10.17 True or false? When a list is passed to a function, a new list is created and passed to the function.

MyProgrammingLab™

10.18 Show the output of the following two programs:

```
def main():
    number = 0
    numbers = [10]

    m(number, numbers)

    print("number is", number,
        "and numbers[0] is",
        numbers[0])

def m(x, y):
    x = 3
    y[0] = 3

main()
```
(a)

```
def main():
    lst = [1, 2, 3, 4, 5]
    reverse(lst)
    for value in lst:
        print(value, end = ' ')

def reverse(lst):
    newLst = len(lst) * [0]

    for i in range(len(lst)):
        newLst[i] = lst[len(lst) - 1 - i]

    lst = newLst

main()
```
(b)

10.19 Show the output of the following two programs:

```
def main():
    list1 = m(1)
    print(list1)
    list2 = m(1)
    print(list2)

def m(x, lst = [1, 1, 2, 3]):
    if x in lst:
        lst.remove(x)
    return lst

main()
```
(a)

```
def main():
    list1 = m(1)
    print(list1)
    list2 = m(1)
    print(list2)

def m(x, lst = None):
    if lst == None:
        lst = [1, 1, 2, 3]

    if x in lst:
        lst.remove(x)
    return lst

main()
```
(b)

10.9 Case Study: Counting the Occurrences of Each Letter

The program in this section counts the occurrence of each letter among 100 letters.

**Key
Point**

Listing 10.8 presents a program that counts the occurrences of each letter in a list of characters. The program does the following:

1. Generates 100 lowercase letters randomly and assigns them to a list of characters, named **chars**, as shown in Figure 10.8a. You can obtain a random letter by using the **getRandomLowerCaseLetter()** function in the **RandomCharacter** module in Listing 6.11.

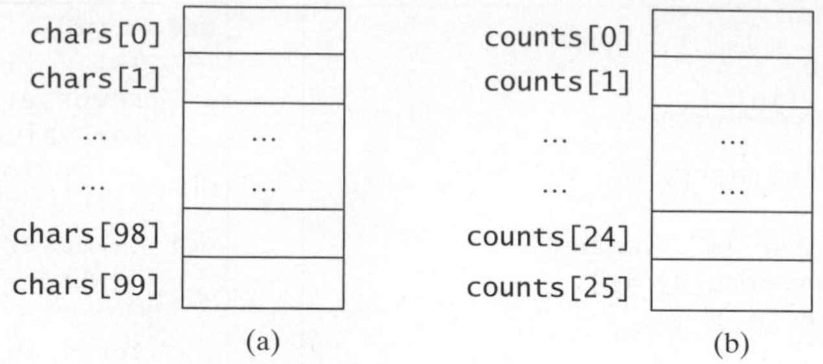

FIGURE 10.8 The **chars** list stores 100 characters, and the **counts** list stores 26 counts, each of which counts the occurrences of a letter.

2. Counts the occurrences of each letter in the list. To do so, it creates a list named **counts** that has 26 **int** values, each of which counts the occurrences of a letter, as shown in Figure 10.8b. That is, **counts[0]** counts the number of times **a** appears in the list, **counts[1]** counts the number of time **b** appears, and so on.

LISTING 10.8 CountLettersInList.py

```
1   import RandomCharacter # Defined in Listing 6.11
2
3   def main():
4       # Create a list of characters
5       chars = createList()
6
7       # Display the list
8       print("The lowercase letters are:")
9       displayList(chars)
10
11      # Count the occurrences of each letter
12      counts = countLetters(chars)
13
14      # Display counts
15      print("The occurrences of each letter are:")
16      displayCounts(counts)
17
18  # Create a list of characters
19  def createList():
20      # Create an empty list
21      chars = []
22
23      # Create lowercase letters randomly and add them to the list
24      for i in range(100):
25          chars.append(RandomCharacter.getRandomLowerCaseLetter())
26
27      # Return the list
28      return chars
29
30  # Display the list of characters
31  def displayList(chars):
32      # Display the characters in the list with 20 on each line
33      for i in range(len(chars)):
34          if (i + 1) % 20 == 0:
35              print(chars[i])
```

create list

pass list chars

return list counts

pass list counts

```
36            else:
37                print(chars[i], end = ' ')
38
39    # Count the occurrences of each letter
40    def countLetters(chars):
41        # Create a list of 26 integers with initial value 0
42        counts = 26 * [0]
43
44        # For each lowercase letter in the list, count it
45        for i in range(len(chars)):
46            counts[ord(chars[i]) - ord('a')] += 1
47
48        return counts
49
50    # Display counts
51    def displayCounts(counts):
52        for i in range(len(counts)):
53            if (i + 1) % 10 == 0:
54                print(counts[i], chr(i + ord('a')))
55            else:
56                print(counts[i], chr(i + ord('a')), end = ' ')
57
58    main() # Call the main function
```

counts

```
The lowercase letters are:
e y l s r i b k j v j h a b z n w b t v
s c c k r d w a m p w v u n q a m p l o
a z g d e g f i n d x m z o u l o z j v
h w i w n t g x w c d o t x h y v z y z
q e a m f w p g u q t r e n n w f c r f
The occurrences of each letter are:
5 a 3 b 4 c 4 d 4 e 4 f 4 g 3 h 3 i 3 j
2 k 3 l 4 m 6 n 4 o 3 p 3 q 4 r 2 s 4 t
3 u 5 v 8 w 3 x 3 y 6 z
```

The **createList** function (lines 19–28) generates a list of 100 random lowercase letters. Line 5 invokes the function and assigns the list to **chars**. What would be wrong if you rewrote the code as follows?

```
chars = 100 * [' ']
chars = createList()
```

You would be creating two lists. The first line would create a list by using **100 * [' ']**. The second line would create a list by invoking **createList()** and assign the reference of the list to **chars**. The list created in the first line would become garbage because it would no longer be referenced. Python automatically collects garbage behind the scenes. Your program would compile and run correctly, but it would create a list unnecessarily.

Invoking **getRandomLowerCaseLetter()** (line 25) returns a random lowercase letter. This function is defined in the **RandomCharacter** class in Listing 6.11.

The **countLetters** function (lines 40–48) returns a list of 26 **int** values, each of which stores the number of occurrences of a letter. The function processes each letter in the list and increases its count by one. A brute-force approach to count the occurrences of each letter might be as follows:

```
for i in range(len(chars)):
    if chars[i] == 'a':
        counts[0] += 1
    elif chars[i] == 'b':
        counts[1] += 1
    ...
```

But a better solution is given in lines 45–46.

```
for i in range(len(chars)):
    counts[ord(chars[i]) - ord('a')] += 1
```

If the letter (**chars[i]**) is **a**, the corresponding count is **counts[ord('a') - ord('a')]** (i.e., **counts[0]**). If the letter is **b**, the corresponding count is **counts[ord('b') - ord('a')]** (i.e., **counts[1]**), since the Unicode of **b** is one more than that of **a**. If the letter is **z**, the corresponding count is **counts[ord('z') - ord('a')]** (i.e., **counts[25]**), since the Unicode of **z** is 25 more than that of **a**.

10.10 Searching Lists

Key Point

If a list is sorted, a binary search is more efficient than a linear search for finding an element in the list.

Searching is the process of looking for a specific element in a list—for example, discovering whether a certain score is included in a list of scores. The **list** class provides the **index** method for searching and returning the index of a matching element from a list. It also supports the **in** and **not in** operators for determining whether an element is in a list.

Searching is a common task in computer programming. Many algorithms are devoted to searching. This section discusses two commonly used approaches: *linear searches* and *binary searches*.

VideoNote

Search a list

linear searches
binary searches

10.10.1 The Linear Search Approach

The linear search approach compares the key element **key** sequentially with each element in the list. It continues to do so until the key matches an element in the list or the list is exhausted without a match being found. If a match is found, the linear search returns the matching element's index in the list. If no match is found, the search returns **-1**. The **linearSearch** function in Listing 10.9 illustrates this approach.

linear search animation on
Companion Website

LISTING 10.9 LinearSearch.py

```
1  # The function for finding a key in the list
2  def linearSearch(lst, key):
3      for i in range(len(lst)):
4          if key == lst[i]:
5              return i
6
7      return -1
```

[0] [1] [2] ...

ith [ ][ ][ ][ ][ ][ ][ ]

key Compare key with lst[i] for i = 0, 1, ...

To better understand this function, trace it with the following statements:

```
lst = [1, 4, 4, 2, 5, -3, 6, 2]
i = linearSearch(lst, 4)   # Returns 1
j = linearSearch(lst, -4)  # Returns -1
k = linearSearch(lst, -3)  # Returns 5
```

The linear search function compares the key with each element in the list. The elements can be in any order. On average, the algorithm will have to examine half of the elements in a list before finding the key, if it exists. Since the execution time of a linear search increases linearly as the number of list elements increases, doing a linear search is inefficient for a large list.

10.10.2 The Binary Search Approach

A binary search is the other common search approach for a list of values. For a binary search to work, the elements in the list must already be ordered. Assume that the list is in ascending order. A binary search first compares the key with the element in the middle of the list. Consider the following three cases:

binary search animation on Companion Website

- If the key is less than the list's middle element, you need to continue to search for the key only in the first half of the list.

- If the key is equal to the list's middle element, the search ends with a match.

- If the key is greater than the list's middle element, you need to continue to search for the key only in the second half of the list.

Note

Clearly, the binary search function eliminates half of the list after each comparison. Sometimes you eliminate half of the elements, and sometimes you eliminate half plus one. Suppose that the list has n elements. For convenience, let n be a power of 2. After the first comparison, n/2 elements are left for further search; after the second comparison, (n/2)/2 elements are left. After the kth comparison, $n/2^k$ elements are left for further search. When k = $\log_2 n$, only one element is left in the list, and you need only one more comparison. Therefore, in the worst-case scenario when using the binary search approach, you need $\log_2 n + 1$ comparisons to find an element in the sorted list. In the worst case for a list of 1024 (2^{10}) elements, the binary search requires only 11 comparisons, whereas a linear search requires 1,023 comparisons in the worst case.

The portion of the list being searched shrinks by half after each comparison. Let **low** and **high** denote, respectively, the first index and last index of the list that is currently being searched. Initially, **low** is **0** and **high** is **len(lst)-1**. Let **mid** denote the index of the middle element, so **mid** is **(low + high) // 2**. Figure 10.9 shows how to find the key **11** in the list [2, 4, 7, 10, 11, 45, 50, 59, 60, 66, 69, 70, 79] using a binary search.

You now know how a binary search works. The next task is to implement it in Python. Don't rush to create a complete implementation. Develop it incrementally, one step at a time. You can start with the first iteration of the search, as shown in Figure 10.10a. It compares the key with the middle element in the list, whose **low** index is **0** and **high** index is **len(lst) - 1**. If **key < lst[mid]**, set the **high** index to **mid - 1**; if **key == lst[mid]**, a match is found and the program returns **mid**; if **key > lst[mid]**, set the **low** index to **mid + 1**.

Next, consider implementing the function to perform a search repeatedly by adding a loop, as shown in Figure 10.10b. The search ends if the key is found, or if the key is not found when **low > high**.

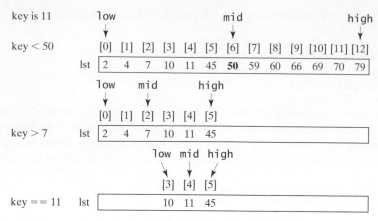

FIGURE 10.9 A binary search eliminates half of the list from further consideration after each comparison.

```
def binarySearch(lst, key):
    low = 0
    high = len(lst) - 1

    mid = (low + high) // 2
    if key < lst[mid]:
        high = mid - 1
    elif key == lst[mid]:
        return mid
    else:
        low = mid + 1
```

(a) Version 1

```
def binarySearch(lst, key):
    low = 0
    high = len(lst) - 1

    while high >= low:
        mid = (low + high) // 2
        if key < lst[mid]:
            high = mid - 1
        elif key == lst[mid]:
            return mid
        else:
            low = mid + 1

    return -1  # Not found
```

(b) Version 2

FIGURE 10.10 A binary search is implemented incrementally.

why not –1?

When the key is not found, **low** is the insertion point where a key would be inserted to maintain the order of the list. It is more useful to return the insertion point than **-1**. The function must return a negative value to indicate that the key is not in the list. Can it simply return **–low**? No. If the key is less than **lst[0]**, **low** would be **0**. **-0** is **0**. This would indicate that the key matches **lst[0]**. A good choice is to let the function return **–low – 1** if the key is not in the list. Returning **–low – 1** indicates not only that the key is not in the list, but also where the key would be inserted.

The complete program appears in Listing 10.10.

LISTING 10.10 BinarySearch.py

```
1   # Use binary search to find the key in the list
2   def binarySearch(lst, key):
3       low = 0
4       high = len(lst) - 1
5
6       while high >= low:
7           mid = (low + high) // 2
8           if key < lst[mid]:
```

```
 9                high = mid - 1
10           elif key == lst[mid]:
11                return mid
12           else:
13                low = mid + 1
14
15       return -low - 1 # Now high < low, key not found
```

first half

matched

second half

The binary search returns the index of the matching element if it is contained in the list (line 11). Otherwise, it returns **-low - 1** (line 15).

What would happen if we replaced **(high >= low)** in line 6 with **(high > low)**? The search would miss a possible matching element. Consider a list with just one element: The search would miss the element.

Does the function still work if there are duplicate elements in the list? Yes, as long as the elements are sorted in increasing order, the function returns the index of one of the matching elements if the element is in the list.

To better understand this function, trace it with the following statements and identify **low** and **high** when the function returns.

```
lst = [2, 4, 7, 10, 11, 45, 50, 59, 60, 66, 69, 70, 79]
i = binarySearch(lst, 2) # Returns 0
j = binarySearch(lst, 11) # Returns 4
k = binarySearch(lst, 12) # Returns -6
l = binarySearch(lst, 1) # Returns -1
m = binarySearch(lst, 3) # Returns -2
```

The following table shows the **low** and **high** values when the function exits and also shows the value returned from invoking the function.

Function	Low	High	Value Returned
binarySearch(lst, 2)	0	1	0
binarySearch(lst, 11)	3	5	4
binarySearch(lst, 12)	5	4	-6
binarySearch(lst, 1)	0	-1	-1
binarySearch(lst, 3)	1	0	-2

Note

Linear searches are useful for finding an element in a small list or an unsorted list, but they are inefficient for large lists. Binary searches are more efficient, but they require that the list be presorted.

binary search benefits

10.11 Sorting Lists

There are many strategies for sorting elements in a list. Selection sorts and insertion sorts are two common approaches.

Key Point

Sorting, like searching, is a common task in computer programming. The **list** class provides the **sort** method for sorting a list.

Many different algorithms have been developed for sorting. This section introduces two simple, intuitive sorting algorithms: *selection sort* and *insertion sort*. By using these algorithms, you will learn valuable techniques for developing and implementing other algorithms.

selection sort

insertion sort

10.11.1 Selection Sort

Suppose that you want to sort a list in ascending order. A selection sort finds the smallest element in the list and swaps it with the first element. It then finds the smallest element remaining and swaps it with the first element in the remaining list, and so on, until only a single element remains. Figure 10.11 shows how to sort the list [**2**, **9**, **5**, **4**, **8**, **1**, **6**] using a selection sort.

Select 1 (the smallest) and swap it with 2 (the first) in the list.

swap
2 9 5 4 8 1 6

The number 1 is now in the correct position and thus no longer needs to be considered.

swap
1 9 5 4 8 2 6

Select 2 (the smallest) and swap it with 9 (the first) in the remaining list.

The number 2 is now in the correct position and thus no longer needs to be considered.

swap
1 2 5 4 8 9 6

Select 4 (the smallest) and swap it with 5 (the first) in the remaining list.

The number 4 is now in the correct position and thus no longer needs to be considered.

1 2 4 5 8 9 6

5 is the smallest and in the right position. No swap is necessary.

The number 5 is now in the correct position and thus no longer needs to be considered.

swap
1 2 4 5 8 9 6

Select 6 (the smallest) and swap it with 8 (the first) in the remaining list.

The number 6 is now in the correct position and thus no longer needs to be considered.

swap
1 2 4 5 6 9 8

Select 8 (the smallest) and swap it with 9 (the first) in the remaining list.

The number 8 is now in the correct position and thus no longer needs to be considered.

1 2 4 5 6 8 9

Since there is only one element remaining in the list, the sort is completed.

FIGURE 10.11 A selection sort repeatedly selects the smallest element and swaps it with the first element in the remaining list.

It can be difficult to develop a complete sorting solution on the first attempt. Start by writing the code for the first iteration to find the smallest element in the list and swap it with the first element, and then observe what would be different for the second iteration, the third, and so on. The insight this gives you will enable you to write a loop that generalizes all the iterations.

The solution can be described as follows:

```
for i in range(len(lst)-1):
    select the smallest element in lst[i : len(lst)]
    swap the smallest with lst[i], if necessary
    # lst[i] is in its correct position.
    # The next iteration applies to lst[i+1 : len(lst)]
```

Listing 10.11 implements the solution.

LISTING 10.11 SelectionSort.py

```
1  # The function for sorting elements in ascending order
2  def selectionSort(lst):
3      for i in range(len(lst) - 1):
```

```
 4               # Find the minimum in the lst[i : len(lst)]
 5               currentMin = lst[i]
 6               currentMinIndex = i
 7
 8               for j in range(i + 1, len(lst)):                        select
 9                   if currentMin > lst[j]:
10                       currentMin = lst[j]
11                       currentMinIndex = j
12
13               # Swap lst[i] with lst[currentMinIndex] if necessary
14               if currentMinIndex != i:
15                   lst[currentMinIndex] = lst[i]                       swap
16                   lst[i] = currentMin
```

The **selectionSort(lst)** function sorts any list of elements. The function is implemented with a nested **for** loop. The outer loop (with the loop control variable **i**) (line 3) is iterated in order to find the smallest element in the list, which ranges from **lst[i]** to **lst[len(lst)-1]**, and exchanges it with **lst[i]**.

The variable **i** is initially **0**. After each iteration of the outer loop, **lst[i]** is in the right place. Eventually, all the elements are put in the right place; therefore, the whole list is sorted.

To understand this function better, trace it with the following statements:

```
lst = [1, 9, 4.5, 10.6, 5.7, -4.5]
selectionSort(lst)
```

10.11.2 Insertion Sort

Suppose that you want to sort a list in ascending order. The insertion-sort algorithm sorts a list of values by repeatedly inserting a new element into a sorted sublist until the whole list is sorted. Figure 10.12 shows how to sort the list [**2, 9, 5, 4, 8, 1, 6**] using an insertion sort.

insertion sort animation on Companion Website

Step 1: Initially, the sorted sublist contains the first element in the list. Insert 9 into the sublist.

2   9   5   4   8   1   6

Step 2: The sorted sublist is [2, 9]. Insert 5 into the sublist.

2   9 → 5   4   8   1   6

Step 3: The sorted sublist is [2, 5, 9]. Insert 4 into the sublist.

2   5 → 9 → 4   8   1   6

Step 4: The sorted sublist is [2, 4, 5, 9]. Insert 8 into the sublist.

2   4   5   9 → 8   1   6

Step 5: The sorted sublist is [2, 4, 5, 8, 9]. Insert 1 into the sublist.

2 → 4 → 5 → 8 → 9 → 1   6

Step 6: The sorted sublist is [1, 2, 4, 5, 8, 9]. Insert 6 into the sublist.

1   2   4   5   8 → 9 → 6

Step 7: The entire list is now sorted.

1   2   4   5   6   8   9

FIGURE 10.12   An insertion sort repeatedly inserts a new element into a sorted sublist.

The algorithm can be described as follows:

```
for i in range(1, len(lst)):
    insert lst[i] into a sorted sublist lst[0 : i] so that
    lst[0..i+1] is sorted.
```

To insert `lst[i]` into `lst[0..i-1]`, save `lst[i]` into a temporary variable, say `currentElement`. Move `lst[i-1]` to `lst[i]` if `lst[i-1] > currentElement`; move `lst[i-2]` to `lst[i-1]` if `lst[i-2] > currentElement`; and so on, until `lst[i-k] <= currentElement` or `k > i` (we pass the first element of the sorted list). Assign `currentElement` to `lst[i-k+1]`. For example, to insert **4** into [**2**, **5**, **9**] in Step 3 in Figure 10.13, move `lst[2]` (**9**) to `lst[3]` since **9** > **4**, and move `lst[1]` (**5**) to `lst[2]` since **5** > **4**. Finally, move `currentElement` (**4**) to `lst[1]`.

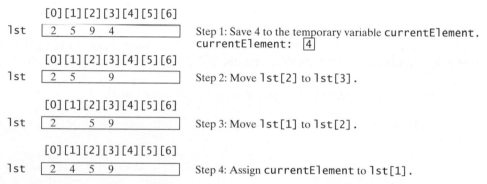

FIGURE 10.13 A new element is inserted into a sorted sublist.

The algorithm can be expanded and implemented as in Listing 10.12.

LISTING 10.12 InsertionSort.py

```
1   # The function for sorting elements in ascending order
2   def insertionSort(lst):
3       for i in range(1, len(lst)):
4           # insert lst[i] into a sorted sublist lst[0 : i] so that
5           #   lst[0 : i+1] is sorted.
6           currentElement = lst[i]
7           k = i - 1
8           while k >= 0 and lst[k] > currentElement:
9               lst[k + 1] = lst[k]
10              k -= 1
11
12          # Insert the current element into lst[k + 1]
13          lst[k + 1] = currentElement
```

shift

insert

The **insertionSort(lst)** function sorts any list of elements. The function is implemented with a nested **for** loop. The outer loop (with the loop control variable **i**) (line 3) is iterated in order to obtain a sorted sublist, which ranges from `lst[0]` to `lst[i]`. The inner loop (with the loop control variable **k**) inserts `lst[i]` into the sublist from `lst[0]` to `lst[i-1]`.

To better understand this function, trace it with the following statements:

```
lst = [1, 9, 4.5, 10.6, 5.7, -4.5]
insertionSort(lst)
```

10.20 Use Figure 10.8 as an example to show how to apply the binary search approach to a search for key **10** and key **12** in the list [**2, 4, 7, 10, 11, 45, 50, 59, 60, 66, 69, 70, 79**].

10.21 If the binary search function returns **−4**, is the key in the list? Where should the key be inserted if you wish to insert the key into the list?

10.22 Use Figure 10.10 as an example to show how to apply the selection-sort approach to sort [**3.4, 5, 3, 3.5, 2.2, 1.9, 2**].

10.23 Use Figure 10.11 as an example to show how to apply the insertion-sort approach to sort [**3.4, 5, 3, 3.5, 2.2, 1.9, 2**].

10.24 How do you modify the **selectionSort** function in Listing 10.11 to sort elements in decreasing order?

10.25 How do you modify the **insertionSort** function in Listing 10.12 to sort elements in decreasing order?

10.12 Case Study: Bouncing Balls

The program in this section displays bouncing balls stored in a list.

Now let's put things we have learned into developing an interesting project. The program we'll write in this section displays bouncing balls, as shown in Figure 10.14a.

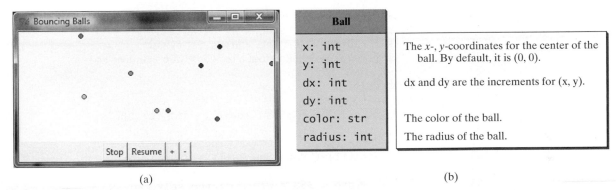

(a)   (b)

FIGURE 10.14 (a) The program displays bouncing balls with control buttons. (b) The **Ball** class encapsulates information about the ball.

The program enables the user to click the + and − buttons to add a ball or remove a ball from the canvas, and click the *Stop* and *Resume* buttons to stop the ball movements or resume them.

Each ball has its own center location (**x, y**), **radius**, **color**, and next increment for its center position, **dx** and **dy**. You can define a class to encapsulate all this information, as shown in Figure 10.14b. Initially, the ball is centered at (0, 0), and **dx = 2** and **dy = 2**. In the animation, the ball is moved to (**x + dx, y + dy**). When the ball reaches the right boundary, change **dx** to **-2**. When the ball reaches the bottom boundary, change **dy** to **-2**. When the ball reaches the left boundary, change **dx** to **2**. When the ball reaches the top boundary, change **dy** to **2**. The program simulates a bouncing ball by changing the **dx** or **dy** values when the ball touches the boundary of the canvas.

When the + button is clicked, a new ball is created. How do you store the ball in the program? You can store the balls in a list. When the − button is clicked, the last ball in the list is removed.

the Ball class

The complete program is given in Listing 10.13.

LISTING 10.13 BounceBalls.py

```
1   from tkinter import * # Import all definitions from tkinter
2   from random import randint
3
4   # Return a random color string in the form #RRGGBB
5   def getRandomColor():
6       color = "#"
7       for j in range(6):
8           color += toHexChar(randint(0, 15)) # Add a random digit
9       return color
10
11  # Convert an integer to a single hex digit in a character
12  def toHexChar(hexValue):
13      if 0 <= hexValue <= 9:
14          return chr(hexValue + ord('0'))
15      else:  # 10 <= hexValue <= 15
16          return chr(hexValue - 10 + ord('A'))
17
18  # Define a Ball class
19  class Ball:
20      def __init__(self):
21          self.x = 0 # Starting center position
22          self.y = 0
23          self.dx = 2 # Move right by default
24          self.dy = 2 # Move down by default
25          self.radius = 3 # The radius is fixed
26          self.color = getRandomColor() # Get random color
27
28  class BounceBalls:
29      def __init__(self):
30          self.ballList = [] # Create a list for balls
31
32          window = Tk() # Create a window
33          window.title("Bouncing Balls") # Set a title
34
35          self.width = 350 # Width of the self.canvas
36          self.height = 150 # Height of the self.canvas
37          self.canvas = Canvas(window, bg = "white",
38              width = self.width, height = self.height)
39          self.canvas.pack()
40
41          frame = Frame(window)
42          frame.pack()
43          btStop = Button(frame, text = "Stop", command = self.stop)
44          btStop.pack(side = LEFT)
45          btResume = Button(frame, text = "Resume",
46              command = self.resume)
47          btResume.pack(side = LEFT)
48          btAdd = Button(frame, text = "+", command = self.add)
49          btAdd.pack(side = LEFT)
50          btRemove = Button(frame, text = "-", command = self.remove)
51          btRemove.pack(side = LEFT)
52
53          self.sleepTime = 100 # Set a sleep time
54          self.isStopped = False
55          self.animate()
56
```

Margin notes:
random color
random hex number
Ball class
ball list
create canvas
create buttons
sleep time
isStopped?

```
57        window.mainloop() # Create an event loop
58
59    def stop(self): # Stop animation                              stop
60        self.isStopped = True
61
62    def resume(self): # Resume animation                          resume
63        self.isStopped = False
64        self.animate()
65
66    def add(self): # Add a new ball                               add
67        self.ballList.append(Ball())
68
69    def remove(self): # Remove the last ball                      remove
70        self.ballList.pop()
71
72    def animate(self): # Animate ball movements                   animate
73        while not self.isStopped:
74            self.canvas.after(self.sleepTime) # Sleep
75            self.canvas.update() # Update self.canvas
76            self.canvas.delete("ball")
77
78            for ball in self.ballList:
79                self.redisplayBall(ball)
80
81    def redisplayBall(self, ball):                                display ball
82        if ball.x > self.width or ball.x < 0:
83            ball.dx = -ball.dx
84
85        if ball.y > self.height or ball.y < 0:
86            ball.dy = -ball.dy
87
88        ball.x += ball.dx
89        ball.y += ball.dy
90        self.canvas.create_oval(ball.x - ball.radius,
91            ball.y - ball.radius, ball.x + ball.radius,
92            ball.y + ball.radius, fill = ball.color, tags = "ball")
93
94 BounceBalls() # Create GUI                                       create GUI
```

The program creates a canvas for displaying balls (lines 35–39), creates the buttons *Stop*, *Resume*, +, and − (lines 43–51), and starts the animation (line 57).

The **animate** method repaints the canvas every **100** milliseconds (lines 72–79). It redisplays every ball in the ball list (lines 78–79). The **redisplayBall** method changes the direction for **dx** and **dy** if the ball touches any boundaries of the canvas (lines 82–86), sets a new center position for the ball (lines 88–89), and redisplays the ball on the canvas (lines 90–92).

When the *Stop* button is clicked, the **stop** method is invoked to set the **isStopped** variable to **True** (line 60) and the animation stops (line 73). When the *Resume* button is clicked, the **resume** method is invoked to set the **isStopped** variable to **False** (line 63) and the animation resumes (line 73).

When the + button is clicked, the **add** method is invoked to add a new ball to the ball list (line 67). When the − button is clicked, the **remove** method is invoked to remove the last ball from the ball list (line 70).

When a ball is created (line 67), the **Ball**'s **__init__** method is invoked to create and initialize the properties **x**, **y**, **dx**, **dy**, **radius**, and **color**. The color is a string **#RRGGBB**, where **R**, **G**, **B** is a hex digit. Each hex digit is randomly generated (line 26). The **toHexChar(hexValue)** method returns a hex character for the value between **0** and **15** (lines 12–16).

KEY TERMS

CHAPTER SUMMARY

1. You can use the Python built-in functions **len**, **max**, **min**, and **sum** to return the length of a list, the maximum and minimum elements in a list, and the sum of all the elements in a list.

2. You can use the **shuffle** function in the **random** module to shuffle the elements in a list.

3. You can use the index operator **[]** to reference an individual element in a list.

4. Programmers often mistakenly reference the first element in a list with index **1**, but it should be **0**. This is called the *index off-by-one error*.

5. You can use the concatenation operator + to concatenate two lists, the repetition operator * to duplicate elements, the *slicing operator* **[:]** to get a sublist, and the **in** and **not in** operators to check whether an element is in a list.

6. You can use a **for** loop to traverse all elements in a list.

7. You can use the comparison operators to compare the elements of two lists.

8. A list object is mutable. You can use the methods **append**, **extend**, **insert**, **pop**, and **remove** to add and remove elements to and from a list.

9. You can use the **index** method to get the *index* of an element in a list, and the **count** method to return the count of the element in the list.

10. You can use the **sort** and **reverse** methods to sort or reverse the elements in a list.

11. You can use the **split** method to split a string into a list.

12. When a function is invoked with a list argument, the reference of the list is passed to the function.

13. If a list is sorted, a binary search is more efficient than a linear search for finding an element in the list.

14. A selection sort finds the smallest number in the list and swaps it with the first element. It then finds the smallest number remaining and swaps it with the first element in the remaining list, and so on, until only a single number remains.

15. The *insertion-sort algorithm* sorts a list of values by repeatedly inserting a new element into a sorted sublist until the whole list is sorted.

TEST QUESTIONS

Do test questions for this chapter online at www.cs.armstrong.edu/liang/py/test.html.

PROGRAMMING EXERCISES

MyProgrammingLab™

Note

If the program prompts the user to enter a list of values, enter the values from one line separated by spaces.

Sections 10.2–10.3

*10.1 (*Assign grades*) Write a program that reads a list of scores and then assigns grades based on the following scheme:

The grade is A if score is $>=$ best $- 10$.
The grade is B if score is $>=$ best $- 20$.
The grade is C if score is $>=$ best $- 30$.
The grade is D if score is $>=$ best $- 40$.
The grade is F otherwise.

Here is a sample run:

```
Enter scores: 40 55 70 58  ↵Enter
Student 0 score is 40 and grade is C
Student 1 score is 55 and grade is B
Student 2 score is 70 and grade is A
Student 3 score is 58 and grade is B
```

10.2 (*Reverse the numbers entered*) Write a program that reads a list of integers and displays them in the reverse order in which they were read.

**10.3 (*Count occurrence of numbers*) Write a program that reads some integers between 1 and 100 and counts the occurrences of each. Here is a sample run of the program:

```
Enter integers between 1 and 100: 2 5 6 5 4 3 23 43 2  ↵Enter
2 occurs 2 times
3 occurs 1 time
4 occurs 1 time
5 occurs 2 times
6 occurs 1 time
23 occurs 1 time
43 occurs 1 time
```

Note that if a number occurs more than one time, the plural word "times" is used in the output.

10.4 (*Analyze scores*) Write a program that reads an unspecified number of scores and determines how many scores are above or equal to the average and how many scores are below the average. Assume the input numbers are separated by one space in one line.

10.5 (*Print distinct numbers*) Write a program that reads in numbers separated by a space in one line and displays distinct numbers (i.e., if a number appears multiple times, it is displayed only once). (Hint: Read all the numbers and store them in **list1. Create a new list **list2**. Add a number in **list1** to **list2**. If the number is already in the list, ignore it.) Here is the sample run of the program:

```
Enter ten numbers: 1 2 3 2 1 6 3 4 5 2  ↵Enter
The distinct numbers are: 1 2 3 6 4 5
```

*10.6 (*Revise Listing 5.13, PrimeNumber.py*) Listing 5.13 determines whether a number **n** is prime by checking whether **2, 3, 4, 5, 6, ..., n/2** is a divisor for **n**. If a divisor is found, **n** is not prime. A more efficient approach is to check whether any of the prime numbers less than or equal to $\sqrt{n}$ can divide **n** evenly. If not, **n** is prime. Rewrite Listing 5.13 to display the first 50 prime numbers using this approach. You need to use a list to store the prime numbers and later use them to check whether they are possible divisors for **n**.

*10.7 (*Count single digits*) Write a program that generates 1,000 random integers between 0 and 9 and displays the count for each number. (Hint: Use a list of ten integers, say **counts**, to store the counts for the number of 0s, 1s, ..., 9s.)

Sections 10.4–10.7

10.8 (*Find the index of the smallest element*) Write a function that returns the index of the smallest element in a list of integers. If the number of such elements is greater than 1, return the smallest index. Use the following header:

def indexOfSmallestElement(lst):

Write a test program that prompts the user to enter a list of numbers, invokes this function to return the index of the smallest element, and displays the index.

*10.9 (*Statistics: compute deviation*) Exercise 5.46 computes the standard deviation of numbers. This exercise uses a different but equivalent formula to compute the standard deviation of **n** numbers.

$$mean = \frac{\sum_{i=1}^{n} x_i}{n} = \frac{x_1 + x_2 + \ldots + x_n}{n} \qquad deviation = \sqrt{\frac{\sum_{i=1}^{n}(x_i - mean)^2}{n-1}}$$

To compute the standard deviation with this formula, you have to store the individual numbers using a list, so that they can be used after the mean is obtained.

Your program should contain the following functions:

```
# Compute the standard deviation of values
def deviation(x):

# Compute the mean of a list of values
def mean(x):
```

Write a test program that prompts the user to enter a list of numbers and displays the mean and standard deviation, as shown in the following sample run:

```
Enter numbers: 1.9 2.5 3.7 2 1 6 3 4 5 2   ↵Enter
The mean is 3.11
The standard deviation is 1.55738
```

*10.10 (*Reverse a list*) The **reverse** function in Section 10.8 reverses a list by copying it to a new list. Rewrite the function that reverses the list passed in the argument and returns this list. Write a test program that prompts the user to enter a list of numbers, invokes the function to reverse the numbers, and displays the numbers.

Section 10.8

*10.11 (*Random number chooser*) You can shuffle a list using **random.shuffle(lst)**. Write your own function without using **random.shuffle(lst)** to shuffle a list and return the list. Use the following function header:

```
def shuffle(lst):
```

Write a test program that prompts the user to enter a list of numbers, invokes the function to shuffle the numbers, and displays the numbers.

10.12 (*Compute GCD*) Write a function that returns the greatest common divisor (GCD) of integers in a list. Use the following function header:

```
def gcd(numbers):
```

Write a test program that prompts the user to enter five numbers, invokes the function to find the GCD of these numbers, and displays the GCD.

Sections 10.9–10.12

10.13 (*Eliminate duplicates*) Write a function that returns a new list by eliminating the duplicate values in the list. Use the following function header:

```
def eliminateDuplicates(lst):
```

Write a test program that reads in a list of integers, invokes the function, and displays the result. Here is the sample run of the program:

```
Enter ten numbers: 1 2 3 2 1 6 3 4 5 2   ↵Enter
The distinct numbers are: 1 2 3 6 4 5
```

*10.14 (*Revise selection sort*) In Section 10.11.1, you used selection sort to sort a list. The selection-sort function repeatedly finds the smallest number in the current list and swaps it with the first one. Rewrite this program by finding the largest number and swapping it with the last one. Write a test program that reads in ten numbers, invokes the function, and displays the sorted numbers.

**10.15 (*Sorted?*) Write the following function that returns true if the list is already sorted in increasing order:

```
def isSorted(lst):
```

Write a test program that prompts the user to enter a list and displays whether the list is sorted or not. Here is a sample run:

```
Enter list: 1 1 3 4 4 5 7 9 10 30 11  ↵Enter
The list is not sorted
```

```
Enter list: 1 1 3 4 4 5 7 9 10 30  ↵Enter
The list is already sorted
```

**10.16 (*Bubble sort*) Write a sort function that uses the bubble-sort algorithm. The bubble-sort algorithm makes several passes through the list. On each pass, successive neighboring pairs are compared. If a pair is in decreasing order, its values are swapped; otherwise, the values remain unchanged. The technique is called a *bubble sort* or *sinking sort* because the smaller values gradually "bubble" their way to the top and the larger values "sink" to the bottom. Write a test program that reads in ten numbers, invokes the function, and displays the sorted numbers.

10.17 (*Anagrams*) Write a function that checks whether two words are anagrams. Two words are anagrams if they contain the same letters. For example, **silent and **listen** are anagrams. The header of the function is:

def isAnagram(s1, s2):

(Hint: Obtain two lists for the two strings. Sort the lists and check if two lists are identical.)

Write a test program that prompts the user to enter two strings and, if they are anagrams, displays **is an anagram**; otherwise, it displays **is not an anagram**.

***10.18 (*Game: Eight Queens*) The classic Eight Queens puzzle is to place eight queens on a chessboard such that no two queens can attack each other (i.e., no two queens are in the same row, same column, or same diagonal). There are many possible solutions. Write a program that displays one such solution. A sample output is shown below:

```
|Q| | | | | | | |
| | | | |Q| | | |
| | | | | | | |Q|
| | | | | |Q| | |
| | |Q| | | | | |
| | | | | | |Q| |
| |Q| | | | | | |
| | | |Q| | | | |
```

***10.19 (*Game: bean machine*) The bean machine, also known as a quincunx or the Galton box, is a device for statistics experiments named after English scientist Sir Francis Galton. It consists of an upright board with evenly spaced nails (or pegs) in a triangular pattern, as shown in Figure 10.15.

Balls are dropped from the opening of the board. Every time a ball hits a nail, it has a 50% chance of falling to the left or to the right. The piles of balls are accumulated in the slots at the bottom of the board.

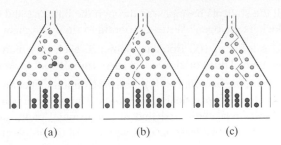

(a)   (b)   (c)

FIGURE 10.15 Each ball takes a random path and falls into a slot.

Write a program that simulates the bean machine. Your program should prompt the user to enter the number of the balls and the number of the slots in the machine. Simulate the falling of each ball by printing its path. For example, the path for the ball in Figure 10.15b is LLRRLLR and the path for the ball in Figure 10.15c is RLRRLRR. Display the final buildup of the balls in the slots in a histogram. Here is a sample run of the program:

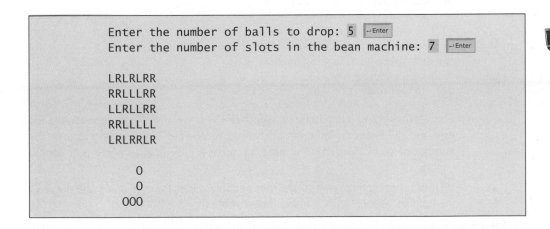

```
Enter the number of balls to drop: 5 ↵Enter
Enter the number of slots in the bean machine: 7 ↵Enter

LRLRLRR
RRLLLRR
LLRLLRR
RRLLLLL
LRLRRLR

    0
    0
   000
```

(Hint: Create a list named **slots**. Each element in **slots** stores the number of balls in a slot. Each ball falls into a slot via a path. The number of *R*s in a path is the position of the slot where the ball falls. For example, for the path LRLRLRR, the ball falls into **slots[4]**, and for the path is RRLLLLL, the ball falls into **slots[2]**.)

***10.20 (*Game: multiple Eight Queens solutions*) Exercise 10.18 has you find one solution for the Eight Queens puzzle. Write a program to count all possible solutions for the Eight Queens problem and display all the solutions.

**10.21 (*Game: locker puzzle*) A school has 100 lockers and 100 students. All lockers are closed on the first day of school. As the students enter, the first student, denoted S1, opens every locker. Then the second student, S2, begins with the second locker, denoted L2, and closes every other locker. Student S3 begins with the third locker and changes every third locker (closes it if it was open, and opens it if it was closed). Student S4 begins with locker L4 and changes every fourth locker. Student S5 starts with L5 and changes every fifth locker, and so on, until student S100 changes L100.

After all the students have passed through the building and changed the lockers, which lockers are open? Write a program to find your answer.

(Hint: Use a list of 100 Boolean elements, each of which indicates whether a locker is open (**True**) or closed (**False**). Initially, all lockers are closed.)

**10.22 (*Simulation: coupon collector's problem*) Coupon Collector is a classic statistics problem with many practical applications. The problem is to pick objects from a set of objects repeatedly and find out how many picks are needed for all the objects to be picked at least once. A variation of the problem is to pick cards from a shuffled deck of 52 cards repeatedly and find out how many picks are needed before you see one of each suit. Assume a picked card is placed back in the deck before picking another. Write a program to simulate the number of picks needed to get four cards, one from each suit and display the four cards picked (it is possible a card may be picked twice). Here is a sample run of the program:

```
Queen of Spades
5 of Clubs
Queen of Hearts
4 of Diamonds
Number of picks: 12
```

10.23 (*Algebra: solve quadratic equations*) Write a function for solving a quadratic equation using the following header:

def solveQuadratic(eqn, roots):

The coefficients of a quadratic equation $ax^2 + bx + c = 0$ are passed to the list **eqn** and the noncomplex roots are stored in **roots**. The function returns the number of roots. See Programming Exercise 4.1 on how to solve a quadratic equation.

Write a program that prompts the user to enter values for a, b, and c and displays the number of roots and all noncomplex roots.

*10.24 (*Math: combinations*) Write a program that prompts the user to enter 10 integers and displays all the combinations of picking two numbers from the 10.

*10.25 (*Game: pick four cards*) Write a program that picks four cards from a deck of 52 cards and computes their sum. An ace, king, queen, and jack represent **1**, **13**, **12**, and **11**, respectively. Your program should display the number of picks that yield the sum of **24**.

**10.26 (*Merge two sorted lists*) Write the following function that merges two sorted lists into a new sorted list:

def merge(list1, list2):

Implement the function in a way that takes **len(list1) + len(list2)** comparisons. Write a test program that prompts the user to enter two sorted lists and displays the merged list. Here is a sample run:

```
Enter list1: 1 5 16 61 111  ↵Enter
Enter list2: 2 4 5 6  ↵Enter
The merged list is 1 2 4 5 5 6 16 61 111
```

*10.27   (*Pattern recognition: four consecutive equal numbers*) Write the following function that tests whether the list has four consecutive numbers with the same value:

```
def isConsecutiveFour(values):
```

Write a test program that prompts the user to enter a series of integers and reports whether the series contains four consecutive numbers with the same value.

**10.28   (*Partition of a list*) Write the following function that partitions the list using the first element, called a *pivot*:

```
def partition(lst):
```

After the partition, the elements in the list are rearranged so that all the elements before the pivot are less than or equal to the pivot and the element after the pivot are greater than the pivot. The function also returns the index where the pivot is located in the new list. For example, suppose the list is [**5**, **2**, **9**, **3**, **6**, **8**]. After the partition, the list becomes [**3**, **2**, **5**, **9**, **6**, **8**]. Implement the function in a way that takes **len(lst)** comparisons. Write a test program that prompts the user to enter a list and displays the list after the partition. Here is a sample run:

```
Enter a list: 10 1 5 16 61 9 11 1  ↵Enter
After the partition, the list is 9 1 5 1 10 61 11 16
```

***10.29   (*Game: hangman*) Write a hangman game that randomly generates a word and prompts the user to guess one letter at a time, as shown in the sample run. Each letter in the word is displayed as an asterisk. When the user makes a correct guess, the actual letter is then displayed. When the user finishes a word, display the number of misses and ask the user whether to continue playing. Create a list to store the words, as follows:

```
# Use any words you wish
words = ["write", "that", "program", ...]
```

```
(Guess) Enter a letter in word ******* > p  ↵Enter
(Guess) Enter a letter in word p****** > r  ↵Enter
(Guess) Enter a letter in word pr**r** > p  ↵Enter
    p is already in the word
(Guess) Enter a letter in word pr**r** > o  ↵Enter
(Guess) Enter a letter in word pro*r** > g  ↵Enter
(Guess) Enter a letter in word progr** > n  ↵Enter
    n is not in the word
(Guess) Enter a letter in word progr** > m  ↵Enter
(Guess) Enter a letter in word progr*m > a  ↵Enter
The word is program. You missed 1 time

Do you want to guess another word? Enter y or n>
```

*10.30   (*Culture: Chinese Zodiac*) Simplify Listing 4.5, ChineseZodiac.py, using a list of strings to store the animals' names.

10.31 (*Occurrences of each digit in a string*) Write a function that counts the occurrences of each digit in a string using the following header:

```
def count(s):
```

The function counts how many times a digit appears in the string. The return value is a list of ten elements, each of which holds the count for a digit. For example, after executing **counts = count("12203AB3")**, **counts[0]** is **1**, **counts[1]** is **1**, **counts[2]** is **2**, and **counts[3]** is **2**.

Write a test program that prompts the user to enter a string and displays the number of occurrences of each digit in the string. Here is a sample run of the program:

```
Enter a string: 232534312  ↵Enter
1 occurs 1 time
2 occurs 3 times
3 occurs 3 times
4 occurs 1 time
5 occurs 1 time
```

10.32 (*Turtle: draw a line*) Write the following function that draws a line from point p1 ([x1, y1]) to point p2 ([x2, y2]).

```
# Draw a line
def drawLine(p1, p2):
```

10.33 (*Tkinter: draw histograms*) Write a program that generates 1,000 lowercase letters randomly, counts the occurrence of each letter, and displays a histogram for the occurrences, as shown in Figure 10.16a.

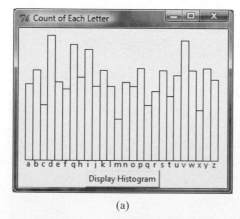

(a)

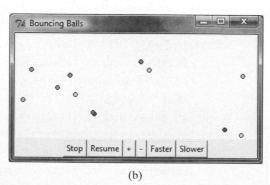

(b)

FIGURE 10.16 (a) A histogram is drawn for the count of each letter. (b) Two buttons are added to control the ball speed.

10.34 (*Turtle: draw histograms*) Rewrite the preceding program using Turtle.

*10.35 (*Tkinter: bouncing balls*) Revise Listing 10.13 to add two buttons—*Faster* and *Slower*, as shown in Figure 10.16b—to speed up or slow down the ball movements.

**10.36 (*Tkinter: linear search animation*) Write a program that animates the linear search algorithm. Create a list that consists of 20 distinct numbers from 1 to 20 in a random order. The elements are displayed in a histogram, as shown in Figure 10.17. You need to enter a search key in the text field. Clicking the *Step* button causes the program to perform one comparison in the algorithm and repaints the histogram with a bar indicating the search position. When the algorithm is finished, display a dialog box to inform the user. Clicking the *Reset* button creates a new random list for a new start.

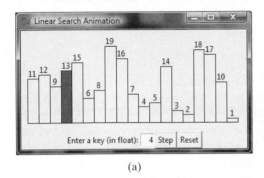 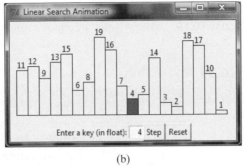

(a)   (b)

FIGURE 10.17   The program animates a linear search.

**10.37 (*Tkinter: binary search animation*) Write a program that animates the binary search algorithm. Create a list with the numbers from 1 to 20 in this order. The elements are displayed in a histogram, as shown in Figure 10.18. You need to enter a search key in the text field. Clicking the *Step* button causes the program to perform one comparison in the algorithm. Use a light-gray color to paint the bars for the numbers in the current search range and use a red color to paint the bar indicating the middle number in the search range. When the algorithm is finished, display a dialog box to inform the user. Clicking the *Reset* button enables a new search to start. This button also makes the text field editable.

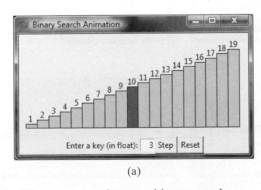 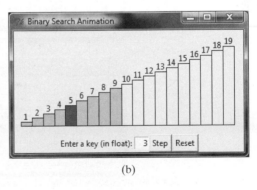

(a)   (b)

FIGURE 10.18   The program animates a binary search.

*10.38 (*Tkinter: selection-sort animation*) Write a program that animates the selection-sort algorithm. Create a list that consists of 20 distinct numbers from 1 to 20 in a random order. The elements are displayed in a histogram, as shown in Figure 10.19. Clicking the *Step* button causes the program to perform an iteration of the outer loop in the algorithm and repaints the histogram for the new list. Color the last bar in the sorted sublist. When the algorithm is finished, display a dialog box to inform the user. Clicking the *Reset* button creates a new random list for a new start.

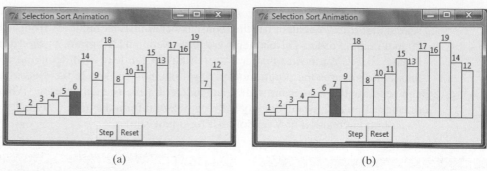

(a)   (b)

FIGURE 10.19 The program animates a selection sort.

*10.39 (*Tkinter: the 24-point card game*) The 24-point card game involves picking any four cards from 52 cards, as shown in Figure 10.20. Note that the jokers are excluded. Each card represents a number. An ace, king, queen, and jack represent 1, 13, 12, and 11, respectively. Enter an expression that uses the four numbers from the four selected cards. Each card number can be used only once in each expression, and each card must be used. You can use the operators (+, −, *, and /) and parentheses in the expression. The expression must evaluate to 24. After entering the expression, click the *Verify* button to check whether the numbers in the expression are currently selected and whether the result of the expression is correct. Display the verification in a dialog box. You can click the *Refresh* button to get another set of four cards. Assume that images are stored in files named 1.gif, 2.gif, ..., 52.gif, in the order of spades, hearts, diamonds, and clubs. So, the first 13 images are for spades 1, 2, 3, ..., and 13.

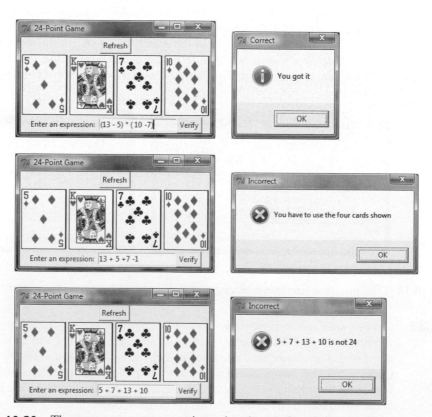

FIGURE 10.20 The user enters an expression using the numbers in the cards.

*10.40 (*Tkinter: insertion-sort animation*) Write a program that animates the insertion-sort algorithm. Create a list that consists of 20 distinct numbers from 1 to 20 in a random order. The elements are displayed in a histogram, as shown in Figure 10.21. Clicking the *Step* button causes the program to perform an iteration of the outer loop in the algorithm and repaints the histogram for the new list. Color the last bar in the sorted sublist. When the algorithm is finished, display a dialog box to inform the user. Clicking the *Reset* button creates a new random list for a new start.

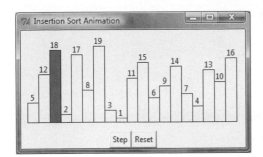 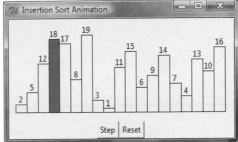

FIGURE 10.21   The program animates an insertion sort.

10.41 (*Display five circles*) Write a program that displays five circles, as shown in Figure 10.22a. Enable the user to drag each circle using the mouse, as shown in Figure 10.22b.

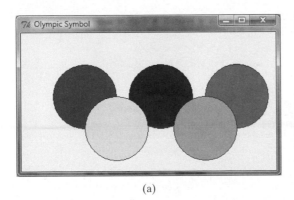 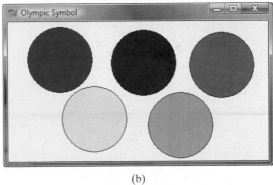

(a)   (b)

FIGURE 10.22   Each circle can be dragged with the mouse.

MULTIDIMENSIONAL LISTS

Objectives

- To learn how a two-dimensional list can represent two-dimensional data (§11.1).

- To access elements in a two-dimensional list by using row and column indexes (§11.2).

- To program common operations for two-dimensional lists (displaying lists, summing all elements, finding min and max elements, random shuffling, and sorting) (§11.2).

- To pass two-dimensional lists to functions (§11.3).

- To write a program for grading multiple-choice questions by using two-dimensional lists (§11.4).

- To solve the closest-pair problem by using two-dimensional lists (§§11.5–11.6).

- To check a Sudoku solution by using two-dimensional lists (§§11.7–11.8).

- To use multidimensional lists (§11.9).

11.1 Introduction

Key
Point

two-dimensional list

VideoNote
Process a matrix

Data in a table or a matrix can be stored in a two-dimensional list.

A *two-dimensional list* is a list that contains other lists as its elements. The preceding chapter introduced how to use a list to store linear collections of elements. You can use a list to store two-dimensional data, such as a matrix or a table, as well. For example, the following table, which provides the distances between cities, can be stored in a list named **distances**.

Distance Table (in miles)

	Chicago	Boston	New York	Atlanta	Miami	Dallas	Houston
Chicago	0	983	787	714	1,375	967	1,087
Boston	983	0	214	1,102	1,505	1,723	1,842
New York	787	214	0	888	1,549	1,548	1,627
Atlanta	714	1,102	888	0	661	781	810
Miami	1,375	1,505	1,549	661	0	1,426	1,187
Dallas	967	1,723	1,548	781	1,426	0	239
Houston	1,087	1,842	1,627	810	1,187	239	0

```
distances = [
    [0, 983, 787, 714, 1375, 967, 1087],
    [983, 0, 214, 1102, 1505, 1723, 1842],
    [787, 214, 0, 888, 1549, 1548, 1627],
    [714, 1102, 888, 0, 661, 781, 810],
    [1375, 1505, 1549, 661, 0, 1426, 1187],
    [967, 1723, 1548, 781, 1426, 0, 239],
    [1087, 1842, 1627, 810, 1187, 239, 0]
]
```

nested list

Each element in the **distances** list is another list, so **distances** is considered a *nested list*. In this example, a two-dimensional list is used to store two-dimensional data.

11.2 Processing Two-Dimensional Lists

Key
Point

row index
column index

A value in a two-dimensional list can be accessed through a row and column index.

You can think of a two-dimensional list as a list that consists of rows. Each row is a list that contains the values. The rows can be accessed using the index, conveniently called a *row index*. The values in each row can be accessed through another index, called a *column index*. A two-dimensional list named **matrix** is illustrated in Figure 11.1.

```
matrix = [
    [1, 2, 3, 4, 5],
    [6, 7, 0, 0, 0],
    [0, 1, 0, 0, 0],
    [1, 0, 0, 0, 8],
    [0, 0, 9, 0, 3],
]
```

matrix[0] is [1, 2, 3, 4, 5]
matrix[1] is [6, 7, 0, 0, 0]
matrix[2] is [0, 1, 0, 0, 0]
matrix[3] is [1, 0, 0, 0, 8]
matrix[4] is [0, 0, 9, 0, 3]

matrix[0][0] is 1
matrix[4][4] is 3

FIGURE 11.1 The values in a two-dimensional list can be accessed through row and column indexes.

Each value in matrix can be accessed using `matrix[i][j]`, where `i` and `j` are the row and column indexes.

The following sections give some examples of using two-dimensional lists.

11.2.1 Initializing Lists with Input Values

The following loop initializes the matrix with user input values:

```
matrix = [] # Create an empty list

numberOfRows = eval(input("Enter the number of rows: "))
numberOfColumns = eval(input("Enter the number of columns: "))
for row in range(numberOfRows):
    matrix.append([]) # Add an empty new row
    for column in range(numberOfColumns):
        value = eval(input("Enter an element and press Enter: "))
        matrix[row].append(value)

print(matrix)
```

11.2.2 Initializing Lists with Random Values

The following loop initializes a list that stores random values between **0** and **99**:

```
import random

matrix = [] # Create an empty list

numberOfRows = eval(input("Enter the number of rows: "))
numberOfColumns = eval(input("Enter the number of columns: "))
for row in range(numberOfRows):
    matrix.append([]) # Add an empty new row
    for column in range(numberOfColumns):
        matrix[row].append(random.randint(0, 99))

print(matrix)
```

11.2.3 Printing Lists

To print a two-dimensional list, you have to print each element in the list by using a loop like the following:

```
matrix = [[1, 2, 3], [4, 5, 6], [7, 8, 9]] # Assume a list is given

for row in range(len(matrix)):
    for column in range(len(matrix[row])):
        print(matrix[row][column], end = " ")
    print() # Print a new line
```

Or you can write:

```
matrix = [[1, 2, 3], [4, 5, 6], [7, 8, 9]] # Assume a list is given

for row in matrix:
    for value in row:
        print(value, end = " ")
    print() # Print a new line
```

11.2.4 Summing All Elements

Use a variable named **total** to store the sum. Initially, **total** is **0**. Add each element in the list to **total** by using a loop like this:

```
matrix = [[1, 2, 3], [4, 5, 6], [7, 8, 9]] # Assume a list is given

total = 0
for row in matrix:
    for value in row:
        total += value

print("Total is", total) # Print the total
```

11.2.5 Summing Elements by Column

For each column, use a variable named **total** to store its sum. Add each element in the column to **total** using a loop like this:

```
matrix = [[1, 2, 3], [4, 5, 6], [7, 8, 9]] # Assume a list is given

for column in range(len(matrix[0])):
    total = 0
    for row in range(len(matrix)):
        total += matrix[row][column]
    print("Sum for column", column, "is", total)
```

11.2.6 Finding the Row with the Largest Sum

To find the row with the largest sum, you may use the variables **maxRow** and **indexOfMaxRow** to track the largest sum and the index of the row. For each row, compute its sum and update **maxRow** and **indexOfMaxRow** if the new sum is greater.

```
matrix = [[1, 2, 3], [4, 5, 6], [7, 8, 9]] # Assume a list is given

maxRow = sum(matrix[0]) # Get sum of the first row in maxRow
indexOfMaxRow = 0

for row in range(1, len(matrix)):
    if sum(matrix[row]) > maxRow:
        maxRow = sum(matrix[row])
        indexOfMaxRow = row

print("Row", indexOfMaxRow, "has the maximum sum of", maxRow)
```

11.2.7 Random Shuffling

You can shuffle the elements in a one-dimensional list by using the **random.shuffle(list)** function, introduced in Section 10.2.3. How do you shuffle all the elements in a two-dimensional list? To accomplish this, for each element **matrix[row][column]**, randomly generate indexes **i** and **j** and swap **matrix[row][column]** with **matrix[i][j]**, as follows:

```
import random

matrix = [[1, 2, 3], [4, 5, 6], [7, 8, 9]] # Assume a list is given

for row in range(len(matrix)):
    for column in range(len(matrix[row])):
        i = random.randint(0, len(matrix) - 1)
```

```
        j = random.randint(0, len(matrix[row]) - 1)

        # Swap matrix[row][column] with matrix[i][j]
        matrix[row][column], matrix[i][j] = \
            matrix[i][j], matrix[row][column]

print(matrix)
```

11.2.8 Sorting

You can apply the **sort** method to sort a two-dimensional list. It sorts the rows on their first elements. For the rows with the same first element, they are sorted on the second elements. If the first and second elements in the rows are the same, their third elements are sorted, and so on. For example,

```
points = [[4, 2], [1, 7], [4, 5], [1, 2], [1, 1], [4, 1]]
points.sort()
print(points)
```

displays [[1, 1], [1, 2], [1, 7], [4, 1], [4, 2], [4, 5]].

11.1 How do you create a list for a two-dimensional set of data with three rows and four columns with values **0**?

✓Check Point

11.2 Can you create a list for two-dimensional data with a different number of elements in a row?

MyProgrammingLab™

11.3 What is the output of the following code?

```
matrix = []
matrix.append(3 * [1])
matrix.append(3 * [1])
matrix.append(3 * [1])
matrix[0][0] = 2
print(matrix)
```

11.4 What is the output of the following code?

```
matrix = []
matrix.append([3 * [1]])
matrix.append([3 * [1]])
matrix.append([3 * [1]])
print(matrix)
matrix[0] = 3
print(matrix)
```

11.5 What is the output of the following code?

```
matrix = []
matrix.append([1, 2, 3])
matrix.append([4, 5])
matrix.append([6, 7, 8, 9])
print(matrix)
```

11.3 Passing Two-Dimensional Lists to Functions

When passing a two-dimensional list to a function, the list's reference is passed to the function.

🔑Key Point

You can pass a two-dimensional list to a function just as you pass a one-dimensional list. You can also return a two-dimensional list from a function. Listing 11.1 gives an example with two functions. The first function, **getMatrix()**, returns a two-dimensional list, and the second function, **accumulate(m)**, returns the sum of all the elements in a matrix.

LISTING 11.1 PassTwoDimensionalList.py

getMatrix function

```
1  def getMatrix():
2      matrix = [] # Create an empty list
3
4      numberOfRows = eval(input("Enter the number of rows: "))
5      numberOfColumns = eval(input("Enter the number of columns: "))
6      for row in range(numberOfRows):
7          matrix.append([]) # Add an empty new row
8          for column in range(numberOfColumns):
9              value = eval(input("Enter a value and press Enter: "))
10             matrix[row].append(value)
11
12     return matrix
13
14 def accumulate(m):
15     total = 0
16     for row in m:
17         total += sum(row)
18
19     return total
20
21 def main():
22     m = getMatrix() # Get a list
23     print(m)
24
25     # Display sum of elements
26     print("\nSum of all elements is", accumulate(m))
27
28 main() # Invoke main function
```

return matrix

accumulate function

get matrix

invoke accumulate function

```
Enter the number of rows: 2 ↵Enter
Enter the number of columns: 2 ↵Enter
Enter a value and press Enter: 1 ↵Enter
Enter a value and press Enter: 2 ↵Enter
Enter a value and press Enter: 3 ↵Enter
Enter a value and press Enter: 4 ↵Enter
[[1, 2], [3, 4]]
Sum of all elements is 10
```

The function **getMatrix** (lines 1–12) prompts the user to enter values for the matrix (line 9), and returns the list (line 12).

The function **accumulate** (lines 14–19) has a two-dimensional list argument. It returns the sum of all elements in the list (line 26).

Check Point

11.6 Show the output of the following code:

```
def f(m):
    for i in range(len(m)):
        for j in range(len(m[i])):
            m[i][j] += 1
```

```
def printM(m):
    for i in range(len(m)):
        for j in range(len(m[i])):
            print(m[i][j], end = "")
        print()

m = [[0, 0], [0, 1]]

printM(m)
f(m)
printM(m)
```

11.4 Problem: Grading a Multiple-Choice Test

The problem is to write a program that grades multiple-choice tests.

Key Point

Suppose there are eight students and ten questions, and the answers are stored in a two-dimensional list. Each row records a student's answers to the questions, as shown in the following illustration.

```
              Students' Answers to the Questions:
                  0 1 2 3 4 5 6 7 8 9

    Student 0     A B A C C D E E A D
    Student 1     D B A B C A E E A D
    Student 2     E D D A C B E E A D
    Student 3     C B A E D C E E A D
    Student 4     A B D C C D E E A D
    Student 5     B B E C C D E E A D
    Student 6     B B A C C D E E A D
    Student 7     E B E C C D E E A D
```

The key is stored in a one-dimensional list:

```
              Key to the Questions:
              0 1 2 3 4 5 6 7 8 9
      Key     D B D C C D A E A D
```

The program grades the test and displays the result. To do this, the program compares each student's answers with the key, counts the number of correct answers, and displays it. Listing 11.2 shows the program.

LISTING 11.2 GradeExam.py

```
 1  def main():
 2      # Students' answers to the questions
 3      answers = [                                              2-D list
 4          ['A', 'B', 'A', 'C', 'C', 'D', 'E', 'E', 'A', 'D'],
 5          ['D', 'B', 'A', 'B', 'C', 'A', 'E', 'E', 'A', 'D'],
 6          ['E', 'D', 'D', 'A', 'C', 'B', 'E', 'E', 'A', 'D'],
 7          ['C', 'B', 'A', 'E', 'D', 'C', 'E', 'E', 'A', 'D'],
 8          ['A', 'B', 'D', 'C', 'C', 'D', 'E', 'E', 'A', 'D'],
 9          ['B', 'B', 'E', 'C', 'C', 'D', 'E', 'E', 'A', 'D'],
10          ['B', 'B', 'A', 'C', 'C', 'D', 'E', 'E', 'A', 'D'],
11          ['E', 'B', 'E', 'C', 'C', 'D', 'E', 'E', 'A', 'D']]
12
13      # Key to the questions
14      keys = ['D', 'B', 'D', 'C', 'C', 'D', 'A', 'E', 'A', 'D']     1-D list
```

```
15
16        # Grade all answers
17        for i in range(len(answers)):
18            # Grade one student
19            correctCount = 0
20            for j in range(len(answers[i])):
21                if answers[i][j] == keys[j]:
22                    correctCount += 1
23
24            print("Student", i, "'s correct count is", correctCount)
25
26    main() # Call the main function
```

compare with key

```
Student 0's correct count is 7
Student 1's correct count is 6
Student 2's correct count is 5
Student 3's correct count is 4
Student 4's correct count is 8
Student 5's correct count is 7
Student 6's correct count is 7
Student 7's correct count is 7
```

The statement in lines 3–11 creates a two-dimensional list of characters and assigns the reference to **answers**.

The statement in line 14 creates a list of keys and assigns the reference to **keys**.

Each row in the list **answers** stores a student's answers, which are graded by comparing them with the keys in the list **keys**. The result is displayed immediately after a student's answers are graded (lines 19–22).

11.5 Problem: Finding the Closest Pair

Key Point

This section presents a geometric problem for finding the closest pair of points.

Given a set of points, the closest-pair problem is to find the two points that are nearest to each other. In Figure 11.2, for example, points **(1, 1)** and **(2, 0.5)** are closest to each other. There are several ways to solve this problem. An intuitive approach is to compute the distances between all pairs of points and find the one with the minimum distance, as implemented in Listing 11.3.

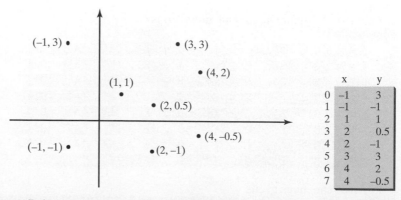

FIGURE 11.2 Points can be represented in a nested list.

LISTING 11.3 NearestPoints.py

```
1   # Compute the distance between two points (x1, y1) and (x2, y2)
2   def distance(x1, y1, x2, y2):
3       return ((x2 - x1) * (x2 - x1) + (y2 - y1) * (y2 - y1)) ** 0.5
4
5   def nearestPoints(points):
6       # p1 and p2 are the indexes in the points list
7       p1, p2 = 0, 1  # Initial two points
8
9       shortestDistance = distance(points[p1][0], points[p1][1],
10          points[p2][0], points[p2][1]) # Initialize shortestDistance
11
12      # Compute distance between every two points
13      for i in range(len(points)):
14          for j in range(i + 1, len(points)):
15              d = distance(points[i][0], points[i][1],
16                           points[j][0], points[j][1])  # Find distance
17
18              if shortestDistance > d:
19                  p1, p2 = i, j # Update p1, p2
20                  shortestDistance = d # New shortestDistance
21
22      return p1, p2
```

distance between two points

track two points

track shortestDistance

for each point i
for each point j
distance between i and j

update shortestDistance

This module defines the **nearestPoints(points)** function, which returns the indexes of the two nearest points in the two-dimensional list **points**. The program uses the variable **shortestDistance** (line 9) to store the distance between the two nearest points, and the indexes of these two points in the **points** list are stored in **p1** and **p2** (line 19).

For each point at index **i**, the program computes the distance between **points[i]** and **points[j]** for all **j > i** (lines 15–16). Whenever a shorter distance is found, the variable **shortestDistance** and **p1** and **p2** are updated (lines 19–20).

The distance between two points **(x1, y1)** and **(x2, y2)** can be computed using the formula $\sqrt{(x_2 - x_1)^2 + (y_2 - y_1)^2}$ (lines 2–3).

Note that there might be more than one closest pair of points with the same minimum distance. The program finds one such pair. You can modify the program to find all the closest pairs in Programming Exercise 11.8.

multiple closest pairs

The program in Listing 11.4 prompts the user to enter the points and then displays the nearest two points.

LISTING 11.4 FindNearestPoints.py

```
1   import NearestPoints
2
3   def main():
4       numberOfPoints = eval(input("Enter the number of points: "))
5
6       # Create a list to store points
7       points = []
8       print("Enter", numberOfPoints, "points:", end = '')
9       for i in range(numberOfPoints):
10          point = 2 * [0]
11          point[0], point[1] = \
12              eval(input("Enter coordinates separated by a comma: "))
13          points.append(point)
14
15      # p1 and p2 are the indexes in the points list
```

import NearestPoints

number of points

2-D list

read points

append a point

get nearest points

```
16      p1, p2 = NearestPoints.nearestPoints(points)
17
18      # Display result
19      print("The closest two points are (" +
20          str(points[p1][0]) + ", " + str(points[p1][1]) + ") and (" +
21          str(points[p2][0]) + ", " + str(points[p2][1]) + ")")
22
23  main() # Call the main function
```

```
Enter the number of points: 8  ↵Enter
Enter coordinates separated by a comma: -1, 3  ↵Enter
Enter coordinates separated by a comma: -1, -1  ↵Enter
Enter coordinates separated by a comma: 1, 1  ↵Enter
Enter coordinates separated by a comma: 2, 0.5  ↵Enter
Enter coordinates separated by a comma: 2, -1  ↵Enter
Enter coordinates separated by a comma: 3, 3  ↵Enter
Enter coordinates separated by a comma: 4, 2  ↵Enter
Enter coordinates separated by a comma: 4, -0.5  ↵Enter
The closest two points are (1, 1) and (2, 0.5)
```

The program prompts the user to enter the number of points (line 4). The points are read from the console and stored in a two-dimensional list named **points** (line 11). The program invokes the **nearestPoints(points)** function to return the indexes of the two nearest points in the list (line 16).

The program assumes that the plane has at least two points. You can easily modify the program in case the plane has zero or one point.

input file

 Tip

It is cumbersome to enter all points from the keyboard. You may store the input in a file, with a name such as FindNearestPoints.txt, and run the program using the following command from a command window:

python FindNearestPoints < FindNearestPoints.txt

11.6 GUI: Finding the Closest Pair

 Key Point

This section displays the points in a canvas, finds the closest pair of points, and draws a line to connect these two points.

The preceding section described a program that prompts the user to enter points and then finds the closest pair. This section presents a GUI program (Listing 11.5) that enables the user to create a point in the canvas with a left-mouse click, and it then dynamically finds the closest pair of points in the canvas and draws a line to connect these two points, as shown in Figure 11.3.

LISTING 11.5 NearestPointsGUI.py

import NearestPoints

```
1  import NearestPoints
2  from tkinter import * # Import all definitions from tkinter
3
```

```
4   RADIUS = 2 # Radius of the point                                point radius
5
6   class NearestPointsGUI:
7       def __init__(self):
8           self.points = [] # Store self.points                    points list
9           window = Tk() # Create a window
10          window.title("Find Nearest Points") # Set title
11
12          self.canvas = Canvas(window, width = 400, height = 200)  create canvas
13          self.canvas.pack()
14
15          self.canvas.bind("<Button-1>", self.addPoint)           bind event handler
16
17          window.mainloop() # Create an event loop
18
19      def addPoint(self, event):
20          if not self.isTooCloseToOtherPoints(event.x, event.y):  check mouse position
21              self.addThisPoint(event.x, event.y)                 add a point
22
23      def addThisPoint(self, x, y):
24          # Display this point
25          self.canvas.create_oval(x - RADIUS, y - RADIUS,
26              x + RADIUS, y + RADIUS)
27          # Add this point to self.points list
28          self.points.append([x, y])                              add to list
29          if len(self.points) > 2:
30              p1, p2 = NearestPoints.nearestPoints(self.points)   nearest points
31              self.canvas.delete("line")
32              self.canvas.create_line(self.points[p1][0],         draw a line
33                  self.points[p1][1], self.points[p2][0],
34                  self.points[p2][1], tags = "line")
35
36      def isTooCloseToOtherPoints(self, x, y):
37          for i in range(len(self.points)):
38              if NearestPoints.distance(x, y,                     check mouse position
39                  self.points[i][0], self.points[i][1]) <= RADIUS + 2:
40                  return True
41
42          return False
43
44  NearestPointsGUI() # Create GUI                                 create GUI
```

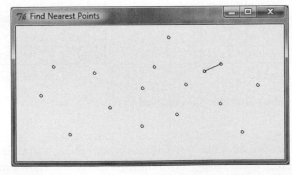

Figure 11.3 You can add a point by clicking the left-mouse button. The two nearest points are connected with a line.

The program creates and displays a canvas (lines 12–13) and binds the left-mouse click event to the callback function **addPoint** (line 15). When the user clicks the left mouse button on the canvas, the **addPoint** handler is invoked (lines 19–21). The **isTooCloseToOtherPoints(x, y)** method determines whether the mouse point is too close to any of the existing points on the canvas (line 20). If not, the point is added to the canvas by invoking **addThisPoint(x, y)** (line 21).

The **isTooCloseToOtherPoints(x, y)** method (lines 36–42) determines whether the point **(x, y)** is too close to other points in the canvas. If so, the program returns **True** (line 40); otherwise, it returns **False** (line 42).

The **addThisPoint(x, y)** method (lines 23–34) displays the point on the canvas (lines 25–26), adds the point to the points list (line 28), finds the new nearest points (line 30), and draws a line to connect the points (lines 32–34).

Note that every time a new point is added, the **nearestPoints** function is invoked to find a pair of nearest points. This function computes the distance between every pair of two points. This will be very time-consuming as more points are added. For a more efficient approach, see Programming Exercise 11.50.

11.7 Problem: Sudoku

Key
Point

The problem is to determine whether a given Sudoku solution is correct.

This section presents an interesting kind of problem that appears in the newspaper every day: the number-placement puzzle commonly known as *Sudoku*. This is a very challenging programming problem. To make it more accessible to novice programmers, this section presents a solution to a simplified version of the Sudoku problem, which is to verify whether a solution is correct. The complete solution for solving the Sudoku problem is presented in Supplement III.A.

fixed cells

free cells

Sudoku is a 9 × 9 grid divided into smaller 3 × 3 boxes (also called *regions* or *blocks*), as shown in Figure 11.4a. Some cells, called *fixed cells*, are populated with numbers from 1 to 9. The objective is to fill the empty cells, also called *free cells*, with the numbers 1 to 9 so that every row, column, and 3 × 3 box contains the numbers 1 to 9, as shown in Figure 11.4b.

5	3			7				
6			1	9	5			
	9	8					6	
8				6				3
4			8		3			1
7				2				6
	6							
			4	1	9			5
				8			7	9

(a) Puzzle

Solution →

5	3	4	6	7	8	9	1	2
6	7	2	1	9	5	3	4	8
1	9	8	3	4	2	5	6	7
8	5	9	7	6	1	4	2	3
4	2	6	8	5	3	7	9	1
7	1	3	9	2	4	8	5	6
9	6	1	5	3	7	2	8	4
2	8	7	4	1	9	6	3	5
3	4	5	2	8	6	1	7	9

(b) Solution

FIGURE 11.4 The Sudoku puzzle in (a) is solved in (b).

representing a grid

For convenience, we use the value **0** to indicate a free cell, as shown in Figure 11.5a. The grid can be naturally represented using a two-dimensional list, as shown in Figure 11.5b.

To find a solution for the puzzle, we must replace each **0** in the grid with an appropriate number from **1** to **9**. For the solution in Figure 11.4b, the list **grid** should be as shown in Figure 11.6.

5	3	0	0	7	0	0	0	0
6	0	0	1	9	5	0	0	0
0	9	8	0	0	0	0	6	0
8	0	0	0	6	0	0	0	3
4	0	0	8	0	3	0	0	1
7	0	0	0	2	0	0	0	6
0	6	0	0	0	0	0	0	0
0	0	0	4	1	9	0	0	5
0	0	0	0	8	0	0	7	9

```
grid =
  [[5, 3, 0, 0, 7, 0, 0, 0, 0],
   [6, 0, 0, 1, 9, 5, 0, 0, 0],
   [0, 9, 8, 0, 0, 0, 0, 6, 0],
   [8, 0, 0, 0, 6, 0, 0, 0, 3],
   [4, 0, 0, 8, 0, 3, 0, 0, 1],
   [7, 0, 0, 0, 2, 0, 0, 0, 6],
   [0, 6, 0, 0, 0, 0, 2, 8, 0],
   [0, 0, 0, 4, 1, 9, 0, 0, 5],
   [0, 0, 0, 0, 8, 0, 0, 7, 9]
  ]
```

(a)   (b)

FIGURE 11.5   A grid can be represented using a two-dimensional list.

```
A solution grid is
  [[5, 3, 4, 6, 7, 8, 9, 1, 2],
   [6, 7, 2, 1, 9, 5, 3, 4, 8],
   [1, 9, 8, 3, 4, 2, 5, 6, 7],
   [8, 5, 9, 7, 6, 1, 4, 2, 3],
   [4, 2, 6, 8, 5, 3, 7, 9, 1],
   [7, 1, 3, 9, 2, 4, 8, 5, 6],
   [9, 6, 1, 5, 3, 7, 2, 8, 4],
   [2, 8, 7, 4, 1, 9, 6, 3, 5],
   [3, 4, 5, 2, 8, 6, 1, 7, 9]
  ]
```

FIGURE 11.6   A solution is stored in **grid**.

Suppose a solution to a Sudoku puzzle is entered. How do you determine whether the solution is correct? Here are two approaches:

- One way to check the solution is to verify that every row, column, and box has the numbers from **1** to **9**.

- The other way is to check each cell. Each cell must contain a number from **1** to **9**, and the cell must be unique in every row, column, and box.

The program in Listing 11.6 prompts the user to enter a solution and reports whether it is valid. We use the second approach to determine whether the solution is correct. We place the **isValid** function in the separate module in Listing 11.7 so that it can be used by other programs.

LISTING 11.6   TestCheckSudokuSolution.py

```
1  from CheckSudokuSolution import isValid
2
3  def main():
4      # Read a Sudoku solution
5      grid = readASolution()                          read input
6
7      if isValid(grid):                               solution valid?
8          print("Valid solution")
9      else:
10         print("Invalid solution")
11
```

read solution

```
12   # Read a Sudoku solution from the console
13   def readASolution():
14       print("Enter a Sudoku puzzle solution:")
15       grid = []
16       for i in range(9):
17           line = input().strip().split()
18           grid.append([eval(x) for x in line])
19
20       return grid
21
22   main() # Call the main function
```

```
Enter a Sudoku puzzle solution:
9 6 3 1 7 4 2 5 8   ⏎Enter
1 7 8 3 2 5 6 4 9   ⏎Enter
2 5 4 6 8 9 7 3 1   ⏎Enter
8 2 1 4 3 7 5 9 6   ⏎Enter
4 9 6 8 5 2 3 1 7   ⏎Enter
7 3 5 9 6 1 8 2 4   ⏎Enter
5 8 9 7 1 3 4 6 2   ⏎Enter
3 1 7 2 4 6 9 8 5   ⏎Enter
6 4 2 5 9 8 1 7 3   ⏎Enter
Valid solution
```

LISTING 11.7 CheckSudokuSolution.py

solution valid?

```
1    # Check whether a solution is valid
2    def isValid(grid):
3        for i in range(9):
4            for j in range(9):
5                if grid[i][j] < 1 or grid[i][j] > 9 \
6                        or not isValidAt(i, j, grid):
7                    return False
8        return True # The fixed cells are valid
9
10   # Check whether grid[i][j] is valid in the grid
11   def isValidAt(i, j, grid):
12       # Check whether grid[i][j] is valid in i's row
```

check columns

```
13       for column in range(9):
14           if column != j and grid[i][column] == grid[i][j]:
15               return False
16
17       # Check whether grid[i][j] is valid in j's column
```

check rows

```
18       for row in range(9):
19           if row != i and grid[row][j] == grid[i][j]:
20               return False
21
22       # Check whether grid[i][j] is valid in the 3-by-3 box
```

check small boxes

```
23       for row in range((i // 3) * 3, (i // 3) * 3 + 3):
24           for col in range((j // 3) * 3, (j // 3) * 3 + 3):
25               if row != i and col != j and \
26                       grid[row][col] == grid[i][j]:
27                   return False
28
29       return True # The current value at grid[i][j] is valid
```

In Listing 11.6, the program invokes the **readASolution()** function (line 5) to read a Sudoku solution and return a two-dimensional list representing a Sudoku grid.

The **isValid(grid)** function determines whether the values in the grid are valid. It checks whether each value is between **1** and **9** and whether each value is valid in the grid (lines 7–10).

isValid function

The **isValidAt(i, j, grid)** function in Listing 11.7 checks whether the value at **grid[i][j]** is valid. It checks whether **grid[i][j]** appears more than once in row **i** (lines 18–20), in column **j** (lines 13–15), and in the 3 × 3 box (lines 23–27).

isValidAt function

How do you locate all the cells in the same box? For any **grid[i][j]**, the starting cell of the 3 × 3 box that contains it is **grid[(i // 3) * 3][(j // 3) * 3]**, as illustrated in Figure 11.7.

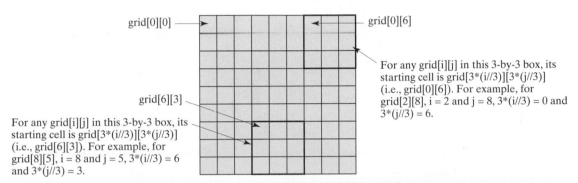

FIGURE 11.7 The location of the first cell in a 3 × 3 box determines the locations of the other cells in the box.

With this insight, you can easily identify all the cells in the box. For example, if **grid[r][c]** is the starting cell of a 3 × 3 box, the cells in the box can be traversed in a nested loop as follows:

```
# Get all cells in a 3-by-3 box starting at grid[r][c]
for row in range(r, r + 3):
    for col in range(c, c + 3):
        # grid[row][col] is in the box
```

It is cumbersome to enter 81 numbers from the console. When you test the program, you may store the input in a file, say CheckSudokuSolution.txt (see www.cs.armstrong.edu/liang/data/CheckSudokuSolution.txt), and run the program using the following command from a command window:

input file

```
python TestCheckSudokuSolution.py < CheckSudokuSolution.txt
```

11.8 Case Study: Sudoku GUI

This section shows how to create a GUI program that checks whether a given Sudoku solution is correct.

Key
Point

The program in the preceding section reads a Sudoku solution from the console and checks whether the solution is correct. This section presents a GUI program that lets the user enter the solution from the **Entry** widget and click the *Validate* button to check if the solution is correct, as shown in Figure 11.8.

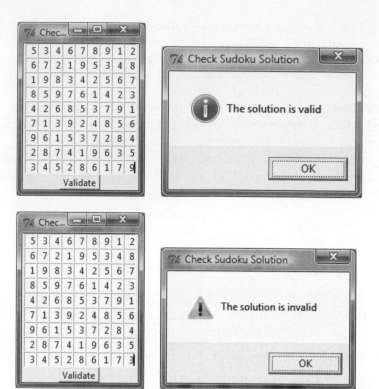

FIGURE 11.8 You can enter the numbers in the **Entry** widget and click the *Validate* button to see if the solution is correct.

The complete program is given in Listing 11.8.

LISTING 11.8 SudokuGUI.py

```
1  from tkinter import * # Import all definitions from tkinter
2  import tkinter.messagebox # Import tkinter.messagebox
3  from CheckSudokuSolution import isValid # Defined in Listing 11.7
4
5  class SudokuGUI:
6      def __init__(self):
7          window = Tk() # Create a window
8          window.title("Check Sudoku Solution") # Set title
9
10         frame = Frame(window) # Hold entries
11         frame.pack()
12
13         self.cells = [] # A list of variables tied to entries
14         for i in range(9):
15             self.cells.append([])
16             for j in range(9):
17                 self.cells[i].append(StringVar())
18
19         for i in range(9):
20             for j in range(9):
21                 Entry(frame, width = 2, justify = RIGHT,
22                     textvariable = self.cells[i][j]).grid(
23                     row = i, column = j)
24
```

import isValid

entries 2-D list

create entries

```
25        Button(window, text = "Validate",
26            command = self.validate).pack()
27
28        window.mainloop() # Create an event loop
29
30    # Check if the numbers entered are a valid solution
31    def validate(self):
32        # Get the numbers from the entries
33        values = [[eval(x.get())
34                    for x in self.cells[i]] for i in range(9)]
35
36        if isValid(values):
37            tkinter.messagebox.showinfo("Check Sudoku Solution",
38                                        "The solution is valid")
39        else:
40            tkinter.messagebox.showwarning("Check Sudoku Solution",
41                                           "The solution is invalid")
42
43  SudokuGUI() # Create GUI
```

create a button
callback handler

validate method

The program creates a two-dimensional list **cells** (lines 13–17). Each element in **cells** corresponds to a value in the entry (lines 19–23). The entries are created and placed using a grid manager in a frame. A button is created to be placed below the frame (lines 25–26). When the button is clicked, the callback handler **validate** is invoked (lines 31–41). The function obtains the values from the entries and puts them into the two-dimensional list **values** (lines 33–34), and then invokes the **isValid** function (defined in Listing 11.7) to check whether the numbers entered from the entries form a valid solution (line 36). The Tkinter's standard dialog boxes are used to display whether a solution is valid (lines 36–41).

11.9 Multidimensional Lists

A two-dimensional list consists of a list of one-dimensional lists and a three-dimensional list consists of a list of two-dimensional lists.

 Key Point

In the preceding sections, you used two-dimensional lists to represent a matrix or a table. Occasionally, you need to represent *n*-dimensional data. You can create *n*-dimensional lists for any integer *n*. For example, you can use a three-dimensional list to store exam scores for a class of six students with five exams, and each exam has two parts (multiple-choice and essay). The following syntax creates a three-dimensional list named **scores**.

```
scores = [
    [[11.5, 20.5], [11.0, 22.5], [15, 33.5], [13, 21.5], [15, 2.5]],
    [[4.5, 21.5], [11.0, 22.5], [15, 34.5], [12, 20.5], [14, 11.5]],
    [[6.5, 30.5], [11.4, 11.5], [11, 33.5], [11, 23.5], [10, 2.5]],
    [[6.5, 23.5], [11.4, 32.5], [13, 34.5], [11, 20.5], [16, 11.5]],
    [[8.5, 26.5], [11.4, 52.5], [13, 36.5], [13, 24.5], [16, 2.5]],
    [[11.5, 20.5], [11.4, 42.5], [13, 31.5], [12, 20.5], [16, 6.5]]]
```

scores[0][1][0] refers to the multiple-choice score for the first student's second exam, which is **11.0**. **scores[0][1][1]** refers to the essay score for the first student's second exam, which is **22.5**. The following figure depicts the meaning of the values in the list.

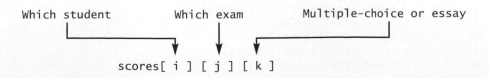

multidimensional list

A *multidimensional list* is a list in which each element is another list. More specifically, a *three-dimensional list* consists of a list of two-dimensional lists, and a *two-dimensional list* consists of a list of one-dimensional lists. For example, `scores[0]` and `scores[1]` are two-dimensional lists, while `scores[0][0]`, `scores[0][1]`, `scores[1][0]`, and `scores[1][1]` are one-dimensional lists and each contains two elements. `len(scores)` is 6, `len(scores[0])` is 5, and `len(scores[0][0])` is 2.

11.9.1 Problem: Daily Temperature and Humidity

Suppose a meteorological station records the temperature and humidity at each hour of every day and stores the data for the past ten days in a text file named weather.txt (see www.cs.armstrong.edu/liang/data/weather.txt). Each line of the file consists of four numbers that indicate the day, hour, temperature, and humidity. The contents of the file may look like the one in (a):

```
1 1 76.4 0.92
1 2 77.7 0.93
...
10 23 97.7 0.71
10 24 98.7 0.74
```

(a)

```
10 24 98.7 0.74
1 2 77.7 0.93
...
10 23 97.7 0.71
1 1 76.4 0.92
```

(b)

Note that the lines in the file are not necessarily in order. For example, the file may appear as shown in (b).

Your task is to write a program that calculates the average daily temperature and humidity for the 10 days. You can use input redirection to read the data from the file and store the data in a three-dimensional list named **data**. The first index of **data** ranges from **0** to **9** and represents the 10 days; the second index ranges from **0** to **23** and represents the 24-hour periods; and the third index ranges from **0** to **1** and represents temperature and humidity, respectively. Note that the days are numbered from **1** to **10** and hours from **1** to **24** in the file. Since the list index starts from **0**, `data[0][0][0]` stores the temperature in day **1** at hour **1** and `data[9][23][1]` stores the humidity in day **10** at hour **24**.

The program is given in Listing 11.9.

LISTING 11.9 Weather.py

three-dimensional list

```
 1  def main():
 2      NUMBER_OF_DAYS = 10
 3      NUMBER_OF_HOURS = 24
 4
 5      # Initialize data
 6      data = []
 7      for i in range(NUMBER_OF_DAYS):
 8          data.append([])
 9          for j in range(NUMBER_OF_HOURS):
10              data[i].append([])
11              data[i][j].append(0) # Temperature value
12              data[i][j].append(0) # Humidity value
13
14      # Read input using input redirection from a file
15      for k in range(NUMBER_OF_DAYS * NUMBER_OF_HOURS):
16          line = input().strip().split()
17          day = eval(line[0])
18          hour = eval(line[1])
19          temperature = eval(line[2])
20          humidity = eval(line[3])
```

```
21              data[day - 1][hour - 1][0] = temperature
22              data[day - 1][hour - 1][1] = humidity
23
24      # Find the average daily temperature and humidity
25      for i in range(NUMBER_OF_DAYS):
26          dailyTemperatureTotal = 0
27          dailyHumidityTotal = 0
28          for j in range(NUMBER_OF_HOURS):
29              dailyTemperatureTotal += data[i][j][0]
30              dailyHumidityTotal += data[i][j][1]
31
32          # Display result
33          print("Day " + str(i) + "'s average temperature is "
34              + str(dailyTemperatureTotal / NUMBER_OF_HOURS))
35          print("Day " + str(i) + "'s average humidity is "
36              + str(dailyHumidityTotal / NUMBER_OF_HOURS))
37
38  main() # Call the main function
```

```
Day 0's average temperature is 77.7708
Day 0's average humidity is 0.929583
Day 1's average temperature is 77.3125
Day 1's average humidity is 0.929583
...
Day 9's average temperature is 79.3542
Day 9's average humidity is 0.9125
```

You can use the following command to run the program:

```
python Weather.py < Weather.txt
```

A three-dimensional list for storing the temperature and humidity is created in lines 6–12 with initial values 0. The loop in lines 15–22 reads the input to the list. You can enter the input from the keyboard, but doing so will be awkward. For convenience, we store the data in a file and use input redirection to read the data from the file. The program reads one line of input as a string and splits it into a list (line 16) to obtain the day, hour, temperature, and humidity (lines 17–20). The loop in lines 25–30 adds all temperatures for each hour in a day to **dailyTemperatureTotal** and all humidity for each hour to **dailyHumidityTotal**. The average daily temperature and humidity are displayed in lines 33–36.

11.9.2 Problem: Guessing Birthdays

Listing 4.3, GuessBirthday.py, is a program that guesses a birthday. The program can be simplified by storing the numbers in a three-dimensional list and prompting the user for the answers using a loop, as shown in Listing 11.10. The sample run of the program can be the same as shown in Listing 4.3.

LISTING 11.10 GuessBirthdayUsingList.py

```
1  def main():
2      day = 0 # Day to be determined
3
4      dates = [
5          [[ 1,  3,  5,  7],
6           [ 9, 11, 13, 15],
7           [17, 19, 21, 23],
```

three-dimensional list

```
 8              [25, 27, 29, 31]],
 9             [[ 2,  3,  6,  7],
10              [10, 11, 14, 15],
11              [18, 19, 22, 23],
12              [26, 27, 30, 31]],
13             [[ 4,  5,  6,  7],
14              [12, 13, 14, 15],
15              [20, 21, 22, 23],
16              [28, 29, 30, 31]],
17             [[ 8,  9, 10, 11],
18              [12, 13, 14, 15],
19              [24, 25, 26, 27],
20              [28, 29, 30, 31]],
21             [[16, 17, 18, 19],
22              [20, 21, 22, 23],
23              [24, 25, 26, 27],
24              [28, 29, 30, 31]]]
25
26      for i in range(5):
27          print("Is your birthday in Set" + str(i + 1) + "?")
28          for j in range(4):
29              for k in range(4):
30                  print(format(dates[i][j][k], "4d"), end = " ")
31              print()
32
33          answer = eval(input("Enter 0 for No and 1 for Yes: "))
34
35          if answer == 1:
36              day += dates[i][0][0]
37
38      print("Your birthday is " + str(day))
39
40  main() # Call the main function
```

display a question

A three-dimensional list **dates** is created in Lines 4–24. This list stores five two-dimensional lists of numbers, each of which is a four-by-four, two-dimensional list.

The loop starting from line 26 displays the numbers in each two-dimensional list and prompts the user to answer whether the birthday is in the list (line 33). If the day is in the set, the first number (**dates[i][0][0]**) in the set is added to variable **day** (line 36). This program is identical to the one in Listing 4.3, except that this program places the five data sets in a list. This is a preferred way to organize data, because data can be reused and processed in loops.

11.7 Show the output of the following code:

```
def f(m):
    for i in range(len(m)):
        for j in range(len(m[i])):
            for k in range(len(m[j])):
                m[i][j][k] += 1

def printM(m):
    for i in range(len(m)):
        for j in range(len(m[i])):
            for k in range(len(m[j])):
                print(m[i][j][k], end = "")
        print()

m = [[[0, 0], [0, 1]], [[0, 0], [0, 1]]]
```

```
printM(m)
f(m)
printM(m)
```

KEY TERMS

column index   362
multidimensional list   378
nested list   362

row index   362
two-dimensional list   362

CHAPTER SUMMARY

1. A *two-dimensional list* can be used to store two-dimensional data such as a table and a matrix.

2. A two-dimensional list is a list. Each of its elements is a list.

3. An element in a two-dimensional list can be accessed using the following syntax: `listName[rowIndex][columnIndex]`.

4. You can use lists of lists to form *multidimensional lists* for storing multidimensional data.

TEST QUESTIONS

Do test questions for this chapter online at www.cs.armstrong.edu/liang/py/test.html.

PROGRAMMING EXERCISES

MyProgrammingLab™

Sections 11.2–11.3

*11.1 (*Sum elements column by column*) Write a function that returns the sum of all the elements in a specified column in a matrix using the following header:

```
def sumColumn(m, columnIndex):
```

Write a test program that reads a 3 × 4 matrix and displays the sum of each column. Here is a sample run:

```
Enter a 3-by-4 matrix row for row 0: 1.5 2 3 4  ⏎Enter
Enter a 3-by-4 matrix row for row 1: 5.5 6 7 8  ⏎Enter
Enter a 3-by-4 matrix row for row 2: 9.5 1 3 1  ⏎Enter
Sum of the elements for column 0 is 16.5
```

```
Sum of the elements for column 1 is 9.0
Sum of the elements for column 2 is 13.0
Sum of the elements for column 3 is 13.0
```

*11.2 *(Sum the major diagonal in a matrix)* Write a function that sums all the numbers of the major diagonal in an $n \times n$ matrix of integers using the following header:

def sumMajorDiagonal(m):

The major diagonal is the diagonal that runs from the top left corner to the bottom right corner in the square matrix. Write a test program that reads a 4×4 matrix and displays the sum of all its elements on the major diagonal. Here is a sample run:

```
Enter a 4-by-4 matrix row for row 1: 1 2 3 4  ↵Enter
Enter a 4-by-4 matrix row for row 2: 5 6.5 7 8  ↵Enter
Enter a 4-by-4 matrix row for row 3: 9 10 11 12  ↵Enter
Enter a 4-by-4 matrix row for row 4: 13 14 15 16  ↵Enter

Sum of the elements in the major diagonal is 34.5
```

*11.3 *(Sort students by grades)* Rewrite Listing 11.2, GradeExam.py, to display the students in increasing order of the number of correct answers.

**11.4 *(Compute the weekly hours for each employee)* Suppose the weekly hours for all employees are stored in a table. Each row records an employee's seven-day work hours with seven columns. For example, the following table stores the work hours for eight employees. Write a program that displays employees and their total hours in decreasing order of the total hours.

	Su	M	T	W	Th	F	Sa
Employee 0	2	4	3	4	5	8	8
Employee 1	7	3	4	3	3	4	4
Employee 2	3	3	4	3	3	2	2
Employee 3	9	3	4	7	3	4	1
Employee 4	3	5	4	3	6	3	8
Employee 5	3	4	4	6	3	4	4
Employee 6	3	7	4	8	3	8	4
Employee 7	6	3	5	9	2	7	9

11.5 *(Algebra: add two matrices)* Write a function to add two matrices. The header of the function is:

def addMatrix(a, b):

In order to be added, the two matrices must have the same dimensions and the same or compatible types of elements. Let **c** be the resulting matrix. Each element c_{ij} is $a_{ij} + b_{ij}$. For example, for two 3×3 matrices **a** and **b**, **c** is

$$
\begin{pmatrix} a_{11} & a_{12} & a_{13} \\ a_{21} & a_{22} & a_{23} \\ a_{31} & a_{32} & a_{33} \end{pmatrix} + \begin{pmatrix} b_{11} & b_{12} & b_{13} \\ b_{21} & b_{22} & b_{23} \\ b_{31} & b_{32} & b_{33} \end{pmatrix} = \begin{pmatrix} a_{11} + b_{11} & a_{12} + b_{12} & a_{13} + b_{13} \\ a_{21} + b_{21} & a_{22} + b_{22} & a_{23} + b_{23} \\ a_{31} + b_{31} & a_{32} + b_{32} & a_{33} + b_{33} \end{pmatrix}
$$

Write a test program that prompts the user to enter two 3×3 matrices and displays their sum. Here is a sample run:

```
Enter matrix1: 1 2 3 4 5 6 7 8 9  ↵Enter
Enter matrix2: 0 2 4 1 4.5 2.2 1.1 4.3 5.2  ↵Enter
The matrices are added as follows:
  1.0 2.0 3.0        0.0 2.0 4.0       1.0 4.0 11.0
  4.0 5.0 6.0     +  1.0 4.5 2.2   =   5.0 11.5 8.2
  11.0 8.0 11.0      1.1 4.3 5.2       8.1 12.3 14.2
```

**11.6 (*Algebra: multiply two matrices*) Write a function to multiply two matrices. The header of the function is:

def multiplyMatrix(a, b)

To multiply matrix **a** by matrix **b**, the number of columns in **a** must be the same as the number of rows in **b**, and the two matrices must have elements of the same or compatible types. Let **c** be the result of the multiplication. Assume the column size of matrix **a** is **n**. Each element c_{ij} is $a_{i1} \times b_{1j} + a_{i2} \times b_{2j} + \ldots + a_{in} \times b_{nj}$. For example, for two 3×3 matrices **a** and **b**, **c** is

$$
\begin{pmatrix} a_{11} & a_{12} & a_{13} \\ a_{21} & a_{22} & a_{23} \\ a_{31} & a_{32} & a_{33} \end{pmatrix} \times \begin{pmatrix} b_{11} & b_{12} & b_{13} \\ b_{21} & b_{22} & b_{23} \\ b_{31} & b_{32} & b_{33} \end{pmatrix} = \begin{pmatrix} c_{11} & c_{12} & c_{13} \\ c_{21} & c_{22} & c_{23} \\ c_{31} & c_{32} & c_{33} \end{pmatrix}
$$

where $c_{ij} = a_{i1} \times b_{1j} + a_{i2} \times b_{2j} + a_{i3} \times b_{3j}$.

Write a test program that prompts the user to enter two 3×3 matrices and displays their product. Here is a sample run:

```
Enter matrix1: 1 2 3 4 5 6 7 8 9  ↵Enter
Enter matrix2: 0 2 4 1 4.5 2.2 1.1 4.3 5.2  ↵Enter
The multiplication of the matrices is
  1 2 3        0 2.0 4.0          5.3 23.9 24
  4 5 6    *   1 4.5 2.2     =    11.6 56.3 58.2
  7 8 9        1.1 4.3 5.2        111.9 88.7 92.4
```

*11.7 (*Points nearest to each other*) The program in Listing 11.3 finds the two points in a two-dimensional space nearest to each other. Revise the program so that it finds the two points in a three-dimensional space nearest to each other. Use a two-dimensional list to represent the points. Test the program using the following points:

```
points = [[-1, 0, 3], [-1, -1, -1], [4, 1, 1],
   [2, 0.5, 9], [3.5, 2, -1], [3, 1.5, 3], [-1.5, 4, 2],
   [5.5, 4, -0.5]]
```

The formula for computing the distance between two points (x_1, y_1, z_1) and (x_2, y_2, z_2) in a three-dimensional space is $\sqrt{(x_2 - x_1)^2 + (y_2 - y_1)^2 + (z_2 - z_1)^2}$.

**11.8 (*All closest pairs of points*) Revise Listing 11.4, FindNearestPoints.py, to find all the nearest pairs of points that have the same minimum distance.

***11.9 (*Game: play a tic-tac-toe game*) In a game of tic-tac-toe, two players take turns marking an available cell in a 3 × 3 grid with their respective tokens (either X or O). When one player has placed three tokens in a horizontal, vertical, or diagonal row on the grid, the game is over and that player has won. A draw (no winner) occurs when all the cells in the grid have been filled with tokens and neither player has achieved a win. Create a program for playing tic-tac-toe.

The program prompts two players to alternately enter an X token and an O token. Whenever a token is entered, the program redisplays the board on the console and determines the status of the game (win, draw, or continue). Here is a sample run:

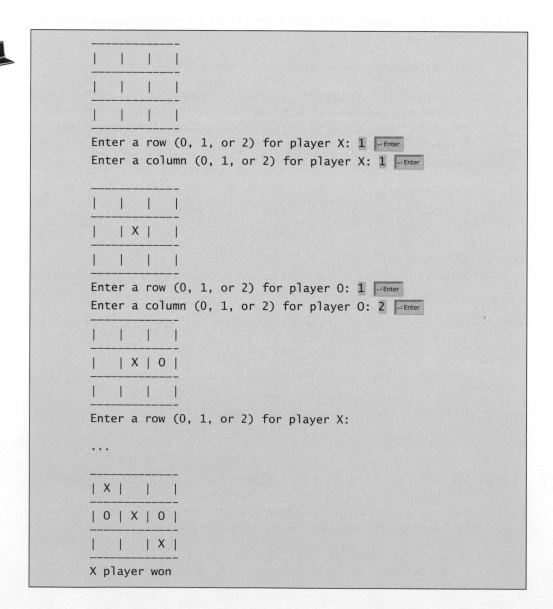

```
-----------
|   |   |   |
-----------
|   |   |   |
-----------
|   |   |   |
-----------
Enter a row (0, 1, or 2) for player X: 1 ↵Enter
Enter a column (0, 1, or 2) for player X: 1 ↵Enter

-----------
|   |   |   |
-----------
|   | X |   |
-----------
|   |   |   |
-----------
Enter a row (0, 1, or 2) for player O: 1 ↵Enter
Enter a column (0, 1, or 2) for player O: 2 ↵Enter
-----------
|   |   |   |
-----------
|   | X | O |
-----------
|   |   |   |
-----------
Enter a row (0, 1, or 2) for player X:

...

-----------
| X |   |   |
-----------
| O | X | O |
-----------
|   |   | X |
-----------
X player won
```

*11.10 (*Largest rows and columns*) Write a program that randomly fills in 0s and 1s into a 4 × 4 matrix, prints the matrix, and finds the rows and columns with the most 1s. Here is a sample run of the program:

```
0011
0011
1101
1010
The largest row index: 2
The largest column index: 2, 3
```

**11.11 (*Game: nine heads and tails*) Nine coins are placed in a 3 × 3 matrix with some face up and some face down. You can represent the state of the coins with the values 0 (heads) and 1 (tails). Here are some examples:

```
0 0 0    1 0 1    1 1 0    1 0 1    1 0 0
0 1 0    0 0 1    1 0 0    1 1 0    1 1 1
0 0 0    1 0 0    0 0 1    1 0 0    1 1 0
```

Each state can also be represented using a binary number. For example, the preceding matrices correspond to the numbers:

```
000010000 101001100 110100001 101110100 100111110
```

There are a total of 512 possibilities. So, you can use the decimal numbers 0, 1, 2, 3, ..., and 511 to represent all states of the matrix. Write a program that prompts the user to enter a number between 0 and 511 and displays the corresponding 3 × 3 matrix with the characters H and T. Here is a sample run:

```
Enter a number between 0 and 511: 7  ↵Enter
H H H
H H H
T T T
```

The user entered 7, which corresponds to 000000111. Since 0 stands for H and 1 for T, the output is correct.

**11.12 (*Financial application: compute tax*) Rewrite Listing 4.7, ComputeTax.py, using lists. For each filing status, there are six tax rates. Each rate is applied to a certain amount of taxable income. For example, from the taxable income of \$400,000 for a single filer, \$8,350 is taxed at 10%, (33,950 – 8,350) at 15%, (82,250 – 33,950) at 25%, (171,550 – 82,250) at 28%, (372,950 – 171,550) at 33%, and (400,000 – 372,950) at 35%. The six rates are the same for all filing statuses, which can be represented in the following list:

```
rates = [0.10, 0.15, 0.25, 0.28, 0.33, 0.35]
```

The brackets for each rate for all the filing statuses can be represented in a two-dimensional list as follows:

```
brackets = [
  [8350, 33950, 82250, 171550, 372950],    # Single filer
  [16700, 67900, 137050, 208850, 372950],  # Married jointly
  [8350, 33950, 68525, 104425, 186475],    # Married separately
  [11950, 45500, 117450, 190200, 372950]   # Head of household
]
```

Suppose the taxable income is $400,000 for single filers. The tax can be computed as follows:

```
tax = brackets[0][0] * rates[0] +
   (brackets[0][1] - brackets[0][0]) * rates[1] +
   (brackets[0][2] - brackets[0][1]) * rates[2] +
   (brackets[0][3] - brackets[0][2]) * rates[3] +
   (brackets[0][4] - brackets[0][3]) * rates[4] +
   (400000 - brackets[0][4]) * rates[5]
```

*11.13 (*Locate the largest element*) Write the following function that returns the location of the largest element in a two-dimensional list:

def locateLargest(a):

The return value is a one-dimensional list that contains two elements. These two elements indicate the row and column indexes of the largest element in the two-dimensional list. Write a test program that prompts the user to enter a two-dimensional list and displays the location of the largest element in the list. Here is a sample run:

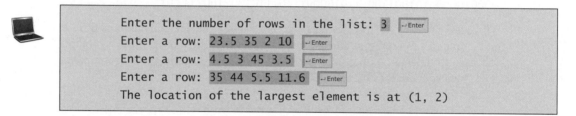

```
Enter the number of rows in the list: 3  ⏎Enter
Enter a row: 23.5 35 2 10  ⏎Enter
Enter a row: 4.5 3 45 3.5  ⏎Enter
Enter a row: 35 44 5.5 11.6  ⏎Enter
The location of the largest element is at (1, 2)
```

11.14 (*Explore matrix*) Write a program that prompts the user to enter the length of a square matrix, randomly fills in **0s and **1**s into the matrix, prints the matrix, and finds the rows, columns, and major diagonal with all **0**s or all **1**s. Here is a sample run of the program:

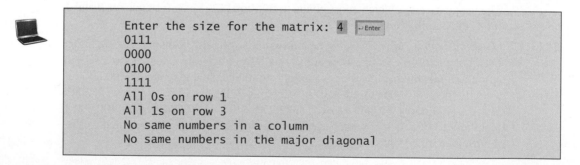

```
Enter the size for the matrix: 4  ⏎Enter
0111
0000
0100
1111
All 0s on row 1
All 1s on row 3
No same numbers in a column
No same numbers in the major diagonal
```

Sections 11.4–11.9

*11.15 (*Geometry: same line?*) Exercise 6.19 gives a function for testing whether three points are on the same line. Write the following function to test whether all the points in the **points** list are on the same line:

def sameLine(points):

Write a program that prompts the user to enter five points and displays whether they are on the same line. Here are sample runs:

```
Enter five points: 3.4 2 6.5 11.5 2.3 2.3 5.5 5 -5 4  ↵Enter
The five points are not on the same line
```

```
Enter five points: 1 1 2 2 3 3 4 4 5 5  ↵Enter
The five points are on the same line
```

*11.16 (*Sort a list of points on y-coordinates*) Write the following function to sort a list of points on their y-coordinates. Each point is a list of two values for x- and y-coordinates.

```
# Returns a new list of points sorted on the y-coordinates
def sort(points):
```

For example, the points [[4, 2], [1, 7], [4, 5], [1, 2], [1, 1], [4, 1]] will be sorted to [[1, 1], [4, 1], [1, 2], [4, 2], [4, 5], [1, 7]]. Write a test program that displays the sorted result for points [[4, 34], [1, 7.5], [4, 8.5], [1, -4.5], [1, 4.5], [4, 6.6]] using **print(list)**.

***11.17 (*Financial tsunami*) Banks lend money to each other. In tough economic times, if a bank goes bankrupt, it may not be able to pay back the loan. A bank's total assets are its current balance plus its loans to other banks. The diagram in Figure 11.9 shows five banks. The banks' current balances are **25, 125, 175, 75,** and **181** million dollars, respectively. The directed edge from node 1 to node 2 indicates that bank 1 lends **40** million dollars to bank 2.

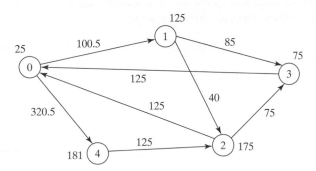

FIGURE 11.9 Banks lend money to each other.

If a bank's total assets are under a certain limit, the bank is unsafe. The money it borrowed cannot be returned to the lender, and the lender cannot count the loan in its total assets. Consequently, the lender may also be unsafe if its total assets are under the limit. Write a program to find all unsafe banks. Your program should read the input as follows. It first reads two integers **n** and **limit**, where **n** indicates the number of banks and **limit** is the minimum total assets for keeping a bank safe. It then reads **n** lines that describe the information for **n** banks with ids from **0** to **n - 1**. The first number in the line is the bank's balance, the second number indicates the number of banks that borrowed money from the bank, and the rest are pairs of two numbers. Each pair describes a borrower. The first number in the pair is the borrower's id and the second is the amount borrowed. For example, the input for the five banks in Figure 11.9 is as follows (note that the limit is **201**):

```
5 201
25 2 1 100.5 4 320.5
```

```
125 2 2 40 3 85
175 2 0 125 3 75
75 1 0 125
181 1 2 125
```

The total assets of bank 3 are (**75** + **125**), which is under **201**, so bank 3 is unsafe. After bank 3 becomes unsafe, the total assets of bank 1 fall below the limit (**125** + **40**), so bank 1 also becomes unsafe. The output of the program should be:

```
Unsafe banks are 3 1
```

(Hint: Use a two-dimensional list **borrowers** to represent loans. **borrowers[i][j]** indicates the loan that bank *i* loans to bank *j*. Once bank *j* becomes unsafe, **borrowers[i][j]** should be set to **0**.)

*11.18 (*Shuffle rows*) Write a function that shuffles the rows in a two-dimensional list using the following header:

def shuffle(m):

Write a test program that shuffles the following matrix:

m = [[1, 2], [3, 4], [5, 6], [7, 8], [9, 10]]

**11.19 (*Pattern recognition: four consecutive equal numbers*) Write the following function that tests whether a two-dimensional list has four consecutive numbers of the same value, either horizontally, vertically, or diagonally:

def isConsecutiveFour(values):

Write a test program that prompts the user to enter the number of rows and columns of a two-dimensional list and then the values in the list. The program displays **True** if the list contains four consecutive numbers with the same value; otherwise, it displays **False**. Here are some examples of the **True** cases:

```
0 1 0 3 1 6 1     0 1 0 3 1 6 1     0 1 0 3 1 6 1     0 1 0 3 1 6 1
0 1 6 8 6 0 1     0 1 6 8 6 0 1     0 1 6 8 6 0 1     0 1 6 8 6 0 1
5 6 2 1 8 2 9     5 5 2 1 8 2 9     5 6 2 1 6 2 9     9 6 2 1 8 2 9
6 5 6 1 1 9 1     6 5 6 1 1 9 1     6 5 6 6 1 9 1     6 9 6 1 1 9 1
1 3 6 1 4 0 7     1 5 6 1 4 0 7     1 3 6 1 4 0 7     1 3 9 1 4 0 7
3 3 3 3 4 0 7     3 5 3 3 4 0 7     3 6 3 3 4 0 7     3 3 3 9 4 0 7
```

***11.20 (*Game: Connect Four*) Connect Four is a two-player board game in which the players alternately drop colored disks into a seven-column, six-row vertically suspended grid, as shown at cs.armstrong.edu/liang/ConnectFour/ConnectFour.html.

The objective of the game is to connect four same-colored disks in a row, column, or diagonal before your opponent does. The program prompts two players to drop a red or yellow disk alternately. Whenever a disk is dropped, the program redisplays the board on the console and determines the status of the game (win, draw, or continue). Here is a sample run:

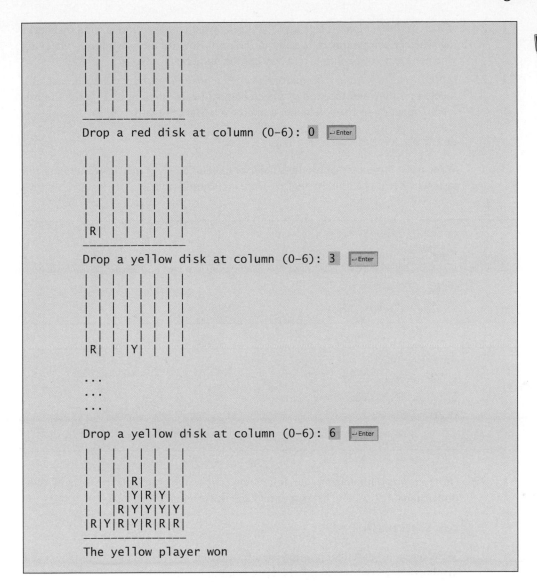

```
| | | | | | | |
| | | | | | | |
| | | | | | | |
| | | | | | | |
| | | | | | | |
| | | | | | | |
_____
Drop a red disk at column (0-6): 0  ↵Enter

| | | | | | | |
| | | | | | | |
| | | | | | | |
| | | | | | | |
| | | | | | | |
|R| | | | | | |
_____
Drop a yellow disk at column (0-6): 3  ↵Enter

| | | | | | | |
| | | | | | | |
| | | | | | | |
| | | | | | | |
| | | | | | | |
|R| | |Y| | | |

...
...
...

Drop a yellow disk at column (0-6): 6  ↵Enter

| | | | | | | |
| | | | | | | |
| | | |R| | | |
| | | |Y|R|Y| |
| | |R|Y|Y|Y|Y|
|R|Y|R|Y|R|R|R|
_____
The yellow player won
```

***11.21   (*Game: multiple Sudoku solutions*) The complete solution for the Sudoku problem is given in Supplement III.A. A Sudoku problem may have multiple solutions. Modify Sudoku.py in Supplement III.A to display the total number of the solutions. Display two solutions if multiple solutions exist.

**11.22   (*Even number of 1s*) Write a program that generates a 6 × 6 two-dimensional matrix filled with 0s and 1s, displays the matrix, and checks to see if every row and every column has an even number of 1s.

*11.23   (*Game: find the flipped cell*) Suppose you are given a 6 × 6 matrix filled with 0s and 1s. All rows and all columns have the even number of 1s. Let the user flip one cell (i.e., flip from 1 to 0 or from 0 to 1) and write a program to find which cell was flipped. Your program should prompt the user to enter a 6 × 6 two-dimensional list with 0s and 1s and find the first row **r** and first column **c** where the even number of 1s property is violated. The flipped cell is at (**r**, **c**).

*11.24 (*Check Sudoku solution*) Listing 11.7 checks whether a solution is valid by checking whether every number is valid in the grid. Rewrite the program by checking whether every row, column, and box has the numbers **1** to **9**.

*11.25 (*Markov matrix*) An $n \times n$ matrix is called a *positive Markov matrix* if each element is positive and the sum of the elements in each column is **1**. Write the following function to check whether a matrix is a Markov matrix:

def isMarkovMatrix(m):

Write a test program that prompts the user to enter a 3×3 matrix of numbers and tests whether it is a Markov matrix. Here are sample runs:

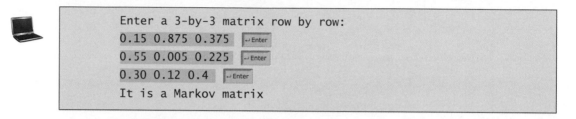

```
Enter a 3-by-3 matrix row by row:
0.15 0.875 0.375  ↵Enter
0.55 0.005 0.225  ↵Enter
0.30 0.12 0.4  ↵Enter
It is a Markov matrix
```

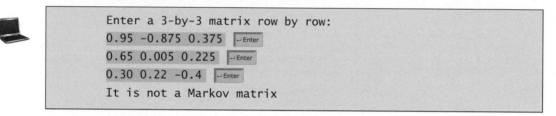

```
Enter a 3-by-3 matrix row by row:
0.95 -0.875 0.375  ↵Enter
0.65 0.005 0.225  ↵Enter
0.30 0.22 -0.4  ↵Enter
It is not a Markov matrix
```

*11.26 (*Row sorting*) Implement the following function to sort the rows in a two-dimensional list. A new list is returned and the original list is intact.

def sortRows(m):

Write a test program that prompts the user to enter a 3×3 matrix of numbers and displays a new row-sorted matrix. Here is a sample run:

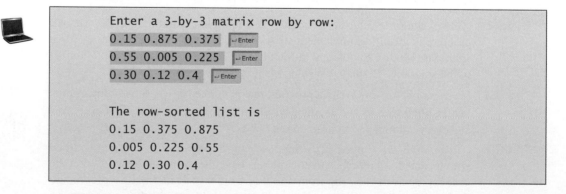

```
Enter a 3-by-3 matrix row by row:
0.15 0.875 0.375  ↵Enter
0.55 0.005 0.225  ↵Enter
0.30 0.12 0.4  ↵Enter

The row-sorted list is
0.15 0.375 0.875
0.005 0.225 0.55
0.12 0.30 0.4
```

*11.27 (*Column sorting*) Implement the following function to sort the columns in a two-dimensional list. A new list is returned and the original list is intact.

def sortColumns(m):

Write a test program that prompts the user to enter a 3 × 3 matrix of numbers and displays a new column-sorted matrix. Here is a sample run:

```
Enter a 3-by-3 matrix row by row:
0.15 0.875 0.375  ↵Enter
0.55 0.005 0.225  ↵Enter
0.30 0.12 0.4  ↵Enter

The column-sorted list is
0.15 0.005 0.225
0.3  0.12  0.375
0.55 0.875 0.4
```

11.28 (*Strictly identical lists*) The two-dimensional lists **m1** and **m2** are *strictly identical* if their corresponding elements are equal. Write a function that returns **True** if **m1** and **m2** are strictly identical, using the following header:

def equals(m1, m2):

Write a test program that prompts the user to enter two 3 × 3 lists of integers and displays whether the two are strictly identical. Here are the sample runs:

```
Enter m1: 51 22 25 6 1 4 24 54 6  ↵Enter
Enter m2: 51 22 25 6 1 4 24 54 6  ↵Enter
The two lists are strictly identical
```

```
Enter m1: 51 25 22 6 1 4 24 54 6  ↵Enter
Enter m2: 51 22 25 6 1 4 24 54 6  ↵Enter
The two lists are not strictly identical
```

11.29 (*Identical lists*) The two-dimensional lists **m1** and **m2** are *identical* if they have the same contents. Write a function that returns **True** if **m1** and **m2** are identical, using the following header:

def equals(m1, m2):

Write a test program that prompts the user to enter two lists of integers and displays whether the two are identical. Here are the sample runs:

```
Enter m1: 51 25 22 6 1 4 24 54 6  ↵Enter
Enter m2: 51 22 25 6 1 4 24 54 6  ↵Enter
The two lists are identical
```

```
Enter m1: 51 5 22 6 1 4 24 54 6  ↵Enter
Enter m2: 51 22 25 6 1 4 24 54 6  ↵Enter
The two lists are not identical
```

*11.30 (*Algebra: solve linear equations*) Write a function that solves the following 2×2 system of linear equations:

$$\begin{aligned} a_{00}x + a_{01}y &= b_0 \\ a_{10}x + a_{11}y &= b_1 \end{aligned} \qquad x = \frac{b_0 a_{11} - b_1 a_{01}}{a_{00} a_{11} - a_{01} a_{10}} \qquad y = \frac{b_1 a_{00} - b_0 a_{10}}{a_{00} a_{11} - a_{01} a_{10}}$$

The function header is:

def linearEquation(a, b):

The function returns **None** if $a_{00}a_{11} - a_{01}a_{10}$ is **0**; otherwise, it returns the solution for x and y in a list. Write a test program that prompts the user to enter a_{00}, a_{01}, a_{10}, a_{11}, b_0, and b_1 and displays the result. If $a_{00}a_{11} - a_{01}a_{10}$ is **0**, report that **The equation has no solution**. Here are the sample runs:

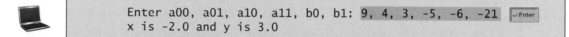
```
Enter a00, a01, a10, a11, b0, b1: 9, 4, 3, -5, -6, -21  ⏎Enter
x is -2.0 and y is 3.0
```

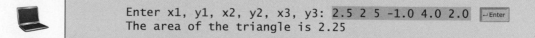
```
Enter a00, a01, a10, a11, b0, b1: 1, 2, 2, 4, 40, 5  ⏎Enter
The equation has no solution
```

*11.31 (*Geometry: intersecting point*) Write a function that returns the intersecting point of two lines. The intersecting point of the two lines can be found by using the formula shown in Exercise 4.25. Assume that (**x1**, **y1**) and (**x2**, **y2**) are the two points on line 1 and (**x3**, **y3**) and (**x4**, **y4**) are the two points on line 2. The function header is:

def getIntersectingPoint(points):

The points are stored in the 4×2 two-dimensional list **points**, with (**points[0][0]**, **points[0][1]**) for (**x1**, **y1**). The function returns the intersecting point (x, y) in a list, and **None** if the two lines are parallel. Write a program that prompts the user to enter four points and displays the intersecting point. See Exercise 4.25 for a sample run.

*11.32 (*Geometry: area of a triangle*) Write a function that returns the area of a triangle using the following header:

def getTriangleArea(points):

The points are stored in the 3×2 two-dimensional list **points**, with (**points[0][0]**, **points[0][1]**) for (**x1**, **y1**). The triangle area can be computed using the formula in Exercise 2.14. The function returns **None** if the three points are on the same line. Write a program that prompts the user to enter three points and displays the area of the triangle. Here is a sample run:

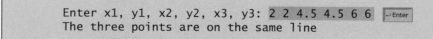
```
Enter x1, y1, x2, y2, x3, y3: 2.5 2 5 -1.0 4.0 2.0  ⏎Enter
The area of the triangle is 2.25
```

```
Enter x1, y1, x2, y2, x3, y3: 2 2 4.5 4.5 6 6  ⏎Enter
The three points are on the same line
```

*11.33 (*Geometry: polygon subareas*) A convex four-vertex polygon is divided into four triangles, as shown in Figure 11.10.

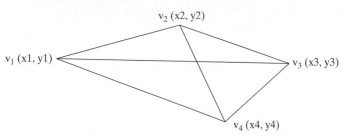

FIGURE 11.10 A four-vertex polygon is defined by four vertices.

Write a program that prompts the user to enter the coordinates of four vertices and displays the areas of the four triangles in increasing order. Here is a sample run:

```
Enter x1, y1, x2, y2, x3, y3, x4, y4: -2.5 2 4 4 3 -2 -2 -3.5  ↵Enter
The areas are 6.17 7.96 8.08 10.42
```

*11.34 (*Geometry: rightmost lowest point*) In computational geometry, often you need to find the rightmost lowest point in a set of points. Write the following function that returns the rightmost lowest point in a set of points:

```
# Return a list of two values for a point
def getRightmostLowestPoint(points):
```

Write a test program that prompts the user to enter the coordinates of six points and displays the rightmost lowest point. Here is a sample run:

```
Enter 6 points: 1.5 2.5 -3 4.5 5.6 -7 6.5 -7 8 1 10 2.5  ↵Enter
The rightmost lowest point is (6.5, -7)
```

*11.35 (*Central city*) Given a set of cities, the central point is the city that has the shortest total distance to all other cities. Write a program that prompts the user to enter the number of the cities and the locations of the cities (that is, their coordinates), and finds the central city.

```
Enter the number of cities: 5  ↵Enter
Enter the coordinates of the
  cities: 2.5 5 5.1 3 1 9 5.4 54 5.5 2.1  ↵Enter
The central city is at (2.5, 5)
```

**11.36 (*Simulation using Turtle: self-avoiding random walk*) A self-avoiding walk in a lattice is a path from one point to another that does not visit the same point twice. Self-avoiding walks have applications in physics, chemistry, and mathematics. They can be used to model chainlike entities such as solvents and polymers. Write a Turtle program that displays a random path that starts from the center and ends at a point on the boundary, as shown in Figure 11.11a, or ends at a dead-end point (i.e., surrounded by four points that have already been visited), as shown in Figure 11.11b. Assume the size of the lattice is 16 × 16.

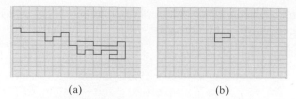

FIGURE 11.11   (a) A path ends at a boundary point. (b) A path ends at dead-end point.

**11.37 (*Simulation: self-avoiding random walk*) Write a simulation program to show that the chance of getting dead-end paths increases as the grid size increases. Your program simulates lattices with sizes from 10 to 80. For each lattice size, simulate a self-avoiding random walk 10,000 times and display the probability of the dead-end paths, as shown in the following sample output:

```
For a lattice of size 10, the probability of dead-end paths is 11.6%
For a lattice of size 11, the probability of dead-end paths is 14.0%
...
For a lattice of size 80, the probability of dead-end paths is 99.5%
```

**11.38 (*Turtle: draw a polygon/polyline*) Write the following functions that draw a polygon/polyline to connect all points in the list. Each element in the list is a list of two coordinates.

```
# Draw a polyline to connect all the points in the list
def drawPolyline(points):

# Draw a polygon to connect all the points in the list and
# close the polygon by connecting the first point with the last point
def drawPolygon(points):

# Fill a polygon by connecting all the points in the list
def fillPolygon(points):
```

VideoNote
Chessboard

**11.39 (*Tkinter: four consecutive equal numbers*) Write a GUI program for Exercise 11.19, as shown in Figure 11.12. Let the user enter the numbers in the text fields in a grid of six rows and seven columns. The user can click the *Solve* button to highlight a sequence of four equal numbers, if it exists.

FIGURE 11.12   Clicking the *Solve* button highlights the four consecutive numbers in a diagonal, a row, or a column.

**11.40 (*Guess the capitals*) Write a program that repeatedly prompts the user to enter a capital for a state. Upon receiving the user input, the program reports whether the answer is correct. Assume that 50 states and their capitals are stored in a two-dimensional list, as shown in Figure 11.13. The program prompts the user to answer all the states' capitals and displays the total correct count. The user's answer is not case sensitive. Implement the program using a list to represent the data in the following table.

```
Alabama        Montgomery
Alaska         Juneau
Arizona        Phoenix
...            ...
...            ...
```

FIGURE 11.13 A two-dimensional list stores states and their capitals.

Here is a sample run:

```
What is the capital of Alabama? Montogomery  ↵Enter
The correct answer should be Montgomery
What is the capital of Alaska? Juneau  ↵Enter
Your answer is correct
What is the capital of Arizona? ...
...
The correct count is 35
```

***11.41 (*Tkinter: Sudoku solutions*) The complete solution for the Sudoku problem is given in Supplement III.A. Write a GUI program that enables the user to enter a Sudoku puzzle and click the *Solve* button to display a solution, as shown in Figure 11.14.

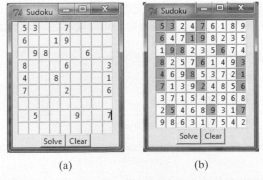

(a)   (b)

FIGURE 11.14 The user can enter a Sudoku puzzle in (a) and click the Solve button to display the solution in (b).

*11.42 (*Tkinter: plot the sine function*) Exercise 5.52 draws a sine function using Turtle. Rewrite the program to draw a sine function using Tkinter, as shown in Figure 11.15a.

> **Hint**
>
> The Unicode for π is **\u03c0**. To display -2π use **turtle.write("-2\u03c0")**. For a trigonometric function like **sin(x)**, **x** is in radians. Use the following loop to add the points to a polygon **p**:
>
> ```
> p = []
> for x in range(-175, 176):
>     p.append([x, -50 * math.sin((x / 100.0) * 2 *
>     math.pi)])
> ```
>
> -2π is displayed at (**-100, -15**), the center of the axis is at (**0, 0**), and 2π is displayed at (**100, -15**).

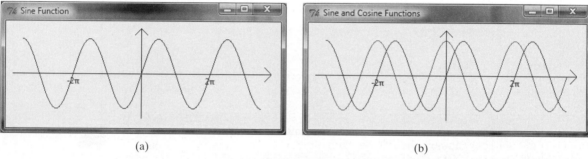

(a)   (b)

FIGURE 11.15 (a) The program plots a sine function. (b) The program plots a sine function in blue and a cosine function in red.

*11.43 (*Tkinter: plot the sine and cosine functions*) Exercise 5.53 draws sine and cosine functions using Turtle. Rewrite the program to draw the sine and cosine functions using Tkinter, as shown in Figure 11.15b.

11.44 (*Tkinter: draw a polygon*) Write a program that prompts the user to enter the coordinates of six points and fills the polygon that connects the points, as shown in Figure 11.16a. Note that you can draw a polygon using **canvas.create_polygon(points)**, where **points** is a two-dimensional list that stores the *x*- and *y*-coordinates of the points.

*11.45 (*Tkinter: plot the square function*) Exercise 5.54 draws a square function. Rewrite the program to draw the square function using Tkinter, as shown in Figure 11.16b.

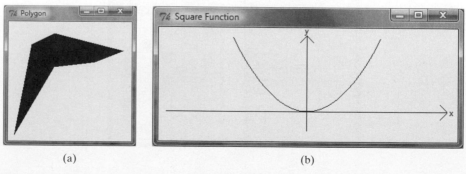

(a)   (b)

FIGURE 11.16 (a) A polygon is drawn from a list of values. (b) The program plots a diagram for function $f(x) = x^2$.

*11.46 (*Tkinter: display a STOP sign*) Write a program that displays a STOP sign, as shown in Figure 11.17a. The hexagon is in red and the text is in black.

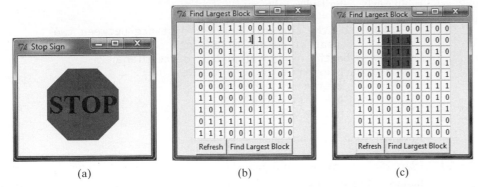

(a)   (b)   (c)

FIGURE 11.17 (a) The program displays a STOP sign. (b–c) The program displays 0s and 1s randomly with a click of the *Refresh* button.

*11.47 (*Tkinter: largest block*) Write a program that displays a 10 × 10 square matrix, as shown in Figure 11.17b. Each element in the matrix is a 0 or 1, randomly generated with a click of the *Refresh* button. Display each number centered in a text box. Allow the user to change the entry value. Click the *Find Largest Block* button to find a largest square submatrix that consists of 1s. Highlight the numbers in the block, as shown in Figure 11.17c.

**11.48 (*Geometry: find the bounding rectangle*) Write a program that enables the user to add and remove points in a two-dimensional plane dynamically, as shown in Figure 11.18. A minimum bounding rectangle is updated as the points are added and removed. Assume the radius of each point is 10 pixels.

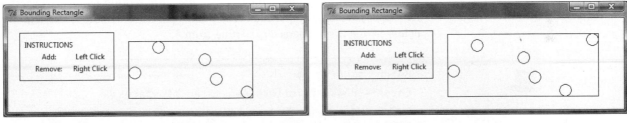

FIGURE 11.18 The program enables the user to add and remove points dynamically and display the bounding rectangle.

11.49 (*Game: display a tic-tac-toe board*) Revise Exercise 9.6 to display a new tic-tac-toe board with a click of the *Refresh* button, as shown in Figure 11.19.

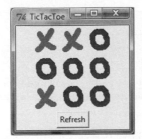

FIGURE 11.19 The program displays a new tic-tac-toe board upon clicking the *Refresh* button.

11.50 (*Geometry: find nearest points*) When a new point is added to the plane, Listing 11.5 finds the pair of two nearest points by examining the distance between every pair of two points. This approach is correct, but not efficient. A more efficient algorithm can be described as follows:

```
Let d be the current shortest distance between two
        nearest points p1 and p2
Let p be the new point added to the plane
For each existing point t:
    if distance(p, t) < d:
        d = distance(p, t)
        p1, p2 = p, t
```

Rewrite Listing 11.5 using this new approach.

11.51 (*Sort students*) Write a program that prompts the user to enter the students' names and their scores on one line, and prints student names in increasing order of their scores. (Hint: Create a list. Each element in the list is a sublist with two elements: score and name. Apply the **sort method to sort the list. This will sort the list on scores.)

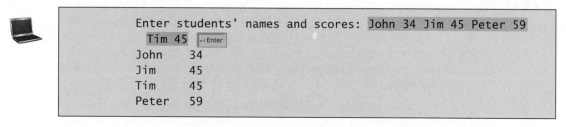

```
Enter students' names and scores: John 34 Jim 45 Peter 59
   Tim 45 ↵Enter
John    34
Jim     45
Tim     45
Peter   59
```

11.52 (*Latin square*) A Latin square is an **n by **n** list filled with **n** different Latin letters, each occurring exactly once in each row and once in each column. Write a program that prompts the user to enter the number **n** and the list of characters, as shown in the sample output and check if the input list is a Latin square. The characters are the first **n** characters starting from **A**.

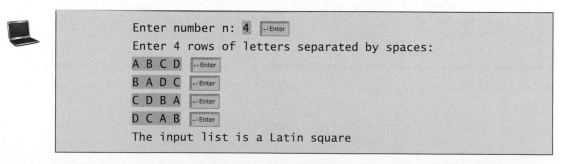

```
Enter number n: 4 ↵Enter
Enter 4 rows of letters separated by spaces:
A B C D ↵Enter
B A D C ↵Enter
C D B A ↵Enter
D C A B ↵Enter
The input list is a Latin square
```

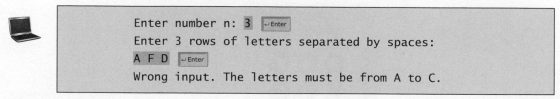

```
Enter number n: 3 ↵Enter
Enter 3 rows of letters separated by spaces:
A F D ↵Enter
Wrong input. The letters must be from A to C.
```

INHERITANCE AND POLYMORPHISM

Objectives

- To define a subclass from a superclass through inheritance (§12.2).

- To override methods in a subclass (§12.3).

- To explore the **object** class and its methods (§12.4).

- To understand polymorphism and dynamic binding (§12.5).

- To determine whether an object is an instance of a class by using the **isinstance** function (§12.6).

- To design a GUI class for displaying a reusable clock (§12.7).

- To discover relationships among classes (§12.8).

- To design classes by using composition and inheritance relationships (§§12.9–12.11).

12.1 Introduction

Object-oriented programming (OOP) allows you to define new classes from existing classes. This is called inheritance.

As discussed earlier in the book, the procedural paradigm focuses on designing functions and the object-oriented paradigm couples data and methods together into objects. Software design using the object-oriented paradigm focuses on objects and operations on objects. The object-oriented approach combines the power of the procedural paradigm with an added dimension that integrates data with operations into objects.

inheritance

Inheritance extends the power of the object-oriented paradigm by adding an important and powerful feature for reusing software. Suppose that you want to define classes to model circles, rectangles, and triangles. These classes have many common features. What is the best way to design these classes to avoid redundancy and make the system easy to comprehend and maintain? The answer is to use inheritance.

12.2 Superclasses and Subclasses

Key Point

Inheritance enables you to define a general class (a superclass) and later extend it to more specialized classes (subclasses).

You use a class to model objects of the same type. Different classes may have some common properties and behaviors that you can generalize in a class, which can then be shared by other classes. Inheritance enables you to define a general class and later extend it to define more specialized classes. The specialized classes inherit the properties and methods from the general class.

why inheritance?

VideoNote
Inheritance
and polymorphism

Consider geometric objects. Suppose you want to design classes to model geometric objects such as circles and rectangles. Geometric objects have many common properties and behaviors; for example, they can be drawn in a certain color, and they can be either filled or unfilled. Thus, a general class **GeometricObject** can be used to model all geometric objects. This class contains the properties **color** and **filled** and their appropriate **get** and **set** methods. Assume that this class also contains the **dateCreated** property and the **getDateCreated()** and **__str__()** methods. The **__str__()** method returns a string description for the object.

Because a circle is a special type of geometric object, it shares common properties and methods with other geometric objects. For this reason, it makes sense to define a **Circle** class that extends the **GeometricObject** class. Similarly, you can define **Rectangle** as a subclass of **GeometricObject**. Figure 12.1 shows the relationship among these classes. A *triangular arrow* pointing to the superclass is used to denote the inheritance relationship between the two classes involved.

triangular arrow

 Note

In OOP terminology, a class **C1** extended from another class **C2** is called a *derived class*, *child class*, or *subclass*, and **C2** is called a *base class*, *parent class*, or *superclass*. For consistency, this book uses the terms "subclass" and "superclass."

subclass
superclass

A subclass inherits accessible data fields and methods from its superclass, but it can also have other data fields and methods. In our example:

■ The **Circle** class inherits all accessible data fields and methods from the **GeometricObject** class. In addition, it has a new data field, **radius**, and its associated **get** and **set** methods. It also contains the **getArea()**, **getPerimeter()**, and **getDiameter()** methods for returning the area, perimeter, and diameter of a circle. The **printCircle()** method is defined to print the information about the circle.

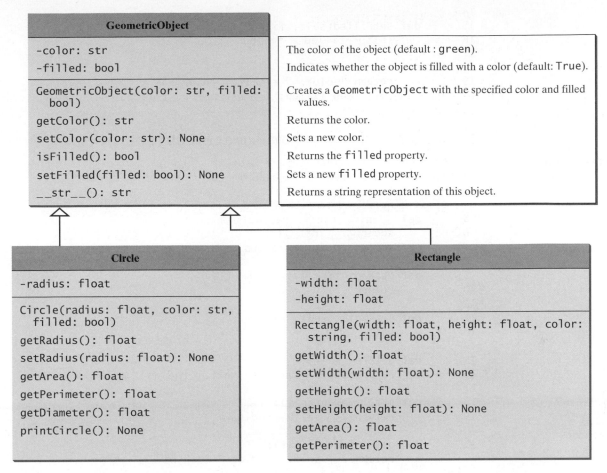

FIGURE 12.1 The **GeometricObject** class is the superclass for **Circle** and **Rectangle**.

■ The **Rectangle** class inherits all accessible data fields and methods from the **GeometricObject** class. In addition, it has the data fields **width** and **height** and the associated **get** and **set** methods. It also contains the **getArea()** and **getPerimeter()** methods for returning the area and perimeter of the rectangle.

The **GeometricObject**, **Circle**, and **Rectangle** classes are shown in Listings 12.1, 12.2, and 12.3.

LISTING 12.1 GeometricObject.py

```
1  class GeometricObject:
2      def __init__(self, color = "green", filled = True):
3          self.__color = color
4          self.__filled = filled
5
6      def getColor(self):
7          return self.__color
8
9      def setColor(self, color):
10         self.__color = color
11
12     def isFilled(self):
13         return self.__filled
```

GeometricObject class
initializer
data fields

getColor

setColor

isFilled

<table>
<tr><td>setFilled</td></tr>
</table>

setFilled

```
14
15      def setFilled(self, filled):
16          self.__filled = filled
17
18      def __str__(self):
19          return "color: " + self.__color + \
20              " and filled: " + str(self.__filled)
```

__str__ at line 18.

LISTING 12.2 CircleFromGeometricObject.py

import GeometricObject

extend GeometricObject
initializer
superclass initializer

```
1   from GeometricObject import GeometricObject
2   import math # math.pi is used in the class
3
4   class Circle(GeometricObject):
5       def __init__(self, radius):
6           super().__init__()
7           self.__radius = radius
8
9       def getRadius(self):
10          return self.__radius
11
12      def setRadius(self, radius):
13          self.__radius = radius
14
15      def getArea(self):
16          return self.__radius * self.__radius * math.pi
17
18      def getDiameter(self):
19          return 2 * self.__radius
20
21      def getPerimeter(self):
22          return 2 * self.__radius * math.pi
23
24      def printCircle(self):
25          print(self.__str__() + " radius: " + str(self.__radius))
```

The **Circle** class is derived from the **GeometricObject** class (Listing 12.1), based on the following syntax:

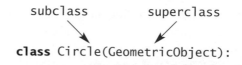

subclass   superclass

class Circle(GeometricObject):

This tells Python that the **Circle** class inherits the **GeometricObject** class, thus inheriting the methods **getColor**, **setColor**, **isFilled**, **setFilled**, and **__str__**. The **printCircle** method invokes the **__str__()** method defined to obtain properties defined in the superclass (line 25).

super().__init__() calls the superclass's **__init__** method (line 6). This is necessary to create data fields defined in the superclass.

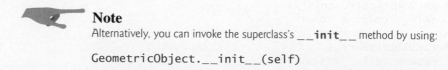

Note

Alternatively, you can invoke the superclass's **__init__** method by using:

```
GeometricObject.__init__(self)
```

This is an old style of syntax that is still supported in Python, but it isn't the preferred style. **super()** refers to the superclass. Using **super()** lets you avoid referring the superclass explicitly. When invoking a method using **super()**, don't pass **self** in the argument. For example, you should use

```
super().__init__()
```

rather than

```
super().__init__(self)
```

The **Rectangle** class, derived from the **GeometricObject** class (Listing 12.1), is defined similarly in Listing 12.3.

```
       class Rectangle(GeometricObject):
```

LISTING 12.3   RectangleFromGeometricObject.py

```
1   from GeometricObject import GeometricObject
2
3   class Rectangle(GeometricObject):               extend superclass
4       def __init__(self, width = 1, height = 1):    initializer
5           super().__init__()                         superclass initializer
6           self.__width = width
7           self.__height = height
8
9       def getWidth(self):                            methods
10          return self.__width
11
12      def setWidth(self, width):
13          self.__width = width
14
15      def getHeight(self):
16          return self.__height
17
18      def setHeight(self, height):
19          self.__height = self.__height
20
21      def getArea(self):
22          return self.__width * self.__height
23
24      def getPerimeter(self):
25          return 2 * (self.__width + self.__height)
```

The code in Listing 12.4 creates **Circle** and **Rectangle** objects and invokes the **getArea()** and **getPerimeter()** methods on these objects. The **__str__()** method is inherited from the **GeometricObject** class and is invoked from a **Circle** object (line 5) and a **Rectangle** object (line 11).

LISTING 12.4   TestCircleRectangle.py

```
1   from CircleFromGeometricObject import Circle
2   from RectangleFromGeometricObject import Rectangle
3
```

Circle object
invoke __str__

Rectangle object
invoke __str__

```
 4  def main():
 5      circle = Circle(1.5)
 6      print("A circle", circle)
 7      print("The radius is", circle.getRadius())
 8      print("The area is", circle.getArea())
 9      print("The diameter is", circle.getDiameter())
10
11      rectangle = Rectangle(2, 4)
12      print("\nA rectangle", rectangle)
13      print("The area is", rectangle.getArea())
14      print("The perimeter is", rectangle.getPerimeter())
15
16  main() # Call the main function
```

```
A circle color: green and filled: True
The radius is 1.5
The area is 7.06858347058
The diameter is 3.0

A rectangle color: green and filled: True
The area is 8
The perimeter is 12
```

Line 6 invokes the **print** function to print a circle. Recall from Section 8.5, this is the same as

```
print("A circle", circle.__str__())
```

The __str__() method is not defined in the **Circle** class, but is defined in the **GeometricObject** class. Since **Circle** is a subclass of **GeometricObject**, __str__() can be invoked from a **Circle** object.

The __str__() method displays the **color** and **filled** properties of a **GeometricObject** (lines 18–20 in Listing 12.1). The default **color** for a **GeometricObject** object is **green** and **filled** is **True** (line 2 Listing 12.1). Since a **Circle** inherits from **GeometricObject**, the default **color** for a **Circle** object is green and the default value for **filled** is **True**.

The following points regarding inheritance are worthwhile to note:

more in subclass

- Contrary to the conventional interpretation, a subclass is not a subset of its superclass. In fact, a subclass usually contains more information and methods than its superclass.

is-a relationships

nonextensible is-a

- Inheritance models the is-a relationships, but not all is-a relationships should be modeled using inheritance. For example, a square is a rectangle, but you should not extend a **Square** class from a **Rectangle** class, because the **width** and **height** properties are not appropriate for a square. Instead, you should define a **Square** class to extend the **GeometricObject** class and define the **side** property for the side of a square.

no blind extension

- Do not blindly extend a class just for the sake of reusing methods. For example, it makes no sense for a **Tree** class to extend a **Person** class, even though they share common properties such as height and weight. A subclass and its superclass must have the is-a relationship.

multiple inheritance

- Python allows you to derive a subclass from several classes. This capability is known as *multiple inheritance*. To define a class derived from multiple classes, use the following syntax:

```
class Subclass(SuperClass1, SuperClass2, ...):
    initializer
    methods
```

12.1 How do you define a class that extends a superclass? What is **super()**? How do you invoke the superclass's initializer?

Check Point

MyProgrammingLab™

12.2 What problem arises in running the following program? How do you fix it?

```python
class A:
    def __init__(self, i = 0):
        self.i = i

class B(A):
    def __init__(self, j = 0):
        self.j = j

def main():
    b = B()
    print(b.i)
    print(b.j)

main() # Call the main function
```

12.3 True or false? A subclass is a subset of a superclass.

12.4 Does Python support multiple inheritance? How do you define a class that extends multiple classes?

12.3 Overriding Methods

To override a method, the method must be defined in the subclass using the same header as in its superclass.

Key Point

A subclass inherits methods from a superclass. Sometimes it is necessary for the subclass to modify the implementation of a method defined in the superclass. This is referred to as *method overriding*.

override

The __str__ method in the **GeometricObject** class returns the string describing a geometric object. This method can be overridden to return the string describing a circle. To override it, add the following new method in Listing 12.2, CircleFromGeometricObject.py:

```python
1  class Circle(GeometricObject):
2      # Other methods are omitted
3
4      # Override the __str__ method defined in GeometricObject
5      def __str__(self):
6          return super().__str__() + " radius: " + str(radius)
```

__str__ in superclass

The __str__() method is defined in the **GeometricObject** class and modified in the **Circle** class. Both methods can be used in the **Circle** class. To invoke the __str__ method defined in the **GeometricObject** class from the **Circle** class, use **super().__str__()** (line 6).

Similarly, you can override the __str__ method in the **Rectangle** class as follows:

```python
def __str__(self):
    return super().__str__() + " width: " + \
        str(self.__width) + " height: " + str(self.__height)
```

For the rest of the book, we assume that the __str__() method in **GeometricObject** class has been overridden in the **Circle** and **Rectangle** classes.

Note

Recall that you can define a private method in Python by adding two underscores in front of a method name (see Chapter 7). A private method cannot be overridden. If a method defined in a subclass is private in its superclass, the two methods are completely unrelated, even though they have the same name.

MyProgrammingLab

12.5 True or false?

(a) You can override a nonprivate method defined in a superclass.

(b) You can override a private method defined in a superclass.

(c) You can override the initializer defined in a superclass.

(d) When constructing an object from a subclass, its superclass's initializer is automatically invoked.

12.6 Show the printout of the following program:

```python
class A:
    def __init__(self, i = 0):
        self.i = i

    def m1(self):
        self.i += 1

class B(A):
    def __init__(self, j = 0):
        super().__init__(3)
        self.j = j

    def m1(self):
        self.i += 1

def main():
    b = B()
    b.m1()
    print(b.i)
    print(b.j)

main() # Call the main function
```

12.4 The **object** Class

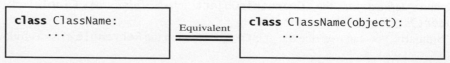
Key Point

*Every class in Python is descended from the **object** class.*

The **object** class is defined in the Python library. If no inheritance is specified when a class is defined, its superclass is **object** by default. For example, the following two class definitions are the same:

`class ClassName:` `    ...`	Equivalent	`class ClassName(object):` `    ...`

The **Circle** class is derived from **GeometricObject** and the **Rectangle** class is derived from **GeometricObject**. The **GeometricObject** class is actually derived from **object**. It is important to be familiar with the methods provided by the **object** class so that you can use them in your classes. All methods defined in the **object** class are special methods with two leading underscores and two trailing underscores. We discuss four methods—__new__(), __init__(), __str__(), and __eq__(other)—in this section.

The __**new**__() method is automatically invoked when an object is constructed. This method then invokes the __**init**__() method to initialize the object. Normally you should only override the __**init**__() method to initialize the data fields defined in the new class.

__new__()
__init__()

The __**str**__() method returns a string description for the object. By default, it returns a string consisting of a class name of which the object is an instance and the object's memory address in hexadecimal format. For example, consider the following code for the **Loan** class, which was defined in Listing 7.8:

__str__()

```
loan = Loan(1, 1, 1, "Smith")
print(loan) # Same as print(loan.__str__())
```

The code displays something like **<Loan.Loan object at 0x01B99C10>**. This message is not very helpful or informative. Usually you should override the __**str**__() method so that it returns an informative description for the object. For example, the __**str**__() method in the **object** class was overridden in the **GeometricObject** class in lines 18–20 in Listing 12.1 as follows:

```
def __str__(self):
    return "color: " + self.__color + \
        " and filled: " + str(self.__filled)
```

The __**eq**__(other) method returns **True** if two objects are the same. So, x.__**eq**__(x) is **True**, but x.__**eq**__(y) returns **False**, because x and y are two different objects even though they may have the same contents. Recall that x.__**eq**__(y) is same as x == y (see Section 8.5).

__eq__(other)

You can override this method to return **True** if two objects have the same contents. The __**eq**__ method is overridden in many Python built-in classes such as **int**, **float**, **bool**, **string**, and **list** to return **True** if two objects have the same contents.

12.7 True or false?

(a) Every object is an instance of the **object** class.

(b) If a class does not extend a superclass explicitly, it extends **object** by default.

12.8 Show the printout of the following code:

```
class A:
    def __init__(self, i = 0):
        self.i = i

    def m1(self):
        self.i += 1

    def __str__(self):
        return str(self.i)

x = A(8)
print(x)
```

12.9 Show the printout of the following program:

```
class A:
    def __new__(self):
        print("A's __new__() invoked")

    def __init__(self):
        print("A's __init__() invoked")
```

```
class B(A):
    def __new__(self):
        print("B's __new__() invoked")

    def __init__(self):
        print("B's __init__() invoked")

def main():
    b = B()
    a = A()

main() # Call the main function
```

12.10 Show the printout of the following program:

```
class A:
    def __new__(self):
        self.__init__(self)
        print("A's __new__() invoked")

    def __init__(self):
        print("A's __init__() invoked")

class B(A):
    def __new__(self):
        self.__init__(self)
        print("B's __new__() invoked")

    def __init__(self):
        print("B's __init__() invoked")

def main():
    b = B()
    a = A()

main() # Call the main function
```

12.11 Show the printout of the following program:

```
class A:
    def __init__(self):
        print("A's __init__() invoked")

class B(A):
    def __init__(self):
        print("B's __init__() invoked")

def main():
    b = B()
    a = A()

main() # Call the main function
```

12.12 Show the printout of the following program:

```
class A:
    def __init__(self, i):
        self.i = i
```

```
        def __str__(self):
            return "A"

    class B(A):
        def __init__(self, i, j):
            super().__init__(i)
            self.j = j

    def main():
        b = B(1, 2)
        a = A(1)
        print(a)
        print(b)

    main() # Call the main function
```

12.13 Show the printout of the following program:

```
    class A:
        def __init__(self, i):
            self.i = i

        def __str__(self):
            return "A"

        def __eq__(self, other):
            return self.i == other.i

    def main():
        x = A(1)
        y = A(1)
        print(x == y)

    main() # Call the main function
```

12.5 Polymorphism and Dynamic Binding

Polymorphism means that an object of a subclass can be passed to a parameter of a superclass type. A method may be implemented in several classes along the inheritance chain. Python decides which method is invoked at runtime. This is known as dynamic binding.

The three pillars of object-oriented programming are *encapsulation*, *inheritance*, and *polymorphism*. You have already learned the first two. This section introduces polymorphism.

The inheritance relationship enables a subclass to inherit features from its superclass with additional new features. A subclass is a specialization of its superclass; every instance of a subclass is also an instance of its superclass, but not vice versa. For example, every circle is a geometric object, but not every geometric object is a circle. Therefore, you can always pass an instance of a subclass to a parameter of its superclass type. Consider the code in Listing 12.5.

Key Point

polymorphism

VideoNote

Dynamic binding

LISTING 12.5 PolymorphismDemo.py

```
1  from CircleFromGeometricObject import Circle
2  from RectangleFromGeometricObject import Rectangle
3
4  def main():
5      # Display circle and rectangle properties
```

```
 6        c = Circle(4)
 7        r = Rectangle(1, 3)
 8        displayObject(c)
 9        displayObject(r)
10        print("Are the circle and rectangle the same size?",
11            isSameArea(c, r))
12
13    # Display geometric object properties
14    def displayObject(g) :
15        print(g.__str__())
16
17    # Compare the areas of two geometric objects
18    def isSameArea(g1, g2) :
19        return g1.getArea() == g2.getArea()
20
21    main() # Call the main function
```

polymorphic call (line 8)
polymorphic call (line 9)

polymorphic call (line 11)

```
color: green and filled: True radius: 4
color: green and filled: True width: 1 height: 3
Are the circle and rectangle the same size? False
```

The **displayObject** method (line 14) takes a parameter of the **GeometricObject** type. You can invoke **displayObject** by passing any instance of **GeometricObject** (for example, **Circle(4)** and **Rectangle(1, 3)** in lines 8–9). An object of a subclass can be used wherever its superclass object is used. This is commonly known as *polymorphism* (from a Greek word meaning "many forms").

what is polymorphism?

As seen in this example, **c** is an object of the **Circle** class. **Circle** is a subclass of **GeometricObject**. The **__str__()** method is defined in both classes. So, which **__str__()** method is invoked by **g** in the **displayObject** method (line 15)? The **__str__()** method invoked by **g** is determined using *dynamic binding*.

dynamic binding

Dynamic binding works as follows: Suppose an object **o** is an instance of classes $C_1, C_2, ...,$ C_{n-1}, and C_n, where C_1 is a subclass of C_2, C_2 is a subclass of $C_3, ...,$ and C_{n-1} is a subclass of C_n, as shown in Figure 12.2. That is, C_n is the most general class, and C_1 is the most specific class. In Python, C_n is the **object** class. If **o** invokes a method **p**, Python searches the implementation for the method **p** in $C_1, C_2, ..., C_{n-1}$, and C_n, in this order, until it is found. Once an implementation is found, the search stops and the first-found implementation is invoked.

Listing 12.6 provides an example that demonstrates dynamic binding.

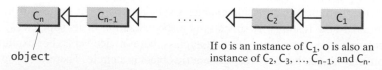

If **o** is an instance of C_1, **o** is also an instance of $C_2, C_3, ..., C_{n-1}$, and C_n.

FIGURE 12.2   The method to be invoked is dynamically bound at runtime.

LISTING 12.6   DynamicBindingDemo.py

```
1    class Student:
2        def __str__(self):
3            return "Student"
```

override __str__()

```
4
5       def printStudent(self):
6           print(self.__str__())
7
8   class GraduateStudent(Student):
9       def __str__(self):                                    override __str__()
10          return "Graduate Student"
11
12  a = Student()
13  b = GraduateStudent()
14  a.printStudent()
15  b.printStudent()
```

```
Student
Graduate Student
```

Since **a** is an instance of **Student**, the **printStudent** method in the **Student** class is invoked for **a.printStudent()** (line 14), which invokes the **Student** class's **__str__()** method to return **Student**.

No **printStudent** method is defined in **GraduateStudent**. However, since it is defined in the **Student** class and **GraduateStudent** is a subclass of **Student**, the **printStudent** method in the **Student** class is invoked for **b.printStudent()** (line 15). The **printStudent** method invokes **GraduateStudent**'s **__str__()** method to display **Graduate Student**, since the object **b** that invokes **printStudent** is **GraduateStudent** (lines 6 and 10).

12.6 The **isinstance** Function

*The **isinstance** function can be used to determine whether an object is an instance of a class.*

Key Point

Suppose you want to modify the **displayObject** function in Listing 12.5 to perform the following tasks:

- Display the area and perimeter of a **GeometricObject** instance.

- Display the diameter if the instance is a **Circle**, and the width and height if the instance is a **Rectangle**.

How can this be done? You might be tempted to write the function as:

```
def displayObject(g):
    print("Area is", g.getArea())
    print("Perimeter is", g.getPerimeter())
    print("Diameter is", g.getDiameter())
    print("Width is", g.getWidth())
    print("Height is", g.getHeight())
```

This won't work, however, because not all **GeometricObject** instances have the **getDiameter()**, **getWidth()**, or **getHeight()** methods. For example, invoking **display(Circle(5))** will cause a runtime error because **Circle** does not have the **getWidth()** and **getHeight()** methods, and invoking **display(Rectangle(2, 3))** will cause a runtime error because **Rectangle** does not have the **getDiameter()** method.

You can fix this problem by using Python's built-in **isinstance** function. This function determines whether an object is an instance of a class by using the following syntax:

```
isinstance(object, ClassName)
```

For example, **isinstance("abc", str)** returns **True** because **"abc"** is an instance of the **str** class, but **isinstance(12, str)** returns **False** because **12** is not an instance of the **str** class.

Using the **isinstance** function, you can implement the **displayObject** function as shown in Listing 12.7.

LISTING 12.7 IsinstanceDemo.py

```
1   from CircleFromGeometricObject import Circle
2   from RectangleFromGeometricObject import Rectangle
3
4   def main():
5       # Display circle and rectangle properties
6       c = Circle(4)
7       r = Rectangle(1, 3)
8       print("Circle...")
9       displayObject(c)
10      print("Rectangle...")
11      displayObject(r)
12
13  # Display geometric object properties
14  def displayObject(g):
15      print("Area is", g.getArea())
16      print("Perimeter is", g.getPerimeter())
17
18      if isinstance(g, Circle):
19          print("Diameter is", g.getDiameter())
20      elif isinstance(g, Rectangle):
21          print("Width is", g.getWidth())
22          print("Height is", g.getHeight())
23
24  main() # Call the main function
```

polymorphic call (line 9)

polymorphic call (line 11)

isinstance? (line 18)

isinstance? (line 20)

```
Circle...
Area is 50.26548245743669
Perimeter is 25.132741228718345
Diameter is 8
Rectangle...
Area is 3
Perimeter is 8
Width is 1
Height is 3
```

Invoking **displayObject(c)** passes **c** to **g** (line 9). **g** is now an instance of **Circle** (line 18). The program displays the circle's diameter (line 19).

Invoking **displayObject(r)** passes **r** to **g** (line 11). **g** is now an instance of **Rectangle** (line 20). The program displays the rectangle's width and height (lines 21–22).

12.14 Explain encapsulation, inheritance, and polymorphism.

12.15 Show the output of the following code:

```python
class Person:
    def getInfo(self):
        return "Person"

    def printPerson(self):
        print(self.getInfo())

class Student(Person):
    def getInfo(self):
        return "Student"

Person().printPerson()
Student().printPerson()
```

(a)

```python
class Person:
    def __getInfo(self):
        return "Person"

    def printPerson(self):
        print(self.__getInfo())

class Student(Person):
    def __getInfo(self):
        return "Student"

Person().printPerson()
Student().printPerson()
```

(b)

12.16 Suppose that **Fruit**, **Apple**, **Orange**, **GoldenDelicious**, and **McIntosh** are defined in the inheritance hierarchy as follows:

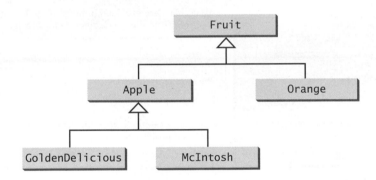

Assume that the following statements are given:

```python
goldenDelicious = GoldenDelicious()
orange = Orange()
```

Answer the following questions:

(a) Is **goldenDelicious** an instance of **Fruit**?

(b) Is **goldenDelicious** an instance of **Orange**?

(c) Is **goldenDelicious** an instance of **Apple**?

(d) Is **goldenDelicious** an instance of **GoldenDelicious**?

(e) Is **goldenDelicious** an instance of **McIntosh**?

(f) Is **orange** an instance of **Orange**?

(g) Is **orange** an instance of **Fruit**?

(h) Is **orange** an instance of **Apple**?

(i) Suppose the method **makeAppleCider** is defined in the **Apple** class. Can **goldenDelicious** invoke this method? Can **orange** invoke this method?

(j) Suppose the method **makeOrangeJuice** is defined in the **Orange** class. Can **orange** invoke this method? Can **goldenDelicious** invoke this method?

12.7 Case Study: A Reusable Clock

Key
Point

This section designs a GUI class for displaying a clock.

Suppose you want to display a clock on a canvas and later reuse the clock in other programs. You need to define a clock class to make the clock reusable. Furthermore, in order to display the clock graphically, you should define it as a widget. Your best option is to define a clock class that extends **Canvas** so that a clock object can be used in the same way as a **Canvas** object.

The contract of the class is shown in Figure 12.3.

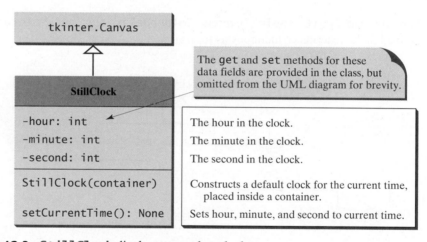

FIGURE 12.3 **StillClock** displays an analog clock.

Listing 12.8 is a test program that uses the **StillClock** class to display an analog clock. The program enables the user to enter a new hour, minute, and second from the **Entry** fields, as shown in Figure 12.4a.

LISTING 12.8 DisplayClock.py

```
1  from tkinter import * # Import all definitions from tkinter
2  from StillClock import StillClock
3
4  class DisplayClock:
5      def __init__(self):
6          window = Tk() # Create a window
7          window.title("Change Clock Time") # Set title
8
9          self.clock = StillClock(window) # Create a clock
10         self.clock.pack()
11
12         frame = Frame(window)
13         frame.pack()
```

import StillClock

create a clock

```
14        Label(frame, text = "Hour: ").pack(side = LEFT)
15        self.hour = IntVar()
16        self.hour.set(self.clock.getHour())
17        Entry(frame, textvariable = self.hour,                create entries
18            width = 2).pack(side = LEFT)
19        Label(frame, text = "Minute: ").pack(side = LEFT)
20        self.minute = IntVar()
21        self.minute.set(self.clock.getMinute())
22        Entry(frame, textvariable = self.minute,
23            width = 2).pack(side = LEFT)
24        Label(frame, text = "Second: ").pack(side = LEFT)
25        self.second = IntVar()
26        self.second.set(self.clock.getMinute())
27        Entry(frame, textvariable = self.second,
28            width = 2).pack(side = LEFT)
29        Button(frame, text = "Set New Time",                 create button
30            command = self.setNewTime).pack(side = LEFT)     callback handler
31
32        window.mainloop() # Create an event loop
33
34    def setNewTime(self):                                    setNewTime
35        self.clock.setHour(self.hour.get())
36        self.clock.setMinute(self.minute.get())
37        self.clock.setSecond(self.second.get())
38
39 DisplayClock() # Create GUI                                 create GUI
```

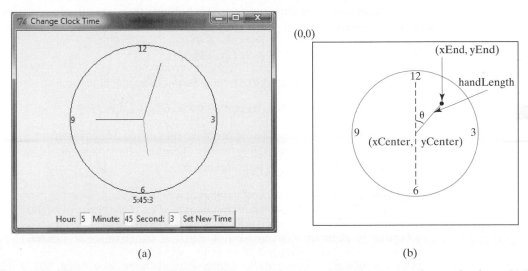

(a)   (b)

FIGURE 12.4 (a) The **DisplayClock** program displays a clock and enables the user to change the time. (b) The endpoint of a clock hand can be determined, given the spanning angle, the hand length, and the center point.

The rest of this section explains how to implement the **StillClock** class. Since you can use the class without knowing how it is implemented, you may skip the implementation if you wish.

How do you obtain the current time? Python provides the **datetime** class, which can be used to obtain the current computer time. You can use the **now()** function to return an instance of **datetime** for the current time, and use the data fields **year**, **month**, **day**, **hour**,

skip implementation?

obtain current time

minute, and **second** to extract date and time information from the object, as shown in the following code:

```
from datetime import datetime

d = datetime.now()
print("Current year is", d.year)
print("Current month is", d.month)
print("Current day of month is", d.day)
print("Current hour is", d.hour)
print("Current minute is", d.minute)
print("Current second is", d.second)
```

draw a clock

To draw a clock, you need to draw a circle and three hands for the second, minute, and hour. To draw a hand, you need to specify the two ends of the line. As shown in Figure 12.4b, one end is at the center of the clock at **(xCenter, yCenter)**; the other end, at **(xEnd, yEnd)**, is determined by the following formula:

```
xEnd = xCenter + handLength × sin(θ)
yEnd = yCenter - handLength × cos(θ)
```

Since there are 60 seconds in one minute, the angle θ (see Figure 12.4b) for the second hand is:

```
θ = second × (2π/60)
```

The position of the minute hand is determined by the minute and second. The exact minute value combined with seconds is **minute + second/60**. For example, if the time is 3 minutes and 30 seconds, the total minutes are 3.5. Since there are 60 minutes in one hour, the angle for the minute hand is:

```
θ = (minute + second/60) × (2π/60)
```

Since one circle is divided into 12 hours, the angle for the hour hand is:

```
θ = (hour + minute/60 + second/(60 × 60)) × (2π/12)
```

For simplicity in computing the angles of the minute hand and hour hand, you can omit the seconds, because they are negligibly small. Therefore, the endpoints for the second hand, minute hand, and hour hand can be computed as:

```
xSecond = xCenter + secondHandLength × sin(second × (2π/60))
ySecond = yCenter - secondHandLength × cos(second × (2π/60))
xMinute = xCenter + minuteHandLength × sin(minute × (2π/60))
yMinute = yCenter - minuteHandLength × cos(minute × (2π/60))
xHour = xCenter + hourHandLength × sin((hour + minute/60) × (2π/12))
yHour = yCenter - hourHandLength × cos((hour + minute/60) × (2π/12))
```

The **StillClock** class is implemented in Listing 12.9.

LISTING 12.9 StillClock.py

extend Canvas
initializer

```
1  from tkinter import * # Import all definitions from tkinter
2  import math
3  from datetime import datetime
4
5  class StillClock(Canvas):
6      def __init__(self, container):
7          super().__init__(container)
```

```
 8              self.setCurrentTime()
 9
10          def getHour(self):                                                    getHour
11              return self.__hour
12
13          def setHour(self, hour):                                              setHour
14              self.__hour = hour
15              self.delete("clock")
16              self.drawClock()
17
18          def getMinute(self):
19              return self.__minute
20
21          def setMinute(self, minute):
22              self.__minute = minute
23              self.delete("clock")
24              self.drawClock()
25
26          def getSecond(self):
27              return self.__second
28
29          def setSecond(self, second):
30              self.__second = second
31              self.delete("clock")
32              self.drawClock()
33
34          def setCurrentTime(self):                                             set current time
35              d = datetime.now()
36              self.__hour = d.hour
37              self.__minute = d.minute
38              self.__second = d.second
39              self.delete("clock")
40              self.drawClock()
41
42          def drawClock(self):                                                  draw clock
43              width = float(self["width"])
44              height = float(self["height"])
45              radius = min(width, height) / 2.4
46              secondHandLength = radius * 0.8
47              minuteHandLength = radius * 0.65
48              hourHandLength = radius * 0.5
49
50              self.create_oval(width / 2 - radius, height / 2 - radius,
51                  width / 2 + radius, height / 2 + radius, tags = "clock")
52              self.create_text(width / 2 - radius + 5, height / 2,
53                              text = "9", tags = "clock")
54              self.create_text(width / 2 + radius - 5, height / 2,
55                              text = "3", tags = "clock")
56              self.create_text(width / 2, height / 2 - radius + 5,
57                              text = "12", tags = "clock")
58              self.create_text(width / 2, height / 2 + radius - 5,
59                              text = "6", tags = "clock")
60
61              xCenter = width / 2
62              yCenter = height / 2
63              second = self.__second
64              xSecond = xCenter + secondHandLength \
65                  * math.sin(second * (2 * math.pi / 60))
66              ySecond = yCenter - secondHandLength \
67                  * math.cos(second * (2 * math.pi / 60))
```

```
68              self.create_line(xCenter, yCenter, xSecond, ySecond,
69                            fill = "red", tags = "clock")
70
71          minute = self.__minute
72          xMinute = xCenter + \
73              minuteHandLength * math.sin(minute * (2 * math.pi / 60))
74          yMinute = yCenter - \
75              minuteHandLength * math.cos(minute * (2 * math.pi / 60))
76          self.create_line(xCenter, yCenter, xMinute, yMinute,
77                            fill = "blue", tags = "clock")
78
79          hour = self.__hour % 12
80          xHour = xCenter + hourHandLength * \
81              math.sin((hour + minute / 60) * (2 * math.pi / 12))
82          yHour = yCenter - hourHandLength * \
83              math.cos((hour + minute / 60) * (2 * math.pi / 12))
84          self.create_line(xCenter, yCenter, xHour, yHour,
85                            fill = "green", tags = "clock")
86
87          timestr = str(hour) + ":" + str(minute) + ":" + str(second)
88          self.create_text(width / 2, height / 2 + radius + 10,
89                            text = timestr, tags = "clock")
```

The **StillClock** class extends the **Canvas** widget (line 5), so a **StillClock** is a **Canvas**. You can use **StillClock** just like a canvas.

The **StillClock** class's initializer invokes the **Canvas** initializer (line 7), then sets the data fields **hour**, **minute**, and **second** using the current time by invoking the **setCurrentTime** method (line 8).

The data fields **hour**, **minute**, and **second** are accompanied by the get and set methods to retrieve and set these data fields (lines 10–32). When a new value is set for the hour, minute, or second, the **drawClock** method is invoked to redraw the clock (lines 16, 24, and 32).

The **setCurrentTime** method gets the current time by invoking **datetime.now()** (line 35) to obtain the current hour, minute, and second (lines 36–38), and invokes the **drawClock** method to redraw the clock (line 40).

The **drawClock** method obtains the width and height of the canvas (lines 43–44) and sets the appropriate size for the hour hand, minute hand, and second hand (lines 45–48). It then uses **Canvas**'s drawing methods to draw a circle, lines, and text strings for displaying a clock (lines 50–89).

12.8 Class Relationships

Key Point

To design classes, you need to explore the relationships among classes. The common relationships among classes are association, aggregation, composition, *and* inheritance.

You have already used inheritance to model the *is-a* relationship. We now explore other relationships.

12.8.1 Association

association

Association is a general binary relationship that describes an activity between two classes. For example, a student taking a course is an association between the **Student** class and the **Course** class, and a faculty member teaching a course is an association between the **Faculty** class and the **Course** class. These associations can be represented in UML graphical notation, as shown in Figure 12.5.

FIGURE 12.5 This UML diagram shows that a student may take any number of courses, a faculty member may teach at most three courses, a course may have from five to sixty students, and a course is taught by only one faculty member.

An association is illustrated by a solid line between two classes with an optional label that describes the relationship. In Figure 12.5, the labels are *Take* and *Teach*. Each relationship may have an optional small black triangle that indicates the direction of the relationship. In this figure, the direction indicates that a student takes a course (as opposed to a course taking a student).

Each class involved in the relationship may have a role name that describes the role it plays in the relationship. In Figure 12.5, *teacher* is the role name for **Faculty**.

Each class involved in an association may specify a *multiplicity*. A multiplicity could be a number or an interval that specifies how many of the class's objects are involved in the relationship. The character ***** means an unlimited number of objects, and the interval **m..n** indicates that the number of objects is between **m** and **n**, inclusively. In Figure 12.5, each student may take any number of courses, and each course must have at least five and at most sixty students. Each course is taught by only one faculty member, and a faculty member may teach from zero to three courses per semester.

multiplicity

In Python code, you can implement associations by using data fields and methods. For example, the relationships in Figure 12.5 may be implemented using the classes in Figure 12.6. The relation "a student takes a course" is implemented using the **addCourse** method in the **Student** class and the **addStudent** method in the **Course** class. The relation "a faculty teaches a course" is implemented using the **addCourse** method in the **Faculty** class and the **setFaculty** method in the **Course** class. The **Student** class may use a list to store the courses that the student is taking, the **Faculty** class may use a list to store the courses that the faculty is teaching, and the **Course** class may use a list to store students enrolled in the course and a data field to store the instructor who teaches the course.

```
class Student:
    # Add course to a list
    def addCourse(self,
        course):
```

```
class Course:
    # Add student to a list
    def addStudent(self,
        student):
    def setFaculty(self, faculty):
```

```
class Faculty:
    # Add course to a list
    def addCourse(self,
        course):
```

FIGURE 12.6 The association relations are implemented using data fields and methods in classes.

12.8.2 Aggregation and Composition

Aggregation is a special form of association that represents an ownership relationship between two objects. Aggregation models *has-a* relationships. The owner object is called an *aggregating object*, and its class is called an *aggregating class*. The subject object is called an *aggregated object*, and its class is called an *aggregated class*.

aggregation

aggregating object
aggregating class
aggregated object
aggregated class
composition

An object can be owned by several other aggregating objects. If an object is exclusively owned by an aggregating object, the relationship between the object and its aggregating object is referred to as a *composition*. For example, "a student has a name" is a composition relationship between the **Student** class and the **Name** class, whereas "a student has an address" is an aggregation relationship between the **Student** class and the **Address** class, since an address can be shared by several students. In UML, a filled diamond is attached to an aggregating class (in this case, **Student**) to denote the composition relationship with an aggregated class (**Name**), and an empty diamond is attached to an aggregating class (**Student**) to denote the aggregation relationship with an aggregated class (**Address**), as shown in Figure 12.7.

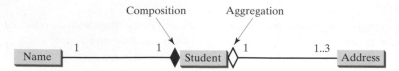

FIGURE 12.7 Each student has a name and an address.

In Figure 12.7, each student has only one multiplicity—address—and each address can be shared by up to **3** students. Each student has one name, and a name is unique for each student.

An aggregation relationship is usually represented as a data field in the aggregating class. For example, the relationships in Figure 12.7 may be implemented using the classes in Figure 12.8. The relation "a student has a name" and "a student has an address" are implemented in the data field **name** and **address** in the **Student** class.

FIGURE 12.8 The composition relations are implemented using data fields in classes.

Aggregation can exist between objects of the same class. For example, Figure 12.9a illustrates that a person can have a supervisor.

```
          ┌─────────┐╲│ 1                      ┌─────────┐╲│ 1
          │ Person  │ ╱├────────┐              │ Person  │ ╱├────────┐
          └─────────┘╱           │ Supervisor  └─────────┘╱           │ Supervisor
              1  └────────────────┘                 m  └────────────────┘
                     (a)                                    (b)
```

FIGURE 12.9 (a) A person can have a supervisor. (b) A person can have several supervisors.

The relationship "a person has a supervisor" can be represented as a data field in the **Person** class, as follows:

```
class Person:
    # The type for the data is the class itself
    def __init__(self, supervisor)
        self.supervisor = supervisor

    ...
```

If a person has several supervisors, as shown in Figure 12.9b, you can use a list to store supervisors.

> **Note**
> Because aggregation and composition relationships are both implemented in classes in similar ways, for simplicity, we refer to both as compositions.

aggregation or composition

12.17 What are the common types of relationships among classes? Describe the UML graphical notation for modeling the relationships among classes.

Check Point

MyProgrammingLab™

12.18 What relationship is appropriate for the following classes? Draw the relationships using UML diagrams.

- Company and Employee

- Course and Faculty

- Student and Person

- House and Window

- Account and Savings Account

12.9 Case Study: Designing the **Course** Class

This section designs a class for modeling courses.

Key Point

Suppose you need to process course information. Each course has a name and has students enrolled. You want to be able to add/drop a student to/from the course. You can use a class to model the courses, as shown in Figure 12.10.

Course	
-courseName: str	The name of the course.
-students: list	A list to store the students in the course.
Course(courseName: str)	Creates a course with the specified name.
getCourseName(): str	Returns the course name.
addStudent(student: str): None	Adds a new student to the course.
dropStudent(student: str): None	Drops a student from the course.
getStudents(): list	Returns the students in the course.
getNumberOfStudents(): int	Returns the number of students in the course.

FIGURE 12.10 The **Course** class models the courses.

A **Course** object can be created using the constructor **Course(name)** by passing a course name. You can add students to the course using the **addStudent(student)** method, drop a student from the course using the **dropStudent(student)** method, and return the names of all the students in the course using the **getStudents()** method. Suppose the **Course** class is available. Listing 12.10 gives a test program that creates two courses and adds students to them.

LISTING 12.10 TestCourse.py

```
1  from Course import Course
2
3  def main():
```

create a course

```
 4    course1 = Course("Data Structures")
 5    course2 = Course("Database Systems")
 6
```

add a student

```
 7    course1.addStudent("Peter Jones")
 8    course1.addStudent("Brian Smith")
 9    course1.addStudent("Anne Kennedy")
10
11    course2.addStudent("Peter Jones")
12    course2.addStudent("Steve Smith")
13
14    print("Number of students in course1:",
```

number of students

return students

```
15        course1.getNumberOfStudents())
16    students = course1.getStudents()
17    for student in students:
18        print(student, end = ", ")
19
20    print("\nNumber of students in course2:",
21        course2.getNumberOfStudents())
22
23 main() # Call the main function
```

```
Number of students in course1: 3
Peter Jones, Brian Smith, Anne Kennedy,
Number of students in course2: 2
```

The **Course** class is implemented in Listing 12.11. It uses a list to store the students for the course in line 4. The **addStudent** method (line 6) adds a student to the list. The **getStudents** method returns the list (line 9). The **dropStudent** method (line 18) is left as an exercise.

LISTING 12.11 Course.py

```
 1 class Course:
 2     def __init__(self, courseName):
 3         self.__courseName = courseName
```

students list

```
 4         self.__students = []
 5
 6     def addStudent(self, student):
```

add a student

```
 7         self.__students.append(student)
 8
 9     def getStudents(self):
```

return students

```
10         return self.__students
11
12     def getNumberOfStudents(self):
```

number of students

```
13         return len(self.__students)
14
15     def getCourseName(self):
16         return self.__courseName
17
18     def dropStudent(student):
19         print("Left as an exercise")
```

When you create a **Course** object, a list object is created. A **Course** object contains a reference to the list. For simplicity, you can say that the **Course** object contains the list.

The user can create a **Course** and manipulate it through the public methods **addStudent**, **dropStudent**, **getNumberOfStudents**, and **getStudents**. However, the user doesn't need to know how these methods are implemented. The **Course** class encapsulates the internal implementation. This example uses a list to store the names of students. You may use a different data type to store student names. The program that uses **Course** does not need to change as long as the contract of the public methods remains unchanged.

12.10 Designing a Class for Stacks

This section designs a class for modeling stacks.

Key
Point

Recall that a stack (see Chapter 6) holds data in a last-in, first-out fashion, as shown in Figure 12.11.

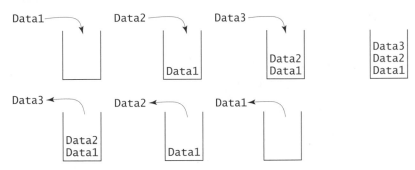

FIGURE 12.11 Data1, Data2, and Data3 are pushed onto the stack in this order and popped out in the reversed order.

Stacks have many applications. For example, a computer uses a stack to process function invocations. When a function is invoked, an activation record that stores its parameters and local variables is pushed onto a stack. When a function calls another function, the new function's activation record is pushed onto the stack. When a function finishes its work and returns to its caller, its activation record is removed from the stack.

stack

You can define a class to model stacks and use a list to store the elements in a stack. There are two ways to design a stack class:

- Using inheritance, you can define a stack class by extending **list**, as shown in Figure 12.12a.

inheritance

- Using composition, you can create a list as a data field in the **Stack** class, as shown in Figure 12.12b.

composition

(a) Using inheritance   (b) Using composition

FIGURE 12.12 **Stack** may be implemented using inheritance or composition.

Both designs are fine, but using composition is better because it enables you to define a completely new stack class without inheriting the unnecessary and inappropriate methods from the **list** class. We use the composition approach in this section and leave you to implement the inheritance approach in Exercise 12.16. The UML diagram for the **Stack** class is shown in Figure 12.13.

composition
inheritance

Suppose that the **Stack** class is available. The test program in Listing 12.12 uses the class to create a stack (line 3), store ten integers **0, 1, 2**, ..., and **9** (lines 5–6), and display them in reverse order (line 9).

Stack	
-elements: list	A list to store the elements in the stack.
Stack()	Constructs an empty stack.
isEmpty(): bool	Returns True if the stack is empty.
peek(): object	Returns the element at the top of the stack without removing it from the stack.
push(value: object): None	Stores an element at the top of the stack.
pop(): object	Removes the element at the top of the stack and returns it.
getSize(): int	Returns the number of elements in the stack.

FIGURE 12.13 The **Stack** class encapsulates the stack storage and provides the operations for manipulating the stack.

LISTING 12.12 TestStack.py

```
1  from Stack import Stack
2
3  stack = Stack()
4
5  for i in range(10):
6      stack.push(i)
7
8  while not stack.isEmpty():
9      print(stack.pop(), end = " ")
```

create a stack

push onto stack

pop from stack

```
9 8 7 6 5 4 3 2 1 0
```

How do you implement the **Stack** class? You can use a list to store the elements in a stack, as shown in Listing 12.13.

LISTING 12.13 Stack.py

```
1  class Stack:
2      def __init__(self):
3          self.__elements = []
4
5      # Return True if the stack is empty
6      def isEmpty(self):
7          return len(self.__elements) == 0
8
9      # Return the element at the top of the stack
10     # without removing it from the stack.
11     def peek(self):
12         if self.isEmpty():
13             return None
14         else:
15             return self.__elements[len(elements) - 1]
16
17     # Store an element at the top of the stack
18     def push(self, value):
19         self.__elements.append(value)
```

list to store elements

isEmpty

peek

push

```
20
21        # Remove the element at the top of the stack and return it
22        def pop(self):                                                    pop
23            if self.isEmpty():
24                return None
25            else:
26                return self.__elements.pop()
27
28        # Return the size of the stack
29        def getSize(self):                                                getSize
30            return len(self.__elements)
```

In line 3, the data field **elements** is defined as private with two leading underscores.
elements is a list, but the client is not aware that the elements in the stack are stored in a list.
The client accesses the stack through the methods **isEmpty()**, **peek()**, **push(element)**,
pop(), and **getSize()**.

12.11 Case Study: The **FigureCanvas** Class

This case study develops the **FigureCanvas** *class for displaying various figures.*

Key
Point

The **FigureCanvas** class enables the user to set the figure type, specify whether the figure is
filled, and display the figure on a canvas. The UML diagram for the class, which can display
lines, rectangles, ovals, and arcs, is shown in Figure 12.14. The **figureType** property
decides which figure to display. If the **filled** property is **True**, the rectangle, oval, or arc is
filled with a color.

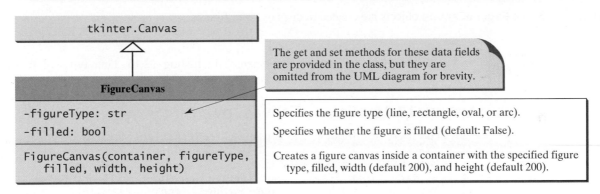

FIGURE 12.14 The **FigureCanvas** class displays various types of figures on the panel.

The UML diagram serves as the contract for the **FigureCanvas** class. The user can use
the class without knowing how the class is implemented. We will begin by writing the program in Listing 12.14 that uses the class to display seven figures in a panel, as shown in
Figure 12.15.

LISTING 12.14 DisplayFigures.py

```
1   from tkinter import * # Import all definitions from tkinter
2   from FigureCanvas import FigureCanvas                              import FigureCanvas
3
4   class DisplayFigures:
5       def __init__(self):
6           window = Tk() # Create a window
7           window.title("Display Figures") # Set title
```

create figure

place figure

```
  8
  9  figure1 = FigureCanvas(window, "line", width = 100, height = 100)
 10  figure1.grid(row = 1, column = 1)
 11  figure2 = FigureCanvas(window, "rectangle", False, 100, 100)
 12  figure2.grid(row = 1, column = 2)
 13  figure3 = FigureCanvas(window, "oval", False, 100, 100)
 14  figure3.grid(row = 1, column = 3)
 15  figure4 = FigureCanvas(window, "arc", False, 100, 100)
 16  figure4.grid(row = 1, column = 4)
 17  figure5 = FigureCanvas(window, "rectangle", True, 100, 100)
 18  figure5.grid(row = 1, column = 5)
 19  figure6 = FigureCanvas(window, "oval", True, 100, 100)
 20  figure6.grid(row = 1, column = 6)
 21  figure7 = FigureCanvas(window, "arc", True, 100, 100)
 22  figure7.grid(row = 1, column = 7)
 23
 24  window.mainloop() # Create an event loop
 25
```

create GUI

```
 26  DisplayFigures() # Create GUI
```

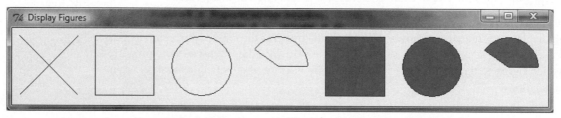

FIGURE 12.15 Seven **FigureCanvas** objects are created to display seven figures.

The **FigureCanvas** class is implemented in Listing 12.15. Four types of figures are drawn according to the **figureType** property (lines 26–34).

LISTING 12.15 FigureCanvas.py

```
  1  from tkinter import * # Import all definitions from tkinter
  2
```

extend Canvas

```
  3  class FigureCanvas(Canvas):
  4      def __init__(self, container, figureType, filled = False,
  5                      width = 100, height = 100):
```

superclass initializer

```
  6          super().__init__(container,
  7                          width = width, height = height)
  8          self.__figureType = figureType
  9          self.__filled = filled
```

draw figure

```
 10          self.drawFigure()
 11
 12      def getFigureType(self):
 13          return self.__figureType
 14
 15      def getFilled(self):
 16          return self.__filled
 17
```

set figure type

```
 18      def setFigureType(self, figureType):
 19          self.__figureType = figureType
 20          self.drawFigure()
 21
```

set fill

```
 22      def setFilled(self, filled):
```

```
23              self.__filled = filled
24              self.drawFigure()
25
26          def drawFigure(self):                                    draw figure
27              if self.__figureType == "line":
28                  self.line()
29              elif self.__figureType == "rectangle":
30                  self.rectangle()
31              elif self.__figureType == "oval":
32                  self.oval()
33              elif self.__figureType == "arc":
34                  self.arc()
35
36          def line(self):                                          draw lines
37              width = int(self["width"])
38              height = int(self["height"])
39              self.create_line(10, 10, width - 10, height - 10)
40              self.create_line(width - 10, 10, 10, height - 10)
41
42          def rectangle(self):
43              width = int(self["width"])
44              height = int(self["height"])
45              if self.__filled:
46                  self.create_rectangle(10, 10, width - 10, height - 10,    fill a rectangle
47                              fill = "red")
48              else:
49                  self.create_rectangle(10, 10, width - 10, height - 10)     draw a rectangle
50
51          def oval(self):
52              width = int(self["width"])
53              height = int(self["height"])
54              if self.__filled:
55                  self.create_oval(10, 10, width - 10, height - 10,    fill an oval
56                              fill = "red")
57              else:
58                  self.create_oval(10, 10, width - 10, height - 10)     draw an oval
59
60          def arc(self):
61              width = int(self["width"])
62              height = int(self["height"])
63              if self.__filled:
64                  self.create_arc(10, 10, width - 10, height - 10,    fill an arc
65                          start = 0, extent = 145, fill = "red")
66              else:
67                  self.create_arc(10, 10, width - 10, height - 10,    draw an arc
68                          start = 0, extent = 145)
```

The **FigureCanvas** class extends the **Canvas** widget (line 3). Thus, a **FigureCanvas** is a canvas, and you can use **FigureCanvas** just like a canvas. You can construct a **FigureCanvas** by specifying the container, figure type, whether the figure is filled, and the canvas width and height (lines 4–5).

The **FigureCanvas** class's initializer invokes the **Canvas** initializer (lines 6–7), sets the data field's **figureType** and **filled** properties (lines 8–9), and invokes the **drawFigure** method (line 10) to draw a figure.

The **drawFigure** method draws a figure based on the **figureType** and **filled** properties (lines 26–34).

The methods **line**, **rectangle**, **oval**, and **arc** draw lines, rectangles, ovals, and arcs (lines 36–68).

Key Terms

aggregation 419	is-a relationships 404
association 418	multiple inheritance 404
composition 419	override 405
dynamic binding 410	polymorphism 409
inheritance 400	

Chapter Summary

1. You can derive a new class from an existing class. This is known as *class inheritance*. The new class is called a *subclass*, *child class* or *extended class*. The existing class is called a *superclass*, *parent class*, or *base class*.

2. To *override* a method, the method must be defined in the subclass using the same header as in its superclass.

3. The **object** class is the root class for all Python classes. The methods **__str__()** and **__eq__(other)** are defined in the **object** class.

4. *Polymorphism* means that an object of a subclass can be passed to a parameter of a superclass type. A method may be implemented in several classes along the inheritance chain. Python decides which method is invoked at runtime. This is known as *dynamic binding*.

5. The **isinstance** function can be used to determine whether an object is an instance of a class.

6. The common relationships among classes are *association*, *aggregation*, *composition*, and *inheritance*.

Test Questions

Do test questions for this chapter online at www.cs.armstrong.edu/liang/py/test.html.

Programming Exercises

MyProgrammingLab™

Sections 12.2–12.6

12.1 (*The Triangle class*) Design a class named **Triangle** that extends the **GeometricObject** class. The **Triangle** class contains:

- Three float data fields named **side1**, **side2**, and **side3** to denote the three sides of the triangle.
- A constructor that creates a triangle with the specified **side1**, **side2**, and **side3** with default values **1.0**.
- The accessor methods for all three data fields.
- A method named **getArea()** that returns the area of this triangle.
- A method named **getPerimeter()** that returns the perimeter of this triangle.
- A method named **__str__()** that returns a string description for the triangle.

For the formula to compute the area of a triangle, see Exercise 2.14. The `__str__()` method is implemented as follows:

```
return "Triangle: side1 = " + str(side1) + " side2 = " +
    str(side2) + " side3 = " + str(side3)
```

Draw the UML diagrams for the classes **Triangle** and **GeometricObject**. Implement the **Triangle** class. Write a test program that prompts the user to enter the three sides of the triangle, a color, and **1** or **0** to indicate whether the triangle is filled. The program should create a **Triangle** object with these sides and set the color and filled properties using the input. The program should display the triangle's area, perimeter, color, and **True** or **False** to indicate whether the triangle is filled or not.

12.2 (*The Location class*) Design a class named **Location for locating a maximal value and its location in a two-dimensional list. The class contains the public data fields **row**, **column**, and **maxValue** that store the maximal value and its indexes in a two-dimensional list, with **row** and **column** as **int** types and **maxValue** as a float type.

Write the following method that returns the location of the largest element in a two-dimensional list.

def Location locateLargest(a):

The return value is an instance of **Location**. Write a test program that prompts the user to enter a two-dimensional list and displays the location of the largest element in the list. Here is a sample run:

```
Enter the number of rows and columns in the list: 3, 4  ↵Enter
Enter row 0: 23.5 35 2 10  ↵Enter
Enter row 1: 4.5 3 45 3.5  ↵Enter
Enter row 2: 35 44 5.5 12.6  ↵Enter
The location of the largest element is 45 at (1, 2)
```

12.3 (*Game: ATM machine*) Use the **Account class created in Exercise 7.3 to simulate an ATM machine. Create ten accounts in a list with the ids **0, 1, ..., 9**, and an initial balance of $100. The system prompts the user to enter an id. If the id is entered incorrectly, ask the user to enter a correct id. Once an id is accepted, the main menu is displayed as shown in the sample run. You can enter a choice of **1** for viewing the current balance, **2** for withdrawing money, **3** for depositing money, and **4** for exiting the main menu. Once you exit, the system will prompt for an id again. So, once the system starts, it won't stop.

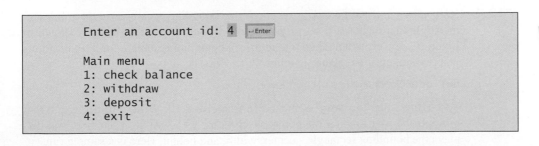

```
Enter an account id: 4  ↵Enter

Main menu
1: check balance
2: withdraw
3: deposit
4: exit
```

```
Enter a choice: 1  ⏎Enter
The balance is 100.00

Main menu
1: check balance
2: withdraw
3: deposit
4: exit
Enter a choice: 2  ⏎Enter
Enter an amount to withdraw: 3  ⏎Enter

Main menu
1: check balance
2: withdraw
3: deposit
4: exit
Enter a choice: 1  ⏎Enter
The balance is 97.00

Main menu
1: check balance
2: withdraw
3: deposit
4: exit
Enter a choice: 3  ⏎Enter
Enter an amount to deposit: 10  ⏎Enter

Main menu
1: check balance
2: withdraw
3: deposit
4: exit
Enter a choice: 1  ⏎Enter
The balance is 107.00

Main menu
1: check balance
2: withdraw
3: deposit
4: exit
Enter a choice: 4  ⏎Enter

Enter an account id:
```

*12.4 (*Geometry: find the bounding rectangle*) A bounding rectangle is the minimum rectangle that encloses a set of points in a two-dimensional plane, as shown in Figure 12.16. Write a method that returns a bounding rectangle for a set of points in a two-dimensional plane, as follows:

def getRectangle(points):

You defined the **Rectangle2D** class in Exercise 8.19. Write a test program that prompts the user to enter the points as x1 y1 x2 y2 x3 y3 ... in one line, and displays the bounding rectangle's center, width, and height. Here is a sample run:

Enter the points: 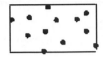 ⏎Enter
The bounding rectangle is centered at (5.0, 6.25) with width
8.0 and height 7.5

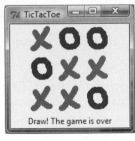

FIGURE 12.16 Points are enclosed inside a rectangle.

Sections 12.7–12.11

**12.5 (*Game: Tic-tac-toe*) Write a program that plays the tic-tac-toe game. Two players take turns clicking an available cell in a 3 × 3 grid with their respective tokens (either X or O). When one player has placed three tokens in a horizontal, vertical, or diagonal row on the grid, the game is over and that player has won. A draw (no winner) occurs when all the cells in the grid have been filled with tokens and neither player has achieved a win. Figure 12.17 shows the representative sample runs of the example.

(a) The X player won the game

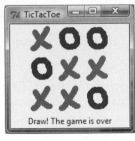

(b) Draw—no winners

(c) The O player won the game

FIGURE 12.17 Two players play a tic-tac-toe game.

Assume that all the cells are initially empty, and that the first player takes the X token and the second player the O token. To mark a cell, the player points the mouse to the cell and clicks it. If the cell is empty, the token (X or O) is displayed. If the cell is already filled, the player's action is ignored.

Define a custom class named **Cell** that extends **Label** for displaying a token and for responding to the button-click event. The class contains a data field token with three possible values—**' '**, **X**, and **O**—that denote whether the cell has been occupied and which token is used in the cell if it is occupied.

The three image files x.gif, o.gif, and empty.gif can be obtained from **cs.armstrong.edu/liang/py/book.zip** in the **image** folder. Use these three images to display the X, O, and empty cells.

12.6 (*Tkinter: two circles intersect?*) Using the **Circle2D class you defined in Exercise 8.18, write a program that enables the user to point the mouse inside a circle and drag it. As the circle is being dragged, the label displays whether two circles overlap, as shown in Figure 12.18.

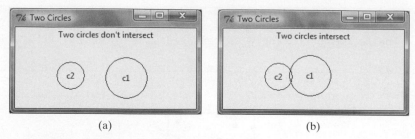

FIGURE 12.18 Check whether two circles are overlapping.

12.7 (*Tkinter: two rectangles intersect?*) Using the **Rectangle2D class you defined in Exercise 8.19, write a program that enables the user to point the mouse inside a rectangle and drag it. As the rectangle is being dragged, the label displays whether two rectangles overlap, as shown in Figure 12.19.

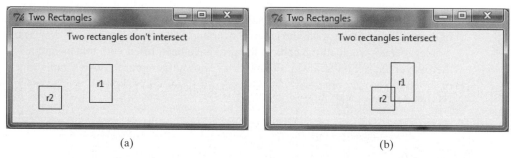

FIGURE 12.19 Check whether two rectangles are overlapping.

12.8 (*Tkinter: two circles intersect?*) Using the **Circle2D class you defined in Exercise 8.18, write a program that enables the user to specify the location and size of two circles and displays whether the circles intersect, as shown in Figure 12.20. Enable the user to point the mouse inside a circle and drag it. As a circle is being dragged, the program updates the circle's center coordinates and its radius in the text fields.

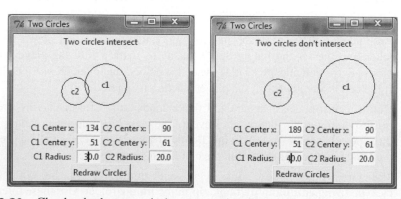

FIGURE 12.20 Check whether two circles are overlapping.

12.9 (*Tkinter: two rectangles intersect?*) Using the **Rectangle2D class you defined in Exercise 8.19, write a program that enables the user to specify the location and size of the rectangles and displays whether the two rectangles intersect, as shown in Figure 12.21. Enable the user to point the mouse inside a rectangle and drag it. As a rectangle is being dragged, the program updates the rectangle's center coordinates, width, and height in the text fields.

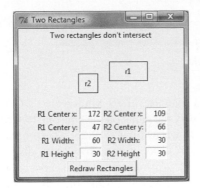
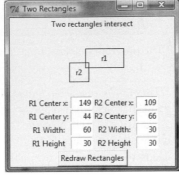

FIGURE 12.21 Check whether two rectangles are overlapping.

12.10 (*Tkinter: four cars*) Write a program that simulates four cars racing, as shown in Figure 12.22. You should define a subclass of **Canvas to display a car.

FIGURE 12.22 The program simulates four cars racing.

**12.11 (*Tkinter: guess birthday*) Listing 4.3, GuessBirthday.py, gives a program for guessing a birthday. Create a program for guessing birthdays as shown in Figure 12.23. The program prompts the user to check whether the date is in any of the five sets. The date is displayed in a message box upon clicking the *Guess Birthday* button.

*12.12 (*Tkinter: a group of clocks*) Write a program that displays four clocks, as shown in Figure 12.24.

FIGURE 12.23 This program guesses the birthdays.

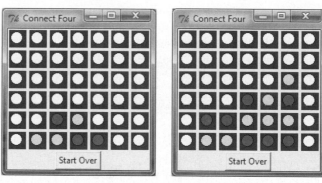

FIGURE 12.24 The program displays four clocks.

***12.13 (*Tkinter: Connect Four game*) In Exercise 11.20, you created a Connect Four game that enables two players to play the game on the console. Rewrite the program using a GUI program, as shown in Figure 12.25. The program enables two players to place red and yellow disks in turn. To place a disk, the player needs to click on an available cell. An *available cell* is unoccupied and its downward neighbor is occupied. The program flashes the four winning cells if a player wins, and reports no winners if all cells are occupied with no winners.

FIGURE 12.25 The program enables two players to play the Connect Four game.

**12.14 (*Tkinter: Mandelbrot fractal*) The Mandelbrot fractal is a well-known image created from a Mandelbrot set (see Figure 12.26a). A Mandelbrot set is defined using the following iteration:

$$z_{n+1} = z_n^2 + c$$

c is a complex number, and the starting point of the iteration is $z_0 = 0$. (For information on complex numbers, see Exercise 8.21.) For a given c, the iteration will produce a sequence of complex numbers: $[z_0, z_1, \ldots, z_n, \ldots]$. It can be shown that the sequence either tends to infinity or stays bounded, depending on the value of c. For example, if c is **0**, the sequence is $[0, 0, \ldots]$, which is bounded. If c is i, the sequence is $[0, i, -1 + i, -i, -1 + i, i, \ldots]$, which is bounded. If c is $1 + i$, the sequence is $[0, 1 + i, 1 + 3i, \ldots]$, which is unbounded. It is known that if the absolute value of a complex value z_i in the sequence is greater than **2**, then the sequence is unbounded. The Mandelbrot set consists of the c value such that the sequence is bounded. For example, **0** and i are in the Mandelbrot set. A Mandelbrot image can be created using the following code:

```
1  COUNT_LIMIT = 60
2
3  # Paint a Mandelbrot image in the canvas
```

```
 4  def paint():
 5      x = -2.0
 6      while x < 2.0:
 7          y = -2.0
 8          while y < 2.0:
 9              c = count(complex(x, y))
10              if c == COUNT_LIMIT:
11                  color = "red" # c is in a Mandelbrot set
12              else:
13                  # get hex value RRGGBB that is dependent on c
14                  color = "#RRGGBB"
15
16              # Fill a tiny rectangle with the specified color
17              canvas.create_rectangle(x * 100 + 200, y * 100 + 200,
18                  x * 100 + 200 + 5, y * 100 + 200 + 5, fill = color)
19              y += 0.05
20          x += 0.05
21
22  # Return the iteration count
23  def count(c):
24      z = complex(0, 0) # z0
25
26      for i in range(COUNT_LIMIT):
27          z = z * z + c # Get z1, z2, ...
28          if abs(z) > 2: return i # The sequence is unbounded
29
30      return COUNT_LIMIT # Indicate a bounded sequence
```

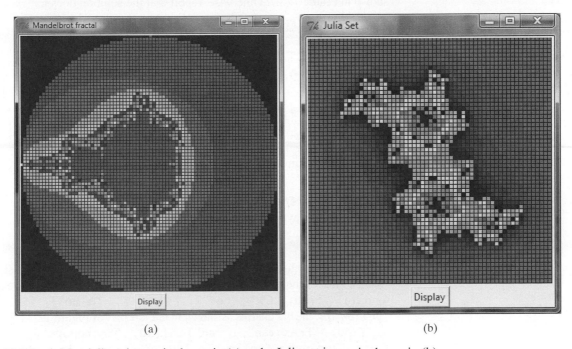

FIGURE 12.26   A Mandelbrot image is shown in (a) and a Julia set image is shown in (b).

The **count(c)** function (lines 23–28) computes $z_1, z_2, \ldots, z_{60}$. If none of their absolute values exceeds **2**, we assume **c** is in the Mandelbrot set. Of course, there could always be an error, but **60** (**COUNT_LIMIT**) iterations usually are enough. Once we find that the sequence is unbounded, the method returns the iteration count (line 28). The method returns **COUNT_LIMIT** if the sequence is bounded (line 30).

The loop in lines 6–20 examines each point (x, y) for $-2 < x < 2$ and $-2 < y < 2$ with interval 0.01 to see if its corresponding complex number $c = x + yi$ is in the Mandelbrot set (line 9). If so, paint the point red (line 11). If not, set a color that is dependent on its iteration count (line 14). Note that the point is painted in a square with width **5** and height **5**. All the points are scaled and mapped to a grid of 400×400 pixels (lines 17–18).

Complete the program to draw a Mandelbrot image, as shown in Figure 12.26a.

12.15 (*Tkinter: Julia set*) The preceding exercise describes Mandelbrot sets. The Mandelbrot set consists of the complex c value such that the sequence $z_{n+1} = z_n^2 + c$ is bounded with z_0 fixed and c varying. If we fix c and vary $z_0 (= x + yi)$, the point (x, y) is said to be in a *Julia set* for a fixed complex value c if the function $z_{n+1} = z_n^2 + c$ stays bounded. Write a program that draws a Julia set as shown in Figure 12.26b. Note that you only need to revise the **count method in Exercise 12.14 by using a fixed c value $(-0.3 + 0.6i)$.

*12.16 (*Implement* **Stack** *using inheritance*) In Listing 12.13, the **Stack** class is implemented using composition. Define a new **Stack** class using inheritance that extends **list**.

Draw UML diagrams of the new class. Implement it. Write a test program that prompts the user to enter five strings and displays them in reverse order.

***12.17 (*Tkinter: the 24-point card game*) Enhance Exercise 10.37 to enable the computer to display the expression for a 24-point game solution if one exists, as shown in Figure 12.27. Otherwise, report that the solution does not exist.

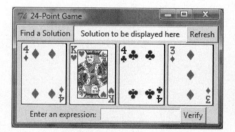 

FIGURE 12.27 The program can automatically find a solution if one exists.

12.18 (*Tkinter: the* **BarChart *class*) Develop a class named **BarChart** that extends **Canvas** for displaying a bar chart:

```
BarChart(parent, data, width = 400, height = 300)
```

Where **data** is a list, each element in the list is a nested list that consists of a value, a title for the value, and a color for the bar in the bar chart. For example, for **data = [[40, "CS", "red"], [30, "IS", "blue"], [50, "IT", "yellow"]]**, the bar chart is as shown in the left part of Figure 12.28. For **data = [[140, "Freshman", "red"], [130, "Sophomore", "blue"], [150, "Junior", "yellow"], [80, "Senior", "green"]]**, the bar chart is as shown in the right part of Figure 12.28. Write a test program that displays two bar charts, as shown in Figure 12.28.

12.19 (*Tkinter: the* **PieChart *class*) Develop a class named **PieChart** that extends **Canvas** for displaying a pie chart using the following constructor:

```
PieChart(parent, data, width = 400, height = 300)
```

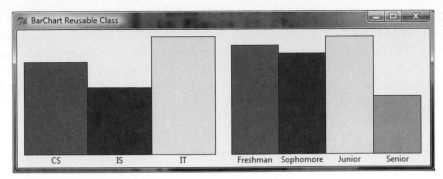

FIGURE 12.28   The program uses the **BarChart** class to display bar charts.

Where **data** is a list, each element in the list is a nested list that consists of a value, a title for the value, and a color for the wedge in the pie chart. For example, for **data = [[40, "CS", "red"], [30, "IS", "blue"], [50, "IT", "yellow"]]**, the pie chart is as shown in the left part of Figure 12.29. For **data = [[140, "Freshman", "red"], [130, "Sophomore", "blue"], [150, "Junior", "yellow"], [80, "Senior", "green"]]**, the pie chart is as shown in the right part of Figure 12.29. Write a test program that displays two pie charts, as shown in Figure 12.29.

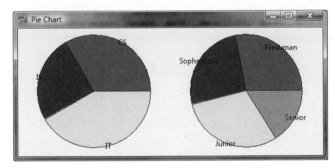

FIGURE 12.29   The program uses the **PieChart** class to display pie charts.

12.20   (*Tkinter: The RegularPolygonCanvas Class*) Define a subclass of **Canvas, named **RegularPolygonCanvas**, to paint an *n*-sided regular polygon. The class contains a property named **numberOfSides**, which specifies the number of sides in the polygon. The polygon is centered in the canvas, and the polygon's size is proportional to the size of the canvas. Create a triangle, square, pentagon, hexagon, heptagon, and octagon from **RegularPolygonCanvas** and display them, as shown in Figure 12.30.

FIGURE 12.30   The program displays several *n*-sided polygons.

*12.21 (*Tkinter:* *display an n-sided regular polygon*) In Exercise 12.20 you created the **RegularPolygonCanvas** subclass for displaying an *n*-sided regular polygon. Write a program that displays a regular polygon and uses two buttons named +1 and −1 to increase or decrease the size of the polygon, as shown in Figure 12.31a–b. Also enable the user to increase or decrease the size by clicking the right or left mouse button and by pressing the *UP* and *DOWN* arrow keys.

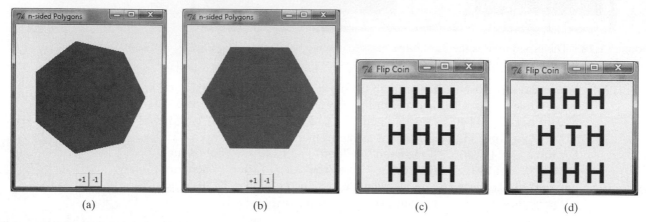

(a) (b) (c) (d)

FIGURE 12.31 (a–b) Clicking the +1 or −1 button increases or decreases the number of sides of a regular polygon. (c–d) The program enables the user to click a cell to flip a coin.

*12.22 (*Flip coins*) Write a program that displays heads (**H**) or tails (**T**) for each of nine coins, as shown in Figure 12.31c–d. When a cell is clicked, the coin is flipped. Write a custom cell class that extends **Label**. In the initializer of the class, bind the event **<Button-1>** with the method for flipping the coin. When the program starts, all cells initially display **H**.

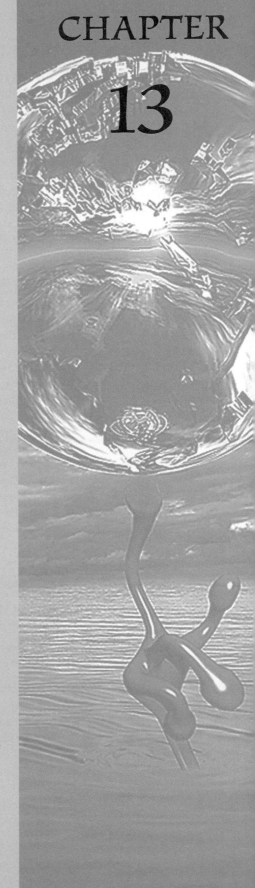

CHAPTER

13

FILES AND EXCEPTION HANDLING

Objectives

- To open a file using the **open** function for reading and writing data (§13.2.1).

- To write data to a file using the **write** method in a file object (§13.2.2).

- To test the existence of a file using the **os.path.isfile** function (§13.2.3).

- To read data from a file using the **read**, **readline**, and **readlines** methods in a file object (§§13.2.4–13.2.5).

- To append data to a file by opening the file in the append mode (§13.2.6).

- To read and write numeric data (§13.2.7).

- To display open and save file dialogs for getting file names for reading and writing data (§13.3).

- To develop applications with files (§13.4).

- To read data from a Web resource (§13.5).

- To handle exceptions by using the **try**, **except**, and **finally** clauses (§13.6).

- To raise exceptions by using the **raise** statements (§13.7).

- To become familiar with Python's built-in exception classes (§13.8).

- To access an exception object in the handler (§13.8).

- To define custom exception classes (§13.9).

- To perform binary IO using the **load** and **dump** functions in the **pickle** module (§13.10).

- To create an address book using binary IO (§13.11).

13.1 Introduction

Key Point

You can use a file to store data permanently; you can use exception handling to make your programs reliable and robust.

why files?

Data used in a program is temporary; unless the data is specifically saved, it is lost when the program terminates. To permanently store the data created in a program, you need to save it in a file on a disk or some other permanent storage device. The file can be transported and can be read later by other programs. In this chapter, you learn how to read and write data from and to a file.

why exception handling?

What happens if your program tries to read data from a file but the file does not exist? Your program will be abruptly terminated. In this chapter you will learn how to write the program to handle this exception so the program can continue to execute.

13.2 Text Input and Output

Key Point

*To read and write data from or to a file, use the **open** function to create a file object and use the object's **read** and **write** methods to read and write data.*

absolute filename

A file is placed in a directory in the file system. An *absolute filename* contains a filename with its complete path and drive letter. For example, **c:\pybook\Scores.txt** is the absolute filename for the file **Scores.txt** on the Windows operating system. Here, **c:\pybook** is referred to as the

directory path

directory path to the file. Absolute filenames are machine dependent. On the UNIX platform, the absolute filename may be **/home/liang/pybook/Scores.txt**, where **/home/liang/pybook** is the directory path to the file **Scores.txt**.

relative filename

A relative filename is relative to its current working directory. The complete directory path for a relative file name is omitted. For example, **Scores.py** is a relative filename. If its current working directory is **c:\pybook**, the absolute filename would be **c:\pybook\Scores.py**.

Files can be classified into text or binary files. A file that can be processed (that is, read,

text file

created, or modified) using a text editor such as Notepad on Windows or vi on UNIX is called

binary file

a *text file*. All the other files are called *binary files*. For example, Python source programs are stored in text files and can be processed by a text editor, but Microsoft Word files are stored in binary files and are processed by the Microsoft Word program.

Although it is not technically precise and correct, you can envision a text file as consisting of a sequence of characters and a binary file as consisting of a sequence of bits. Characters in a text file are encoded using a character encoding scheme such as ASCII and Unicode. For example, the decimal integer **199** is stored as the sequence of the three characters **1**, **9**, and **9**,

why binary file?

in a text file, and the same integer is stored as a byte-type value **C7** in a binary file, because decimal **199** equals hex **C7** ($199 = 12 \times 16^1 + 7$). The advantage of binary files is that they are more efficient to process than text files.

> **Note**
> Computers do not differentiate between binary files and text files. All files are stored in binary format, and thus all files are essentially binary files. Text IO (input and output) is built upon binary IO to provide a level of abstraction for character encoding and decoding.

This section shows you how to read and write strings from and to a text file. Binary files are introduced in Section 13.10.

13.2.1 Opening a File

How do you write data to a file and read the data back from a file? You need to first create a file object that is associated with a physical file. This is called *opening a file*. The syntax for opening a file is:

```
fileVariable = open(filename, mode)
```

The **open** function returns a file object for *filename*. The **mode** parameter is a string that specifies how the file will be used (for reading or writing), as shown in Table 13.1.

TABLE 13.1 File Modes

Mode	Description
`"r"`	Opens a file for reading.
`"w"`	Opens a new file for writing. If the file already exists, its old contents are destroyed.
`"a"`	Opens a file for appending data from the end of the file.
`"rb"`	Opens a file for reading binary data.
`"wb"`	Opens a file for writing binary data.

For example, the following statement opens a file named **Scores.txt** in the current directory for reading:

```
input = open("Scores.txt", "r")
```

You can also use the absolute filename to open the file in Windows, as follows:

```
input = open(r"c:\pybook\Scores.txt", "r")
```

The statement opens the file **Scores.txt** that is in the **c:\pybook** directory for reading. The **r** prefix before the absolute filename specifies that the string is a *raw string*, which causes the Python interpreter to treat backslash characters as literal backslashes. Without the **r** prefix, you would have to write the statement using an escape sequence as:

```
input = open("c:\\pybook\\Scores.txt", "r")
```

raw string

13.2.2 Writing Data

The **open** function creates a file object, which is an instance of the **_io.TextIOWrapper** class. This class contains the methods for reading and writing data and for closing the file, as shown in Figure 13.1.

_io.TextIOWrapper	
read([number.int]): str	Returns the specified number of characters from the file. If the argument is omitted, the entire remaining contents in the file are read.
readline(): str	Returns the next line of the file as a string.
readlines(): list	Returns a list of the remaining lines in the file.
write(s: str): None	Writes the string to the file.
close(): None	Closes the file.

FIGURE 13.1 A file object contains the methods for reading and writing data.

After a file is opened for writing data, you can use the **write** method to write a string to the file. In Listing 13.1, the program writes three strings to the file Presidents.txt.

LISTING 13.1 WriteDemo.py

```
1  def main():
2      # Open file for output
3      outfile = open("Presidents.txt", "w")
```

open file for writing

```
      4
      5        # Write data to the file
      6        outfile.write("Bill Clinton\n")
      7        outfile.write("George Bush\n")
      8        outfile.write("Barack Obama")
      9
     10        outfile.close() # Close the output file
     11
     12   main() # Call the main function
```

write data *(margin note at line 6)*

close file *(margin note at line 10)*

The program opens a file named **Presidents.txt** using the **w** mode for writing data (line 3). If the file does not exist, the **open** function creates a new file. If the file already exists, the contents of the file will be overwritten with new data. You can now write data to the file.

file pointer *(margin note)*

When a file is opened for writing or reading, a special marker called a *file pointer* is positioned internally in the file. A read or write operation takes place at the pointer's location. When a file is opened, the file pointer is set at the beginning of the file. When you read or write data to the file, the file pointer moves forward.

The program invokes the **write** method on the file object to write three strings (lines 6–8). Figure 13.2 shows the position of the file pointer after each write.

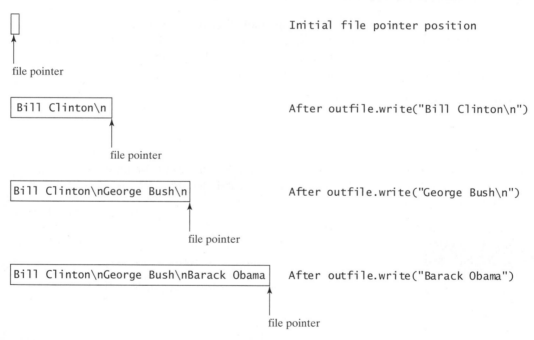

Initial file pointer position

file pointer

Bill Clinton\n   After outfile.write("Bill Clinton\n")

file pointer

Bill Clinton\nGeorge Bush\n   After outfile.write("George Bush\n")

file pointer

Bill Clinton\nGeorge Bush\nBarack Obama   After outfile.write("Barack Obama")

file pointer

Figure 13.2 Three strings are written to the file.

The program closes the file to ensure that data is written to the file (line 10). After this program is executed, three names are written to the file. You can view the file in a text editor, as shown in Figure 13.3.

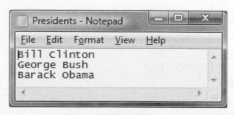

Figure 13.3 A file named Presidents.txt contains three names.

Note

When you invoke **print(str)**, the function automatically inserts the newline character **\n** after displaying the string. However, the **write** function does not automatically insert the newline character. You have to explicitly write the newline character to the file.

Warning

If you open an existing file for writing, the original contents of the file will be destroyed/overwritten with the new text.

13.2.3   Testing a File's Existence

To prevent the data in an existing file from being erased by accident, you should test to see if the file exists before opening it for writing. The **isfile** function in the **os.path** module can be used to determine whether a file exists. For example:

```
import os.path
if os.path.isfile("Presidents.txt"):
    print("Presidents.txt exists")
```

Here **isfile("Presidents.txt")** returns **True** if the file Presidents.txt exists in the current directory.

13.2.4   Reading Data

VideoNote

Process text file

After a file is opened for reading data, you can use the **read** method to read a specified number of characters or all characters from the file and return them as a string, the **readline()** method to read the next line, and the **readlines()** method to read all the lines into a list of strings.

   Suppose the file Presidents.txt contains the three lines shown in Figure 13.3. The program in Listing 13.2 reads the data from the file.

LISTING 13.2   ReadDemo.py

```
 1  def main():
 2      # Open file for input
 3      infile = open("Presidents.txt", "r")
 4      print("(1) Using read(): ")
 5      print(infile.read())
 6      infile.close() # Close the input file
 7
 8      # Open file for input
 9      infile = open("Presidents.txt", "r")
10      print("\n(2) Using read(number): ")
11      s1 = infile.read(4)
12      print(s1)
13      s2 = infile.read(10)
14      print(repr(s2))
15      infile.close() # Close the input file
16
17      # Open file for input
18      infile = open("Presidents.txt", "r")
19      print("\n(3) Using readline(): ")
20      line1 = infile.readline()
21      line2 = infile.readline()
22      line3 = infile.readline()
23      line4 = infile.readline()
24      print(repr(line1))
25      print(repr(line2))
26      print(repr(line3))
27      print(repr(line4))
28      infile.close() # Close the input file
```

open file for reading

read all data
close file

open file for reading

read characters

read characters
raw string

read a line

read all lines

```
29
30      # Open file for input
31      infile = open("Presidents.txt", "r")
32      print("\n(4) Using readlines(): ")
33      print(infile.readlines())
34      infile.close() # Close the input file
35
36  main() # Call the main function
```

```
(1) Using read():
Bill Clinton
George Bush
Barack Obama

(2) Using read(number):
Bill
' Clinton\nG'

(3) Using readline():
'Bill Clinton\n'
'George Bush\n'
'Barack Obama'
''

(4) Using readlines():
['Bill Clinton\n', 'George Bush\n', 'Barack Obama']
```

using read()

The program first opens the file Presidents.txt using the **r** mode for reading through the file object **infile** (line 3). Invoking the **infile.read()** method reads all characters from the file and returns them as a string (line 5). The file is closed (line 6).

using read(number)

The file is reopened for reading (line 9). The program uses the **read(number)** method to read the specified number of characters from the file. Invoking **infile.read(4)** reads **4** characters (line 11) and **infile.read(10)** reads **10** characters (line 13). The **repr(s)** function returns a raw string for **s**, which causes the escape sequence to be displayed as literals, as shown in the output.

repr function

Figure 13.4 shows the file pointer's position after each read.

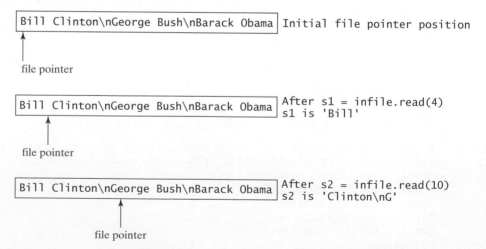

FIGURE 13.4 The file pointer moves forward as characters are read from the file.

using readline()

The file is closed (line 15) and reopened for reading (line 18). The program uses the **readline()** method to read a line (line 20). Invoking **infile.readline()** reads a line that ends with **\n**. All characters in a line are read including the **\n**. When the file pointer is positioned at the end of the file, invoking **readline()** or **read()** returns an empty string **''**.

Figure 13.5 shows the file pointer's position after each **readline** method is called.

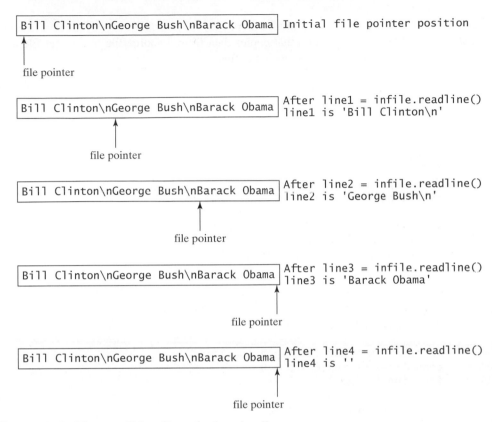

FIGURE 13.5 The **readline()** method reads a line.

The file is closed (line 28) and reopened for reading (line 31). The program uses the **readlines()** method to read all lines and return a list of strings. Each string corresponds to a line in the file.

using readlines()

13.2.5 Reading All Data from a File

Programs often need to read all data from a file. Here are two common approaches to accomplishing this task:

1. Use the **read()** method to read all data from the file and return it as one string.

2. Use the **readlines()** method to read all data and return it as a list of strings.

These two approaches are simple and appropriate for small files, but what happens if the file is so large that its contents cannot be stored in the memory? You can write the following loop to read one line at a time, process it, and continue reading the next line until it reaches the end of the file:

```
line = infile.readline() # Read a line
while line != '':
    # Process the line here ...
    # Read next line
    line = infile.readline()
```

Note that when the program reaches the end of the file, **readline()** returns **''**.

Python also lets you read all lines by using a **for** loop, as follows:

```
for line in infile:
    # Process the line here ...
```

This is much simpler than using a **while** loop.

Listing 13.3 illustrates a program that copies data from a source file to a target file and counts the number of lines and characters in the file.

LISTING 13.3 CopyFile.py

| | ```
1   import os.path
2   import sys
3
4   def main():
5       # Prompt the user to enter filenames
6       f1 = input("Enter a source file: ").strip()
7       f2 = input("Enter a target file: ").strip()
8
9       # Check if target file exists
10      if os.path.isfile(f2):
11          print(f2 + " already exists")
12          sys.exit()
13
14      # Open files for input and output
15      infile = open(f1, "r")
16      outfile = open(f2, "w")
17
18      # Copy from input file to output file
19      countLines = countChars = 0
20      for line in infile:
21          countLines += 1
22          countChars += len(line)
23          outfile.write(line)
24      print(countLines, "lines and", countChars, "chars copied")
25
26      infile.close()  # Close the input file
27      outfile.close() # Close the output file
28
29  main() # Call the main function
``` |

Margin notes (left column):
input file
output file

check file existence

open file for input
open file for output

initialize countLines and
  countChars
read a line
increase countLines
increase countChars
write a line

close input file
close output file

```
Enter a source file: input.txt  ↵Enter
Enter a target file: output1.txt  ↵Enter
output1.txt already exists
```

```
Enter a source file: input.txt  ↵Enter
Enter a target file: output2.txt  ↵Enter
3 lines and 73 characters copied
```

The program prompts the user to enter a source file **f1** and a target file **f2** (lines 6–7) and determines whether **f2** already exists (lines 10–12). If so, the program displays a message that the file already exists (line 11) and exits (line 12). If the file doesn't already exist, the program opens file **f1** for input and **f2** for output (lines 15–16). It then uses a **for** loop to read each line from file **f1** and write each line into file **f2** (lines 20–23). The program tracks the number
```

of lines and characters read from the file (lines 21–22). To ensure that the files are processed properly, you need to close the files after they are processed (lines 26–27).

13.2.6 Appending Data

You can use the **a** mode to open a file for appending data to the end of an existing file. Listing 13.4 gives an example of appending two new lines into a file named **Info.txt**.

LISTING 13.4 AppendDemo.py

```
1  def main():
2      # Open file for appending data
3      outfile = open("Info.txt", "a")          open file for appending
4      outfile.write("\nPython is interpreted\n")  write data
5      outfile.close() # Close the file          close file
6
7  main() # Call the main function
```

The program opens a file named Info.txt using the **a** mode for appending data to the file through the file object **outfile** (line 3). Assume the existing file contains the text "Programming is fun." Figure 13.6 shows the position of the file pointer after the file is opened and after each write. When the file is opened, the file pointer is positioned at the end of the file.

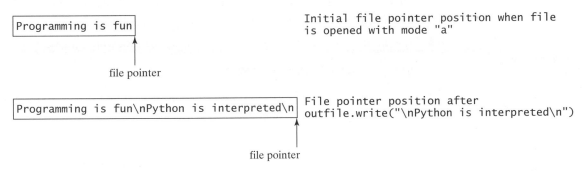

FIGURE 13.6 The data is appended to the file.

The program closes the file to ensure that the data is properly written to the file (line 5).

13.2.7 Writing and Reading Numeric Data

To write numbers to a file, you must first convert them into strings and then use the **write** method to write them to the file. In order to read the numbers back correctly, separate them with whitespace characters, such as **" "** or **\n**.

In Listing 13.5, the program writes ten random single digits to a file and reads them back from the file.

LISTING 13.5 WriteReadNumbers.py

```
1  from random import randint
2
3  def main():
4      # Open file for writing data
5      outfile = open("Numbers.txt", "w")        open file for writing
6      for i in range(10):
7          outfile.write(str(randint(0, 9)) + " ")  write data
```

close file

```
 8        outfile.close() # Close the file
 9
10        # Open file for reading data
```
open file for reading
```
11        infile = open("Numbers.txt", "r")
12        s = infile.read()
```
convert to numbers
```
13        numbers = [eval(x) for x in s.split()]
14        for number in numbers:
15            print(number, end = " ")
```
close file
```
16        infile.close() # Close the file
17
18   main() # Call the main function
```

```
8 1 4 1 2 5 5 1 3 2
```

The program opens a file named **Numbers.txt** using the **w** mode for writing data to that file using the file object **outfile** (line 5). The **for** loop writes ten numbers into the file, separated by spaces (lines 6–7). Note that the numbers are converted to strings before being written to the file.

The program closes the output file (line 8) and reopens it using the **r** mode for reading data through the file object **infile** (line 11). The **read()** method reads all data as a string (line 12). Since the numbers are separated by spaces, the string's **split** method splits the string into a list (line 13). The numbers are obtained from the list and displayed (lines 14–15).

13.1   How do you open a file for reading, for writing, and for appending, respectively?

13.2   What is wrong about creating a file object using the following statement?

```
infile = open("c:\book\test.txt", "r")
```

13.3   When you open a file for reading, what happens if the file does not exist? When you open a file for writing, what happens if the file already exists?

13.4   How do you determine whether a file exists?

13.5   What method do you use to read 30 characters from a file?

13.6   What method do you use to read all data into a string?

13.7   What method do you use to read a line?

13.8   What method do you use to read all lines into a list?

13.9   Will your program have a runtime error if you invoke **read()** or **readline()** at the end of the file?

13.10   When reading data, how do you know if it is the end of the file?

13.11   What function do you use to write data to a file?

13.12   How do you denote a raw string literal in the program?

13.13   How do you write and read numeric data?

13.3 File Dialogs

The **tkinter.filedialog** *module contains the functions* **askopenfilename** *and* **asksaveasfilename** *for displaying the file Open and Save As dialog boxes.*

Tkinter provides the **tkinter.filedialog** module with the following two functions:

```
# Display a file dialog box for opening an existing file
filename = askopenfilename()
```

```
# Display a file dialog box for specifying a file for saving data
filename = asksaveasfilename()
```

Both functions return a filename. If the dialog is cancelled by the user, the function returns **None**. Here is an example of using these two functions:

```
1   from tkinter.filedialog import askopenfilename
2   from tkinter.filedialog import asksaveasfilename
3
4   filenameforReading = askopenfilename()                         file dialog for opening
5   print("You can read from " + filenameforReading)
6
7   filenameforWriting = asksaveasfilename()                       file dialog for saving
8   print("You can write data to " + filenameforWriting)
```

When you run this code, the **askopenfilename()** function displays the Open dialog box for specifying a file to open, as shown in Figure 13.7a. The **asksaveasfilename()** function displays the Save As dialog for specifying the name of the file to save, as shown in Figure 13.7b.

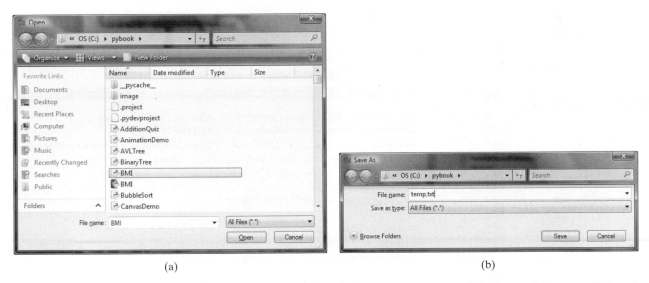

(a)   (b)

FIGURE 13.7   The **askopenfilename()** function displays the Open dialog (a) and the **asksaveasfilename()** function displays the Save As dialog (b).

Now let's create a simple text editor that uses menus, toolbar buttons, and file dialogs, as shown in Figure 13.8. The editor enables the user to open and save text files. Listing 13.6 shows the program.

LISTING 13.6   FileEditor.py

```
1   from tkinter import *
2   from tkinter.filedialog import askopenfilename                 import file dialogs
3   from tkinter.filedialog import asksaveasfilename
4
5   class FileEditor:
6       def __init__(self):
7           window = Tk()
8           window.title("Simple Text Editor")
```

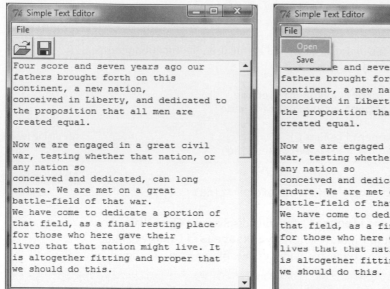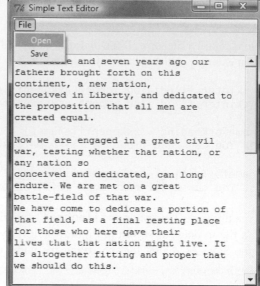

FIGURE 13.8 The editor enables you to open and save files from the File menu or from the toolbar.

	9
	10 `# Create a menu bar`
menu bar	11 `menubar = Menu(window)`
	12 `window.config(menu = menubar) # Display the menu bar`
	13
	14 `# Create a pull-down menu and add it to the menu bar`
	15 `operationMenu = Menu(menubar, tearoff = 0)`
add menu	16 `menubar.add_cascade(label = "File", menu = operationMenu)`
	17 `operationMenu.add_command(label = "Open",`
open file handler	18 `    command = self.openFile )`
	19 `operationMenu.add_command(label = "Save",`
save file handler	20 `    command = self.saveFile )`
	21
	22 `# Add a tool bar frame`
	23 `frame0 = Frame(window) # Create and add a frame to window`
	24 `frame0.grid(row = 1, column = 1, sticky = W)`
	25
	26 `# Create images`
	27 `openImage = PhotoImage(file = "image/open.gif")`
	28 `saveImage = PhotoImage(file = "image/save.gif")`
	29
toolbar buttons	30 `Button(frame0, image = openImage, command =`
	31 `    self.openFile).grid(row = 1, column = 1, sticky = W)`
	32 `Button(frame0, image = saveImage,`
	33 `    command = self.saveFile).grid(row = 1, column = 2)`
	34
	35 `frame1 = Frame(window) # Hold editor pane`
	36 `frame1.grid(row = 2, column = 1)`
	37
scrollbar	38 `scrollbar = Scrollbar(frame1)`
	39 `scrollbar.pack(side = RIGHT, fill = Y)`
text	40 `self.text = Text(frame1, width = 40, height = 20,`
	41 `    wrap = WORD, yscrollcommand = scrollbar.set)`
	42 `self.text.pack()`
handle scrolling	43 `scrollbar.config(command = self.text.yview)`
	44

```
45          window.mainloop() # Create an event loop
46
47      def openFile(self):                                          open file
48          filenameforReading = askopenfilename()
49          infile = open(filenameforReading, "r")
50          self.text.insert(END, infile.read()) # Read all from the file
51          infile.close()  # Close the input file
52
53      def saveFile(self):                                          save file
54          filenameforWriting = asksaveasfilename()
55          outfile = open(filenameforWriting, "w")
56          # Write to the file
57          outfile.write(self.text.get(1.0, END))
58          outfile.close() # Close the output file
59
60  FileEditor() # Create GUI                                         create GUI
```

The program creates the File menu (lines 15–20). The File menu contains the menu commands *Open* for loading a file (line 18) and *Save* for saving a file (line 20). When the *Open* menu is clicked, the **openFile** method (lines 47–51) is invoked to display the Open dialog to open a file using the **askopenfilename** function (line 48). After the user selects a file, the filename is returned and used to open the file for reading (line 49). The program reads the data from the file and inserts it into the **Text** widget (line 50).

When the *Save* menu is clicked, the **saveFile** method (lines 53–58) is invoked to display the Save As dialog to save a file using the **asksaveasfilename** function (line 54). After the user enters or selects a file, the filename is returned and used to open the file for writing (line 55). The program reads the data from the **Text** widget and writes it to the file (line 57).

The program also creates toolbar buttons (lines 30–33) and places them in a frame. The toolbar buttons are the buttons with image icons. When the *Open* toolbar button is clicked, the callback method **openFile** is invoked (line 31). When the *Save* toolbar button is clicked, the callback method **saveFile** is invoked (line 33).

The program creates a text area using the **Text** widget tied with a scroll bar (lines 38–43). The **Text** widget and scrollbar are placed inside **frame1**.

13.14 How do you display a file dialog for opening a file?

13.15 How do you display a file dialog for saving a file?

Check
Point

MyProgrammingLab™

13.4 Case Study: Counting Each Letter in a File

The problem in this case study is to write a program that prompts the user to enter a filename and counts the number of occurrences of each letter in the file regardless of case.

Key
Point

Here are the steps to solve this problem:

1. Read each line from the file as a string.

2. Use the string's **lower()** method to convert all the uppercase letters in the string to lowercase.

3. Create a list named **counts** that has **26 int** values, each of which counts the occurrences of a letter. That is, **counts[0]** counts the number of times **a** appears, **counts[1]** counts the number of **b**s, and so on.

4. For each character in the string, determine whether it is a lowercase letter. If so, increment the corresponding count in the list.

5. Finally, display the count.

Listing 13.7 shows the complete program.

LISTING 13.7 CountEachLetter.py

enter a filename
open file

create a list
read a line

count letters in line

display results

count letters
count a letter

```
1  def main():
2      filename = input("Enter a filename: ").strip()
3      infile = open(filename, "r") # Open the file
4
5      counts = 26 * [0] # Create and initialize counts
6      for line in infile:
7          # Invoke the countLetters function to count each letter
8          countLetters(line.lower(), counts)
9
10         # Display results
11     for i in range(len(counts)):
12         if counts[i] != 0:
13             print(chr(ord('a') + i) + " appears " + str(counts[i])
14                 + (" time" if counts[i] == 1 else " times"))
15
16     infile.close() # Close file
17
18 # Count each letter in the string
19 def countLetters(line, counts):
20     for ch in line:
21         if ch.isalpha() :
22             counts[ord(ch) - ord('a')] += 1
23
24 main() # Call the main function
```

```
Enter a filename: input.txt  ↵Enter
a appears 3 times
b appears 3 times
x appears 1 time
```

The main function prompts the user to enter a filename (line 2) and opens the file (line 3). It creates a list with **26** elements initialized to **0** (line 5). The **for** loop (lines 6–8) reads each line from the file, converts the letters to lowercase, and passes them to invoke **countLetters**.

The **countLetters(line, counts)** function examines each character in **line**. If it is a lowercase letter, the program adds **1** to its corresponding **counts** (lines 21–22).

After all the lines are processed, the program displays each letter contained in the file and its count, if the count is greater than **0** (lines 11–14).

13.5 Retrieving Data from the Web

Key Point

You can use the urlopen function to open a Uniform Resource Locator (URL) and read data from the Web.

Using Python, you can write simple code to read data from a Web site. All you need to do is to open a URL by using the **urlopen** function, as follows:

```
infile = urllib.request.urlopen("http://www.yahoo.com")
```

The **urlopen** function (defined in the **urllib.request** module) opens a URL resource like a file. Here is an example that reads and displays the Web content for a given URL:

```
import urllib.request
```

```
infile = urllib.request.urlopen("http://www.yahoo.com/index.html")
print(infile.read().decode())
```

The data read from the URL using **infile.read()** is raw data in bytes. Invoking the **decode()** method converts the raw data to a string.

Let's rewrite the program in Listing 13.7 to prompt the user to enter a file from a URL on the Internet rather than from a local system. The program is given in Listing 13.8.

LISTING 13.8   CountEachLetterURL.py

```
 1  import urllib.request
 2
 3  def main():
 4      url = input("Enter a URL for a file: ").strip()          enter a URL
 5      infile = urllib.request.urlopen(url)                      open a URL
 6      s = infile.read().decode() # Read the content as string   read data from URL
 7
 8      counts = countLetters(s.lower())                          count letters in line
 9
10      # Display results
11      for i in range(len(counts)):
12          if counts[i] != 0:
13              print(chr(ord('a') + i) + " appears " + str(counts[i])   display results
14                  + (" time" if counts[i] == 1 else " times"))
15
16  # Count each letter in the string
17  def countLetters(s):
18      counts = 26 * [0] # Create and initialize counts           count letters
19      for ch in s:
20          if ch.isalpha():
21              counts[ord(ch) - ord('a')] += 1                    count a letter
22      return counts
23
24  main() # Call the main function
```

```
Enter a filename: http://cs.armstrong.edu/liang/data/Lincoln.txt  ↵Enter
a appears 102 times
b appears 14 times
c appears 31 times
d appears 58 times
e appears 165 times
f appears 27 times
g appears 28 times
h appears 80 times
i appears 68 times
k appears 3 times
l appears 42 times
m appears 13 times
n appears 77 times
o appears 92 times
p appears 15 times
q appears 1 time
r appears 79 times
s appears 43 times
t appears 126 times
u appears 21 times
v appears 24 times
w appears 28 times
y appears 10 times
```

The main function prompts the user to enter a URL (line 4), opens the URL (line 5), and reads data from the URL into a string (line 6). The program converts the string to lowercase and invokes the **countLetters** function to count the occurrences of each letter in the string (line 8). The function returns a list showing how many times each letter occurs.

The **countLetters(s)** function creates a list of 26 elements with an initial value of **0** (line 18). The function examines each character in **s**. If it is a lowercase letter, the program adds **1** to its corresponding **counts** (lines 20–21).

Note

The **http://** prefix is required in the URL for the **urlopen** function to recognize a valid URL. It would be wrong if you enter a URL like this:

cs.armstrong.edu/liang/data/Lincoln.txt

Check
Point

MyProgrammingLab™

13.16 How do you open a Web page from a Python program?

13.17 What function can be used to return a raw string from a normal string?

13.6 Exception Handling

Key
Point

Exception handling enables a program to deal with exceptions and continue its normal execution.

why exception handling?

VideoNote

Handle exceptions

When running the programs in the preceding sections, what happens if the user enters a file or a URL that does not exist? The program would be aborted and raise an error. For example, if you try to run Listing 13.7 by entering a nonexistent filename, the program would report this **IOError**:

```
c:\pybook\python CountEachLetter.py
Enter a filename: NonexistentOrIncorrectFile.txt  ↵Enter
Traceback (most recent call last):
  File "C:\pybook\CountEachLetter.py", line 23, in <module>
    main()
  File "C:\pybook\CountEachLetter.py", line 4, in main
    infile = open(filename, "r") # Open the file
IOError: [Errno 22] Invalid argument: 'NonexistentOrIncorrectFile.txt\r'
```

traceback

The lengthy error message is called a *stack traceback* or *traceback*. The traceback gives information on the statement that caused the error by tracing back to the function calls that led to this statement. The line numbers of the function calls are displayed in the error message for tracing the errors.

An error that occurs at runtime is also called an *exception*. How can you deal with an exception so that the program can catch the error and prompt the user to enter a correct filename? This can be done using Python's exception handling syntax.

try ... except

The syntax for exception handling is to wrap the code that might raise (or throw) an exception in a **try** clause, as follows:

```
try:
    <body>
except <ExceptionType>:
    <handler>
```

Here, **<body>** contains the code that may raise an exception. When an exception occurs, the rest of the code in **<body>** is skipped. If the exception matches an exception type, the corresponding handler is executed. **<handler>** is the code that processes the exception. Now you can insert new code for exception handling into lines 2 and 3 in Listing 13.7 to let the user enter a new filename if the input is incorrect, as shown in Listing 13.9.

LISTING 13.9 CountEachLetterWithExceptionHandling.py

```
 1  def main():
 2      while True:
 3          try:
 4              filename = input("Enter a filename: ").strip()
 5              infile = open(filename, "r") # Open the file
 6              break
 7          except IOError:
 8              print("File " + filename + " does not exist. Try again")
 9
10      counts = 26 * [0] # Create and initialize counts
11      for line in infile:
12          # Invoke the countLetters function to count each letter
13          countLetters(line.lower(), counts)
14
15      # Display results
16      for i in range(len(counts)):
17          if counts[i] != 0:
18              print(chr(ord('a') + i) + " appears " + str(counts[i])
19                  + (" time" if counts[i] == 1 else " times"))
20
21      infile.close() # Close file
22
23  # Count each letter in the string
24  def countLetters(line, counts):
25      for ch in line:
26          if ch.isalpha():
27              counts[ord(ch) - ord('a')] += 1
28
29  main()
```

Annotations (right margin):
- try clause (line 3)
- enter a filename (line 4)
- open file (line 5)
- create a list (line 10)
- read a line (line 11)
- count letters in line (line 13)
- display results (line 18)
- count letters (line 24)
- count a letter (line 27)

Annotations (left margin): if an exception occurs (pointing from line 5 to line 7)

```
Enter a filename: NonexistentOrIncorrectFile  ↵Enter
File NonexistentOrIncorrectFile does not exist. Try again
Enter a filename: Lincoln.dat  ↵Enter
File Lincoln.dat does not exist. Try again
Enter a filename: Lincoln.txt  ↵Enter
a appears 102 times
b appears 14 times
...
...
w appears 28 times
y appears 10 times
```

The program uses a **while** loop to repeatedly prompt the user to enter a filename (lines 2–8). If the name is correct, the program exits the loop (line 6). If an **IOError** exception is raised by invoking the **open** function (line 5), the **except** clause is executed to process the exception (lines 7–8) and the loop continues.

The **try/except** block works as follows:

try ... except

- First, the statements in the body between **try** and **except** are executed.

- If no exception occurs, the **except** clause is skipped. In this case, the **break** statement is executed to exit the **while** loop.

- If an exception occurs during execution of the **try** clause, the rest of the clause is skipped. In this case, if the file does not exist, the **open** function raises an exception and the **break** statement is skipped.

- When an exception occurs, if the exception type matches the exception name after the **except** keyword, the **except** clause is executed, and then the execution continues after the **try** statement.

- If an exception occurs and it does not match the exception name in the **except** clause, the exception is passed on to the caller of this function; if no handler is found, it is an *unhandled exception* and execution stops with an error message displayed.

A **try** statement can have more than one **except** clause to handle different exceptions. The statement can also have an optional **else** and/or **finally** statement, in a syntax like this:

```
 1  try:
 2      <body>
 3  except <ExceptionType1>:
 4      <handler1>
 5  ...
 6  except <ExceptionTypeN>:
 7      <handlerN>
 8  except:
 9      <handlerExcept>
10  else:
11      <process_else>
12  finally:
13      <process_finally>
```

multiple excepts

The multiple **except**s are similar to **elif**s. When an exception occurs, it is checked to match an exception in an **except** clause after the **try** clause sequentially. If a match is found, the handler for the matching case is executed and the rest of the **except** clauses are skipped. Note that the **<ExceptionType>** in the last **except** clause may be omitted. If the exception does not match any of the exception types before the last **except** clause (line 8), the **<handlerExcept>** (line 9) for the last **except** clause is executed.

else

A **try** statement may have an optional **else** clause, which is executed if no exception is raised in the **try** body.

finally clause

A **try** statement may have an optional **finally** clause, which is intended to define cleanup actions that must be performed under all circumstances. Listing 13.10 gives an example of using exception handling.

LISTING 13.10   TestException.py

```
 1  def main():
 2      try:
 3          number1, number2 = eval(
 4              input("Enter two numbers, separated by a comma: "))
 5          result = number1 / number2
 6          print("Result is", result)
 7      except ZeroDivisionError:
 8          print("Division by zero!")
 9      except SyntaxError:
10          print("A comma may be missing in the input")
11      except:
12          print("Something wrong in the input")
13      else:
14          print("No exceptions")
15      finally:
```

enter two numbers

except ZeroDivisionError

except SyntaxError

except

else

finally

```
16          print("The finally clause is executed")
17
18  main() # Call the main function
```

```
Enter two numbers, separated by a comma: 3, 4  ↵Enter
Result is 0.75
No exceptions
The finally clause is executed
```

```
Enter two numbers, separated by a comma: 2, 0  ↵Enter
Division by zero!
The finally clause is executed
```

```
Enter two numbers, separated by a comma: 2 3  ↵Enter
A comma may be missing in the input
The finally clause is executed
```

```
Enter two numbers, separated by a comma: a, v  ↵Enter
Something wrong in the input
The finally clause is executed
```

When you enter **3, 4**, the program computes the division and displays the result, then the **else** clause is executed, and finally the **finally** clause is executed.

When you enter **2, 0**, a **ZeroDivisionError** is raised when executing the division (line 5). The **except** clause in line 7 caught this exception and processed it, and the **finally** clause is then executed.

When you enter **2 3**, a **SyntaxError** is raised. The **except** clause in line 9 caught this exception and processed it, and the **finally** clause is then executed.

When you enter **a, v**, an exception is raised. This exception is processed by the **except** clause in line 11, and the **finally** clause is then executed.

13.7 Raising Exceptions

Exceptions are wrapped in objects, and objects are created from classes. An exception is raised from a function.

Key Point

You learned how to write the code to handle exceptions in the preceding section. Where does an exception come from? How is an exception created? The information pertaining to an exception is wrapped in an object. An exception is raised from a function. When a function detects an error, it creates an object from an appropriate exception class and throws the exception to the caller of the function, using the following syntax:

```
raise ExceptionClass("Something is wrong")
```

Here's how this works. Suppose the program detects that an argument passed to a function violates the function's contract; for example, the argument must be nonnegative, but a negative argument is passed. The program can create an instance of **RuntimeError** and raise the exception, as follows:

```
ex = RuntimeError("Wrong argument")
raise ex
```

Or, if you prefer, you can combine the preceding two statements in one like this:

```
raise RuntimeError("Wrong argument")
```

You can now modify the **setRadius** method in the **Circle** class in Listing 12.2 to raise a **RuntimeError** exception if the radius is negative. The revised **Circle** class is given in Listing 13.11.

LISTING 13.11 CircleWithException.py

```
1  from GeometricObject import GeometricObject
2  import math
3
4  class Circle(GeometricObject):
5      def __init__(self, radius):
6          super().__init__()
7          self.setRadius(radius)
8
9      def getRadius(self):
10         return self.__radius
11
12     def setRadius(self, radius):
13         if radius < 0:
14             raise RuntimeError("Negative radius")
15         else:
16             self.__radius = radius
17
18     def getArea(self):
19         return self.__radius * self.__radius * math.pi
20
21     def getDiameter(self):
22         return 2 * self.__radius
23
24     def getPerimeter(self):
25         return 2 * self.__radius * math.pi
26
27     def printCircle(self):
28         print(self.__str__() + " radius: " + str(self.__radius))
```

Margin notes:
- import GeometricObject
- extend GeometricObject
- initialize radius
- raise exception
- set radius

The test program in Listing 13.12 creates circle objects using the new **Circle** class in Listing 13.11.

LISTING 13.12 TestCircleWithException.py

```
1  from CircleWithException import Circle
2
3  try:
4      c1 = Circle(5)
5      print("c1's area is", c1.getArea())
6      c2 = Circle(-5)
7      print("c2's area is", c2.getArea())
8      c3 = Circle(0)
9      print("c3's area is", c3.getArea())
10 except RuntimeException:
11     print("Invalid radius")
```

Margin notes:
- create a circle
- handle exception

```
c1's area is 78.53981633974483
Invalid radius
```

When attempting to create a **Circle** object with a negative radius (line 6), a **RuntimeError** is raised. The exception is caught in the **except** clause in lines 10–11.

Now you know how to raise exceptions and how to handle exceptions. So what are the benefits of using exception handling? It enables a function to throw an exception to its caller. The caller can handle this exception. Without this capability, the called function itself must handle the exception or terminate the program. Often the called function does not know what to do in case of an error. This is typically the case for library functions. The library function can detect the error, but only the caller knows what needs to be done when an error occurs. The essential benefit of exception handling is to separate the detection of an error (done in a called function) from the handling of an error (done in the calling method).

exception handling benefits

Many library functions raise exceptions, such as **ZeroDivisionError**, **TypeError**, and **IndexError**. You can use the **try-except** syntax to catch and process the exceptions.

Functions may invoke other functions in a chain of function calls. Consider an example involving multiple function calls. Suppose the **main** function invokes **function1**, **function1** invokes **function2**, **function2** invokes **function3**, and **function3** raises an exception, as shown in Figure 13.9. Consider the following scenario:

- If the exception type is **Exception3**, it is caught by the **except** block for handling this exception in **function2**. **statement5** is skipped, and **statement6** is executed.

- If the exception type is **Exception2**, **function2** is aborted, the control is returned to **function1**, and the exception is caught by the **except** block for handling **Exception2** in **function1**. **statement3** is skipped, and **statement4** is executed.

- If the exception type is **Exception1**, **function1** is aborted, the control is returned to the **main** function, and the exception is caught by the **except** block for handling **Exception1** in the **main** function. **statement1** is skipped, and **statement2** is executed.

- If the exception is not caught in **function2**, **function1**, or **main**, the program terminates, and **statement1** and **statement2** are not executed.

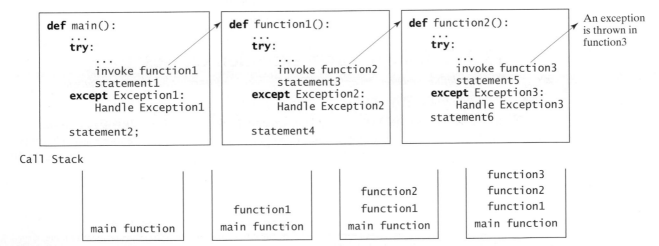

FIGURE 13.9 If an exception is not caught in the current function, it is passed to its caller. The process is repeated until the exception is caught or passed to the **main** function.

13.8 Processing Exceptions Using Exception Objects

Key Point

*You can access an exception object in the **except** clause.*

As stated earlier, an exception is wrapped in an object. To throw an exception, you first create an exception object and then use the **raise** keyword to throw it. Can this exception object be accessed from the **except** clause? Yes. You can use the following syntax to assign the exception object to a variable:

```
try
    <body>
except ExceptionType as ex:
    <handler>
```

With this syntax, when the **except** clause catches the exception, the exception object is assigned to a variable named **ex**. You can now use the object in the handler.

Listing 13.13 gives an example that prompts the user to enter a number and displays the number if the input is correct. Otherwise, the program displays an error message.

LISTING 13.13 ProcessExceptionObject.py

read a number
catch exception

```
1  try:
2      number = eval(input("Enter a number: "))
3      print("The number entered is", number)
4  except NameError as ex:
5      print("Exception:", ex)
```

```
Enter a number: 34  ↵Enter
The number entered is 34
```

```
Enter a number: one  ↵Enter
Exception: name 'one' is not defined
```

When you enter a nonnumeric value, an object of **NameError** is thrown from line 2. This object is assigned to variable **ex**. So, you can access it to handle the exception. The **__str__()** method in **ex** is invoked to return a string that describes the exception. In this case the string is **name 'one' is not defined**.

13.9 Defining Custom Exception Classes

Key Point

*You can define a custom exception class by extending **BaseException** or a subclass of **BaseException**.*

So far we have used Python's built-in exception classes such as **ZeroDivisionError**, **SyntaxError**, **RuntimeError**, and **NameError** in this chapter. Are there any other types of exceptions you can use? Yes, Python has many more built-in exceptions. Figure 13.10 shows some of them.

Note

The class names **Exception**, **StandardError**, and **RuntimeError** are somewhat confusing. All three of these classes are exceptions, and all of the errors occur at runtime.

The **BaseException** class is the root of exception classes. All Python exception classes inherit directly or indirectly from **BaseException**. As you can see, Python provides quite a

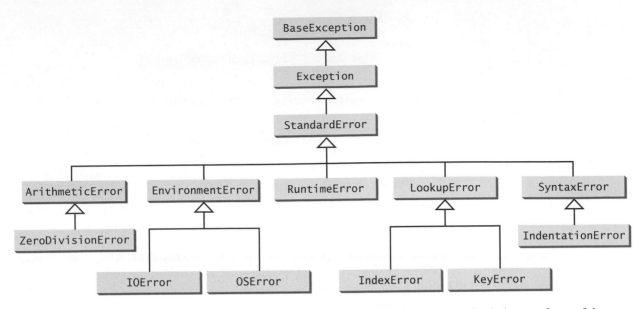

Figure 13.10 Exceptions raised are instances of the classes shown in this diagram, or of subclasses of one of these classes.

few exception classes. You can also define your own exception classes, derived from **BaseException** or from a subclass of **BaseException**, such as **RuntimeError**.

The **setRadius** method in the **Circle** class in Listing 13.11 throws a **RuntimeError** exception if the radius is negative. The caller can catch this exception, but the caller does not know what radius caused this exception. To fix this problem, you can define a custom exception class to store the radius, as shown in Listing 13.14.

LISTING 13.14 InvalidRadiusException.py

```
1  class InvalidRadiusException(RuntimeError):
2      def __init__(self, radius):
3          super().__init__()
4          self.radius = radius
```

extend RuntimeError

This custom exception class extends **RuntimeError** (line 1). The initializer simply invokes the superclass's initializer (line 3) and sets the radius in the data field (line 4).

Now let's modify the **setRadius(radius)** method in the **Circle** class to raise an **InvalidRadiusException** if the radius is negative, as shown in Listing 13.15.

LISTING 13.15 CircleWithCustomException.py

```
1  from GeometricObject import GeometricObject
2  from InvalidRadiusException import InvalidRadiusException
3  import math
4
5  class Circle(GeometricObject):
6      def __init__(self, radius):
7          super().__init__()
8          self.setRadius(radius)
9
10     def getRadius(self):
11         return self.__radius
12
13     def setRadius(self, radius):
```

import GeometricObject
import
  InvalidRadiusException

extend GeometricObject

initialize radius

setRadius

```
14              if radius >= 0:
15                  self.__radius = radius
16              else:
17                  raise InvalidRadiusException(radius)
18
19      def getArea(self):
20          return self.__radius * self.__radius * math.pi
21
22      def getDiameter(self):
23          return 2 * self.__radius
24
25      def getPerimeter(self):
26          return 2 * self.__radius * math.pi
27
28      def printCircle(self):
29          print(self.__str__(), "radius:", self.__radius)
```

The **setRadius** method raises an **InvalidRadiusException** if the radius is negative (line 17). Listing 13.16 gives a test program that creates circle objects using the new **Circle** class in Listing 13.15.

LISTING 13.16 TestCircleWithCustomException.py

```
1   from CircleWithCustomException import Circle
2   from InvalidRadiusException import InvalidRadiusException
3
4   try:
5       c1 = Circle(5)
6       print("c1's area is", c1.getArea())
7       c2 = Circle(-5)
8       print("c2's area is", c2.getArea())
9       c3 = Circle(0)
10      print("c3's area is", c3.getArea())
11  except InvalidRadiusException as ex:
12      print("The radius", ex.radius, "is invalid")
13  except Exception:
14      print("Something is wrong")
```

get radius

```
c1's area is 78.53981633974483
The radius -5 is invalid
```

When creating a **Circle** object with a negative radius (line 7), an **InvalidRadiusException** is raised. The exception is caught in the **except** clause in lines 11–12.

order of exception handlers

The order in which exceptions are specified in **except** blocks is important, because Python finds a handler in this order. If an **except** block for a superclass type appears before an **except** block for a subclass type, the **except** block for the subclass type will never be executed. Thus, it would be wrong to write the code as follows:

```
try:
    ....
except Exception:
    print("Something is wrong")
except InvalidRadiusException:
    print("Invalid radius")
```

13.18 Suppose that `statement2` causes an exception in the following `try-except` block:

```
try:
    statement1
    statement2
    statement3
except Exception1:
    # Handle exception 1
except Exception2:
    # Handle exception 2

statement4
```

Answer the following questions:

- Will `statement3` be executed?

- If the exception is not caught, will `statement4` be executed?

- If the exception is caught in the `except` block, will `statement4` be executed?

13.19 What is displayed when the following program is run?

```
try:
    list = 10 * [0]
    x = list[10]
    print("Done ")
except IndexError:
    print("Index out of bound")
```

13.20 What is displayed when the following program is run?

```
def main():
    try:
        f()
        print("After the function call")
    except ZeroDivisionError:
        print("Divided by zero!")
    except:
        print("Exception")

def f():
    print(1 / 0)

main() # Call the main function
```

13.21 What is displayed when the following program is run?

```
def main():
    try:
        f()
        print("After the function call")
    except IndexError:
        print("Index out of bound")
    except:
        print("Exception in main")

def f():
    try:
        s ="abc"
        print(s[3])
```

```
        except ZeroDivisionError:
            print("Divided by zero!")

main()  # Call the main function
```

13.22 Suppose that **statement2** causes an exception in the following statement:

```
try:
    statement1
    statement2
    statement3
except Exception1:
    # Handle exception
except Exception2:
    # Handle exception
except Exception3:
    # Handle exception
finally:
    statement4

statement5
```

Answer the following questions:

- Will **statement5** be executed if the exception is not caught?

- If the exception is of type **Exception3**, will **statement4** be executed, and will **statement5** be executed?

13.23 How do you raise an exception in a function?

13.24 What are the benefits of using exception handling?

13.25 What is displayed when the following program is run?

```
try:
    lst = 10 * [0]
    x = lst[9]
    print("Done")
except IndexError:
    print("Index out of bound")
else:
    print("Nothing is wrong")
finally:
    print("Finally we are here")

print("Continue")
```

13.26 What is displayed when the following program is run?

```
try:
    lst = 10 * [0]
    x = lst[10]
    print("Done ")
except IndexError:
    print("Index out of bound")
else:
    print("Nothing is wrong")
finally:
    print("Finally we are here")

print("Continue")
```

13.27 What is wrong in the following code?

```
try:
    # Some code here
    ...
except ArithmeticError:
    print("ArithmeticError")
except ZeroDivisionError:
    print("ZeroDivisionError")

print("Continue")
```

13.28 How do you define a custom exception class?

13.10 Binary IO Using Pickling

To perform binary IO using pickling, open a file using the mode **rb** *or* **wb** *for reading binary or writing binary and invoke the* **pickle** *module's* **dump** *and* **load** *functions to write and read data.*

Key Point

You can write strings and numbers to a file. Can you write any object such as a list directly to a file? Yes. This would require binary IO. There are many ways to perform binary IO in Python. This section introduces binary IO using the **dump** and **load** functions in the **pickle** module.

The Python **pickle** module implements the powerful and efficient algorithms for serializing and deserializing objects. *Serializing* is the process of converting an object into a stream of bytes that can be saved to a file or transmitted on a network. *Deserializing* is the opposite process that extracts an object from a stream of bytes. Serializing/deserializing is also known as *pickling/unpickling* or *dumping/loading* objects in Python.

pickle module
serializing
deserializing

13.10.1 Dumping and Loading Objects

As you know, all data in Python are objects. The **pickle** module enables you to write and read any data using the **dump** and **load** functions. Listing 13.17 demonstrates these functions.

LISTING 13.17 BinaryIODemo.py

```
1  import pickle
2
3  def main():
4      # Open file for writing binary
5      outfile = open("pickle.dat", "wb")
6      pickle.dump(45, outfile)
7      pickle.dump(56.6, outfile)
8      pickle.dump("Programming is fun", outfile)
9      pickle.dump([1, 2, 3, 4], outfile)
10     outfile.close() # Close the output file
11
12     # Open file for reading binary
13     infile = open("pickle.dat", "rb")
14     print(pickle.load(infile))
15     print(pickle.load(infile))
16     print(pickle.load(infile))
17     print(pickle.load(infile))
18     infile.close() # Close the input file
19
20  main() # Call the main function
```

open for binary write
dump an int
dump a float
dump a string
dump a list
close file

open for binary read
load an object

close file

```
45
56.6
Programming is fun
[1, 2, 3, 4]
```

To use pickle, you need to import the **pickle** module (line 1). To write objects to a file, open the file using the mode **wb** for writing binary (line 5) and use the **dump(object)** method to write the object into the file (lines 6–9). This method serializes the object into a stream of bytes and stores them in the file.

The program closes the file (line 10) and opens it for reading binary (line 13). The **load** method is used to read the objects (lines 14–17). This method reads a stream of bytes and deserializes them into an object.

13.10.2 Detecting the End of File

If you don't know how many objects are in the file, how do you read all the objects? You can repeatedly read an object using the **load** function until it throws an **EOFError** (end of file) exception. When this exception is raised, catch it and process it to end the file-reading process.

The program in Listing 13.18 stores an unspecified number of integers in a file by using object IO, and then it reads all the numbers back from the file.

LISTING 13.18 DetectEndOfFile.py

```
1  import pickle
2
3  def main():
4      # Open file for writing binary
5      outfile = open("numbers.dat", "wb")
6
7      data = eval(input("Enter an integer (the input exits " +
8          "if the input is 0): "))
9      while data != 0:
10         pickle.dump(data, outfile)
11         data = eval(input("Enter an integer (the input exits " +
12             "if the input is 0): "))
13
14     outfile.close() # Close the output file
15
16     # Open file for reading binary
17     infile = open("numbers.dat", "rb")
18
19     end_of_file = False
20     while not end_of_file:
21         try:
22             print(pickle.load(infile), end = " ")
23         except EOFError:
24             end_of_file = True
25
26     infile.close() # Close the input file
27
28     print("\nAll objects are read")
29
30 main() # Call the main function
```

Margin notes:
- open for binary write (line 5)
- dump an int (line 10)
- close file (line 14)
- open for binary read (line 17)
- load an object (line 22)
- handle exception (line 23)
- set end_of_file (line 24)

```
Enter an integer (the input exits if the input is 0): 4  ↵Enter
Enter an integer (the input exits if the input is 0): 5  ↵Enter
Enter an integer (the input exits if the input is 0): 7  ↵Enter
Enter an integer (the input exits if the input is 0): 9  ↵Enter
Enter an integer (the input exits if the input is 0): 0  ↵Enter
4 5 7 9
All objects are read
```

The program opens the file for writing binary (line 5) and repeatedly prompts the user to enter an integer and saves it to the file using the **dump** function (line 10) until the integer is **0**.

The program closes the file (line 14) and reopens it for reading binary (line 17). It repeatedly reads an object using the **load** function (line 22) in a **while** loop until an **EOFError** exception occurs. When an **EOFError** exception occurs, **end_of_file** is to set to **True**, which terminates the **while** loop (line 20).

As shown in the sample output, the user entered four integers and they are saved and then read back and displayed on the console.

13.29 How do you open a file for writing objects and reading objects?

13.30 How do you invoke the function to write an object and to read an object?

13.31 What is wrong if the code in lines 20–24 in Listing 13.18 is replaced by the following code?

```
while not end_of_file:
    try:
        print(pickle.load(infile), end = " ")
    except EOFError:
        end_of_file = True
    finally:
        infile.close() # Close the input file
```

13.32 Can you replace the code in lines 20–24 in Listing 13.18 with the following code?

```
try:
    while not end_of_file:
        print(pickle.load(infile), end = " ")
except EOFError:
    print("\nAll objects are read")
finally:
    infile.close() # Close the input file
```

✓ **Check Point**

MyProgrammingLab™

13.11 Case Study: Address Book

The problem in this case study is to create an address book using binary IO.

🔑 **Key Point**

Now we will use object IO to create a useful project for storing and viewing an address book. The user interface of the program is shown in Figure 13.11. The *Add* button stores a new

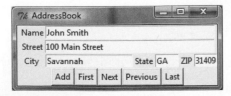

FIGURE 13.11 **AddressBook** stores and retrieves addresses from a file.

address at the end of the file. The *First*, *Next*, *Previous*, and *Last* buttons retrieve the first, next, previous, and last addresses from the file, respectively.

We will define a class named **Address** to represent an address and use a list to store all the addresses. When the *Add* button is clicked, the program creates an **Address** object with the name, street, city, state, and ZIP code collected from the user input, appends the object to the list, and stores the list to a file using binary IO. Assume that the file is named **address.dat**.

When the program is launched, it first reads the list from the file and displays the first address from the list in the user interface. If the file is empty, it displays empty entries. The program is given in Listing 13.19.

LISTING 13.19 AddressBook.py

```
1   import pickle
2   import os.path
3   from tkinter import * # Import all definitions from tkinter
4   import tkinter.messagebox
5
6   class Address:
7       def __init__(self, name, street, city, state, zip):
8           self.name = name
9           self.street = street
10          self.city = city
11          self.state = state
12          self.zip = zip
13
14   class AddressBook:
15       def __init__(self):
16           window = Tk() # Create a window
17           window.title("AddressBook") # Set title
18
19           self.nameVar = StringVar()
20           self.streetVar = StringVar()
21           self.cityVar = StringVar()
22           self.stateVar = StringVar()
23           self.zipVar = StringVar()
24
25           frame1 = Frame(window)
26           frame1.pack()
27           Label(frame1, text = "Name").grid(row = 1,
28               column = 1, sticky = W)
29           Entry(frame1, textvariable = self.nameVar,
30               width = 40).grid(row = 1, column = 2)
31
32           frame2 = Frame(window)
33           frame2.pack()
34           Label(frame2, text = "Street").grid(row = 1,
35               column = 1, sticky = W)
36           Entry(frame2, textvariable = self.streetVar,
37               width = 40).grid(row = 1, column = 2)
38
39           frame3 = Frame(window)
40           frame3.pack()
41           Label(frame3, text = "City", width = 5).grid(row = 1,
42               column = 1, sticky = W)
43           Entry(frame3,
44               textvariable = self.cityVar).grid(row = 1, column = 2)
45           Label(frame3, text = "State").grid(row = 1,
46               column = 3, sticky = W)
47           Entry(frame3, textvariable = self.stateVar,
```

Address class

entry variables

create UI

```
48              width = 5).grid(row = 1, column = 4)
49          Label(frame3, text = "ZIP").grid(row = 1,
50              column = 5, sticky = W)
51          Entry(frame3, textvariable = self.zipVar,
52              width = 5).grid(row = 1, column = 6)
53
54          frame4 = Frame(window)
55          frame4.pack()
56          Button(frame4, text = "Add",                          create buttons
57              command = self.processAdd).grid(row = 1, column = 1)
58          btFirst = Button(frame4, text = "First",
59              command = self.processFirst).grid(row = 1, column = 2)
60          btNext = Button(frame4, text = "Next",
61              command = self.processNext).grid(row = 1, column = 3)
62          btPrevious = Button(frame4, text = "Previous", command =
63              self.processPrevious).grid(row = 1, column = 4)
64          btLast = Button(frame4, text = "Last",
65              command = self.processLast).grid(row = 1, column = 5)
66
67          self.addressList = self.loadAddress()                 load addresses
68          self.current = 0                                      initialize current
69
70          if len(self.addressList) > 0:                         setAddress
71              self.setAddress()
72
73          window.mainloop() # Create an event loop
74
75      def saveAddress(self):                                    saveAddress
76          outfile = open("address.dat", "wb")
77          pickle.dump(self.addressList, outfile)                store list
78          tkinter.messagebox.showinfo(
79              "Address saved", "A new address is saved")
80          outfile.close()
81
82      def loadAddress(self):                                    loadAddress
83          if not os.path.isfile("address.dat"):
84              return [] # Return an empty list                  return empty list
85
86          try:
87              infile = open("address.dat", "rb")
88              addressList = pickle.load(infile)                 read list
89          except EOFError:
90              addressList = []
91
92          infile.close()
93          return addressList                                    return list
94
95      def processAdd(self):                                     processAdd
96          address = Address(self.nameVar.get(),                 create address
97              self.streetVar.get(), self.cityVar.get(),
98              self.stateVar.get(), self.zipVar.get())
99          self.addressList.append(address)                      append address
100         self.saveAddress()                                    store address list
101
102     def processFirst(self):                                   processFirst
103         self.current = 0                                      initialize current
104         self.setAddress()                                     set address
105
106     def processNext(self):                                    processNext
107         if self.current < len(self.addressList) - 1:
```

```
108                        self.current += 1
109                        self.setAddress()
110
processPrevious   111        def processPrevious(self):
                  112            print("Left as exercise")
                  113
processLast       114        def processLast(self):
                  115            print("Left as exercise")
                  116
setAddress        117        def setAddress(self):
                  118            self.nameVar.set(self.addressList[self.current].name)
                  119            self.streetVar.set(self.addressList[self.current].street)
                  120            self.cityVar.set(self.addressList[self.current].city)
                  121            self.stateVar.set(self.addressList[self.current].state)
                  122            self.zipVar.set(self.addressList[self.current].zip)
                  123
create GUI        124    AddressBook() # Create GUI
```

The **Address** class is defined with the __init__ method that creates an **Address** object with a name, street, city, state, and ZIP code (lines 6–12).

The __init__ method in **AddressBook** creates the user interface for displaying and processing addresses (lines 25–65). It reads the address list from the file (line 67) and sets the current index for the address in the list to **0** (line 68). If the address list is not empty, the program displays the first address (lines 70–71).

The **saveAddress** method writes the address list to the file (line 77) and displays a message dialog to alert the user that a new address has been added (lines 78–79).

The **loadAddress** method reads the address list to the file (line 88). If the file does not exist, the program returns an empty list (lines 83–84).

The **processAdd** method creates an **Address** object using the values from the entries. It appends the object to the list (line 99) and invokes the **saveAddress** method to store the newly updated list to the file (line 100).

The **processFirst** method resets **current** to **0**, which points to the first address in the address list (line 103). It then sets the address in the entries by invoking the **setAddress** method (line 104).

The **processNext** method moves **current** to point to the next address in the list (line 108) if **current** is not pointing to the last address in the list (line 107) and resets the address in the entries (line 109).

The **setAddress** method sets the address fields for the entries (lines 117–122). The methods **processPrevious** and **processLast** are left as an exercise.

KEY TERMS

absolute filename 440	raw string 441
binary file 440	relative filename 440
deserializing 465	serializing 465
directory path 440	text file 440
file pointer 442	traceback 454

CHAPTER SUMMARY

1. You can use file objects to read/write data from/to files. You can open a file to create a file object with mode **r** for reading, **w** for writing, and **a** for appending.

2. You can use the **os.path.isfile(f)** function to check if a file exists.

3. Python has a file class that contains the methods for reading and writing data, and for closing a file.

4. You can use the `read()`, `readline()`, and `readlines()` methods to read data from a file.

5. You can use the `write(s)` method to write a string to a file.

6. You should close the file after the file is processed to ensure that the data is saved properly.

7. You can read a Web resource just like reading data from a file.

8. You can use exception handling to catch and handle runtime errors. You place the code that may raise an exception in the `try` clause, list the exceptions in the `except` clauses, and process the exception in the `except` clause.

9. Python provides built-in exception classes such as `ZeroDivisionError`, `SyntaxError`, and `RuntimeError`. All Python exception classes inherit directly or indirectly from `BaseException`. You can also define your own exception class derived from `BaseException` or from a subclass of `BaseException`, such as `RuntimeError`.

10. You can use the Python `pickle` module to store objects in a file. The `dump` function writes an object to the file and the `load` function reads an object from the file.

TEST QUESTIONS

Do test questions for this chapter online at www.cs.armstrong.edu/liang/py/test.html.

PROGRAMMING EXERCISES

MyProgrammingLab™

Sections 13.2–13.5

**13.1 (*Remove text*) Write a program that removes all the occurrences of a specified string from a text file. Your program should prompt the user to enter a filename and a string to be removed. Here is a sample run:

```
Enter a filename: test.txt  ↵Enter
Enter the string to be removed: morning  ↵Enter
Done
```

*13.2 (*Count characters, words, and lines in a file*) Write a program that will count the number of characters, words, and lines in a file. Words are separated by a white-space character. Your program should prompt the user to enter a filename. Here is a sample run:

```
Enter a filename: test.txt  ↵Enter
1777 characters
210 words
71 lines
```

*13.3 (*Process scores in a text file*) Suppose that a text file contains an unspecified number of scores. Write a program that reads the scores from the file and displays their total and average. Scores are separated by blanks. Your program should prompt the user to enter a filename. Here is a sample run:

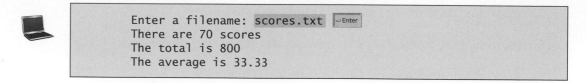

```
Enter a filename: scores.txt  ⏎Enter
There are 70 scores
The total is 800
The average is 33.33
```

*13.4 (*Write/read data*) Write a program that writes 100 integers created randomly into a file. Integers are separated by a space in the file. Read the data back from the file and display the sorted data. Your program should prompt the user to enter a filename. If the file already exists, do not override it. Here is a sample run:

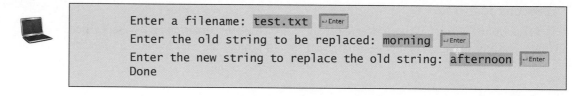

```
Enter a filename: test.txt  ⏎Enter
The file already exists
```

```
Enter a filename: test1.txt  ⏎Enter
20 34 43 ... 50
```

**13.5 (*Replace text*) Write a program that replaces text in a file. Your program should prompt the user to enter a filename, an old string, and a new string. Here is a sample run:

```
Enter a filename: test.txt  ⏎Enter
Enter the old string to be replaced: morning  ⏎Enter
Enter the new string to replace the old string: afternoon  ⏎Enter
Done
```

*13.6 (*Count words*) Write a program that counts the number of words in President Abraham Lincoln's Gettysburg Address from http://cs.armstrong.edu/liang/data/Lincoln.txt.

**13.7 (*Game: hangman*) Rewrite Exercise 10.29. The program reads the words stored in a text file named hangman.txt. Words are delimited by spaces.

13.8 (*Encrypt files*) Encode the file by adding 5 to every byte in the file. Write a program that prompts the user to enter an input filename and an output filename and saves the encrypted version of the input file to the output file.

13.9 (*Decrypt files*) Suppose a file is encrypted using the scheme in Exercise 13.8. Write a program to decode an encrypted file. Your program should prompt the user to enter an input filename and an output filename and should save the unencrypted version of the input file to the output file.

Sections 13.6–13.9

13.10 (The `Rational` class) Modify the `Rational` class in Listing 8.4, Rational.py, to throw a `RuntimeError` exception if the denominator is `0`.

13.11 (The `Triangle` class) Modify the `Triangle` class in Programming Exercise 12.1 to throw a `RuntimeError` exception if the three given sides cannot form a triangle.

13.12 (The `TriangleError` class) Define an exception class named `TriangleError` that extends `RuntimeError`. The `TriangleError` class contains the private data fields `side1`, `side2`, and `side3` with accessor methods for the three sides of a triangle. Modify the `Triangle` class in Exercise 12.1 to throw a `TriangleError` exception if the three given sides cannot form a triangle.

Sections 13.10–13.11

13.13 (*Tkinter: display a graph*) A graph consists of vertices and edges that connect vertices. Write a program that reads a graph from a file and displays it on a panel. The first line in the file contains a number that indicates the number of vertices (n**). The vertices are labeled as **0, 1, ..., n-1**. Each subsequent line, with the format **u x y v1, v2, ...**, describes that the vertex **u** is located at position (**x, y**) with the edges (**u, v1**), (**u, v2**), and so on. Figure 13.12a gives an example of the file for a graph. Your program prompts the user to enter the name of the file, reads data from the file, and displays the graph on a panel, as shown in Figure 13.12b.

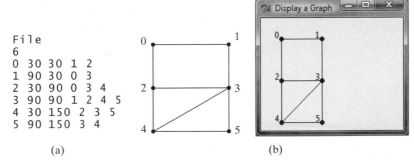

(a)   (b)

FIGURE 13.12   The program reads the information about the graph and displays it visually.

13.14 (*Tkinter: display a graph*) Rewrite Exercise 13.13 to read data from a Web URL such as **http://cs.armstrong.edu/liang/data/graph.txt. The program should prompt the user to enter the URL for the file.

**13.15 (*Tkinter: address book*) Rewrite the address book case study in Section 13.11 with the following improvements, as shown in Figure 13.13:

(a) Add a new button named *Update*. Clicking it enables the user to update the address that is currently displayed.

(b) Add a label below the buttons to display the current address location and the total number of addresses in the list.

(c) Implement the unfinished `processPrevious` and `processLast` methods in Listing 13.19.

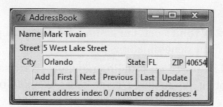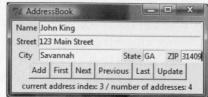

FIGURE 13.13 The new Update button and status label are added in the AddressBook UI.

**13.16 (*Create large dataset*) Create a data file with 1000 lines. Each line in the file consists of a faculty first name, last name, rank, and salary. Faculty's first name and
last name for the *i*th line are **FirstName*i*** and **LastName*i***. The rank is randomly
generated as assistant, associate, and full. The salary is randomly generated as a
number with two digits after the decimal point. The salary for assistant professor
should be in the range from 50,000 to 80,000, for associate professor from 60,000
to 110,000, and for full professor from 75,000 to 130,000. Save the file in
Salary.txt. Here are some sample data:.

```
FirstName1 LastName1 assistant 60055.95
FirstName2 LastName2 associate 81112.45
. . .
FirstName1000 LastName1000 full 92255.21
```

*13.17 (*Process large dataset*) A university posts its employee salary at **http://cs
.armstrong.edu/liang/data/Salary.txt**. Each line in the file consists of faculty first
name, last name, rank, and salary (see Exercise 13.16). Write a program to display
the total salary for assistant professors, associate professors, full professors, and
all faculty, respectively, and display the average salary for assistant professors,
associate professors, full professors, and all faculty, respectively.

CHAPTER

14

TUPLES, SETS, AND DICTIONARIES

Objectives

- To create tuples (§14.2).
- To use tuples as fixed lists to prevent elements from being added, deleted, or replaced (§14.2).
- To apply common sequence operations for tuples (§14.2).
- To create sets (§14.3.1).
- To add and remove elements in a set using the **add** and **remove** methods (§14.3.2).
- To use the **len**, **min**, **max**, and **sum** functions for a set of elements (§14.3.2).
- To use the **in** and **not in** operators to determine whether an element is in a set (§14.3.2).
- To traverse the elements in a set using a **for** loop (§14.3.2).
- To test whether a set is a subset or a superset of another set using the **issubset** or **issuperset** method (§14.3.3).
- To test whether two sets have the same contents using the == operator (§14.3.4).
- To perform set union, intersection, difference, and symmetric difference using the operators **|**, **&**, **-**, and **∧** (§14.3.5).
- To compare the performance differences between sets and lists (§14.4).
- To use sets to develop a program that counts the keywords in a Python source file (§14.5).
- To create dictionaries (§14.6.1).
- To add, modify, and retrieve elements in a dictionary using the syntax **dictionaryName[key]** (§14.6.2).
- To delete items in a dictionary using the **del** keyword (§14.6.3).
- To traverse keys in a dictionary using a **for** loop (§14.6.4).
- To obtain the size of a dictionary using the **len** function (§14.6.5).
- To test whether a key is in a dictionary using the **in** or **not in** operator (§14.6.6).
- To test whether two dictionaries have the same content using the == operator (§14.6.7).
- To use the **keys**, **values**, **items**, **clean**, **get**, **pop**, and **popitem** methods on a dictionary (§14.6.8).
- To use dictionaries to develop applications (§14.7).

14.1 Introduction

You can use a tuple for storing a fixed list of elements, a set for storing and quickly accessing nonduplicate elements, and a dictionary for storing key/value pairs and for accessing elements quickly using the keys.

problem

data structure

The "**No-Fly**" **list** is a list, created and maintained by the U.S. government's Terrorist Screening Center, of people who are not permitted to board a commercial aircraft for travel in or out of the United States. Suppose we need to write a program that checks whether a person is on the No-Fly list. You can use a Python list to store names in the No-Fly list. However, a more efficient data structure for this application is a *set*. In computer science, a *data structure* is a particular way of storing and organizing data in a computer so that it can be used efficiently for certain applications.

This chapter introduces sets along with two additional useful data structures—tuples and dictionaries.

14.2 Tuples

Tuples are like lists, but their elements are fixed; that is, once a tuple is created, you cannot add new elements, delete elements, replace elements, or reorder the elements in the tuple.

tuple

If the contents of a list in your application shouldn't change, you can use a tuple to prevent elements from being added, deleted, or replaced accidentally. A *tuple* is very much like a list, except that its elements are fixed. Furthermore, tuples are more efficient than lists due to Python's implementations.

creating tuples

You create a tuple by enclosing its elements inside a pair of parentheses. The elements are separated by commas. You can create an empty tuple and create a tuple from a list, as shown in the following example:

```
t1 = () # Create an empty tuple

t2 = (1, 3, 5) # Create a tuple with three elements

# Create a tuple from a list
t3 = tuple([2 * x for x in range(1, 5)])
```

You can also create a tuple from a string. Each character in the string becomes an element in the tuple. For example:

```
# Create a tuple from a string
t4 = tuple("abac") # t4 is ['a', 'b', 'a', 'c']
```

tuple operations

Tuples are sequences. The common operations for sequences in Table 10.1 can be used for tuples. You can use the functions **len**, **min**, **max**, and **sum** on a tuple. You can use a **for** loop to traverse all elements in a tuple, and can access the elements or slices of the elements using an index operator. You can use the **in** and **not in** operators to determine whether an element is in a tuple, and can also compare the elements in tuples using the comparison operators.

Listing 14.1 gives an example of using tuples.

Listing 14.1   TupleDemo.py

create a tuple

```
1  tuple1 = ("green", "red", "blue") # Create a tuple
2  print(tuple1)
3
4  tuple2 = tuple([7, 1, 2, 23, 4, 5]) # Create a tuple from a list
5  print(tuple2)
6
```

```
7   print("length is", len(tuple2)) # Use function len
8   print("max is", max(tuple2)) # Use max
9   print("min is", min(tuple2)) # Use min
10  print("sum is", sum(tuple2)) # Use sum
11
12  print("The first element is", tuple2[0]) # Use index operator
13
14  tuple3 = tuple1 + tuple2 # Combine two tuples
15  print(tuple3)
16
17  tuple3 = 2 * tuple1 # Duplicate a tuple
18  print(tuple3)
19
20  print(tuple2[2 : 4]) # Slicing operator
21  print(tuple1[-1])
22
23  print(2 in tuple2) # in operator
24
25  for v in tuple1:
26      print(v, end = ' ')
27  print()
28
29  list1 = list(tuple2) # Obtain a list from a tuple
30  list1.sort()
31  tuple4 = tuple(list1)
32  tuple5 = tuple(list1)
33  print(tuple4)
34  print(tuple4 == tuple5) # Compare two tuples
```

use functions

index operator

+

*

slicing

in operator

for loop

create a list from tuple

compare

```
('green', 'red', 'blue')
(7, 1, 2, 23, 4, 5)
length is 6
max is 23
min is 1
sum is 42
The first element is 7
('green', 'red', 'blue', 7, 1, 2, 23, 4, 5)
('green', 'red', 'blue', 'green', 'red', 'blue')
(2, 23)
blue
True
green red blue
(1, 2, 4, 5, 7, 23)
True
False
```

The program creates tuple **tuple1** with some strings (line 1) and tuple **tuple2** from a list (line 4). It applies the **len**, **max**, **min**, and **sum** functions on **tuple2** (lines 7–10). You can use the index operator to access elements in a tuple (line 12), the + operator to combine two tuples (line 14), the * operator to duplicate a tuple (line 17), and the slicing operator to get a portion of the tuple (lines 20–21). You can use the **in** operator to determine whether a specific element is in a tuple (line 23). The elements in a tuple can be traversed using a **for** loop (lines 25–26).

The program creates a list (line 29), sorts the list (line 30), and then creates two tuples from this list (lines 31–32). The comparison operator == is used to compare tuples (line 34).

Tuples have fixed elements. So wouldn't the statement in line 17 throw an error since **tuple3** has already been defined in line 14? Line 17 is fine, though, because it assigns a new tuple to variable **tuple3**. Now **tuple3** points to the new tuple. "Tuples have fixed elements" means that you cannot add new elements, delete elements, replace the elements, or shuffle the elements in a tuple.

Note

A tuple contains a fixed list of elements. An individual element in a tuple may be mutable. For example, the following code creates a tuple of circles (line 2), and changes the first circle's radius to **30** (line 3).

```
1  >>> from CircleFromGeometricObject import Circle
2  >>> circles = (Circle(2), Circle(4), Circle(7))
3  >>> circles[0].setRadius(30)
4  >>> circles[0].getRadius()
5  >>> 30
6  >>>
```

immutable tuple

In this example, each element in the tuple is a circle object. Even though you cannot add, delete, or replace circle objects in the tuple, you can change a circle's radius, since a circle object is mutable. If a tuple contains immutable objects, the tuple is said to be immutable. For example, a tuple of numbers or a tuple of strings is immutable.

Check Point

MyProgrammingLab™

14.1 What are the differences between a list and a tuple? How do you create a tuple from a list? How do you create a list from a tuple?

14.2 What is wrong in the following code?

```
t = (1, 2, 3)
t.append(4)
t.remove(0)
t[0] = 1
```

14.3 Is the following code correct?

```
t1 = (1, 2, 3, 7, 9, 0, 5)
t2 = (1, 2, 5)
t1 = t2
```

14.4 Show the printout of the following code:

```
t = (1, 2, 3, 7, 9, 0, 5)
print(t)
print(t[0])
print(t[1: 3])
print(t[-1])
print(t[ : -1])
print(t[1 : -1])
```

14.5 Show the printout of the following code:

```
t = (1, 2, 3, 7, 9, 0, 5)
print(max(t))
print(min(t))
print(sum(t))
print(len(t))
```

14.6 Show the printout of the following code:

```
t1 = (1, 2, 3, 7, 9, 0, 5)
t2 = (1, 3, 22, 7, 9, 0, 5)
print(t1 == t2)
print(t1 != t2)
print(t1 > t2)
print(t1 < t2)
```

14.3 Sets

Sets are like lists in that you use them for storing a collection of elements. Unlike lists, however, the elements in a set are nonduplicates and are not placed in any particular order.

Key Point

If your application does not care about the order of the elements, using a set to store elements is more efficient than using lists due to Python's implementations. This section introduces how to use sets.

set

14.3.1 Creating Sets

You can create a set of elements by enclosing the elements inside a pair of curly braces ({}). The elements are separated by commas. You can create an empty set, or you can create a set from a list or a tuple, as shown in the following examples:

VideoNote
Use sets

```
s1 = set() # Create an empty set
s2 = {1, 3, 5} # Create a set with three elements
s3 = set([1, 3, 5]) # Create a set from a tuple

# Create a set from a list
s4 = set([x * 2 for x in range(1, 10)])
```

Likewise, you can create a list or a tuple from a set by using the syntax `list(set)` or `tuple(set)`.

You can also create a set from a string. Each character in the string becomes an element in the set. For example:

```
# Create a set from a string
s5 = set("abac") # s5 is {'a', 'b', 'c'}
```

Note that although the character **a** appears twice in the string, it appears only once in the set because a set does not store duplicate elements.

A set can contain the elements of the same type or mixed types. For example, s = {1, 2, 3, "one", "two", "three"} is a set that contains numbers and strings. Each element in a set must be hashable. Each object in Python has a hash value and an object is *hashable* if its hash value never changes during its lifetime. All types of objects introduced so far except lists are hashable. Why set elements must be hashable is explained in bonus Web Chapter 21, Hashing: Implementing Sets and Dictionaries.

hashable

14.3.2 Manipulating and Accessing Sets

You can add an element to a set or remove an element by using the **add(e)** or **remove(e)** method. You can use the **len**, **min**, **max**, and **sum** functions on a set, and a **for** loop to traverse all elements in a set.

You can use the **in** or **not in** operator to determine whether an element is in the set. For example:

```
>>> s1 = {1, 2, 4}
>>> s1.add(6)
>>> s1
{1, 2, 4, 6}
>>> len(s1)
4
>>> max(s1)
6
```

```
>>> min(s1)
1
>>> sum(s1)
13
>>> 3 in s1
False
>>> s1.remove(4)
>>> s1
{1, 2, 6}
>>>
```

Note

The **remove(e)** method will throw a **KeyError** exception if the element to be removed is not in the set.

14.3.3 Subset and Superset

issubset

A set **s1** is a subset of **s2** if every element in **s1** is also in **s2**. You can use the **s1.issubset(s2)** method to determine whether **s1** is a subset of **s2**, as shown in the following code:

```
>>> s1 = {1, 2, 4}
>>> s2 = {1, 4, 5, 2, 6}
>>> s1.issubset(s2) # s1 is a subset of s2
True
>>>
```

issuperrset

A set **s1** is a superset of set **s2** if every element in **s2** is also in **s1**. You can use the **s1. issuperset(s2)** method to determine whether **s1** is a superset of **s2**, as shown in the following code:

```
>>> s1 = {1, 2, 4}
>>> s2 = {1, 4, 5, 2, 6}
>>> s2.issuperset(s1) # s2 is a superset of s1
True
>>>
```

14.3.4 Equality Test

You can use the == and != operators to test if two sets contain the same elements. For example:

```
>>> s1 = {1, 2, 4}
>>> s2 = {1, 4, 2}
>>> s1 == s2
True
>>> s1 != s2
False
>>>
```

In this example, **s1** and **s2** contain the same elements regardless of the order of the elements in the sets.

Note that it makes no sense to compare the sets using the conventional comparison operators (>, >=, <=, and <), because the elements in a set are not ordered. However, these operators have special meanings when used for sets:

- **s1** < **s2** returns **True** if **s1** is a proper subset of **s2**.

- **s1** <= **s2** returns **True** if **s1** is a subset of **s2**.

- **s1** > **s2** returns **True** if **s1** is a proper superset of **s2**.

- **s1** >= **s2** returns **True** if **s1** is a superset of **s2**.

Note

If **s1** is a proper subset of **s2**, every element in **s1** is also in **s2**, and at least one element in **s2** is not in **s1**. If **s1** is a proper subset of **s2**, **s2** is a proper superset of **s1**.

14.3.5 Set Operations

Python provides the methods for performing set union, intersection, difference, and symmetric difference operations.

The *union* of two sets is a set that contains all the elements from both sets. You can use the **union** method or the | operator to perform this operation. For example:

set union
union |

```
>>> s1 = {1, 2, 4}
>>> s2 = {1, 3, 5}
>>> s1.union(s2)
{1, 2, 3, 4, 5}
>>>
>>> s1 | s2
{1, 2, 3, 4, 5}
>>>
```

The *intersection* of two sets is a set that contains the elements that appear in both sets. You can use the **intersection** method or the & operator to perform this operation. For example:

set intersection
intersection &

```
>>> s1 = {1, 2, 4}
>>> s2 = {1, 3, 5}
>>> s1.intersection(s2)
{1}
>>>
>>> s1 & s2
{1}
>>>
```

The *difference* between **set1** and **set2** is a set that contains the elements in **set1** but not in **set2**. You can use the **difference** method or the – operator to perform this operation. For example:

set difference
difference -

```
>>> s1 = {1, 2, 4}
>>> s2 = {1, 3, 5}
>>> s1.difference(s2)
```

```
{2, 4}
>>>
>>> s1 - s2
{2, 4}
>>>
```

set symmetric_difference

symmetric_difference ∧

The *symmetric difference* (or *exclusive or*) of two sets is a set that contains the elements in either set, but not in both sets. You can use the **symmetric_difference** method or the ∧ operator to perform this operation. For example:

```
>>> s1 = {1, 2, 4}
>>> s2 = {1, 3, 5}
>>> s1.symmetric_difference(s2)
{2, 3, 4, 5}
>>>
>>> s1 ∧ s2
{2, 3, 4, 5}
>>>
```

Note that these set methods return a resulting set, but they do not change the elements in the sets.

Listing 14.2 illustrates a program that uses sets.

LISTING 14.2 SetDemo.py

create a set

create a set from list

is in set?

union |

difference -

intersection &

exclusive or ∧

create a list from set
compare

```
 1  set1 = {"green", "red", "blue", "red"} # Create a set
 2  print(set1)
 3
 4  set2 = set([7, 1, 2, 23, 2, 4, 5]) # Create a set from a list
 5  print(set2)
 6
 7  print("Is red in set1?", "red" in set1)
 8
 9  print("length is", len(set2)) # Use function len
10  print("max is", max(set2)) # Use max
11  print("min is", min(set2)) # Use min
12  print("sum is", sum(set2)) # Use sum
13
14  set3 = set1 | {"green", "yellow"} # Set union
15  print(set3)
16
17  set3 = set1 - {"green", "yellow"} # Set difference
18  print(set3)
19
20  set3 = set1 & {"green", "yellow"} # Set intersection
21  print(set3)
22
23  set3 = set1 ∧ {"green", "yellow"} # Set exclusive or
24  print(set3)
25
26  list1 = list(set2) # Obtain a list from a set
27  print(set1 == {"green", "red", "blue"}) # Compare two sets
28
29  set1.add("yellow")
```

```
30  print(set1)
31
32  set1.remove("yellow")
33  print(set1)
```

```
{'blue', 'green', 'red'}
{1, 2, 4, 5, 7, 23}
Is red in set1? True
length is 6
max is 23
min is 1
sum is 42
{'blue', 'green', 'yellow', 'red'}
{'blue', 'red'}
{'green'}
{'blue', 'red', 'yellow'}
True
{'blue', 'green', 'yellow', 'red'}
{'blue', 'green', 'red'}
```

The program creates **set1** as **{"green", "red", "blue", "red"}** (line 1). Because a set does not contain any duplicates, only one element **red** is stored in **set1**. The program creates **set2** from a list using the **set** function (line 4).

The program applies the **len**, **max**, **min**, and **sum** functions on the sets (lines 9–12). Note that you cannot use the index operator to access elements in a set, because the elements are not in any particular order.

len, max, min, sum

The program performs the set union, difference, intersection, and symmetric difference operations in lines 14–24.

|, -, &, ^

```
Set union:  {"green", "red", "blue"} | {"green", "yellow"})
            => {"green", "red", "blue", "yellow"} (line 14)

Set difference:  {"green", "red", "blue"} - {"green", "yellow"})
                 => {"red", "blue"} (line 17)

Set intersection:  {"green", "red", "blue"} & {"green", "yellow"})
                   => {"green"} (line 20)

Set symmetric_difference:  {"green", "red", "blue"} ^ {"green", "yellow"})
                           => {"red", "blue", "yellow"} (line 23)
```

The program uses **==** to determine whether the two sets have the same elements (line 27).

comparisons

The program uses the **add** and **remove** methods to add and remove an element in the set (lines 29 and 32).

add
remove

14.7 How do you create an empty set?

14.8 Can a list, set, or tuple have elements of different types?

14.9 Which of the following sets are created correctly?

```
s = {1, 3, 4}
s = {{1, 2}, {4, 5}}
s = {[1, 2], [4, 5]}
s = {(1, 2), (4, 5)}
```

14.10 What are the differences between a list and a set? How do you create a set from a list? How do you create a list from a set? How do you create a tuple from a set?

✓Check
Point
MyProgrammingLab™

14.11 Show the printout of the following code:

```
students = {"peter", "john"}
print(students)
students.add("john")
print(students)
students.add("peterson")
print(students)
students.remove("peter")
print(students)
```

14.12 Will the following code have a runtime error?

```
students = {"peter", "john"}
students.remove("johnson")
print(students)
```

14.13 Show the printout of the following code:

```
student1 = {"peter", "john", "tim"}
student2 = {"peter", "johnson", "tim"}
print(student1.issuperset({"john"}))
print(student1.issubset(student2))
print({1, 2, 3} > {1, 2, 4})
print({1, 2, 3} < {1, 2, 4})
print({1, 2} < {1, 2, 4})
print({1, 2} <= {1, 2, 4})
```

14.14 Show the printout of the following code:

```
numbers = {1, 4, 5, 6}
print(len(numbers))
print(max(numbers))
print(min(numbers))
print(sum(numbers))
```

14.15 Show the printout of the following code:

```
s1 = {1, 4, 5, 6}
s2 = {1, 3, 6, 7}
print(s1.union(s2))
print(s1 | s2)
print(s1.intersection(s2))
print(s1 & s2)
print(s1.difference(s2))
print(s1 - s2)
print(s1.symmetric_difference(s2))
print(s1 ^ s2)
```

14.16 Show the printout of the following code:

```
set1 = {2, 3, 7, 11}
print(4 in set1)
print(3 in set1)
print(len(set1))
print(max(set1))
print(min(set1))
print(sum(set1))
print(set1.issubset({2, 3, 6, 7, 11}))
print(set1.issuperset({2,3, 7, 11}))
```

14.17 Show the output of the following code:

```
set1 = {1, 2, 3}
set2 = {3, 4, 5}

set3 = set1 | set2
```

```
print(set1, set2, set3)

set3 = set1 - set2
print(set1, set2, set3)

set3 = set1 & set2
print(set1, set2, set3)

set3 = set1 ^ set2
print(set1, set2, set3)
```

14.4 Comparing the Performance of Sets and Lists

Sets are more efficient than lists for the in *and* not in *operator and for the* remove *method.*

Key Point

The elements in a list can be accessed using the index operator. However, sets do not support the index operator, because the elements in a set are unordered. To traverse all elements in a set, use a for loop. We now conduct an interesting experiment to test the performance of sets and lists. The program in Listing 14.3 shows the execution time of (1) testing whether an element is in a set and a list, and (2) removing elements from a set and a list.

LISTING 14.3   SetListPerformanceTest.py

```
 1  import random
 2  import time
 3
 4  NUMBER_OF_ELEMENTS = 10000
 5
 6  # Create a list
 7  lst = list(range(NUMBER_OF_ELEMENTS))                              create a list
 8  random.shuffle(lst)
 9
10  # Create a set from the list
11  s = set(lst)                                                      create a set
12
13  # Test if an element is in the set
14  startTime = time.time() # Get start time
15  for i in range(NUMBER_OF_ELEMENTS):
16      i in s                                                        number in set?
17  endTime = time.time() # Get end time
18  runTime = int((endTime - startTime) * 1000) # Get test time       get run time
19  print("To test if", NUMBER_OF_ELEMENTS,
20      "elements are in the set\n",
21      "The runtime is", runTime, "milliseconds")
22
23  # Test if an element is in the list
24  startTime = time.time() # Get start time
25  for i in range(NUMBER_OF_ELEMENTS):
26      i in lst                                                      number in list?
27  endTime = time.time() # Get end time
28  runTime = int((endTime - startTime) * 1000) # Get test time
29  print("\nTo test if", NUMBER_OF_ELEMENTS,
30      "elements are in the list\n",
31      "The runtime is", runTime, "milliseconds")
32
33  # Remove elements from a set one at a time
34  startTime = time.time() # Get start time
```

remove from set

```
35    for i in range(NUMBER_OF_ELEMENTS):
36        s.remove(i)
37    endTime = time.time() # Get end time
38    runTime = int((endTime - startTime) * 1000) # Get test time
39    print("\nTo remove", NUMBER_OF_ELEMENTS,
40        "elements from the set\n",
41        "The runtime is", runTime, "milliseconds")
42
43    # Remove elements from a list one at a time
44    startTime = time.time() # Get start time
45    for i in range(NUMBER_OF_ELEMENTS):
46        lst.remove(i)
47    endTime = time.time() # Get end time
48    runTime = int((endTime - startTime) * 1000) # Get test time
49    print("\nTo remove", NUMBER_OF_ELEMENTS,
50        "elements from the list\n",
51        "The runtime is", runTime, "milliseconds")
```

remove from list

```
To test if 10000 elements are in the set
The runtime is 5 milliseconds

To test if 10000 elements are in the list
The runtime is 4274 milliseconds

To remove 10000 elements from the set
The runtime is 7 milliseconds

To remove 10000 elements from the list
The runtime is 1853 milliseconds
```

In line 7, the **range(NUMBER_OF_ELEMENTS)** function returns a sequence of numbers from **0** to **NUMBER_OF_ELEMENTS - 1**. So **list(range(NUMBER_OF_ELEMENTS))** returns a list of integers from **0** to **NUMBER_OF_ELEMENTS - 1** (line 7). The program shuffles the list (line 8), and creates a set from the list (line 11). Now the set and the list contain the same elements.

The program obtains the runtime for testing whether the elements **0** to **NUMBER_OF_ELEMENTS - 1** are in the set (lines 14–21) and in the list (lines 24–31). As you can see in the output, it takes 5 milliseconds to test this for the set and 4,274 milliseconds for the list.

The program obtains the runtime for removing the elements **0** to **NUMBER_OF_ELEMENTS - 1** from the set (lines 34–41) and in the list (lines 44–51). Again, you can see in the output that it takes 7 milliseconds for the set and 1,853 milliseconds for the list.

sets are better

As these runtimes illustrate, sets are much more efficient than lists for testing whether an element is in a set or a list. So, the "No-Fly" list mentioned at the beginning of this chapter should be implemented using a set instead of a list, because it is much faster to test whether an element is in a set than in a list.

bonus chapters

You may wonder why sets are more efficient than lists. To get the answers, read the online bonus chapters on developing efficient algorithms, linked lists, and hashing.

14.5 Case Study: Counting Keywords

 Key Point

This section presents an application that counts the number of the keywords in a Python source file.

For each word in a Python source file, we need to determine whether the word is a keyword. To handle this efficiently, store all the keywords in a set and use the **in** operator to test if a word is in the keyword set. Listing 14.4 gives this program.

LISTING 14.4 CountKeywords.py

```
 1  import os.path
 2  import sys
 3
 4  def main():
 5      keyWords = {"and", "as", "assert", "break", "class",          keyword set
 6                  "continue", "def", "del", "elif", "else",
 7                  "except", "False", "finally", "for", "from",
 8                  "global", "if", "import", "in", "is", "lambda",
 9                  "None", "nonlocal", "not", "or", "pass", "raise",
10                  "return", "True", "try", "while", "with", "yield"}
11
12      filename = input("Enter a Python source code filename: ").strip()   enter a filename
13
14      if not os.path.isfile(filename): # Check if file exists         file exists?
15          print("File", filename, "does not exist")
16          sys.exit()
17
18      infile = open(filename, "r") # Open files for input            open file
19
20      text = infile.read().split() # Read and split words from the file   read and split words
21
22      count = 0
23      for word in text:
24          if word in keyWords:                                       is a keyword?
25              count += 1                                             count keyword
26
27      print("The number of keywords in", filename, "is", count)
28
29  main()
```

```
Enter a Python source code filename: GuessNumber.py  ⏎Enter
The number of keywords in GuessNumber.py is 7
```

```
Enter a Python source file: TTT.py  ⏎Enter
File TTT.py does not exist
```

The program creates a set for keywords (lines 5–10) and prompts the user to enter a Python source filename (line 12). It checks if the file exists (line 14). If not, exit the program (line 16).

The program opens the file and splits the words from the text (line 20). For each word, the program checks if the word is a keyword (line 24). If so, increase the count by **1** (line 25).

14.6 Dictionaries

A dictionary is a container object that stores a collection of key/value pairs. It enables fast retrieval, deletion, and updating of the value by using the key.

Key Point

Suppose your program needs to store the detailed information on terrorists in the "No-Fly" list. A *dictionary* is an efficient data structure for such a task. A dictionary is a collection that

dictionary

what is a dictionary?

stores the values along with the keys. The keys are like an index operator. In a list, the indexes are integers. In a dictionary, the key must be a hashable object. A dictionary cannot contain duplicate keys. Each key maps to one value. A key and its corresponding value form an *item* (or *entry*) stored in a dictionary, as shown in Figure 14.1a. The data structure is a called a "dictionary" because it resembles a word dictionary, where the words are the keys and the words' definitions are the values. A dictionary is also known as a *map*, which maps each key to a value.

key/value pair
dictionary item
dictionary entry
map

VideoNote
Use dictionaries

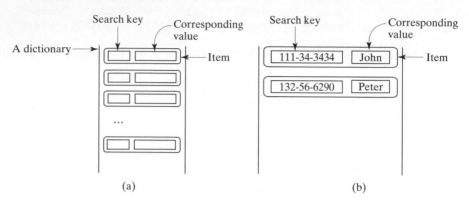

(a) (b)

FIGURE 14.1 A dictionary's item is a key/value pair.

14.6.1 Creating a Dictionary

You can create a dictionary by enclosing the items inside a pair of curly braces ({}). Each item consists of a key, followed by a colon, followed by a value. The items are separated by commas. For example, the following statement:

```
students = {"111-34-3434":"John", "132-56-6290":"Peter"}
```

creates a dictionary with two items, as shown in Figure 14.1b. The item is in the form **key:value**. The key in the first item is **111-34-3434**, and its corresponding value is **John**. The key must be of a hashable type such as numbers and strings. The value can be of any type.

You can create an empty dictionary by using the following syntax:

```
students = {} # Create an empty dictionary
```

 Note

Python uses curly braces for sets and dictionaries. The syntax **{}** denotes an empty dictionary. To create an empty set, use **set()**.

14.6.2 Adding, Modifying, and Retrieving Values

To add an item to a dictionary, use the syntax:

```
dictionaryName[key] = value
```

For example:

```
students["234-56-9010"] = "Susan"
```

If the key is already in the dictionary, the preceding statement replaces the value for the key.

To retrieve a value, simply write an expression using **dictionaryName[key]**. If the key is in the dictionary, the value for the key is returned. Otherwise, a **KeyError** exception is raised.

For example:

```
1  >>> students = {"111-34-3434":"John", "132-56-6290":"Peter"}
2  >>> students["234-56-9010"] = "Susan" # Add a new item
3  >>> students["234-56-9010"]
4  "Susan"
5  >>> students["111-34-3434"] = "John Smith"
6  >>> students["111-34-3434"]
7  "John Smith"
8  >>> student["343-45-5455"]
9  Traceback (most recent call last):
10   File "<stdin>", line 1, in <module>
11  KeyError: '343-45-5455'
12  >>>
```

Line 1 creates a dictionary with two items. Line 2 adds a new item with the key **234-56-9010** and the value **Susan**. The value associated with the key **234-56-9010** is returned in line 3. Line 5 modifies the item for the key **111-34-3434** with the new value **John Smith**, and line 8 retrieves the value for a nonexistent key **343-45-5455**, which raises a **KeyError** exception.

14.6.3 Deleting Items

To delete an item from a dictionary, use the syntax:

del dictionaryName[key]

For example:

del students["234-56-9010"]

This statement deletes an item with the key **234-56-9010** from the dictionary. If the key is not in the dictionary, a **KeyError** exception is raised.

14.6.4 Looping Items

You can use a **for** loop to traverse all keys in the dictionary. For example:

```
1  >>> students = {"111-34-3434":"John", "132-56-6290":"Peter"}
2  >>> for key in students:
3  ...      print(key + ":" + str(students[key]))
4  ...
5  "111-34-3434":"John"
6  "132-56-6290":"Peter"
7  >>>
```

The **for** loop iterates on keys in dictionary **students** (line 2). **students[key]** returns the value for the key (line 3).

14.6.5 The **len** Function

len(dictionary)

You can find the number of the items in a dictionary by using **len(dictionary)**. For example:

```
1  >>> students = {"111-34-3434":"John", "132-56-6290":"Peter"}
2  >>> len(students)
3  2
4  >>>
```

In line 2, **len(students)** returns the number of items in dictionary **students**.

14.6.6 Testing Whether a Key Is in a Dictionary

in operator

You can use the **in** or **not in** operator to determine whether a key is in the dictionary. For example:

```
1  >>> students = {"111-34-3434":"John", "132-56-6290":"Peter"}
2  >>> "111-34-3434" in students
3  True
4  >>> "999-34-3434" in students
5  False
6  >>>
```

In line 2, **"111-34-3434" in students** checks whether the key **111-34-3434** is in dictionary **students**.

14.6.7 Equality Test

You can use the == and != operators to test whether two dictionaries contain the same items. For example:

```
>>> d1 = {"red":41, "blue":3}
>>> d2 = {"blue":3, "red":41}
>>> d1 == d2
True
>>> d1 != d2
False
>>>
```

In this example, **d1** and **d2** contain the same items regardless of the order of the items in a dictionary.

Note

You cannot use the comparison operators (>, >=, <=, and <) to compare dictionaries because the items are not ordered.

14.6.8 The Dictionary Methods

The Python class for dictionaries is **dict**. Figure 14.2 lists the methods that can be invoked from a dictionary object.

dict	
keys(): tuple	Returns a sequence of keys.
values(): tuple	Returns a sequence of values.
items(): tuple	Returns a sequence of tuples. Each tuple is (key, value) for an item.
clear(): None	Deletes all entries.
get(key): value	Returns the value for the key.
pop(key): value	Removes the item for the key and returns its value.
popitem(): tuple	Returns a randomly selected key/value pair as a tuple and removes the selected item.

FIGURE 14.2 The **dict** class provides methods for manipulating a dictionary object.

The **get(key)** method is similar to **dictionaryName[key]** except that the **get** method returns **None** if the key is not in the dictionary rather than raising an exception. The **pop(key)** method is the same as **del dictionaryName[key]**.

Here are some examples that show these methods in use:

```
1  >>> students = {"111-34-3434":"John", "132-56-6290":"Peter"}
2  >>> tuple(students.keys())
3  ("111-34-3434", "132-56-6290")
4  >>> tuple(students.values())
5  ("John", "Peter")
6  >>> tuple(students.items())
7  (("111-34-3434", "John"), ("132-56-6290", "Peter"))
8  >>> students.get("111-34-3434")
9  "John"
10 >>> print(students.get("999-34-3434"))
11 None
12 >>> students.pop("111-34-3434")
13 "John"
14 >>> students
15 {"132-56-6290":"Peter"}
16 >>> students.clear()
17 >>> students
18 {}
19 >>>
```

The dictionary **students** is created in line 1, and **students.keys()** in line 2 returns the keys in the dictionary. In line 4, **students.values()** returns the values in the dictionary, and **students.items()** in line 6 returns items as tuples in the dictionary. In line 10, invoking **students.get("999-34-3434")** returns the student name for the key **999-34-3434**. Invoking **students.pop("111-34-3434")** in line 12 removes the item in the dictionary with the key **111-34-3434**. In line 16, invoking **students.clear()** removes all items from the dictionary.

MyProgrammingLab™

14.18 How do you create an empty dictionary?

14.19 Which of the following dictionaries are created correctly?

```
d = {1:[1, 2], 3:[3, 4]}
d = {[1, 2]:1, [3, 4]:3}
d = {(1, 2):1, (3, 4):3}
d = {1:"john", 3:"peter"}
d = {"john":1, "peter":3}
```

14.20 Each item in a dictionary has two parts. What are they called?

14.21 Suppose a dictionary named **students** is {"john":3, "peter":2}. What do the following statements do?

(a) `students["susan"] = 5`

(b) `students["peter"] = 5`

(c) `students["peter"] += 5`

(d) `del students["peter"]`

14.22 Suppose a dictionary named **students** is {"john":3, "peter":2}. What do the following statements do?

(a) `print(len(students))`

(b) `print(students.keys())`

(c) `print(students.values())`

(d) `print(students.items())`

14.23 Show the output of the following code:

```
def main():
    d = {"red":4, "blue":1, "green":14, "yellow":2}
    print(d["red"])
    print(list(d.keys()))
    print(list(d.values()))
    print("blue" in d)
    print("purple" in d)
    d["blue"] += 10
    print(d["blue"])

main() # Call the main function
```

14.24 Show the output of the following code:

```
def main():
    d = {}
    d["susan"] = 50
    d["jim"] = 45
    d["joan"] = 54
    d["susan"] = 51
    d["john"] = 53
    print(len(d))

main() # Call the main function
```

14.25 For a dictionary **d**, you can use **d[key]** or **d.get(key)** to return the value for the key. What are the differences between them?

14.7 Case Study: Occurrences of Words

This case study writes a program that counts the occurrences of words in a text file and displays ten most frequently used words in decreasing order of their occurrence counts.

The program in this case study uses a dictionary to store an item consisting of a word and its count. The program determines whether each word is already a key in the dictionary. If not, the program adds a dictionary item with the word as the key and the value **1**. Otherwise, the program increases the value for the word (key) by **1** in the dictionary. Assume the words are case-insensitive (for example, **Good** is treated the same as **good**). The program displays the ten most frequently used words in the file in decreasing order of their count.

Listing 14.5 shows the solution to the problem.

LISTING 14.5 CountOccurrenceOfWords.py

```
 1  def main():
 2      # Prompt the user to enter a file
 3      filename = input("Enter a filename: ").strip()
 4      infile = open(filename, "r") # Open the file
 5
 6      wordCounts = {} # Create an empty dictionary to count words
 7      for line in infile:
 8          processLine(line.lower(), wordCounts)
 9
10      pairs = list(wordCounts.items()) # Get pairs from the dictionary
11
12      items = [[x, y] for (y, x) in pairs] # Reverse pairs in the list
13
14      items.sort() # Sort pairs in items
15
16      for i in range(len(items) - 1, len(items) - 11, -1):
17          print(items[i][1] + "\t" + str(items[i][0]))
18
19  # Count each word in the line
20  def processLine(line, wordCounts):
21      line = replacePunctuations(line) # Replace punctuation with space
22      words = line.split() # Get words from each line
23      for word in words:
24          if word in wordCounts:
25              wordCounts[word] += 1
26          else:
27              wordCounts[word] = 1
28
29  # Replace punctuation in the line with a space
30  def replacePunctuations(line):
31      for ch in line:
32          if ch in "~@#$%^&*()_-+=~<>?/,.;:!{}[]|'\"":
33              line = line.replace(ch, " ")
34
35      return line
36
37  main() # Call the main function
```

enter a file
open file

create a dictionary

process each line

get pairs to list

reverse pair

display item

replace punctuation
extract words

increase word count

new word

replace punctuation

```
Enter a filename: Lincoln.txt  ⏎Enter
that      13
the       11
we        10
to        8
here      8
a         7
and       6
```

```
of        5
nation    5
it        5
```

The program prompts the user to enter a filename (line 3) and opens the file (line 4). It creates a dictionary **wordCounts** (line 6) to store pairs of words and their occurrence counts. The words serve as the keys.

The program reads each line from the file and invokes **processLine(line, wordCounts)** to count the occurrence of each word in the line (lines 7–8). Suppose the **wordCounts** dictionary is **{"red":7, "blue":5, "green":2}**. How do you sort it? The dictionary object does not have the **sort** method. But the **list** object has it, so you can get the pairs into a list and then sort that list. The program obtains the list of pairs in line 10. If you apply the **sort** method to the list, the pairs will be sorted on their first element, but we need to sort each pair on their count (the second element). How can we do this? The trick is to reverse the pair. The program creates a new list with all the pairs reversed (line 12), and then applies the **sort** method (line 14). Now the list is sorted like this: **[[2, "green"], [5, "blue"], [7, "red"]]**.

sort pairs

The program displays the last ten pairs from the list to show the words with the highest count (lines 16–17).

processLine

The **processLine(line, wordCounts)** function invokes **replacePunctuations(line)** to replace all punctuation marks by spaces (line 21), then extracts words by using the **split** method (line 22). If a word is already in the dictionary, the program increases its count (line 25); otherwise, the program adds a new pair to the dictionary (line 27).

replacePunctuations (line)

The **replacePunctuations(line)** method checks each character in each line. If it is a punctuation mark, the program replaces it with a space (lines 32–33).

Now sit back and think how you would write this program without using a dictionary. You could use a nested list such as **[[key1, value1], [key2, value2], ...]**, but your new program would be longer and more complex. You will find that a dictionary is a very efficient and powerful data structure for solving problems such as this.

KEY TERMS

data structure   476
dictionary   487
dictionary entry   488
dictionary item   488
hashable   479
immutable tuple   478
key/value pair   488

map   488
set   479
set difference   481
set intersection   481
set union   481
set symmetric difference   482
tuple   476

CHAPTER SUMMARY

1. A *tuple* is a fixed list. You cannot add, delete, or replace elements in a tuple.

2. Since a tuple is a sequence, the common operations for sequences can be used for tuples.

3. Though you cannot add, delete, or replace elements in a tuple, you can change the content of individual elements if the elements are mutable.

4. A tuple is *immutable* if all its elements are immutable.

5. *Sets* are like lists in that you use them for storing a collection of elements. Unlike lists, however, the elements in a set are nonduplicates and are not placed in any particular order.

6. You can add an element to a set using the **add** method and remove an element from the list using the **remove** method.

7. The **len**, **min**, **max**, and **sum** functions can be applied to a set.

8. You can use a **for** loop to traverse the elements in a set.

9. You can use the **issubset** or **issuperset** method to test whether a set is a subset or a superset of another set, and use the **|**, **&**, **−**, and **^** operators to perform set union, intersection, difference, and symmetric difference.

10. Sets are more efficient than lists for testing whether an element is in a set or a list as well as for removing elements from a set or a list.

11. A *dictionary* can be used to store *key/value pairs*. You can retrieve a value using a *key*. The keys are like an index operator. In a list, the indexes are integers. In a dictionary, the keys can be any hashable objects such as numbers and strings.

12. You can use **dictionaryName[key]** to retrieve a value in the dictionary for the given key and use **dictionaryName[key] = value** to add or modify an item in a dictionary.

13. You can use **del dictionaryName[key]** to delete an item for the given key.

14. You can use a **for** loop to traverse all keys in a dictionary.

15. You can use the **len** function to return the number of items in a dictionary.

16. You can use the **in** and **not in** operators to test if a key is in a dictionary and use the **==** and **!=** operator to test if two dictionaries are the same.

17. You can use the methods **keys()**, **values()**, **items()**, **clear()**, **get(key)**, **pop(key)**, and **popitem()** on a dictionary.

TEST QUESTIONS

Do test questions for this chapter online at **www.cs.armstrong.edu/liang/py/test.html**.

PROGRAMMING EXERCISES

MyProgrammingLab™

Sections 14.2–14.6

*14.1 (*Display keywords*) Revise Listing 14.4 CountKeywords.py to display the keywords in a Python source file as well as to count the number of the keywords.

*14.2 (*Count occurrences of numbers*) Write a program that reads an unspecified number of integers and finds the ones that have the most occurrences. For example, if you enter **2 3 40 3 5 4 −3 3 3 2 0**, the number **3** occurs most often. Enter all numbers in one line. If not one but several numbers have the most occurrences, all of them should be reported. For example, since **9** and **3** appear twice in the list **9 30 3 9 3 2 4**, both occurrences should be reported.

*14.3 (*Count the occurrences of each keyword*) Write a program that reads in a Python source code file and counts the occurrence of each keyword in the file. Your program should prompt the user to enter the Python source code filename.

*14.4 (*Tkinter: Count the occurrences of each letter*) Rewrite Listing 14.5 using a GUI program to let the user enter the file from an entry field, as shown in Figure 14.3a. You can also select a file by clicking the *Browse* button to display an Open file dialog box, as shown in Figure 14.3b. The file selected is then displayed in the entry field. Clicking the *Show Result* button displays the result in a text widget. You need to display a message in a message box if the file does not exist.

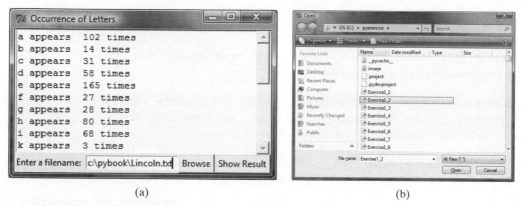

(a)   (b)

FIGURE 14.3 The program lets the user select a file and displays the occurrence counts of the letters in the file.

*14.5 (*Tkinter: Count the occurrences of each letter*) Revise the preceding exercise to display a histogram for the result, as shown in Figure 14.4. You need to display a message in a message box if the file does not exist.

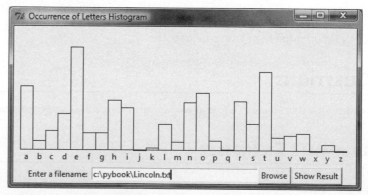

FIGURE 14.4 The program lets the user select a file and displays the occurrence counts in a histogram.

*14.6 (*Tkinter: Count the occurrences of each letter*) Rewrite Listing 14.5 using a GUI program to let the user enter the URL from an entry field, as shown in Figure 14.5. Clicking the *Show Result* button displays the result in a text widget. You need to display a message in a message box if the URL does not exist.

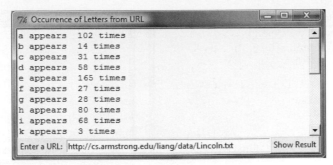

FIGURE 14.5 The program lets the user enter a URL for a file and displays the occurrence counts of the letters in the file.

*14.7 (*Tkinter: Count the occurrences of each letter*) Revise the preceding exercise to display a histogram for the result, as shown in Figure 14.6. You need to display a message in a message box if the URL does not exist.

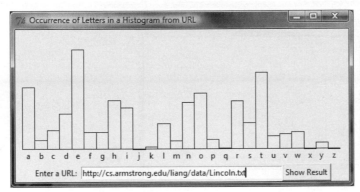

FIGURE 14.6 The program lets the user enter a URL for a file and displays the occurrence counts of the letters in a histogram.

14.8 (*Display nonduplicate words in ascending order*) Write a program that prompts the user to enter a text file, reads words from the file, and displays all the nonduplicate words in ascending order.

***14.9 (*Game: hangman*) Write the hangman game with a graphics display, as shown in Figure 14.7. After seven misses, the program displays the word. The user can press the *Enter* key to continue to guess another word.

*14.10 (*Guess the capitals*) Rewrite Exercise 11.40 using a dictionary to store the pairs of states and capitals so that the questions are randomly displayed.

*14.11 (*Count consonants and vowels*) Write a program that prompts the user to enter a text filename and displays the number of vowels and consonants in the file. Use a set to store the vowels **A, E, I, O**, and **U**.

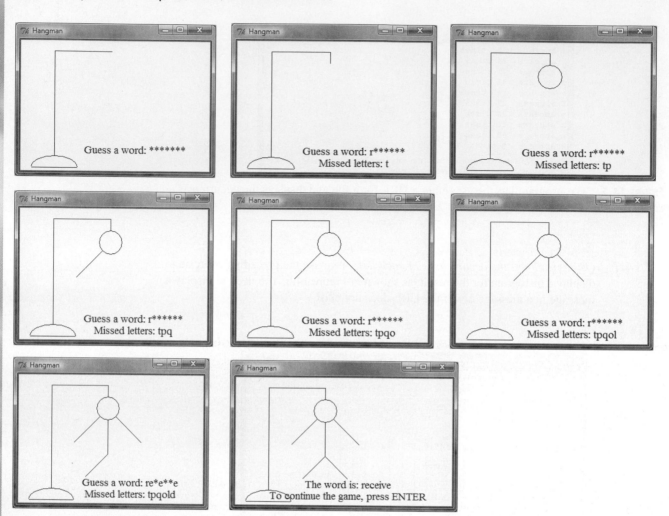

FIGURE 14.7 The hangman game lets the user enter letters to guess a word.

RECURSION

Objectives

- To explain what a recursive function is and describe the benefits of using recursion (§15.1).

- To develop recursive programs for recursive mathematical functions (§§15.2–15.3).

- To explain how recursive function calls are handled in a call stack (§§15.2–15.3).

- To solve problems using recursion (§15.4).

- To use a helper function to design a recursive function (§15.5).

- To implement a selection sort using recursion (§15.5.1).

- To implement a binary search using recursion (§15.5.2).

- To get a directory's size using recursion (§15.6).

- To solve the Towers of Hanoi problem using recursion (§15.7).

- To draw fractals using recursion (§15.8).

- To solve the Eight Queens problem using recursion (§15.9).

- To explain the relationship and differences between recursion and iteration (§15.10).

- To understand tail-recursive functions and explain why they are desirable (§15.11).

15.1 Introduction

Key Point

Recursion is a technique that leads to elegant solutions to problems that are difficult to program using simple loops.

search word problem

Suppose you want to find all the files in a directory that contain a particular word. How do you solve this problem? There are several ways to do so. An intuitive and effective solution is to use recursion by searching the files in each subdirectory recursively.

H-tree problem

The H-tree shown in Figure 15.1 is used in a very large-scale integration (VLSI) design as a clock distribution network for routing timing signals to all parts of a chip with equal propagation delays. How do you write a program to display the H-tree? A good approach is to use recursion by exploring the recursive pattern.

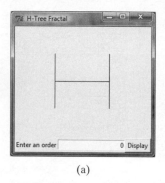
(a)

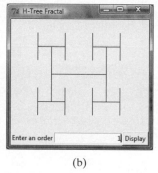
(b)

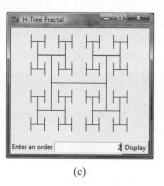
(c)

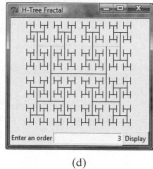
(d)

FIGURE 15.1   An H-tree can be displayed using recursion.

recursive function

To use recursion is to program by using *recursive functions*—functions that invoke themselves. Recursion is a useful programming technique. In some cases, it enables you to develop a natural, straightforward, simple solution to an otherwise difficult problem. This chapter introduces the concepts and techniques of recursive programming and presents examples that show you how to "think recursively."

15.2 Case Study: Computing Factorials

VideoNote
Function sum

Key Point

A recursive function is one that invokes itself.

Many mathematical functions are defined using recursion. Let's begin with a simple example. The factorial of a number n can be recursively defined as follows:

```
0! = 1;
n! = n × (n - 1)!; n > 0
```

How do you find $n!$ for a given n? To find $1!$ is easy, because you know that $0!$ is 1, and $1!$ is $1 \times 0!$. Assuming that you know $(n - 1)!$, you can obtain $n!$ immediately by using $n \times (n - 1)!$. Thus, the problem of computing $n!$ is reduced to computing $(n - 1)!$. When computing $(n - 1)!$, you can apply the same idea recursively until n is reduced to 0.

Let `factorial(n)` be the function for computing $n!$. If you call the function with $n = 0$, it immediately returns the result. The function knows how to solve the simplest case, which is referred to as the *base case* or the *stopping condition*. If you call the function with $n > 0$, it reduces the problem into a subproblem for computing the factorial of $n - 1$. The *subproblem* is essentially the same as the original problem, but it is simpler or smaller. Because the subproblem has the same property as the original problem, you can call the function with a different argument, which is referred to as a *recursive call*.

base case or stopping condition

recursive call

The recursive algorithm for computing **factorial(n)** can be simply described as follows:

```
if n == 0:
    return 1
else:
    return n * factorial(n - 1)
```

A recursive call can result in many more recursive calls, because the function keeps on dividing a subproblem into new subproblems. For a recursive function to terminate, the problem must eventually be reduced to a stopping case, at which point the function returns a result to its caller. The caller then performs a computation and returns the result to its own caller. This process continues until the result is passed back to the original caller. The original problem can now be solved by multiplying **n** by the result of **factorial(n - 1)**.

Listing 15.1 is a complete program that prompts the user to enter a nonnegative integer and displays the factorial for the number.

LISTING 15.1 ComputeFactorial.py

```
1  def main():
2      n = eval(input("Enter a nonnegative integer: "))
3      print("Factorial of", n, "is", factorial(n))
4
5  # Return the factorial for the specified number
6  def factorial(n):
7      if n == 0: # Base case                                base case
8          return 1
9      else:
10         return n * factorial(n - 1) # Recursive call      recursion
11
12 main() # Call the main function
```

```
Enter a nonnegative integer: 4  ↵Enter
Factorial of 4 is 24
```

```
Enter a nonnegative integer: 10  ↵Enter
Factorial of 10 is 3628800
```

The **factorial** function (lines 6–10) is essentially a direct translation of the recursive mathematical definition for the factorial into Python code. The call to **factorial** is recursive because it calls itself. The parameter passed to **factorial** is decremented until it reaches the base case of **0**.

Now that you have seen how to write a recursive function, let's see how recursion works. how does it work? Figure 15.2 illustrates the execution of the recursive calls, starting with **n = 4**. The use of stack for recursive calls is shown in Figure 15.3.

Pedagogical Note

It is simpler and more efficient to implement the **factorial** function by using a loop. However, we use the recursive **factorial** function here to demonstrate the concept of recursion. Later in this chapter, we will present some problems that are inherently recursive and are difficult to solve without using recursion.

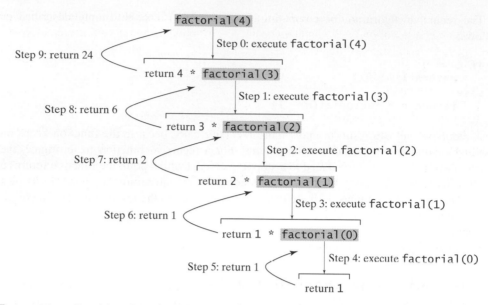

FIGURE 15.2 Invoking `factorial(4)` spawns recursive calls to `factorial`.

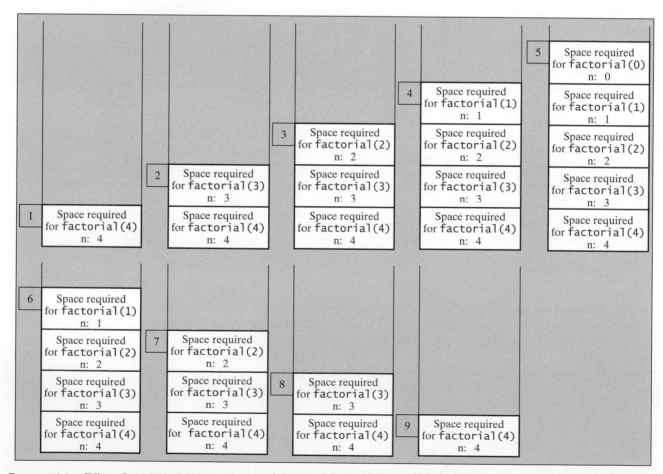

FIGURE 15.3 When `factorial(4)` is being executed, the `factorial` function is called recursively, causing stack space to dynamically change.

If recursion does not reduce the problem in a manner that allows it to eventually converge into the base case, *infinite recursion* can occur. For example, suppose you mistakenly write the **factorial** function as follows:

infinite recursion

```
def factorial(n):
    return n * factorial(n - 1)
```

The function runs infinitely and causes a **RuntimeError**.

The example discussed so far shows a recursive function that invokes itself. This is known as *direct recursion*. It is also possible to create *indirect recursion*. This occurs when function **A** invokes function **B**, which in turn invokes function **A**. There can even be several more functions involved in the recursion. For example, function **A** invokes function **B**, which invokes function **C**, which invokes function **A**.

direct recursion
indirect recursion

15.1 What is a recursive function?

15.2 How many times would the **factorial** function in Listing 15.1 be invoked for **factorial(6)**?

15.3 Write a recursive mathematical definition for computing 2^n for a positive integer n.

15.4 Write a recursive mathematical definition for computing x^n for a positive integer n and a real number x.

15.5 Write a recursive mathematical definition for computing $1 + 2 + 3 + \ldots + n$ for a positive integer.

15.6 What is an infinite recursion? What is a direct recursion? What is an indirect recursion?

✓**Check
Point**

MyProgrammingLab

15.3 Case Study: Computing Fibonacci Numbers

In some cases, recursion enables you to create an intuitive, straightforward, simple solution to a problem.

🔑**Key
Point**

The **factorial** function in the preceding section could easily be rewritten without using recursion. In this section, we show an example for creating an intuitive, straightforward, simple solution to a problem using recursion that would otherwise be difficult to solve. Consider the well-known Fibonacci-series problem:

```
The series: 0  1  1  2  3  5  8  13  21  34  55  89 . . .
   indexes: 0  1  2  3  4  5  6  7   8   9   10  11
```

The Fibonacci series begins with **0** and **1**, and each subsequent number is the sum of the preceding two. The series can be recursively defined as follows:

```
fib(0) = 0
fib(1) = 1
fib(index) = fib(index - 2) + fib(index - 1); index >= 2
```

> **Note**
> The Fibonacci series was named for Leonardo Fibonacci, a medieval mathematician who originated it to model the growth of the rabbit population. It can be applied in numeric optimization and in various other areas.

How do you find **fib(index)** for a given **index**? It is easy to find **fib(2)**, because you know **fib(0)** and **fib(1)**. Assuming that you know **fib(index - 2)** and **fib(index - 1)**, you can obtain **fib(index)** immediately. Thus, the problem of computing **fib(index)** is reduced to computing **fib(index - 2)** and **fib(index - 1)**. When doing so, you apply the idea recursively until **index** is reduced to **0** or **1**.

The base case is **index = 0** or **index = 1**. If you call the function with **index = 0** or **index = 1**, it immediately returns the result. If you call the function with **index >= 2**, it divides the problem into two subproblems for computing **fib(index - 1)** and **fib(index - 2)** using recursive calls. The recursive algorithm for computing **fib(index)** can be simply described as follows:

```
if index == 0:
    return 0
elif index == 1:
    return 1
else:
    return fib(index - 1) + fib(index - 2)
```

Listing 15.2 is a complete program that prompts the user to enter an index and computes the Fibonacci number for that index.

LISTING 15.2 ComputeFibonacci.py

```
 1  def main():
 2      index = eval(input("Enter an index for a Fibonacci number: "))
 3      # Find and display the Fibonacci number
 4      print("The Fibonacci number at index", index, "is", fib(index))
 5
 6  # The function for finding the Fibonacci number
 7  def fib(index):
 8      if index == 0: # Base case
 9          return 0
10      elif index == 1: # Base case
11          return 1
12      else:  # Reduction and recursive calls
13          return fib(index - 1) + fib(index - 2)
14
15  main() # Call the main function
```

base case (line 8)

base case (line 10)

recursion (line 13)

```
Enter an index for a Fibonacci number: 1 ↵Enter
The Fibonacci number at index 1 is 1
```

```
Enter an index for a Fibonacci number: 6 ↵Enter
The Fibonacci number at index 6 is 8
```

```
Enter an index for a Fibonacci number: 7 ↵Enter
The Fibonacci number at index 7 is 13
```

The program does not show the considerable amount of work done behind the scenes by the computer. Figure 15.4, however, shows the successive recursive calls for evaluating **fib(4)**. The original function, **fib(4)**, makes two recursive calls, **fib(3)** and **fib(2)**, and then returns **fib(3) + fib(2)**. But in what order are these functions called? In Python, operands are evaluated from left to right, so **fib(2)** is called after **fib(3)** is completely evaluated. The labels in Figure 15.4 show the order in which the functions are called.

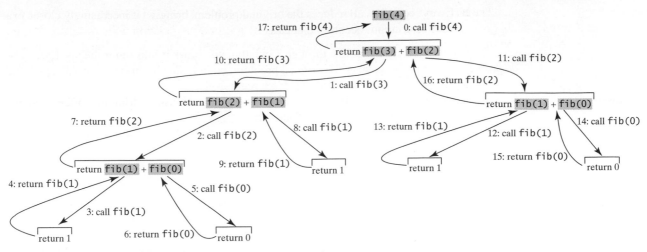

FIGURE 15.4   Invoking **fib(4)** spawns recursive calls to **fib**.

As shown in Figure 15.4, there are many duplicated recursive calls. For instance, **fib(2)** is called twice, **fib(1)** three times, and **fib(0)** twice. In general, computing **fib(index)** requires roughly twice as many recursive calls as does computing **fib(index - 1)**. As you try larger index values, the number of calls substantially increases, as shown in Table 15.1.

TABLE 15.1   Number of Recursive Calls in **fib(n)**

n	2	3	4	10	20	30	40	50
# of calls	3	5	9	177	21891	2692537	331160281	2075316483

Pedagogical Note

The recursive implementation of the **fib** function is very simple and straightforward, but it isn't efficient. See Programming Exercise 15.2 for an efficient solution using loops. Though it is not practical, the recursive **fib** function is a good example of how to write recursive functions.

15.7   How many times would the **fib** function in Listing 15.2 be invoked for **fib(6)**?

15.8   Show the output of the following programs and identify their base cases and recursive calls.

```
def f(n):
    if n == 1:
        return 1
    else:
        return n + f(n - 1)

print("Sum is", f(5))
```

```
def f(n):
    if n > 0:
        print(n % 10)
        f(n // 10)

f(1234567)
```

15.4 Problem Solving Using Recursion

If you think recursively, many problems can be solved using recursion.

Key Point

The preceding sections presented two classic recursion examples. All recursive functions have the following characteristics:

- The function is implemented using an **if-else** or a **switch** statement that leads to different cases.

- One or more base cases (the simplest case) are used to stop recursion.

recursion characteristics

if-else

base cases

reduction

■ Every recursive call reduces the original problem, bringing it increasingly closer to a base case until it becomes that case.

In general, to solve a problem through recursion, you break it into subproblems. Each subproblem is almost the same as the original problem, but it is smaller in size. You can apply the same approach to each subproblem to solve it recursively.

think recursively

Recursion is everywhere. It is fun to *think recursively*. Consider drinking coffee. You can describe the procedure recursively, as follows:

```
def drinkCoffee(cup):
    if cup is not empty:
        cup.takeOneSip() # Take one sip
        drinkCoffee(cup)
```

VideoNote

Function print numbers

Assume **cup** is an object for a cup of coffee with the instance functions **isEmpty()** and **takeOneSip()**. You can break the problem into two subproblems: one is to drink one sip of coffee, and the other is to drink the rest of the coffee in the cup. The second problem is the same as the original problem but smaller in size. The base case for the problem is when the cup is empty.

Consider the problem of printing a message **n** times. You can break the problem into two subproblems: one is to print the message one time, and the other is to print it **n** - **1** times. The second problem is the same as the original problem but it is smaller in size. The base case for

recursive call

the problem is **n** == **0**. You can solve this problem using recursion as follows:

```
def nPrintln(message, n):
    if n >= 1:
        print(message)
        nPrintln(message, n - 1)
    # The base case is n == 0
```

Note that the **fib** function in the preceding section returns a value to its caller, but the **nPrintln** function is void and does not.

think recursively

If you *think recursively*, you can use recursion to solve many of the problems presented in earlier chapters of this book. Consider the palindrome problem in Listing 8.1. Recall that a string is a palindrome if it reads the same from the left and from the right. For example, "mom" and "dad" are palindromes, but "uncle" and "aunt" are not. The problem of determining whether a string is a palindrome can be divided into two subproblems:

■ Determine whether the first character and the last character of the string are equal.

■ Ignore the two end characters and see if the rest of the substring is a palindrome.

The second subproblem is the same as the original problem but smaller in size. There are two base cases: (1) the two end characters are not the same, and (2) the string size is **0** or **1**. In case 1, the string is not a palindrome; in case 2, the string is a palindrome. The recursive function for this problem can be implemented as shown in Listing 15.3.

LISTING 15.3 RecursivePalindromeUsingSubstring.py

function header
base case

base case

recursive call

```
1  def isPalindrome(s):
2      if len(s) <= 1: # Base case
3          return True
4      elif s[0] != s[len(s) - 1]: # Base case
5          return False
6      else:
7          return isPalindrome(s[1 : len(s) - 1])
8
```

```
 9  def main():
10      print("Is moon a palindrome?", isPalindrome("moon"))
11      print("Is noon a palindrome?", isPalindrome("noon"))
12      print("Is a a palindrome?", isPalindrome("a"))
13      print("Is aba a palindrome?", isPalindrome("aba"))
14      print("Is ab a palindrome?", isPalindrome("ab"))
15
16  main() # Call the main function
```

```
Is moon a palindrome? False
Is noon a palindrome? True
Is a a palindrome? True
Is aba a palindrome? True
Is ab a palindrome? False
```

The string slicing operator in line 7 creates a new string that is the same as the original string except without the first and last characters. Checking whether a string is a palindrome is equivalent to checking whether the substring is a palindrome if the two end characters in the original string are the same.

Check Point

MyProgrammingLab™

15.9 Describe the characteristics of recursive functions.

15.10 Show the call stacks for **isPalindrome("abcba")** using the functions defined in Listing 15.3.

15.11 Show the output of the following two programs:

```
def f(n):
    if n > 0:
        print(n, end = ' ')
        f(n - 1)

f(5)
```

```
def f(n):
    if n > 0:
        f(n - 1)
        print(n, end = ' ')

f(5)
```

15.12 What is wrong in the following function?

```
def f(n):
    if n != 0:
        print(n, end = ' ')
        f(n / 10)

f(1234567)
```

15.5 Recursive Helper Functions

Sometimes you can find a recursive solution by slightly changing the original problem. This new function is called a recursive helper function. *The original problem can be solved by invoking the recursive helper function.*

Key Point

The preceding recursive **isPalindrome** function is not efficient, because it creates a new string for every recursive call. To avoid creating new strings, you can use the low and high indexes to indicate the range of the substring. These two indexes must be passed to the recursive function.

Since the original function is **isPalindrome(s)**, you have to create the new function **isPalindromeHelper(s, low, high)** to accept additional information on the string, as shown in Listing 15.4.

LISTING 15.4 RecursivePalindrome.py

```
1  def isPalindrome(s):
2      return isPalindromeHelper(s, 0, len(s) - 1)
3
4  def isPalindromeHelper(s, low, high):
5      if high <= low: # Base case
6          return True
7      elif s[low] != s[high]: # Base case
8          return False
9      else:
10         return isPalindromeHelper(s, low + 1, high - 1)
11
12 def main():
13     print("Is moon a palindrome?", isPalindrome("moon"))
14     print("Is noon a palindrome?", isPalindrome("noon"))
15     print("Is a a palindrome?", isPalindrome("a"))
16     print("Is aba a palindrome?", isPalindrome("aba"))
17     print("Is ab a palindrome?", isPalindrome("ab"))
18
19 main() # Call the main function
```

helper function
base case

base case

The **isPalindrome(s)** function checks whether a string **s** is a palindrome, and the **isPalindromeHelper(s, low, high)** function checks whether a substring **s[low : high + 1]** is a palindrome. The **isPalindrome(s)** function passes the string **s** with **low = 0** and **high = len(s) – 1** to the **isPalindromeHelper** function, which can be invoked recursively to check a palindrome in an ever-shrinking substring. It is a common design technique in recursive programming to define a second function that receives additional parameters. Such a function is known as a *recursive helper function*.

recursive helper function

Helper functions are very useful in designing recursive solutions for problems involving strings and lists. The sections that follow give two more examples.

15.5.1 Selection Sort

Selection sort was introduced in Section 10.11.1. Recall that it finds the smallest element in a list and swaps it with the first element. It then finds the smallest element remaining and swaps it with the first element in the remaining list, and so on until the remaining list contains only a single element. The problem can be divided into two subproblems:

- Find the smallest element in the list and swap it with the first element.

- Ignore the first element and sort the remaining smaller list recursively.

The base case is that the list contains only one element. Listing 15.5 gives the recursive sort function.

LISTING 15.5 RecursiveSelectionSort.py

```
1  def sort(lst):
2      sortHelper(lst, 0, len(lst) - 1) # Sort the entire list
3
4  def sortHelper(lst, low, high):
5      if low < high:
6          # Find the smallest element and its index in lst[low .. high]
7          indexOfMin = low
```

helper function
base case

```
8              min = lst[low]
9              for i in range(low + 1, high + 1):
10                 if lst[i] < min:
11                     min = lst[i]
12                     indexOfMin = i
13
14             # Swap the smallest in lst[low .. high] with lst[low]
15             lst[indexOfMin] = lst[low]
16             lst[low] = min
17
18             # Sort the remaining lst[low+1 .. high]
19             sortHelper(lst, low + 1, high)                              recursive call
20
21  def main():
22      lst = [3, 2, 1, 5, 9, 0]
23      sort(lst)
24      print(lst)
25
26  main() # Call the main function
```

The **sort(lst)** function sorts a list in **lst[0..len(lst) - 1]** and the **sortHelper(lst, low, high)** function sorts a sublist in **lst[low..high]**. The second function can be invoked recursively to sort an ever-shrinking sublist.

15.5.2   Binary Search

Binary search was introduced in Section 10.10.2. For a binary search to work, the elements in the list must already be ordered. The binary search first compares the key with the element in the middle of the list. Consider the following three cases:

- Case 1: If the key is less than the middle element, the program recursively searches for the key in the first half of the list.

- Case 2: If the key is equal to the middle element, the search ends with a match.

- Case 3: If the key is greater than the middle element, the program recursively searches for the key in the second half of the list.

Case 1 and Case 3 reduce the search to a smaller list. Case 2 is a base case when there is a match. Another base case is that the search is exhausted without a match. Listing 15.6 gives a simple solution for the binary search problem using recursion.

LISTING 15.6   RecursiveBinarySearch.py

```
1   def recursiveBinarySearch(lst, key):
2       low = 0
3       high = len(lst) - 1
4       return recursiveBinarySearchHelper(lst, key, low, high)
5
6   def recursiveBinarySearchHelper(lst, key, low, high):                 helper function
7       if low > high:  # The list has been exhausted without a match     base case
8           return -low - 1
9
10      mid = (low + high) // 2
11      if key < lst[mid]:
12          return recursiveBinarySearchHelper(lst, key, low, mid - 1)    recursive call
13      elif key == lst[mid]:                                             base case
14          return mid
15      else:
16          return recursiveBinarySearchHelper(lst, key, mid + 1, high)   recursive call
```

```
17
18  def main():
19      lst = [3, 5, 6, 8, 9, 12, 34, 36]
20      print(recursiveBinarySearch(lst, 3))
21      print(recursiveBinarySearch(lst, 4))
22
23  main() # Call the main function
```

The **recursiveBinarySearch** function finds a key in the whole list (lines 1–4). The **recursiveBinarySearchHelper** function finds a key in the list with the index from **low** to **high** (lines 6–16).

The **recursiveBinarySearch** function passes the initial list with **low = 0** (line 2) and **high = len(lst) - 1** (line 3) to the **recursiveBinarySearchHelper** function, which is invoked recursively to find the key in an ever-shrinking sublist.

MyProgrammingLab™

15.13 What is a recursive helper function?

15.14 Show the call stack for **sort([2, 3, 5, 1])** using the function defined in Listing 15.5.

15.6 Case Study: Finding the Directory Size

Key Point

Recursive functions can efficiently solve problems with recursive structures.

The preceding examples can easily be solved without using recursion. This section presents a problem that is difficult to solve without using recursion. The problem is to find the size of a directory. The size of a directory is the sum of the sizes of all the files in the directory. A directory *d* may contain subdirectories. Suppose a directory contains files $f_1, f_2, \ldots, f_m$ and subdirectories $d_1, d_2, \ldots, d_n$, as shown in Figure 15.5.

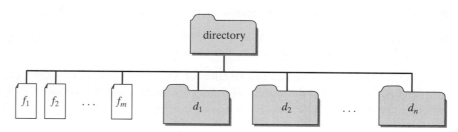

FIGURE 15.5 A directory contains files and subdirectories.

The size of the directory can be defined recursively as follows:

$$size(d) = size(f_1) + size(f_2) + \ldots + size(f_m) + size(d_1) + size(d_2) + \ldots + size(d_n)$$

To implement the program, you need the following three functions from the **os** module:

- **os.path.isfile(s)**, which returns **True** if **s** is a filename. Recall that this function was introduced in §13.2.3 to check if a file exists.

- **os.path.getsize(filename)**, which returns the size of the file.

- **os.listdir(directory)**, which returns a list of the subdirectories and files under the directory.

The program in Listing 15.7 prompts the user to enter a directory or a filename and displays its size.

LISTING 15.7 DirectorySize.py

```
1   import os
2
3   def main():
4       # Prompt the user to enter a directory or a file
5       path = input("Enter a directory or a file: ").strip()
6
7       # Display the size
8       try:
9           print(getSize(path), "bytes")                          invoke function
10      except:
11          print("Directory or file does not exist")
12
13  def getSize(path):                                             getSize function
14      size = 0 # Store the total size of all files
15
16      if not os.path.isfile(path):                               is directory?
17          lst = os.listdir(path) # All files and subdirectories   all subitems
18          for subdirectory in lst:
19              size += getSize(path + "\\" + subdirectory)         recursive call
20      else: # Base case, it is a file
21          size += os.path.getsize(path) # Accumulate file size    base case
22
23      return size
24
25  main() # Call the main function
```

```
Enter a directory or a file: c:\pybook  ⏎Enter
619631 bytes
```

```
Enter a directory or a file: c:\pybook\Welcome.py  ⏎Enter
76 bytes
```

```
Enter a directory or a file: c:\book\NonExistentFile  ⏎Enter
Directory or file does not exist
```

If the **path** is a directory (line 16), each subitem (file or subdirectory) in the directory is recursively invoked to obtain its size (line 19). If the **path** is a file (line 20), the file size is obtained (line 21).

If the user enters an incorrect or a nonexistent file or directory, the program throws an exception (line 11).

Tip

To avoid mistakes, it is a good practice to test base cases. For example, you should test the program for an input of a filename, an empty directory, a nonexistent directory, and a nonexistent filename.

testing base cases

15.15 What function do you use to test if a filename exists? What function do you use to return the size of a file? What function do you use to return all files and subdirectories under a directory?

15.7 Case Study: Towers of Hanoi

Key Point

The Towers of Hanoi problem is a classic problem that can be solved easily by using recursion, but it is difficult to solve otherwise.

The Towers of Hanoi problem is a classic recursion problem that every computer scientist knows. The problem involves moving a specified number of disks of distinct sizes from one tower to another while observing the following rules:

■ There are n disks labeled 1, 2, 3, . . ., n, and three towers labeled A, B, and C.

■ No disk can be on top of a smaller disk at any time.

■ All the disks are initially placed on tower A.

■ Only one disk can be moved at a time, and it must be the top disk on a tower.

The objective of the problem is to move all the disks from tower A to tower B with the assistance of tower C. For example, if you have three disks, the steps to move all of the disks from tower A to B are shown in Figure 15.6.

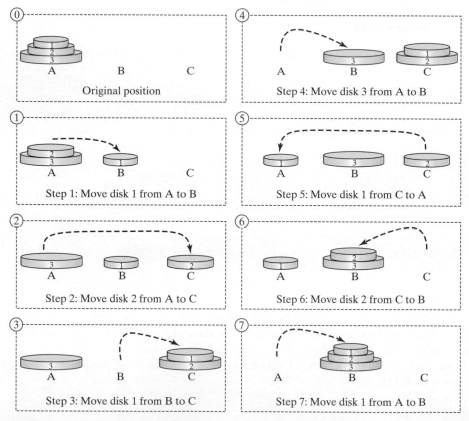

FIGURE 15.6 The goal of the Towers of Hanoi problem is to move disks from tower A to tower B without breaking the rules.

Note

The Towers of Hanoi is a classic computer-science problem, to which many Web sites are devoted. One of them worth looking at is **www.cut-the-knot.com/recurrence/hanoi.shtml**.

In the case of three disks, you can find the solution manually. For a larger number of disks, however—even for four—the problem is quite complex. Fortunately, the problem has an inherently recursive nature, which leads to a straightforward recursive solution.

The base case for the problem is **n = 1**. If **n == 1**, you could simply move the disk from A to B. When **n > 1**, you could split the original problem into three subproblems and solve them sequentially, as follows:

1. Move the first **n - 1** disks from A to C with the assistance of tower B, as shown in Step 1 in Figure 15.7.

2. Move disk **n** from A to B, as shown in Step 2 in Figure 15.7.

3. Move **n - 1** disks from C to B with the assistance of tower A, as shown in Step 3 in Figure 15.7.

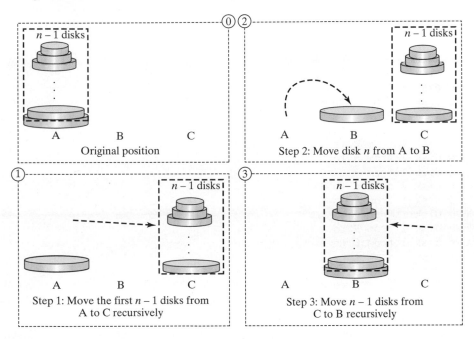

FIGURE 15.7 The Towers of Hanoi problem can be decomposed into three subproblems.

The following function moves *n* disks from the **fromTower** to the **toTower** with the assistance of the **auxTower**:

```
def moveDisks(n, fromTower, toTower, auxTower):
```

The algorithm for the function can be described as follows:

```
if n == 1: # Stopping condition
    Move disk 1 from the fromTower to the toTower
else:
    moveDisks(n - 1, fromTower, auxTower, toTower)
    Move disk n from the fromTower to the toTower
    moveDisks(n - 1, auxTower, toTower, fromTower)
```

The program in Listing 15.8 prompts the user to enter the number of disks and invokes the recursive function **moveDisks** to display the solution for moving the disks.

LISTING 15.8 TowersOfHanoi.py

```
1  def main():
2      n = eval(input("Enter number of disks: "))
3
```

```
4      # Find the solution recursively
5      print("The moves are:")
6      moveDisks(n, 'A', 'B', 'C')
7
8  # The function for finding the solution to move n disks
9  #    from fromTower to toTower with auxTower
10 def moveDisks(n, fromTower, toTower, auxTower):
11     if n == 1: # Stopping condition
12         print("Move disk", n, "from", fromTower, "to", toTower)
13     else:
14         moveDisks(n - 1, fromTower, auxTower, toTower)
15         print("Move disk", n, "from", fromTower, "to", toTower)
16         moveDisks(n - 1, auxTower, toTower, fromTower)
17
18 main() # Call the main function
```

base case

recursion

recursion

```
Enter number of disks: 4  ⏎ Enter
The moves are:
Move disk 1 from A to C
Move disk 2 from A to B
Move disk 1 from C to B
Move disk 3 from A to C
Move disk 1 from B to A
Move disk 2 from B to C
Move disk 1 from A to C
Move disk 4 from A to B
Move disk 1 from C to B
Move disk 2 from C to A
Move disk 1 from B to A
Move disk 3 from C to B
Move disk 1 from A to C
Move disk 2 from A to B
Move disk 1 from C to B
```

Consider tracing the program for **n** = 3. The successive recursive calls are shown in Figure 15.8. As you can see, writing the program is easier than tracing the recursive calls. The system uses stacks to trace the calls behind the scenes. To some extent, recursion provides a level of abstraction that hides iterations and other details from the user.

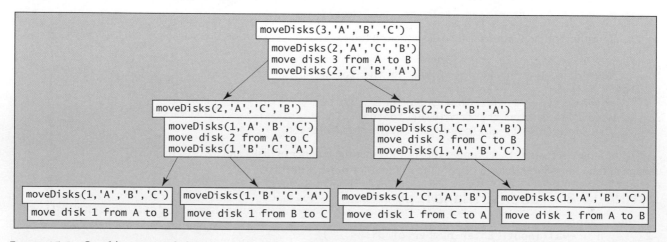

FIGURE 15.8 Invoking **moveDisks(3, 'A', 'B', 'C')** spawns calls to **moveDisks** recursively.

15.16 How many times would the `moveDisks` function in Listing 15.8 be invoked for `moveDisks(5, 'A', 'B', 'C')`?

15.8 Case Study: Fractals

Recursion is ideal for displaying fractals, because fractals are inherently recursive.

A *fractal* is a geometrical figure, but unlike triangles, circles, and rectangles, fractals can be divided into parts, each of which is a reduced-size copy of the whole. There are many interesting examples of fractals. This section introduces a simple fractal, the *Sierpinski triangle*, named after a famous Polish mathematician.

A Sierpinski triangle is created as follows:

1. Begin with an equilateral triangle, which is considered to be a Sierpinski fractal of *order* (or *level*) **0**, as shown in Figure 15.9a.

2. Connect the midpoints of the sides of the triangle of order **0** to create a Sierpinski triangle of order **1** (Figure 15.9b).

3. Leave the center triangle intact. Connect the midpoints of the sides of the three other triangles to create a Sierpinski triangle of order **2** (Figure 15.9c).

4. You can repeat the same process recursively to create a Sierpinski triangle of order **3**, **4**, and so on (Figure 15.9d).

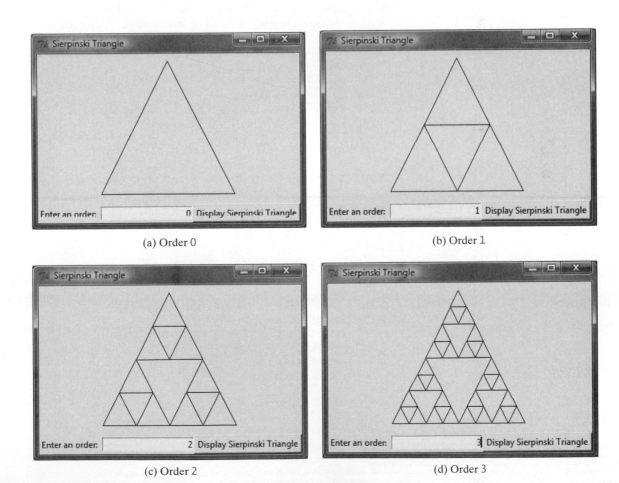

(a) Order 0

(b) Order 1

(c) Order 2

(d) Order 3

FIGURE 15.9 A Sierpinski triangle is a pattern of recursive triangles.

The problem is inherently recursive. How do you develop a recursive solution for it? Consider the base case when the order is **0**. It is easy to draw a Sierpinski triangle of order **0**. How do you draw a Sierpinski triangle of order **1**? The problem can be reduced to drawing three Sierpinski triangles of order **0**. How do you draw a Sierpinski triangle of order **2**? The problem can be reduced to drawing three Sierpinski triangles of order **1**, so the problem of drawing a Sierpinski triangle of order **n** can be reduced to drawing three Sierpinski triangles of order **n** - **1**.

Listing 15.9 is a program that displays a Sierpinski triangle of any order, as shown in Figure 15.9. You can enter an order in a text field to display a Sierpinski triangle of the specified order.

LISTING 15.9 SierpinskiTriangle.py

```python
from tkinter import * # Import all definition from tkinter

class SierpinskiTriangle:
    def __init__(self):
        window = Tk() # Create a window
        window.title("Sierpinski Triangle") # Set a title

        self.width = 200
        self.height = 200
        self.canvas = Canvas(window,
            width = self.width, height = self.height)
        self.canvas.pack()

        # Add a label, an entry, and a button to frame1
        frame1 = Frame(window) # Create and add a frame to window
        frame1.pack()

        Label(frame1,
            text = "Enter an order: ").pack(side = LEFT)
        self.order = StringVar()
        entry = Entry(frame1, textvariable = self.order,
                justify = RIGHT).pack(side = LEFT)
        Button(frame1, text = "Display Sierpinski Triangle",
            command = self.display).pack(side = LEFT)

        window.mainloop() # Create an event loop

    def display(self):
        self.canvas.delete("line")
        p1 = [self.width / 2, 10]
        p2 = [10, self.height - 10]
        p3 = [self.width - 10, self.height - 10]
        self.displayTriangles(int(self.order.get()), p1, p2, p3)

    def displayTriangles(self, order, p1, p2, p3):
        if order == 0: # Base condition
            # Draw a triangle to connect three points
            self.drawLine(p1, p2)
            self.drawLine(p2, p3)
            self.drawLine(p3, p1)
        else:
            # Get the midpoint of each triangle's edge
            p12 = self.midpoint(p1, p2)
            p23 = self.midpoint(p2, p3)
            p31 = self.midpoint(p3, p1)

            # Recursively display three triangles
            self.displayTriangles(order - 1, p1, p12, p31)
```

create a canvas (line 10)

create an entry (line 21)

create a button (line 23)

display triangle (line 28)

recursive triangles (line 35)

draw one triangle (line 38)

get midpoints (line 43)

top subtriangle (line 48)

```
49                self.displayTriangles(order - 1, p12, p2, p23)         left subtriangle
50                self.displayTriangles(order - 1, p31, p23, p3)         right subtriangle
51
52        def drawLine(self, p1, p2):                                    draw a line
53            self.canvas.create_line(
54                p1[0], p1[1], p2[0], p2[1], tags = "line")
55
56        # Return the midpoint between two points
57        def midpoint(self, p1, p2):                                    midpoint
58            p = 2 * [0]
59            p[0] = (p1[0] + p2[0]) / 2
60            p[1] = (p1[1] + p2[1]) / 2
61            return p
62
63    SierpinskiTriangle() # Create GUI                                  create GUI
```

When you enter an order in the text field and then click the *Display Sierpinski Triangle* button, the callback **display** function is invoked to create three points and display the triangle (lines 30–33). display function

The three points of the triangle are passed to invoke **displayTriangles** (line 35). If **order == 0**, the **displayTriangles(order, p1, p2, p3)** function displays a triangle that connects three points **p1**, **p2**, and **p3** in lines 38–40, as shown in Figure 15.10a. Otherwise, it performs the following tasks: displayTriangles function

1. Obtains a midpoint between **p1** and **p2** (line 43), a midpoint between **p2** and **p3** (line 44), and a midpoint between **p3** and **p1** (line 45), as shown in Figure 15.10b.

2. Recursively invokes **displayTriangles** with a reduced order to display three smaller Sierpinski triangles (lines 48–50). Note that each small Sierpinski triangle is structurally identical to the original big Sierpinski triangle except that the order of a small triangle is one less, as shown in Figure 15.10b.

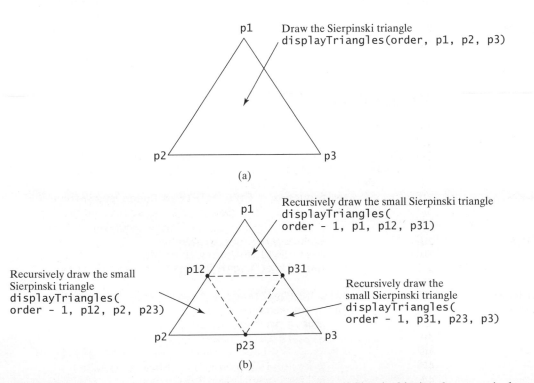

FIGURE 15.10 Drawing a Sierpinski triangle spawns calls to draw three small Sierpinski triangles recursively.

15.9 Case Study: Eight Queens

The Eight Queens problem is to find a solution to place a queen in each row on a chessboard so that no two queens can attack each other.

This case study creates a program that arranges eight queens on a chessboard. There can only be one queen in each row, and the queens must be positioned such that no two queens can take the other. You need to use a two-dimensional list to represent the chessboard, but because each row can have only one queen, it is sufficient to use a one-dimensional list to denote the queen's position in the row. So, create a list named **queens** as follows:

```
queens = 8 * [-1]
```

Assign **j** to **queens[i]** to denote that a queen is placed in row **i** and column **j**. Figure 15.11a shows the contents of the list **queens** for the chessboard in Figure 15.11b. Initially, **queens[i]** = -1 indicates that row **i** is not occupied.

queens[0]	0
queens[1]	4
queens[2]	7
queens[3]	5
queens[4]	2
queens[5]	6
queens[6]	1
queens[7]	3

(a)   (b)

FIGURE 15.11 **queens[i]** denotes the position of the queen in row **i**.

The program in Listing 15.10 displays a solution for the Eight Queens problem.

LISTING 15.10 EightQueens.py

initialize queens
start search

create queen image
display chessboard

display queen

```
1  from tkinter import * # Import all definitions from tkinter
2
3  SIZE = 8 # The size of the chessboard
4  class EightQueens:
5      def __init__(self):
6          self.queens = SIZE * [-1] # Queen positions
7          self.search(0) # Search for a solution from row 0
8
9          # Display solution in queens
10         window = Tk() # Create a window
11         window.title("Eight Queens") # Set a title
12
13         image = PhotoImage(file = "image/queen.gif")
14         for i in range(SIZE):
15             for j in range(SIZE):
16                 if self.queens[i] == j:
17                     Label(window, image = image).grid(
18                         row = i, column = j)
```

```
19                       else:
20                           Label(window, width = 5, height = 2,
21                               bg = "red").grid(row = i, column = j)
22
23              window.mainloop() # Create an event loop
24
25      # Search for a solution starting from a specified row
26      def search(self, row):                                          search this row
27          if row == SIZE: # Stopping condition
28              return True # A solution found to place 8 queens
29
30          for column in range(SIZE):                                  search columns
31              self.queens[row] = column # Place it at (row, column)   place a queen
32              if self.isValid(row, column) and self.search(row + 1):  recursive call
33                  return True # Found and exit for loop               found
34
35              # No solution for a queen placed at any column of this row
36          return False                                                not found
37
38      # Check if a queen can be placed at row i and column j
39      def isValid(self, row, column):                                 check validity
40          for i in range(1, row + 1):
41              if (self.queens[row - i] == column # Check column       check column
42                  or self.queens[row - i] == column - i               check upleft diagonal
43                  or self.queens[row - i] == column + i):             check upright diagonal
44                  return False # There is a conflict
45          return True # No conflict
46
47  EightQueens() # Create GUI
```

The program initializes the list **queens** with eight values −1 to indicate that no queens have been placed on the chessboard (line 6). The program invokes **search(0)** (line 7) to start a search for a solution from row **0**, which recursively invokes **search(1)**, **search(2)**, ..., and **search(7)** (line 32).

After a solution is found, the program displays 64 labels in the window (8 per row) and places a queen image in the cell at **queens[i]** for each row **i** (line 17).

The recursive **search(row)** function returns **True** if all the rows are filled (lines 27–28). The function checks whether a queen can be placed in column **0, 1, 2, ..., and 7** in a **for** loop (line 30). The program places a queen in the column (line 31). If the placement is valid, the program recursively searches for the next row by invoking **search(row + 1)** (line 32). If this search is successful, the program returns **True** (line 33) to exit the **for** loop. In this case, there is no need to look for the next column in the row. If there is no solution that allows a queen to be placed in any column in this row, the function returns **False** (line 36).

Suppose you invoke **search(row)** for **row 3**, as shown in Figure 15.12a. The function tries to fill in a queen in column **0, 1, 2**, and so on in this order. For each trial, the **isValid(row, column)** function (line 32) is called to check whether placing a queen at the specified position causes a conflict with the queens placed earlier. It also ensures that no queen is placed in the same column (line 41), upper left diagonal (line 42), or upper right diagonal (line 43), as shown in Figure 15.12b. If **isValid(row, column)** returns **False**, the program checks the next column, as shown in Figure 15.12c. If **isValid(row, column)** returns **True**, the program recursively invokes **search(row + 1)**, as shown in Figure 15.12d. If **search(row + 1)** returns **False**, the program checks the next column on the preceding row, as shown Figure 15.12c.

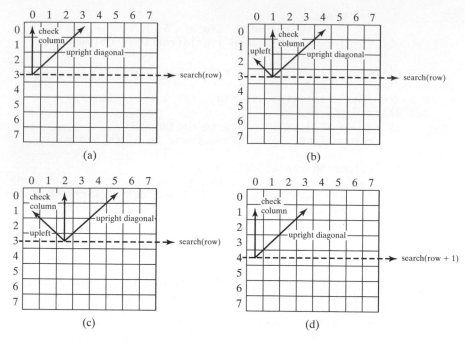

FIGURE 15.12 Invoking `search(row)` fills in a queen in a column in the row.

15.10 Recursion vs. Iteration

Key Point

Recursion is an alternative form of program control. It is essentially repetition without a loop.

When you use loops, you specify a loop body. The repetition of the loop body is controlled by the loop control structure. In recursion, the function itself is called repeatedly. A selection statement must be used to control whether to call the function recursively or not.

recursion overhead

Recursion bears substantial overhead. Each time the program calls a function, the system must allocate memory for all of the function's local variables and parameters. This can consume considerable computer memory and requires extra time to manage the additional memory.

recursion advantages

Any problem that can be solved recursively can be solved nonrecursively with iterations. Recursion has at least one negative aspect: that is, it uses up too much time and memory. Why, then, should you use it? In some cases, using recursion enables you to specify a clear, simple solution for an inherently recursive problem that would otherwise be difficult to achieve. For example, the directory-size problem, the Towers of Hanoi problem, and the fractal problem are rather cumbersome to solve without using recursion.

recursion or iteration?

The decision whether to use recursion or iteration should be based on the nature of, and your understanding of, the problem you are trying to solve. The rule of thumb is to use whichever approach can best develop an intuitive solution that naturally mirrors the problem. If an iterative solution is obvious, use it—it will generally be more efficient than the recursive option.

Caution

stack overflow

Recursive programs can run out of memory, causing a stack-overflow exception.

Tip

performance concern

Avoid using recursion if you are concerned about your program's performance, because it takes more time and consumes more memory than iteration. In general, recursion can be used to solve the inherent recursive problems such as Towers of Hanoi, Directory size, and Sierpinski triangles.

15.17 Which of the following statements are true?

- Any recursive function can be converted into a nonrecursive function.

- Recursive functions take more time and memory to execute than nonrecursive functions.

- Recursive functions are *always* simpler than nonrecursive functions.

- There is always a selection statement in a recursive function to check whether a base case is reached.

15.18 What is a cause for a stack-overflow exception?

Check Point

MyProgrammingLab™

15.11 Tail Recursion

A tail recursive function is efficient for reducing stack size.

A recursive function is said to be *tail recursive* if there are no pending operations to be performed on return from a recursive call, as illustrated in Figure 15.13a. However, function **B** in Figure 15.13b is not tail recursive because there are pending operations after a function call is returned.

Key Point

tail recursive

```
Recursive function A
    ...
    ...

    ...
    Invoke function A recursively
```
(a) Tail recursion

```
Recursive function B
    ...
    ...
    Invoke function B recursively
    ...
    ...
```
(b) Nontail recursion

FIGURE 15.13 A tail-recursive function has no pending operations after a recursive call.

For example, the recursive **isPalindromeHelper** function (lines 4–10) in Listing 15.4 is tail recursive because there are no pending operations after recursively invoking **isPalindromeHelper** in line 10. However, the recursive **factorial** function (lines 6–10) in Listing 15.1 is not tail recursive, because there is a pending operation, namely multiplication, to be performed on return from each recursive call.

Tail recursion may be desirable: Because the function ends when the last recursive call ends, there is no need to store the intermediate calls in the stack.

A nontail-recursive function can often be converted to a tail-recursive function by using auxiliary parameters. These parameters are used to contain the result. The idea is to incorporate the pending operations into the auxiliary parameters in such a way that the recursive call no longer has a pending operation. You may define a new auxiliary recursive function with the auxiliary parameters. For example, the **factorial** function in Listing 15.1 can be written in a tail-recursive way as follows:

```
1  # Return the factorial for a specified number
2  def factorial(n):
3      return factorialHelper(n, 1) # Call auxiliary function
4
5  # Auxiliary tail-recursive function for factorial
6  def factorialHelper(n, result):
```

original function
invoke auxiliary function

auxiliary function

```
recursive call
```

```
7     if n == 0:
8         return result
9     else:
10        return factorialHelper(n - 1, n * result)
```

The first **factorial** function simply invokes the auxiliary function (line 3). In line 6, the auxiliary function contains the auxiliary parameter **result** that stores the result for a factorial of **n**. This function is invoked recursively in line 10. There is no pending operation after a call is returned. The final result is returned in line 8, which is also the return value from invoking **factorialHelper(n, 1)** in line 3.

Check Point

MyProgrammingLab™

15.19 What is tail recursion?

15.20 Why is tail recursion desirable?

15.21 Is the recursive selection function in Listing 15.5 tail recursive?

15.22 Rewrite the **fib** function in Listing 15.2 using tail recursion.

KEY TERMS

base case 500	recursive function 500
direct recursion 503	recursive helper function 508
indirect recursion 503	stopping condition 500
infinite recursion 503	tail recursive 521

CHAPTER SUMMARY

1. A *recursive function* is one that directly or indirectly invokes itself. For a recursive function to terminate, there must be one or more *base cases*.

2. Recursion is an alternative form of program control. It is essentially repetition without a loop control. It can be used to specify simple, clear solutions for inherently recursive problems that would otherwise be difficult to solve.

3. Sometimes the original function needs to be modified to receive additional parameters in order to be invoked recursively. A *recursive helper function* can be defined for this purpose.

4. Recursion bears substantial overhead. Each time the program calls a function, the system must allocate memory for all of the function's local variables and parameters. This can consume considerable computer memory and requires extra time to manage the additional memory.

5. A recursive function is said to be *tail recursive* if there are no pending operations to be performed on return from a recursive call. Tail recursion is efficient.

TEST QUESTIONS

Do test questions for this chapter online at www.cs.armstrong.edu/liang/py/test.html.

PROGRAMMING EXERCISES

Sections 15.2–15.3

*15.1 (*Sum the digits in an integer using recursion*) Write a recursive function that computes the sum of the digits in an integer. Use the following function header:

```
def sumDigits(n):
```

For example, **sumDigits(234)** returns $2 + 3 + 4 = 9$. Write a test program that prompts the user to enter an integer and displays its sum.

*15.2 (*Fibonacci numbers*) Rewrite the **fib** function in Listing 15.2 using iterations.

(Hint: To compute **fib(n)** without recursion, you need to obtain **fib(n - 2)** and **fib(n - 1)** first.) Let **f0** and **f1** denote the two previous Fibonacci numbers. The current Fibonacci number would then be **f0 + f1**. The algorithm can be described as follows:

```
f0 = 0 # For fibs(0)
f1 = 1 # For fib(1)

for i in range(2, n + 1):
    currentFib = f0 + f1
    f0 = f1
    f1 = currentFib

# After the loop, currentFib is fib(n)
```

Write a test program that prompts the user to enter an index and displays its Fibonacci number.

*15.3 (*Compute greatest common divisor using recursion*) The **gcd(m, n)** can also be defined recursively as follows:

- If **m % n** is **0**, **gcd(m, n)** is **n**.
- Otherwise, **gcd(m, n)** is **gcd(n, m % n)**.

Write a recursive function to find the GCD. Write a test program that prompts the user to enter two integers and displays their GCD.

15.4 (*Sum series*) Write a recursive function to compute the following series:

$$m(i) = 1 + \frac{1}{2} + \frac{1}{3} + \ldots + \frac{1}{i}$$

Write a test program that displays $m(i)$ for $i = 1, 2, \ldots, 10$.

15.5 (*Sum series*) Write a recursive function to compute the following series:

$$m(i) = \frac{1}{3} + \frac{2}{5} + \frac{3}{7} + \frac{4}{9} + \frac{5}{11} + \frac{6}{13} + \ldots + \frac{i}{2i + 1}$$

Write a test program that displays $m(i)$ for $i = 1, 2, \ldots, 10$.

*15.6 (*Summing series*) Write a recursive function to compute the following series:

$$m(i) = \frac{1}{2} + \frac{2}{3} + \ldots + \frac{i}{i + 1}$$

Write a test program that prompts the user to enter an integer for i and displays $m(i)$.

*15.7 (*Fibonacci series*) Modify Listing 15.2 so that the program finds the number of times the **fib** function is called. (Hint: Use a global variable and increment it every time the function is called.)

Section 15.4

*15.8 (*Print the digits in an integer reversely*) Write a recursive function that displays an integer value reversely on the console using the following header:

```
def reverseDisplay(value):
```

For example, invoking **reverseDisplay(12345)** displays **54321**. Write a test program that prompts the user to enter an integer and displays its reversal.

*15.9 (*Print the characters in a string reversely*) Write a recursive function that displays a string reversely on the console using the following header:

```
def reverseDisplay(value):
```

For example, **reverseDisplay("abcd")** displays **dcba**. Write a test program that prompts the user to enter a string and displays its reversal.

*15.10 (*Occurrences of a specified character in a string*) Write a recursive function that finds the number of occurrences of a specified letter in a string using the following function header.

```
def count(s, a):
```

For example, **count("Welcome", 'e')** returns 2. Write a test program that prompts the user to enter a string and a character, and displays the number of occurrences for the character in the string.

Section 15.5

15.11 (*Print the characters in a string reversely*) Rewrite Exercise 15.9 using a helper function to pass the substring for the **high index to the function. The helper function header is:

```
def reverseDisplayHelper(s, high):
```

*15.12 (*Find the largest number in a list*) Write a recursive function that returns the largest integer in a list. Write a test program that prompts the user to enter a list of integers and displays the largest element.

*15.13 (*Find the number of uppercase letters in a string*) Write a recursive function to return the number of uppercase letters in a string using the following function headers:

```
def countUppercase(s):
def countUppercaseHelper(s, high):
```

Write a test program that prompts the user to enter a string and displays the number of uppercase letters in the string.

*15.14 (*Occurrences of a specified character in a string*) Rewrite Exercise 15.10 using a helper function to pass the substring of the **high** index to the function. The helper function header is:

```
def countHelper(s, a, high):
```

*15.15 (*Find the number of uppercase letters in a list*) Write a recursive function to return the number of uppercase letters in a list of characters. You need to define the following two functions. The second one is a recursive helper function.

```
def count(chars):
def countHelper(chars, high):
```

Write a test program that prompts the user to enter a list of characters in one line and displays the number of uppercase letters in the list.

*15.16 (*Occurrences of a specified character in a list*) Write a recursive function that finds the number of occurrences of a specified character in a list. You need to define the following two functions. The second one is a recursive helper function.

```
def count(chars, ch):
def countHelper(chars, ch, high):
```

Write a test program that prompts the user to enter a list of characters in one line, and a character, and displays the number of occurrences of the character in the list.

Sections 15.6–15.11

*15.17 (*Tkinter: Sierpinski triangle*) Revise Listing 15.9 to let the user use left-mouse/right-mouse clicks to increase/decrease the current order by 1. The initial order is 0.

*15.18 (*Towers of Hanoi*) Modify Listing 15.8, TowersOfHanoi.py, so that the program finds the number of moves needed to move *n* disks from tower A to tower B. (Hint: Use a global variable and increment it for every move.)

*15.19 (*Decimal to binary*) Write a recursive function that converts a decimal number into a binary number as a string. The function header is as follows:

```
def decimalToBinary(value):
```

Write a test program that prompts the user to enter a decimal number and displays its binary equivalent.

*15.20 (*Decimal to hex*) Write a recursive function that converts a decimal number into a hex number as a string. The function header is as follows:

```
def decimalToHex(value):
```

Write a test program that prompts the user to enter a decimal number and displays its hex equivalent.

*15.21 (*Binary to decimal*) Write a recursive function that parses a binary number as a string into a decimal integer. The function header is as follows:

```
def binaryToDecimal(binaryString):
```

Write a test program that prompts the user to enter a binary string and displays its decimal equivalent.

*15.22 (*Hex to decimal*) Write a recursive function that parses a hex number as a string into a decimal integer. The function header is as follows:

```
def hexToDecimal(hexString):
```

Write a test program that prompts the user to enter a hex string and displays its decimal equivalent.

15.23 (*String permutation*) Write a recursive function to print all the permutations of a string. For example, for the string **abc, the printout is:

```
abc
acb
bac
bca
cab
cba
```

(Hint: Define the following two functions. The second function is a helper function.

```
def displayPermuation(s):
def displayPermuationHelper(s1, s2):
```

The first function simply invokes **displayPermuation(" ", s)**. The second function uses a loop to move a character from **s2** to **s1** and recursively invokes it with a new **s1** and **s2**. The base case is that **s2** is empty and prints **s1** to the console.)

Write a test program that prompts the user to enter a string and displays all its permutations.

*15.24 (*Number of files in a directory*) Write a program that prompts the user to enter a directory and displays the number of files in the directory.

**15.25 (*Tkinter: Koch snowflake fractal*) Section 15.8 presented the Sierpinski triangle fractal. In this exercise, you will write a program to display another fractal, called the *Koch snowflake*, named after a famous Swedish mathematician. A Koch snowflake is created as follows:

1. Begin with an equilateral triangle, which is considered to be the Koch fractal of order (or level) **0**, as shown in Figure 15.14a.
2. Divide each line in the shape into three equal line segments and draw an outward equilateral triangle with the middle line segment as the base to create a Koch fractal of order **1**, as shown in Figure 15.14b.
3. Repeat Step 2 to create a Koch fractal of order **2**, **3**, ..., and so on, as shown in Figure 15.14c–d.

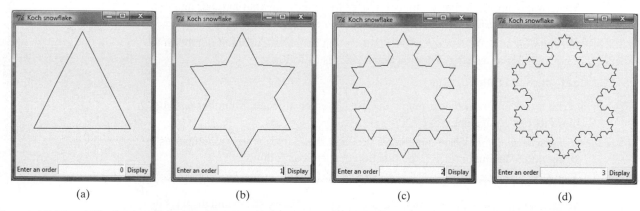

| (a) | (b) | (c) | (d) |

FIGURE 15.14 A Koch snowflake is a fractal starting with a triangle.

**15.26 (*Turtle: Koch snowflake fractal*) Rewrite the *Koch snowflake* program in Exercise 15.25 using Turtle, as shown in Figure 15.15. Your program should prompt the user to enter the order and display the corresponding fractal for the order.

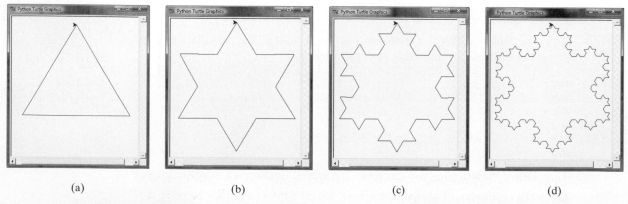

| (a) | (b) | (c) | (d) |

FIGURE 15.15 The Koch snowflake fractal is drawn using Turtle.

**15.27 (*All eight queens*) Modify Listing 15.10, EightQueens.py, to find all the possible solutions to the Eight Queens problem.

**15.28 (*Find words*) Write a program that finds all the occurrences of a word in all the files under a directory, recursively. Your program should prompt the user to enter a directory name.

**15.29 (*Tkinter: H-tree fractal*) An *H-tree* is a fractal defined as follows:

1. Begin with a letter H. The three lines of the H are of the same length, as shown in Figure 15.1a.
2. The letter H (in its sans-serif form, H) has four endpoints. Draw an H centered at each of the four endpoints to an H-tree of order 1, as shown in Figure 15.1b. These Hs are half the size of the H that contains the four endpoints.
3. Repeat Step 2 to create an H-tree of order 2, 3, ..., and so on, as shown in Figure 15.1c–d.

Write a Python program that draws an H-tree, as shown in Figure 15.1.

**15.30 (*Turtle: H-tree fractal*) Rewrite the H-tree fractal in Exercise 15.29 using Turtle, as shown in Figure 15.16. Your program should prompt the user to enter the order and display the corresponding fractal for the order.

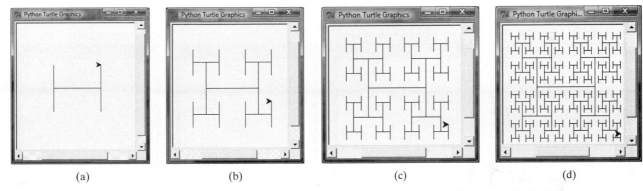

(a) (b) (c) (d)

FIGURE 15.16 An H-tree fractal is drawn using Turtle for order of 0 in (a), 1 in (b), 2 in (c), and 3 in (d).

**15.31 (*Tkinter: Recursive tree*) Write a program to display a recursive tree, as shown in Figure 15.17.

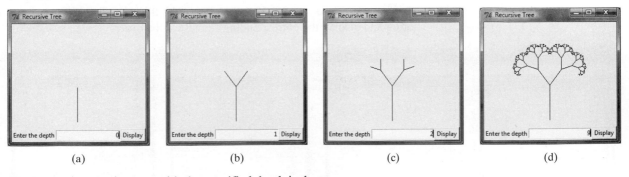

(a) (b) (c) (d)

FIGURE 15.17 A recursive tree with the specified depth is drawn.

**15.32 (*Turtle: Recursive tree*) Rewrite the recursive tree in Exercise 15.31 using Turtle, as shown in Figure 15.18. Your program should prompt the user to enter the order and display the corresponding fractal for the order.

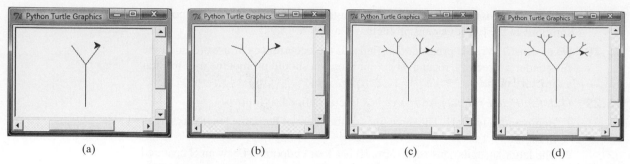

(a)　　　　(b)　　　　(c)　　　　(d)

FIGURE 15.18　A recursive tree is drawn using Turtle with depth 0 in (a), 1 in (b), 2 in (c), and 3 in (d).

**15.33　(*Tkinter: Hilbert curve*) The Hilbert curve, first described by German mathematician David Hilbert in 1891, is a space-filling curve that visits every point in a square grid with a size of 2×2, 4×4, 8×8, 16×16, or any other power of 2. Write a program that displays a Hilbert curve for the specified order, as shown in Figure 15.19.

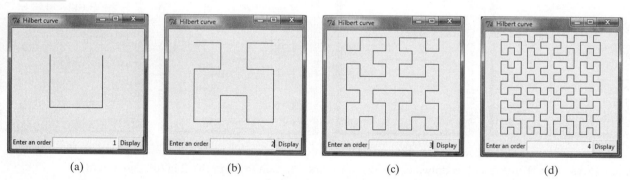

(a)　　　　(b)　　　　(c)　　　　(d)

FIGURE 15.19　A Hilbert curve with the specified order is drawn.

**15.34　(*Turtle: Hilbert curve*) Rewrite the Hilbert curve in Exercise 15.33 using Turtle, as shown in Figure 15.20. Your prsogram should prompt the user to enter the order and display the corresponding fractal for the order.

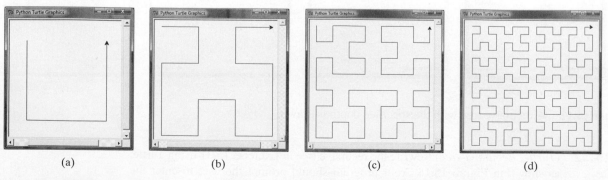

(a)　　　　(b)　　　　(c)　　　　(d)

FIGURE 15.20　A Hilbert curve is drawn using Turtle with order 0 in (a), 1 in (b), 2 in (c), and 3 in (d).

15.35 (*Tkinter: Sierpinski triangle*) Revise Listing 15.9, SierpinskiTriangle.py, to display the filled Sierpinski triangles, as shown in Figure 15.21.

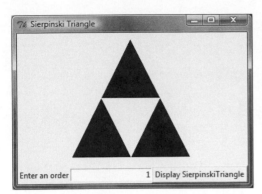 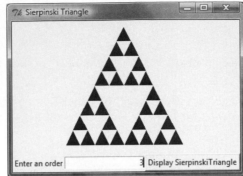

FIGURE 15.21 Filled Sierpinski triangles are displayed.

15.36 (*Turtle: Sierpinski triangle*) Rewrite Listing 15.9, SierpinskiTriangle.py, using Turtle.

APPENDIXES

Appendix A
Python Keywords

Appendix B
The ASCII Character Set

Appendix C
Number Systems

Python Keywords

The following keywords are reserved by the Python language. They should not be used for anything other than their predefined purpose in Python.

and	else	in	return
as	except	is	True
assert	False	lambda	try
break	finally	None	while
class	for	nonlocal	with
continue	from	not	yield
def	global	or	
del	if	pass	
elif	import	raise	

APPENDIX B

The ASCII Character Set

Tables B.1 and B.2 show ASCII characters and their respective decimal and hexadecimal codes. The decimal or hexadecimal code of a character is a combination of its row index and column index. For example, in Table B.1, the letter A is at row 6 and column 5, so its decimal equivalent is 65; in Table B.2, letter A is at row 4 and column 1, so its hexadecimal equivalent is 41.

TABLE B.1   ASCII Character Set in the Decimal Index

	0	1	2	3	4	5	6	7	8	9
0	nul	soh	stx	etx	eot	enq	ack	bel	bs	ht
1	nl	vt	ff	cr	so	si	dle	dc1	dc2	dc3
2	dc4	nak	syn	etb	can	em	sub	esc	fs	gs
3	rs	us	sp	!	"	#	$	%	&	'
4	(	)	*	+	,	-	.	/	0	1
5	2	3	4	5	6	7	8	9	:	;
6	<	=	>	?	@	A	B	C	D	E
7	F	G	H	I	J	K	L	M	N	O
8	P	Q	R	S	T	U	V	W	X	Y
9	Z	[	\	]	^	_	`	a	b	c
10	d	e	f	g	h	i	j	k	l	m
11	n	o	p	q	r	s	t	u	v	w
12	x	y	z	{	|	}	~	del		

TABLE B.2   ASCII Character Set in the Hexadecimal Index

	0	1	2	3	4	5	6	7	8	9	A	B	C	D	E	F
0	nul	soh	stx	etx	eot	enq	ack	bel	bs	ht	nl	vt	ff	cr	so	si
1	dle	dc1	dc2	dc3	dc4	nak	syn	etb	can	em	sub	esc	fs	gs	rs	us
2	sp	!	"	#	$	%	&	'	(	)	*	+	,	-	.	/
3	0	1	2	3	4	5	6	7	8	9	:	;	<	=	>	?
4	@	A	B	C	D	E	F	G	H	I	J	K	L	M	N	O
5	P	Q	R	S	T	U	V	W	X	Y	Z	[	\	]	^	_
6	`	a	b	c	d	e	f	g	h	i	j	k	l	m	n	o
7	p	q	r	s	t	u	v	w	x	y	z	{	|	}	~	del

APPENDIX C

Number Systems

C.1 Introduction

binary numbers

Computers use binary numbers internally, because computers are made naturally to store and process 0s and 1s. The binary number system has two digits, 0 and 1. A number or character is stored as a sequence of 0s and 1s. Each 0 or 1 is called a *bit* (binary digit).

decimal numbers

In our daily life we use decimal numbers. When we write a number such as 20 in a program, it is assumed to be a decimal number. Internally, computer software is used to convert decimal numbers into binary numbers, and vice versa.

hexadecimal number

We write computer programs using decimal numbers. However, to deal with an operating system, we need to reach down to the "machine level" by using binary numbers. Binary numbers tend to be very long and cumbersome. Often hexadecimal numbers are used to abbreviate them, with each hexadecimal digit representing four binary digits. The hexadecimal number system has 16 digits: 0–9 and A–F. The letters A, B, C, D, E, and F correspond to the decimal numbers 10, 11, 12, 13, 14, and 15.

The digits in the decimal number system are 0, 1, 2, 3, 4, 5, 6, 7, 8, and 9. A decimal number is represented by a sequence of one or more of these digits. The value that each digit represents depends on its position, which denotes an integral power of 10. For example, the digits 7, 4, 2, and 3 in decimal number 7423 represent 7000, 400, 20, and 3, respectively, as shown below:

$$\boxed{7 \mid 4 \mid 2 \mid 3} = 7 \times 10^3 + 4 \times 10^2 + 2 \times 10^1 + 3 \times 10^0$$

$$10^3 \ 10^2 \ 10^1 \ 10^0 = 7000 + 400 + 20 + 3 = 7423$$

base
radix

The decimal number system has ten digits, and the position values are integral powers of 10. We say that 10 is the *base* or *radix* of the decimal number system. Similarly, since the binary number system has two digits, its base is 2, and since the hex number system has 16 digits, its base is 16.

If 1101 is a binary number, the digits 1, 1, 0, and 1 represent 1×2^3, 1×2^2, 0×2^1, and 1×2^0, respectively:

$$\boxed{1 \mid 1 \mid 0 \mid 1} = 1 \times 2^3 + 1 \times 2^2 + 0 \times 2^1 + 1 \times 2^0$$

$$2^3 \ 2^2 \ 2^1 \ 2^0 = 8 + 4 + 0 + 1 = 13$$

If 7423 is a hex number, the digits 7, 4, 2, and 3 represent 7×16^3, 4×16^2, 2×16^1, and 3×16^0, respectively:

$$\boxed{7 \mid 4 \mid 2 \mid 3} = 7 \times 16^3 + 4 \times 16^2 + 2 \times 16^1 + 3 \times 16^0$$

$$16^3 \ 16^2 \ 16^1 \ 16^0 = 28672 + 1024 + 32 + 3 = 29731$$

C.2 Conversions Between Binary and Decimal Numbers

Given a binary number $b_n b_{n-1} b_{n-2} \ldots b_2 b_1 b_0$, the equivalent decimal value is

binary to decimal

$$b_n \times 2^n + b_{n-1} \times 2^{n-1} + b_{n-2} \times 2^{n-2} + \ldots + b_2 \times 2^2 + b_1 \times 2^1 + b_0 \times 2^0$$

Here are some examples of converting binary numbers to decimals:

Binary	Conversion Formula	Decimal
10	$1 \times 2^1 + 0 \times 2^0$	2
1000	$1 \times 2^3 + 0 \times 2^2 + 0 \times 2^1 + 0 \times 2^0$	8
10101011	$1 \times 2^7 + 0 \times 2^6 + 1 \times 2^5 + 0 \times 2^4 + 1 \times 2^3 + 0 \times 2^2 +$ $1 \times 2^1 + 1 \times 2^0$	171

To convert a decimal number d to a binary number is to find the bits $b_n, b_{n-1}, b_{n-2}, \ldots, b_2, b_1,$ and b_0 such that

decimal to binary

$$d = b_n \times 2^n + b_{n-1} \times 2^{n-1} + b_{n-2} \times 2^{n-2} + \ldots + b_2 \times 2^2 + b_1 \times 2^1 + b_0 \times 2^0$$

These bits can be found by successively dividing d by 2 until the quotient is 0. The remainders are $b_0, b_1, b_2, \ldots, b_{n-2}, b_{n-1},$ and b_n.

For example, the decimal number 123 is 1111011 in binary. The conversion is done as follows:

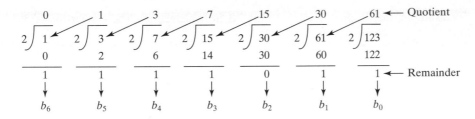

Tip

The Windows Calculator, as shown in Figure C.1, is a useful tool for performing number conversions. To run it, search for *Calculator* from the *Start* button and launch Calculator, then under *View* select *Scientific*.

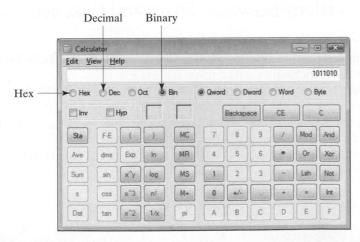

FIGURE C.1 You can perform number conversions using the Windows Calculator.

C.3 Conversions Between Hexadecimal and Decimal Numbers

hex to decimal

Given a hexadecimal number $h_n h_{n-1} h_{n-2} \ldots h_2 h_1 h_0$, the equivalent decimal value is

$$h_n \times 16^n + h_{n-1} \times 16^{n-1} + h_{n-2} \times 16^{n-2} + \ldots + h_2 \times 16^2 + h_1 \times 16^1 + h_0 \times 16^0$$

Here are some examples of converting hexadecimal numbers to decimals:

Hexadecimal	Conversion Formula	Decimal
7F	$7 \times 16^1 + 15 \times 16^0$	127
FFFF	$15 \times 16^3 + 15 \times 16^2 + 15 \times 16^1 + 15 \times 16^0$	65535
431	$4 \times 16^2 + 3 \times 16^1 + 1 \times 16^0$	1073

decimal to hex

To convert a decimal number d to a hexadecimal number is to find the hexadecimal digits $h_n, h_{n-1}, h_{n-2}, \ldots, h_2, h_1$, and h_0 such that

$$d = h_n \times 16^n + h_{n-1} \times 16^{n-1} + h_{n-2} \times 16^{n-2} + \ldots + h_2 \times 16^2$$
$$+ h_1 \times 16^1 + h_0 \times 16^0$$

These numbers can be found by successively dividing d by 16 until the quotient is 0. The remainders are $h_0, h_1, h_2, \ldots, h_{n-2}, h_{n-1}$, and h_n.

For example, the decimal number 123 is 7B in hexadecimal. The conversion is done as follows:

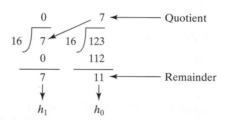

C.4 Conversions Between Binary and Hexadecimal Numbers

hex to binary

To convert a hexadecimal to a binary number, simply convert each digit in the hexadecimal number into a four-digit binary number, using Table C.1.

For example, the hexadecimal number 7B is 1111011, where 7 is 111 in binary, and B is 1011 in binary.

binary to hex

To convert a binary number to a hexadecimal, convert every four binary digits from right to left in the binary number into a hexadecimal number.

For example, the binary number 1110001101 is 38D, since 1101 is D, 1000 is 8, and 11 is 3, as shown below.

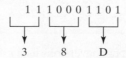

TABLE C.1 Converting Hexadecimal to Binary

Hexadecimal	Binary	Decimal
0	0000	0
1	0001	1
2	0010	2
3	0011	3
4	0100	4
5	0101	5
6	0110	6
7	0111	7
8	1000	8
9	1001	9
A	1010	10
B	1011	11
C	1100	12
D	1101	13
E	1110	14
F	1111	15

 Note

Octal numbers are also useful. The octal number system has eight digits, 0 to 7. A decimal number 8 is represented in the octal system as 10.

Here are some good online resources for practicing number conversions:

- http://forums.cisco.com/CertCom/game/binary_game_page.htm
- http://people.sinclair.edu/nickreeder/Flash/binDec.htm
- http://people.sinclair.edu/nickreeder/Flash/binHex.htm

REVIEW QUESTIONS

1. Convert the following decimal numbers into hexadecimal and binary numbers:

100; 4340; 2000

2. Convert the following binary numbers into hexadecimal and decimal numbers:

1000011001; 100000000; 100111

3. Convert the following hexadecimal numbers into binary and decimal numbers:

FEFA9; 93; 2000

INDEX

CREDITS

Cover and chapter opener art: "Life Aquatic" © Arthur Xanthopoulos from Damaged Photography

Figure 1.1 (CPU): © Shutterstock/Studio 37

Figure 1.1 (Memory): © Shutterstock/Arno van Dulmen

Figure 1.1 (Storage Devices/hard drive): © Shutterstock/Péter Gudella

Figure 1.1 (Storage Devices/USB flash drive): © Shutterstock/Vasilius

Figure 1.1 (Storage Devices/DVD): © Shutterstock/Nata-Lia

Figure 1.1 (Input Devices/keyboard): © Shutterstock/Dmitry Rukhlenko

Figure 1.1 (Input Devices/mouse): © Fotolia/Andrey Khrobostov

Figure 1.1 (Input Devices/joystick): © Shutterstock/George Dolgikh

Figure 1.1 (Output Devices/monitor): © Shutterstock/Nikola Spasenoski

Figure 1.1 (Output Devices/laser printer): © Shutterstock/restyler

Figure 1.1 (Communication Devices/cable modem): © Shutterstock/prism68

Figure 1.1 (Communication Devices/network interface card): © Shutterstock/moritorus

Figure 1.1 (Communication Devices/wireless modem): © Shutterstock/tuanyick

Figure 1.2: © Shutterstock/Xavier P

Figure 1.4: © Shutterstock/Péter Gudella

Figure 1.5 (USB flash drive/plugged in): © Shutterstock/xj

Figure 1.5 (USB flash drive/unplugged/cap off): © Shutterstock/Vasilius

Figure 1.6 (keyboard): © Shutterstock/Dmitry Rukhlenko

Figure 1.7 (network interface card): © Shutterstock/moritorus

Figure 1.7 (server): © Shutterstock/Madlen

Figure 1.7 (PC): © Shutterstock/Dmitry Melnikov

Figures 1.11, 1.12, 1.14–1.20, 2.3, 2.4, 3.1, 3.3–3.7, 4.7, 4.13–4.16, 5.2–5.6, 6.10–6.13, 7.1, 9.1, 9.3–9.6, 9.9–9.40, 10.5, 10.13, 10.15–10.21, 11.3, 11.8, 11.12, 11.14–11.19, 12.4, 12.15, 12.17–12.31, 13.3, 13.7, 13.8, 13.11–13.13, 14.9–14.12, 14.14, 15.1, 15.9, 15.14–15.21: Python, Turtle Graphics, and Tkinter are Copyright © 2001–2011 Python Software Foundation. All rights reserved.

Console Input

```
string = input("Enter a string: ")
number = eval(input("Enter a number: "))
number1, number2, number3 = eval(input("Enter three numbers, separated by commas: ")
```

Console Output

```
print(item1, item2, ...)
print(item1, item2, ..., end = "ending string")
```

Random Numbers

```
random.randint(a, b) # Return a random integer between a and b
random.randrange(a, b) # Return a random integer between a and b - 1
random.random() # Return a random float between 0.0 and 1.0, excluding 1.0
```

range Functions

```
range(a, b) # Returns a sequence a, a + 1, ..., b - 1
range(b) # Same as range(0, b)
range(a, b, k) # Returns a sequence a, a + k, a + 2k, ..., with the last number
               # in the sequence less than b
```

Arithmetic Operators

```
+       addition
-       subtraction
*       multiplication
/       float division
//      integer division
%       remainder
**      exponent
```

Augmented Assignment Operators

```
=       assignment
+=      addition assignment
-=      subtraction assignment
*=      multiplication assignment
/=      float division assignment
//=     integer division assignment
%=      remainder assignment
**=     exponent assignment
```

Relational Operators

```
<       less than
<=      less than or equal to
>       greater than
>=      greater than or equal to
==      equal to
!=      not equal
```

Logical Operators

```
and     logical conjunction
or      logical disjunction
not     logical negation
```

Simultaneous Assignment

```
x, y = y, x # Swap x with y
```

Conditional Expression

```
v = v1 if condition else v2
```

Defining Functions

```
def functionName(parameters):
    statements
```

loop statements

```
while condition:
    statements

# strings, lists, tuples
# are examples of sequences
for e in sequence:
    statements

for line in file:
    statements

for key in dictionary:
    statements
```

selection statements

```
if condition:
    statements

if condition:
    statements
else:
    statements

if condition1:
    statements
elif condition2:
    statements
else:
    statements
```

Companion Web site: www.pearsonhighered.com/liang